People in
Crisis

危機

People in Crisis

Clinical and Diversity Perspectives

SIXTH EDITION

Lee Ann Hoff

Bonnie Joyce Hallisey ◆ Miracle Hoff

Routledge
Taylor & Francis Group

New York   London

Routledge
Taylor & Francis Group
711 Third Avenue
New York, NY 10017

Routledge
Taylor & Francis Group
2 Park Square
Milton Park, Abingdon
Oxon OX14 4RN

International Standard Book Number-13: 978-0-415-99075-2 (Softcover)

Library of Congress Cataloging-in-Publication Data

Hoff, Lee Ann.
   People in crisis : clinical and diversity perspectives / Lee Ann Hoff, Bonnie Joyce Hallisey, and Miracle Hoff. -- 6th ed.
       p. ; cm.
   Includes bibliographical references and indexes.
   ISBN 978-0-415-99075-2 (pbk. : alk. paper)
   1. Crisis intervention (Mental health services) I. Hallisey, Bonnie Joyce. II. Hoff, Miracle. III. Title.
   [DNLM: 1. Crisis Intervention--methods. 2. Life Change Events. 3. Violence. WM 401 H698pa 2009]

RC480.6.H64 2009
616.89'025--dc22   2008029121

Visit the Taylor & Francis Web site at
http://www.taylorandfrancis.com

and the Routledge Web site at
http://www.routledge.com

Xueling Cen

CRISIS: DANGER and OPPORTUNITY

Danger . . . of health decline, suicide, violence, sustance abuse
Opportunity . . . for growth, development, and strength during future crises

To People in Crisis across cultures and generations
who have inspired us with their strength, vision, and the
meaning of life through suffering, crisis, and beyond.

Contents

ix

PART III Suicide, Violence, and Catastrophic Events

List of Figures

List of Tables

List of Exhibits

Preface

Since the birth of *People in Crisis* over thirty years ago, the aims have remained constant: First, to understand the universal experience of crisis—how people feel, think, and act when upset, fearful, or threatened with their life; and based on this insight, to help distressed persons and their significant others by sharing strategies and resources to weather the storm of acute anxiety, emotional pain, or a full-blown crisis. Crisis intervention today is widely accepted as an integral facet of comprehensive mental health services as envisioned in *Action for Mental Health*, the 1961 final Report of the Congressional Joint Commission on Mental Illness and Health in the United States. One result of the national research published by the Commission was this: Community based 24/7 crisis care is an *essential* component of community mental health services. Before that designation, crisis intervention was primarily the work of mental health specialists treating acutely psychotic persons or people who are a danger to themselves and others in the back wards of psychiatric institutions, or the police containing violent people at home and on the streets.

From these limited domains, crisis care moved to the national radar screen through hundreds of suicide prevention and crisis hotline programs. Initially, this pioneering work was derided by some as a mere "psychological band aid." Beyond this *front line* development of the crisis field, early *theoretical* underpinnings of crisis intervention drew heavily from work with disaster survivors and soldiers suffering "shell shock" following the extraordinary emotional trauma of fighting wars. Signficantly, in just a few decades, we have come "full circle" from the beginnings of crisis theory and intervention as a formal body of knowledge, to its current prominence in our responses to national and global disasters, seemingly unending war, and tragic violence at home, in our schools, the streets, and workplace.

The sixth edition of this book, *People in Crisis: Clinical and Diversity Perspectives*, builds on and refines the "crisis paradigm" introduced in the book's second edition. Based on research with abused women and their families, the Crisis Paradigm serves as an integrated theoretical framework for the entire book. It reframes hazardous life events and developmental transition states *not* as "crises" in themselves, but as *origins* of crisis. Further, it adds *sociocultural* factors (values, inequalities based on race, class, gender, ethnicity, or sexual identity, and violence by individuals or state-sponsored) as frequent origins of crisis. Research and clinical experience reveal the significant influence of these sociocultural factors on crisis outcomes, particularly if occurring during vulnerable transition states or when dealing with serious losses. The book situates the vast majority of emotional crises within the *normal* range of life cycle events (e.g., birth, marriage, and death) since the beginning of recorded time. But it also addresses acute emotional trauma arising from events that fall *outside* the range of everyday human experience (for example, repeated exposure to battlefield trauma, or a life-threatening rape) without ascribing a psychiatric diagnosis to the person suffering such extraordinary traumas.

Audience

Continuing to address the intended readers of previous editions, *People in Crisis*, 6th edition, reflects the fact that crisis care is *everybody's business*, not just the specialty of any one helping profession. Across cultures, we can grow and learn from one another in the art of helping people in crisis. The comprehensiveness, theoretical integration, a multi-cultural perspective, interdisciplinary approach, and examples illustrating the diversity of crisis experience in this book suggest these potential readers:

- Students (undergraduate and graduate) in health, mental health, social services, pastoral counseling, and criminal justice programs
- Front line crisis workers in health and social service agencies—counselors, social workers, nurses (basic and advanced practice), primary care providers (physicians, nurse practitioners, physician assistants), clergy, police, teachers, rescue workers
- Mental health professionals and specialized crisis workers, paid and volunteer
- Health and mental health educators who train counselors, nurses, social workers, physicians, and clinical psychologists (in special crisis courses, or integrated into standard curricula)
- Human service administrators and program coordinators who must plan and develop crisis programs, and supervise the clinicians who staff them
- Social science teachers and researchers who are interested in the study and application of crisis theory and socio-cultural concepts in health and other human service practice
- The general reader who seeks a better understanding of personal crises

New in Sixth Edition

This edition continues earlier editions' grounding in holism and an interdisciplinary approach underscoring a key premise of successful crisis care in today's human services arena: Working in a collaborative team relationship is not only essential for best practice outcomes, but also for the safety and self-care of crisis workers themselves. Following are several areas that have been expanded or updated for this edition:

1. As the book's new sub-title indicates, diversity content is broadened, including key diversity concepts and human rights principles applied to new case examples that reveal commonalities and differences across cultures in the origin and experience of crisis. This includes the assertion that an "outsider" will rarely if ever be "competent" in a culture

other than one's own, but that all of us can enhance our "sensitivity" to the perspective of those "different" clients appearing in the global community of crisis care practice.

2. Cited throughout the book is recent research and practice regarding the concept of "resilience" which complements a basic premise of crisis theory not only as *danger,* but as an *opportunity* for growth and development that has informed all editions of the book.

3. Readers fluent in Chinese or who are familiar with earlier editions will note the change in the Chinese word for crisis, "danger and opportunity," that has graced the cover and chapter notations since the third edition in 1989. (See Appreciation section for the astute Chinese student responsible for this change.) No matter what psychiatric diagnostic labels might be attached to a person in crisis, the perspective of both danger and opportunity underscores what every person can learn, and what life-threatening dangers can be avoided, when timely, sensitive support, and professional expertise are available and sensitively applied.

4. Widely disseminated humanitarian and institutional responses and disaster research (from Hurricane Katrina and the Asian Tsunami) support the reaffirmation in Chapter 13 of basic public health principles revealed in earlier disaster research: The vast majority of disaster survivors do not have psychological "disorders" and are not candidates for psychiatric treatment; they do not usually welcome a formal "psychological de-briefing" so much as a cup of coffee, a blanket or tent to substitute for a lost home, and some concrete practical information about available survival and recovery resources.

5. The Comprehensive Mental Health Assessment (CMHA) 21-item tool (Chapter 3) is continued and elaborated from its testing and implementation in a large New York county mental health system; this includes, in a case illustration, the addition of a service plan based on assessment of basic life functions and signals of distress that integrates crisis care with mental health practice protocols. As in earlier editions, Operational Definitions for CMHA items assessing risk of *victimization, suicide, and assault/homicide* are included with case illustrations. Operational Definitions for the tool's remaining 18 items are now available in the Online Resources accompanying this edition, with an invitation to clinicians and researchers to collaborate in further development and testing of this tool. Chapter 3 also introduces the work of psychiatrist Paul McHugh that is used at the Johns Hopkins University Department of Psychiatry for training psychiatric residents. The increasing "professionalization" of basic crisis services and psychiatric labeling of everyday problems as "disorders" makes the CMHA tool more relevant than ever for its attention to life-threatening danger and the larger context of social and/or psychiatric problems that increase one's vulnerability to crisis in the first place.

6. Workplace and school-based violence topics are elaborated in Chapter 12, drawing on a six-year NIOSH-based interdisciplinary multi-methods study at the University of Massachusetts-Lowell focusing on injuries of healthcare workers, and on my ongoing efforts to engage university personnel in well-documented measures designed to prevent the personal and community-wide effects of violence by distressed and alienated students, as in the Virginia Tech and related massacres. (See Online Resources for Web links and opportunities to collaborate in replicating survey research on student stress and crisis.) This chapter also cites new research regarding the presumed correlation between psychiatric illness and rates of violence.

7. Besides updated references, a Glossary and Online Resources have been added to this edition—including teaching aids and student study guides. Also online—for students, faculty, or others who need to consult further resources—are references from the 5th edition of this book and international crisis networking information.

8. Chapters in Parts II and III have been re-ordered (see Organization).

9. The importance of connection among primary care, public health and human rights vis-à-vis people in crisis worldwide has been strengthened. This includes essential collaboration between front-line crisis workers and psychiatric clinicians, which can sometimes be compromised in an era of *pathologizing* everyday life—an occurrence explained in part because health insurance, especially in the United States, does not readily support the professional service people in crisis may need without a "diagnosis" based on the *DSM-IV-R*, the "Bible of Psychiatry," although non-stigmatizing assessment approaches are available.

Sources

As in previous editions, concepts are illustrated with examples from major ethnic, racial, and socioeconomic groups receiving crisis services in the United States and Canada, from literature reviews, clinical experience, and from cross-cultural teaching and travel experience in university and continuing education settings. I have also used my experience, research, and consultation work in urban and rural settings in the United States and abroad, including volunteer work with abused women and people with HIV/AIDS. The cases are real but disguised to protect persons' identity.

The theory and research informing this book reflect the interdisciplinary facet of the crisis field and its relevance to social work, nursing, psychology, public health, medicine, and the applied social sciences of anthropology and sociology. Put another way, crisis care is everyone's business, not the specialty of any one discipline. I have therefore tried to avoid technical jargon and write in a language understandable to student, professional, and lay readers alike.

Organization

The book consists of three parts:

Part I: The Understanding and Practice of Crisis Intervention. The five chapters in this part present the basic concepts and strategies necessary to understand, identify, and provide skilled assistance to people in distress or acute crisis. It includes individual as well as social and family-focused strategies. This part lays the foundation for considering major crisis experiences in greater depth across all other chapters.

Part II: Crises Related to Developmental and Situational Transition States. For this edition the three chapters in this part (in earlier editions, Part III) were moved forward, especially to address student readers. Since students—whether in late adolescence, or as adult learners returning to college—are typically in a major transition state themselves, they might more easily digest and apply major concepts in relation to their own experience before addressing the potentially harrowing topics of suicide and violence in Part III. The theme in this part is passage, cultural context, and the need for "contemporary rites of passage" to assist individuals through these normal life events and the final passage to death.

Part III: Suicide, Violence, and Catastrophic Events. The five chapters in this part deal with violence toward self and others both as an *origin* of crisis (for example, victimization and war) and as a *response* to crisis (for example, suicide or abuse and homicide). The needs of victim-survivors as well as assailants are addressed, with major emphasis on risk assessment and prevention. The fearsome presence of violence—at home, in schools, the streets, and workplace—not only in U.S. society but throughout the world, has informed the book's continued attention to topics such as the routine assessment for self-injury and suicide; victimization; assault/homicide danger; and disasters originating from human and technological factors, disparities between rich and poor, and violence among ethnic, religious, and other groups and nations that leave so many victims in its wake.

More detailed part and chapter descriptions are presented in the introductions to each part.

Final Word

Crisis is intrinsic to life, but it is not a mental illness, although a person with psychiatric illness is usually more vulnerable than others in the face of life's challenges and traumatic events. Nor is formal crisis intervention a panacea for all of life's problems. The Chinese word for crisis signifies both the *danger* and *opportunity* of crisis—violence toward self and others, substance abuse and depression, *or* building on human resilience and capacity for growing toward greater strength in the face of future challenges. With determination and timely support, we can come through a crisis enriched and stronger or stagnating and hopeless. We can attain new awareness and coping ability, or lose our emotional and physical health and the opportunity to live a purposeful life and die a peaceful death. It is my hope that this book will make a difference for all those who read it.

Appreciation

As this sixth edition goes to press, I thank all the students, their teachers, crisis workers and reviewers who have critiqued previous editions. You have thereby contributed to making this book a continued source of inspiration and guidance in our work with people in crisis. Most of what any of us have learned in this field can be traced to the wounded and suffering people who have trusted us by sharing their pain. Their courage and strength in navigating serious life crises have inspired me to keep going with a new edition. I am mindful, especially for those new to the field who want to master the concepts and skills necessary to grow and learn from the challenging and often life-threatening events people worldwide face in life's journey toward the final passage. In the health and social sciences, people's "stories" or "case studies" are central to eliciting the empathy necessary for engaging helpfully with a client in distress or emotional crisis. For this I offer special thanks to my teachers and mentors in the liberal arts, psychiatric/mental health nursing, psychiatry, and social sciences for what they have taught me about the human condition and how we can alleviate suffering and pain as the examples in this text illustrate.

Most specially, I thank Miracle Hoff and Bonnie Joyce Hallisey, without whose help this most certainly would be a "lesser" book. While crisis care by definition is interdisciplinary, your insights to advance its application in social work and counseling psychology are deeply appreciated. I have the sense that when you enthusiastically agreed to partner with me for this sixth edition—despite my honest presentation of the work entailed—you did not anticipate a "baptism by fire" so to speak in the grit and determination required for the birth of a presentable manuscript. You have given new meaning to "family as friends" and "friends as family"—happily, in this case, without "baggage" or conflict. My profound thanks to each of you! I also thank Eliza Hutchinson who stood with me through thick and thin with the challenges of new technology for manuscript production and delivery. Eliza, you will go far in your vision and pursuit of health care in the global community!

At Routledge, my deep appreciation goes to publisher George Zimmar, who grasped the vision and mission of this book from its beginning, and to my editor, Dana Bliss, for his astute and gracious guidance toward completion of this sixth edition. Dana, may you never forget how valuable editorial wisdom is, even for an already published author! Special thanks also go to Xueling Cen, a California State University Family Studies student, who observed the "wrong" translation of the Chinese word for "danger and opportunity" in the fifth edition, and produced the corrected translation in traditional Chinese as it appears here. And thank you, Professor Reginald Clark, for introducing Xueling for her contribution to this book.

I also thank Fred Coppersmith who supervised design and template features for the book; Elise Weinger for the cover design; Chris Tominich for assisting with design and keeping me on schedule with all the finishing pieces for production; Karen Simon for supervising the production process; marketing managers Jennifer Schilling and Kenya Pierre, and all others who have contributed to making this book a venture we can all be proud of. Without your patience, endurance and belief in the venture, this book would not have seen the light of day. Thank you. I also offer special thanks to those who have graciously agreed to endorse this sixth edition. Your belief in the book and its place in crisis care education and training is a tremendous boon to the advancement of crisis care as an essential facet of health, counseling, and social services.

Finally and once again, I thank my family and friends who already know how to "stand by until it's over" when another edition of *People in Crisis* takes center stage in my life.

Lee Ann Hoff
January 2009
Boston, Massachusetts

I would like to send a very special thank you to Lee Ann Hoff for entrusting in me a piece of her legacy. Your contribution to this world cannot be described with words. I am very proud to have you as my mentor.

I would also like to thank my family for their support. David, you have supported me through thick and thin with your patience and generous heart; I love you dearly. Kyle, Joe, Brandon, Mason and Jasmine, you are my inspiration; thank you for sharing me and understanding when mom needed some alone time to do her "homework." To my extended family and friends, thank you for words of support for the hectic life I chose to lead.

Miracle Hoff
Fargo, North Dakota

Lee Ann, it is a great honor to join with you in continuing your vital work. After 15 years of teaching at Curry College in Milton, Massachusetts, there is not a course, nor a text that is closer to my heart, mind and professional philosophy than *People in Crisis*. This book offers life skills knowledge with tremendous professional application. The interdisciplinary approach, multicultural dimensions, human rights philosophy, and clinical wisdom are invaluable to all of us who seek to help our fellow human beings.

May my children, Meaghan, Matthew and Elizabeth Hallisey, my best and lasting legacy, continue to develop well through their own life passages, living life fully and accomplishing good in the world.

Bonnie Joyce Hallisey
Boston, Massachusetts

About the Authors

Lee Ann Hoff is a nurse-anthropologist and mental health professional with extensive clinical, management, teaching, research, and consulting experience in crisis and mental health care, women's health, and sociocultural issues affecting health. Following graduate study in psychiatric/mental health nursing at Catholic University of America, and an interdisciplinary fellowship in suicidology and crisis at Johns Hopkins University, Lee Ann pioneered in the 1960s and '70s in developing community mental health centers, specialized crisis services, and standards for the certification of crisis centers and their workers. In recognition of this work, she was honored by the American Association of Suicidology with its first national service award, and received an Honorary Recognition award from the American Nurses Association.

Dr. Hoff's teaching experience spans undergraduate, graduate, and continuing education programs across health, social service, women's studies, and police departments nationally and internationally, most recently as Professor at the University of Massachusetts-Lowell (now, as Research Associate), Visiting Professor at ISPA (Institute for Applied Psychology) in Lisbon, Portugal, and Adjunct Professor, University of Ottawa, Faculty of Health Sciences. She is founding director of the Life Crisis Institute, affiliated with the University of Massachusetts-Lowell.

Hoff's other major publications include *Battered Women as Survivors* (1990), Routledge; *Psychiatric & Mental Health Essentials in Primary Care* (co-author, Betty Morgan), (in press); and *Violence and Abuse Issues: Cross-Cultural Perspectives for Health and Social Services*, Routledge (in press). See Online Resources for Dr. Hoff's other publications, educational background, professional achievements, and contact information for collaborative research, education, and human rights projects.

Miracle Hoff is a mental health, crisis, and substance abuse counselor. She has clinical and administrative experience in outpatient services for both adolescents and adults. Miracle holds a master's degree in community counseling. Her professional special interests include adolescence, resiliency, substance abuse, client empowerment, and preventive intervention. She lives in eastern North Dakota with her husband and five children.

Bonnie Joyce Hallisey is a social worker with an M.S.W. from Boston University and B.A. from Marquette University. After her initial work as a child welfare specialist, the Commonwealth of Massachusetts sponsored her through graduate school. Bonnie went on to do community mental health with diverse populations in Boston, to consult with business and human service agencies and have a private clinical practice. She teaches sociology and psychology courses at Curry College in Milton, Massachusetts.

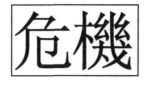

PART I

THE UNDERSTANDING AND PRACTICE OF CRISIS INTERVENTION

The concepts and strategies that form the nucleus of crisis theory and practice are fundamental to understanding and helping people in crisis. Chapter 1 sets the concepts in historical context, linking contemporary crisis care to the theories and practices that preceded it. A psychosociocultural perspective is highlighted in a research-based Crisis Paradigm, which is introduced in Chapter 1, is discussed in detail in Chapter 2, and provides the theoretical framework of the entire book. In Chapter 3, the concepts are applied to the process of assessing individuals and families for crisis—including life-threatening risk. Chapter 4 focuses on planning and implementing crisis care strategies based on assessment, and Chapter 5 extends the helping process to family, group, and community crisis situations. The concepts and strategies addressed in Part 1 constitute the foundation for all remaining chapters.

Part I

THE UNDERSTANDING AND PRACTICE OF CRISIS INTERVENTION

Crisis Theory and Practice
Introduction and Overview

Deborah, age 50, is married and the mother of two teenage children. One day at work, she had a heart attack and was taken to the hospital by an ambulance. This is clearly a medical emergency and a source of stress for Deborah and her family. However, a life-threatening event like this may also precipitate an emotional crisis for Deborah and for everyone involved. Chronic stress following Deborah's physical illness could lead to an emotionally troubled family or to the mental breakdown of individual family members, depending on the various psychological, social, and cultural factors involved in the crisis. Whether this hazardous situation results in growth and enrichment for Deborah and her loved ones, or in a lower level of functioning for one or all of them, depends largely on their problem-solving abilities, cultural values regarding illness and health, and current levels of social and economic support.

Deborah, it turns out, is a health care executive who has just received a promotion. She comes from a working-class family. One of her major life ambitions is to achieve professional success while also maintaining a stable family life. Deborah's husband and children are devoted to her, but she feels constant pressure to set an example of strength and to perform to an exacting standard. Being a responsible wife and mother and a successful professional are all-important goals to Deborah. These facts of Deborah's life and the lives of people like her signify the *subjectivity* of the crisis experience—that is, how each individual interprets a distressful event. This subjectivity contributes to the difficulty of scientific research and theory-building about crisis (Antonvosky, 1987; Hoff, 1990).

What Is Crisis and Crisis Intervention?

There are meaningful differences and relationships among the key terms *stress, predicament, emergency, crisis,* and *emotional or mental disturbance* or *breakdown*.[1] Stress is not crisis; stress is tension, strain, or pressure. Predicament is not crisis either; predicament is a condition or situation that is unpleasant, dangerous, or embarrassing. Emergency is not crisis; emergency is an unforeseen combination of circumstances that calls for immediate action, often with life-or-death implications. Finally, crisis is not emotional or mental illness. *Crisis* may be defined as a serious occasion or turning point presenting both danger and opportunity.

If Deborah or members of her family become extremely upset as a result of her heart attack and feel emotionally unable to handle the event, they are said to be in crisis. In this book, *crisis,* in a clinical context, refers to an acute emotional upset arising from situational, developmental, or sociocultural sources and resulting in a temporary inability to cope by means of one's usual problem-solving devices. A crisis does not last long and is self-limiting. *Crisis management* refers to the entire process of working through the crisis to its end point of *crisis resolution,* a process that usually includes activities not only of the individual in crisis but also of various members of the person's natural and institutional social network. It is an integral facet of psychosocial health care.

Whether the resolution of a crisis is positive or negative often depends on *crisis intervention*—that aspect of health service carried out by a crisis worker—nurse, social worker, police officer, physician, counselor, or minister. Crisis intervention is a short-term helping process. It focuses on resolution of the immediate problem through the use of personal, social, and environmental resources. *Crisis counseling* is a time-limited aspect of crisis resolution focusing on the emotional, cognitive, and behavioral ramifications of the crisis. It is usually done by providers with formal preparation in counseling techniques. *Psychotherapy* is a helping process, brief or over a longer term, directed toward changing a person's feelings and patterns of thought and behavior.

Crisis intervention is related to but differs from psychotherapy. Thus, for example, a primary care provider whose assessment of a patient reveals high risk for suicide would arrange immediate referral to an agency's 24/7 crisis service or to a mental health specialist on call. Psychotherapists, on the other hand, who face a similar high-risk situation typically are prepared to integrate the crisis intervention process into an established therapy contract (Hoff & Morgan, in press). *Emergency psychiatry* is a branch of medicine that deals with acute behavioral disturbances related to severe cognitive impairment or emotional instability. It may overlap with crisis intervention, but it also implies the need for distinct medical intervention such as psychotropic medication or admission to an inpatient psychiatric service. The paradigm for this helping process and the theory supporting it constitute the *crisis model.* For related definitions, see the Glossary.

---

[1] The terms emotional or mental *breakdown, disturbance, illness,* and *disorder* are used interchangeably. This usage recognizes that the psychosocial, crisis, and psychiatric assessment processes are not exact science. See Chapter 3 for elaboration and discussion of psychiatric diagnosis and labeling.

Predicaments, conflicts, and emergencies such as Deborah's lead to stress that can evolve into a crisis state. But stress is a common denominator in everyone's passage from infancy through childhood to adolescence, adulthood, and old age, and its effects vary. For example, your son finds himself in turmoil during adolescence; your son's friend does not. You face midlife as a normal part of human development; your friend becomes depressed; a neighbor becomes suicidal. Part of the beauty of life, though, is the rebirth of peace following turmoil and pain; few escape the lows—and the subsequent highs—of living through stressful events or victimization by violence.

Although stressful events, emotional upsets, and emergency situations are parts of life that have a potential for crisis, a crisis does not necessarily follow a traumatic event. Nor does crisis imply or inevitably lead to emotional or mental breakdown. Something that is a crisis for one person may not be for another. As long as we are able to handle stressful life events, we will not experience a crisis. But if stress overwhelms us, and we are unable to find a way out of our predicament, a crisis may result. Crises must be resolved constructively or emotional or mental illness, addictions, suicide, or violence against others can be the unfortunate outcome. And once emotional breakdown occurs, a person is more vulnerable to other stressful life events, thus beginning an interacting cycle of stress, crisis, and destructive crisis outcomes. Crisis does not occur in isolation but is usually experienced in dynamic interplay with stress and illness in particular cultural contexts, as elaborated in Chapter 2.

Note that the events of our lives do not themselves activate crisis. Crisis occurs when our interpretation of these events, our coping ability, and the limitations of our social resources lead to stress so severe that we cannot find relief. Accordingly, understanding people in crisis and knowing how to help them involves attention not only to the emotional tension experienced, but also to the social, cultural, and material factors that influence how people respond to stressful life events. The heart of successful crisis resolution consists of reducing one's vulnerability while enhancing one's resilience and capacity for emotional growth (Hoff, M., 2005; Gitterman, 2001).

Key concepts and strategies necessary to understand and effectively assist people in crisis form the core of this text. They can be summarized broadly in the following aspects of crisis theory and practice:

1. The nature of the person in crisis (Chapter 1)
2. The crisis experience (Chapter 2)
3. The environment and context of crisis care and resolution (Chapters 1 and 2)
4. The formal process of crisis care—assessment, planning, implementation, and follow-up with diverse individuals and groups (all remaining chapters)

Widespread Views about People in Crisis and How to Help Them

People have been experiencing stress, predicaments, and life crises from the beginning of time. They have also found a variety of ways to resolve predicaments and live through crises. People have always helped others cope with life events as well. Hansell (1976, pp. 15–19) cites the biblical Noah anticipating the great flood as an example of how our ancestors handled crises. Noah was warned of the serious predicament he and his family would be facing shortly. They prepared for the event, and through various clever maneuvers, they avoided being overwhelmed by the floodwaters.

Insights developed through the psychological and social sciences have helped people understand themselves and others in crisis. The advent of a more enlightened view of people in crisis has helped put to rest some old myths about "upset people." It is not so easy anymore to write off as "crazy" and institutionalize people who seem to be behaving strangely in the face of an upsetting event. However, the constraints of health care restructuring in the United States and the continuing bias against those needing psychosocial care and residential psychiatric treatment can result in serious consequences in both human and economic terms when necessary treatment is shortchanged (Ustan, 1999). The growing acceptance of crisis care as an essential facet of comprehensive health services is a promising development for people with problems or who are experiencing acute emotional distress.

Views about people in crisis and how to help them vary according to one's value system and the philosophical assumptions guiding practice. But whatever these values and assumptions are, they must be made explicit. People who are involved in crisis intervention—parents, spouses, social workers, nurses, counselors, teachers—can be most helpful if they recognize that everyone has vast potential for growth and that crisis is a point of *opportunity* as well as *danger*, as depicted by the Chinese symbol displayed on this book's cover and chapter openers. For most of us, our healthiest human growth and greatest achievements can often be traced to the trust and hopeful expectations of significant others. Successful crisis intervention involves helping people take advantage of the opportunity and avoid the danger inherent in crisis. Our success in this task may hinge on our values and beliefs about the nature of the person experiencing the crisis. In this book, the following values are assumed.

■ People in crisis, while in a state of high tension and anxiety, are basically *normal* from the standpoint of diagnosable illness. However, the precrisis state for some persons in crisis may be that of emotional turmoil or mental illness. In these instances, the person can be viewed as ill while simultaneously experiencing a crisis. In some cases, emotional or mental breakdown is the result of a negative resolution of crisis, often because of inadequate social support. So even though crisis is related to emotional or mental disturbance, it is important to distinguish between crisis and diagnosable emotional and mental states—that is, *disorders* in the biomedical paradigm.

■ People in crisis are social by nature and live in specific cultural communities by necessity. Their psychological response to hazardous events therefore cannot be properly understood apart from a sociocultural context. "Cultural competence" by crisis workers does not imply detailed knowledge of another's cultural system (Diversity), but it does include withholding judgment about behaviors that may appear "strange" and instead inquiring sensitively about the meaning of customs and beliefs that inform one's interpretation of and response to life events.

■ People in crisis generally want to and are capable of helping themselves, although this capacity may be impaired to varying degrees. Their need for self-mastery and their capacity for growth from the crisis experience are usually enhanced with timely help from friends, family, neighbors, and sometimes from trained crisis workers. Conversely, failure to receive such help when needed can result in diminished growth and disastrous crisis resolution in the form of addictions, self-harm, suicide, assault on others, or mental breakdown. The strength of a person's desire for self-determination and growth, one's resilience, and available help from others will usually influence the outcome of crisis in a favorable direction.

■ The prevention of burnout in human service workers is tied to their recognition of people's basic need for self-determination, even when in crisis. This implies resisting the tendency to rescue or "save" distressed people. Such tactics compromise the possibilities of a healthy crisis outcome. In contrast, actively fostering self-sufficiency contributes to an upset person's sense of control needed for positive crisis resolution. This is true especially when a fear of losing control is a major part of the crisis experience.

■ The greatest economy and effectiveness of crisis care in terms of health promotion and the prevention of suffering occurs when practice with individuals is contextualized in a public health and human rights framework (see Farmer, 1999). Crisis intervention is recognized as the third of three revolutionary phases that have occurred since the turn of the century in the mental and public health fields: (1) Freud's discovery of the unconscious, (2) the discovery of psychotropic drugs in the 1950s, and (3) crisis intervention in the 1960s and after.

■ Although crisis intervention is not merely a Band-Aid (as it was formerly deemed) or simply a necessary preliminary action trivial in comparison with real treatment carried out by professional psychotherapists, neither is it psychotherapy. The fact that some of the same techniques, such as listening, are used by both psychotherapists and crisis workers does not mean that psychotherapy and crisis intervention are equated, any more than either can be equated with friendship or consultation, which also employ listening. Crisis intervention focuses on problem solving around hazardous life events and avoids probing into unconscious conflict and deep-seated psychological problems—the province of psychotherapy.

Growing numbers of counselors, family members, and others regard the stress and crises of human life as normal, as opportunities to advance from one level of maturity to another. Such was the case for the self-actualized individuals studied by Maslow (1970). His study, unique in its time for its focus on normal rather than disturbed people, revealed that people are resilient and capable of virtually limitless growth and development. Growth, rather than stagnation and emotional breakdown, occurred for these people in the midst of pain, adversity, and turmoil of events such as divorce and physical illness. This optimistic view of people and their problems is becoming a viable alternative to the popular view of life and human suffering in an illness paradigm. Interpreting crisis as illness implies treatment or tranquilization, whereas viewing it as opportunity invites a human, growth-promoting response to people in crisis.

The Evolution of Crisis Theory and Intervention Contexts

In the broadest sense, crisis and crisis intervention are as old as humankind. Helping distressed people is intrinsic to the nurturing side of human character. The capacity for creating a culture of caring and concern for those in emotional or physical pain is implicit in the social nature of humans. In a sense, then, crisis intervention is human action embedded in our cultural heritage of learning how to live successfully through stressful life events among one's fellow human beings.

When considered in the context of professional human services, however, crisis intervention is fairly recent. As an organized body of knowledge and practice, crisis intervention is based on humanistic foundations. However, knowledge and experience from the social and health sciences enhance our ability to help others.

Today, crisis intervention is widely accepted as an integral facet of health and human service delivery systems. In this text, the focus is on the interdisciplinary foundation of contemporary crisis theory and practice, and on the distinctive contributions of each area or pioneer in the field, along with critiques of current issues and differences.

Freud and Psychoanalytic Theory

Decades ago, Freud made pioneering contributions to the study of human behavior and the treatment of emotional conflict. He laid the foundation for a view of people as complex beings capable of self-discovery and change. Through extensive case studies, he demonstrated the profound effect that early life experiences can have on later development and happiness. He also found that people can resolve conflicts stemming from traumatic events of childhood and thereby live fuller, happier lives. His conclusions, however, are based largely on the study of disturbed rather than normal individuals. Also, Freud's interpretation of childhood sexual abuse as mere fantasy resulted in an unfortunate legacy: many children and adults still are not believed when they disclose the trauma of abuse. Psychoanalysis, the treatment method developed from Freud's theory, is costly, lengthy, available to few, and generally not applicable to the person in crisis.

Another limitation of Freudian theory is its foundation in biology, resulting in a mechanistic model of personality. Freud's model states that the three-part system of personality—id, ego, and superego—must be kept in balance (*equilibrium*) to avoid unhealthy defense mechanisms and psychopathology. Most analysts today reject the concept of *determinism* inherent in classical psychoanalytic theory. Determinism is based on the idea that our personalities and later life problems are firmly set by early childhood experiences. However, Freud's concept of equilibrium is commonplace in earlier crisis literature, and even today it can be traced to the scientific method in the helping professions and the search for laws (as in the natural sciences) to explain human behavior. In spite of the limitations of Freudian theory, certain psychoanalytic techniques, such as listening and *catharsis* (the expression of feelings about a traumatic event), are useful in human helping processes, including crisis intervention and brief psychotherapy.

Ego Psychology and Resilience

Awareness of the static nature of Freudian theory led to the development of new, less deterministic views of human beings. In the last several decades, ego psychologists such as Fromm (1941), Erikson (1963), and Maslow (1970) did much to lay the philosophical base for crisis theory. They stressed the person's ability to learn and grow throughout life, a developmental concept used throughout this book. Their views about people and human problems are based on the study of normal rather than disturbed individuals. However, the traditional patriarchal family structures implied in Erikson's theory produce increased stress for women, partly because they require women to bear disproportionately the burden of caretaking roles throughout their lives—a pattern that is changing but nevertheless dominant.

Highly complementary to crisis and life-span development theory is the concept of resilience. Broadly defined, *resilience* includes the ability to bounce back and quickly recover one's strength when faced with challenging or even horrific life events (Kaminsky et al., 2007). It addresses the question of how people differ in their response to an array of stressful but similar circumstances that test a person's coping ability: One may resort to substance abuse or violence; another "rises to the occasion," seeks and accepts available help, and moves on to the next challenge. Put another way, resilient people use the "danger" of crisis as an "opportunity" to learn new coping skills. Success in facing adversity and growth in resilience, however, is deeply embedded in the quality of one's social network (see Chapter 5).

Wolin and Wolin (1993) typify a common theme in resilience literature—a focus on people's strengths rather than their deficits. The deficit or at-risk focus can lay the foundation for labeling a person, a process with potentially harmful results that can last a lifetime, as is well established in social science literature (see Chapter 3). As M. Hoff (2005, p. 9) notes: It depends on how labels are used. History is replete with heroic life stories of people who faced the most daunting of odds such as torture, war, or a concentration camp, but who effectively rebounded from psychological terror and massive losses, and went on to productive, even celebrated lives; for example, Elie Wiesel, a holocaust survivor, and Dith Pran, who escaped and brought to world attention the Cambodian genocide of the Khmer Rouge, featured in an award-winning film, *The Killing Fields*. This does not mean that individual, family, school, and environmental risk factors should be ignored. Rather, it highlights the importance of shifting from the "at-risk" paradigm to one of "at promise," which underscores people's strengths and their innate potential for growth, health, and competence while fulfilling developmental and other tasks across the life span (Brendtrow, Brokenleg, & Van Bockern, 1990; Gitterman, 2001; Hoff, M., 2005; Marshall, 2001; Sanders, 2008). Such resiliency is facilitated by personal, family, community, and political advocacy (Collishawa, 2005).

Resilience research builds on the pioneering work of giants in social psychology, philosophy, and holocausts and disaster studies who are cited throughout this book. It also bolsters the importance of focusing on prevention rather than on "fixing" people after the damage is done. In our approach to crisis assessment, and through case examples in subsequent chapters, we illustrate the fruits of an "at promise" approach to crisis care across cultures. Of course, deeply wounded people, from whatever source, often require help beyond what their families can provide; i.e., the services of professional crisis workers and mental health specialists, but the costs in both human and economic terms are very steep when prevention and early intervention through education, consultation, and 24/7 access to crisis care are compromised in the misguided attempt to "save" money that should be wisely invested in a nation's future—its children, its soldiers, and all who contribute to society when not disabled by neglect or lack of needed health and social services.

Military Psychiatry

During World War II and the Korean War, members of the military who felt distressed were treated at the front lines whenever possible rather than being sent back home to psychiatric hospitals. Studies reveal that the majority of these men were able to return to combat duty rapidly as a result of receiving immediate help, that is, crisis intervention, individually or in a group (Glass, 1957). This approach to psychiatric practice in the military assumed that active combat was the normal place for a soldier and that the soldier would return to duty in spite of temporary problems. So even though military psychiatrists used crisis intervention primarily to expedite institutional goals, they made a useful discovery for the crisis field as a whole.

Today, however, this historic foundation of crisis care for traumatized soldiers—not to mention lessons learned from the Vietnam War veterans who were mistreated—appear to have been erased from ethical and evidence-based decision making in providing needed services to many war veterans. In numbers straining statistical norms, soldiers returning from the Afghanistan and Iraq wars commit suicide or find themselves homeless, divorced, addicted to alcohol and other drugs, or abandoned as they try to survive horrific traumas of the battlefield (see Chapter 3 on labeling and Chapter 13 on posttraumatic stress disorder [PTSD]). The case of a veteran denied benefits and given a diagnosis of preexisting "personality disorder" extended all the way to an investigative committee of the U.S. Congress.

Preventive Psychiatry and Public Health

In 1942, a terrible fire raged through the Cocoanut Grove Melody Lounge in Boston, killing 492 people. Lindemann's classic study (1944) of bereavement following this disaster defined the grieving process that people went through after the sudden death of a relative. Lindemann found that the survivors of this disaster who developed serious psychopathologies had failed to go through the normal process of grieving. His findings can be applied to working with anyone suffering a serious loss. Because loss is a common theme in the crisis experience, Lindemann's work constitutes one of the most important foundations of contemporary crisis theory. Unfortunately, decades later, many others still lack the assistance and social approval necessary for grief work following loss and instead are offered medication (see in Chapter 4 the sections on "Loss, Change, and Grief Work" and "Psychotropic Drugs: What Place in Crisis Intervention?"). Grief work consists of the process of mourning one's loss, experiencing the pain of such loss, and eventually accepting the reality of loss and adjusting to life without the loved person or object. Encouraging and supporting people to experience the normal process of grieving can prevent negative outcomes of crises due to loss.

Tyhurst (1957), another pioneer in preventive psychiatry, has helped us understand a person's response to community crises such as natural disasters. During the 1940s and 1950s, Tyhurst studied transition states such as migration, parenthood, and retirement. His work examined many crisis states that occur as a result of social mobility or cultural change.

Among all the pioneers in the preventive psychiatry field, perhaps none is more outstanding or more frequently quoted than Gerald Caplan. In 1964, he developed a conceptual framework for understanding crisis, including especially the process of crisis development (discussed in detail in Chapter 2). Caplan also emphasized a community-wide—that is, public health—approach to crisis intervention. Public education programs and consultation with various caretakers, such as teachers, police officers, and public health nurses, were cited as important ways to prevent destructive outcomes of crises. In his classic work *Principles of Preventive Psychiatry* (1964), Caplan's focus on prevention, mastery, and the importance of social, cultural, and material "supplies" to avoid crisis seems highly suitable to explaining the development and resolution of crisis. This public health framework resonates with a current emphasis on human rights and with the intrinsic connections among health and economic and political developments and social justice (Rodriguez-Garcia & Akhter, 2000).

Caplan's contribution to the development of crisis theory and practice is so basic that virtually all writers in the field rely on or adapt his major concepts. However, because of the centrality of Caplan's work in the entire crisis field, as well as the controversy surrounding his work and its disease-focused model (for instance, Brandt & Gardner, 2000), a brief examination of his work is in order.

Caplan's conceptual framework can be questioned for its reliance on disease rather than on health concepts. This limitation is offset, however, by his emphasis on prevention rather than treatment of disease. A critique of what should probably be preserved and what should be questioned lays the foundation for the next chapter, which relies heavily on Caplan in explaining the phases of crisis development, and will be supported by analysis and case examples throughout the text.

Caplan grounds his work in the mechanistic concepts set forth by Freud and in one of the most popular theories in the social and health sciences—*general systems theory*. The concepts of *homeostasis* and *equilibrium* are central to general systems theory. They are more suited to explaining physical disease processes than emotional crisis, yet they are pivotal in much of crisis theory. Systems authority Ludwig von Bertalanffy (1968), a biologist, cites several limitations to the systems concept of homeostasis as applied in psychology and psychiatry. For example, homeostasis does not apply to processes of growth, development, creation, and the like (p. 210). Nor does it account for resilience as an innate capacity portending one's "promise" in addressing adversity versus passive acceptance of what appears on life's journey.

A homeostatic interpretation of the crisis experience implies that people in crisis are unable to take charge of their lives. People who accept this view of themselves when in crisis—that is, have a weak *internal locus of control*—will be less likely to participate actively in the crisis resolution process and will thereby diminish their potential for growth. General systems theory and the static concept of equilibrium comes from consensus theory in the social sciences, which states that people in disequilibrium are out of kilter in respect to both their personality and the social system; they are unbalanced rather than in the ideal state of equilibrium. When a system is in equilibrium, people and behavior fit according to established norms (*consensus*). Parsons's (1951) definition of the "sick role" as a state of "deviance" is one of the most classic and controversial examples of consensus theory (Levine & Kozloff, 1978). Systems theory appeals to our desire and need for precision and a sense of order in our lives. However, the reality of our lives and the world at large suggests that dynamic, interactional theories correspond more closely to the way people actually feel, think, behave, and make sense of the crises they experience. The concept of *chaos* (Ramsay, 1997), recognizes the complexity of the human condition. Its notion of sensitive dependence on initial conditions resonates with the concept of subjectivity and the need for reassessment during the chaos of the crisis experience.

Another major criticism of the concept of equilibrium in crisis theory is that it is reductionist. It attempts to explain a complex human phenomenon in the framework of a single discipline, psychology, whereas the explanation of human behavior demands more than psychological concepts. Existential philosophy, learning, and other humanistic frameworks are ignored by this deterministic notion borrowed from mathematics, engineering, and the natural sciences (McKinlay & Marceau, 1999; Weed, 1998). For example, how can the concept of equilibrium explain the different responses of people to the crises encountered in concentration camps and atomic bomb blasts or dislocation from wars of "ethnic cleansing"? Or after the death of a child, a parent's equilibrium may still waver at the thought of the tragic loss, yet a resilient parent may have resolved this crisis within a religious framework.

Still another problem with the concept of equilibrium in crisis theory is its implications for practice; for example, in attempts to help abused women in crisis (Bograd, 1984). A systems approach here implies the importance of keeping the family intact in spite of abuse and often with heavy reliance on psychotropic drugs. Chemical restoration of homeostasis with these drugs is common. Other rationales might explain the pervasive use of medication in crisis situations, yet attention to the theory underlying this practice might reduce this prevalent but misguided approach to upset people. Chemical tranquilization practiced without humanistic crisis intervention is related to *iatrogenesis*—that is, illness induced by physicians and other health providers (McKinlay, 1990). Indeed, general systems theory supports the notion that within the complementary health delivery and economic systems, budgets can be balanced and higher profits secured if a sufficient number of drugs (in addition to other technological devices) are sold, regardless of clinical contraindications for their use (Dubovsky & Dubovsky, 2007). Other frameworks, such as conflict and change theory, are needed to support the awareness and social action necessary to address some of these damaging practices in agencies serving distressed people.

In summary, since human beings are more than their bodies, one might ask: Why rely so heavily on natural science models when philosophy, the humanities, and political science are also available to help explain human behavior?

Community Mental Health

Caplan's concepts about crisis emerged during the same period in which the community mental health movement was born. An important influence on crisis intervention during this era was the 1961 report of the Congressional Joint Commission on Mental Illness and Health in the United States. This report, *Action for Mental Health*, laid the foundation for the community mental health movement in the United States. It documented, through 5 years of study, the crucial fact that people were not getting the help they needed, when they needed it, and where they needed it—close to their natural social setting. The report revealed that (1) people in crisis were tired of waiting lists, (2) professionals were tired of lengthy and expensive therapy that often did not help, (3) large numbers of people (42%) went initially to a physician or to clergy for any problem, (4) long years of training were not necessary to learn how to help distressed people, and (5) volunteers and community caretakers (for example, police officers, teachers, and ministers) were a large untapped source for helping people in distress.

One of the many recommendations in this report was that every community should have a local emergency mental health program. In 1963 and 1965, legislation made federal funds available to provide comprehensive mental health services through community mental health centers. Hansell (1976) refined many of the findings of Caplan, Tyhurst, military psychiatry, and community mental health studies into a systemwide response to the distressed person. His work is especially important to crisis workers in community mental health agencies and primary care settings, where many people in high-risk groups go for help. However, some communities still do not have comprehensive crisis programs. Even among those that do, emergency and other services are often far from ideal. Political and fiscal policies in recent decades resulted in further departures from community mental health ideals worldwide (Hoff, 1993; Marks & Scott, 1990). Reform movements in Canada, Europe, and the United States have attempted to reverse this trend (e.g., McKee, Ferlie, & Hyde, 2008; Mosher & Burti, 1994; Rachlis & Kushner, 1994).

Primary Health Care

Since the Alma Ata Declaration by the World Health Organization (WHO) in 1978, international and national agencies, both public and private, have committed themselves to the concept of primary health care as fundamental to the health status of citizens (U.S. Department of Health and Human Services, 2000). WHO's original declaration focuses on immunization, sanitation, nutrition, and maternal and child health, as well as on the economic, occupational, and educational underpinnings of health status, but health planners and policymakers are increasingly recognizing that mental health status is tied to socioeconomic and other macro factors affecting individuals in various population groups. One of the most serious implications of this interrelationship is the socioeconomic and cultural context in which violence is used as a response to individual and interpersonal stressors (Hoff, 2000). Fiscal constraints worldwide have forced even greater attention to the centrality of primary health care in various health reform efforts. However, despite savings in cost and human pain, crisis intervention as part of primary care is still not fully recognized for its contribution to preventing illness and maintaining health. In the United States, this can be traced in part to several historical themes: (1) the mind–body split in health practice, (2) an individual versus population-based focus in health service delivery, and (3) a bias against and disparity in health insurance coverage for those with mental or emotional illness (Hoff, 1993; Ustun, 1999). Australia, however, has integrated a mental health liaison team into its mainstream health system, including hospitals, general practice, and community support services such as police (Webster & Harrison, 2004).

Crisis Care and Psychiatric Stabilization

Similar to the growing emphasis on primary health care is the integration of crisis approaches on behalf of those suffering from acute psychotic episodes. Typically, such persons are seen in the crisis unit of community mental health centers or in the emergency service of general hospitals, where the emphasis is on triage and rapid disposition. Psychopharmacologic agents are often used to stabilize distressed people. The strong medical orientation in such units warrants greater caution than usual by providers to ensure that crisis intervention techniques are not supplanted rather than supplemented by chemical stabilization of acutely upset persons (Dubovsky & Dubovsky, 2007). When these units are not tightly integrated with other services, staff burnout and rapid turnover are two of the costly results. Ideally, all mental health staff should be trained in crisis intervention. Clark and Hughes (2002) note that staffing by psychiatric emergency nurses (PENs) increased interdisciplinary staff efficiency, as well as patient and family satisfaction. Similarly, initial emergency department treatment of acutely psychotic patients may affect future patient and staff attitudes—either inhibiting or enhancing the treatment process (Sturis, 2002).

Crisis Care and Chronic Problems

People with chronic problems (medical and psychiatric) are more vulnerable to crisis episodes in general, and their vulnerability is exacerbated by fiscal and other policies that have left thousands of seriously disturbed people without the mental health services they need after years of institutionalization (Hoff, 1993; Johnson, 1990; Perese, 1997). One result of these actions is that community-based crisis hotlines may serve by default as the routine support service to seriously disturbed people whose care is not always well coordinated among an array of agencies and providers. Another result is the expectation that primary care health providers offer the support and continued treatment needed by these individuals, whose mental status exacerbates their often precarious medical status. Routine training in crisis and psychosocial care for those serving this vulnerable population would prevent (1) a misuse of hotlines, (2) excessive prescription of psychotropic drugs by those without specialized psychiatric training, and (3) frequent readmissions to costly psychiatric services (Hoff & Morgan, in press). Frequently, crisis intervention programs lack outcome measures or an evaluation component, thereby shortchanging research. Use of the Comprehensive Mental Health Assessment (CMHA) tool with its Likert-like rating scale addresses some of these shortcomings (see Chapter 3).

Suicide Prevention and Other Specialized Crisis Services

Another influence to be noted is the suicide prevention movement. McGee (1974) has documented in detail the work of the Los Angeles Suicide Prevention Center and other groups in launching the suicide prevention and crisis intervention movement in the United States. The Los Angeles Suicide Prevention Center was born out of the efforts of Norman Farberow and Edwin Shneidman. In the late 1950s, these two psychologists led the movement by studying suicide notes. Through their many projects and those of numerous colleagues, suicide prevention and crisis centers were established throughout North America and Western Europe. The Samaritans, founded in 1953 in London by Chad Varah, and its counterpart, Befrienders International, are the most widespread and visible suicide prevention groups, with hundreds of branches in the United Kingdom and other countries. Another group, Lifeline Contact Teleministry (now Contact USA), was founded in 1963 in Sydney, Australia. Contact USA now has over 40 centers in 20 states, with 10,000 volunteers committed to a vision of reaching all who seek someone to listen, someone who cares.

The suicide prevention and crisis movement emerged in the United States during the decade when professional mental health workers had a mandate (Congressional Joint Commission on Mental Illness and Health, 1961) and massive federal funding to provide emergency services along with other mental health care. Remarkably, however, most crisis centers were staffed by volunteers and often were started by volunteer citizen groups, such as mental health or ministerial associations. Despite political and other controversy, there is now improved collaboration between volunteer and professionally staffed mental health agencies (Levine, 1981). Some crisis centers in the United States have shut down because of insufficient funds or inadequate leadership, and others have merged with community mental health programs. Still others have adapted and expanded their services or have begun new programs to meet the special needs of rape victims, abused children, runaway youths, battered women, or people with HIV-AIDS.

Currently, suicide prevention and crisis services exist in a variety of organizational frameworks. For example, many shelters for battered women that offer 24-hour telephone response and physical refuge avoid traditional hierarchies in favor of a collective structure. Regardless of the models used, however, every community should have a comprehensive crisis program, including mobile crisis services for suicide emergencies, discharged mental patients, and victims of violence (Ferris et al., 2003).

Increasing recognition of the need for comprehensive crisis services has resulted in some relief from the dichotomy in practice between traditional psychiatric emergency care and grassroots suicide prevention, along with other specialized crisis services. The separation and territorial conflicts between these two aspects of crisis service are at best artificial and at worst a disservice to people experiencing life crises or psychiatric emergencies, the boundaries of which often overlap. For example, if an abused woman in a refuge run by volunteers becomes suicidal or psychotic, staff members without crisis intervention training usually must call on psychiatric professionals for assistance. Conversely, a health or mental health professional treating a battered woman in a hospital emergency facility may compound the problem by exhibiting victim-blaming attitudes and practices.

Sociological Influences

Discussion of the evolution of crisis theory and practice thus far suggests that the momentum has come largely from psychological, psychiatric, or community sources. It is true that the strongest influences on crisis theory and practice have stressed individual rather than social aspects of crisis. Nevertheless, the relative neglect of social factors in crisis theory does not reflect their unimportance, but rather represents a serious omission. Caplan (1964, pp. 31–34) refers to the psychological, social, cultural, and material supplies necessary to maintain equilibrium and avoid crisis. Yet in practice, while acknowledging the place of social support in the crisis development and resolution process, most writers focus on reducing psychological tension and returning to precrisis equilibrium, without emphasizing how social factors influence these processes (see Chapter 5). Among earlier writers, psychiatrist Hansell (1976) has done the most to stress social influences on the development of crisis and its positive resolution, with particular application to the seriously and persistently mentally ill. His social-psychological approach to crisis theory and practice is explained further in Chapters 2 and 3, in concert with cross-cultural influences in the field.

Cross-Cultural Influences

Political, social, and technological developments have contributed to more permeable national boundaries and at the same time have sharpened cultural awareness, unique ethnic identities, and sensitivity to diversity issues. For instance, international relations are becoming more critical; refugees from war-torn countries are received in countries where the hosts may not know the refugees' language, and familiar supports are often minimal at best; cross-continental travel and communication are more accessible; gay, lesbian, bisexual, and transgendered activists have made visible the toll of discrimination on suicide rates among youth in this group. These observations have implications for cross-cultural and diversity issues in the experience of crisis, as well as the variance in response to distressed people. The rich data on rites of passage marking human transition states in traditional societies are another significant contribution of social anthropology to the understanding of life crises. These insights from other cultures are particularly relevant to crises around transition states, as discussed in Chapter 6. In North American society, distinct contributions to crisis theory from First Nations people, from immigrant ethnic groups, and from women have illuminated the significance of crises arising out of the social structure, associated values, and various discriminatory practices (see Chapter 2).

Key Concepts Regarding Diversity

Our sensitive application of insights from the social sciences (especially anthropology and sociology) rests on several key concepts underpinning crisis care with diverse groups. *Ethnicity* is tied to the notion of shared origin and culture. In multicultural societies such as the United States and Canada, ethnic identities can shift and change based on power distribution and factors like language, skin color, religion, or country of origin, while some groups may define themselves as *bicultural* within a dominant culture of a particular society (Loustaunau & Sobo, 1997). An internationally renowned cellist, Yo-Yo Ma (2008) said about his tricultural identity—French, Chinese, and American—"I explore what I don't understand."

Ethnocentrism is the emotional attitude that one's own ethnic group, nation, or culture is superior to that of others. Exaggerated ethnocentrism can lead to prejudice, bias, and discrimination toward others based on their ethnic identity, e.g., "Jews are greedy," or "Blacks are lazy," and "Mexicans are dirty" (see Chapter 4, Communication and Rapport, for ethnocentrism's influence on communication and empowerment in crisis care). *Stereotyping* refers to an unvarying pattern of thinking and pigeonholing a person or group in a box that does not allow for individuality, critical judgment, and basic respect for people different from ourselves—thus putting a damper on positive crisis care outcomes.

Cultural relativism is a more complex concept. It requires that instead of prejudging others, we consider various actions, beliefs, or traits within their cultural *context* in order to better understand them. Cultural relativism presents difficulties, however, especially in health care practice, in that some cultural practices may be harmful to physical and emotional health and welfare. It allows outsiders to ignore or dismiss certain human rights violations, such as woman battering, as "that's just part of their culture." A dramatic and controversial example illustrating cultural relativism is female genital mutilation, FGM, which in one folk language is called *tahara*, or "purity," implying that girls and women who have not undergone this procedure are "impure." Of particular significance here is that the WHO has defined FGM as a human rights violation. In both Canada and the United States, medical professionals can be charged with assault for performing FGM; furthermore, parents requesting the operation in the United States and Canada can be charged with aiding and abetting the assault. Based on the WHO definition, FGM is also grounds for claiming political asylum in some countries.

Commonalities and Cross-Cultural Differences in Crisis Care

These sociocultural concepts underscore two major points in the crisis experience and our goal of helping people in crisis across cultures:

1. No matter where we travel or whether we study or are fluent in another language, most of us will never completely understand or be comfortable except in our own ancestral culture with its values, beliefs, and so forth. This is generally true despite how much we might rail against and perhaps despise some aspects of our own cultural heritage. This speaks to the *positive* aspect of ethnocentrism—that is, the love of and adherence to our own culture as the presumed "best," at least for us in our particular here-and-now circumstances. Without such attachment to one's cultural heritage and some degree of ethnocentrism, we most likely would have global chaos, with masses of people rushing to reside in the perceived "best" culture. It also speaks to the "longing for home" that some refugees from war, torture, or natural disaster express in the safer haven of an adopted country.

2. Despite ethnocentrism and one's natural tendency to accept and adhere to our own cultural heritage (good and not so good), alongside the *distinctions* among the world's cultures, there obviously is much that we share with all members of the global community.

In crisis work, this is the juncture point that presents great challenges and involves a twofold task: (1) For the individual client encountered today or tomorrow, we must uncover what is *unique* about that person's *definition of and response to critical life events*. (2) Among the observations we make about this client, and without overgeneralizing, we must ascertain what she or he has *in common* with other people worldwide who have suffered a loss, serious illness, or catastrophic events such as torture or disaster.

This clinical challenge is magnified by the political, social, and technological developments that contribute to more permeable national boundaries today, and have their impact on particular individuals in distress or crisis. As if this were not enough, ethnic conflict and war leave many injured and homeless people who are forced into refugee status in foreign lands.

Currently a popular term in health and social science literature is the *cultural competence* required of providers to respond appropriately to the diverse clients seeking help in multicultural societies like the United Kingdom, Canada, and the United States. Such competency presents a daunting challenge for many providers who face a multitude of languages and belief systems among their clients. Instead of cultural competence, we prefer the phrase *cultural awareness and sensitivity* to diversity issues, because—as noted above—we can never be truly "competent" (i.e., well qualified or adequate) in any culture but our own. Regardless of terminology, most important in crisis care is to recognize the wisdom and clinical relevance of this *key principle* in working with anyone different from ourselves: Whatever our ethnic or cultural identity, we should never assume that—even with extensive study and exposure—we can ever be fully knowledgeable about people whose culture and beliefs are different from ours.

In other chapters we will illustrate with case examples what is *common* and what is *unique* among people cross-culturally in their response to critical life events. Our elaboration on this introduction will include assessment questions in Chapter 3 that do not presume upon a medicocentric approach to understanding and helping a distressed person whose beliefs about healing do not coincide with Western protocols (Dobkin de Rios, 2002; Fadiman, 1997; Loustanunau & Sobo, 1997; Kleinman et al., 1978; see also Pedersen et al., 1996).

Feminist and Victim/Survivor Influences

Women increasingly reject theories and practices that damage them outright or prevent their human growth and development (Boston Women's Health Book Collective, 2005; Mirkin, 1994). The influence of feminism on crisis theory has increased considerably, along with the growing literature on violence, as women and children are the primary objects of abuse worldwide (Hoff, 2000; Mawby & Walklate, 1994). In particular, feminist and complementary critical analysis reveals dramatically the intersection of violence, victimization, crisis, and suicide. Thus, although cross-cultural, ethnic, and feminist experiences are the newest in the historical development of contemporary crisis theory and practice, in a real sense they are also the oldest influences, as suggested earlier by the origins of crisis intervention. We thus come full circle in this historical review, but the value and urgency of feminist and human rights activism are more relevant than ever when observing, for example, that rape of women and girls as the "spoils of war" over many centuries continues unabated during current wars.

Life Crises: A Psychosociocultural Perspective

Our review of the diverse sources of crisis theory and practice suggests that understanding and helping people in crisis is a complex, interdisciplinary endeavor. Because human beings encompass physical, emotional, social, and spiritual functions, no one theory is adequate to explain the crisis experience, its origins, or the most effective approach to helping people in crisis.

Accordingly, this book draws on insights, concepts, and strategies from psychology, nursing, sociology, psychiatry, anthropology, philosophy, political science, and critical analysis to propose a dynamic theory and practice framework emphasizing the following:[2]

- Individual, social, cultural, and material origins of crisis
- Development of the psychological crisis state
- Emotional, behavioral, and cognitive manifestations of crisis

---

[2] The late Sol Levine, a medical sociologist, referred to this approach as "creative integrationism," not to be confused with superficial eclecticism (personal communication, 1983).

- Interactive relationships among stress, crisis, and illness (physical and mental)
- Issues involved and skills needed to deal with transition states, suicidal crises, violence against others, and disaster
- Resolution of crises by use of psychological, social, material, and cultural resources
- Collaboration among the person or family in crisis and various significant others in the positive resolution of crisis
- The global social-political task of reducing the crisis vulnerability of various disadvantaged groups through social change strategies and advocacy for health in a public health and human rights framework

These elements of crisis theory and practice are illustrated relationally in the Crisis Paradigm (Figure 1.1) as a preview of Chapter 2. The Crisis

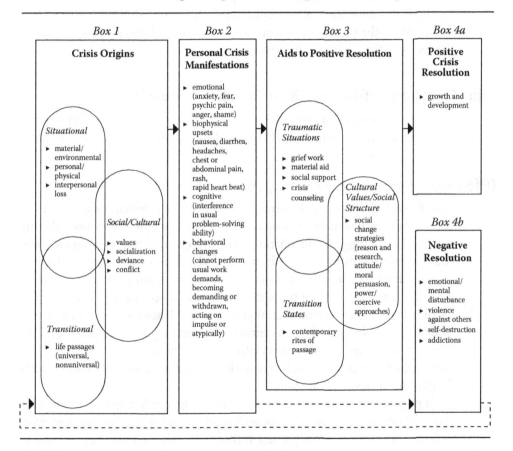

FIGURE 1.1 Crisis Paradigm. Crisis origins, manifestations, and outcomes and the respective functions of crisis care have interactional relationships. The intertwined circles represent the distinct yet interrelated origins of crisis and aids to positive resolution, even though personal manifestations are often similar. The arrows pointing from origins to positive resolution illustrate the *opportunity for growth and development* through crisis. The broken line at the bottom depicts the potential *danger of crisis* in the absence of appropriate aids. The loop between Box 4b and Box 1 denotes the *vulnerability* to future crisis episodes following negative resolution.

Paradigm depicts (1) the *crisis process* experienced by the distressed person from origin through resolution and (2) the place of natural and formal crisis intervention in promoting growth and avoiding negative crisis outcomes. This paradigm draws on research and clinical experience with survivors of violence (Hoff, 1990), other life event research (for example, Antonovsky, 1980), and work with survivors of man-made disasters. The inclusion of sociocultural origins of crisis extends the traditional focus of crisis intervention to situational and developmental life events, a framework found inadequate to guide practice with people intentionally injured through violence, prejudice, neglect, or disaster.

The paradigm suggests a tandem approach to crisis care—that is, attending to the immediate problem while not losing sight of the social change and public health strategies needed to address the complex sociocultural origins of certain crisis situations. This psychosociocultural perspective serves as the framework for examining life crisis situations throughout this book. Concepts in the paradigm that are shaded in other chapters depict a particular focus in the crisis care process.

Crisis Care: Intersection with Other Therapeutic Models

Approaches to crisis intervention used by helpers will vary according to their exposure to historical influences, their values, and their professional preparation in various disciplines.

Differentiating Approaches to Helping People in Distress

The following discussion illustrates the differences, overlap, and similarities among approaches to assist people who are acutely upset or emotionally disturbed. It also suggests the relationship between crisis intervention and other ways of helping distressed people, some of whom suffer serious mental illness.

Certainly, we should not regard crisis intervention as a panacea for all social, emotional, and mental problems. While crisis care is not synonymous with psychotherapy, some techniques, such as listening and catharsis, are used in both. Nor is crisis intervention intended only for poor people, reserving psychotherapy for the financially secure. The occurrence of crisis does not depend on a person's socioeconomic status, and crisis intervention can be helpful regardless of that status.

It may be just as damaging to use a crisis intervention approach when it is inapplicable as *not* to use the approach when it does apply. For example, when suicide and crisis hotlines are not linked with other mental health services, there can be negative side effects, sometimes referred to as "systems problems." Callers seeking help from crisis centers know that they must at least *act* as though they are in crisis in order to get attention and help. Thus, some callers may appear to be in crisis when they are not. For example, a person who is crying may or may not be in crisis. Judgment of crisis should be based on assessment of the person's total situation.

If workers are unskilled in crisis assessment, they may unwittingly encourage crisis-like behavior by discounting what distressed people say—much as the little boy crying wolf in the fable was discounted because he had cried wolf so many times when there was no wolf that no one believed him when there was. In other words, if workers assume that a person is exaggerating or pretending—crying wolf—and therefore fail to accurately assess the situation through questioning, they could miss the real and urgent message the person is trying to convey. Suicide or violence toward others may be the unfortunate outcome.

Table 1.1 illustrates the range of services and differences among various services available to people with psychosocial problems or psychiatric illness. Crisis care is just one of the many services people need. Effective crisis intervention can be an important link to a person's acceptance of a referral for psychotherapy. This is because during crisis, people are more likely than at other times to consider getting help for chronic problems that made them crisis prone in the first place. Crisis intervention is also a significant means of avoiding last-resort measures such as institutional care. Crisis approaches, although necessary, are usually insufficient for people with serious mental and social disabilities. Such individuals need long-term rehabilitation programs as well, including, for example, training for jobs, instruction in home management, and support in transitional facilities such as the Fountain House model (Cella, Besancon, & Zipple, 1997; Johnson, 1990).

The limitations of crisis intervention and the need to see it in a larger sociocultural and political perspective are dramatically illustrated in the following vignette. McKinlay (1990, p. 502) discusses the "manufacture of illness" and the futility of tinkering with "downstream" versus "upstream" endeavors:

> My friend, Irving Zola, relates the story of a physician trying to explain the dilemmas of the modern practice of medicine: "You know," he said, "sometimes it feels like this. There I am standing by the shore of a swiftly flowing river and I hear the cry of a drowning man. So, I jump into the river, put my arms around him, pull him to shore and apply artificial respiration. Just when he begins to breathe, another cry for help. So back in the river again, reaching, pulling, applying, breathing and then another yell. Again and again, without end, goes the sequence. You know, I am so busy jumping in, pulling them to shore, applying artificial respiration, that I have no time to see who the hell is upstream pushing them all in."

This story underscores the need for crisis practitioners to take the time to consider their work in a broader "upstream" public health perspective, not only for the sake of people in crisis but also to prevent burnout and a loss of meaning in their work. Within the array of services available to distressed people, the different helping modes obviously overlap (see Table 1.1).

But charts and models are intended to clarify points in theoretical discussion rather than represent an exact picture of reality. Also, while the Crisis Paradigm presented in this book is strongly linked to public and community

TABLE 1.1   Comparison of Therapies and the Crisis Intervention Model

Psychotherapy	Medical-Institutional Therapy	Social-Service Rehabilitation Therapy	Crisis Intervention
Type of People Served			
Those who wish to correct neurotic personality or behavior patterns	People with serious mental or emotional breakdowns	Those who are chronically disabled	Individuals and families in crisis or precrisis states
Service Goals			
Work through unconscious conflicts	Manage, adjust, stabilize	Rehabilitation; return to normal functioning in society insofar as possible	Promote growth
Reconstruct behavior and personality patterns	Recover from acute disturbance		Promote personal and social integration
Grow personally and socially			
Service Methods			
Introspection	Medication	Work training	Social and environmental manipulation
Catharsis	Behavior modification	Resocialization	
Interpretation	Electric shock	Training in activities of daily living	Focus on feelings and problem solving
Free association	Group activities	Peer and counselor support and advocacy	Possible use of medication to promote goals
(Use of additional techniques depends on philosophy and training of therapist.)	(Use of additional techniques depends on philosophy of institution.)		Decision counseling
Activity of Workers			
Exploratory	Direct, noninvolved or indirect	Structured but less so than in crisis intervention	Active/direct (depends on functional level of client)
Nondirective interpretive			
Length of Service			
Usually long term	Short or long term (depends on degree of disability and approach of psychiatrist)	Long term—a few months to 2–3 years	Short term—usually 6 sessions or fewer
	High repeat rate		
Beliefs About People			
Individualistic or social (depends on philosophy of therapist)	Individualistic—social aspect secondary	Hopeful—people can change	Social—people are capable of growth and self-mastery
	Institutional needs and order may overshadow the needs of people	Mental disability or a diagnosis should not spell hopelessness	

Psychotherapy	Medical-Institutional Therapy	Social-Service Rehabilitation Therapy	Crisis Intervention
Attitudes toward Service			
Emphasis on wisdom of therapist and 50-minute hour	Scheduled	Willingness to stick with it and observe only slow change	Flexible, any hour
	Staff attitudes may become rigid and institutionalized		
Flexibility varies with individual therapist		Hopefulness and expectation of goal achievement	

services, the intervention strategies outlined can be applied using telephone, face-to-face, and outreach modes in various settings: homes in different cultural milieus, primary care clinics, hospitals, and social agencies. In spite of hazy boundaries between crisis and other service models, there are fundamental differences among their purposes and assumptions about people needing help. For example, in the biomedical model, intervention consists of treatment directed toward cure or alleviation of symptoms of a person presumed ill or diseased. The focus is on the *individual*, who is generally assumed to harbor the source of difficulty within himself or herself (Barney, 1994). In contrast, the crisis model proposed in this book is embedded in the public health perspective and therefore stresses the following:

- Social, cultural, and environmental factors in addition to personal origins of crisis
- Prevention of destructive crisis outcomes such as suicide or mental breakdown (or if psychopathology was present prior to the crisis, the prevention of further breakdown and chronic psychopathology)
- Psychosocial growth and development as the ideal outcome of crisis—a possibility greatly enhanced through social support, environmental factors, and other crisis care strategies

Prevention strategies are usually associated conceptually with public health and primary care models. In growth and development theory, the term *enhancement* is preferred for describing preventive activities that promote health and development. Until recently, relatively little theorizing and research have gone into positive psychology. However, it has become clearer to many clinicians that normal and supernormal functioning cannot be understood within a purely problem-oriented framework. The resulting shift in emphasis is toward a set of assumptions and attributions about health, motivation, and the strengths perspective, including a person's capacity and potential for healthy social functioning (Strumpfer, 2006). These concepts are considered together in the next section, on the assumption that crisis intervention is relevant for preventing disease (and other negative outcomes) as well as for enhancing the growth, development, and resilience of individuals and, by extension, the health status of population groups (Gitterman, 2001).

Crisis Prevention and Promoting Emotional Growth and Resilience

Viewing crisis as both an opportunity and a danger means that knowing what lies ahead can allow us to prepare for normal life events and usually prevent the development of crises. For many people, however, these normal events do lead to hazard or danger rather than to opportunity. Although we cannot predict events such as the sudden death of a loved one, the birth of a premature child, or natural disaster, we can anticipate how people will react to them. In his study of survivors of the Cocoanut Grove fire, Lindemann (1944) demonstrated the importance of recognizing crisis responses and preventing negative outcomes of crisis. Once a population or individual is identified as being at risk of crisis, we can use a number of time-honored approaches to prevent crisis and enhance growth.

Primary Prevention and Enhancement

Primary prevention, in the form of education, consultation, and crisis intervention, is designed to reduce the occurrence of mental disability and promote growth, development, and crisis resistance in a community. There are several means of doing this:

1. *Eliminate or modify the hazardous situation.* The practice of immunizing children against smallpox and diphtheria, for example, is based on the fact that failure to immunize can expose large numbers of people to the hazards of disease. Knowledge of sociopsychological hazards should inspire similar efforts to eliminate or modify these hazards. For example, we can alter hospital structures and practices to reduce the risk of crisis for hospitalized children and adults, eliminate substandard housing for crisis-prone older people and others disadvantaged by poverty, and educate people about the nature and effects of these hazards.

2. *Reduce exposure to hazardous situations.* For example, a flood warning allows people to escape disaster. In the psychosocial sphere, crisis prevention includes advising and screening people entering potentially stressful situations such as college, an unusual occupation such as working in a foreign country, or a demanding occupation such as nursing, policing, and fire fighting. Many colleges offer seminars to help new students adapt to college life and alert them to dangers such as substance abuse and sexual assault, which are common in the first year. With respect to the AIDS pandemic, education and physical and psychosocial preventive practices must be combined (see Chapter 7).

3. *Reduce vulnerability by increasing coping ability.* In the physical health sector, people with certain diseases are directed to obtain extra rest, eat certain foods, and take prescribed medicines. In the psychosocial

sphere, older people, the poor, and refugees are most often exposed to the risk of urban or homeland dislocation. Extra physical resources, social services, and social action skills can counter the negative social and emotional effects of hazardous situations like ethnic conflict in a housing complex. New parents will feel less vulnerable and less prone to abuse or neglect if they are prepared for the challenge of rearing their first child or one with special needs. Programs such as the Childrens' Trust Fund in Boston reduce vulnerability in children by teaching them about inappropriate touching, e.g., what's covered by a bathing suit and their right to privacy. Marriage, retirement, or geographical relocation are other important life transitions that we can prepare for so that they become occasions for continued growth rather than deterioration.

The success of anticipatory preventive measures for target groups is heavily influenced by a person's resilience, openness to learning, cultural values, previous problem-solving success, and general social supports. Anticipatory prevention is similar to the developmental notion of using education to assist people at risk to better handle stressful life events.

When hazardous events or a person's vulnerability to events cannot be accurately predicted or when people are unable to respond to generic, anticipatory prevention, participatory techniques are indicated for the person or family in crisis (Caplan, 1974). These involve a thorough psychosocial assessment and counseling of individuals or families by skilled crisis workers, as elaborated in later chapters. In developmental frameworks, the individual and the family participate actively in resolving the crisis. Such active participation assumes the basic human need for self-determination and the importance of providers' avoiding rescue pitfalls.

Secondary Prevention

The term *secondary prevention* implies that some form of mental disability has already occurred because of the absence of primary activities or because a person is unable to profit from those activities. The aim of secondary prevention is to shorten the duration of disability, often by providing sustained support and easy access to crisis services. If such services are offered, emotionally disturbed and mentally ill people may not need psychiatric hospitalization. Veterans suffering from physical and psychic war trauma need ready access to services to prevent long-term disabling effects or suicide. The disabling effects of institutional life and the increased cost are thereby avoided, as are the destructive results of removal from one's natural community. Because mentally disturbed individuals are more crisis prone than others, they need more active help during crisis than others might. When psychiatric inpatient treatment is necessary, premature discharge on financial grounds is usually counterproductive; it defeats therapeutic goals and sets in motion a vicious cycle of repeat hospital admissions. The thousands of homeless mentally ill persons illustrate this principle.

Tertiary Prevention

The goal of *tertiary prevention* is to reduce long-term disabling effects for those who are recovering from a mental disorder. Social and rehabilitation programs are an important means of helping these people return to former social and occupational roles or learn new ones. Crisis intervention is also important for the same reasons noted in the discussion of secondary prevention. The recovery process includes learning new ways of coping with stress through positive crisis resolution. Thus, even if the precrisis state is one of mental disability, it is never too late to learn new coping devices, as implied in a growth-and-development model.

Crisis Services in a Continuum Perspective

Anticipatory and participatory techniques can be viewed as a continuum of services for people with different kinds of psychosocial problems or mental illness (see Figure 1.2). The continuum suggests that people with problems vary in their dependency on other people and agencies for help. It also illustrates the economic implications of crisis intervention in addition to its clinical and humanistic benefits. However, in the United States, health and human service workers trying to implement community-based crisis approaches in their individual practices are often frustrated by insurance reimbursement policies that underscore disparities in coverage for those needing mental health care (Sabin, 2000).

The five essential services illustrated in the continuum were originally mandated by the Community Mental Health Acts of 1963 and 1965 in the United States. Later federal guidelines for basic services include rehabilitation, addiction services, victim services, specialized services for the elderly and children, and evaluation programs, although policy decisions have curtailed many of these programs. Crisis intervention is now considered a key part of these mental health and social services.

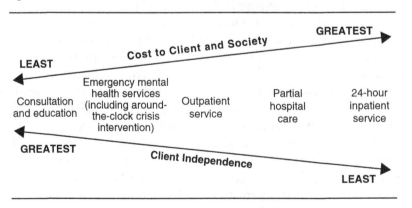

FIGURE 1.2 Continuum of Mental Health Services: Cost and Client Independence. Assisting distressed people in their natural social roles (homemaker, paid worker, student) through consultation, education, and crisis services is the *least* costly means of service and allows the *greatest* client independence; institution-based care is the *most* costly means and allows the *least* client independence.

Among the crisis intervention approaches and settings encompassed in this continuum, consultation and education come under the general umbrella of primary prevention and enhancement. Twenty-four-hour crisis services can also be seen as primary prevention, depending on the precrisis state of the individual in crisis. Emergency mental health is most closely related to traditional psychiatry and the management of behavioral emergencies in hospital settings (Goldman, 2000), which ideally should be linked to crisis and suicide prevention agencies. Outpatient care, partial hospital care, and 24-hour inpatient care (residential) services incorporate crisis intervention while focusing on underlying emotional and mental disorders (that is, secondary and tertiary prevention).

To underscore the social and cultural concepts central to the Crisis Paradigm presented here and to affirm current emphasis on community-based crisis intervention, let us consider the economy of crisis intervention in the home and its smooth linkage to other elements of comprehensive service.

For a person already in crisis, admission to a hospital for the purpose of receiving help during the crisis can itself be a hazardous event. Polak (1967) illustrated this fact in his study of 104 men admitted to a psychiatric hospital in Scotland. Polak found that these men or their families had typically requested psychiatric hospital admission following previous unresolved crises around separation, physical illness, death, and migration. However, although it offered temporary relief, admission also was frequently the occasion for another crisis because family patterns of interaction were disrupted, and the patient and the family often had disturbing and unrealistic fantasies and expectations about the purpose and meaning of hospitalization. Now, with some premature insurance-driven discharges, other crises are precipitated (Johnson, 1990).

Hansell (1976) notes how inviting a hospital environment seems to a person deprived of normal community supports. Hospitalization can also be misused by families who lack personal and social resources for relating to disturbed members. Hansell suggests that crisis can just as well lead to improved friendships as to "asylum" (see also Scott, 2000.) However, in the United States, a much publicized dramatic swing of the pendulum has occurred as a result of failed policies around "deinstitutionalization." The original goal was to provide community-based services for the mentally ill and use psychiatric hospitalization only when there was serious danger of suicide or homicide and cognitive impairment resulting in life-threatening neglect of basic self-care due to serious mental illness with which a family member could no longer cope. A key factor in this failed policy is that money (public funding of mental health services) did not follow the discharged patients to the community. The tragic result is confinement of thousands of mentally ill persons to the street, jails, and prisons under deplorable conditions (Early, 2006).

Research thus not only supports the hazards of being uprooted from natural social settings but also provides a sober reminder of this social reality: agencies are indeed subcultures of the larger society in which crisis intervention by family members, friends, and neighbors is an everyday occurrence.

This does not preclude the need for formal crisis intervention by persons specially trained for this task. Rather, it highlights the fact that the prospects for positive crisis resolution by individuals, families, and peer groups are enhanced and negative complications are reduced when formal crisis care occurs as close as possible to natural settings. It also means that when crisis assessment reveals the need for psychiatric in-patient treatment, the crisis worker and family members should not be burdened with insurance and other obstacles such as Pete Early (2006) encountered in trying to get help for his son stricken by a serious mental illness. These points are illustrated in the following account of a counselor doing crisis work in a home.

Case Example: Ray

Last week, another counselor and I made a home visit to a family that was very upset because the parents thought their 22-year-old son Ray had "flipped out" on drugs. The parents had called with the express purpose of getting their son into psychiatric hospital care, even though he had refused to go before. I had said when they called that we would not automatically put Ray in the hospital but that we would come over to assess the situation and help the entire family through the crisis. We worked out a strategy for telling Ray directly and clearly the reasons for our visit. Ray refused to come to the phone, shouting, "They're the people who will take me to the hospital in an ambulance." When we got there, a family session revealed that Ray was the scapegoat for many other family problems. We worked out a crisis service plan, and Ray started to show some trust in us after about two hours with the whole family. He could see that we didn't just come to whisk him off to a mental hospital. In the end, even Ray's family was relieved that he didn't have to go to the hospital. Before our home visit, they had seen no other way out. They had talked with several therapists before, but no one had ever come to the house or worked with the whole family.

Although psychiatric hospital treatment is necessary in some cases, its cost in both human and economic terms may be even greater if discharge is premature and community and family supports are inadequate. Besides people like Ray, many patients with first-episode psychosis can be successfully helped by an intensive home treatment team (Tomar, Brimblecombe, & Sullivan, 2003). Figure 1.3 illustrates these points and contrasts medical and developmental approaches in an acute situation like that of Ray and his family. We believe the prognosis for Ray is more positive with a growth and development approach. In the event that psychotropic medication is indicated, the long-term results will almost certainly be enhanced if used in combination with crisis counseling, an intensive home treatment plan, and possibly rehabilitation services (Dubovsky & Dubovsky, 2007; Tomar, Brimblecombe, & O'Sullivan, 2003).

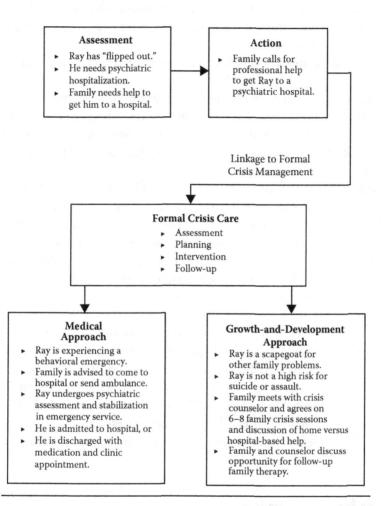

Natural Crisis Care

Assessment
▸ Ray has "flipped out."
▸ He needs psychiatric hospitalization.
▸ Family needs help to get him to a hospital.

Action
▸ Family calls for professional help to get Ray to a psychiatric hospital.

Linkage to Formal Crisis Management

Formal Crisis Care
▸ Assessment
▸ Planning
▸ Intervention
▸ Follow-up

Medical Approach
▸ Ray is experiencing a behavioral emergency.
▸ Family is advised to come to hospital or send ambulance.
▸ Ray undergoes psychiatric assessment and stabilization in emergency service.
▸ He is admitted to hospital, or
▸ He is discharged with medication and clinic appointment.

Growth-and-Development Approach
▸ Ray is a scapegoat for other family problems.
▸ Ray is not a high risk for suicide or assault.
▸ Family meets with crisis counselor and agrees on 6–8 family crisis sessions and discussion of home versus hospital-based help.
▸ Family and counselor discuss opportunity for follow-up family therapy.

FIGURE 1.3 Natural and Formal Crisis Care. The medical approach is compared with the growth-and-development approach to formal crisis care.

Basic Steps in Crisis Care

Because of the emotional pain of crisis, resolution will occur with or without the assistance of others. Crisis intervention can be carried out in a variety of settings, some natural, some institutional. Regardless of the context or variations in personal style, the probability of positive crisis outcomes is greatly enhanced by attention to the basic steps of crisis care. These steps include the following:

1. Psychosocial assessment of the individual or family crisis, including evaluation of victimization trauma and the risk of suicide or assault on others[3]
2. Development of a plan with the person or family in crisis
3. Implementation of the plan, drawing on personal, social, and material resources
4. Follow-up and evaluation of the crisis intervention process and outcomes

The example of Ray and his family illustrates these steps.

Broadly these basic steps of crisis care correspond to the problem-solving process used in medical, nursing, and social work practice, as well as in other human service protocols. The example of Ray and his family illustrates both "natural" crisis intervention as employed by his family, as well as a formal, structured process (see Crisis Paradigm, Figure 1.1). It underscores the fact that everyone recognizes when someone is "crazy," that is, not acting according to commonly accepted social norms. Assessment of this situation revealed the family's inability to handle the crisis alone. They managed the crisis by calling for and receiving professional help. In sharp contrast, Pete Early's son landed in the criminal justice system, explicitly traceable to denial of the psychiatric treatment he needed. (See Chapter 12 for further discussion of violence and the mentally ill.)

A focus on early intervention and prevention of negative outcomes would include providing the average person, through public education programs, with more skills in detecting victimization and suicide or assault potential, as well as in assessing the advantages and limits of psychiatric hospitalization. Professional providers would then be less likely to simply discount what people in crisis say. After all, professional assessments must, in the end, rely on data presented by the traumatized, suicidal, or disturbed person, the family, police, and other laypersons.

Standards for Crisis Services

The importance of basic principles of crisis care was highlighted in 1976 by the launching of a program in the United States to certify comprehensive crisis services, including community-based agencies and programs in hospitals or community mental health centers. This program was developed by the American Association of Suicidology (AAS), a standard-setting body for suicide prevention and crisis services (Hoff & Wells, 1989). In an age when consumers are increasingly conscious of the quality of service they receive, certification is a step in the direction of ensuring such quality. (See Online Resources for further information regarding crisis training and service standards.)

---

[3] Some health professionals may wish to include a diagnosis following this step. See Chapter 3 on diagnosis and labeling theory.

Summary and Discussion Questions

The development of crisis theory and practice has sprung from diverse sources in the health field and social sciences. Approaches to crisis intervention vary with the needs of the person in crisis and the training and experience of helpers. Preventing crises, especially the negative outcomes of crises, is central to the approach of this book. Formal crisis care consists of four steps—assessment, planning, intervention, and follow-up—carried out in a psychosociocultural framework. The development of national standards for crisis services and workers attests to the growing maturity of formal crisis intervention as a recognized field grounded in knowledge and practice.

1. Considering the origins of crisis theory and practice, discuss the relevance of an historical perspective regarding current critical events in one global community.
2. How does *resilience* differ from a "stiff upper lip" approach to life's hazards and misfortunes?
3. Identify an example of using both "at-risk" and "at promise" factors in helping a person in distress.
4. Using a personal or professional example, compare and contrast contemporary crisis care practice with the claim that it is essentially an interdisciplinary service model requiring teamwork.

References

Antonovsky, A. (1980). *Health, stress, and coping.* San Francisco: Jossey-Bass.

Antonovsky, A. (1987). *Unraveling the mystery of health: How people manage stress and stay well.* San Francisco: Jossey-Bass.

Barney, K. (1994). Limitations of the critique of the medical model. *Journal of Mind and Behavior, 15*(1, 2), 19–34.

Bertalanffy, L. von. (1968). *General systems theory* (Rev. ed.). New York: Braziller.

Bograd, M. (1984). Family systems approaches to wife battering: A feminist critique. *American Journal of Orthopsychiatry, 54*(4), 558–568.

Boston Women's Health Book Collective. (2005). *Our bodies, ourselves: A new edition for a new era.* New York: Simon & Schuster.

Brandt, A. M., & Gardner, M. (2000). Antagonism and accommodation: Interpreting the relationship between public health and medicine in the United States during the 20th century. *American Journal of Public Health, 90*(5), 707–715.

Brendtro, L., Brokenleg, M., & Van Bockern, S. (1990). *Reclaiming youth at risk.* Bloomington, IN: National Educational Service.

Caplan, G. (1964). *Principles of preventive psychiatry.* New York: Basic Books.

Caplan, G. (1974). *Support systems and community mental health.* New York: Behavioral Publications.

Caplan, G. (1981). Mastery of stress: Psychosocial aspects. *American Journal of Psychiatry, 138*(4), 413–420.

Cella, E. P., Besancon, V., & Zipple, A. M. (1997). Expanding the role of clubhouses: Guidelines for establishing a system of integrated day services. *Psychiatric Rehabilitation Journal, 21*(1), 10–15.

Clark, D., & Hughes, L. (2002). Psychiatric nurses in hospital emergency departments. *Canadian Nurse, 98*(10), 23–26.

Collishawa, S., Pickles, A., Messer, J., Rutter, M., Shearer, C., & Maughana, B. (2005). Resilience to adult psychopathology following childhood maltreatment: Evidence from a community sample. *Child Abuse & Neglect, 31,* 211–229.

Congressional Joint Commission on Mental Illness and Health. (1961). *Action for mental health.* New York: Basic Books.

Dobkin de Rios, M. (2002). What we can learn from shamanic healing: Brief psychotherapy with Latino immigrants. *American Journal of Public Health, 92*(10), 1576–1578.

Dubovsky, S. L., & Dubovsky, A. N (2007). *Psychotropic drug prescriber's survival guide: Ethical mental health treatment in the age of Big Pharma.* New York: W.W. Norton.

Early, P. (2006). *Crazy: A father's search through America's mental health madness.* New York: Berkley Books.

Erikson, E. (1963). *Childhood and society* (2nd ed.). New York: Norton.

Fadiman, A. (1997). *The spirit catches you and you fall down.* New York: The Noonday Press, Farrar, Straus and Giroux.

Farmer, P. (1999). Pathologies of power: Rethinking health and human rights. *American Journal of Public Health, 89*(10), 1486–1496.

Ferris, L., De Siato, C., Sandercock, J., Williams, J., & Shulman, K. (2003). A descriptive analysis of two mobile crisis programs for client with severe mental illness. *Canadian Journal of Public Health, 94*(3), 233–237.

Fromm, E. (1941). *Escape from freedom.* Austin, TX: Holt, Rinehart, and Winston.

Gitterman, A. (2001). Social work practice with vulnerable and resilient populations. In A. Gitterman (Ed.), *Handbook of social work practice with vulnerable and resilient populations* (2nd ed., pp. 1–36). New York: Columbia University Press.

Glass, A. T (1957). Observations upon the epidemiology of mental illness in troops during warfare. In *Symposium on prevention and social psychiatry.* Washington, DC: Walter Reed Army Institute of Research and the National Research Council.

Goldman, H. H. (2000). *Review of general psychiatry* (5th ed.). New York: Lange Medical Books and McGraw-Hill.

Hansell, N. (1976). *The person in distress.* New York: Human Sciences Press.

Hoff, L. A. (1990). *Battered women as survivors.* London: Routledge.

Hoff, L. A. (1993). Review essay: Health policy and the plight of the mentally ill. *Psychiatry, 56*(4), 400–419.

Hoff, L. A. (2000). Interpersonal violence. In C. E. Koop, C. E. Pearson, & M. R. Schwarz (Eds.), *Critical issues in global health* (pp. 260–271). San Francisco: Jossey-Bass.

Hoff, L. A., & Morgan, B. (in press). *Psychiatric and mental health essentials in primary care.*

Hoff, L. A., & Wells, J. O. (Eds.). (1989). *Certification standards manual* (4th ed.). Denver: American Association of Suicidology.

Hoff, M. (2005). *Resilience: A paradigm of promise.* Unpublished master's thesis. Fargo: North Dakota State University, Department of Counselor Education.

Johnson, A. B. (1990). *Out of bedlam: The truth about deinstitutionalization.* New York: Basic Books.

Kaminsky, M., McCabe, O. L., Langlieb, A. M., & Everly, G. S. (2007). An evidence-informed model of human resistance, resilience, and recovery: The Johns Hopkins' outcome-driven paradigm for disaster mental health services. *Brief Treatment and Crisis Intervention, 7*(1), 1–11.

Kleinman, A. et al. (1978). Culture, illness, and care: Clinical lessons from anthropologic and cross-cultural research. *Annals of Internal Medicine*, 88.

Levine, M. (1981). *The history and politics of community mental health.* New York: Oxford University Press.

Levine, S., & Kozloff, M. A. (1978). The sick role: Assessment and overview. *Annual Review of Sociology, 4*, 317–343.

Lindemann, E. (1944). Symptomatology and management of acute grief. *American Journal of Psychiatry, 101*, 101–148. [Reprinted in H. J. Parad (Ed.), *Crisis intervention: Selected readings.* (1965). New York: Family Service Association of America.]

Loustaunau, M. O., & Sobo, E. J. (1997). *The cultural context of health, illness, and healing.* Westport, CT: Bergin & Garvey.

Marks, I., & Scott, R. (Eds.). (1990). *Mental health care delivery: Innovations, impediments and implementation.* Cambridge: Cambridge University Press.

Marshall, K. (2001). Bridging the resilience gap: Research and practice. Retrieved February 7, 2005 from http://www.cce.umn.edu/pdfs/nrrc/capt pdf/bridge.pdg.

Maslow, A. (1970). *Motivation and personality* (2nd ed.). New York: HarperCollins.

Mawby, R. I., & Walklate, S. (1994). *Critical victimology.* Thousand Oaks, CA: Sage.

McGee, R. K. (1974). *Crisis intervention in the community.* Baltimore, MD: University Park Press.

McKee, L., Ferlie, E., & Hyde, P. (2008). Organizing and reorganizing: Power and change in health care organizations. Houndmills, Basingstoke, Hampshire, U.K.: Palgrave MacMillan.

McKinlay, J. B. (1990). A case for refocusing upstream: The political economy of illness. In P. Conrad & R. Kern (Eds.), *The sociology of health and illness: Critical perspectives* (3rd ed., pp. 502–516). New York: St. Martin's Press.

McKinlay, J. B., & Marceau, L. D. (1999). A tale of three tails. *American Journal of Public Health, 89*(3), 295–298.

Mirkin, M. P. (Ed.). (1994). *Women in context: Toward a feminist reconstruction of psychotherapy.* New York: Guilford Press.

Mosher, L. R., & Burti, L. (1994). *Community mental health: A practical guide.* New York: Norton.

Parsons, T. (1951). Social structure and the dynamic process: The case of modern medical practice. In *The social system* (pp. 428–479). New York: Free Press.

Pedersen, P. B., Draguns, J. G., Lonner, W. J., & Trimble, J. E. (Eds.). (1996). *Counseling across cultures.* Thousand Oaks, CA: Sage Publications.

Perese, E. F. (1997). Unmet needs of persons with chronic mental illnesses: Relationship to their adaptation to community living. *Issues in Mental Health Nursing, 18*(1), 19–34.

Polak, P. (1967). The crisis of admission. *Social Psychiatry, 2*, 150–157.

Rachlis, M., & Kushner, C. (1994). *Strong medicine: How to save Canada's health care system.* New York: HarperCollins.

Ramsay, R. (1997). Chaos theory and crisis intervention: Toward a new meaning of equilibrium in understanding and helping people in crisis. *Child and Family, 1*(3), 23–35.

Roberts, A. R. & Everly, G. S. (2006). A meta-analysis of 36 crisis intervention studies. *Brief Treatment and Crisis Intervention, 6*, 10–21.

Rodriguez-Garcia, R., & Akhter, M. N. (2000). Human rights: The foundation of public health practice. *American Journal of Public Health, 90*(5), 693–694.

Sabin, J. E. (2000). Managed care and health care reform: Comedy, tragedy, and lessons. *Psychiatric Services, 51*(11), 1392–1396.

Sanders, S. (2008). Understanding resilience. New York: Routledge.

Scheper-Hughes, N., & Lovell, A. M. (1986). Breaking the circuit of social control: Lessons in public psychiatry from Italy and Franco Basaglia. *Social Science and Medicine, 23*(2), 159–178.

Scott, R. L. (2000). Evaluation of a mobile crisis program: Effectiveness, efficiency, and consumer satisfaction. *Psychiatric Services 51*(9), 1153–1156.

Strumpfer, D. J. W. (2006). The strengths perspective: Fortigenesis in adult life. *Social Indicators Research, 77,* 11–36.

Sturis, I. (2002). Nursing intervention and treatment of the acutely psychotic patient in the emergency department. *Journal of the American Psychiatric Nurses Association,* 8(6), S36–S39.

Tomar, R., Brimblecombe, N., & O'Sullivan, S. (2003). Service innovations: Home treatment for first-episode psychosis. *Psychiatric Bulletin, 27,* 148–157.

Tyhurst, J. S. (1957). The role of transition states—including disasters—in mental illness. In *Symposium on preventive and social psychiatry.* Washington, DC: Walter Reed Army Institute of Research and the National Research Council.

U.S. Department of Health and Human Services. (2000). *Healthy people 2010: Understanding and improving health.* Washington, DC: Author.

Ustun, T. B. (1999). The global burden of mental disorders. *American Journal of Public Health, 89*(9), 1315–1321.

Webster, S., & Harrison, L. (2004). The multidisciplinary approach to mental health crisis management: An Australian example. *Journal of Psychiatric and Mental Health Nursing, 11,* 21–29.

Weed, D. L. (1998). Beyond black box epidemiology. *American Journal of Public Health, 88*(1), 12–14.

Wolin, S. J., & Wolin, S. (1993). *The resilient self: How survivors of troubled families rise above adversity.* New York: Villard Books.

Yo-Yo Ma (2008, March 10). Essay: This I believe. Boston: WGBH, National Public Radio.

See Online Resources for additional references.

危機
CHAPTER 2

Understanding People in Crisis

Understanding people in crisis is the foundation for assessment, planning, intervention, and follow-up—steps intrinsic to the crisis care process. A recurring problem in the social sciences is that theories are often formulated without sufficient grounding in reality. Conversely, practitioners frequently do not study the values and theoretical assumptions implicit in research. For example, census figures reveal that mothers are awarded custody of their children in most cases. If fathers are routinely denied custody without examining the comparative parenting abilities of each parent, then a belief in biological determinism (for example, women are naturally better parents, or men lack nurturing capacity) is implied. In another example, the use of psychotropic drugs, predominantly for women in crisis, suggests theoretical assumptions about the nature of crisis and the people receiving the drugs. Also, crisis theories may rely too exclusively on the experience of ill rather than healthy individuals. As Antonovsky (1980, pp. 35–37) suggests, the crucial question may be, Why do people stay healthy? (*salutogenesis*) rather than, What makes them sick? (*pathogenesis*).

An examination of the central concepts of crisis theory provides the building blocks for understanding the crisis experience and its resolution. These concepts help answer the following questions about theory-based crisis care:

1. What are the origins of crisis?
2. How are the origins related to prediction, prevention, and resolution of crisis?
3. How is crisis related to stress and illness?
4. How does the crisis state develop, and how is it manifested?
5. How do different people resolve crises?
6. How does the interaction between natural and formal crisis intervention work to produce positive crisis outcomes?

In Chapter 1, crisis was broadly linked to stress, emergencies, and emotional and mental disturbance. This chapter shows the interrelationship among human distress situations and addresses key questions about the crisis experience.

The Origins of Crisis

Examining the origins of crisis is important because insight into how a problem begins enhances our chances of dealing with it effectively. Here we use the term *origin* in the sense of the root source or beginning of a phenomenon—in this case, crisis. Considerations of origins may or may not include speculation about causes, because such an examination is associated with the so-called hard determinism found in the natural sciences. A search for cause-and-effect laws is questionable in a humanistic framework. This interpretation of origin also suggests that instead of asking what causes crisis, one would examine, for example, how some people respond resiliently to stressful events and avoid full-blown crisis while others do not. Uncovering crisis origins also reveals the reasons that some people resolve crisis through problem solving and growth, some by suicide, and others by chronic emotional illness (Vaillant, 1993). The following discussion clarifies the relationships among crisis origins, risk factors, manifestations, and intervention strategies, in terms of origins and development. Broadly speaking, crisis origins fall into three categories: *situational* (traditional term is *unanticipated*), *transitional state* (traditional term is *anticipated*), and *cultural and social-structural*.

Situational Origins

Crises defined as situational originate from three sources: (1) material or environmental (for example, fire or natural disaster), (2) personal or physical (for example, heart attack, diagnosis of fatal illness, loss of limb or other bodily disfigurement from accidents or disease), and (3) interpersonal or social (for example, death of a loved one or divorce) (see Figure 2.1, upper circle, Box 1). Such situations are usually unanticipated. Because the traumatic event leading to possible crisis is unforeseen, one generally can do nothing to prepare for it except in an indirect sense: careful driving habits can reduce the risk of accident; changing risky lifestyle practices such as smoking can reduce the risk of heart attack or cancer; open communication may lessen the chance of divorce; a change in sexual behavior can reduce the risk of contracting HIV-AIDS. Crises arising from such situations originate, at least indirectly, from personal life choices. For example, keeping in good physical and psychological health, nurturing a social support system, and avoiding too many changes at one time prepare one indirectly to better handle unforeseen events (Turner & Avison, 1992).

In a classic example of an unanticipated traumatic event—loss of a child by sudden infant death syndrome (SIDS)—research (Hogberg & Bergstrom, 2000) suggests that the medically advised prone (on stomach) sleeping position has often been a major factor in SIDS (see Chapter 6); therefore, if despite this research finding, parents inappropriately blame themselves in their crisis response, crisis counseling and grief work will usually alleviate self-blame and result in a positive outcome (unless psychopathology was present before the crisis or the death is mistakenly attributed to parental abuse). At the other end of the spectrum, in crises originating from complex sociocultural or interrelated sources, the implications for intervention are

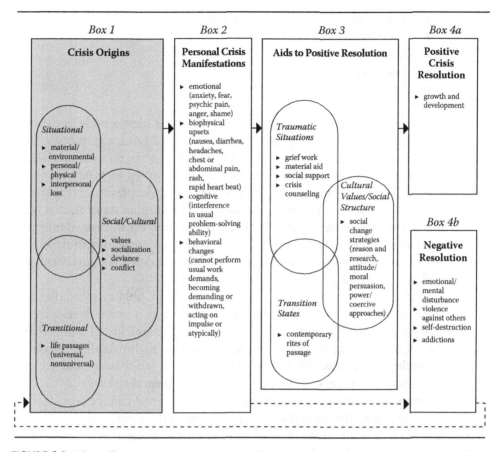

FIGURE 2.1 Crisis Paradigm. Crisis origins, manifestations, and outcomes and the respective functions of crisis care have interactional relationships. The intertwined circles represent the distinct yet interrelated origins of crisis and aids to positive resolution, even though personal manifestations are often similar. The arrows pointing from origins to positive resolution illustrate the *opportunity for growth and development* through crisis; the broken line at the bottom depicts the potential *danger of crisis* in the absence of appropriate aids. The loop between Box 4b and Box 1 denotes the *vulnerability* to future crisis episodes following negative resolution.

also more complex. The stress and possible crisis originating from a natural event, such as being struck and injured by lightning, might be the easiest to handle, depending on the degree and type of physical injury.

Transition State Origins

The next broad category of crisis origins, transition states, consists of two types: (1) *universal*—life-cycle or normal transitions consisting of human development phases from conception to death and (2) *nonuniversal*—passages signaling a shift in social status (see Figure 2.1, lower circle, Box 1). The first type is universal in that no one escapes life passages, at least not the first and last phases. Erikson (1963) and other developmental psychologists have identified human transition states as follows:

- Prenatal to infancy
- Infancy to childhood

- Childhood to puberty and adolescence
- Adolescence to adulthood
- Maturity to middle age
- Middle age to old age
- Old age to death

During each phase, a person is subject to unique stressors. He or she faces the challenge of completing specific developmental tasks; e.g., moving from mistrust to trust, from inferiority to identity. Failure to do so stunts human growth, and one's personality does not mature according to its natural potential. Although growth toward maturity is exciting, people usually experience a higher level of anxiety during developmental transition states than at other times. The natural change in roles, body image, physical and sexual functioning, and attitudes toward oneself and the world may create inner turmoil and restlessness. Successful completion of developmental tasks requires energy as well as nurturance and social approval from others.

With appropriate support, a person is normally able to meet the challenge of growth from one life stage to another. In this sense, developmental crises are considered normal and therefore can be anticipated and prepared for. Developmental transition states need not be nightmarish; they can be rewarding times in which people enjoy a sense of self-mastery and achievement from the successful completion of developmental tasks.

Stress and turmoil can occur during developmental change periods if the individual lacks the normal social supports needed for the process of maturation. And each successive stage of development is affected by what took place in the previous phase. For some, the challenge of human growth is indeed a nightmare; life's turning points become crises with destructive effects rather than normal periods of change and challenge. Some people greet adolescence, middle age, and old age with suicide attempts, depression, or withdrawal to a closed, more secure, and familiar world. They approach life with a deep rejection of self and suspicion of the surrounding world.

Our unique challenge in life is to move forward, not to stagnate or regress. For some, however, various situational factors make this a seemingly impossible task. Developmental challenges are particularly acute for young people who grow up in communities where economic security and other dreams are never borne or are quickly dashed by multiple stressors, loss of family members or friends by violence, and other tragic events.

The second type of transition state, nonuniversal, includes turning points such as the change from student to worker and worker (including homemaker) to student, migration, and retirement. Crises originating from such sources differ from those arising from unanticipated hazardous events. Like the developmental transition states, nonuniversal passages are usually anticipated and can therefore be prepared for. Unlike developmental transitions, however, everyone does not experience them. And some transitions, such as relocation because of refugee status in a war-torn country, are complicated by cultural and economic factors in one's homeland (see Chapter 8). The transition states (universal and nonuniversal) from which some crises stem can be seen not only as markers along life's pathway but also as processes that can develop in positive or negative directions (Hoff, M., 2005; see also Chapter 6).

Crises developing from situational and transitional states are the easiest to understand and to handle successfully. One's personal values involved in resolving such crises generally do not clash with common interpretations of life's experiences. For example, if a person loses precious possessions and is left homeless by a fire caused by arson, one's ability to handle the stress involved is generally assisted by knowledge that there are laws designed to bring the arsonist to justice, and by insurance, which may partially compensate for the material loss. To summarize, crises arising from hazardous situations and from transition states are distinct yet related. An individual in a major transition state is usually vulnerable. When the stress of an unanticipated traumatic event is added, the person is even more likely to experience a crisis because one's usual coping capacity may be strained to the limit by these combined stressors.

To illustrate, let us consider Carol and Jim, who demonstrate a capacity for growth and development around divorce.

Case Example: Carol and Jim

Carol, age 38, and Jim, age 36, decide mutually to obtain a divorce. They have been married 13 years and have two children—Dean, age 12, and Cindy, age 9. Together they work out a custody and visiting agreement, satisfying their desires and taking the children's wishes into consideration. Carol and Jim had essentially untroubled childhoods and feel secure and confident as individuals. They can, therefore, avoid the common tactic of using their children as weapons against each other. The divorce is decidedly a source of stress to Dean and Cindy, but neither of the children (although they are not happy about the divorce) experiences it as a crisis. Both parents are mature in their marital and parental roles and do not deny their children the nurturance they continue to need from both parents. The divorce is also not the occasion of a crisis for either spouse. In fact, they both saw their marriage as stagnating their personal growth. Their decision to divorce is not a crisis; rather, as Maslow (1970) shows, it is an occasion for further self-actualization, or growth.

Many divorces, however, are more tumultuous than this couple's, and may become tragic. For example, in an abusive marriage, a man may greet the news of divorce with a threat to kill first his wife and then himself (see Chapters 11 and 12). Such cases, in their contrasting manifestations, illustrate (1) the highly subjective nature of the crisis experience, (2) the various factors that influence the development of a crisis state, and (3) the intrinsic relationships among transitional, situational, and sociocultural influences on the crisis experience.

Cultural and Social-Structural Origins

Crises arising from cultural values and the social structure include job loss stemming from discrimination on the basis of age, race, gender, disability, or sexual identity. In contrast, job loss from illness or poor personal performance can be viewed as a result of a prior crisis or illness. Job loss occurring from discriminatory treatment in the workforce is rooted in cultural values about the diversity issues already noted—values that are embedded in culture and the social structure (see Chapter 1). Also in this category are crises resulting from the deviant acts of others, behavior that violates accepted social norms: robbery, rape, incest, marital infidelity, and physical abuse (see Figure 2.1, right circle, Box 1). Crises from these sources are never truly expected; there is something shocking and catastrophic about them. Yet in a sense they are predictable. An older infirm woman living in a high-crime area is more vulnerable to attack than a stronger and younger person. Other examples of crises arising from sociocultural sources include violence against children and women (related to values about discipline, the role of women, and social-structural factors in the family) and residential dislocation (related to disaster, economic, class, and ethnic issues, such as *gentrification*—the displacement of the poor by the "gentry" during the "upgrading" of urban centers). In New Orleans, epicenter of Hurricane Katrina, while the tourist industry has recovered, hundreds of the poor and homeless are still struggling (see Chapter 13).

In general, crises originating from sociocultural sources are less amenable to control by individuals than are crises arising from personal action. Thus, a person of a racial minority group facing a housing crisis due to suspected discrimination and a woman in job crisis due to alleged gender discrimination must be prepared to deal with the bureaucratic justice system. To avoid the downward spiral discussed later in this chapter, *social* factors should not be misconstrued as *personal* liabilities producing crises. Consider the challenge of resolving a crisis originating from the following twist in justice: a woman is brutally beaten and threatened with her life; she and her children are left homeless, while the man who has committed the crime enjoys the comfort and security of the marital dwelling. This example of battering also illustrates the interrelationships among crisis origins. That is, an abused woman may suffer physical injury and loss of home (situational events) and be forced into a status change from married to single (transitional), but the *primary* origin of her crisis can be traced to cultural values about women, the socialization of men toward aggression, violation of basic human rights, diversity regarding communitarian values, and a widespread cultural climate approving of violence (for example, war, capital punishment, pornography) (Hoff, 2000b; Mawby & Walklate, 1994). Therefore, intervention strategies focused only on the upper and lower circles (see Figure 2.1, Box 3), without attention to social change strategies and public compensation for the woman's injuries, usually will not be sufficient.[1] Interrelated crisis origins are also apparent in the high suicide rates of gay, lesbian, bisexual, or transgendered youth, and in people with AIDS, their families, and caretakers.

---

[1] The Crisis Paradigm, or theoretical framework underpinning this entire book evolved from ethnographic research with abused women and their children (Hoff, 1990).

To illustrate further, note the difference in the element of *control* in two different crisis situations: (1) A heavy cigarette smoker with full knowledge of the evidence linking smoking to lung cancer receives a diagnosis of lung cancer. More than likely, insurance benefits will be available in spite of this self-chosen high-risk lifestyle. (2) A Japanese-American survivor of the nuclear bomb blast at Hiroshima receives a diagnosis of leukemia. The victim is refused insurance coverage for the required medical care by both private insurers and the U.S. government (WGBH Educational Foundation, 1982, pp. 17–18). For most people it is a greater challenge to face bureaucratic obstacles to needed services than to reflect on one's personal decisions influencing a crisis situation.

A more complex example of crisis from sociocultural sources involves the perpetrators of deviant acts. Here, social and personal elements are intertwined. For example, the parents of an infant whom they have abused and brought to a hospital for treatment will probably be in crisis, as will a mother who loses custody of her children because of drug abuse. Such child abuse and neglect may be rooted in cultural values about physical discipline, mothers (as opposed to mothers and fathers together) as primary child rearers, and socioeconomic status. Although such deviance may be strongly influenced by social and cultural factors, individual perpetrators of violence against others need to be carefully considered for personal liability.

These illustrations provide a preview of the relationship between origins of crisis and strategies of intervention (to be discussed further in later chapters). In short, whenever a crisis originates outside the individual, it is usually beyond the individual *alone* to resolve the crisis successfully while not relinquishing our basic need for power and control over our own lives. In such situations, the person is usually more vulnerable and has greater difficulty making sense of the traumatic event and avoiding negative coping strategies (Herman, 1992; Sanders, 2008). Public, social strategies, therefore, need to accompany any individual interventions on behalf of people whose crises originate in the sociocultural milieu.

Interrelationships between Crisis Origins and Development

Identifying the origins of a crisis, important as it is, is only one step toward effective crisis resolution. Various situational, developmental, and sociocultural factors do not in themselves constitute a crisis state. The factors placing people at risk vary and interact to produce a crisis that is manifested in emotional, cognitive, behavioral, and biophysical responses to traumatic life events (see Figure 2.1, Box 2).

Developmentalists Danish et al. (1980, pp. 342–345) cite several factors that affect how a person responds to life events:

- *Timing.* For example, first marriage at age 16 or 50 may be more stressful than at other times.
- *Duration.* This refers to the process aspect of life events such as pregnancy or retirement.

- *Sequencing.* For example, the birth of a child before marriage is usually more stressful than after.
- *Cohort specificity.* For example, in a reversal of traditional roles, a man becomes a househusband and a woman a corporate executive.
- *Contextual purity.* This refers to how the event relates to other events and the lives of other people.
- *Probability of occurrence.* For example, the majority of married women will become widows.

The clinical relevance of these factors can be seen in Schulberg and Sheldon's (1968, pp. 553–558) probability formulation for assessing which persons are most crisis prone:

1. *The probability that a disturbing and hazardous event will occur.* Death of close family members is highly probable, whereas natural disasters are very improbable.
2. *The probability that an individual will be exposed to the event.* Every adolescent faces the challenge of adult responsibilities, whereas fewer people face the crisis of an unwanted move from their settled dwelling.
3. *The vulnerability of the individual to the event.* The mature adult can adapt more easily to the stress of moving than can a child in the first year of school or a retired person who has lived a long time in one community.

In assessing risk, then, one should consider (1) the degree of stress stemming from a hazardous event, (2) the risk of a person being exposed to that event, and (3) the person's vulnerability or ability to adapt to the stress. Our awareness of these risk factors in individuals and groups enhances the success of crisis prevention and health promotion, as discussed in Chapter 1.

Case Example: Dorothy

Dorothy, age 38, has been treated for depression three times during the past 9 years. Before her marriage and the birth of her three children, Dorothy held a job as a secretary and is now employed part-time. Dorothy's husband, a company executive, accepted a job transfer to a new location in another city. This city is known for its hostile attitudes toward African American families like Dorothy's. Dorothy dreaded the move and considered joining her husband a few months later. She thought this might allow her some time to see whether her husband's job placement might be permanent. However, she abandoned the idea because she dreaded being away from her husband for that length of time. One month after the move, Dorothy made a suicide attempt and was taken to a mental health agency by her husband.

In this case, the initial probability of the occurrence of the hazardous event, the move, was small. The probability of Dorothy's exposure to the event was high, considering her marital status and her dependence on her husband. Her racial identity made her more vulnerable to stress from sociocultural sources such as housing discrimination. Her vulnerability in view of her past history was also very high. Taken together, these factors made Dorothy a high risk for crisis. Research on vulnerability to life events underscores the emotional cost of caretaking roles for women like Dorothy. Women are more exposed to acute life stressors because of traditional role expectations, including their response to events affecting significant others in their social network, with a consequent increased risk of depression (Conger, Lorenz, Elder, & Simons, 1993; Turner & Avison, 1992). For women like Dorothy, the risk increases if they are faced with a hazardous event such as the death of a husband.

The case of a family in crisis as a result of a teenager's suicide attempt also suggests the interactional aspect of crisis origins. Although the teenager's crisis may stem directly from personal feelings of failure and worthlessness and indirectly from family conflict, the family's crisis of dealing with a suicidal member is usually affected by the culturally situated stigma still attached to self-destructive behavior (see Chapter 9).

These examples underscore the fact that life events in themselves are not crises. Rather, the *origins* of crisis to life events, their linkage to one's sociocultural milieu, personal values, resilience, and related factors vary among individuals and influence the development and subjective manifestations of crisis in different people. Identifying specific crisis origins during assessment and tailoring intervention strategies to distinct or interrelated origins increases the probability of positive crisis resolution and growth (see Figure 2.1, Box 3). Details of such assessment and intervention strategies are presented in the remainder of the book.

Stress, Resilience, Crisis, and Illness

Theories and research on stress and coping occupy a prominent position in the literature of psychology, sociology, anthropology, nursing, medicine, and epidemiology (Brown, 1993; Brown & Harris, 1978; Loustaunau & Sobo, 1997; Selye, 1956). The issue of coping with stressful life events often revolves around the relationship between stress and illness; virtually all authorities agree that stress and illness are related. The questions considered in this book are:

- Do stressful life events cause illness, and if so, what is the process involved?
- Do sick people experience more stressful life events than the healthy?
- To what extent do social and psychological resources and resilience buffer the impact of stressful life events?
- What effect, if any, do "resistance resources" (Antonovsky, 1980) have on stress arising from the social structure—for example, race, class, gender, or age disparity?
- What is the relationship between stress and the concept and experience of crisis?

Imprecise definitions can create problems in answering these questions; sometimes the concepts of stress, crisis, and illness are used interchangeably (see Chapter 3 on psychiatric labeling). The following definitions may clarify the discussion:

- *Stress* is described by Selye (1956, p. 15) as a specific syndrome that is nonspecifically induced. Stress can also be viewed as a relationship between the person and the environment (McElroy & Townsend, 1985). For this book, stress is defined as the discomfort, pain, or troubled feeling arising from emotional, social, cultural, or physical sources and that results in the need to relax, be treated, or otherwise seek relief. Stress can be grouped into two types. *Acute stress* is brief in duration and occurs with fairly predictable manifestations and results, one of which may be crisis. *Insidious stress* is longer in duration (weeks, months, or years), with less awareness by the person experiencing it and with long-range cumulative but less clearly certain effects, which may include burnout and disease (Landy, 1977, p. 311). Stress is inherent in the process of living and may be experienced from any source: invasion of the body by organisms, trauma, internal psychological turmoil, brain disease, cultural values, and social organization.
- *Burnout,* a related concept, includes emotional exhaustion, usually stemming from work-related stressors. It is manifested in physical signs and symptoms; feelings of cynicism, anger, and resentment; a defeatist attitude as in "What's the use? I give up"; and poor social performance at home and at work. Burnout is distinguished from crisis by its chronic rather than acute character. Also, people suffering from burnout often are not aware of the connections among their feelings, their behavior, and the chronic stress they are under.
- *Disease* is a pathological concept describing a condition that can be objectively verified through physical examination, observation, and various laboratory tests. The "diseased" person may or may not be aware of objective organic lesions or behavioral disturbances observable by others, e.g., Alzheimer's disease or schizophrenia.
- *Illness* is related to disease but is distinguished by its subjective character. It is a cultural concept that implies the social recognition that one cannot carry out expected social roles. For instance, a person may have an early cancerous lesion but not feel ill. Once the lesion is diagnosed as cancer, though, the person is considered ill, and the social, psychological, and cultural dimensions of the disease surface: stigma, denial, fear of death. Illness may be claimed subjectively as a reason for inability to perform normally. For example, a person may say, "I don't feel well. I have a backache" (a condition not easily diagnosed), although no objective indicators of disease may be present. Illness can therefore be seen as
  - *Punishment*—for example, "What did I do to deserve cancer?"
  - *Deviance*—for example, using the "sick role" to evade responsibilities

- *An indicator of social system performance*—for example, absenteeism due to "illness," although the real reason is job dissatisfaction
- *A social control device*—for example, attaching a psychiatric label such as *borderline personality disorder* to patients whose histories (often including childhood sexual abuse) are poorly understood (Hoff, 2000a)
- *A response to stress*—from physical, environmental, social, psychological, or cultural sources

- *Emotional breakdown* is an inability to manage one's feelings to the point of chronic interference in normal functioning; it is manifested in depression, anger, fear, and the like.
- *Mental breakdown* is a disturbance in cognitive functioning; it is manifested in the general inability to think and act normally. Brain disease, biochemical imbalance, and exposure to serious social stressors may be involved. It progresses to the point of interference in problem-solving ability and the appropriate expression of feelings, everyday behavior, and interaction with others.
- *Crisis* is an acute emotional upset; it is manifested in an inability to cope emotionally, cognitively, or behaviorally and to solve problems by usual devices.

Research on stress, crisis, and emotional and mental breakdown reveals a lack of integration between clinical and social science insights. The imbalance between a clinical and a developmental-social analysis of coping with stressful life events needs correction. Researchers trained clinically in health promotion and primary prevention, and in social science are bridging some of these gaps (e.g., Clark, 2006; Green & Diaz, 2007; Meyer & Schwartz, 2000). However, the medicalization and causal scientific models in all branches of human service practice have dominated the stress research field (McKinlay & Marceau, 1999). Conclusions from much of the research on stress point to the limitations of causal models in the analysis of stress. Since the September 11, 2001 terrorist attacks, increasing attention is being directed to considering macro-level stressors in our understanding of the stress process and its relationship to hazardous events, illness, coping, and social support. Richman et al. (2008) found significant distress levels and problematic alcohol use after the 9/11 attacks. In contrast to studies initiated after 9/11, their longitudinal study included pre-9/11 assessments of mental health, which were compared with assessments in 2003 and 2005.

Overly simplistic reductionist psychological accounts of stress and illness are not the only problem in the crisis intervention field. Durkheim's (1897/1951) notion that people's positions in the social structure—lack of social integration and a sense of attachment to society—are *causes* of anomic and egoistic suicides is a prime example of sociological reductionism; it fails to account for differences in the way individuals interpret and cope with stressful life events from various sources. Although cause-and-effect laws certainly operate in regard to the physical stressors of a gunshot wound to the heart or the repeated inhalation of carcinogens—these stressors do cause death or lung cancer, respectively—a *social act*, such as suicide or violence against others, cannot be explained within the same causal framework (Hoff, 1990). What is the relevance of reductionist causal reasoning to crisis response and intervention?

Acute or chronic stress does not automatically lead to emotional imbalance or mental incompetence, abuse of alcohol and other drugs, suicide, or assault on others. If it did, humans, who by nature are rational, conscious, and responsible for their behavior, could routinely attribute their behavior to causes external to themselves and be excused from accountability. This, in fact, is the case in certain instances in which mitigating circumstances allow an excuse for some behaviors that might otherwise be punishable.

In general, however, responses to stress vary. Increasingly, researchers are recognizing the importance of *context* in explaining behavior (Dobash & Dobash, 1998, pp. 9–10). Maslow's (1970) research, for example, underscores the apparent growth-promoting function of high-stress situations for achieving self-actualization, not destruction of self and others. Antonovsky's (1980) cross-cultural research on concentration camp survivors and women in menopause suggests similar conclusions. He proposes the concept of "resistance resources" (pp. 99–100), including social network support and a "sense of coherence" (SOC), as intervening variables in stressful situations. SOC includes the person's perception of events as comprehensible, manageable, and meaningful. It is highly compatible with resilience and protective factors that aid in positive crisis resolution, while its strength-based perspective can mitigate negative effects of the deficit and pathology models so prevalent in U.S. society (Hoff, M., 2005).

Applied to crisis response, a person with a strong SOC will define social stressors as social rather than assuming blame for trouble that did not originate from oneself. One's resistance resources can make the difference between positive or negative responses to developmental transitions or to extreme stress (which a clinician might define as crisis), such as the catastrophic experience of concentration camp survivors. Research with battered women (Hoff, 1990) supports these views and the position taken in this book: stress, crisis, and illness (physical, emotional, and mental) are interactionally, not causally, related.

The Crisis–Psychiatric Illness Interface

Another argument about the relationships among stress, crisis, and illness concerns traditional victim blaming around crises of interpersonal violence (Ryan, 1971). The battering of women, for example, was attributed to a woman's provocative behavior, presumably arising from her own emotional or mental disturbance. This view is now widely rejected, as the global epidemic of violence against women has taken center stage and continues unabated among refugees in Darfur, Sudan (Hoff, 2000b). Psychiatric and social analysis (for example, Hoff, 1990; Rieker & Carmen, 1986) reveals that the woman's emotional symptoms do not *cause* battering; rather, they occur almost invariably in the *context* of having been victimized both physically and psychologically.

Figure 2.2 illustrates this process in the downward spiral toward illness, a process that for assault victims especially usually begins with the misassignment of responsibility for the violence and abuse. Such a descent toward maladaptation can also occur in cases of oppression and discrimination based on race or sexual identity, for example. Key to this downward, possibly self-destructive or violent course is the process of *internalizing* blame or oppression originating from sociocultural sources. Once a person or group inappropriately absorbs blame for others' actions and takes on the identity of victim, helplessness or horizontal violence—venting rage or violence on people of one's own group—may prevent the proper channeling of anger toward personal healing and social change (see Figure 2.1, Box 3).

It is therefore crucial to simultaneously acknowledge the pain of victimization and oppression and keep sight of the fact that a downward spiral is not inevitable. Most important, then, for survival and growth beyond victimhood, are recognizing the deep-seated roots of violence, stopping victim-blaming at

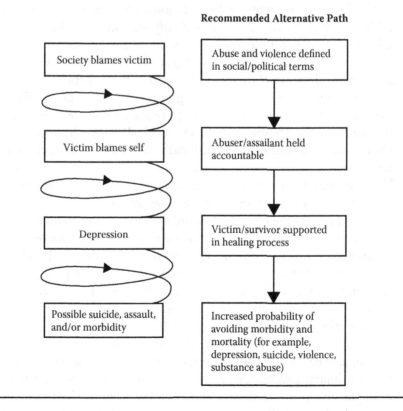

FIGURE 2.2   Abuse, the Downward Spiral, and Alternative Path. *Primary* prevention is ideal, but intervention at *secondary* and *tertiary* levels can also prevent morbidity and save lives.

its sociocultural source, offering social support, and engaging in social change strategies that interrupt the downward spiral toward preventable morbidity and mortality (Hoff, 1990; McCullough, 1995). Note that Figure 2.2 includes these alternatives to the downward spiral.

One of the most popular notions surrounding women's crises stemming from violence is that the violent man is under high stress. To the extent that this explanation is accepted, the person's violence is excused on the basis of presumed mental incompetence. Although it is true that the extreme stress and anxiety associated with a crisis state can distort cognitive functions such as memory and decision making, mental incompetence would not be assumed if history revealed that the perpetrator's mental faculties were intact *before* the crisis (see Chapter 3). A person's decision to hit or kill his or her spouse during the high tension of a marital fight is therefore neither wise nor excusable. Social research over several decades supports the proposition that temporary insanity claims are really excuses used to evade responsibility for one's own violent behavior. This does not negate recognition that some crimes are committed by people who are diagnosed as mentally ill according to commonly accepted criteria, such as having delusions, hallucinations, or exhibiting bizarre behavior.

Yet despite a common tendency to associate violent behavior with mental illness, such a generalization is clearly unfounded (Friedman, 2006; see Chapter 12 for further discussion). Some recent jury acquittals of women who killed their abusive partners suggest that these women were not viewed as mentally ill; rather, the stress and danger of their circumstances after years of abuse were considered sufficient grounds for acquittal. Similarly, many men are excused from their battering, though some are convicted. One of the most striking findings of Hoff's research (1990) with abused women was their tendency to excuse their husband's violence but not their own retaliatory violence, even if the wives were under the influence of drugs or alcohol. When women are convicted of murdering their husbands, however, research suggests discriminatory practices (Browne, 1987).

These findings are remarkably similar to Erich Lindemann's classic study (1944): survivors of the Cocoanut Grove disaster might have been spared the negative experience of serious psychopathology if they had had assistance, such as with grief work, at the time of the crisis. Abused women and others without resources and assistance for constructive crisis resolution may start the downward course and become suicidal, homicidal, addicted, or emotionally disturbed, especially after repeated abuse. The reciprocal relationships among stress, crisis, and illness are observed further in the multifaceted stressors an abused woman must deal with while in crisis after a violent attack: physical injury, psychological upset, or change in her social situation—for example, disrupted marriage or residential or economic loss (see Chapter 11, Figure 11.2, for an illustration of this relationship). Similarly, the crisis–illness relationship can be observed among the homeless. Considering how basic home and shelter are for all, the most remarkable evidence of human resilience is the survival of so many people against the greatest of odds and continuing stressors, even with the burden of serious mental disturbance (Hoff, 1993).

In a scientific sense, then, concepts of crisis, stress, and illness are imprecise and complexly associated with the political economy, a biomedical approach to people in distress, social inequality, and dominant values about people and illness in the cultural milieu—essentially an interactional, rather than causal, relationships among stress, crisis, and illness. What simplistic models miss is the influence of the distinctive individual experience of stress, crisis, and illness. Table 2.1 illustrates the distinctions and relationships between

TABLE 2.1   Distress Differentiation

Type of Distress or Problem	Origins	Possible Manifestations
Stress (acute)	Hazardous life events (such as heart attack, accident, death of loved one, violent attack, sudden job loss, natural disaster)	Emotional crisis General Adaptation Syndrome General Adaptation Syndrome Disease process
	Invasion by microorganisms	
	Man-made disaster	Annihilation of present civilization
Stress (chronic)	Strain in social relationships (such as marriage)	Burnout Psychosomatic or stress-related illness
	Position in social structure (age, sex, race, class)	Emotional or mental breakdown
	Socioeconomic problems (such as unemployment)	
	Chronic ill health	
	Developmental transition states	
Crisis	Traumatic situations (material, personal/physical, interpersonal)	Emotional Behavioral
	Transition states (developmental and other)	Cognitive ⎫ Changes Biophysical ⎭
	Cultural values, social structure	
Emotional or mental breakdown	Failure of positive response to acute stress and/or crisis	Neurotic and/or psychotic symptoms (such as learned helplessness or self-denigration by an abused woman)
	Continuation of chronic stress from various sources	

Possible Responses

Positive	Negative	Duration
Grief work	Failure to ask for and accept help	Brief
Adaptation, emotional and social growth through healthy coping	Suicide, assault, addiction, emotional/mental breakdown	

(continued)

TABLE 2.1 Distress Differentiation (continued)

Positive	Negative	Duration
Medical treatment, rest, exercise	Refusal of treatment, complications, possible premature death	
Prevention: Political action	Denial of possibility	Weeks, months, years, or lifetime
Lifestyle changes (such as diet, rest, exercise, leisure)	Exacerbation of burnout	
Social change strategies	All of the above, and mystification by and response to symptoms versus sources of chronic stress	
Transition state preparation		
Grief work	Inability to accomplish new role tasks	Few days to 6 weeks
Crisis coping and resolution by use of personal, social, and material resources	Same as for acute stress	
Prevention: Education about sources of crisis and appropriate preventive action (such as contemporary rites of passage, action to reduce social disparities)		
Reorganization or change of ineffective emotional, cognitive, and behavioral responses to stress and crisis (usually with help of therapy)	Same as all of above, and increased vulnerability to crisis and inability to cope with acute and chronic stress	Weeks, months, years, or lifetime
Action to change social sources of chronic stress		

these concepts. It also links the concepts with their origins, providing a preview of the next section and remaining chapters.

Development and Individual Manifestations of Crisis

We have seen how crisis originates from physical, material, personal, social, and cultural sources, as well as how it fits into the larger picture of life's ups and downs. Let us now consider the experience of crisis at the individual, personal level.

Why People Go into Crisis

People in crisis are, by definition, emotionally upset; they are unable to solve life's problems in their usual way. A happy, healthy life implies an ability to solve problems effectively. It also implies that basic human needs are fulfilled. Our basic needs include a sense of physical and psychological well-being; a supportive network of friends, family, and associates; and a sense of identity and belonging to one's society and cultural heritage. Hansell (1976, pp. 31–49) describes our essential needs as the "seven basic attachments." All of us have a stable arrangement of transactions between ourselves and our environment. Essentially, we are attached to

1. Food, oxygen, and other physical supplies necessary to life
2. A strong sense of self-identity
3. At least one other person in a close, mutually supportive relationship
4. At least one group that accepts us as a member
5. One or more roles in which we feel self-respect and can perform with dignity
6. Financial security or a means of participating in an exchange of the goods and services we need and value
7. A comprehensive system of meaning—that is, a set of values that help us set goals and understand ourselves and the world around us

Typically, people in crisis suffer a sudden loss or threat of loss of a person or thing considered essential and important. One or several of their basic attachments are severed or are at risk of being severed. For example, the shock of the unexpected death of a loved one by car accident or heart attack can leave a person feeling incomplete and at a loss about what to do, where to turn. The individual's familiar source of support and comfort disappears without warning, with no time to adjust to the change. Similar shock occurs in response to the suicide or murder of a friend or family member, the threat of divorce, a diagnosis of a terminal illness such as AIDS, or an operation such as a mastectomy, which seriously alters one's body. A person with AIDS, for example, not only loses health and faces the probability of a shortened life cycle but also may be abandoned by friends and family and scorned by would-be helpers.

Case Example: Edward

Edward, age 45, has been an outstanding assistant director of his company. When he is promoted to the vacated position of executive director, he becomes depressed and virtually nonfunctional. Edward, in spite of external signs of success, lacks basic self-confidence; he cannot face the challenge of the new job. The possibility of failure in his new position is unbearable. His anxiety about success prevents him from achieving the success he desires. Edward is one of the many people who, with the help of family and friends, and perhaps a crisis counselor, can avoid possible failure and depression. He has his whole past career, including many successes, to draw on profitably in his present job. With help, he might see that failure in his present position need not mean the end of a happy and productive life.

Caplan (1964) and Tyhurst (1957) note that for some people a crisis is triggered when they face a particularly challenging psychosocial event. A crisis for such individuals represents a call to new action that they cannot face with their present resources. Shock and a resulting crisis state can also occur at the time of normal role transitions. For instance, events like graduation can signal the need for young people to balance their dependence on parents with the young adult responsibilities of finding employment and establishing sexual identity.

How a Crisis Develops

A crisis does not occur instantaneously. There are identifiable phases of development—psychosocial in character—that lead to an active crisis state. These phases were first described by Tyhurst (1957) in his study of individual responses to community disaster. Survivors experience three overlapping phases: (1) a period of impact, (2) a period of recoil, and (3) a posttraumatic period. This breakdown of phases is applied most appropriately to crises originating from catastrophic, shocking events, such as rape and other violent attacks, war-related devastation, or sometimes the news of a terminal disease (see "Individual Responses to Disaster" in Chapter 13 for a detailed description of these phases).

Caplan (1964) describes four phases in the development of extreme anxiety and crisis. His description of phases is applicable to crises occurring in a more gradual process from less catastrophic stressors. Recognizing these phases of crisis development is useful in the important task of preventing stressful life events from spiraling into crises.

Case Example: John—Phases of Crisis Development

PHASE ONE

A traumatic event causes an initial rise in one's level of anxiety. The person is in a predicament and responds with familiar problem-solving mechanisms to reduce or eliminate the stress and discomfort stemming from excessive anxiety. John, age 34, is striving toward a career as an executive in his company when he receives a diagnosis of multiple sclerosis. His wife, Nancy, is very supportive. He adjusts to this unexpected disturbing event by continuing to work as long as he can. John also has the advantage of the most advanced medical treatment available for multiple sclerosis. In addition, John's physician is skillful in applying medical knowledge of the emotional impact of John's diagnosis. At this stage, John's traumatic event does not result in a crisis for him.

PHASE TWO

In this phase, the person's usual problem-solving ability fails, and the stimulus that caused the initial rise in tension continues. To continue with the illustration of John's case: the disease process is advancing despite excellent medical treatment. John's wife, Nancy, begins to participate less in some of her own interests, including volunteer work, so she can spend more time with her husband. The accumulating medical expenses and loss of work time strain the family's financial resources. John and Nancy receive a report from school that their son, Larry, age 14, is having behavioral problems. At this stage, because there is greater stress, the possibility of a crisis state for John increases, but a crisis is not inevitable. Whether it occurs or not depends on what happens next in John's life.

PHASE THREE

In this phase, the individual's anxiety level rises further. The increased tension moves the person to use every resource available, including unusual or new means, to solve the problem and reduce the increasingly painful state of anxiety. In John's case, he fortunately has enough inner strength, resilience, and sensitivity to recognize the strain of his illness on his wife and child. He looks for new ways to cope with his increasing stress. First, he confides in his physician, who responds by taking time to listen and offer emotional support. His physician also arranges for home health services through a visiting nurse agency. This outside health assistance frees Nancy from some of her steadily increasing responsibilities. The physician also encourages John and Nancy to seek help from the school guidance counselor regarding their son, Larry, which they do.

Another way to prevent a crisis state at this phase is to redefine or change one's goals. This means of avoiding crisis is not usually possible for someone who is emotionally isolated from others and feels locked into solving a problem alone. With the help of his physician, John could accept his illness as something that changed his capacity to function in predefined, expected ways. However, he does not have to alter his fundamental ability to live a meaningful, rewarding life because of illness. As John's illness progresses, it becomes necessary to change his role as the sole financial provider in the family. John and Nancy talk openly with each other about the situation. Together they decide that Nancy will take a job to ease the financial strain. They also ask the nursing agency to increase the home health services, as Nancy is beginning to resent her confinement to the house and the increasing demands of being nurse to her husband.

PHASE FOUR

This is the state of active crisis that results when the following conditions exist:

- Internal strength and social support are lacking.
- The person's problem remains unresolved.
- Tension and anxiety rise to an unbearable degree.

An active crisis does not occur in John's case because he is able to respond constructively to his unanticipated illness. John has natural social supports and is resilient enough to use available help, so his stress does not become unbearable. The example of John illustrates how a full-blown crisis (phase four) can be avoided by various decisions and actions taken during any one of the three preceding phases.

The following example of George Sloan is in sharp contrast to that of John. George's case will be continued and discussed in subsequent chapters.

Case Example: George Sloan—Phases of Crisis Development

George Sloan, age 48, works as a machinist with a construction company. Six evenings a week, he works a second job as a taxi driver in a large metropolitan area; his beat includes high-crime sections of the city. He has just come home from the hospital after his third heart attack. The first occurred at age 44 and the second at age 47.

PHASE ONE

George is advised by his physician to cut down on his work hours. Specifically, the doctor recommends that he give up his second job and spend more time relaxing with family and friends. George's physician recognizes his patient's vulnerability to heart attacks, especially in relation to his lifestyle. George rarely slows down. He is chronically angry about things going wrong and about not being able to get ahead financially. He receives his physician's advice with mixed feelings. On the one hand, he sees the relationship between his heavy work schedule and his heart attacks; on the other hand, he resents what he acknowledges as a necessary change to reduce further risk of death by heart attack.

In any case, his health and financial problems markedly increase his usual level of anxiety. He talks superficially to his wife, Marie, about his dilemma, but receives little support or understanding from her; their marital relationship is already strained. Marie suggests that in place of George's second job, she increase her part-time job to full-time. George resents this because of what it implies about his image of himself as the chief provider.

George's discouragement and anger about not getting ahead are aggravated by Marie's complaints of never having enough money for the things she wants. George also resents what he perceives as the physician's judgment that he is not strong enough to do two jobs. At this stage, George is in a precrisis state, with a high degree of stress and anxiety.

PHASE TWO

George fails to obtain relief from his anxiety by talking with his wife. He does not feel comfortable talking with his physician about his reluctance to cut down the work stress as advised. When attempting to do so, he senses that the physician is rushed. So he concludes that his doctor is only concerned about giving technical advice, not about how George handles the advice. The prospect of quitting his second job and bringing home less money leaves George feeling like a failure. His initial conflict and rise in tension continue. If he quits his second job, he cannot preserve his image as adequate family provider; yet he cannot reduce the risk of death by heart disease if he continues his present pace. Help from other resources seems out of his reach.

PHASE THREE

George's increased anxiety moves him to try talking with his wife again. Ordinarily, he would have abandoned the idea based on the response he received earlier. This action therefore constitutes an unusual effort for him, but he fails again in getting the help he needs. To make matters worse, George and Marie learn that their 16-year-old son, Arnold, has been suspended from school for a week due to suspected drug involvement. This leaves George feeling like even more of a failure, as he is seldom home during normal family hours. In addition, Marie nags him about not spending enough time with the children. George's high level of anxiety becomes so obvious that Marie finally suggests, "Why don't you talk to the doctor about whatever's bothering you?" George knows that this is a good idea but cannot bring himself to do it, as he has always taken pride in solving his own problems. For the same reason, he cannot accept his wife's proposal to start working full-time. Personality and social factors block him from redefining or changing his goals as a means of problem resolution and crisis prevention. Financial concerns, along with the new problem of his son, further increase his anxiety level. George is in a predicament that he does not know how to resolve.

PHASE FOUR

George is at a complete loss about how to deal with all the stress in his life—the threat to his health and life if he continues his present pace, the threat to his self-image if he quits the second job, the failure to communicate with his wife, and the sense of failure and guilt in his role as a parent. His anxiety increases to the breaking point:

- He feels hopeless.
- He does not know where to turn.
- He is in a state of active crisis.

George's case illustrates situational (heart disease), maturational (adolescent changes), and sociocultural (sex-role stereotyping) factors in the development of life crises. It also highlights the subjective elements that contribute to a crisis state at different times in people's lives. George's heart disease was clearly an unanticipated, stressful—even life-threatening—event. The threat of his son's being suspended was unanticipated and a source of added stress. Yet Arnold's adolescence was anticipated as a normal phase of human development. If George's heart disease had developed at a time when his marriage was less strained, he might have received more help and support. And Arnold might have made it through adolescence without school suspension if there had been regular support from both parents. As it turned out, George and Marie had received the first report of Arnold's behavior problems in school shortly after George's first heart attack 4 years earlier. They were advised at that time to seek family or marital counseling; they did, but only for a single session. Finally, the socialization of George and Marie to stereotypical male and female roles was an added source of stress and a barrier to constructive crisis resolution. These contextual factors underscore the subjectivity of the crisis experience.

For another person, such as John in the previous case, or for George at another time of life, the same medical diagnosis and the same advice could have had an altogether different effect. This is also true for Arnold. A different response from his parents when he had given his first signals of distress, or a more constructive approach from school officials and counselors, might have prevented the additional stress of Arnold's school suspension.

Or different cultural expectations for husbands and wives could have altered each person's interpretation of the stressful situation. (George's case will be continued in Chapter 3.)

The Duration and Outcomes of Crisis

People cannot stay in crisis forever. The state of crisis and the accompanying anxiety are too painful. There is a natural time limitation to the crisis experience because the individual cannot survive indefinitely in such a state of psychological pain and turmoil. The emotional distress stemming from extreme anxiety moves the person toward action to reduce the anxiety to an endurable level as soon as possible. This aspect of the crisis experience underscores the *danger* and the *opportunity* that crisis presents.

Experience with people in crisis has led to the observation that the acute emotional upset lasts from a few days to a few weeks. The person must then move toward some sort of resolution—either temporary or permanent. This is often expressed in terms such as, "I can't go on like this anymore. Something has got to give," or "Please, tell me what to do to get out of this mess. I can't stand it," or "I feel like I'm losing my mind."

What, then, happens to the person in crisis? Several outcomes are possible.

1. The person can return to the precrisis state. This happens as a result of effective problem solving, made possible by internal strength, values, and social supports. Such an outcome does not necessarily imply new psychological growth as a result of the experience; the person simply returns to his or her usual state of being.
2. The person may not only return to the precrisis state but also can grow from the crisis experience through discovery of new resources and ways of solving problems. These discoveries result from the crisis experience itself. John's case (with multiple sclerosis) is a good example of such growth. He took advantage of resources available to him and his family, such as his physician and the school guidance counselor. He found new ways of solving problems. The result for John was a process of growth: (a) His concept of himself as a worthwhile person was reinforced in spite of the loss of physical integrity from his illness. (b) He strengthened his marriage and his ability to relate to his wife regarding a serious problem. This produced growth for both of them. (c) He developed in his role as a father by constructively handling the problem with his son in addition to his own personal stress.
3. The person responds to the problem by lapsing into neurotic, psychotic, or destructive patterns of behavior. For example, the individual may become very withdrawn, suspicious, or depressed. A person's distorted perception of events may be exaggerated to the point of blaming others inappropriately for the misfortunes experienced. Some people in crisis resolve their problems, at least temporarily, by excessive drinking or other drug abuse or by impulsive disruptive behavior. Others resort

to more extreme measures by attempting or committing suicide or by abusing or killing others.

All of these negative and destructive outcomes of the crisis experience occur when the individual lacks constructive ways of solving life's problems and relieving intolerable anxiety. George (with a heart attack) for example, came to the conclusion in his despair that he was worth more dead than alive. Consequently, he was brought to the hospital emergency department after a car crash. George crashed his car deliberately but did not die as he had planned. This was his chosen method of suicidal death, which he thought would spare his family the stigma of suicide. He felt that he had already over-burdened them. George's case will be continued in Chapters 3 and 4 with respect to his treatment in the emergency service and his follow-up care.

Considering all of the possible outcomes of a crisis experience, the following goals become obvious.

- To help people in crisis return at least to their precrisis state
- To do all that is possible to help people grow and become stronger as a result of the crisis and effective problem solving
- To be alert to danger signals in order to prevent negative, destructive outcomes of a crisis experience

The last goal is achieved by recognizing that negative results of crisis are often not necessary, but occur because of insufficient personal and family strengths or because of insensitivity and a lack of appropriate resources and crisis intervention skills in the human service sector (see Figure 2.1, Boxes 4a and 4b).

The Sociocultural Context of Personal Crisis

The contrasting cases of John (with multiple sclerosis) and George (with a heart attack) illustrate both the success and the limitations of individual approaches to life crises. Let us suppose that John and George each had identical help available from human services agencies. If George's crisis response is rooted partially in social and cultural sources—as seems to be the case—then intervention must consciously address these factors in order to be successful. Otherwise, unattended social and cultural issues can form a barrier to a strictly psychological crisis counseling approach. They also underscore McKinlay's argument (1990, p. 502) about "downstream" versus "upstream" endeavors and link individual crisis intervention efforts to complementary preventive and social change strategies.

Preventive strategies were discussed in the previous chapter. Individual and social network crisis intervention approaches are considered in detail in the remaining chapters. Social action ideas are incorporated in relevant cases throughout the book. The social change aspects of comprehensive crisis work belong to the follow-up phase of the total process (see Figure 1.3, Growth and Development Approach box). In the Crisis Paradigm (Figure 2.1), such social change strategies are illustrated in the right circle of Box 3, corresponding to sociocultural crisis origins in Box 1. However, the foundation for such action is laid in one of the cognitive aspects of healthy crisis resolution—*understanding* the traumatic event, its sources, and how it affects the way one feels during crisis. For example, a rape victim can be helped to understand that she feels guilty and dirty about being raped—not because she is in fact guilty and dirty—but because of the widely accepted social value that women are responsible if they are raped because they dress provocatively, hitchhike, or in a similar way allegedly provoke the attack (see Figure 2.2).

The tradition among human service workers of claiming "value neutrality" may lead some to object to including social change strategies as a formal part of service. Yet to offer only short-term crisis counseling or psychotherapy for problems stemming from cultural and social origins is value-laden in itself—that is, it suggests that the person should merely adjust to a disadvantaged position in society rather than develop and act on an awareness of the underlying factors contributing to depression or suicidal feelings (see, for example, McNamee & Gergen, 1992). As Johnson (1990, p. 230) points out, professionals who focus solely on purportedly neutral "clinical" material and avoid "this policy stuff," shortchange themselves and their clients whose crises are linked to various policy issues. It is therefore not a question of whether crisis workers are value-free, as such work is almost invariably affected by our values. Rather, values should be made explicit, so that clients can make their own choices (such as accepting or acting on their disadvantaged position) from a more enlightened base. For example, if international bodies such as the United Nations (UN) or Human Rights Watch publicly condemn torture or unfair economic policies, disadvantaged people are less likely to blame themselves when sociopolitical origins are thus made visible.

Social Change Strategies in Comprehensive Crisis Care

As readers are perhaps less familiar with social change strategies than with other aspects of crisis care follow-up, such as psychotherapy for underlying personality problems, the following summary is offered. It highlights the principles of social change agentry as presented in the Crisis Paradigm and is adapted from the classic work of Chin and Benne (1969). These strategies are central to positive crisis resolution, particularly those crises originating from sociocultural sources.

Strategies Based on Reason and Research

Foremost among these strategies are research findings, new concepts, and the clarification of language to more closely represent reality as experienced by people, not as theorized by academics. These strategies rest on the assumption that people are reasonable and when presented with evidence will take appropriate action to bring about needed change. However, this strategy alone is usually not enough to move people toward change, such as enacting workplace policies that affect staff safety and injury prevention on the job.

Strategies Based on Reeducation and Attitude Change

These approaches to change are based on the assumption that people are guided by internalized values and habits and that they act according to institutionalized roles and perceptions of self. For example, some parents need help to balance their personal happiness with parental responsibility for the children they brought into the world. This group of strategies includes an activity central to contemporary crisis theory—fostering learning and growth in the persons who make up the system to be changed. This includes people who are in crisis because of greater vulnerability stemming from a disadvantaged position in society. This change strategy is also relevant to people whose usual coping devices leave something to be desired, such as people with learned helplessness, excessive drinking, or those who abuse others (see Figure 2.2). Prominent illustrations of this strategy include (1) the mediation and nonviolent conflict resolution programs being instituted to stem the tide of youth violence (Jenkins & Bell, 1992; Kottler, 1994) and (2) programs aimed at reclaiming values of respect for the environment and for people different from ourselves. An example of this kind of program is the Teaching Tolerance program of the Southern Poverty Law Center. Through such programs, experiencing and dealing openly with the psychic pain of the crisis experience (in contrast to resorting to violence or chronic unhealthy coping) often moves people to learn new ways of coping with life's problems.

Power-Coercive Strategies

The emphasis in these strategies is on political and economic sanctions in the exercise of power, along with such moral power moves as playing on sentiments of guilt, shame, and a sense of what is just and right. It is assumed that political action approaches will probably not succeed apart from reeducation and attitude changes. New action, such as strikes by nurses who have been traditionally socialized to a subservient role in the health care system, demands by ethnic minorities to end housing and job discrimination, or protests against harassment and violence based on sexual identity, usually requires "new knowledge, new skills, new attitudes, and new value orientations" (Chin & Benne, 1969, p. 42; Holland, 1994).

In a similar vein, Marris (1987, pp. 156–164) proposes that new formulations of social meaning should accompany struggles to assert the ideals of society and to implement social justice policies. This presumes collective planning by people concerned with those who are distressed or in crisis because of discrimination and repressive policies—for example, feminists; racial equity groups; immigrants; gay, lesbian, bisexual, and transgendered activists; and disabled persons.

Prevention of such crises and their aftermath demands civic involvement and planned engagement with powerful government bodies to resolve contested immigration and related issues through the voting booth and an orderly reform process versus a "show of force" tactic, for example, raiding a workplace whose immigrant laborers were stitching armored vests and back packs for U.S. solders in Iraq.

Unique Cultural Resources and Constraints in Change Agentry

The incorporation of social change strategies into a comprehensive approach to crisis work underscores the importance of tailoring intervention strategies to correspond with the origins of stress and crisis, as illustrated in the Crisis Paradigm. Some of these origins are clearly cultural in character. As noted in Chapter 1, deeply held beliefs, norms, and rules about appropriate behavior and customs (as in "cultural relativism," see Chapter 1) can lead to violation of universal human rights including everyone's right to bodily integrity, health care, freedom of movement, and physical safety. When this seems to be the case in some crisis situations, a mutually respectful and collaborative relationship is crucial to positive crisis resolution. For example, if parents cite their religious beliefs as a basis for corporal punishment of children or the marriage of underage minors, principles of basic human rights must prevail in the state's responsibility to protect children from physical and sexual abuse. Not to do so evokes the concept of "cultural relativism" as an excuse to look the other way with "that's just part of their religion" (see Lowery, 1984).

Some women have been socialized to accept their culturally prescribed role in society; for example, the view that their vulnerability and constraints on their behavior are necessary because of their biologically based and therefore natural psychic weakness (Sayers, 1982). Women may therefore expect to simply *endure* what nature offers—not unlike survivors of natural disaster. However, social cultural sources of stress can be *resisted*, as can the threat of man-made disaster.

On the other hand, people in crisis across cultures can rely on traditional beliefs in the role of the family in caring for distressed members, and various healing ceremonies such as Shamanism in some Latino societies (Dobkin de Rios, 2002). Another important resource in multicultural societies is the availability of crisis workers who speak the language of clients served. It is said that language is the window to culture. The lack of language resources can result in tragic crisis outcomes—especially among refugees from disaster and war.

These ideas support the importance of raising consciousness and employing human rights and public health perspectives in crisis work. It is now common for health and mental health professionals to recommend that victims of intimate partner violence, rape victims, and survivors of war and disaster trauma participate in support groups that assist them in addressing these kinds of social and political issues in the healing process.

Table 2.2 illustrates how these ideas are encompassed in a comprehensive approach with respect to the various elements of the crisis experienced by George and his family. (See Chapter 5, Social Network and Group Process, for an illustration of this comprehensive approach to an abused woman, Ramona.) The approaches can be grouped as preventive and enhancement, immediate or short-term, and long-range (follow-up). This diagram suggests

TABLE 2.2   Comprehensive Crisis Care

	Approaches to Crisis Care and Resolution		
Crisis Element	**Preventive and Enhancement**	**Immediate or Short-Term**	**Long-Range (Follow-Up)**
Heart attack	Lifestyle factors (such as diet, exercise, relaxation)	Life-support measures	Lifestyle factors
Marital and role strain	Marriage preparation Communication	Marriage counseling	Normative reeducative change
Midlife change and marital strain	Rites of passage (such as a support group)[a]	Women's support group Men's support group	Normative reeducative change strategies
Arnold's school suspension	Rites of passage (such as adolescent support group)	Family and social network crisis counseling	Family counseling or therapy
George's suicide attempt	Family support and normative reeducative change following first heart attack	Individual and family crisis counseling	Family counseling Normative reeducative change Lifestyle factors

[a] Contemporary substitutes for traditional rites of passage are discussed in Chapter 6.

that primary prevention and enhancement activities can abort a destructive crisis outcome like premature death. It demonstrates, too, the interactions and relationship (not necessarily an orderly sequence) between strategies, as well as the fact that various elements of comprehensive crisis care may be included in a single encounter with a person in crisis. The diagram illustrates that it is never too late to consider preventive and enhancement approaches (such as at secondary and tertiary levels), even if a suicide attempt has been made; nor is it ever too late to learn from the experience of others (Hoff & Resing, 1982).

The case of George suggests the intersection of responses relevant to crises originating from three sources: traumatic personal situations, transition states, and gender-role strain related to socialization. This case also underscores the fact that people will resolve their crises with or without the help of significant others. People rich in personal, social, and material resources are often able to resolve crises positively in a natural (as opposed to institutional) context with the help of family, friends, and neighbors. Many, however, lack such resources or for personal, cultural, and political reasons cannot mobilize them successfully during crisis. In these instances, more formal help from trained crisis workers is needed to see them through this potentially dangerous period and promote positive crisis resolution (see Figure 2.1, Box 4a). The rest of this book is devoted to the principles and strategies necessary for effective crisis intervention—assessment, planning, implementation of plan, and follow-up—the formal aspect of crisis care.

Summary and Discussion Questions

Success in crisis assessment and intervention depends on our understanding (1) the origins of crisis, (2) how crisis differs from stress and illness, and (3) the development and individual manifestations of crisis. Regardless of the origin of crisis, people in crisis have a number of characteristics in common. The probability of preventing negative outcomes for these individuals is increased by our sensitivity to the origins of crisis and the application of appropriate intervention strategies in distinct sociocultural contexts. These concepts are illustrated in the Crisis Paradigm, which provides the theoretical framework of this book.

1. Compare and contrast the growth-and-development and medical models of crisis intervention in terms of cost containment and recidivism among mentally ill persons in crisis.
2. Consider the various reasons why violence and abuse are rampant worldwide despite advocacy from groups such as the United Nations and Amnesty International.
3. Why are "reductionist" theories of stress of limited value in understanding crisis care?
4. Identify an example that reveals the intertwined origins of crisis as the basis for assessment and intervention.
5. Why is it important to distinguish between stress, crisis, and mental illness?

References

Antonovsky, A. (1980). *Health, stress, and coping*. San Francisco: Jossey-Bass.

Brown, G. W. (1993). Life events and affective disorder: Replications and limitations. *Psychosomatic Medicine, 55*(3), 248–259.

Brown, G. W., & Harris, T. (1978). *The social origins of depression*. London: Tavistock.

Browne, A. (1987). *When battered women kill*. New York: Free Press.

Caplan, G. (1964). *Principles of preventive psychiatry*. New York: Basic Books.

Chin, R., & Benne, K. D. (1969). General strategies for effecting change in human systems. In W. G. Bennis, K. D. Benne, & R. Chin (Eds.), *The planning of change* (2nd ed., pp. 32–57). Austin, TX: Holt, Rinehart and Winston.

Clark, A. T. (2006). Coping with interpersonal stress and psychosocial health among children and adolescents: A meta-analysis. *Journal of Youth and Adolescence, 35*(1), 11–24.

Conger, R. D., Lorenz, F. O., Elder, G. H., & Simons, R. L. (1993). Husband and wife differences in response to undesirable life events. *Journal of Health and Social Behavior, 34*(1), 71–88.

Danish, S. J., Smyer, M. A., & Nowak, C. A. (1980). Developmental intervention: Enhancing life-event processes. *Life-Span Development and Behavior, 3*, 339–366.

Dobash, R. E., & Dobash, R. P. (Eds.). (1998). *Rethinking violence against women*. Thousand Oaks, CA: Sage.

Dobkin de Rios, M. (2002). What we can learn from hamanic healing: Brief psychotherapy with Latino immigrant clients. *American Journal of Public Health*, 92(10), 1576–1578.

Durkheim, E. (1951). *Suicide* (2nd ed.). New York: Free Press. (Original work published 1897.)

Erikson. E. (1963). *Childhood and society* (2nd ed.). New York: Norton.

Friedman, R. A. (2006). Violence and mental illness—How strong is the link? *New England Journal of Medicine, 355*(20), 2064–2066.

Green, D. L., & Diaz, N. (2007). Predictions of emotional stress in crime victims: Implications for treatment. *Brief Treatment and Crisis Intervention, 7*, (194–205).

Hansell, N. (1976). *The person in distress.* New York: Human Sciences Press.

Herman, J. (1992). *Trauma and recovery: The aftermath of violence.* New York: Basic Books.

Hoff, L. A. (1990). *Battered women as survivors.* London: Routledge.

Hoff, L. A. (1993). Review essay: Health policy and the plight of the mentally ill. *Psychiatry, 56*(4), 400–419.

Hoff, L. A. (2000a). Crisis care. In B. Everett & R. Gallop (Eds.), *The link between childhood trauma and mental illness: Effective interventions for mental health professionals* (pp. 227–251). Thousand Oaks, CA: Sage.

Hoff, L. A. (2000b). Interpersonal violence. In C. E. Koop, C. E. Pearson, & M. R. Schwarz (Eds.), *Critical issues in global health* (pp. 260–271). San Francisco: Jossey-Bass.

Hoff, L. A., & Resing, M. (1982). Was this suicide preventable? *American Journal of Nursing, 82*(7), 1106–1111. (Also reprinted in B. A. Backer, P. M. Dubbert, & E. J. P. Eisenman, Eds. 1985. *Psychiatric/mental health nursing: Contemporary readings*, pp. 169–180. Belmont, CA: Wadsworth.)

Hoff, M. (2005). *Resilience: A paradigm of promise.* Unpublished master's thesis. Fargo: North Dakota State University, Department of Counselor Education.

Hogberg, U., & Bergstrom, E. (2000). Suffocated prone: The iatrogenic tragedy of SIDS. *American Journal of Public Health, 90*(4), 527–531.

Holland, H. (1994). *Born in Soweto.* Harmondsworth, England: Penguin Books.

Jenkins, E. J., & Bell, C. C. (1992). Adolescent violence: Can it be curbed? *Adolescent Medicine: State of the Art Reviews, 3*(1), 71–86.

Johnson, A. B. (1990). *Out of bedlam: The truth about deinstitutionalization.* New York: Basic Books.

Kottler, J. A. (1994). *Beyond blame: A new way of resolving conflicts in relationships.* San Francisco: Jossey-Bass.

Landy, D. (Ed.). (1977). *Culture, disease, and healing: Studies in medical anthropology.* Old Tappan, NJ: Macmillan.

Lindemann, E. (1944). Symptomatology and management of acute grief. *American Journal of Psychiatry, 101*, 101–148. (Also reprinted in H. J. Parad, Ed. 1965. *Crisis intervention: Selected readings.* New York: Family Service Association of America.)

Loustaunau, M. O., & Sobo, E. J. (1997). *The cultural context of health, illness, and medicine.* New York: Bergin & Garvey.

Lowery, C. R. (1984). The wisdom of Solomon: Criteria for child custody from the legal and clinical points of view. *Law and Human Behavior, 8*(3/4), 371–380.

Marris, P. (1987). *Meaning and action: Community action and conceptions of change* (2nd ed.). London: Routledge.

Maslow, A. (1970). *Motivation and personality* (2nd ed.). New York: HarperCollins.

Mawby, R. I., & Walklate, S. (1994). *Critical victimology.* Thousand Oaks, CA: Sage.

McCullough, C. J. (1995). *Nobody's victim*. New York: Clarkson/Potter.

McElroy, A., & Townsend, P. K. (1985). *Medical anthropology in ecological perspective*. Boulder, CO: Westview Press.

McKinlay, J. B. (1990). A case for refocusing upstream: The political economy of illness. In P. Conrad & R. Kern (Eds.), *The sociology of health and illness: Critical perspectives* (3rd ed., pp. 502–516). New York: St. Martin's Press.

McKinlay, J. B., & Marceau, L. D. (1999). A tale of 3 tails. *American Journal of Public Health, 89*(3), 295–298.

McNamee, S., & Gergen, K. J. (Eds.). (1992). *Therapy as social construction*. Thousand Oaks, CA: Sage.

Meyer, I. H., & Schwartz, S. (2000). Social issues as public health: Promise and peril. *American Journal of Public Health, 90*(8), 1189–1191.

Richman, J. A., Cloninger, L., & Rospenda, K. M. (2008). Macrolevel stressors, terrorism, and mental health outcomes: Broadening the stress paradigm. *American Journal of Public Health, 98*(2), 323–329.

Rieker, P. P., & Carmen, E. H. (1986). The victim-to-patient process: The disconfirmation and transformation of abuse. *American Journal of Orthopsychiatry, 56*, 360–371.

Ryan, W. (1971). *Blaming the victim*. New York: Vintage Books.

Sanders, S. (2008). *Understanding resilience*. New York: Routledge.

Sayers, J. (1982). *Biological politics*. London: Tavistock.

Schulberg, H. C., & Sheldon, A. (1968). The probability of crisis and strategies for preventive intervention. *Archives of General Psychiatry, 18*, 553–558.

Selye, H. (1956). *The stress of life*. New York: McGraw-Hill.

Turner, R. J., & Avison, W. R. (1992). Innovations in the measurement of life stress: Crisis theory and the significance of event resolution. *Journal of Health and Social Behavior, 33*(1), 36–50.

Tyhurst, J. S. (1957). The role of transition states—including disasters—in mental illness. In *Symposium on preventive and social psychiatry*. Washington, DC: Walter Reed Army Institute of Research and the National Research Council.

Vaillant, G. E. (1993). *The wisdom of the ego: Sources of resilience in adult life*. Cambridge, MA: Harvard University Press.

WGBH Educational Foundation. *Survivors* [Public television documentary]. (1982). Boston: Author.

See Online Resources for additional references.

危機

CHAPTER 3

Identifying People at Risk

We know, generally, how crises originate, and we know how to predict and prevent many crises or destructive crisis outcomes in large population groups. This general knowledge, however, must be made accessible for use with individuals in actual or potential crisis. Crises from some sources are predictable and therefore more easily prepared for; preparation helps reduce the risk of crisis as well as the possibility of damaging outcomes. Common sources of predictable crises are developmental states and the role changes marking adolescence, adulthood, marriage, midlife, retirement, and old age. Typically, a person may first go to school, then get a job, find a life partner, become a parent, and reach the age of retirement. Because role changes usually are anticipated, precautions can be taken to avoid a crisis. But some people do not or cannot prepare themselves for these events; the possibility of crisis for them is increased. For example, a young person whose parents have been overindulgent and inconsistent in their responses will find it difficult to move from adolescence to adulthood. Overprotective parents stifle a child's normal development, so the move to adulthood becomes a risk and a hazard rather than an opportunity for further challenge and growth. Also, a person need not rush into marriage but can thoughtfully consider what such a major role change implies. Yet many do rush, and crises result.

Another factor affecting these predictable role changes is the element of timing (see Chapters 2 and 6). For example, a man or woman marrying for the first time at age 40 may have planned very carefully for this life change, but altering an established pattern of living alone and being independent may lead to unanticipated stress. In addition, parental and other social supports for newlyweds are less likely to be available in later marriages. In contrast, although a planned event such as a return to school at midlife can be hazardous due to atypical timing, an older student may be less vulnerable to crisis. This is because a more mature student or life partner often has the advantage of experience, financial security, and clear-cut goals—valuable resources that younger people may possess in lesser measure.

Another aspect of a potentially hazardous role transition, even if prepared for, is its timing in connection with other life events. Many life changes are in one's control (for example, marriage or returning to school in midlife), whereas others are not (for example, menopause or death of an elderly parent). Careful planning around controllable changes can reduce a person's cumulative stress and the hazards of crisis, illness, and accidents.

Other life events are less predictable: sudden death of a loved one; serious physical illness; urban dislocation; personal and financial loss through flood, hurricane, or fire; birth of a premature infant. When these unanticipated events occur during transition states or when they originate from cultural values and one's disadvantaged social position, the probability of crisis is increased.

These examples and the interactive nature of crisis origins (discussed in Chapters 1 and 2) underscore the subjective nature of the crisis experience and the need to identify individuals at risk. Regardless of how predictable crisis responses might be among groups, it is important to translate *general* risk factors into an assessment of the issues and problems faced by *this* person or family at *this* particular time. Such an assessment—and assistance based on it—implies the need for precise information about individuals and families who may be at risk. For example,

1. In what developmental phase is the person or family?
2. What recent hazardous events have occurred in the life of this person or family?
3. How has this person or family interpreted these events?
4. Is there actual or potential threat to life? How urgent is the need for intervention?
5. What is the sociocultural context in which all of this is happening?

The ramifications of answers to these and related questions form the basis of this chapter on identifying and assessing people in precrisis or crisis states, the focus of Box 2 in Figure 3.1, the Crisis Paradigm.

The Importance of Crisis Assessment

Observers may think that an emotionally upset person is obviously in a state of crisis. This is not necessarily so; thorough assessment should precede such a judgment. Still, an untrained observer may quickly dismiss the need for assessment in order to proceed to a seemingly more urgent task—to *help* the individual. Such well-intentioned help sometimes has the opposite effect, however. This is most likely to happen if the urge to help springs from a helper's excessive need to be needed, thereby obscuring the distressed person's basic need for mastery and self-determination. One way to avoid misplaced helping is to be aware of and not indulge in rescue fantasies. Another is to identify people at risk through a careful assessment process that includes the intersections of life events with transition states.

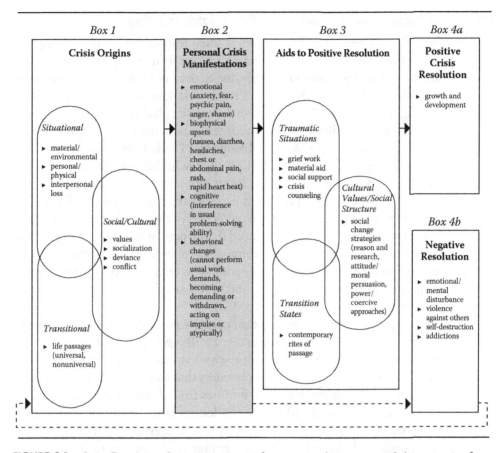

Box 1	Box 2	Box 3	Box 4a
Crisis Origins	**Personal Crisis Manifestations**	**Aids to Positive Resolution**	**Positive Crisis Resolution**

Situational

▶ material/ environmental
▶ personal/ physical
▶ interpersonal loss

Social/Cultural

▶ values
▶ socialization
▶ deviance
▶ conflict

Transitional

▶ life passages (universal, nonuniversal)

▶ emotional (anxiety, fear, psychic pain, anger, shame)
▶ biophysical upsets (nausea, diarrhea, headaches, chest or abdominal pain, rash, rapid heart beat)
▶ cognitive (interference in usual problem-solving ability)
▶ behavioral changes (cannot perform usual work demands, becoming demanding or withdrawn, acting on impulse or atypically)

Traumatic Situations

▶ grief work
▶ material aid
▶ social support
▶ crisis counseling

Cultural Values/Social Structure

▶ social change strategies (reason and research, attitude/ moral persuasion, power/ coercive approaches)

Transition States

▶ contemporary rites of passage

▶ growth and development

Box 4b

Negative Resolution

▶ emotional/ mental disturbance
▶ violence against others
▶ self-destruction
▶ addictions

FIGURE 3.1 Crisis Paradigm. Crisis origins, manifestations, and outcomes and the respective functions of crisis care have interactional relationships. The intertwined circles represent the distinct yet interrelated origins of crisis and aids to positive resolution, even though personal manifestations are often similar. The arrows pointing from origins to positive resolution illustrate the *opportunity for growth and development* through crisis; the broken line at the bottom depicts the potential *danger of crisis* in the absence of appropriate aids. The loop between Box 4b and Box 1 denotes the *vulnerability* to future crisis episodes following negative resolution.

Impediments to Adequate Assessment

Assessment can be impeded by the very nature of the crisis intervention process, a humane function that is now standard practice in health and social service settings. Helping people in crisis is immediate and often highly rewarding. However, those human service workers who are most inclined to action and who expect to obtain quick observable results often do not take time to study and evaluate their own work (see Online Resources). When the challenge of self-review is combined with the difficulty of evaluating any human helping process objectively, it is easy to see how comprehensive crisis care can flounder. This is a particularly hazardous approach in the era of managed care and provider time constraints in the United States when psychotropic drugs may be used for psychosocial problems. Without a sound theoretical base and established techniques, there is little to distinguish crisis intervention from intuitive first aid.

Hazards of Inadequate Assessment and Psychiatric Labeling

The failure to assess prior to helping is often responsible for the misapplication of the crisis model. In the human service field, it is particularly unfortunate to misjudge a person in crisis due to poor observation and inadequate assessment. Ultimately, these errors result in failure to help, which can have lifelong, destructive effects. Successful crisis prediction and assessment increase the possibility of preventive intervention and make hospital admission (and its attendant risks) less likely (see "Crisis Care" in Chapter 1). A note from the golden age of social psychiatry highlights the importance of assessment and resolution of crisis as an alternative to psychiatric hospitalization; this observation about what happens after admission is still relevant: "The admission itself tends to promote denial of the social forces in the family and community that have produced it. The patient may then emerge as the scapegoat for these family and community problems, and psychiatric assessment [versus crisis assessment] after admission tends to focus on the patient's symptomatology [versus strengths and problem-solving ability] as the major cause of admission" (Polak, 1967, p. 153).

Inadequate assessment has another negative result. When there is only the *appearance*—not the reality—of crisis, an ill-advised response might reinforce crisis-like behavior by someone who has learned that the only way to get help is to convince health care providers that there is a crisis. This pattern is observed increasingly in calls to hotlines from discharged mental patients or chronically ill people who lack the longer-term treatment and support their condition requires. The complexity and danger of this situation for suicidal people is discussed further in Chapter 9. The person in crisis and the family should be advised, therefore, that there are many alternative ways of resolving life's crises.

Since the widespread deinstitutionalization of the mentally ill, psychotropic drug use is often the chemical restraint substituting for the locked doors of a psychiatric hospital, even for misdiagnosed young children from families with multiple problems—including violence—that cry out for a family-centered comprehensive treatment plan (Gellene, 2007). Or, at the opposite extreme, Pete Earley (2006) was told when seeking treatment of his son for a serious psychotic episode, "If your son isn't going to hurt you or someone else, he doesn't need to be in a locked mental ward" (p. 28).

Crisis: "Normal" Response to Acute Stress and/or Psychiatric "Disorder"

Discussion in this section is particularly relevant to mental health clinicians and primary care providers who are trained in use of the DSM-IV-TR (*Diagnostic and Statistical Manual of Mental Disorders*) and licensed to diagnose and treat people with mental health disorders. However, the controversial points around psychiatric diagnosing are also relevant for frontline crisis personnel, such as social service case workers, who confront serious—even life-threatening—crises in their everyday work, but who do not feel qualified to question medical decisions and/or psychotropic drug prescriptions in complex and highly disturbed family situations. The issues concerning this topic assume the widely recognized mind/body/emotional/spiritual connections in people's responses to life stressors having a much longer history than relatively recent "formal" crisis theory. Discussion also assumes evidence-based findings of the biological and genetic factors contributing to these serious disorders: schizophrenia, dementias, and bipolar illness.[1]

Case Example: Rebecca

The dilemma regarding psychiatric diagnosing and its intersection with serious family problems is highlighted in the tragic death of 4-year-old Rebecca Riley. At age 2, Rebecca was diagnosed with "bipolar disorder." This diagnosis served as a psychiatrist's rationale for prescribing powerful psychotropic drugs for Rebecca (FDA-approved only for adults) under the *off-label* authority of physicians for such use. Autopsy results revealed an overdose of these drugs as the cause of Rebecca's death. Since Rebecca's mother administered the drugs, she was charged with first-degree murder, with the charge later reduced to second-degree murder.

This case provoked national controversy among mental health professionals regarding the assignment of "bipolar disorder" to Rebecca and her prepuberty siblings (Diller, 2007, p. A9; Elliott, 2006). As psychologist Stephen Schlein (2007, p. A11) asked: "How could a child be diagnosed with a bipolar disorder at the age of 2 . . . when there's so much going on in the life of a 2-year-old related to normal problems of human development and ordinary concerns of daily living? . . . We now have a whole culture obsessed with diagnostic labels [with a] focus on taking the right medicine." In a similar vein, even the NIMH (National Institute of Mental Health) director, Dr. Thomas R. Insel, has said that the increase in bipolar diagnoses is "worrisome" (Gellene, 2007, p. A2). A flippant use of the term *bipolar* has also drifted into popular culture, with the expression, "Oh, she's bipolar!" as an excuse for mere bad behavior by someone with a satisfactory work record and enjoying stable relationships—two major life functions that typically are disrupted for someone suffering the serious psychiatric disorder *bipolar illness*.

Of particular significance in this case was the child's presumed "psychopathology" with minimal attention to other serious family issues. While this

---

[1] The DSM-IV-TR, 4th edition, 2000, is an expanded volume of 943 pages, with 10.5 pages of codes. In the DSM-II, depression had 8 subtypes, while in DSM-III and IV, depression subtypes multiplied to over 2000. We might well ask: Does this represent an evidence-based increase in mental illness? Or is it something more complex, including the political-economic and the social construction of mental illness? Readers are referred to Cooksey & Brown (1998) and to Brown & Hoff (in press), for further analyses regarding mental health assessment. See also McHugh (2005) for his description of the DSM as a symptom, appearance-driven manual comparable to bird and botanical field guides. Psychiatrists McHugh and Clark (2006) propose explanatory methods instead, modeled after medicine's *International Statistical Classification of Diseases and Related Health Problems*. Such a model moves beyond symptoms to organize psychiatric disorders as etiopathic clusters such as the "perspectives" approach used at the Johns Hopkins University School of Medicine. This approach distinguishes symptoms from causes, asking as a basis for treatment planning: What does the patient have? Who are they? What do they do? What do they encounter?

family was also on the rolls of the state's Child Protective Services, case workers did not feel qualified to question the treating psychiatrist's drug regimen for Rebecca. The legal ramifications of this case include a lawsuit against the prescribing psychiatrist. While Schlein notes that the "mental health field has regressed in a most dramatic fashion," a partial explanation for his view and that of many others may lie in the fact that the psychiatrist "treating" Rebecca was caught up in an uncritical acceptance of the biological psychiatry paradigm that allowed for overlooking the "elephant in the living room," that is, the failure to address the complex family issues affecting Rebecca and her siblings (Luhrmann, 2000; see also Chapter 5, social network techniques, for an intervention option that might have averted this tragedy).

Psychiatric Labeling and Crisis Assessment

Institutionalization is certainly more expensive than community-based crisis intervention, but that is not the only consideration. The institutionalization of the upset person can possibly make matters worse, and certainly more complicated. After diagnosis, the person takes on the identity of a patient and falls into roles expected by the institution. The classic works of Becker (1963), Goffman (1961), and Lemert (1951) are supported by later research (Link, Phelan, Bresnahan, Stueve, & Pescosolido, 1997) documenting the enduring negative effects of psychiatric labeling, *even* when psychiatric treatment has had positive results. Essentially, the same thing can happen to an adolescent confined to a detention center, with even more negative impact at this stage of life cycle development. But some families do request institutionalization for disturbed or aggressive people when they can no longer care for them at home.

Today, however, those for whom psychiatric inpatient treatment is indicated and truly necessary face triple jeopardy in the United States because of disparity in health insurance for the treatment of emotional and mental illness. (1) They may have to "invent" a life-threatening crisis as a ticket to hospital admission. (2) Once there, they suffer the possible negative fallout of living with the psychiatric diagnosis required for reimbursement of treatment costs. (3) Once discharged and often before recommended treatment is completed, they are at greater risk of repeat crisis episodes and readmission for hospital treatment. The human and financial costs of psychiatric recidivism from this misguided approach are enormous, tragic, and mostly preventable.

This scenario is most acute and potentially most damaging for seriously disturbed or out-of-control children and adolescents in the United States, a situation that has reached crisis proportions nationwide. Admission of these children to general pediatric wards, adult psychiatric units, or detention, combined with the administration of psychotropic drugs never tested for use with children, reveals the need for two policy actions: (1) the provision of special child and adolescent psychiatric inpatient treatment services and (2) the return to the prevention and early intervention ideals of community-based and 24-hour, 7-day-a-week access to comprehensive crisis service and outpatient treatment, as recommended by the Congressional Joint Commission on Mental Health and Illness over a half century ago (1961).

Older adults as well are vulnerable to the hazards of psychiatric labeling. Besides their greater risk for organically based diseases such as Parkinson's or Alzheimer's, many older people suffer from depression (Osgood, 1992). In most instances, their depression is linked to the series of losses that many have endured at this stage of the life cycle—for example, life partner, physical health or mobility, friends who have died or are unable to visit. One gerontologist advised primary care providers to apply *functional* instead of psychiatric diagnostic criteria when assessing such persons (see Comprehensive Mental Health Assessment (CMHA), later in this chapter). As he aptly noted, an 85-year-old man grieving the loss of his spouse and his own failing health does not need to go to his grave with a psychiatric label.

Every society has social norms—that is, expectations of how people are to interact with others. When people deviate from these norms, sanctions are applied or stigmas attached to pressure the deviant member to return to acceptable norms of behavior, suffer the consequences of their deviance, or behave in accord with their stigmatized status. Deviance can therefore be considered from three perspectives as illustrated in the following examples:

1. In Western societies, a widow may be socially ostracized if she mourns the loss of her husband beyond the generally accepted few weeks. If she does so, she deviates from the expected norm for grief and mourning in a death-denying society.
2. A person who is caught and convicted of stealing a car or molesting a child has engaged in behavior that is explicitly forbidden in most societies. Although these are clear-cut examples of deviance, the results of such violations vary. For example, an African American is more likely to be apprehended and judged harshly for the car theft than is a white person in the United States.
3. Some people are considered deviant not for particular actions but for some aspect of their being. Thus, a gay person, a woman in menopause, an old person, or a handicapped individual carries a "mark" and can be stigmatized as a result of a physical, social, or mental attribute. The physical or social mark (difference) may become indistinguishable from the person's identity. Goffman (1963) in his classic work on stigma refers to this as "spoiled identity." Thus, a person does not *suffer* from paraplegia or schizophrenia but *is* a paraplegic or schizophrenic; the person who takes his or her own life does not just *commit* suicide but *is* a suicide; a woman with a tumultuous social history that often includes sexual abuse as a child is not just difficult to treat but *is* a "borderline" (Everett & Gallop, 2000). The person's identity becomes encompassed in a particular behavior or physical or mental characteristic.

Labeling theory, a controversial topic in social science, continues as the subject of lively debate (Link et al., 1997). Briefly, labeling theory proposes the concepts of primary and secondary deviance in an interactive relationship, as illustrated in Figure 3.2. The argument between advocates and critics of

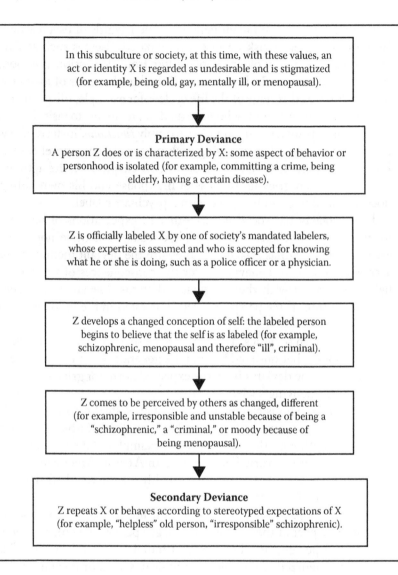

FIGURE 3.2 Relationship between Primary and Secondary Deviance. X = a deviant act or identity; Z = a particular person labeled as deviant. Thanks to John McKinlay for his ideas about representing labeling theory in this format.

labeling theory centers on this question: Would secondary deviance occur if the person who is labeled did not experience both an altered self-concept and a change in the way others perceive him or her? An extreme view is that primary deviance could virtually be dismissed except for the detrimental effects of labeling and secondary deviance following it. In contrast, Gove (1978) suggests that the higher rates of depression among women have nothing to do with the labeling of mental illness. Rather, he says, depression among women is related to their disadvantaged position in society. This may be so, particularly if women are socialized to *endure* rather than *resist* oppression, as Cloward and Piven (1979) suggest. Each of these positions has implications for crisis assessment as well as for general mental health practice. This is because certain personal attributes or behaviors do not fall into the range of behavior and conditions commonly accepted as normal and desirable. This is primary deviance, which exists whether or not it is identified with a label. For example, some people break social rules even though they are not always caught and identified as rule breakers.

There are distinct disadvantages for those who are labeled because of gender, sexual identity, and other bias (Fausto-Sterling, 2000; Holden, 1986). People may try to "pass" or hide their identities because of the prejudices of others. For example, gay, lesbian, bisexual, and transgendered people are very careful about coming out; many women will not reveal their age, or they become avid consumers of beauty aids to keep a youthful appearance; people with a psychiatric problem may not wish to reveal the diagnosis, as they often experience prejudice in the job market. Alternatively, people may feel compelled to act as others expect. For example, misbehaving children inappropriately labeled as disabled may refer to their social security disability checks as "crazy" money; convicted lawbreakers often repeat their offenses; or a person diagnosed with schizophrenia may say, "How do you expect me to succeed in this job? I'm a schizophrenic." Diagnostic labeling has also been critiqued for its inappropriate application cross-culturally (Hagey & McDonough, 1984), its ethical implications (Mitchell, 1991), and its lack of scientific objectivity (Cooksey & Brown, 1998). In cases of domestic abuse, it can obscure the primary *social* issue of violence (Hoff, 2000).

Labeling theory is particularly relevant to crisis assessment practice and in the relationship of crisis to illness. If crisis is viewed as an opportunity for change and growth rather than as an illness or occasion for social or psychiatric labeling, assessment can be an important step toward growth. But crisis assessment should not be confused with traditional psychiatric diagnosis; in the view of many, psychiatry is not highly scientific, and diagnoses can often be contradictory, despite current emphasis on the biological correlates of mental illness (Cohen, 1993). The DSM, sometimes referred to as the "bible" of psychiatric diagnosticians, has come under particular scrutiny for its social biases and the disproportionate power it wields while disparities persist in insurance reimbursement for mental health services (Johnson, 2008; McHugh, 2001; McHugh & Clark, 2006; see also Caplan, 1995).

Psychological evaluation is inherently subjective and often tinged with political considerations, as these authors attest. Another example of this is the contradictory evidence presented by psychiatrists representing the defense and the prosecution in criminal cases with insanity pleas. This does not mean that efforts to improve the objectivity of psychiatric diagnostic procedures should stop. Nor does it deny the fact that some people in crisis are also mentally disturbed and therefore diagnosable in a psychiatric framework. It simply means that a crisis experience should be assessed and approached in a crisis—not an illness—framework, so that negative outcomes such as illness are avoided. If mental illness was present before the crisis, the chances of its recurrence are reduced with timely crisis care. Casting the currently accessible, humane approach of crisis intervention into an illness framework might render it as bureaucratic and inaccessible as some aspects of the traditional health care system. In short, one might ask, why attach a diagnostic label that is actually or potentially damaging, when illness may not be the central issue and when the person's subjective meaning system is central to the crisis resolution process?

Anthropologist Tanya Luhrmann's (2000) extensive field study of medical residents training to be psychiatrists offers some profoundly disturbing answers to this question, many intertwined with theoretical, economic, and moral issues. See also Nehls's research (1999) regarding patients' experience of psychiatric labeling and its stigma, and Rosenhan's (1973) classic study of psychiatric patient identity. Rosenhan demonstrated that the psychiatric professionals charged with the admission and diagnosis of those regarded as insane could not distinguish between pseudo-patients and the truly impaired. Consequently, the pseudo-patients had a difficult time getting released from the hospital even though they had no objective signs of mental illness. The study supports Polak's (1967) observations—now standard for the most part—that psychiatric hospitalization

- Is a crisis in itself
- Is the direct result of previously undetected and unresolved crisis
- Should be avoided whenever possible
- Should be used only as a last resort when all other efforts to help have failed
- Should be substituted, whenever possible, with accurate crisis assessment and intervention in the person's natural social setting

Now that psychiatric hospitalization is less common, and thousands are discharged without housing or adequate community support, mentally disturbed people nevertheless endure similar biases and burdens in life on the streets (Earley, 2006; Hoff, 1993; Johnson, 1990).

This discussion supports the earlier recommendations about assessment and intervention in natural settings (see Chapter 1). It is not that psychiatrists and other mental health professionals do not understand the difference between crisis and mental illness, but once a patient is admitted to a medical or hospital establishment, managed care and insurance policies require diagnosing them. The potentially damaging results of psychiatric labeling occur in the context of continuing cultural bias against the mentally ill. Capponi (1992), for example, describes the challenges faced by "psychiatric survivors" of the system purportedly designed to help them. The tragic continuation of this challenge among veterans of the Afghanistan and Iraq wars is dramatic in ascribing to some of them seeking mental health treatment the diagnosis of "personality disorder" instead of posttraumatic stress disorder (PTSD).

Since the Vietnam War, PTSD has become the lexicon for what heretofore was labeled "shell shock," an essentially *normal* response to the horrific traumas of war; e.g., witnessing and then carrying away the mutilated and dead body of one's comrade—traumas "out of normal range" of everyday human experience. The personality disorder diagnosis serves the purpose of justifying a presumed "preexisting" condition as a basis for denying disability benefits to veterans after putting their lives on the line to support war goals. Public response to this failure in the fundamentals of crisis and mental health care of veterans has extended even to the U.S. Congress (Kors, 2007; Madrigal, 2005; Sennott, 2007). The "social construction" of mental illness has a long and tortured history which sadly continues, not only because of the misuse or overuse of psychiatric labels, but also because it can hinder the important business of diagnosing and appropriately treating serious mental illness, which has biological origins and occurs across cultures (McHugh & Clark, 2006).

Diversity Perspectives on Diagnosis

In a diversity perspective, similar negative consequences were dramatically made visible in Fadiman's (1997) account of a Hmong family in California. The Western medical diagnosis of "epilepsy" did not coincide with the Hmong meaning of a *convulsion*—"The spirit catches you and you fall down"—forming the basis of a major cultural clash between physicians and the Hmong parents' beliefs about what was wrong with their child. Their treatment wishes called for combining Western medicine with folk remedies to coax the child's wandering soul back to her body. Here is an adaptation of questions medical anthropologist Arthur Kleinman recommended to avoid a culture clash like this.

1. What do you call the problem?
2. What do you think has caused the problem?
3. Why do you think it started when it did?
4. What do you think the sickness does? How does it work?
5. How severe is the sickness? Will it have a short or long course?
6. What kind of treatment do you think the patient should have? What are the important results you hope she receives from this treatment?
7. What are the chief problems the sickness has caused you and your family?
8. What do you fear most about the sickness?
9. How do you think we [at this agency, clinic, or hospital] can best help you with this problem?

Asking questions like this can lead to greater cross-cultural understanding and prevention of the tragic outcomes Fadiman (pp. 260–261) described.

Fadiman's account could serve as a primer for exploring the diversity issues discussed in Chapter 1 (see also Loustaunau & Sobo, 1997).

The Distinctiveness of Crisis Assessment

The ability to discriminate, then, between a crisis and a noncrisis state requires prediction and assessment skills. Good intentions are not enough. The development of assessment skills does not take years of intensive study and training. It does require the ability to combine what is known from observing and helping distressed people with the natural tendency to assist someone in trouble. Teachers, parents, nurses, police, physicians, and clergy are on the front lines where life crises occur. In these roles, people can do a great deal to help others and prevent unnecessary casualties, especially when formal training is added to one's natural crisis intervention ability (see Online Resources).

Ivan Illich (1976) asserts that the bureaucratization of medicine has deprived ordinary people of the helping tools they could readily use on behalf of others if the system allowed their use. His point is consistent with the current emphasis on primary care and responsibility for one's own health. Bureaucracies jeopardize the human aspect of the crisis intervention approach, which has made it an accessible, inoffensive way for distressed people to receive help. Similarly, the pervasiveness of individualism and the power of biomedicine (Luhrmann, 2000) present a temptation to medicalize the crisis assessment and intervention process. As many tools as possible should be available to people who are willing and able to help others. By sharpening time-tested assessment and helping strategies, frontline workers become particularly suited for prevention of acute crises. When a full-blown crisis is in progress, frontline workers as primary care providers must collaborate creatively with counselors and mental health professionals, who are trained to do a more comprehensive crisis assessment. The different levels of assessment—grounded in theory and sound principles—are discussed in the next section. The distinctiveness of crisis assessment is summarized as follows:

1. The crisis assessment *process*, unlike traditional psychiatric diagnosis, is intricately tied to crisis *resolution*—another compelling reason why assessment in comprehensive crisis care cannot be overstressed. For example, if a highly anxious person learns during assessment that the fear of "going crazy" is a typical crisis response, fear is relieved, and the person is already helped along the path of positive crisis resolution. Applied to a primary care office setting, this principle implies that within a single visit there must be some preliminary resolution, if only providing support and firm linkage to a mental health professional.
2. Crisis assessment occurs immediately, rather than days or weeks later as in traditional psychiatric practice.
3. The focus in crisis assessment is on immediate, identifiable problems, rather than on personality dynamics or presumed coping deficits. Once the problems are identified, assessment proceeds to ascertain the person's *cognitive, emotional,* and *behavioral functioning* in relation to them.

4. Historical material is dealt with in a special way in crisis assessment. Probing into psychodynamic issues such as unresolved childhood conflicts and repressed emotions is inappropriate. In contrast, it is not only appropriate but also necessary to obtain a person's history of solving problems, resolving crises, and dealing with stressful life events. Such historical material is vital for assessing and mobilizing the personal and social resources needed to effect positive crisis outcomes. It can be obtained by asking, for example, "What have you done in the past that has worked for you when you're upset?"

5. Crisis assessment is not complete without an evaluation of risk to life (see Chapters 9, 11, and 12).

6. Crisis assessment is not something done *to* a person but is a process carried out *with* a person and in active collaboration with significant others. A service contract is therefore a logical outcome of appropriate crisis assessment.

7. Social and cultural factors and community resources are integral to a comprehensive crisis assessment because the origins and manifestations of crisis are sociocultural as often as they are individual. Understanding the interplay between the person and his or her cultural environment provides a foundation for appropriate intervention (Canada et al., 2006).

The Assessment Process

Knowledge of factors that portend crisis guides us in assessing particular distressed individuals. However, health and human service workers encountering an acutely upset person may still have many questions: What do I say? What questions should I ask? How do I find out what's really happening with someone who seems so confused and upset? How do I recognize a person in crisis? If the person in crisis is not crazy, what distinguishes him or her from someone who is mentally disturbed but not in active crisis? What roles do the family and community play on behalf of the person in crisis? In short, as in general medical care, human service workers need a structured framework for the assessment process.

Triage and Levels of Crisis Assessment

Two levels of assessment should be completed through questions specific to each level.

Level I—Risk to Life

Here are the key questions for completing a Level I assessment: Is there an immediate or potential threat to life, either the life of the individual in crisis or the lives of others? In other words, has the person been abused? And what are the risks of suicide, assault, and homicide?

Level I assessment is *critical* and should be done by everyone, including people in their natural roles of friend, neighbor, parent, and spouse, as well as people in various professional positions: physicians, nurses, teachers, police, clergy, welfare workers, and prison officials. It has *life-and-death* dimensions and forms the basis for mobilizing emergency services on behalf of the person, family, or community in crisis.

Every person in crisis should be assessed regarding victimization and danger to self and others. (Techniques for assessment of suicidal danger are presented in detail in Chapter 9. Assessment for victimization trauma is presented in Chapter 11. Assessing the risk of assault or homicide is discussed in Chapter 12.) Here, a key facet of crisis work is emphasized: *no crisis assessment is complete without direct triage questioning about victimization and the danger of suicide and assault or homicide.* Exhibit 3.1, the Triage Tool, offers sample questions to ascertain immediate life-threatening danger. It underscores the interactional relationship between victimization, suicide, and assault risk, and the key place of social resources in preventing death (Hoff & Rosenbaum, 1994).

If a layperson, frontline health worker, or professional without special crisis training ascertains that a person is a probable risk for abuse, suicide, assault, or homicide, an experienced professional crisis worker should be consulted for Level II assessment and follow-through. Some life-threatening situations must be approached collaboratively with the police or forensic psychiatry specialists (see Chapter 12). Most crisis and psychiatric emergency services have such collaborative relationships for handling high-risk crises (see Online Resources).

**EXHIBIT 3.1   SCREENING FOR VICTIMIZATION AND LIFE-
                 THREATENING BEHAVIORS: TRIAGE QUESTIONS**

1. Have you been troubled or injured by any kind of abuse or violence? (for example, hit by partner, forced sex)
   ☐ Yes   ☐ No   ☐ Not sure   ☐ Refused
   If yes, check one of the following:
   ☐ By someone in your family?   ☐ By an acquaintance or stranger?
   Describe:

2. If yes, has something like this ever happened before?
   ☐ Yes   ☐ No   If yes, when? _____
   Describe:

3. Do you have anyone you can turn to or rely on now to protect you from possible further injury?
   ☐ Yes   ☐ No   If yes, who? _____

4. Do you feel so bad now that you have thought of hurting yourself/suicide?
   ☐ Yes   ☐ No   If yes, what have you thought about doing? _____
   Describe:

5. Are you so angry about what's happened that you have considered hurting someone else?
   ☐ Yes   ☐ No
   Describe:

Level II: Comprehensive Mental Health Assessment

This more extensive assessment involves consideration of basic personal and social characteristics of the distressed person and the person's family. Typically, this is done by a trained crisis counselor or mental health professional. This means that besides identifying life-threatening risk, we should also look for resilience and protective factors such as coping strategies, sense of purpose and internal motivation, self-efficacy, family support, and sense of identity that can assist in crisis resolution (Hoff, M., 2005; Solberg et al., 2007).

Questions in Level II assessment make presumptions based on the outcomes of Level I triage questions regarding victimization trauma and risk of harming self and others, plus the following: Is there evidence that the person is unable to function in his or her usual life role? Is the person in danger of being extruded from his or her natural social setting? What are the psychological, socioeconomic, and other factors related to the person's coping with life's stressors? Level II assessment is comprehensive and corresponds to the elements of the total crisis experience:

1. *Identification of crisis origins.* What hazardous events occurred? Is there emotional turmoil associated with a stressful situation or a major transition state? What sociocultural factors are involved?
2. *Development of crisis.* Is the person in the initial or acute phase of crisis? (See "How a Crisis Develops" in Chapter 2.)
3. *Manifestations of crisis.* How does the person interpret hazardous events or situations, and what are the corresponding emotional, cognitive, behavioral, and biophysical responses to them? Are the events perceived as threat, loss, or challenge? Does the person deal with the accompanying stress effectively? What is a person's *usual* functional level in dealing with stressful events?
4. *Identification of resources.* These include personal, family, interpersonal, and material resources.
5. *Determination of the sociocultural milieu.* What environmental factors affect the person or family in crisis?

All professional human service workers should acquire skill in this kind of assessment if they do not already have it. Close friends and family members are often able to make such an assessment as well. The chances for their success depend on their personal level of self-confidence, general experience, and previous success in helping others with problems. In general, however, a person unaccustomed to dealing with acutely distressed people or with no special training in crisis intervention should consult experienced professional crisis counselors. This is especially important in assessing people in complex, multiproblem, life-threatening, or catastrophic situations. The different foci and performances of Level I and Level II assessments are summarized in Table 3.1. Let us now consider the assessment process in detail.

TABLE 3.1   Crisis Assessment Levels

	Focus of Assessment	Assessment Done By
Level I	Risk to life • Victimization • Suicide (self) • Assault and/or homicide (against child, partner, parent, health provider, police officer)	Everyone (natural and formal crisis managers) • Family, friends, neighbors • Hotline workers • Frontline workers: clergy, police officers, nurses, physicians, teachers • Crisis and mental health professionals
Level II	Comprehensive psychological and social aspects of the person's life pertaining to the hazardous event, including assessment of chronic self-harm	Counselors or mental health professionals formally trained in crisis and assessment strategies

Identifying Origins and Phases of Crisis Development: Prevention Focus

A basic step in crisis assessment is identification of the events or situations that led to the person's distress. Golan (1969) elaborates on Caplan's (1964) concept of crisis development in phases that present opportunities for crisis prevention and early intervention. These phases illustrate the hazardous event and the precipitating factor, which along with the person's vulnerability, constitute the components of the crisis state originating from interpersonal sources, transition states, or sociocultural situations.

The *hazardous event* is the initial shock or situation that sets in motion a series of reactions culminating in a crisis (Golan, 1969). If the event is not already apparent, the helping person should ask directly, "What happened?" Sometimes people are so upset or overwhelmed by a series of things that they cannot clearly identify the sequence of events. In these instances, it is helpful to ask when the person began feeling so upset. Simple, direct questions should be asked about the time and circumstances of all upsetting or dangerous events. Putting events in order has a calming effect; the person experiences a certain sense of self-possession in being able to make some order out of confusion. This is particularly true for the highly anxious person who is afraid of losing control or "going crazy."

The experience of stressful, hazardous events *is not in itself a crisis*. It is one of several components of the crisis state. After all, just getting on with our lives implies the everyday management of stressful events. Extensive experience and research with abused women, for example, reveal them as capable survivors despite daunting odds (Hoff, 1990). The question is: How is *this* particular event unusual in terms of its timing, severity, danger, or the person's ability to handle it successfully? Is the person basically thriving or headed for trouble? This component of crisis corresponds to Caplan's (1964) first phase of crisis development, which may or may not develop into a full-blown crisis, depending on personal circumstances and the strength of social attachments (as the example of John, Chapter 2, illustrates). Early prevention and strategic intervention are pivotal in avoiding a full-blown crisis.

Because hazardous events alone are insufficient to constitute a crisis state, we need also to focus our assessment process on the *immediacy* of the person's stress—the precipitating factor. This is the proverbial straw that broke the camel's back—the final, stressful event in a series of such events or a situation that pushes the person from a state of acute vulnerability into crisis. The precipitating event is not always easy to identify, particularly when the presenting problem seems to have been hazardous for a long time.

The *precipitating factor* is often a minor incident. It can nevertheless take on crisis proportions in the context of other stressful events and the person's inability to use usual problem-solving devices. In this sense, it resembles Caplan's third phase of crisis development, following the failure of ordinary problem solving (the second phase). It corresponds to the final event that moves people to seek help because they can no longer cope after a series of antecedent crises. In a series of crises experienced by the same person, the precipitating factor in one crisis episode may be the hazardous event in the next. Thus, in real life, a long-standing hazardous situation leaves one vulnerable to crisis when "just one more thing"—the *precipitating factor* (or proverbial "last straw") can push one over the edge into crisis. Determining the mutual presence of these two components is useful in the assessment process, especially for distinguishing between *chronic stress* and an *acute crisis state*. For example, a chronic problem rather than a crisis is suggested in this interchange:

Question: What brought you here *today*, since these problems have been with you for some time now?

Response: I was watching a television program on depression and finally decided to get help for my problems.

Identifying these components of crisis and one's resilience or vulnerability entails ascertaining whether a person's *usual* functioning is challenged but the individual is "thriving" with basic supports, or is "in trouble" and on the brink of full-blown crisis. (See Online Resources for an illustration of the "thriving" or "in trouble" factor in crisis assessment and resolution.)

Careful assessment also can prevent the mistake of referring to a person experiencing repeated crisis episodes as one in *chronic crisis*—a contradiction in terms. A review of histories revealing repeated crisis experiences suggests that (1) comprehensive crisis care was not implemented, or (2) providers mistakenly assumed that crisis intervention alone would address serious problems demanding longer-term treatment. Such examples underscore a key concept in this book: *crisis care is necessary but not always sufficient*—the limitations of managed care policies notwithstanding.

Identifying Individual Crisis Manifestations

In crisis assessment, the identification of hazardous events or situations and the precipitating factor must be placed in meaningful context. This is done

TABLE 3.2   Assessing Personal Responses

Sample Assessment Questions	Possible Verbal Responses	Interpretation in Terms of Personal Crisis Manifestations (Emotional, Cognitive, Behavioral)
How do you feel about what happened? (for example, divorce, or rape)	*Divorce:* I don't want to live without her. If I kill myself, she'll be sorry.	Feelings of desperation, acute loss, revenge (emotional)
(Or if the feelings have already been expressed spontaneously), I can see you're really upset.	*Rape:* I shouldn't have accepted his invitation to have a drink. I suppose it's my fault for being so stupid.	Guilt, self-blame (emotional, cognitive)
What did you do when she told you about wanting a divorce?	I figured, good riddance. I only stayed for the kids' sake. But now that she's gone, I'm really lonely, and I hate the singles' bar scene.	Relief, ambivalence (emotional, cognitive)
	Or: I went down to the bar and got drunk and have been drinking a lot ever since.	Unable to cope effectively, desire to escape loneliness (emotional, behavioral)
How do you usually handle problems that are upsetting to you?	I generally talk to my closest friend or just get away by myself for a while to think things through.	Generally effective coping ability (behavioral, cognitive)
Why didn't this work for you this time?	My closest friend moved away, and I just haven't found anyone else to talk to that I really trust.	Realization of need for substitute support (cognitive, behavioral)

by ascertaining a person's subjective reaction or vulnerability when facing stressful events, and corresponds to Caplan's second and fourth phases of crisis development. Its focus is on the person's *emotional, biophysical, cognitive*, and *behavioral* responses to recent stressful events. A person's subjective response can be elicited by questions such as those illustrated in Table 3.2. The answers to questions like these are important for several reasons:

- They provide essential information to determine whether a person is thriving as usual or headed toward crisis.
- They suggest whether the person's problem-solving ability and usual coping devices are, for example, healthy or unhealthy, and how these ways of coping are related to what Caplan calls the personal, material, and sociocultural supplies needed to avoid crisis.
- They provide information about the meaning of stressful life events to various people and about the individual's particular definition of the situation, which is essential to a personally tailored intervention plan.
- They link the assessment process to intervention strategies by providing baseline data for action and for learning new ways of coping.

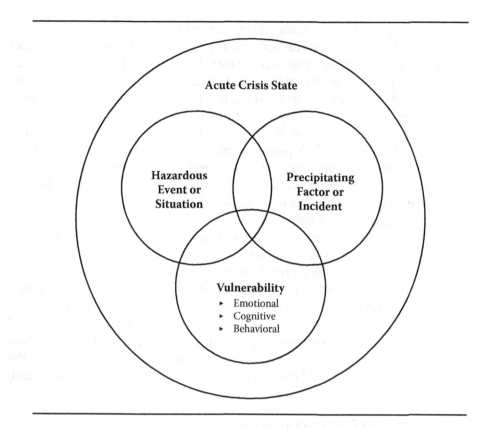

FIGURE 3.3 Components of the Crisis State. The components in the intertwining circles represent the interactional process that characterizes the crisis experience.

The relationships among hazardous events or situations, people's responses to them (their vulnerability), and the precipitating factor comprising a full-blown crisis are illustrated in Figure 3.3.

The answers to our assessment questions provide a broad picture of what Hansell (1976) calls "crisis plumage," the distinguishing characteristics of a person in crisis compared with one who is not. This plumage consists of distress signals that people send to others when they experience a loss or a threat of loss, are abused or in danger, or are challenged to increase their supplies—their basic needs or life attachments. Signals of distress include the following:

1. Difficulty in managing one's feelings
2. Suicidal or homicidal tendencies
3. Alcohol or other drug abuse
4. Trouble with the law
5. Inability to effectively use available help

These signals usually indicate that a person is coping ineffectively with a crisis and needs assistance to forestall negative crisis outcomes. In short, people proceed through life with material, personal, and sociocultural resources, as well as problem-solving devices for dealing with various stressors. When these resources are intact, people generally avoid the possible negative outcomes of stressful life events. For example, in assessing the vulnerability of an assault victim, careful attention must be paid to the *circumstances* of victimization; in contrast, if the attack is linked to the victim's character traits, we are very close to victim blaming, which hampers the person's recovery and may contribute to the downward spiral depicted in Figure 2.2, Chapter 2. A person in crisis usually seeks help from others to compensate for a temporary inability to deal constructively with life's stressors. The help received is crisis intervention. If the help obtained is from human service institutions or professionals, it is known as *formal crisis care*, as distinguished from *natural crisis care.*

However, in order to be part of the crisis solution rather than the problem, crisis workers must assess in greater detail the parameters of the individual's vulnerability and one's cultural beliefs about healing and help seeking, as Fadiman (1997) described in her account of the Hmong family crisis, which culminated in parental loss of child custody. Comprehensive crisis assessment requires understanding the emotional, biophysical, cognitive, and behavioral responses to hazardous events in cultural perspective (see Dobkin de Rios, 2002; Kleinman, 1980; and Chapter 6, on ritual). Let us consider, then, the specific characteristics of crisis plumage—how people in crisis typically feel, think, and act (see Figure 3.1, Box 2).

Emotional and Biophysical Response

People in crisis experience a high degree of anxiety and tension—in short, severe emotional pain. Another common theme is a sense of loss or emptiness. This feeling springs directly from an actual or threatened loss in self-esteem, physical well-being, material goods, social relationships, or a failure to reach a life goal, such as promotion or retirement. Other feelings frequently experienced are fear, shock, anger, guilt, embarrassment, or shame. Fear is often expressed in terms of losing control or not understanding why one is responding in a certain way. Anger may be directed inward for not being able to manage one's life or at a significant other for leaving, dying, or inflicting physical or sexual abuse. Guilt and embarrassment often follow anger that does not seem justified. How can one be angry at a dead person when considering one's luck in being alive from an accident or disaster? Some survivors may feel "death guilt" for having been spared. People who are abused by someone they love often feel ashamed—an outcome of the victim-blaming legacy.

Of all feelings common to the crisis experience, anxiety is probably the most familiar. A certain degree of tension is a normal part of life; it serves to move us to make plans for productive action. Without it, we become nonproductive. For example, Terri, a student, has no anxiety about passing or failing a course. She therefore does not exert the effort required to study and achieve a passing grade. When a person is excessively anxious, however, negative results usually occur. Acute anxiety is one of the most painful experiences a human being can have. However, this does not necessarily imply the presence of a psychiatric disorder.

Anxiety is manifested in a number of ways. Some characteristics will be peculiar to the person concerned. Commonly experienced signs of anxiety are

- Sense of dread
- Fear of losing control
- Inability to focus on one thing
- Physical symptoms—sweating, frequent urination, diarrhea, nausea and vomiting, tachycardia (rapid heartbeat), headache, chest or abdominal pain, rash, menstrual irregularity, and sexual disinterest

---

Case Example: Delaine

Delaine, age 45, feels bereft after the recent death of her husband. Her friends have been supportive since his death from chronic heart disease. She chides herself and feels guilty about not being able to take the loss any better. She knew her husband's condition was precarious; nevertheless, she had depended on him as a readily available source of reassurance. Because she is basically a cheerful person, always on hand to support others in distress, she is embarrassed by what she perceives as weakness following her husband's death.

Because she cries more than usual, Delaine is afraid she may be losing control. At times, she even wonders whether she is going crazy. It should be noted that Delaine is in a major developmental transition to middle age. Also, the oldest of her three children was recently married, leaving her with a sense of loss in her usual mothering role. An additional, but anticipated, loss is the recent news that one of her close friends will soon be leaving town. This threatens to further erode Delaine's base of support. Delaine feels angry about all the losses in her life, asking, "Why does all this have to happen to me all at once?" But she also feels guilty about her anger; after all, her friend deserves the opportunity that the move will afford her and her husband, and Delaine knows her daughter has every right to get married and live her own life.

Complicating Delaine's emotional upheaval, she has developed gastrointestinal symptoms, including bouts of lower abdominal pain and diarrhea. She has avoided her friend's advice to seek counseling but did see her primary care provider about her physical symptoms and requested something to ease her "embarrassing" crying bouts.

What Delaine does not realize are these facts:

- She has a right to her feelings about these disturbing events.
- She has a right and a need to express those feelings.
- Her feelings of loss and anger do not cancel the good feelings and support she can continue to have from her daughter and friend, though in an altered form.
- Her physical symptoms are probably related to the psychosocial facets of her life.

Were it not for these developmental and situational factors, Delaine might not have experienced her husband's death as a crisis. The stability of Delaine's life was disrupted on several counts:

■ Her role as wife was changed to that of widow.
■ Her role as mother of her oldest daughter was altered by her daughter's marriage.
■ Her affectional attachment to her husband was completely severed.
■ Her affectional attachment to her friend will be altered in terms of physical distance and immediacy of support.
■ Her notion of a full life includes marriage, so she must adjust, at least temporarily, to a change in that perception.
■ Her unanticipated physical symptoms need medical attention.

Delaine's case underscores the importance of (1) incorporating crisis assessment strategies—at a minimum, Level I—into primary health care and (2) sorting out, through physical examination and laboratory tests, the separate and interacting relationship between physical and emotional symptoms (Edmands, Hoff, Kaylor, Mower, & Sorrell, 1999). Primary care providers should not assign a psychiatric diagnosis of *anxiety disorder* without a Level II crisis assessment, which typically includes mental health specialty skills. Implications for treatment based on assessment are discussed in the continuation of Delaine's case in Chapter 4.

In short, mental health providers' assessment skills include the necessary *general* knowledge about medical phenomena to make an appropriate initial response followed by referral to medical specialists; primary care (nonpsychiatric) providers' assessment skills include the necessary *general* knowledge of psychosocial and psychiatric phenomena to make an empathic response, apply crisis intervention strategies such as ensuring safety of self and others, and implement referral to crisis or mental health specialists for comprehensive assessment and care. Instead of concluding that a person suffering the emotional and physiological consequences of stressful events and insufficient supports has an anxiety disorder, a crisis-trained provider would realize that emotional pain is the predictable and *normal* response to life's normal upheavals and upsetting events and is experienced by most people over the life span. These responses do not require a DSM-IV-TR diagnosis to warrant a health provider's appropriate response, and they *should not* require such a psychiatric label for health insurance coverage (see Johnson, 2007; Luhrmann, 2000, chap. 6, "The Crisis of Managed Care").

For an overview and critique of mental health assessment tools and the importance of a *functional* assessment approach, see Brown and Hoff (2010, Chapter 2, in press).

Cognitive Response: Thoughts, Perceptions, and Interpretations of Events

Feelings—especially of high anxiety—have great impact on perceptions and thinking processes. In crisis, one's attention is focused on the acute shock and anguish being experienced and a few items concerning the crisis event. As a consequence, the person's usual memory and way of perceiving may be altered. The person may have difficulty sorting things out. The relationship between events may not seem clear. Acutely anxious people feel caught in a maze of events they cannot fit together. They often have trouble defining who they are and what their skills are. The state of anguish and resulting confusion can alter a person's ability to make decisions and solve problems, the very skills needed during acute anxiety states. This disturbance in perceptual processes and problem-solving ability increases the individual's already heightened state of anxiety. Sometimes the person fears losing control.

The distorted perceptual process observed in crisis states should not be confused with mental illness, in which a person's *usual* pattern of thinking is more gravely disturbed, or with acute confusional states (*delirium*), in which altered perceptions are also apparent. In a crisis state, the disturbance arises from and is part of the crisis experience. There is a rapid return to normal perception once the crisis is resolved.

Case Example: Joan

Joan, age 34, called a mental health center stating that her husband had just left the house with his rifle and that she did not know where he was going. She was afraid for her life, as they had had an argument the night before during which she had complained about his drinking and he had threatened her. On further questioning, it turned out that Joan's husband had left the house at his usual time for work in a neighboring town. He had left with the rifle the previous evening after the argument, although on occasion he also took his gun along to work in case he had a chance to go hunting. After 3 hours, he had returned, apparently calmed down, and put away the gun. The gun was still in the house in a safe place when Joan called. There was nothing in the interaction to lead an outside observer to conclude that Joan's husband would not be home as usual after a day at work.

Noteworthy in this example is Joan's disturbed perceptual process. On questioning, she cannot recall certain details without help and cannot put all the facts into logical order. Joan is obviously very anxious about her safety, a factor requiring serious attention, especially given the presence of a gun. Complicating Joan's anxiety is her sense of guilt about her role in precipitating the argument with her husband by mentioning his drinking. Her anxiety is consistent with her perception—not necessarily the reality—of a threat to her safety. The determining factor is how she *perceives* the event. Nevertheless, marital discord and the presence of a gun underscore the importance of assessing thoroughly for a history of abuse and safety resources for a woman like Joan—as already discussed in Level I triage assessment. One of the most common complaints from abused women and their advocates is that people do not believe them or take their stories seriously.

The feelings of people in crisis are usually consistent with their perception of the situation. Recognition of this fact should decrease the possibility of casting people with similar problems into a common mold. The *perception* of the event is one of the factors that makes an event a crisis for one person but not for another. Joan's case illustrates how excessive anxiety can interfere with cognitive functioning and effective problem solving. If Joan were not so anxious, she would probably have arrived at an obvious way to ensure her immediate safety—that is, removing the gun or leaving the house herself and seeking help. Joan probably knows that the use of weapons is intrinsically connected with their availability, but her anxiety prevents her from using that knowledge.

Other aspects of cognitive functioning spring from different socialization processes and value systems that influence how particular events are interpreted. The Hmong story illustrates the different meanings and crisis potential of various ethnic and religious groups (Fadiman, 1997). A state legislator who was jailed for a minor offense killed himself hours after being imprisoned. For this elected figure, the transgression meant loss of reputation, whereas a person arrested for repeated drunken driving may interpret the event differently because of having less to lose. People socialized to feel incomplete without marriage will probably experience the loss of a spouse as an occasion of crisis, whereas others grow from the challenges of greater independence. These examples illustrate the importance of being culturally sensitive and not imposing our own values and behavior norms on others. No situation or disturbance affects two people in the same way, and the same person may respond differently to similar events at different times in life. Thus, interpersonal *process*—not rote mental status examination—should be central as we assess varying subjective interpretations of life events.

Behavioral Responses

Behavior usually follows from what people think and feel and from their interpretations of life events. A person who feels anxious and has a distorted perception of events is likely to behave in unusual ways. However, what may seem unusual, distorted, or crazy to an outsider may be considered normal behavior within certain cultural groups. In order to determine whether a person's behavior is normal or deviant, we need to start with *that* person's cultural definition of what is usual, not our own. This is particularly important if the crisis worker and the person in distress are from different cultures, classes, or ethnic groups. If the distressed person is too upset to provide this kind of information, it should be elicited from family or friends whenever possible. Failing that, a consultation with someone of the person's ethnic or cultural group would be useful.

A significant behavioral sign of crisis is the individual's inability to perform normal vocational functions in the usual manner—for example, when a person cannot do necessary household chores, concentrate on studies, or work at an outside job. Another sign is a change in social behavior, such as withdrawing from friends, making unusual efforts to avoid being alone, or becoming clingy or demanding (Hansell, 1976). As social connections break down, the person may also feel detached or distant from others. Some people in crisis act on impulse. They may drive a car recklessly, make a suicide attempt, or attack others as a desperate means of solving a problem (see Chapters 9 and 12).

Some people will go out of their way to reject the assistance offered by friends. Often this response arises out of the person's sense of helplessness and embarrassment at not being able to cope in the usual manner. The person fears that acceptance of help may be misinterpreted as a confirmation of perceived weakness. To allay such fears, it is paramount that crisis workers examine the attitudes and any biases they may bring to the assessment milieu. People in crisis are also observed to behave in ways that are inconsistent with their thoughts and feelings. For example, a young woman witnessed a shooting accident that caused the death of her boyfriend. Initially, she was visibly upset by the event. She was brought by her family to a mental health emergency clinic. During the interview with a counselor, she laughed inappropriately when talking about the shooting and death she had witnessed, a behavior suggesting very high anxiety. Another behavioral signal of crisis is atypical behavior, such as driving while intoxicated by an individual with no previous record of such behavior.

In summary, when assessing vulnerability, it is important to find out how *this* person is reacting *here and now* to whatever happened. The simplest way to assess a person's vulnerability is to ask, "How do you feel about what happened? What do you usually do when you're upset?" and similar questions suggested in Table 3.3.

Family and Community Factors Influencing Personal Crisis Coping and Resilience

Our discussion of the assessment process thus far has focused primarily on techniques to determine the hazardous events or situations precipitating the crisis and the individual's vulnerability as revealed in personal responses to these events—emotional, cognitive, behavioral, and biophysical. Crisis assessment, however, is incomplete without evaluating the person's social resources and cultural milieu. This includes inquiring whether the person perceives family and other social contacts as real or potential assets or as liabilities.

In this book, social assessment means including the person's social network members deliberately—not just incidentally—in the assessment process. This is not difficult to do, but does require the worker's conviction of its importance and the willingness to make the effort. Often workers cite a lack of time or inaccessibility of the family as reasons for limiting the assessment to the upset individual. But this probably obscures their own lack of conviction or skills in the use of social approaches. Given the centrality of social aspects in crisis responses, we should examine these issues in order to refine crisis assessment and intervention strategies. Including a social approach in crisis assessment reduces misidentifying who is in crisis. That is, sometimes the person who appears or is brought in for help may be upset but not in

TABLE 3.3 Differentiation: Effective and Ineffective Crisis Coping According to Crisis Episode

Crisis Episode		Personal Manifestations	Crisis Coping	
Hazardous Event	Origin		Ineffective	Effective
Loss of child by death	*Situational:* Unexplained physical malfunctioning or death of child, for example, SIDS	Emotional	Depression	Grief work
		Biophysical	Stomach or other ailments	
		Cognitive	Conviction of having done something wrong to cause death of the child	Recognizing and accepting that one used all available knowledge to prevent the death
		Behavioral	Inability to care for other children appropriately (for example, overprotective-ness)	Attending peer support group
Physical battering by partner	*Sociocultural:* Values and other factors affecting relationships	Emotional	Crying, depression, feelings of worthlessness, self-blame, and helplessness	Anger, shock (How could he do this to me?), outrage at the fact that it happened
		Cognitive	Assumption that the beating was justified: inability to decide what to do	Conviction of inappropriateness of violence between men and women, decision to leave and/or otherwise reorder one's life free of violence
		Behavioral	Alcohol abuse, abuse of children, excusing of partner's violence	Seeking refuge in nonviolent shelter, initiating steps toward economic independence, participating in peer group support and social change activities

crisis. A complete assessment could reveal that an entire family is in crisis, as could happen, for example, when a teenager tries to commit suicide, or as the tragic death of Rebecca Riley attests.

The sociocultural context of crisis and community resources are integral to family assessment, and often figure in the origin and resolution of crises, as illustrated in the Crisis Paradigm. Evaluation should include questions about whether the person has received necessary help from community resources, as well as inquiries about cultural and socioeconomic factors that may contribute to the person's vulnerability and ability to resolve crises constructively. For example, negative factors, such as racial unrest, or positive ones, such as opportunities for poor people to become economically self-sufficient, should be considered. These aspects of comprehensive crisis assessment and their implications for intervention are discussed further in Chapter 5.

The individual and sociocultural aspects of crisis assessment are summarized and illustrated with examples in Table 3.3. This diagram elaborates on the concept of healthy and unhealthy coping. It outlines the relationship between crisis origins and personal manifestations of crisis (see Figure 3.1, Boxes 1 and 2). It also links the crisis assessment process to various intervention techniques. For example, if assessment reveals that a person is coping well in general terms—emotional, biophysical, cognitive, and behavioral—the information received can be used to help the person cope more effectively. Careful assessment can also show when not to intervene—in areas where the person's coping is adequate or the person chooses to do without our services. Even a person who is acutely upset can be helped to realize that he or she is coping adequately in *some* aspects of life (for example, at work but not at home or vice versa). In short, a skilled crisis worker avoids doing either too little or too much. An old adage applies here: "If it's not broken, don't fix it."

The next section describes a structured approach to carrying out the assessment process, using the concepts discussed so far.

An Assessment Interview

An interview (see Table 3.4) with George Sloan, age 48, is conducted by an emergency department nurse. George is brought to the hospital by police following an attempt to commit suicide by crashing his car. (This case illustration is continued from Chapter 2, Development of Crisis.)

Besides the technical aspects of asking clear, direct questions, this interview excerpt illustrates another important point. The nurse reveals an understanding of George's problem and empathizes with the despair he must be feeling when she says,

- "So your car accident was really an attempt to kill yourself?"
- "Sounds like you've been having a rough time, George."
- "I can see that your illness and all the other troubles have left you feeling pretty bad."
- "George, I can see that you're feeling desperate about your situation."
- "I'm glad your suicide attempt didn't work."

The nurse clearly comes through as a human being with feelings and concern about a patient who is in despair. Concern is conveyed by a gentle tone of voice and unstylized manner. Furthermore, the nurse is able to express feelings without sounding sentimental and shocked, and apparently is not afraid to be with a person in the acute emotional pain of crisis. As shown by this interview, effective assessment techniques are not highly complicated or veiled in mystery. The techniques require the following:

- A straightforward approach with simple direct questions
- The ability to empathize or appreciate the other person's perspective
- An ability to grasp the depth of another's despair and share the feelings this evokes
- The courage not to run away from frightening experiences like suicide attempts

The interview also shows that ascertaining suicide risk (Level I assessment) is an integral part of thorough crisis assessment. Parents, teachers, friends, and police can augment their natural tendencies to help by learning these assessment techniques. Failure to use the techniques can mean the difference between life and death for someone like George Sloan. It is not uncommon for people in his condition to be treated medically or surgically without anyone finding out about his intention to commit suicide. If he

TABLE 3.4 Assessment Interview Example

Assessment Techniques	Interview between George Sloan and Emergency Department Nurse	
Signals of Distress and Crisis to Be Identified	*Nurse:*	Hello, Mr. Sloan. Would you like to be called Mr. Sloan or George?
	George:	George is fine.
	Nurse:	Will you tell me what happened, George?
	George:	I had a car accident. Can't you see that without asking? (slightly hostile and seemingly reluctant to talk)
	Nurse:	Yes, I know, George. But the police said you were going the wrong way on the expressway. How did that happen?
Active Crisis State: Extreme anxiety to the breaking point	*George:*	Yes, that's right. (hesitates) Well, I just couldn't take it anymore, but I guess it didn't work.
	Nurse:	Sounds like you've been having a rough time, George. Can you tell me what it is you can't take anymore?
Hazardous Event/ Situation: Physical illness	*George:*	Well, I've got heart trouble ...
Vulnerable State: Loss of external social supports or inability to use them		It's gotten to be too much for my wife. I can't expect her to do much more.

Assessment Techniques	Interview between George Sloan and Emergency Department Nurse	
Loss of personal coping ability		We're having trouble with our 16-year-old son, Arnold.
Inability to communicate stress to significant others		I just couldn't take it anymore. I figured I'd do everybody a favor and get rid of myself.
High-lethal suicide attempt	*Nurse:*	So your car accident was really an attempt to kill yourself?
	George:	That's right. That way, at least my wife wouldn't lose the insurance along with everything else she's had to put up with.
	Nurse:	I can see that your heart trouble and all your other troubles have left you feeling pretty bad.
Depression	*George:*	That's about it, too bad I came out alive. I really feel I'm worth more dead than alive.
	Nurse:	I can see that you're feeling desperate about your situation. How long have you felt this way?
	George:	I've had heart trouble for about four years. After my last heart attack, the doctor told me I had to slow down or it would probably kill me. Well, there's no way I can change things that I can see.
Precipitating Factor: Inability to perform in expected role as father	*Nurse:*	What happened this past week that made you decide to end it all?
	George:	Well, our kid Arnold got suspended from school— that did it! I figured if a father can't do any better with his son than that, what's the use?
	Nurse:	I gather from what you say and feel that you just couldn't see any other way out.
State of Active Crisis: Vulnerability: Fixation on role expectations, inability to use outside helping resources	*George:*	That's right. Money is really getting tight; my wife was talking about getting a full-time job, and that really bothers me to think that I can't support my family anymore. And if she starts working more, things might get even worse with Arnold. There was no one to talk to. Suicide's the only thing left.
	Nurse:	With all these problems, George, have you ever thought about suicide before?
History of poor coping ability	*George:*	Yes, once, after my doctor told me to really watch it after my last heart attack. I felt pretty hopeless and thought of crashing my car then. But things weren't so bad then between me and my wife, and she talked me out of it and seemed willing to stick with me.
	Nurse:	I see, but this time you felt there was nowhere else to turn. Anyway, George, I'm glad your suicide attempt didn't work. I'd really like to help you consider some other ways to deal with all these problems.
	George:	I don't know what they could be. I really feel hopeless, but I guess I could see what you've got to offer.
	Nurse:	There are several things we can discuss.

Note: The discussion of George's case will be continued in Chapter 4, "Helping People in Crisis."

receives only medical or surgical treatment and nothing else changes in his life, George Sloan is at risk of committing suicide within 6 to 12 months. He is already in a high-risk category (see Chapter 9).

Another objective of the initial interview is to provide the person in crisis with concrete help. If George had not felt the nurse's acceptance and concern, he would not have dropped his initial resistance to sharing his dilemma. The nurse opened the discussion of alternatives to suicide.

Having identified an individual as being in a state of crisis, the helping person proceeds to give or obtain whatever assistance is indicated. In complex situations or in circumstances involving life and death, the helper should engage the services of professional crisis workers. Once the state of crisis is ascertained, the professional crisis worker engages the person in a comprehensive evaluation (Level II assessment) of his or her problems. Such assessment techniques are currently practiced in many crisis and counseling clinics, community mental health programs, and in mental health professionals' private practice. A framework and a sample tool from an assessment protocol are discussed next.

Comprehensive Crisis Assessment

A well-organized worker uses tools that aid in the assessment process. If a crisis worker lacks direction and a sense of order, this adds to the confusion felt by acutely anxious people. Tools emphasize a structured approach to the assessment process, but no record system or mechanical tool, such as computer analysis, can substitute for the empathy, knowledge, and experience of a skilled clinician. Records are to complement, not displace, clinical judgment and expertise in the psychosocial interview process. Nor should record-keeping procedures be allowed to depersonalize interaction with a distressed person.

Philosophy and Context of a Record System

The framework and sample tool recommended to guide and record the crisis care process as conceived in this book was selected because it was developed with client collaboration and illustrates the principles that should guide any crisis-sensitive record system. The example presented here

- Is based on the understanding of crisis in the psychosociocultural perspective emphasized in this text
- Is client centered in that it includes the person's self-evaluation as an integral aspect of the assessment process
- Assumes that the client is a member of a social network—not simply an individual in psychological disequilibrium—and that disruption or threat of disruption from essential social attachments is often the occasion of crisis and therefore provides significant members of the person's social network an opportunity to participate actively in the assessment process
- Provides a structured, standardized framework for gathering data while including subjective, narrative-style information from the client

- Focuses on a view of the person in crisis as a human being functioning at varying degrees of adequacy or inadequacy, not merely as a DSM diagnostic entity
- Assists in fostering continuity between the various steps of the crisis intervention process (assessment, planning, implementation, follow-up) by providing relevant, organized information so that the client's level of functioning, goals, and methods for attaining these goals can be sharply defined and used as a guide in the course of service
- Provides supervisory staff with information necessary to monitor service and ensure quality care to clients on an ongoing basis
- Provides administrative staff the database needed for monitoring and evaluating service program outcomes in relation to stated objectives

Genesis of a Comprehensive Mental Health Record System

The record system of which an assessment tool is a part was developed by a special task force in the Erie County Mental Health System in Buffalo, New York. Its basic tool, the Comprehensive Mental Health Assessment (CMHA) form is unique in that it incorporates crisis care principles into the assessment and record-keeping requirements of a state and county mental health department, while retaining its client-centered focus. Clients at risk for crisis who were served in this mental health system included (1) people experiencing various unanticipated hazardous life events, who were therefore at risk of extrusion from their natural social setting, and (2) people vulnerable to crisis in relation to chronic mental or emotional disturbance, chemical dependence, or disadvantaged social circumstances. Some of the case examples cited in this book are drawn from people who requested service in this crisis-sensitive mental health system.

A key impetus for developing record system came from the nationwide "deinstitutionalization" policy; that is, the New York State Department of Mental Hygiene needed a reliable means of tracking seriously mentally ill patients who were discharged from state psychiatric facilities and who were to be served in community-based agencies. Another goal was to incorporate crisis intervention into mental health service protocols as an aid to preventing the need for expensive hospital-based psychiatric care in the first place.

The original record system was tested in the 1970s with crisis and mental health workers and people receiving services in the community mental health agencies in the six Erie County catchment areas that adopted the system. Included were the majority of publicly funded programs serving urban, suburban, and rural communities in a metropolitan area with a population of 1.25 million. A client was considered an active partner in developing the clinical record and had full access to it. Examples of client feedback include the following:

- "I'm not as bad off as I thought."
- "This takes some of the mystery out of mental health."
- "Getting help with a problem isn't so magical after all."
- "Now I have a diary of how I worked out my problems and got better."

The revised version presented here was evaluated for validity and interrater reliability in six comparable agencies in Massachusetts and Ontario, Canada.

This record system's philosophical underpinning is in the civil rights movement (including the rights of psychiatric patients) and the nationwide program of deinstitutionalizing the mentally ill and providing community-based, easily accessible services; the goal was to restore and maintain people in noninstitutional settings and thereby prevent readmission to psychiatric facilities whenever possible. Today most public mental hospitals have shut down, and many former patients of these facilities roam the streets homeless and without adequate treatment and social support. Fortunately, however, some ideal community-based services are being developed—for example, the Club House transition service modeled on the empowerment value of the civil rights movement (Cella, Besancon, & Zipple, 1997; Farrell & Deeds, 1997).

For these and other mental health services built on the WHO (World Health Organization) People 2010 goals, which emphasize health promotion, risk prevention, clients' active involvement in their own health, and moving beyond quick-fix drug approaches to complex mental health problems, this record system holds promise. Managed care policies around treatment goals and evidence indicating progress toward achieving them underscore the need for tools that aid in service delivery without compromising the importance of provider–client team efforts. The tool also captures key features of emotional and mental disturbance or disability, and complements the "perspectives" approach to diagnosis proposed by McHugh and Clark (2006). Finally, it underscores our themes of resilience and clients' potential for growth through crisis and other challenges to mental health. The category "violence experienced" was added in 1982 and published in Hoff & Rosenbaum (1994) and in three earlier editions of this text.[2]

Assessment Forms[3]

Because of the life-and-death implications of certain items, specifications (Operational Definitions) and rating scales are included for three of the 21 items: item 13, violence/abuse experienced; item 14, injury to self; and item 15, danger to others. This is essentially a Level I assessment. They are included in Chapters 11, 9, and 12, respectively.

Initial Contact Sheet

This form (see Exhibit 3.2) is intended to provide basic demographic and problem information at the time the client requests service or is presented for service by another person or agency. It should provide the worker with sufficient data to make several key decisions *early* in the crisis care process:

[2] See Brown & Hoff, in press, and Online Resources for Operational Definitions of Assessment Form items. Here we illustrate only forms with the Case Example of George, continued from Chapter 2, and the Child Screening Checklist. For prospective collaboration in ongoing research on this tool, contact the author.

[3] For complete forms and specifications for their use and for information about reliability and validity studies, the reader is referred to the author, who can be contacted through the publisher.

EXHIBIT 3.2   INITIAL CONTACT SHEET

Today's Date: *2-15-09*   I.D.: *101*

Name: *George O. Sloan*

Age: *48*   Relationship Status: Married *X* Single ___ Other ___

Address: *33 Random Avenue, Middletown 01234, Central County*

Telephone: *(444) 123-0987*

Have you talked with anyone about this? No *X* Yes ___

If yes, to whom? _____ Date of last contact: _____

Significant other (name and phone): *wife, Marie Sloan (444) 123-0987*

Are you taking any medication now? No ___ Yes *X*

If yes, what? *nitroglycerine*

How Urgent Is Your Need for Help?

Very Urgent. Request requires an immediate response (within minutes)—for example, crisis outreach; medical emergency requiring an ambulance, such as overdoses, severe drug reaction; or police needed if situation involves extreme danger or weapons.

Urgent. Response should be rapid but not necessarily immediate (within a few hours)—for example, low to moderate risk of suicide or mild drug reaction.

Somewhat Urgent. Response should be made within a day (24 hours)—for example, planning conference in which key persons are not available until the following evening.

Slightly Urgent. Response is required within a few days—for example, client whose funding runs out within a week needs public assistance.

Not Urgent. Situation has existed for a long time and does not warrant immediate intervention (a week or two is unlikely to cause any significant difference)—for example, child with a learning disability; couple that needs marital counseling.

Crisis rating:

1	2	3	4	⑤
Not urgent				Very urgent

Probability of engaging in counseling/treatment contract:

1	2	③	4	5
Very high				Very low

Summary of presenting problem or situation and help-seeking goal: *George Sloan, 48 was brought to the ER (emergency room) by police following a suicide attempt by car crash. His intention was to die, as he saw no way out of his personal and family problems. Has had heart trouble for 4 years. Was urged to quit second job and take office job in Police Dept. His 16-yr-old son's suspension from school adds to his sense of failure. Feels he has no one to talk to. Had considered suicide after last heart attack, but support from his wife prevented him then from crashing his car. While initially reluctant, Mr. Sloan now seems open to counseling assistance.*

Disposition and Recommendation: *Referred to Psychiatric Liaison Service. Recommend Mr. Sloan receive full assessment and crisis counseling while being treated for injuries from suicidal car accident, plus follow-up with entire family.*

Signature (intake/triage person): *Jane Doe, R.N.*   Date: *2/15/09*

- How urgent is the situation?
- Who is to be assigned responsibility for proceeding with the next step?
- What type of response is indicated as the next step?

This form is used chiefly by the worker designated to handle all incoming calls and on-site requests for service during a specified period of time, sometimes called a *triage worker*. The "Crisis Rating" section of the form should be completed according to the guidelines in Exhibit 3.2.

Assessment Worksheet

The Assessment Worksheet (see Exhibit 3.3) can be used in two ways: (1) it can serve as an interview guide in a face-to-face session with the client, or (2) the client (if not acutely upset) can be given the form to complete *on-site*, after which the items are discussed in a face-to-face interview. If the Crisis Rating is 1 or 2 (not urgent), the client can complete the form at home as background for a follow-up visit. Such use of this form assumes that *the record belongs to the client*. This principle needs shoring up because psychiatric groups have used legal channels to keep mental health clients from gaining access to their records. A client-centered record also reflects the view that they are in charge of their lives and that the helping process should not be mysterious to them. The worksheet is *never* to be used without initial client/ provider interaction or as an intake checklist with no follow-up discussion. An abuse victim or a potentially suicidal person could perceive such action as a dismissal of one's immediate concerns. The Child Screening Checklist (see Exhibit 3.4) can be used in a similar fashion. (The complete record system available online includes the Significant Other Worksheet and a more detailed assessment Summary Form and comparative rating scales charting client functioning at intake, interim, discharge, and follow-up points.)

A cautionary note is in order here: forms and rating scales can never substitute for rapport, time, and sensitivity to the unique needs of each distressed person. Clinicians bombarded with management information systems must be careful to avoid recording more and more about doing less and less. A client-centered record system like this, which clearly documents progress in treatment goals based on systematic assessment, may even advance the cause of parity in insurance coverage for mental health services rendered.

Interview Summary: George Sloan

Interview data from the Assessment Worksheet reveals a discrepancy between Mr. Sloan's self-assessment and that of the interviewer, based on information from the emergency nurse (Table 3.4). Clearly, Mr. Sloan is alive not by intent, but by accident and medical intervention. The nurse's interview laid the foundation for the further assessment as shown in this worksheet, and the crisis counseling and detailed service planning that should follow by referral to a mental health specialist. Ratings of 4 and 5 indicating high stress, risk to life, and poor functioning are obvious priorities in next steps (to be continued in Chapter 4, "Developing a Service Contract").

EXHIBIT 3.3   ASSESSMENT WORKSHEET: GEORGE SLOAN

Note: Client response in *italics*; interviewer comment in [brackets]

1. Physical Health: How do you judge your physical health in general?

1	2	☒	4	5
Excellent	Good	Fair	Poor	Very poor

Comments: *No problems except for heart. Feel OK except for chest pain, which is getting more frequent.*
[Appears to underestimate seriousness of heart condition]

2. Self-Acceptance/Self-Esteem: How do you feel about yourself as a person?

1	2	3	☒	5
Very good	Good	Fair	Poor	Very poor

Comments: *Not very good—especially when I think about my son's trouble—that it's probably my fault. Seems like I'm no good at anything lately.*
[Told emergency nurse he was worth more dead than alive]

3. Vocational/Occupational (includes student, homemaker, volunteer): How would you judge your work/school situation?

1	2	☒	4	5
Very good	Good	Fair	Poor	Very poor

Comments: *I can still do patrol work, but the doctor says I should slow down.*
[Needs help adjusting work life to heart health risks]

4. Immediate Family: How would you describe your relationship with your family?

1	2	3	☒	5
Very good	Good	Fair	Poor	Very poor

Comments: *Ever since my first heart attack, we seem to be going from bad to worse, especially with our son Arnold.*
[Recognizes family problems but unable to resolve effectively]

5. Intimacy/Significant Other Relationship(s): Is there anyone you feel really close to and can rely on if you're very upset or in a life-threatening situation?

1	2	3	☒	5
Always	Usually	Sometimes	Rarely	Never

Comments: *Not really. Things used to be better between my wife and me, but we seem to be drifting apart.*
[Could not confide with wife about suicide intent]

6. Residential/Housing: How do you judge your housing situation?

☒	2	3	4	5
Very good	Good	Fair	Poor	Very poor

Comments:

7. Financial Security: How would you describe your financial situation?

1	☒	3	4	5
Very good	Good	Fair	Poor	Very poor

Comments: *As long as I have my second job, it's OK, but I don't like the idea of my wife working full time.*
[Appears not to connect financial constraints with health problems and suicidal danger]

8. Decision-Making Ability: How satisfied are you with your ability to make life decisions?

1	2	☒	4	5
Always very satisfied		Somewhat dissatisfied		Always very dissatisfied

Comments: *Mostly around the problems we have with Arnold.*
[Is also at a loss about how to deal with marital stress]

9. Problem-Solving Ability: How would you judge your ability to solve everyday problems?

1	2	☒	4	5
Very good	Good	Fair	Poor	Very poor

Comments: *I thought I was doing pretty well before this heart trouble got in the way of my second job.*
[Appears to overestimate his problem-solving ability except by suicide]

10. Life Goals/Spiritual Values: How satisfied are you with how your life goals (and things you value most) are working for you?

1	2	☒	4	5
Always very satisfied		Somewhat dissatisfied		Always very dissatisfied

Comments: *I almost always felt satisfied before the heart trouble started 4 years ago.*
[Has been dissatisfied enough to make a serious suicide attempt]

11. Leisure Time/Community Involvement: How satisfied are you with the availability of leisure time and ability to relax and take part in activities beyond everyday duties?

1	2	☒	4	5
Always very satisfied		Somewhat dissatisfied		Always very dissatisfied

Comments: *I don't have much free time, but I really like my work. I suppose our whole family could use more time together.*

12. Feelings: How comfortable are you with your feelings? (For example, do you often feel anxious or fearful?)

1	2	☒	4	5
Always comfortable		Sometimes uncomfortable		Always uncomfortable

Comments: *Just during the last few months I really started feeling depressed. My wife says I bottle everything up.*
[Unable to convey to his wife or physician the depth of his suicidal despair]

13. Violence/Abuse Experienced: To what extent have you been injured or troubled by physical, sexual, or emotional abuse?

☒	2	3	4	5
Never		Several times recently		Routinely (every day or so)

Comments/Describe:

Note: If rating of item 13 is 2 or above, answer items 19, 20, and 21 on the next page.

14. Injury to Self: Do you have any thoughts of suicide or a plan to hurt yourself in any way?

1	2	3	4	☒
No risk whatsoever		Moderate risk		Very serious risk

Comments/Describe: *I still can't find any way out except suicide, but right now I feel a little better from talking with you.*

15. Danger to Other(s): Do you have any thoughts about violence or a plan to physically harm someone?

☒	2	3	4	5
No risk whatsoever		Moderate risk		Very serious risk

Comments/Describe:

16. Substance Use/Abuse (alcohol and/or other drugs): Does the use of alcohol or other drugs concern you or interfere with your life in any way (work, family)?

☒	2	3	4	5
Never	Rarely	Sometimes	Frequently	Constantly

Comments/Describe:

17. Legal: What is your tendency to get in trouble with the law?

☒	2	3	4	5
None	Slight	Moderate	Great	Very great

Comments/Describe:

18. Agency Use: How satisfied are you with getting the help you need from doctors or other health providers?

1	2	3	☒	5
Always very satisfied		Somewhat dissatisfied		Always very dissatisfied

Comments: *I don't like going to doctors and avoid it if at all possible. My heart doctor told me to slow down, but that's easier said than done.*

Note: If item 13, Violence/Abuse Experienced, is rated 2 or higher, answer items 19, 20, and 21.

19. Relationship with Abuser: How would you describe your relationship with the person who has abused you?

1	2	3	4	5
No contact or conflict now		Occasional conflict		Great conflict and turmoil

Comments/Describe:

20. Safety—Self: How safe do you feel now?

1	2	3	4	5
Very safe		Sometimes unsafe		Very unsafe

Comments/Describe:

21. (If there are children) Safety—Children: How safe do you think your children are?

1	2	3	4	5
Very safe		Sometimes unsafe		Very unsafe

Comments:

Additional Items: Do you have any other issues, concerns, or problems that you wish to discuss with a counselor?
No, not really.

Urgency/Importance: Among the items noted, which do you consider the most urgent or in need of immediate attention?
Well, I wish I could do right by my family but I just can't get through to my wife.

Name: *George Sloan*
Address: *33 Random Avenue*
Middletown 01234 Central County
Telephone: *(444) 123-0987*
Date: *2-15-09*

EXHIBIT 3.4   CHILD SCREENING CHECKLIST

Child's Full Name _____ Gender _____
Date of Birth _____

Family Relationship Concerns:

Does not get along with ☐ mother   ☐ father   ☐ brother(s)   ☐ sister(s)
☐ refuses to participate in family activities   ☐ refuses to accept and perform family responsibilities   ☐ frequently absent parent   ☐ marital problems/domestic violence
☐ rotating "parents" (parents' girlfriends or boyfriends)   ☐ inadequate child care arrangements   ☐ family health problems   ☐ financial insecurity/homelessness
☐ family transitions (move, divorce, remarriage, incarceration, death)   ☐ rejection of child   ☐ other

School Concerns:

☐ Poor grades/underachievement   ☐ lack of motivation/disinterest/failure to do homework   ☐ frequent absences or tardiness   ☐ warnings, detentions, suspensions   ☐ does not get along with students   ☐ does not get along with teachers   ☐ other

Peer Relationship Concerns:

☐ Inability to get along with peers   ☐ lack of friends   ☐ prefers to be alone
☐ prefers to be with adults   ☐ does not associate with peers   ☐ not accepted by
peers   ☐ bullied/harassed by peers   ☐ reluctant to leave parent/home   ☐ other

Dyssocial Behavioral Concerns:

☐ Excessive lying   ☐ stealing   ☐ vandalism   ☐ fire setting   ☐ aggression/
fighting/violence   ☐ runaway   ☐ early sexual behavior   ☐ inappropriate sexual
behavior   ☐ substance abuse   ☐ court involvement   ☐ homicidal   ☐ suicidal
☐ other

Personal Adjustment Concerns:

☐ Temper tantrums   ☐ easily upset   ☐ clinging/dependent   ☐ sleep disturbances
☐ nervous mannerisms   ☐ thumb sucking   ☐ speech problems   ☐ eating problems
☐ wetting, soiling, retention   ☐ lacks self-confidence/self-esteem   ☐ other

Emotional Concerns:

☐ Loneliness   ☐ boredom   ☐ being different   ☐ frustration   ☐ anger/hostility
☐ anxiousness   ☐ fearfulness   ☐ negativism   ☐ depression   ☐ other

Medical and Developmental Concerns:

☐ Acute illness   ☐ chronic illness   ☐ disabilities   ☐ allergies   ☐ accident prone
☐ seizures   ☐ physical complaints   ☐ lengthy or frequent clinic/hospital visits
☐ medication   ☐ surgery   ☐ mental retardation   ☐ other

Strengths and assets:

_____

_____

_____

_____

Comments:

_____

_____

_____

_____

Screened by

_____

_____

_____

_____

Summary and Discussion Questions

Some people are at greater risk of crisis than others. Identifying groups of people who are most likely to experience a crisis is helpful in recognizing individuals in crisis. People in crisis have typical patterns of thinking, feeling, and acting. There is no substitute for a thorough assessment of whether a person is or is not in crisis. The assessment is the basis of the helping plan. It can save lives and avoid many later problems, including unnecessary placement of people in institutions, and can address issues of managed care as it affects people in serious need of mental health services.

1. Consider the difference between a "functional assessment" and psychiatric diagnosis in a human rights and client empowerment perspective.
2. Identify scientific evidence and/or other factors that might explain the increased incidence of bi-polar illness in wealthy countries.
3. What are the underlying values in the United States that support the continuing disparity in insurance coverage for people needing mental health services?
4. How do you think use of the CMHA tool and "Child Screening Checklist" might influence crisis and social services for troubled families and children?

References

Becker, H. S. (1963). *Outsiders: Studies in the sociology of deviance.* New York: Free Press.

Brown, L., & Hoff, L. A. (in press). Mental health assessment in primary care. In L. A. Hoff & B. Morgan. *Psychiatric & mental health essentials in primary care.*

Canada, M., Heath, M. A., Money, K., Annandale, N., Fischer, L., & Young, E. L. (2006). Crisis intervention for students of diverse backgrounds: School counselors' concerns. *Brief Treatment and Crisis Intervention, 7,* 12–24.

Caplan, G. (1964). *Principles of preventive psychiatry.* New York: Basic Books.

Caplan, P. (1995). *They say you're crazy: How the world's most powerful psychiatrists decide who's normal.* Reading, MA: Addison-Wesley.

Capponi, P (1992). *Upstairs in the crazy house.* Toronto: Penguin Books.

Cella, E. P., Besancon, V., & Zipple, A. M. (1997). Expanding the role of clubhouses: Guidelines for establishing a system of integrated day services. *Psychiatric Rehabilitation Journal, 21*(1), 10–15.

Cloward, R. A., & Piven, F. F. (1979). Hidden protest: The channeling of female innovations and resistance. *Signs: Journal of Women in Culture and Society, 4,* 651–669.

Cohen, C. I. (1993). The biomedicalization of psychiatry: A critical overview. *Community Mental Health Journal, 29,* 509–521.

Congressional Joint Commission on Mental Health and Illness. (1961). *Action for mental health.* New York: Basic Books.

Cooksey, E. C., & Brown, P. (1998). Spinning on its axes: DSM and the social construction of psychiatric diagnosis. *International Journal of Health Sciences, 28*(3), 525–554.

Diller, L. (2007, June 19). Misguided standards of care. *Boston Globe*, p. A9.

Dobkin de Rios, M. (2002). What we can learn from Shamanic healing: Brief psychotherapy with Latino immigrant clients. *American Journal of Public Health*, 92(10), 1576–1578.

Earley, P. (2006). *Crazy: A father's search through America's mental health madness*. New York: Berkley Books.

Edmands, M. S., Hoff, L. A., Kaylor, L., Mower, L., & Sorrell, S. (1999). Bridging gaps between mind, body and spirit: Healing the whole person. *Journal of Psychosocial Nursing, 37*(10), 1–7.

Elliot, G. R. (2006). *Medicating young minds*. New York: Stewart, Taleori, & Chang.

Everett, B., & Gallop, R. (2000). *The link between childhood trauma and mental illness: Effective interventions for mental health professionals*. Thousand Oaks, CA: Sage.

Fadiman, A. (1997). *The spirit catches you and you fall down: A Hmong child, her American doctors, and the collision of two cultures*. New York: Noonday Press, Farrar, Straus and Giroux.

Farrell, S. P., & Deeds, E. S. (1997). The clubhouse model as exemplar. *Journal of Psychosocial Nursing, 35*(1), 27–34.

Fausto-Sterling, A. (2000). *Sexing the body*, New York: Basic Books.

Gellene, D. (2007, September 4). Bipolar disorder cases boom among youths. *Boston Globe*, p. A2.

Goffman, E. (1961). *Asylums*. New York: Doubleday.

Goffman, E. (1963). *Stigma*. Englewood Cliffs, NJ: Prentice Hall.

Golan, N. (1969). When is a client in crisis? *Social Casework, 50*, 389–394.

Gove, W. (1978). Sex differences in mental illness among adult men and women: An examination of four questions raised regarding whether or not women actually have higher rates. *Social Science and Medicine, 12*, 187–198.

Hagey, R., & McDonough, P. (1984). The problem of professional labeling. *Nursing Outlook, 32*(3), 151–157.

Hansell, N. (1976). *The person in distress*. New York: Human Sciences Press.

Hoff, L. A. (1990). *Battered women as survivors*. London: Routledge.

Hoff, L. A. (1993). Review essay: Health policy and the plight of the mentally ill. *Psychiatry, 56*(4), 400–419.

Hoff, L. A. (2000). Interpersonal violence. In C. E. Koop, C. E. Pearson, & M. R. Schwarz (Eds.), *Critical issues in global health* (pp. 260–271). San Francisco: Jossey-Bass.

Hoff, M. (2005). *Resilience: A paradigm of promise*. Unpublished master's thesis. Fargo: North Dakota State University, department of counselor education.

Hoff, L. A., Hanrahan, P., & Gallop, R. (2000). *Comprehensive mental health assessment: A functional approach*. Unpublished manuscript.

Hoff, L. A., & Rosenbaum, L. (1994). A victimization assessment tool: Instrument development and clinical implications. *Journal of Advanced Nursing, 20*(4), 627–634.

Holden, C. (1986). Proposed new psychiatric diagnoses raise charges of gender bias. *Science, 231*, 327–328.

Illich, I. (1976). *Limits to medicine*. Harmondsworth, England: Penguin Books.

Johnson, A. B. (1990). *Out of bedlam: The truth about deinstitutionalization*. New York: Basic Books.

Johnson, T. D. (December 2007/January 2008). Long fight for mental health parity continues for Americans. *The Nation's Health*, 1, 22–23.

Kleinman, A. (1980). *Patients and healers in the context of culture*. Berkeley: University of California Press.

Kors, J. (2007, October 15). Specialist town takes his case to Washington. *The Nation*, 13–20.

Lemert, W. M. (1951). *Social pathology*. New York: McGraw-Hill.

Link, B. G., Phelan, J. C., Bresnahan, M., Stueve, A., & Pescosolido, B. A. (1997). Public conceptions of mental illness: Labels, causes, dangerousness, and social distance. *American Journal of Public Health, 89*(9), 128–133.

Loustaunau, M. D., & Sobo, E. J. (1997). *The cultural context of health, illness and medicine*. New York: Bergin & Garvey.

Luhrmann, T. M. (2000). *Of two minds: The growing disorder in American psychiatry*. New York: Knopf.

Lyness, J. M. (1997). *Psychiatric pearls*. Philadelphia: F. A. Davis.

Madrigal, K. B. (2005). Treatment beliefs of combat trauma survivors with posttraumatic stress disorder. *Practicing Anthropology, 27*(3), 37–40.

McHugh, P. R. (2001). The DSM: Gaps & essences. *Psychiatric Research Report, 17*(2), 2–3, 14–15.

McHugh, P. R., & Clark, M. R., (2006). Diagnostic and classificatory dilemmas. In M. Blumenfeld & J. J. Strain (Eds.), *Psychosomatic medicine* (pp. 39–45). Philadelphia: Lippincott, Williams, & Wilkins.

Mettugh, P. R. (2005). Striving for coherence: Psychiatry's efforts over classification. *Journal of the American Medical Association, 293*(20), 2526–2528.

Mitchell, G. (1991). Nursing diagnosis: An ethical analysis. *Image: Journal of Nursing Scholarship, 23*(2), 99–103.

Nehls, N. (1999). Borderline personality disorder: The voice of patients. *Research in Nursing and Health, 22*(4), 285–293.

Osgood, N. (1992). *Suicide in later life: Recognizing the warning signs*. San Francisco: New Lexington Press.

Polak, P. (1967). The crisis of admission. *Social Psychiatry, 2*, 150–157.

Polak, P. (1976). A model to replace psychiatric hospitalization. *Journal of Nervous and Mental Disease, 162*, 13–22.

Rosenhan, D. L. (1973). On being sane in insane places. *Science, 179*, 250–258. (Also reprinted in H. D. Schwartz & C. S. Kart. 1976. *Dominant issues in medical sociology*. Reading, MA: Addison-Wesley; and in P. J. Brink (Ed.). 1976. *Transcultural nursing*. Englewood Cliffs, NJ: Prentice Hall.)

Schlein, S. (March 12, 2007). When diagnosis is part of the problem. *Boston Globe*, p. A11.

Sennott, C. M. (2007, November 11). Back but not at home. *Boston Globe*, pp. A1, 22–23.

Solberg, V. S. H., Carlstrom, A. H., Howard, K. A. S., & Jones, J. E. (2007). Classifying at-risk high school youth: The influence of exposure to community violence and protective factors on academic and health outcomes. *Career Development Quarterly, 55*, 313–327.

See Online Resources for additional references.

CHAPTER 4

Helping People in Crisis

Understanding the crisis model lays the foundation for assessing people at risk. The focus in this chapter is on the interpersonal context of crisis care and on specific strategies for assisting people who are acutely upset. Specifically, communication and rapport, planning, contracting, and working through the crisis toward a positive outcome will be discussed. The principles and techniques suggested can be applied in a wide variety of crisis intervention settings: primary care agencies, homes, hospitals, clinics, hotlines, and alternative crisis services. These principles and techniques can be varied and adapted according to professional training, personal preference, and setting, but the fundamental ideas remain the same.

Communication and Rapport: The Immediate Context of Crisis Work

Crisis intervention strategies are not likely to work if a crisis worker has failed to establish rapport with the person in crisis. Just as assessment is part of the helping process, rapport and effective communication are integrated throughout all stages of crisis care: assessment, planning, intervention, and follow-up.

The Nature and Purpose of Communication

Human beings are distinguished from the nonhuman animal kingdom by our ability to produce and use symbols and to create meaning out of the events and circumstances of our lives. Through language and nonverbal communication, we let our fellow humans know what we think and feel about life and about one another. For example, a man might say, "Life is not worth living without her." He may be contemplating suicide after divorce because he sees life without his cherished companion as meaningless. A rape victim or terminally ill woman might say, "What did I do to deserve this?" thus accounting for the situation by blaming herself. Communication is the medium through which we

- Struggle to survive (for example, by giving away prized possessions or saying, "I don't care anymore" as a cry for help after a serious loss)

- Develop meaningful human communion and maintain it (for example, by giving and receiving support during stress and crisis)
- Bring stability and organization into our lives (for example, by sorting out the chaotic elements of a traumatic event with a caring person)
- Negotiate social and political struggles at national and international levels

When communication fails, a person may feel alone, abandoned, worthless, and unloved, or conflict and tension may occur in interpersonal relations. The most tragic result of failed communication is violence toward self and others; at the societal level, this translates into war. Such destructive outcomes of failed communication are more probable in acute crisis situations. Given the importance of communication in the development and resolution of crisis, let us consider some of the factors that influence our interactions with people in crisis.

Factors Influencing Communication in Crisis Work

Many sources provide theoretical knowledge about human communication: psychology, sociology, cultural anthropology, ecology, and sociolinguistics (for example, Loustaunau & Sobo, 1997; Storti, 1994). These sources provide important insights into communication as it applies to crisis work.

Psychology. As noted in Chapter 3, cognitive functions are significant in crisis response and coping. The way a person *perceives* stressful events influences how that person *feels* about these events and communicates feelings about them. When an event and a person's perception of the meaning of the event are incongruous and thus lead to a culturally inappropriate expression of feelings, this may indicate mental impairment and greater vulnerability to stress. For example, a person who feels depressed and unworthy of help will usually have difficulty expressing feelings such as anger, which might be appropriate after a traumatic event such as a violent attack. A human services provider who feels insecure may talk too much or fail to be appropriately active when the situation calls for worker initiative.

Sociology. Sociological factors affecting communication in crisis situations spring from society at large as well as from the subcultures of various crisis service delivery systems. These include status, role, and gender factors, and political and economic factors. For example, a health provider may assume that suicide risk assessment is someone else's responsibility. Or, socioeconomic policies may obscure the fact that community-based help is often more appropriate than hospital care. Similarly, the predominance of individualistic approaches may hinder using the highly effective group medium of helping people in crisis.

Cultural Anthropology. Insights from cultural anthropology underscore the importance of sensitivity to another person's values and beliefs in understanding what life events mean to different people. As discussed in Chapter 1, *ethnocentrism* fosters a person's cultural identity and sense of belonging to a social group. At its worst, exaggerated ethnocentrism can become destructive in resolving community problems among different ethnic groups by imposing their values and customs on others. Ethnocentric attitudes can also interfere with effective communication in crisis situations.

It is important to remember in crisis work that for many people certain values are worth dying for. Needless to say, if an *imposed*—rather than a negotiated—crisis management plan contradicts dearly held values and threatens a person's sense of self-mastery, the chances of success are minimal. Examples of values that may be critical include a person's (1) idea of the meaning of death, illness, and health, (2) feelings about whether to seek and accept help, and (3) opinion about how help should be offered. For example, a person contemplating suicide but seeking one last chance to get help may interpret a prescription for sleeping pills as "an invitation to die" (Jourard, 1970). Crisis workers should also be aware that many human service professionals in the United States and other Western societies hold values of the white, middle-class majority.

Ecology. Environmental factors are intricately tied to cultural values regarding privacy. Examples from previous chapters suggest that the environment in which crisis service is offered influences the outcome of the crisis. If a person lacks privacy, such as in a busy hospital emergency department, the likelihood of successful communication during crisis is reduced. A serious commitment to crisis service delivery in emergency settings, therefore, would provide for separate rooms to facilitate the kind of communication necessary for acutely upset people. A worker's skills are useless if staffing and material factors prevent the effective application of those skills (see Online Resources).

Similarly, in crisis work done by police officers and social service staff, such as mediating a marital fight or parental custody issues, spatial factors can be critical in saving lives. The expression "A man's home is his castle" symbolizes a personalized and defended territory where a crisis worker may be defined as an "outsider" and is thus more vulnerable. Inattention to these unstated but culturally shared experiences can result in violent behavioral—that is, nonverbal—communication about this hidden dimension of public and private life. Police officers often refer to the "sixth sense" they develop through street experience and sensitivity to environmental factors related to crisis. Potential victims in high-crime areas and stressful work environments should also sensitize themselves to elements in their milieu that may signal a crisis of violence, so they can protect themselves. Police or neighborhood associations are good sources of this kind of information. As a lifesaving measure, health and social service staff required to make home visits should not do so without having done a Level I risk assessment (see Chapter 3) by telephone and/or team consultation. Depending on the degree of risk, the worker should *not* go alone or without arranging for police backup in the event of emergency (see Chapter 12, workplace violence).

Sociolinguistics. Sociolinguistics is the study of social theories of language. Scholars examine how social factors such as race, gender, class, region, and religion influence language and how language can both influence health status and condition thought and social action. Language is a window to culture. As the common medium for communication between particular linguistic communities, it is the most observable way to ascertain the ideas, beliefs, and attitudes of various cultural groups. Insensitivity to an individual's linguistic interpretation can reflect a failure to appreciate diverse cultural values. Effective crisis workers should have something in common linguistically with various ethnic groups if they are to serve people in the groups within the framework of their value systems.

Language, then, serves as a pivotal link between individual and social approaches to crisis. For example, in *individual* crisis work with a victim of rape or racially motivated violence, a worker helps the person talk about the event, work through feelings, and develop a plan of action, such as reporting to the police. The *sociocultural* element in this kind of crisis situation is the message that may be conveyed to women and ethnic minority groups that they are responsible for their own victimization (Ryan, 1971). Such cultural messages are revealed in conversation: "Women and blacks are their own worst enemies," or "Why does she [a battered woman] stay?" Such messages influence how victimized people may respond emotionally, cognitively, and behaviorally to violent events.

The written word similarly conveys the beliefs and values of a cultural community. For example, you may have observed many pages ago that the language in this book is nonmedical and nonsexist. This usage is based on the recognition that language is a powerful conveyor of social and cultural norms governing social status and behavior. Intercultural and gender relationships, sexual identity, and theoretical frameworks underpinning practice can be revealed through oral and written language—for example, defining "crisis" as essentially a "normal" experience or a diagnosable psychiatric entity such as *acute stress disorder* (DSM-IV-R 308.3; *Diagnostic and Statistical Manual of Mental Disorders*).

Crisis workers will discover other examples in which sensitivity in communication affects interactions with people in crisis. Communication is not only necessary for carrying out the crisis intervention process, but is also an integral aspect of the helping process itself.

Relationships, Communication, and Rapport

Technically flawless communication skills are useless in the absence of rapport with the person in crisis. Conversely, if our values, attitudes, and feelings about a person are respectful, unprejudiced, and based on true concern, those values will almost always be conveyed to the person, regardless of any technical errors in communication. This point cannot be overemphasized. For example, it is commonplace to hear, "I thought he was suicidal, but I didn't say anything because I was afraid I'd say the wrong thing." This argument represents a gross misconception of the nature of language. If we truly are concerned about whether a person lives or dies, this concern will almost invariably be conveyed in what we say unless we

- Deliberately say the opposite of what we mean
- Are mentally ill, with an accompanying distortion and contradiction between thought and language

- Lack knowledge about suicidal people or feel anxious about how the person will respond to our sincere message and therefore fail to deliver it (see Chapter 9)

Crisis workers therefore must learn the technical aspects of skillful communication with people who are upset. They must avoid asking why and refrain from asking questions that lead to yes or no answers; they must not make judgments or offer unrealistic reassurance. But it is equally important to establish rapport and foster the relationship necessary for a distressed individual to accept help. Although theoretical and technical knowledge is important in facilitating positive outcomes with people in crisis, the quality of the relationship we establish is far more important. In particular, this includes the worker's ability to convey empathy, caring, and sincerity. However, Truax and Carkhuff (1967) found that nonprofessional persons are highly capable of creating such relationships and that mental health professionals' demonstrations of empathy *decrease* as the length of time after their original training *increases*—findings still relevant today. Burnout or lack of team support can negatively affect the helping relationship and help explain this finding.

In our efforts to establish rapport, two objectives are central:

1. We should aim to make the distressed person feel understood. We can convey understanding by using reflective statements such as, "You seem to be very hurt and upset by what has happened," and "Sounds like you're very angry." If our perception of what the person is feeling is incorrect, the words *seem to be* and *sounds like* provide an opening for the person to explain his or her perception of the upsetting or traumatic event. The expression "I understand" should generally be avoided, as it may be perceived as presumptuous; there is always the possibility that we do not truly understand. Parents who suffer the loss of a child say that no one but a similarly grieving parent can truly understand.
2. If we are unclear about the nature or extent of what the person feels or is troubled by, we should convey our wish to understand by asking, for example, "Could you tell me more about that?" or "How do you feel about what has happened?" or "I'm not sure I understand. Could you tell me what you mean by that?"

Besides these techniques for establishing rapport, there are several other means of removing barriers to effective communication (Pluckhan, 1978, pp. 116–128; Arnold & Boggs, 1999):

- Become aware of the internal and external noises that may inhibit our ability to communicate sincerely.
- Avoid double messages. For example, we may convey concern at a verbal level but contradict our message by posture, facial gestures, or failure to give undivided attention. Traditionally, this is known as the "double bind" in communication (Bateson, 1958).

- Avoid unwarranted assumptions about other people's lives, feelings, and values (Kottler, 1994).
- Keep communication clear of unnecessary professional and technical jargon; when technical terminology is unavoidable, translate it.
- Be aware of the trust-risk factor in communication. We must periodically examine whether we are trustworthy and what kind of social, cultural, and personal situations warrant the trust needed to accept help from another (Pluckhan, 1978, pp. 88–89; Northouse & Northouse, 1998). Also keep in mind that some people are distrustful not because of us, but because they have been betrayed by others they trusted.
- Take advantage of opportunities to improve self-awareness, self-confidence, and sensitivity to factors affecting communication (human relations courses, biofeedback training, assertiveness workshops).

These suggestions represent a small part of the communication field as it pertains to crisis work. Because communication is inseparable from culture and human life, its importance in helping people in crisis can hardly be overestimated (Haley, 1987). Keeping in mind these contextual aspects of crisis work, let us proceed to specific strategies of planning, intervention, and follow-up in the crisis care process. In the Crisis Paradigm, these steps are illustrated in the intertwined circles in Box 3 (see Figure 4.1).

Planning with a Person or Family in Crisis

There is no substitute for a good plan for crisis resolution. Without careful planning and direction, a helper can only add to the confusion already experienced by the person in crisis. Some may argue that in certain crisis situations there is no time to plan, as life-and-death issues may be at stake. Rather than excusing the need for planning, this only underscores its urgency. A good plan can be formulated in a few minutes by someone who knows the signs of crisis, is confident in his or her own ability to help, and is able to enlist additional, immediate assistance in cases of impasse or life-and-death emergency.

Case Example: Robert

A police officer was called to the home of Robert, who had recently been discharged from a hospital. He had angrily barricaded himself in the bathroom and was making threatening comments to his family. On arrival, the officer learned that a psychiatrist–social worker team was already at the home. They were frightened by Robert's threats and were unable to persuade him to unlock the door. The officer identified himself and asked Robert to open the door. He refused. The officer then forced the door open. There was no formal discussion between the officer and the mental health team. Robert became frightened and stabbed the officer in the shoulder with a kitchen knife.

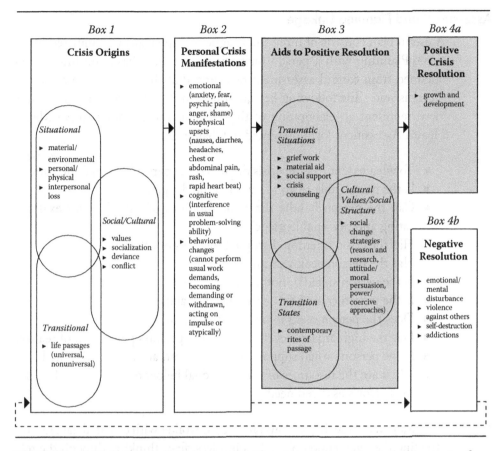

FIGURE 4.1 Crisis Paradigm. Crisis origins, manifestations, and outcomes and the respective functions of crisis care have an interactional relationship. The intertwined circles represent the distinct yet interrelated origins of crisis and aids to positive resolution, even though personal manifestations are often similar. The arrows pointing from origins to positive resolution illustrate the opportunity for growth and development through crisis; the broken line at the bottom depicts the potential danger of crisis in the absence of appropriate aids. The loop between Box 4b and Box 1 denotes the vulnerability to future crisis episodes following negative resolution.

This case illustrates several points:

1. Action occurred *before* planning. As a result, the resources of the professional mental health and police systems were not used to their fullest capacity.
2. When police officers and others are injured by mentally disturbed persons, the injury is often related to the worker's inadequate training in crisis intervention (see Chapter 12). Because most police officer training now includes crisis intervention, police deaths and injuries on the job have declined.
3. The time spent *planning*—even if it is only a few minutes—can prevent injuries and save lives.

Research on similar work-related injuries documents that many of these injuries might have been prevented (Chappell & Di Martino, 1998; Vida, Inc., 2008).

Assessment and Planning Linkage

A useful plan consists of more than vague or haphazardly formulated intentions. Planning with a person for crisis resolution is based on information obtained from careful assessment revealing that the person is in a crisis or precrisis state. The following key questions, in the context of a skilled interview, represent an elaboration of the 21 items the Comprehensive Mental Health Assessment form presented in Chapter 3:

- To what extent has the crisis disrupted the person's normal life pattern?
- Is the person able to go to school or hold a job?
- Can the person handle the responsibilities of daily life, for example, eating and personal hygiene?
- Has the crisis situation disrupted the lives of others?
- Has the person been victimized by crime?
- Is the person suicidal, homicidal, or both?
- Is the person coping through substance abuse?
- Does the person seem to be close to despair?
- Has the high anxiety level distorted the person's perception of reality?
- Is the person's usual support system present, absent, or exhausted?
- What are the resources of the individual helper or agency in relation to the person's assessed needs?

The answers to such questions provide the worker with essential data for constructing the intervention plan. This involves, first, thinking through the relationships between events and the way the person is thinking, feeling, and acting and then formulating some possible solutions with the person and the family.

To ensure that the plan is specific to the person's crisis response and corresponding needs, a worker may set priorities by checking the assessment form for ratings of 3, 4, or 5 (the levels designating ineffective or impaired functioning). The worker should then ask the person which problem or issue seems the most urgent—for example, "It seems there are a lot of things upsetting you right now. Which of these is the most important for you to get help with immediately?" In the event that such questions reveal cognitive or emotional impairment (e.g., hallucinations, paranoid ideation, profound mood swings as in bipolar illness) to the extent that a person cannot be actively engaged in the helping process, a psychiatric consultation is indicated.

Decision Counseling and Client Empowerment

Skill in decision counseling (Hansell, 1970) is intrinsic to the crisis assessment, planning, and intervention process. Decision counseling is cognitively oriented and allows the upset person to put distorted thoughts, chaotic feelings, and disturbed behavior into some kind of order. The person is encouraged to

- Search for the boundaries of the problem. ("How long has this been troubling you?" or "In what kind of situation do you find yourself getting most upset?")
- Appraise the meaning of the problems and how they can be mastered. ("How has your life changed since you were injured during military service?")
- Make a decision about various solutions to the problem. ("What do you think you can do about this?" or "What have you done so far about this problem?")
- Test the solutions in a clear-cut action plan that is documented in a service contract.

In decision counseling, the crisis worker facilitates crisis resolution by helping the person decide the following:

- What problem is to be solved? ("Of the things you are troubled by, what is it you want help with now?")
- How can it be solved? ("What do you think would be most helpful?")
- When should it be solved? ("How about coming in after school today with your husband and your son?")
- Where should it be solved? ("Yes, we do make home visits. Tell me more about your situation, so we can decide if a home or office visit is best.")
- Who should be involved in solving it? ("Have you talked to anyone else about this problem who could be helpful?")

Decision counseling also includes setting goals for the future and forming an alternative action plan to be used if the current plan fails or goals are not achieved. It is also highly complementary to the cognitive behavior approach Madrigal (2005) describes for combat veterans suffering PTSD. This approach underscores a fundamental premise of crisis counseling and the opportunity it affords a person to learn new skills in dealing with troubling symptoms. Madrigal notes that traumatized veterans who may have been placed under a gag order by military supervisors may fear possible punishment for talking about their combat experience with outsiders. If veterans choose to share trauma stories with other veterans to strengthen bonding around a common experience, it should be their decision. At the San Diego Veterans Administration (VA) clinic PTSD program, veterans like this are often relieved to learn that they are not expected to repeatedly talk about their trauma as in the culturally embedded belief that without "exposure-based intervention"—or "spitting it out"—they will not get better (Madrigal, p. 38). Further, Madrigal cites cognitive-behavioral approaches as an aid to protect clinicians from "vicarious traumatization" and burnout from listening to trauma stories all day to the exclusion of action plans and acquiring new coping skills (see Chapter 13, and CISD [critical incident stress debriefing], Community Responses to Disaster, and Williams & Poijula, 2002). Dobkin de Rios (2002) makes similar points about personal control, behavior modification, and cognitive restructuring in Shamanic healing with Latino immigrant clients (see also Dattilio & Freeman, 2007).

In decision counseling, the counselor must have thorough knowledge of the person's functional level and network of social attachments. Used effectively, this technique makes maximum use of client empowerment strategies and learning from the turmoil of crisis to (1) assess one's current coping ability, (2) develop new problem-solving skills, (3) establish more stable emotional attachments, (4) improve one's social skills, and (5) increase personal competence and satisfaction with life patterns.

Developing a Service Contract

Once an action plan is agreed on by the person in crisis and the worker, it is important to confirm the plan in a service contract (see Exhibit 4.1, suggesting next steps and planning focus with Mr. George Sloan, case example in Chapter 3). The nature of the contract is implied in the fact that the plan for crisis intervention is *mutually arrived at by the helper and the distressed person*. If the person comes to the attention of professional crisis counselors or mental health professionals with training in crisis intervention, the service contract should be formalized in writing. The following conditions are implicit in the contract:

- The person is essentially in charge of his or her own life.
- The person is able to make decisions.
- The crisis counseling relationship is one between partners.
- Both parties to the contract, the person in crisis and the crisis counselor, have rights and responsibilities, as spelled out in the contract.
- The relationship between the helper and the person in crisis is complementary rather than hierarchical, as between a supervisor and a subordinate.

Institutional psychiatry and traditional mental health professions in North America have come under serious attack for violating civil rights (Rodriguez-Garcia & Akhter, 2000). Individuals have been locked up, medicated, and given electric shock against their will in mental institutions. Protests and demands for appropriate treatment by human rights and consumer groups have led to certain reforms, although this is still contested terrain (Hoff, 1993; Luhrmann, 2000). For example, if the right to treatment in the "least restrictive environment" is used to deny treatment to a mentally ill person needing a protective hospital environment, something is seriously wrong in the presumably "reformed" mental health system, which has shifted responsibility for protective containment to the criminal justice system (Earley, 2006). Currently, groups like the National Alliance for the Mentally Ill and the Ontario Psychiatric Survivors Association do advocacy work around these issues. The Universal Declaration of Human Rights, adopted by the United Nations in 1948, continues to bring attention to the issue, which makes client service contracts more important than ever as safeguards against abuse of those rights.

People have the right to either use or refuse services; the formal service contract protects that right. In addition, the contract establishes the following:

- What the client can expect from the counselor
- What the counselor can expect from the client
- How the two parties will achieve the goals on which they have agreed
- The target dates for achieving the goals defined in the contract

Nothing goes into a contract that is not mutually developed by client and counselor through decision counseling. Both parties sign the contract and retain copies. Receiving help on a contractual basis has these effects: (1) reducing the possibility that the helping relationship will degenerate into a superior–subject or rescuer–victim stance, (2) enhancing the self-mastery and social skills of the client, (3) facilitating growth through a crisis experience, (4) reducing the incidence of failure in helping a person in crisis, and (5) documenting for insurance purposes the goals and outcomes of crisis care and mental health treatment. Planning and applying emergency mental health services can be additionally challenging if there are cultural clashes with ethnically and linguistically diverse groups (Canada et al., 2006).

Crisis Care in an Emergency Setting: Illustration

Applied to George Sloan (continued from Chapter 3), a crisis counseling service contract builds on interview data from the Emergency Department (ED) illustrated in Table 4.1. Interdepartmental actions following medical emergency treatment after his suicidal car crash include: (1) Clear communication (in medical record and verbally) by ED staff to the surgical recovery unit that Mr. Sloan's injuries resulted from a suicide attempt; (2) placement of Mr. Sloan in a room close to the nurses station; (3) recovery unit medical

TABLE 4.1 Crisis Care in an Emergency Setting

Intervention Techniques	Interview between George Sloan and Emergency Department Nurse
Exploring resources	*Nurse:* You said you really can't talk to your wife about your problems. Is there anyone else you've ever thought about talking with?
	George: Well, I tried talking to my doctor once, but he didn't really have time. Then a few months ago, my minister could see I was pretty down and he stopped by a couple of times, but that didn't help.
Facilitating client empowerment and decision making	*Nurse:* Is there anyone else you think you could talk to?
	George: No, not really—nobody, anyway, that would understand.

(continued)

TABLE 4.1   Crisis Care in an Emergency Setting (continued)

Intervention Techniques	Interview between George Sloan and Emergency Department Nurse
Suggesting new resources	*Nurse:* What about seeing a regular counselor, George? We have connections here in the emergency room with the psychiatric department of our hospital, where a program could be set up to help you work out some of your problems.
	George: What do you mean? You think I'm crazy or something? (defensively) I don't need to see a shrink.
Listening, accepting client's feelings	*Nurse:* No, George, of course I don't think you're crazy. But when you're down and out enough to see no other way to turn but suicide—well, I know things look pretty bleak now, but talking to a counselor usually leads to some other ways of dealing with problems if you're willing to give it a chance.
	George: Well, I could consider it. What would it cost? I sure can't afford any more medical bills.
Involving client in the plan Facilitating client decision making Making the plan concrete and specific Involving significant other	*Nurse:* Here at our hospital clinic, if you can't pay the regular fee, you can apply for medical assistance. How would you like to arrange it? I could call someone now to come over and talk with you and set up a program, or you can call them yourself tomorrow and make the arrangements.
	George: Well, I feel better now, so I think I'd just as soon wait until tomorrow and call them—besides, I guess I should really tell my wife; I don't know how she'd feel about me seeing a counselor. But then I guess suicide is kind of a coward's way out.
Reinforcing coping mechanism Actively encouraging client action	*Nurse:* George, you sound hesitant, and I can understand what you must be feeling. Talking again with your wife sounds like a good idea. Or you and your wife might want to see the counselor together sometime. But I hope you do follow through on this, as I really believe you and your family could benefit from some help like this. After all, you've had a lot of things hit you at one time.
Expressing empathy	*George:* Well, it's hard for me to imagine what anyone could do, but maybe at least my wife and I could get along better and keep our kid out of trouble. I just wish she'd quit insisting on things I can't afford.
Conveying realistic hope that things might get better	*Nurse:* That's certainly a possibility, and that alone might improve things. How about this, George: I'll call you tomorrow afternoon to see how you are and whether you're having any trouble getting through to the counseling service?
Initiating follow-up plan	*George:* That sounds fine. I guess I really should give it another chance. Thanks for everything.
	Nurse: I'm glad we were able to talk, George. I'll be in touch tomorrow.

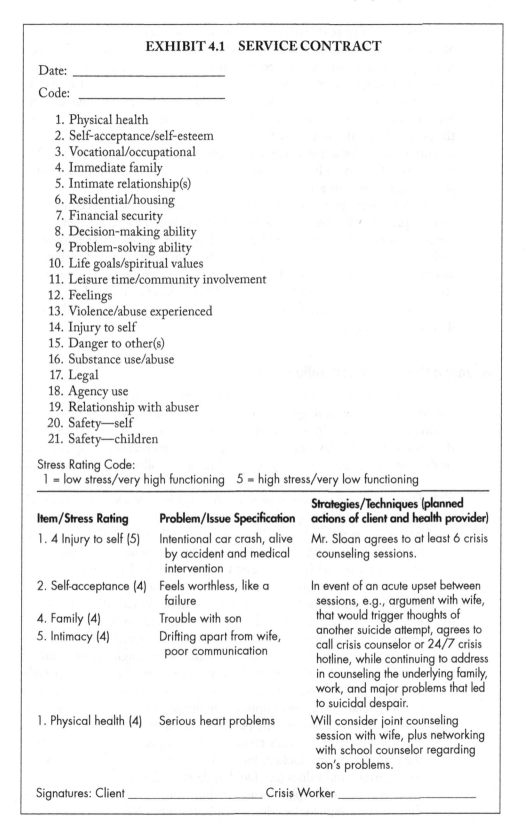

EXHIBIT 4.1   SERVICE CONTRACT

Date: _____

Code: _____

1. Physical health
2. Self-acceptance/self-esteem
3. Vocational/occupational
4. Immediate family
5. Intimate relationship(s)
6. Residential/housing
7. Financial security
8. Decision-making ability
9. Problem-solving ability
10. Life goals/spiritual values
11. Leisure time/community involvement
12. Feelings
13. Violence/abuse experienced
14. Injury to self
15. Danger to other(s)
16. Substance use/abuse
17. Legal
18. Agency use
19. Relationship with abuser
20. Safety—self
21. Safety—children

Stress Rating Code:
 1 = low stress/very high functioning   5 = high stress/very low functioning

Item/Stress Rating	Problem/Issue Specification	Strategies/Techniques (planned actions of client and health provider)
1. 4 Injury to self (5)	Intentional car crash, alive by accident and medical intervention	Mr. Sloan agrees to at least 6 crisis counseling sessions.
2. Self-acceptance (4)	Feels worthless, like a failure	In event of an acute upset between sessions, e.g., argument with wife, that would trigger thoughts of another suicide attempt, agrees to call crisis counselor or 24/7 crisis hotline, while continuing to address in counseling the underlying family, work, and major problems that led to suicidal despair.
4. Family (4)	Trouble with son	
5. Intimacy (4)	Drifting apart from wife, poor communication	
1. Physical health (4)	Serious heart problems	Will consider joint counseling session with wife, plus networking with school counselor regarding son's problems.

Signatures: Client _____ Crisis Worker _____

and nursing staff empathically and openly acknowledge and discuss with Mr. Sloan their knowledge of his failed suicide attempt; (4) engaging Mr. Sloan to accept medical and nursing recommendation of referral to crisis care or a mental health specialist; (5) a crisis counseling specialist has an introductory session with Mr. Sloan while in the hospital to lay a foundation for goal setting and follow-up counseling to deal with suicide prevention, and the personal, family, and related issues contributing to his despair. Without this kind of interdepartmental and interagency collaboration, people like Mr. Sloan may "fall through the cracks" and are at serious risk of future—and perhaps fatal—suicide attempts.

The next steps in a service contract with George Sloan (Exhibit 4.1) include planning for crisis counseling with an initial focus on items from the Assessment Worksheet rated 5 or 4—those needing most attention since he has agreed to a referral for counseling. Specific strategies and techniques would be negotiated between Mr. Sloan and the crisis counselor, drawing on strategies in this chapter and Chapter 10 for persons at serious risk of suicide. This example of a Service Contract form is adapted from the record system described in Chapter 3.

Evaluating the Crisis Intervention Plan

A plan can be used in several ways: (1) as a self-evaluation tool, (2) as a checklist for evaluating what might be missing or determining why progress seems elusive, (3) as a means by which supervisors can monitor client service, (4) as data for consultants who are brainstorming with workers about complex or difficult crisis situations. A good plan should have the following characteristics:

1. *Developed with the person in crisis.* A good intervention plan is developed in active collaboration with the person in crisis and the significant people in the person's life. The underlying philosophy is that people can help themselves with varying degrees of help from others. Doing things to, rather than with, a distressed person can lead to failure in crisis intervention. If the goals for crisis intervention and problem solving are formulated by the helper alone, those goals are practically worthless— no matter how appropriate they appear. Inattention to this important element of the planning process is probably responsible for more failures in healthy crisis resolution than any other single factor. Making decisions *for* rather than *with* the person in crisis violates the growth-and-development concept that is basic to effective crisis intervention. If a worker takes over, this implies that the person cannot participate in matters of vital concern. The person in crisis may feel devalued. Also, when a counselor assumes control, other important characteristics of the plan may be overlooked, for example, attention to the person's cultural pattern and values (see Dobkin de Rios, 2002).

2. *Problem oriented.* The plan focuses on immediate, concrete problems that directly contribute to the crisis—that is, the hazardous event or situation

and the "last straw" precipitating factor. For example, George Sloan says suicide is all that's left, a teenage daughter has run away, a woman gets a diagnosis of breast cancer, or a man learns he has AIDS. The plan should avoid probing into personality patterns or underlying psychological or marital problems contributing to the risk of crisis. These are properly the aim of psychotherapy or ongoing counseling, which the individual may choose after the immediate crisis is resolved. Exploration of previous successes and failures in problem solving is appropriate in the crisis model.

3. *Appropriate to a person's functional level and dependency needs.* The helper assesses how the person is thinking, feeling, and acting. If the individual is too anxious to think straight and make decisions (as assessed through decision counseling), the helper takes a more active role than might otherwise be indicated. In general, a crisis worker should never make a decision for another unless thorough assessment reveals that the person is unable to make decisions independently, as in an acute psychotic state.

If the person is feeling pent up with emotion, the plan should include adequate time to express those feelings. It is legitimate to give directions for action if the person's behavior and thinking are chaotic. Success in this kind of action plan is based on a belief in a person's ability to reassume independence once the acute crisis phase is over. A firm, confident approach, based on accurate assessment and respect for the person, inspires confidence and restores a sense of order and independence to the individual in crisis.

Success in this aspect of planning implies an understanding of human interdependence. Healthy *inter*dependence is keeping a good balance between dependence and independence needs. Some individuals are too dependent most of the time; others are too independent most of the time. The excessively independent person will probably have a hard time accepting the need for more dependence on others during a crisis. Asking for help is viewed as a loss of self-esteem. In contrast, the very dependent person will tend to behave more dependently during a crisis than the situation warrants.

These considerations underscore the need for thorough assessment of a person's strengths, resources, and usual coping abilities. A good rule of thumb is never to do something *for* a person until it is clear that the person cannot do it alone. We all resent extreme dependence on others, as it keeps us from growing to our full potential. It is equally important that helpers not fail to do for a person in crisis what assessment reveals the person cannot do alone. The crisis intervention model calls for active participation by the worker. However, the crisis counselor needs to know when to let go, so the person can once again take charge of his or her life. This is more easily done by workers who are self-aware and self-confident.

4. *Consistent with a person's culture and lifestyle.* Inattention to a person's lifestyle, values, and cultural patterns can result in the failure of a seemingly perfect plan. We must be sensitive to the person's total situation and careful not to impose our own value system on a person

whose lifestyle and values are different. As already noted, various cultural, ethnic, and religious groups have distinct patterns of response to events such as death, physical illness, divorce, and pregnancy out of wedlock. A sincere interest in people different from ourselves conveys respect, elicits information relevant to health, and curbs ethnocentric tendencies.

5. *Inclusive of the person's significant other(s) and social network.* If acutely upset people are viewed as social beings, a plan that excludes their social network is incomplete. Because crises occur when there is a serious disruption in normal social transactions or a person's self-perception in interpersonal situations, planning must attend to these important social factors. This is true even when the closest social contacts are hostile and are contributing significantly to the crisis.

   It is tempting to avoid dealing with family members who appear indifferent to or want a troubled person out of their lives. Still, significant others should be brought into the planning, at least to clarify whether or not they are a future source of help. In the event that the person is no longer wanted (for example, by a divorcing spouse or parents who abandon their children), the plan will include a means of helping the individual accept this reality and identify new social contacts. A child not helped to face such harsh realities may spend years fantasizing about reuniting a broken family. Put another way, our plan should include information about whether the family (or other significant person) is part of the problem or part of the solution (see Chapter 5).

6. *Realistic, time limited, and concrete.* A good crisis intervention plan is realistic about needs and resources. For example, a person who is too sick or who has no transportation or money should not be expected to come to an office for help. The plan should also contain a clear time frame. The person or family in crisis needs to know that client and counselor actions A, B, and C are planned to occur at points X, Y, and Z. This kind of structure is reassuring to someone in crisis. It provides concrete evidence that:

   - Something definite will happen to change the present state of discomfort.
   - The seemingly endless confusion and chaos of the crisis experience can be handled in terms familiar to the person.
   - The entire plan has a clearly anticipated ending point.

For the person who fears going crazy, is threatened with violence, or finds it difficult to depend on others, it is reassuring to look forward to having events under control again within a specified time.

An effective plan is also concrete in terms of place and circumstances—for example, "Family crisis counseling sessions will be held at the crisis clinic at 7:00 pm twice a week; one session will be held at daughter Nancy's school and will include her guidance counselor, the school nurse, and the principal." Or "Police will provide transportation for a victim of violence."

7. *Dynamic and renegotiable.* A dynamic plan is not carved in marble; it is alive, meaningful, and flexible. It is specific to a particular person with unique problems and allows for ongoing changes in the person's life. It should also include a mechanism for dealing with changes if the original plan no longer fits the person's needs, so that expected outcomes will not be perceived as failures. A person who doubts whether anything can be done to help should be assured, "If this doesn't work, we'll examine why and try something else." This feature of a plan is particularly important for people who distrust service agencies or who have experienced repeated disappointment or abandonment in their efforts to obtain help.

8. *Inclusive of follow-up.* Finally, a good plan includes an agreement for follow-up contact after the apparent resolution of the crisis. This feature is too often neglected by crisis and mental health workers. If not initially placed in the plan and the service contract, follow-up may fall by the wayside. In life-threatening crisis situations, a follow-up plan literally can mean the difference between life and death.

Careful attention to these planning criteria reduces the probability of negative crisis outcomes (Figure 4.1, Box 4b). These unhealthy outcomes increase one's vulnerability to future crisis episodes.

Working through a Crisis: Intervention Strategies

Effective crisis care fosters growth and avoids negative, destructive outcomes of traumatic events. Helping a person through healthy crisis resolution means carrying out the plan that was developed after assessment. The worker's crisis intervention techniques should follow from the way the person in crisis is thinking, feeling, and acting and should be tailored to the distinct origins of the crisis (see Figure 4.1, Boxes 1 and 3).

The manifestations of ineffective crisis coping in the case of George Sloan are spelled out on the assessment form illustrated in Chapter 3. The items designating life areas and signals of distress represent a detailed picture of biophysical, emotional, cognitive, and behavioral functioning (see Exhibit 4.1, Service Contract for George Sloan). Ineffective coping in any of these realms can be thought of as a red flag signaling possible negative crisis outcomes. The signals indicate that help is needed and that natural and formal crisis intervention strategies should be mobilized. Using any psychosocial techniques of intervention requires assessing the need for emergency medical services and establishing access to them if necessary. Common instances of such intervention are in the event of self-inflicted injury, victimization by crime, or injury by accident, as discussed in Chapters 10, 11, and 7, respectively. Having assessed the person's coping ability in each of the functional areas, the crisis worker helps the person avoid negative outcomes and move toward growth and development while resolving the crisis. The following crisis intervention strategies are suggested as ways to achieve this goal.

Loss, Change, and Grief Work

No matter what the origin of distress, a common theme observed in people in crisis is that of loss, including loss of

- Spouse, child, or other loved one
- Health, property, and physical security
- Job, home, country, and cultural supports
- A familiar social role
- Freedom, safety, and bodily integrity
- The opportunity to live beyond youth

From this it follows that a pivotal aspect of successful crisis resolution is grief work. Bereavement is the response to any acute loss. Our rational, social nature implies attachment to other human beings and a view of ourselves in relationship to the rest of the world: our family, friends, culture, pets, and home. Death and the changes following any loss are as inevitable as the ocean tide, but because loss is so painful emotionally, our natural tendency is to avoid coming to terms with it immediately and directly.

Grief work, therefore, takes time. Grief is not a set of symptoms to be treated; rather, it is a process of suffering that a bereaved person goes through on the way to a new life without the lost person, status, or object of love. It includes numbness and somatic distress (tightness in the throat, need to sigh, shortness of breath, lack of muscular power), pining and searching, anger and depression, and finally a turning toward recovery (Lindemann, 1944; Parkes, 1975). Care of the bereaved is a communal responsibility. Traditional societies, however, have assisted the bereaved much more effectively than have industrialized ones. Material prosperity and the high value placed on individual strength and accomplishment tend to dull awareness of personal mortality and the need for social support. This issue is discussed more fully in Chapter 6. Because reconciliation with loss is so important in avoiding destructive outcomes of crises, the main features of bereavement reactions are included here.

- A process of realization eventually replaces denial and the avoidance of memory of the lost person, status, or object.
- An alarm reaction sets in, including restlessness, anxiety, and various somatic reactions that leave a person unable to initiate and maintain normal patterns of activity.
- The bereaved has an urge to search for and find the lost person or object in some form. Painful pining, preoccupation with thoughts of the lost person or role and events leading to the loss, and general inattentiveness are common.

- Anger may develop toward the one who has died, or oneself, or others: "Oh John, why did you leave me?" or "Why didn't I insist that he go to the hospital?" are typical reactions.

- Guilt about perceived neglect is typical—neglect by self or others—as is guilt about having said something harsh to the person now dead or guilt about one's own survival—Lifton and Olson's (1976) "death guilt." There may also be outbursts against the people who press the bereaved person to accept the loss before he or she is psychologically ready.

- Feelings of internal loss or mutilation are revealed in remarks such as, "He was a part of me," or "Something of me went when they tore down our homes and neighborhood." The "urban villagers" (Gans, 1962) in Boston's West End mourned the loss of their community to an urban renewal project for several decades.

- By adopting the traits and mannerisms of the lost person or by trying to build another home of the same kind, the bereaved person re-creates a world that has been lost. This task of grief work is monumental for refugees who have lost family members and everything but the clothes on their backs.

- A pathological variant of normal grief may emerge—that is, the reactions just described may be excessive, prolonged, inhibited, or inclined to take a distorted form. This is most apt to happen in the absence of social support. Variants of normal grief also happen in the case of *ambiguous loss,* situations in which it is not clear whether the lost person is dead or a prisoner of war, for example, or cases in which there is delay or uncertainty of ritual closure, such as waiting for recovery of remains after an airliner crash or other catastrophe (see Boss, 1999).

These reactions have been observed in widows, disaster survivors, persons who have lost a body part, or who have lost their homes in urban relocation, and among people who have lost a loved one, especially if the death is an untimely one, as in the case of SIDS or AIDS (Ericsson, 1993; Lindemann, 1944; Marris, 1974; Parkes, 1975).

Both normal and pathological reactions are influenced by factors existing before, during, and after a loss. These are similar to the personal, material, demographic, cultural, and social influences affecting the outcome of any other crisis. Examples of factors affecting the response to loss include an inflexible approach to problem solving, poverty, the dependency of youth or old age, cultural inhibition of emotional expression, and the unavailability of social support. Assisting the bereaved in avoiding pathological outcomes of grief is an essential feature of a preventive and developmental approach to crisis work. Grief work, then, can be viewed as integral to any crisis resolution process in which loss figures as a major theme.

Normal grief work (Harvey, 1998; Lindemann, 1944; Parkes, 1975) consists of the following:

1. *Acceptance of the pain of loss.* This means dealing with memories of the deceased.
2. *Open expression of pain, sorrow, hostility, and guilt.* The person must feel free to mourn the loss openly, usually by weeping, and to express feelings of guilt and hostility.
3. *Understanding of the intense feelings associated with loss.* For example, the fear of going crazy is a normal part of the grieving process. When these feelings of sorrow, fear, guilt, and hostility are worked through in the presence of a caring person, they gradually subside. The ritual expression of grief, as in funerals, greatly aids in this process.
4. *Resumption of normal activities and social relationships without the person lost.* Having worked through the memories and feelings associated with a loss, a person acquires new patterns of social interaction apart from the deceased.

Many bereaved persons find support groups particularly helpful. Being with others who have suffered a similar loss provides understanding as well as some relief of the social isolation that may follow an acute loss. When people do not do grief work following any profound loss, serious emotional, mental, and social problems can occur. All of us can help people grieve without shame over their losses. This is possible if we are sensitized to the importance of expressing feelings openly and to the various factors affecting the bereavement process.

Those whose needs around grief work extend beyond the few crisis counseling sessions should have the benefit of individual or group psychotherapy. This may include persons who have suffered several serious losses in a short time or those with pathological grief reactions accompanied by serious depression. Children are of special concern around loss and grief because they may be overlooked as adults focus on their own grief. Linda Goldman (1994, 1996) has produced informative guides for laypersons and professionals, focusing on the particular needs of grieving children (see also Perschy, 1997, for helping grieving adolescents),

Other Intervention and Counseling Strategies

Some additional crisis care strategies include the following, regarding emotional, cognitive, and behavioral coping with crisis:

1. *Listen actively and with concern.* When a person is ashamed of his or her inability to cope with a problem, or feels that the problem is too minor to be so upset about, a good listener can dispel some of these feelings. Listening helps a person feel important and deserving of help no matter how trivial the problem may appear. Effective listening demands attention to possible listening barriers, such as internal and external noise and the other factors influencing communication discussed

earlier. Comments such as, "Hmm," "I see," and "Go on" are useful in acknowledging what a person says; they also encourage more talking and build rapport and trust. The failure to listen forms a barrier to all other intervention strategies.

2. *Encourage the open expression of feelings.* Listening is a natural forerunner of this important crisis intervention technique. One reason that some people are crisis prone is that they habitually bottle up feelings such as anger, grief, frustration, helplessness, and hopelessness. Negative associations with expressing feelings during childhood seem to put a damper on such expression when traumatic events occur later in life, or may be rooted in cultural norms. (See Madrigal, 2005, regarding this tactic and possible negative effects among combat veterans.) The crisis worker's acceptance of a distressed person's feelings often helps the person feel better immediately. It also can be the beginning of a healthier coping style in the future. This is one of the rewarding growth possibilities for people in crisis who are fortunate enough to get the help they need.

A useful technique for fostering emotional expression is role playing or role modeling. For example, the worker could say, "If that happened to me, I think I'd be very angry," thus giving the distressed person permission to express feelings that one may hesitate to share, perhaps out of misdirected shame. For extreme anxiety and accompanying changes in biophysical function, relaxation techniques and exercise can be encouraged. The increase in energy that follows a crisis experience can be channeled into constructive activity and socially approved outlets, such as assigning tasks to disaster victims or providing athletic facilities in hospitals. The current popular emphasis on self-help techniques, such as physical exercise and leisure for stress reduction, should be encouraged as a wholesome substitute for chemical tranquilizers during crisis.

As important as listening and emotional and physical expression are, they do not constitute crisis intervention in themselves. Without additional strategies, these techniques may not result in positive crisis resolution. Used together, grief work, listening, and facilitating the expression of feelings address the emotional responses to crisis, but the cognitive and behavioral elements of the crisis are equally important. The next several strategies focus on these facets of the crisis resolution process.

3. *Help the person gain an understanding of the crisis.* The individual may ask, "Why did this awful thing have to happen to me?" This perception of a traumatic event implies that the event occurred because the person in crisis was bad and deserving of punishment. The crisis worker can help the person see the many factors that contribute to a crisis situation and thereby curtail self-blaming. The individual is encouraged to examine the total problem, including his or her own behavior or physical symptoms, as they may be related to the crisis. Thoughtful reflection

on oneself and one's behavior can lead to growth and change rather than self-deprecation and self-pity.

4. *Help the person gradually accept reality.* Respond to a person's tendency to adopt a victim role or to blame problems on others. An individual in crisis who adopts the victim role can be helped to escape that role (McCullough, 1995). It may be tempting to agree with the person who is blaming others, especially when the person's story, as well as the reality, reveal especially cruel attacks, rejections, or other unfair treatment. Those whose crises stem primarily from social sources do not just *feel* victimized, they *are* in fact victimized. Such abused people, though, are also survivors (Hoff, 1990); their survival skills can be tapped for constructive crisis resolution by encouraging them to channel their anger into action to change oppressive social arrangements and policies (see Figure 4.1, right circle, Box 3).

The tendency to blame and scapegoat is especially strong in family and marital crises. The crisis counselor should help such people understand that victim-persecutor relationships are not one-sided. This can be done effectively when the counselor has established an appropriate relationship with the person. If the counselor has genuine concern and is not engaging in rescue fantasies, the distressed person is more likely to accept the counselor's interpretation of his or her own role in the crisis event. The victim-rescuer-persecutor syndrome occurs frequently in human relationships of all kinds and is common in many helping relationships. People viewed as victims are not rescued easily, so counselors who try it are usually frustrated when their efforts fail. Their disappointment may move them to "persecute" their "victim" for failure to respond. At this point, the victim turns persecutor and punishes the counselor for a well-intentioned but inappropriate effort to help (Haley, 1969b; James & Jongeward, 1971; McKinlay, 1990). Figure 4.2 illustrates the pitfalls of engaging in rescue or power struggles in crisis work or other human relationships.

In such "meta-complementary" relationships (Haley, 1969a), the egalitarian aspects of the service contract are sabotaged—that is, one person allows or pressures another to define a relationship in a certain way. For example, if Person A acts helpless and provokes Person B to take care of him or her, A is actually in control while being manifestly dependent. Translated to the helping relationship, a counselor may not wish to be controlled any more than a client would, hence the initiation of the troublesome victim-rescuer-persecutor cycle that is so difficult to disrupt once started. (See social network strategies and group process in Chapter 5 for an effective means of interrupting the cycle and Chapter 9 for rescue implications with self-destructive persons.)

5. *Help the person explore new ways of coping with problems.* Instead of responding to loss and crises as helpless victims or with suicide and

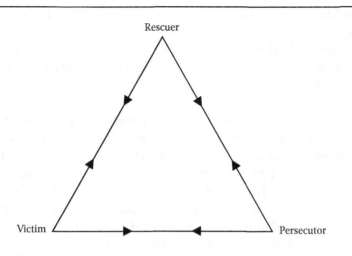

Key Concepts

Rescuer Role:
- Cannot be enacted without a complementary "victim"
- May suggest provider's excessive "need to be needed"
- Impedes growth and empowerment of client

Victim Role:
- Threatens basic need for self-mastery and self-determination
- Even if overt message is demand for rescue, more help covertly leads
  to resentment and role switch to "persecutor"

Practice Implications:
- Emphasize self-awareness and focus on empathy versus sympathy
- Conduct data-based assessment of client's actual needs
- Provide neither more nor less than needed
- Promote interdependence (versus excessive dependence or independence)
- Avoid power and control tactics

FIGURE 4.2   Victim-Rescuer-Persecutor Triangle. Adapted from Transactional Analysis.

homicide attempts, people can learn new responses. Sometimes people have given up on problem-solving devices that used to work for them.

Case Example: Jane

Jane, age 38, was able to weather a lot of storms until her best friend died. After her friend's death, she somehow could not find the energy necessary to establish new friendships. Exploration revealed that Jane had never worked through the grief she had experienced over the death of her friend. The lack of healthy resolution of this crisis left Jane more vulnerable than she might otherwise have been when her daughter, age 18, left home and married. Jane had temporarily given up and stopped using her effective problem-solving devices.

In Jane's case, a crisis worker might ask about previous successful coping devices and find out whether Jane thinks any of these might work for her now. Jane could also be assisted with delayed grief work and with exploring avenues for developing new friendships (see also Littrell, 1998; Walter & Peller, 2000).

6. *Link the person to a social network.* The technique of exploring new coping devices leads naturally to this important facet of crisis care. Just as disruption of social ties is an important precursor of crisis, the restoration of those ties (or if they have been permanently lost, the formation of new ones) is one of the most powerful means of resolving a crisis in a healthy way. The crisis counselor takes an active role in helping a person reestablish valued social network ties, or to sever ties experienced as unhealthy. This aspect of crisis care is also known as *social network intervention*—the ecological approach—and is discussed in detail in the next chapter.

Another way to enhance social network linkage is through "contemporary rites of passage" (see Figure 4.1, lower circle, Box 3). Such ritual support mechanisms are especially important in dealing with the common theme of loss during crisis, whether through unanticipated events or role changes. Chapter 6 discusses this strategy in detail.

7. *Reinforce the newly learned coping devices, evaluate counseling outcomes, and follow up after crisis resolution.* The person is given time to try the proposed solutions to the problem. Successful problem-solving mechanisms are reinforced; unsuccessful solutions are discarded, and new ones are sought. In any case, the person is not cut off abruptly.

A follow-up contact is carried out as agreed to in the initial plan. Some workers argue that follow-up contact maintains people in an unnecessary state of dependency. Others think that contacting a person later constitutes an invasion of privacy and an imposition of therapy on an unwilling client. Rarely does this argument hold when the person being helped has initiated the helping process, and follow-up is included in a mutually negotiated service contract. Unquestionably, premature or pressured referrals for psychotherapy or other services for people who do not want them would be unethical. Yet we need to consider whether the "invasion of privacy" and similar arguments may be covering a dearth of sensitively designed and integrated follow-up programs (see Online Resources). As already noted, in the managed care milieu, the practice of collaboratively developed "contracting"—whether in counseling or primary health care settings—enhances the prospect of client responsibility for self-care and follow-through, while serving as a structured framework for continued service, evaluation of same, and avoidance of recidivism and systems problems (see assessment in Chapter 3).

Follow-up is more likely to be successful and less likely to be interpreted as an unwanted intrusion if:

- It is incorporated into the total service plan rather than added as an afterthought or an unexpected telephone call.
- It is based on the principle of self-determination (even if a person is in crisis) and on the avoidance of "savior" tactics as well as any denigration of others' values and abilities by counselors.

When carefully designed, then, follow-up work can often be the occasion for reaching people who are unable to initiate help for themselves *before* a crisis occurs. This is especially true for people who are suicidal and very depressed, those threatened with violence, those whose medical and emotional problems are complexly intertwined, and those especially vulnerable because of severe psychiatric illness or who have been disappointed in previous help-seeking efforts. In such life-threatening situations, a person often feels worthless and is unable to reach out for help. In Mr. George Sloan's situation, the ED nurse's sensitive questioning and listening laid the foundation, and others followed up with crisis counseling, as illustrated in Exhibit 4.1, Service Contract (see Chapters 9, 10, and 11).

These crisis intervention strategies can be mastered by any helping person who chooses to learn them. Human service workers and community caretakers, volunteer counselors, social workers, nurses, physicians, police officers, teachers, and clergy increasingly incorporate crisis intervention as a part of their professional training in caring for distressed people. Whether in offices, institutions, homes, or mobile outreach programs, effective helping techniques save time and effort spent on problems that can develop from ineffectively resolved crises (Hoff & Morgan, in press). Primary prevention is much less costly in both human and economic terms. These basic strategies can be applied in a variety of settings and circumstances to be discussed in the remaining chapters. In highly charged and potentially violent crisis situations (both individual and group), additional techniques are indicated (see Part 3).

Psychotropic Drugs: What Place in Crisis Intervention?

Advertisements bombard us constantly with the idea that drugs are a solution for many problems. We hear, "Do you feel down or upset? Can't sleep? Can't control your kids? Take pills." The inclusion of a question in this section's title mirrors the controversy and questions that abound in any discussion of drugs among professionals and laypersons alike. These controversies, prominent across media sources, are situated in historical, cultural, and economic realities commonly discussed by patients, their families, health and mental health providers, policymakers, and others. The purpose for this book is *not* a comprehensive review or critique of the issues or individual drugs and their indications. Health providers with prescriptive authority (physicians and some advanced practice nurses) are obliged to keep current on drugs and their use. The focus here is to consider how psychotropic drugs can be used responsibly or misused in crisis work. Some common historical facts, related questions, and results of research and practice with psychotropic agents are therefore presented as context for criteria that should guide drug use for some clients in crisis situations.

1. People have been using mind-altering substances over many centuries. It is therefore unlikely that a particular "war on drugs" will significantly alter this pattern. People in crisis are at higher risk of abusing not only illicit substances such as cocaine, but also legal substances such as alcohol and prescription medications. Moreover, prescription medications for pain or anxiety are frequently obtained through illegal means. Since all substances have the potential to exacerbate a crisis, why are some legal and others illegal?

2. How did so many people, both professionals and the general public, come to believe that chemical tranquilization is a preferred way to deal with life's stresses and crises? For example, some parents and teachers insist on drugs for "attention deficit hyperactivity disordered" children. When confronted with a client's demand for drugs, it is not uncommon to hear practitioners say, "But they want the pills. They don't want to talk about or deal with what's troubling them or what's going on in the family. What am I supposed to do?" Of note here is the fact that the advertising industry and professional practice have enormous influence on what the public comes to accept as a norm. Also of note is the national crisis in the United States resulting from inadequate counseling and psychiatric services for disturbed children, services that would alleviate excessive reliance on drugs for children. Of further policy significance is the requirement of some insurance companies to have a child evaluated for medication very early in the course of treatment as a condition for covering other psychotherapeutic services.

3. The media, as well as some medical and psychiatric professionals, are increasingly addressing the problem of prescription drugs, their overuse, and their escalating costs (Angell, 2005; Dubovsky & Dubovsky, 2007); many Americans go to Canada to purchase an identical drug at a fraction of the cost. What does the profit motive have to do with the overuse of some drugs and the prices U.S. citizens are expected to pay in comparison with others (see Brownlee, 2007)? Given this pattern of dependency on and overuse of prescription drugs, why does the political war on drugs continue to focus on foreign production of illegal drugs rather than on prevention and treatment among users at home? And why—in the United States—are the main victims of this war mostly poor inner-city black youth rather than those profiting from the illegal drug traffic?

4. More than a half century of research-based knowledge and experience regarding psychotropic drugs establishes that their greatest efficacy is

when used in combination with other therapeutic modalities, such as psychotherapy and support in rehabilitation programs. These outcomes have been demonstrated even in the treatment of bipolar illness and schizophrenia, the mental disorders with strong biological correlates. Yet the disparity in insurance coverage for treatment and rehabilitation of the mentally ill beyond psychotropic medications continues.

Clearly, the benefits of psychotropic drugs when used responsibly are accepted by professionals and laypersons alike. It is their misuse and over-dependence that are in dispute. With this overview of the problem, let us consider the criteria for use of psychotropic drugs (usually, antianxiety agents and antidepressants) for distressed people.

Tranquilizers taken during crisis temporarily relieve anxiety but do nothing about the problem's root cause. At best, they are a crutch. At worst, they can be addictive and can displace effective problem solving at the psychosocial level. For the person in crisis, psychotropic drugs should *not* be used as a substitute for crisis counseling and problem solving. However, there are times when an antianxiety agent or sleep aid is indicated in addition to the crisis intervention techniques outlined previously. These instances are (1) when a person is experiencing extreme anxiety, has frequent crying spells, or fears losing control, (2) when a person is so distraught that it is impossible to engage him or her in the problem-solving process, and (3) when a person's extreme anxiety prevents sleep for a significant period of time. Exercise and nonchemical means of relaxation should be encouraged (see Chapter 10, drug treatment for depression). The increasingly popular alternative or complementary medical techniques should also be encouraged—for example, biofeedback, acupuncture, herbal remedies, and so forth, for certain bodily responses to stress.

Apart from these special circumstances, psychotropic drugs should be avoided whenever possible while dealing with a critical life event. By relieving anxiety on a temporary basis, these drugs can have the effect of reducing the person's motivation to effectively resolve a crisis. With chemical tranquilization, the person loses the advantages of increased energy during a crisis state. The *opportunity* for psychosocial growth is often lost due to the temporary tranquility of a drugged psyche, while the *danger* may be increased—including possible overdose or unpleasant and even dangerous side effects from interactions among drugs that are not carefully monitored. Some drugs can complicate rather than alleviate the original symptoms for which they were sought.

Caution is also suggested to crisis workers who have physician or psychiatrist consultants available to them. Sometimes crisis workers ask for psychiatric consultation simply because of their own lack of clinical experience, not because the distinct service of a psychiatrist is needed. As long as the psychiatrist shares the worker's values regarding crisis care and has additional crisis intervention skills, there is no problem. However, this is not true of all psychiatrists; some have little training or experience in crisis intervention but have the legal right to prescribe drugs. A similar dynamic may apply to other health providers with prescriptive authority. Of note is the fact that the majority of psychotropic drug prescriptions are written by providers who lack specialty training in psychopathology and its treatment (Hoff & Morgan, in press; Lessig, 1996), underscoring the importance of consultation by primary care providers with a psychiatrist or advanced practice psychiatric nurse (see Edmands, Hoff, Kaylor, Mower, & Sorrell, 1999).

Although the traditional psychiatric management of behavioral emergencies has some features in common with crisis intervention, it should not be equated with the crisis model if a strictly biomedical approach (relying heavily on chemical stabilization) is used (see Cohen, 1993; Luhrmann, 2000, Chapter 4). The nonmedical crisis worker should remember that a consultation request may result in a distressed person's receiving a drug prescription when actually what is needed is the experience of highly skilled crisis specialists. Such specialists include, but are not limited to, psychiatrists. Conversely, a comprehensive plan for certain individuals in crisis may include measures available only through the professions of medicine and psychiatry. Psychiatrists have a medical degree and the skills and legal powers unique to their training and position in the field of medicine. Unlike nonmedical counselors or psychiatric practitioners—social workers, for example—psychiatrists (in addition to prescriptive authority) can admit people to hospitals, and make distinctions between psychological, psychiatric, and neurological disturbances. Psychiatrists also diagnose and treat the symptoms of drug overdose. In the United States, advanced practice nurses and psychologists can also prescribe medication in some jurisdictions. Ideally, psychiatric stabilization programs, such as those in emergency departments with holding beds, should include the services of skilled crisis counselors.

In short, all steps taken by the crisis intervention movement to reduce the large-scale dependence on drugs for problem solving during crisis and at other times will be steps forward. Professionals licensed to prescribe are urged to consult guides such as those by Dubovsky and Dubovsky (2007) and Elliott (2006). (For further analysis of this issue, see also Barney, 1994; Brownlee, 2007; Breggin & Breggin, 1994; Hamilton, Jensvold, Rothblum, & Cole, 1995; Luhrmann, 2000; Zito et al., 2000).

Crisis and Psychosocial Care in a Primary Care Setting: Illustration

Applying crisis care to Delaine's case (continued from Chapter 3), the primary care provider, either a physician or an advanced practice nurse, would have made a mental connection between her request for something to ease her crying bouts, her gastrointestinal symptoms, and the series of losses she has suffered. Without discounting or minimizing any of Delaine's presenting symptoms, the provider would listen attentively and make an empathic response affirming the realistic basis for her distress—for example, "You've certainly been through a lot in a very short time. It's not surprising that you feel sad and a bit overwhelmed with many losses and big changes from what you're used to."

The provider would also use the office visit to teach about the essential normality of physical symptoms like Delaine's in response to coping with major life stressors. Such teaching would serve as a context for explaining to Delaine the limitations of psychotropic medication if not accompanied by social support and counseling around her many losses.

Delaine's history of coping suggests her positive response to this approach. Ideally, the physician or advanced practice nurse develops the following plan with Delaine.

1. Laboratory tests to aid diagnosis and follow-up treatment of gastrointestinal symptoms
2. A referral to the on-site mental health service (usually staffed by a social worker or advanced practice psychiatric–mental health nurse) for crisis counseling around loss and guilt
3. A one-week prescription of an antianxiety medication to be monitored in concert with follow-up counseling by the mental health specialist
4. A recommendation to consider joining a support group for widows (resource information is given, with the suggestion to discuss this further in follow-up counseling)
5. A follow-up appointment for review of laboratory results and general progress

Exhibit 4.2 sets out the basics for assessment and crisis work in primary care (see also Hoff & Morgan, in press).

Summary and Discussion Questions

Without communication and rapport—the immediate context for crisis work—success will probably elude us. Resolution of crisis should occur in a person's or a family's natural setting whenever possible. Planning well and using good crisis intervention skills are the best ways to avoid extreme

---

EXHIBIT 4.2   BASICS OF PSYCHOSOCIAL ASSESSMENT AND CRISIS WORK IN PRIMARY CARE

1. Detection (implies routine inquiry in health assessment protocols)
2. Assessment of risk (includes emotional trauma from victimization and danger of injury to self and others)
3. Empathic, supportive response (constitutes public recognition of trauma from abuse)
4. Safety planning for self (and for mothers and their children as well)
5. Linkage, effective referral, and follow-up (implies collaboration with crisis, mental health, or trauma specialist)

measures such as hospitalization and lengthy rehabilitation programs. The active involvement of a distressed person in a plan for crisis resolution is essential if crisis intervention is to succeed as a way of helping people. The service contract symbolizes this active involvement. The use of psychotropic drugs may decrease such involvement and can sabotage the growth potential of the crisis experience.

1. With an example, consider the differences between crisis counseling strategies and psychotherapy.
2. Considering the "dangers" of a full-blown crisis state, why is it important to understand the commonalities and differences between crisis intervention and psychotherapy, especially in working with a client whose values and beliefs are different from one's own?
3. Identify the major factors contributing to the victim-rescuer persecution triangle and what strategies can be used to avoid enmeshment in the triangle.
4. Consider the pros and cons of the "war" on drugs in relation to crisis prevention.

References

Angell, M. (2005). *The truth about drug companies: How they deceive us and what to do about it.* New York: Random House.

Arnold, E., & Boggs, K. U. (1999). *Interpersonal relationships: Professional communication skills for nurses* (3rd ed.). Philadelphia: Saunders.

Barney, K. (1994). Limitations of the critique of the medical model. *Journal of Mind and Behavior, 15*(1, 2), 19–34.

Bateson, G. (1958). *Naven* (2nd ed.). Palo Alto, CA: Stanford University Press.

Boss, P. (1999). *Ambiguous loss.* Cambridge, MA: Harvard University Press.

Breggin, P., & Breggin, G. R. (1994). *Talking back to Prozac: What doctors won't tell you about today's most controversial drug.* New York: St. Martin's Press.

Brownlee, S. (2007). *Overtreated: Why too much medicine is making us sicker and poorer.* New York: Bloomsbury.

Chappell, D., & Di Martino, V. (1998). *Violence at work.* Geneva: International Labour Organisation.

Cohen, C. I. (1993). The biomedicalization of psychiatry: A critical overview. *Community Mental Health Journal, 29*, 509–521.

Dattilio, F. M., & Freeman, A. (Eds.). (2007). *Cognitive-behavioral strategies in crisis intervention* (3rd ed.). New York: Guilford Press.

Dobkin de Rios, M. (2002). What we can learn from Shamanic healing: Brief psychotherapy with Latino immigrant clients. *American Journal of Public Health, 92*(10), 1576–1578.

Dubovsky, S. L., & Dubovsky, A. N. (2007). *Psychotropic drug prescribers's survival guide: Ethical mental health treatment in the age of Big Pharma.* New York: W. W. Norton.

Earley, L. (2006). *Crazy: A father's search therough America's mental health madness.* New York: Berkley Books.

Edmands, M. S., Hoff, L. A., Kaylor, L., Mower, L., & Sorrell, S. (1999). Bridging gaps between mind, body and spirit: Healing the whole person. *Journal of Psychosocial Nursing, 37*(10), 1–7.

Elliot, G. R. (2006). *Medicating young minds.* New York: Stewart, Tabori, & Chang.

Ericsson, S. (1993). *Companion through the darkness: Inner dialogues on grief.* New York: Harper-Collins.

Gans, H. (1962). *The urban villagers.* New York: Free Press.

Goldman, L. (1994). *Life and loss: A guide to help grieving children.* Philadelphia: Taylor & Francis.

Goldman, L. (1996). *Breaking the silence: A guide to help children with complicated grief: Suicide, homicide, AIDS, violence and abuse.* Philadelphia: Taylor & Francis.

Haley, J. (1969a). *Strategies of psychotherapy.* Philadelphia: Grune & Stratton.

Haley, J. (1969b). The art of being a failure as a therapist. *American Journal of Orthopsychiatry, 39*(4), 691–695.

Haley, J. (1987). *Problem-solving therapy.* San Francisco: Jossey-Bass.

Hamilton, J. A., Jensvold, M. F., Rothblum, E. D., & Cole, E. (Eds.). (1995). *Psychopharmacology from a feminist perspective.* New York: Harrington Park Press.

Hansell, N. (1970). Decision counseling. *Archives of General Psychiatry, 22*, 462–467.

Harvey, J. H. (Ed.). (1998). *Perspectives on loss: A source book.* Philadelphia: Taylor & Francis.

Hoff, L. A. (1990). *Battered women as survivors.* London: Routledge.

Hoff, L. A. (1993). Review essay: Health policy and the plight of the mentally ill. *Psychiatry, 56*(4), 400–419.

Hoff, L. A., & Morgan, B. (in press). *Psychiatric and mental health essentials in primary care.*

James, M., & Jongeward, D. (1971). *Born to win.* Reading, MA: Addison-Wesley.

Jourard, S. M. (1970). Suicide: An invitation to die. *American Journal of Nursing, 70*(2), 269, 273–275.

Kottler, J. A. (1994). *Beyond blame: A new way of resolving conflicts in relationships.* San Francisco: Jossey-Bass.

Lessig, D. Z. (1996). Primary care diagnosis and pharmacologic treatment of depression in adults. *Nurse Practitioner, 21*(10), 74–87.

Lifton, R. J., & Olson, E. (1976). The human meaning of total disaster: The Buffalo Creek experience. *Psychiatry, 39*, 1–18.

Lindemann, E. (1944). Symptomatology and management of acute grief. *American Journal of Psychiatry, 101*, 101–148. (Also reprinted in H. J. Parad, Ed., 1965. *Crisis intervention: Selected readings.* New York: Family Service Association of America.)

Littrell, J. M. (1998). *Brief counseling in action.* New York: Norton.

Loustaunau, M. O., & Sobo, E. J. (1997). *The cultural context of health, illness, and medicine.* New York: Bergin & Garvey.

Luhrmann, T. M. (2000). *Of two minds: The growing disorder in American psychiatry.* New York: Knopf.

Madrigal, K. B. (2005). Treatment beliefs of combat trauma survivors with posttraumatic stress disorder. *Practicing Anthropology, 27*(3), 37–40.

Marks, I. M., & Scott, R. (Eds.). (1990). *Mental health care delivery: Innovations, impediments, and implementation.* Cambridge: Cambridge University Press.

Marris, P. (1974). *Loss and change.* London: Routledge.

McCullough, C. J. (1995). *Nobody's victim.* New York: Clarkson/Potter.

McKinlay, J. B. (1990). A case for refocusing upstream: The political economy of illness. In P. Conrad & R. Kern (Eds.), *The sociology of health and illness: Critical perspectives* (3rd ed., pp. 502–516). New York: St. Martin's Press.

Northouse, L. L., & Northouse, P. G. (1998). *Health communication: Strategies for health professionals* (3rd ed.). East Norwalk, CT: Appleton & Lang.

Parkes, C. M. (1975). *Bereavement: Studies of grief in adult life.* Harmondsworth, England: Penguin Books.

Perschy, M. K. (1997). *Helping teens work through grief.* Philadelphia: Taylor & Francis.

Pluckhan, M. L. (1978). *Human communication.* New York: McGraw-Hill.

Rodriguez-Garcia, R., & Akhter, M. N. (2000). Human rights: The foundation of public health practice. *American Journal of Public Health, 90*(5), 693–694.

Ryan, W. (1971). *Blaming the victim.* New York: Vintage Books.

Storti, C. (1994). *Cross-cultural dialogues: Seventy-four brief encounters with cultural difference.* Yarmouth, ME: Intercultural Press.

Truax, C. B., & Carkhuff, R. R. (1967). *Toward effective counseling and psychotherapy.* Hawthorne, NY: Aldine de Gruyter.

Walter, J. L., & Peller, J. E. (2000). *Recreating brief therapy.* New York: Norton.

Williams, M. B., & Poijila, S. (2002). *The PTST workbook: Simple, effective techniques for overcoming traumatic stress symptoms.* Oakland, CA: New Harbinger Publishers.

Zito, J. M., Safer, D. J., dos Reis, S., Gardner, J. E., Boles, M., & Lynch, F. (2000). Trends in the prescribing of psychotropic medications to preschoolers. *Journal of the American Medical Association, 283*(8), 1025–1030.

See Online Resources for additional references.

CHAPTER 5

Family and Social Network Strategies during Crisis

We are conceived and born in a social context. We grow and develop among other people. We experience crises around events in our social milieu. People near us—friends, family, community—help or hinder us through crises. And finally, death, even for those who die alone and abandoned, demands some response from the society left behind.

Social Aspects of Human Growth

Multidisciplinary research increasingly supports joining individual and social approaches to helping distressed people (for example, Antonovsky, 1987; Boissevain, 1979; Hoff, 1990; Mitchell, 1969). Despite the prevalence of individual intervention techniques, overwhelming evidence now shows that social networks and support are primary factors in a person's susceptibility to disease, the process of becoming ill and seeking help, the treatment process, and the outcome of illness, whether that is rehabilitation and recovery or death (for example, Berges, 2006; Berkman & Syme, 1979). Sociocultural concepts are especially relevant with persons from diverse ethnic backgrounds (Dresssler, Balieriro, & Dos Santos, 1997; Lin, 2001; Loustaunau & Sobo). The work of clinicians during the golden age of social psychiatry supports the prolific social science literature on social approaches to distressed people (for example, Garrison, 1974; Polak, 1971). After using family and social network approaches, clinicians seldom return to predominantly individual practice (for example, Yalom, 1995). Hansell (1976) casts his entire description of persons in crisis in a social framework. Caplan (1964) laid the foundation for much of Hansell's work. The Crisis Paradigm (see Figure 5.1) in this book similarly stresses the pivotal role of sociocultural factors in the development, manifestation, and resolution of crises. This chapter presents an overview of social approaches to crisis intervention and suggests strategies for family, social network, and group practice.

An interrelated assumption underlies this discussion: People often avoid social approaches because they have not been trained to use them, or their

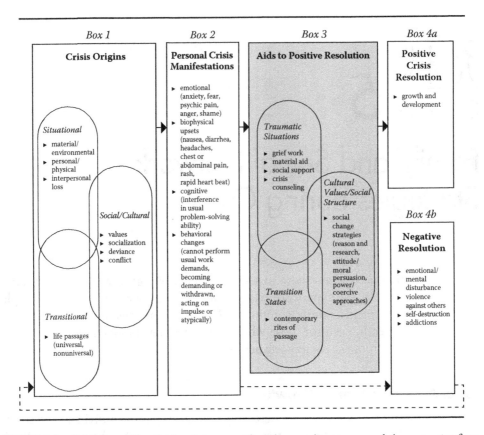

FIGURE 5.1 Crisis Paradigm. Crisis origins, manifestations, and outcomes and the respective functions of crisis care have interactional relationships. The intertwined circles represent the distinct yet interrelated origins of crisis and aids to positive resolution, even though personal manifestations are often similar. The arrows pointing from origins to positive resolution illustrate the *opportunity for growth and development* through crisis; the broken line at the bottom depicts the potential *danger of crisis* in the absence of appropriate aids. The loop between Box 4b and Box 1 denotes the *vulnerability* to future crisis episodes following negative resolution.

usefulness is still questioned. In addition, individual approaches often are not evaluated for either their effectiveness or their underlying assumptions. The treatment bias favoring individualistic measures is compounded by heavy reliance on psychoactive drugs, whereas evidence of sociocultural variables affecting health and illness often takes second place (McKinlay & Marceau, 1999; Meyer & Schwartz, 2000). Social strategies contrast strongly with approaches in which upsets are seen primarily as the result of personality dynamics and internal conflicts. Advocates of the latter view do not entirely disregard social factors, nor do advocates of social-interactional approaches ignore individual factors. Rather, their differences are in emphasis and in their conviction of what constitutes an appropriate helping process.

A social network may consist of a person's family, friends, neighbors, relatives, bartender, employer, hairdresser, teacher, welfare worker, physician, lawyer—anyone with whom a person has regular social intercourse. Different individuals have different networks. The following interview with a cocktail waitress illustrates the diversity of social network support and how the *natural* crisis care process works.

Case Example: The Cocktail Waitress

This is the dumpiest bar I've ever worked in, but I really enjoy it. I like the people. When I quit my last job and came here, a lot of old men followed me. There are all kinds of bars, but if it weren't for bars like this, a lot of old people and "down and outers" wouldn't have any place to go. Our regulars don't have anything or anyone, and they admit it. I feel like a counselor a lot of times. One of my customers, a pretty young woman, has had several children taken away. When her caseworker called me to ask if I thought she was ready to have her child back, I said no—and I told the woman so.

I think the people I feel closest to are the old men who are lonesome or widowed. One guy who shouldn't drink at all stayed on the wagon for quite a while, then went on a 3-week binge. His girlfriend told him that she didn't want him anymore if he didn't stop drinking. So he came in here and got sick after two drinks. He fell on the floor and hurt himself. I called the police and asked them to take him to the hospital. I called the girlfriend, and she and I both convinced him to finally get some help to control his drinking. When he got out, he came in and thanked me. This is really rewarding.

I work hard at helping people get on the right track, and I'm really tough on people who don't do anything with their lives, like these old guys. I know just how much they can drink. Take Ben, he can drink only three and I tell him, "OK, you can have them either all at once, or you can stick around for a while." I was brought up to respect my elders, and I don't want to see these guys go out and fall on their faces. I have a good friend who's a priest. We argued for years about my work in the bar. Finally, he agreed that it wasn't a bad thing to do. Someone has to do it.

The next case example highlights the individual, as opposed to the social, approach to *formal* crisis care.

Case Example: Ellen

Ellen, age 16, ran away from home. Shortly after police returned her, she attempted suicide with approximately 10 aspirin and five of her mother's tranquilizers. Ellen had exhibited many signs of depression. She was seen for individual counseling at a mental health clinic for 12 sessions. Ellen's parents were seen initially for one session as part of the assessment process. The counselor learned that Ellen was always somewhat depressed and withdrawn at home and that she was getting poor grades in school.

Counseling focused on Ellen's feelings of guilt, worthlessness, and anger, centered on her relationship with her parents. She complained that her father was aloof and seldom available when there was a problem. She felt closer to her mother but said her mother was unreasonably strict about her friends and hours out. At the conclusion of the individual counseling sessions, Ellen was less depressed and felt

> less worthless, although things were essentially the same at home and school. Two
> months after termination of counseling, Ellen made another suicide attempt, this
> time with double the amount of aspirin and tranquilizers.

This case reveals that the involvement of Ellen's family and the school counselor—primary people in her social network—was not an integral part of the helping process. In contrast, a social approach to Ellen's problem would have attended to her feelings of depression and worthlessness, but these feelings would have been viewed in the context of her interactions with those closest to her, not as the result of her withdrawn personality. In other words, in crisis intervention, people and their problems are seen in a psychosocial rather than a psychoanalytic context.

Within the psychosocial framework, Ellen's counselor would have included at least her family and the school counselor in the original assessment and counseling plan. This initial move might have revealed still other people who were important to Ellen and would be able to help. For example, when Ellen ran away, she went to her Aunt Dorothy's house; she felt closer to Dorothy than to her parents.

Social support is central to the process of human growth, development, and crisis intervention. Ellen is in a normal transition stage of development. The way she handles the natural stress of adolescence depends on the people in her social network: her parents, brothers and sisters, friends, teachers, and relatives. Her relationship with these people sets the tone for the successful completion of developmental tasks. A counselor with a social view of the situation would say that necessary social supports were lacking at a time in Ellen's life when stress was already high. So instead of normal growth, Ellen experienced a degree of stress that resulted in a destructive outcome—a suicide attempt. This was a clear message that support from members of her social network was weak.

Even when stress becomes so great that suicide seems the only alternative, it is not too late to mobilize a shaky social network on behalf of a person in crisis. Failure to do so can result in the kind of outcome that occurred for Ellen—that is, another crisis within two months. Individual crisis counseling was not necessarily bad for Ellen; it simply was not enough.

Before considering the specifics of how a person's social network is engaged or developed in crisis resolution, let us examine two important facets of the social network—the family and the community in crisis.

Families in Crisis

Although social relations are important for an individual in crisis, often the members of a person's social network are themselves in crisis. The family unit can experience crises just as individuals can. Researchers consider family troubles in terms of sources, effect on family structure, and type of event affecting the family (Hill, 1965; Parad & Caplan, 1965). If the source of trouble is within the family, an event is usually more distressing than if the source is external, such as a flood or racial prejudice. Often an individual in crisis may precipitate a family crisis. For example, if family members make suicide attempts or abuse alcohol, the family usually lacks basic harmony and internal adequacy, as suggested in the case of Ellen, discussed in the previous section.

Family troubles must be assessed according to their effect on the family configuration. Families experience stress from *dismemberment* (loss of family member), *accession* (the unexpected addition of a member), *demoralization* (loss of morale and family unity), or a combination of all three (Hill, 1965). This classification of stressor events casts, in a family context, the numerous traumatic life events associated with crises. Death and hospitalization, which are crisis-precipitating events for individuals, are examples of dismemberment for families. Unwanted pregnancy, a source of crisis for the girl or woman, is also an example of accession to the family, and therefore a possible precipitant of family crisis as well. A person in crisis because of trouble with the law for delinquency or drug addiction may trigger family demoralization and crisis (Bishop & McNally, 1993; Seelig, Goldman-Hall, & Jerrell, 1992). Divorce and acquisition of children by stepparents and stepfamilies also constitute dismemberment and accession. The U.S. Census Bureau reports that stepparents or adoptive parents are an increasingly large component of two-parent families (Kreider & Fields, 2005). Role and relationship loss are sources of significant stress. Divorce, suicide, homicide, illegitimacy, imprisonment, and institutionalizations for mental illness are examples of demoralization and dismemberment or accession.

The nuclear family (father, mother, and children) is the norm in most Western societies, whereas the extended family (including relatives) is the norm in most non-Western societies. Among immigrant Mexican women in the United States, relatives of the family of origin are more important sources of emotional support than friends (Vega, Kolody, Valle, & Weir, 1991). It is now widely recognized and accepted that the traditional form of the nuclear family is being replaced by a variety of family forms. This includes an increasing role of grandparents or other relatives assisting with child rearing.

Communal or "New Age" families may provide more avenues of support for some people than do traditional nuclear families. A current variation on these themes is the cohousing approach, which is designed to address some of the family issues faced by all. Cohousing was initiated by a Danish divorced mother seeking greater support for rearing her children. Developed from the utopian ideal put forth by Thomas More (1516/1965) in the 16th century, the concept encompasses several features intended to

- Provide privacy through separate, self-contained units for individuals and families
- Relieve isolation and alienation and promote community by an arrangement of clustered homes, a shared common house, a shared garden, play and work space, community dinners, and perhaps a computer center
- Encourage diversity by welcoming a broad range of residents and lifestyles
- Promote a sense of ownership and empowerment by participatory planning and design from the start

Pioneered primarily in Denmark during the 1970s and 1980s, the cohousing movement highlights the advantages of traditional village life in contemporary communities (McCamant & Durrett, 1988; www.coho.org). Hundreds of cohousing communities exist in Western Europe and North America or are in start-up stages.

Increasingly, people call on friends and peers for essential material and social support that traditionally came from one's extended family. However, these new family forms can also be the source of unanticipated conflict when lines of authority are unclear, when opinions differ about privacy and intimacy, and when the group cannot reach consensus about how to get necessary domestic work done. Whether or not stressful events lead to crisis depends on a family's resources for handling such events. Hill (1965, p. 33) gives a vivid description of the nuclear family and its burden as a social unit.

> Compared with other associations in society, the family is badly handicapped organizationally. Its age composition is heavily weighted with dependents, and it cannot freely reject its weak members and recruit more competent teammates. Its members receive an unearned acceptance; there is no price for belonging. Because of its unusual age composition and its uncertain gender composition, it is intrinsically a puny work group and an awkward decision-making group. This group is not ideally manned to withstand stress, yet society has assigned to it the heaviest of responsibilities: the socialization and orientation of the young, and the meeting of the major emotional needs of all citizens, young and old.

With its unique position in society, the family is the most natural source of support and understanding, which many of us rely on when in trouble, but it is also the arena in which we may experience our most acute distress or even abuse and violence. All families have problems, and all families have ways of dealing with them. Some are very successful in problem solving; others are less so. Much depends on the resources available in the normal course of family life. Despite the burdens many face that can be traced to family stress, discord, or abuse, crisis workers can enhance individuals' prospects of moving beyond their family troubles. The labeling of so many families as "dysfunctional" can be just as damaging as the psychiatric labeling of individuals (Hoff, M., 2005; Wolin, 1993).

In addition to the ordinary stressors affecting families in recent years, U.S. families have faced extraordinary stress stemming from a laissez-faire approach to public policy affecting families (DeKavas-Watt, Proctor, & Smith, 2007). Note the following:

■ Millions of Americans have no health insurance coverage, while many lack money for the most basic health care (except the very poor who are covered by Medicaid)—this, despite decades of grassroots and legislative efforts addressing health care as a basic human rights issue, not a privilege of those who can pay the price. Astronomical health care bills are the major reason for U.S. citizens to declare bankruptcy.

■ Because affordable, high-quality child care is unavailable for many, millions of children are left alone. Although available on-site child care for employees is increasing, their access to it (or paid family leave) is by no means the norm in the United States, as it is in many Western European countries.

■ Caretakers in day-care centers that do exist typically earn very low wages, and caring for children at home still falls predominantly on mothers—a symbol of gender inequality and the value placed on children as a nation's resource.

■ Millions of families cannot afford to buy a home, and millions of others are homeless (see Chapter 6).

■ The majority of mothers are in the labor force, and most are there not only for personal fulfillment but also because they need the money; yet the discrepancy between North American women's wages compared with similarly qualified men persists despite civil rights legislation decades ago (DeNarvas-Walt, Proctor, & Smith, 2006).

Traditional caretaking patterns in the home are additional sources of stress for families, particularly for women (Sommers & Shields, 1987). James Levine, director of the Fatherhood Project at the Family and Work Institute in New York, urges fathers to assume more active roles in parenting. Despite the guilt many wage-earning mothers often feel for not being home full-time for parenting, family—not day care—is of dominant importance in shaping children. The disproportionate burden of caretaking placed on women is even starker in less industrialized societies. This source of stress on families will only increase with the AIDS crisis and the increasing numbers of elderly people needing care, unless the prevailing attitude and practice regarding the caretaking role shifts radically (see Chapters 6 and 7).

A family's vulnerability to crisis is also determined by how it defines a traumatic event. For some families, a divorce or a pregnancy without marriage is regarded as nearly catastrophic; for others, these are simply new situations to cope with. Much depends on religious and other values. Similarly, financial loss for an upper-middle-class family may not be a source of crisis if there are other reserves to draw on. In contrast, financial loss for a family with very limited material resources can be the last straw; such families are generally more vulnerable. If the loss includes a loss of status, however, the middle-class family that values external respectability will be more vulnerable to crisis than the family with little to lose in prestige.

As important as a family perspective is, one also needs to look beyond the family for influences on family disharmony and crisis. A well-known example of the failure to look further is Senator Daniel Patrick Moynihan's report, *The Negro Family, the Case for National Action* (1965). Moynihan concluded that causal relationships existed between juvenile delinquency and black households headed by women, and between black women wage earners and "emasculated" black men. When these factors were examined in relation to poverty, however, there was no significant difference between black and white female-headed households. This study is now largely discredited for its race bias, but it still represents the need to consider interrelationships among race, class, and gender, which often surface in studies of crime and other social issues.

Current welfare reform policies in most states require mothers with inadequate job skills to work for poverty-level wages, which compounds the issue of affordable child care. If such mothers are also denied education and training opportunities to improve their economic status, children already at risk face even greater odds in healthy development. Overall, draconian policies often fail to recognize the interrelatedness of poverty, race, and gender bias and widespread urban decay—the roots of problems instead of obvious symptoms (Allen & Baber, 1994; Medoff & Sklar, 1994; Wilson, 1987). These policy failures and the continuing pattern in numbers of children born to single mothers is particularly revealing in light of the correlation between falling birthrates and the improvement in women's educational and economic status, regardless of race or ethnicity. This correlation has been established over five generations of women. It is easier, of course, to blame women for their dependency than to address the socioeconomic and cultural origins of welfare dependency.

Such blaming of families that are in crisis due to deeply rooted social problems becomes more significant when considering that the United States is the only industrialized country without a national family policy to deal with issues such as maternity and paternity leaves, child care, and flexible work schedules, even though the two-income family is the norm rather than the exception (see Chapter 6). Although the U.S. Congress passed a bill permitting unpaid family leave in medium to large companies without threat of job loss, few wage-earning parents can afford the loss of a regular paycheck. In contrast, most Western European parents can take such leave *with* pay.

Despite debates about whether day care is harmful or helpful for infants and toddlers, as well as passionate arguments about abortion, the impending collapse of the family (according to some people), and traditional as opposed to alternative family structures, everyone agrees that human beings need other human beings for development and survival. In short, support from social network members—or the lack of it—influences the outcome of everyday stress, crisis, and illness whether the resolution of crisis is human growth or death. The probability, then, of people receiving support during crisis *includes* family issues but is not limited to them. Community stability and resources as well as public policies that affect individuals and families must also be considered (see Chapter 6).

Communities in Crisis

Just as individuals in crisis are entwined with their families, so are families bound up with their community. An entire neighborhood may feel the impact of an individual in crisis. In one small community, a man shot himself in his front yard. The entire community, to say nothing of his wife and small children, was affected by this man's crisis. Of course, the murder or abduction of a child in a small community invariably incites community-wide fear on behalf of other children. A crisis response to the entire community, including special sessions for school children, is indicated in these situations. Incidents of violence targeted at schools and their children and teachers call for planning similar to disaster preparedness, as discussed in Chapter 13. In the United States, most states require a comprehensive plan for crisis preparedness, response, and recovery in crisis situations (Kann, Brener, & Wechsler, 2007).

Clearly, then, communities ranging from small villages to sprawling metropolitan areas experience crisis. In small communal or religious groups, the deprivation of individual needs or rebellion against group norms can mushroom into a crisis for the entire membership. Social and economic inequities among racial and ethnic groups or police brutality can trigger a large-scale community crisis. The risk of crisis for these groups is influenced by:

- Social and economic stability of individual family units within a neighborhood
- Level at which individual and family needs are met within the group or neighborhood
- Adequacy of neighborhood resources to meet social, housing, economic, and recreational needs of individuals and families
- Personality characteristics and personal strengths of the group's members

Psychosocial needs must be met if individuals are to survive and grow. In the context of Maslow's (1970) hierarchy of needs, as a person meets the basic survival needs of hunger, thirst, and protection from the elements, other needs emerge, such as the need for social interaction and pleasant surroundings. We cannot actualize our potential for growth if we are barely surviving and using all our energy just to stay alive. To the extent that people's basic needs are unmet, they are increasingly crisis prone.

This is true, for example, of millions of people worldwide who suffer from hunger, war, and other disasters, and of those living in large, inner-city housing projects. Poverty is rampant. Slum landlords take advantage of people who are already disadvantaged; there is a constant threat of essential utilities being cut off for persons with inadequate resources to meet skyrocketing rates, leaving them vulnerable to death by exposure. An elderly couple in an eastern state, unable to pay their bills, died of exposure after a utility company cut off their heat. Emergency medical and social services are often inadequate or inaccessible through the bureaucratic structure.

The social and economic problems of the urban poor have been complicated further by the recent trend toward gentrification—the upgrading of inner-city property so that it is only affordable by the well-to-do. In a partial reversal of an earlier "white flight" from inner-city neighborhoods, middle-class and upper-middle-class professionals (mostly white) are returning to the city. Housing crises or homelessness are the unfortunate outcome for many who are displaced (see Chapter 8).

Similar deprivations exist on North American Indian reservations, among migrant farm groups, and in sprawling cities with shantytowns (especially in the Southern Hemisphere), where millions of the world's poorest people eke out a way to survive. As a result of the personal, social, and economic deprivations in these communities, crime becomes widespread, adding another threat to basic survival. Another crisis-prone setting is the subculture of the average jail or prison. Physical survival is threatened by poor health services, and there is danger of suicide. Prisoners fear rape and physical attack by fellow prisoners. Social needs of prisoners go unmet to the extent that the term *rehabilitation* does not apply to what happens in prisons. This situation, combined with community attitudes, unemployment, and poverty, makes ex-offenders highly crisis prone after release from prison (see Chapter 12).

Natural disasters such as floods, hurricanes, and severe snowstorms, and real or threatened acts of terrorism are other sources of community crisis (see Chapter 13). This is true not only in internationally publicized cases but also in small communities. In one small town, families and children were threatened and virtually immobilized by an 18-year-old youth suspected of being a child molester. Another small community feared for everyone's safety when three teenagers threatened to bomb the local schools and police station in response to their own crises: The teenagers had been expelled from school and were unemployed.

Communities in crisis have several characteristics in common with those observed in individuals in crisis. First, within the group, an atmosphere of tension and fear is widespread. Second, rumor runs rampant during a community crisis. Individuals in large groups color and distort facts out of fear and lack of knowledge. Third, as with individuals in crisis, normal functioning is inhibited or at a standstill. Schools and businesses are often closed; health and emergency resources may be in short supply. However, as is the case with families, traumatic events such as war, school violence, and terrorist attacks can also mobilize and strengthen a group or nation (see Macy et al., 2004).

Individual, Family, and Community Interaction

Individuals, families, and communities in crisis must be considered in relation to one another. Basic human needs and the prevention of destructive outcomes of crises form an interdependent network.

Privacy, Intimacy, Community

Human needs in regard to the self and the social network are threefold: (1) The need for privacy; (2) the need for intimacy; (3) the need for community. To lead a reasonably happy life free of excessive strain, people should have a balanced fulfillment of needs in each of these three areas. Many people support the cohousing concept because it addresses the problem of meeting those needs. With a suitable measure of privacy, intimate attachments, and a sense of belonging to a community, people can avoid the potentially destructive effects of the life crises they encounter. Figure 5.2 illustrates these needs concentrically.

In the center of the interactional circle is the individual, with his or her personality, attributes and liabilities, view of self, view of the world, and goals, ambitions, and values. The centered person who is self-accepting has a need and a capacity for privacy. Well-adjusted people can retreat to their private world as a means of rejuvenating themselves and coming to terms with self and with the external world.

We all have differing needs and capacities for privacy. However, equally vital needs for intimacy and community affiliation should not be sacrificed to an excess of privacy. The need for privacy can be violated either by a consistent deprivation of normal privacy or by retreat into an excess of privacy, that is, isolation. Privacy deprivation can occur, for example, when families are crowded into inadequate housing or when marriage partners are extremely clingy.

The excessively dependent and clinging person is too insecure to ever be alone in his or her private world. Such an individual usually assumes that there can be no happiness alone; the person's full psychosocial development has been stunted and the capacity for privacy is therefore unawakened. The person does not see how unfulfilling an overly dependent relationship can be.

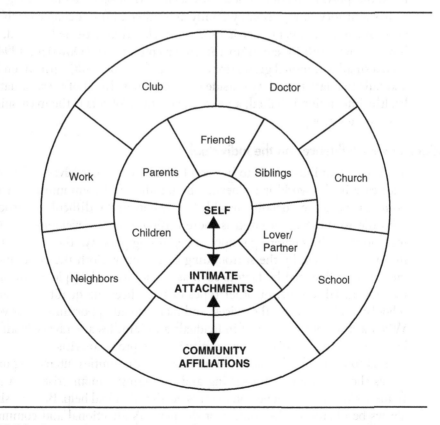

FIGURE 5.2 Privacy, Intimacy, Community Interaction.

For example, a man involved in this kind of relationship is a prime candidate for a suicide attempt when his wife threatens to divorce him; the wife is also deprived of essential privacy and feels exhausted by the demand to relate continually to another person.

The problem of too much privacy leads to a consideration of the needs for intimacy and community. A person can seldom have too much privacy if social needs are being met. An example of social-need deprivation is the isolated person who eventually commits suicide because of extreme loneliness and feelings of rejection by others. The concentric circle of needs illustrates the continuous interaction between privacy, intimacy, and community.

The Individual's Extension beyond Self

Individuals who feel in charge of themselves and capable of living in their private world are at a great advantage as they reach out and establish intimate attachments. They may have a mature marital relationship or a small circle of intimate friends to rely on (see Figure 5.2). Need fulfillment in this second circle enables the individual to establish and enjoy additional relationships in the work world and the larger community. The development of this interactional system can be halted in many situations: (1) if a person feels too insecure to establish intimate or communal attachments, (2) if a person is handicapped by mental illness, has been institutionalized for a long time, or has a history of rejection by family and others, (3) if a couple establishes an intimate attachment that is essentially closed and turned inward, thus limiting need fulfillment from the larger community (Dowrick, 1994), or (4) if a small communal group (for example, a religious cult) turns in on itself and fails to relate to society outside of its confines. In all of these situations, healthy interaction is halted; an extreme example of this is the mass suicides of some cult groups.

Social Network Influences on the Individual

The capacity of individuals to live comfortably with themselves and to move with ease in the world is influenced by families and communities. A child born into a chaotic, socially unstable family may find it difficult to settle into a hostile world. Such a child is more crisis prone at developmental turning points, such as entering school or beginning puberty. The child's family, in turn, is affected by the surrounding community. Both the child and the family are influenced by factors such as economic and employment opportunities; racial, ethnic, or other types of prejudice; the quality of available schools; family and social services; and recreational opportunities for youth. When a sufficient number of individuals and families are adversely affected by these factors, the whole community is more prone to crisis.

This concept of individuals, families, and communities interacting underscores the importance of assessing and managing human crises in a social framework. Certainly, a person in crisis needs individual help. But this should always be offered in the context of the person's affectional and community needs. The psychiatrist Halleck (1971) urged a social approach to human problems and crises that are still relevant today (see Luhrmann, 2000). Halleck suggests that it may be unethical for a therapist to spend professional time focusing on a single individual in prison who has made a suicide attempt. Rather than tending only to the individual in crisis, the therapist would be taking a more responsible approach by using professional skills to influence the prison system that contributes to suicidal crises. As violence escalates and the subcultures of U.S. prisons explode with overcrowding and more violence, the crises in these communities will only increase as long as the socioeconomic and cultural roots of aggression are ignored (see Chapter 12).

Extending this argument to the home, emergency treatment of abused children without explicit attention to family factors (as in the tragic death of Rebecca Riley, discussed in Chapter 3, hazards of inadequate assessment) is a grave departure from the principle of comprehensive family service around the complex issues, including intimate partner abuse. Work with survivors of abuse and sexual assault supports similar conclusions: these individuals' crises originate from society's values about women, marriage, the family, and violence (see Figure 5.1, the Crisis Paradigm).

Social Network and Group Process in Crisis Intervention

The foundations have been laid in the Crisis Paradigm underpinning this book, which stresses the dynamic relationships among individual, family, and sociocultural factors. The task now is to consider the application of this perspective in actual work with distressed people.

A Social Network Framework

Social approaches to crisis intervention never lose sight of the interactional networks among individuals, families, and other social elements. Helping people resolve crises constructively involves helping them reestablish themselves in harmony with intimate associates and with the larger community. In practice, this might mean, for example:

- Relieving the extreme isolation that led to a suicide attempt
- Developing a satisfying relationship to replace the loss of one's partner or a close friend
- Reestablishing ties in the work world and resolving job conflicts
- Returning to normal school tasks after expulsion for truancy, drug abuse, or violence
- Establishing stability and a means of family support after desertion by an alcoholic parent
- Allaying community anxiety concerning bomb threats or child safety
- Identifying why a client complains that "no one is helping me" when, in fact, five agencies (or more) are officially involved

In each of these instances, an individual, psychotherapeutic approach is often used. However, a social strategy, for all of these examples, is so appropriate and evidence supporting it seems so extensive that one wonders why so many practitioners rely primarily on individual approaches—including psychotropic drugs—to crisis resolution. The reasons are complex, of course, and related to issues such as the medicalization of life problems and to the political and economic factors influencing illness and its treatment (see Chapters 1 and 4).

Increasing numbers of practitioners, however, are choosing social strategies for helping distressed people. In an era before biological psychiatry became dominant (Cohen, 1993), the experience of social psychiatrists (for example, Halleck, 1971; Hansell, 1976; Polak, 1971) and nonmedical practitioners (for example, Garrison, 1974) suggested that social network techniques are among the most practical and effective available to crisis workers. Hansell (1976) refers to such network strategies as the *screening-linking-planning conference method*. This method was developed and used extensively in community mental health systems in Chicago and Buffalo on behalf of high-risk former mental patients and others. Polak (1971) called this method *social systems intervention* in his community mental health work in Colorado. The use of network strategies in resolving highly complex crisis situations is unparalleled in mental health practice. Their effectiveness is based on recognition and acceptance of the person's basic social nature. Social network techniques, therefore, are essential crisis worker skills. They should not be neglected in favor of excessive reliance on medications, a pattern traceable in part to cost containment measures and the dominance of biological psychiatry (Luhrmann, 2000; McHugh, 1999). As noted in Chapter 4, psychoactive drugs are often highly effective but rarely are sufficient without other forms of therapy.

An effective crisis worker has faith in members of a person's social network and in the techniques for mobilizing these people on behalf of a distressed person. A worker's lack of conviction translates into a negative self-fulfilling prophecy—that is, the response of social network members is highly dependent on what the worker expects will happen. A counselor skilled in social network techniques approaches people with a positive attitude and conveys an expectation that the person will respond positively and will have something valuable or essential to offer the distressed individual. Workers confident in themselves and in the use of social support and networking techniques can successfully use an assertive approach that yields voluntary participation by those whose help is needed (Elklit et al., 2001).

Social Network Strategies

Besides confidence in the usefulness of social approaches, the crisis worker also needs practice skills. Social network strategies can be used at any time during the course of service: at the beginning of intervention, when an impasse has been reached and evaluation suggests the need for a new strategy,

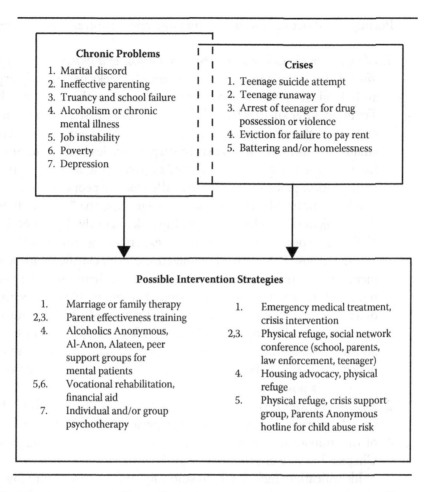

FIGURE 5.3 Comparison of Chronic Problems, Crises, and Intervention Strategies. The permeable boundaries between the two types of distress suggest the mutual influence these situations have on each other.

or at the termination of service. In an era when powerful U.S. health insurance carriers can arbitrate clinical decisions and both patients and clinicians stagger under the weight of paperwork that drives up health care costs, fragmentation of service can be the unfortunate result. This reality in the United States strengthens the importance of social network pioneers like Hansell (1976), Garrison (1974), and Polak (1971), and the role of health care activists and legislative reformers to finally resolve a nearly century-long struggle to achieve healthcare parity regardless of ability to pay. The social network approach is particularly effective when chronic problems and crisis episodes intersect (Evans et al., 2003; see Figure 5.3). Its relevance underscores the worldwide trend toward community-based primary care, as discussed in Chapter 1, even as a shortage of primary care providers looms.

Putting social network strategies into operation involves several steps.

1. *Clarify with the Client and Others the Purpose of a Network Strategy and Their Active Participation in It.* A person who seeks help usually expects an individual approach and may be surprised at the social emphasis. Tradition, after all, dies hard. Educating clients, based on our own convictions, is therefore an essential aspect of success with social network strategies. Similarly, clients may be surprised to learn that they not only have an *opportunity* but are *expected* to participate actively in the crisis resolution process. This is especially true for people who may have developed unhealthy dependencies on agencies: the "agency shopper," the "revolving door client," the multiproblem family (Lynch & Tiedje, 1991), the repeat caller, or the person experiencing chronic stress.

   The purpose of a network conference can be clarified with a statement such as this: "John, you've been coming here for some months now, each time with a new crisis around an old problem, it seems. We don't seem to be helping you with what you need. And you say other agencies aren't helping you either. I think we should all get together and try to figure out what's going wrong. Whatever it is we're doing now doesn't seem to be working." A positive presentation like this usually elicits a positive response.

2. *Identify All Members of the Social Network.* This "laundry list" should include everyone involved with the person either before or because of the individual's crisis. The comprehensive assessment suggested in Chapter 3 is very useful in accomplishing this step.

   Identification includes brainstorming and creative thinking with the client about possible substitutes for missing elements of a support network. This includes social resources that are currently unused but that could lead to successful crisis resolution, for example, transitional housing or support for job training. People who lack a *natural* support network (such as discharged mental patients who have been institutionalized for many years and have little or no family support) may rely extensively on institutional network support. When such support is suddenly withdrawn, they are particularly vulnerable to recurring crises and need substitute sources of support (Farrell & Deeds, 1997; Hoff, 1993; Johnson, 1990). This problem has been particularly acute in U.S. communities where adequate community-based services were not developed in concert with the virtual emptying of state mental institutions (see "Homelessness and Vulnerability to Violence" in Chapter 8). The excerpt from a networking session with Alice illustrates these points. Rather than pressuring Alice to go back home, Mr. Higgins is engaged as a new network member. A network conference about such problems may also yield the necessary evidence for community political action to alleviate these problems.

Case Example: Excerpt from Networking Session with Alice

Mr. Rothman (by telephone): Mrs. Barrett, this is Mr. Rothman at the crisis clinic. Your daughter Alice is here and refuses to go home. Alice and I would like to have you join us in a planning conference.

Mrs. Barrett: So that's where she is. I've done everything I know of to help that girl. There's nothing more I can do.

Mr. Rothman: I know you must feel very frustrated, Mrs. Barrett, but it's important that you join us even if it's agreed that Alice doesn't go back home.

After a few more minutes, Mrs. Barrett agrees to come to the clinic with her husband. (Alice is age 34, has been in and out of mental hospitals, and cannot hold a job. She and her mother had a verbal battle about household chores.) Mrs. Barrett threatened to call the police when Alice started throwing things. Alice left and went to the crisis clinic. During the session at the clinic, the conference leader addresses questions to those attending and facilitates discussion:

To Alice: Alice, will you review for everyone here how you see your problem?

To Mr. Higgins, the counselor from the emergency hostel: Will you explain your emergency housing service, eligibility requirements, and other arrangements to Alice and her parents?

To Alice: How does this housing arrangement sound to you, Alice?

To Alice's parents: What do you think about this proposal?

---

3. *Identify the "Symptom Bearer" for a Family or Social Network.* This is the person whose crisis state is most obvious. Sometimes this individual is called "crazy." Mental health workers often refer to this person as the *identified client*—recognizing that the entire family or community is, in fact, the client, but their role in the individual's crisis is unclear. The symptom bearer is also commonly called the scapegoat for a disturbed social system.

4. *Establish Contact with the Resource People Identified and Explain to Them the Purpose of the Conference.* Elicit the cooperation of these people in helping the person who is stalled in the therapy process and is therefore increasingly vulnerable to repeat crisis episodes. Explain how you perceive the troubling situation and how you think someone can be of help to the distressed person. Finally, arrange the conference at a mutually satisfactory time and place.

If our approach is positive, others involved with a multiagency client will usually express relief that someone is taking the initiative to coordinate services. The families of people with repeated crisis episodes often respond similarly. Problems at this stage may occur because the crisis worker is not convinced that there is a need for the conference, or people from other agencies may raise the issue of confidentiality. This is actually not an issue, because the client has been actively involved in the process of planning the conference: "Why, of course John consents. He's right here with me now." Consent forms should not be a problem if the client participates actively. A straightforward approach is the most successful when using this method.

People may be concerned that conference participants might work together against the client. This is another nonissue, as the purpose of the conference is problem solving for the client's benefit, not punishment. If intentions are sincere, if the purposes of the conference are adhered to, and if the leader is competent, the group process should yield constructive, not destructive, results. People tend to surpass their own expectations in situations like this—even the worker who is frustrated by dependent self-destructive persons. Often the conference represents hope of success. This hope in turn is conveyed to the client. Another recommended strategy for defusing fears about a client being harmed is to appoint a client advocate, someone who will ensure that the client's interests are not sacrificed in any way during the conference. Staff should therefore work in teams of two in conducting these conferences.

5. *Convene the Client and Network Members Conference.* The network conference should be held in a place that is conducive to achieving the conference objectives. This might be the home, office, or hospital emergency department.

6. *Conduct the Network Conference with the Distressed Person and with His or Her Social Network.* During this time, starting with the client's view, the problem is explored as it pertains to everyone involved. The complaints of all parties are aired, and possible solutions are proposed and considered in relation to available resources.

7. *Conclude the Conference with an Action Plan for Resolving the Crisis or Other Problem.* For example, link the troubled person to a social resource such as welfare, emergency or transitional housing, emergency hospitalization, or job training.

   The details of the action plan are clearly defined: everyone knows *who* is to do *what* within a designated time frame. A contingency plan specifies what is to be done if the plan fails (see "Planning with a Person or Family in Crisis" in Chapter 4). This facet of the formal network strategy is what distinguishes it most from a haphazard or unsystematic involvement of a client's family or other network members.

8. *Establish a Follow-up Plan.* This involves determining the time, place, circumstances, membership, and purpose of the next meeting. Experience reveals that many seemingly intractable problems can be traced to a failure to examine why an established action plan did not turn out as anticipated.

9. *Record the Results of the Conference and Distribute Copies to All Participants.* This step is based on the principles of contracting discussed in Chapter 4. It also provides the basis for evaluating progress or for finding out what went wrong if the plan fails. This step is particularly important in cases in which both the client and staff feel hopeless about further progress.

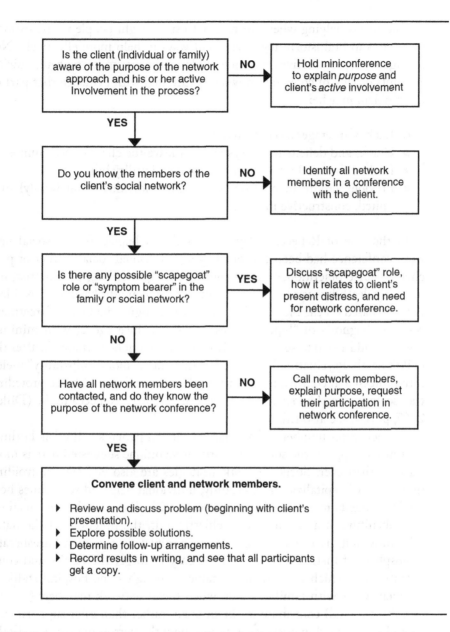

FIGURE 5.4 Steps in Implementing Social Network Strategies.

Success of Social Network Techniques

Workers who have tried social network techniques are very confident in them; the strategy usually yields highly positive results. Its success can be traced to two key factors: (1) the power and effective implementation of *group process* techniques and (2) *active client involvement* in every step of the process. The client's empowerment and responsibility for self-care that are thereby implied are powerful antidotes to hopelessness and a failure to follow through on recommended treatment. For example, a client can scarcely continue to protest that no one is helping when meeting with six to eight people whose explicit purpose is to brainstorm together about ways to help more effectively. Nor can agency representatives continue to blame the victim for repeated suicide attempts or lack of cooperation when confronted with evidence that part of the problem may be:

■ Lack of interagency coordination
■ Cracks and deficits in the system that leave the client's needs unmet
■ Lack of financial resources to pay rent and utility bills
■ Previous failure to confront the client (individuals and family) in a united, constructive manner

In the case of Rebecca Riley (discussed in Chapter 3), if a social network conference had been convened by a professional social worker or psychiatric nurse practitioner and attended by the prescribing psychiatrist, her untimely death by overdose of psychotropic drugs might have been avoided. Instead, based on the biological psychiatry paradigm, the focus of treatment was the diagnosis of "bipolar illness" ascribed since age 2, with minimal attention addressed to serious family issues made public nationwide after the child's death. Psychiatrist Dr. Diller's statement of "moral culpability" fueled intraprofessional controversy regarding the responsibility of those providing the "science" (i.e., biological psychiatry) that allowed Rebecca to die (Diller, 2007, p. A 9; see also Elliott, 2006).

As increasing numbers of discharged mental patients call crisis hotlines for routine support, the social networking technique suggested here is more relevant than ever. Social network strategies are also effective in avoiding unnecessary hospitalization. Certainly, individual help and sometimes hospital treatment are indicated for a person in crisis. But once the person enters the subculture of a hospital or psychiatric unit, the functions of the natural family unit are often disrupted or minimized. In the busy, bureaucratic atmosphere of institutions, it is all too easy to forget the family and community from which the individual came, although some hospital staffs do excellent work with families. Even when social network members (natural and institutional) contribute to the problem rather than offer support, they should be included in crisis resolution to help the person in crisis clarify the positive and negative aspects of social life. Steps of the social network intervention process are illustrated in Figure 5.4.

A final observation is offered for readers who are new to this approach or feel intimidated by it. Social network principles—if not all the steps outlined here—can be applied in varying degrees. In noninstitutional crisis settings, for example, some of the steps may be unnecessary. The example of Ramona illustrates a very simple version of network intervention in a highly charged situation. Years of special training are not required for success in network techniques. Yet professionals and others trained in group process should be comfortable in applying this method even in complex situations.

Case Example: Ramona

Ramona was one of a group of eight abused women in a shelter with no overnight staffing. This shelter, like most, screens its residents for acute suicidal tendencies, addictions, and mental disturbance. Ramona became suicidal nevertheless, and one night she locked herself in the parlor to protect herself from acting on her suicidal tendencies with kitchen knives. When she slept, she did so on the office sofa, so she would not have to be alone. Ramona had not told her fellow house members why she did these things, although the other women did know that she was suicidal. Tension among the residents grew because they did not understand Ramona's behavior. They were afraid that if they asked about it, she would become more suicidal (see Chapter 6 regarding this popular myth). One of the residents said she would leave the house if the staff did not get rid of Ramona.

Assessing the total situation, Diane, a volunteer staffer who was also a registered nurse trained in crisis intervention, called a meeting to discuss the problem. She explained to Ramona that other residents were worried about her and asked, "Are you willing to meet with them and explain what's happening with you?" Ramona replied, "Sure," and eagerly jumped off the sofa. The volunteer added that she had experience with suicidal people and was not afraid to discuss suicide. This brought a sigh of relief and a "Thank God!" from Ramona. (Ramona was on the waiting list for admission to a local hospital psychiatric unit for treatment of other problems.)

In the group meeting, Ramona explained her behavior as self-protection, not hostility, as her fellow residents had perceived, and shared with the group that she felt most protected and least suicidal when another resident had simply gone for a walk with her. Ramona also reassured everyone that in the event she hurt herself or died, it was her responsibility, not theirs. All residents expressed relief at having the problem openly discussed and agreed to keep future communication open with Ramona instead of trying to second-guess her.

Crisis Groups

The idea of helping people in groups developed during and after World War II. Because so many people needed help and resources were limited, it was impossible to serve everyone individually; group therapies were instituted. This experience, along with the success of the method, established the group mode of helping as often the method of choice rather than expediency. Whether or not workers use group modes in crisis intervention is influenced by their training and experience. Attitudes have been strongly influenced by psychiatric practice models that emphasize individual rather than social factors.

The traditional emphasis on individual rather than group approaches has contributed to the relative lack of study of group methods in crisis intervention (Walsh & Phelau, 1974). As is true of social network techniques, success in working with groups depends on workers' conviction that the method is appropriate in the crisis intervention process. Group work is indicated in several instances:

1. *As a means of assessing a person's coping mechanisms.* This can be uniquely revealed through interaction with a group. Direct observation of a person in a group setting can uncover behaviors that may have contributed to the crisis situation. The individual is helped to grasp the reality and impact of his or her behavior in relation to others, which can lead to the discovery of more constructive coping mechanisms. The group is an ideal medium for such a process.

2. *As a means of crisis resolution.* This can be accomplished through the helping process inherent in a well-defined and appropriately led group. For the group members in crisis, the number of helpers is extended from one counselor to the whole group. The process of helping others resolve crises restores a person's confidence and can relieve a member's fear of going crazy or losing control.

3. *As a means of relieving the extreme isolation of some individuals in crisis.* For persons almost completely lacking in social resources or the ability to relate to others, the crisis group can be a first step in reestablishing a vital social network. Madrigal's (2005) description of traumatized combat veterans bonding with other veterans—not "outsiders"—supports the place of group support as one aspect of comprehensive crisis care.

4. *As a means of immediate screening and assessment.* This is especially useful in settings where large numbers of people come for help and the number of counselors is limited. This is the case in some metropolitan areas where the population is more crisis prone due to housing, financial conditions, employment, violence, and physical health problems.

Crisis Assessment in Groups

A crisis assessment group should be used only when individual counseling resources are so limited that the people asking for help would otherwise not be seen at all or would be placed on a waiting list. The chief value of a crisis assessment group is to screen out and assist people in most serious need of help before helping those in less critical need. This kind of screening is often necessary in busy emergency mental health clinics. Not all the people who come to such clinics are in crisis. The crisis assessment group is a means of quickly identifying those persons in need of immediate help. This method of assessment should not be used as a substitute for a comprehensive evaluation of individuals, including active involvement of the person's social network members. In essence, it should be considered a group approach to triage—that is, quickly identifying those whose needs are most urgent.

Suggested Procedure for Group Crisis Assessment

Ideally, crisis assessment group work proceeds as in the following example:

Step 1: Several people appear for service in an emergency mental health clinic within one hour: Joe, age 28; Jenny, age 36; Charles, age 39; and Louise, age 19. Only two counselors are available for assessment, one of whom is involved in an assessment interview.

Step 2: Each person is asked whether he or she is willing to be seen for initial assessment with a group of people who also desire crisis counseling. During this initial presentation, each person is also told that (a) the reason for the group assessment is to give some immediate assistance and prevent a long period of waiting due to staff shortages and (b) the group assessment is not a substitute for individual assessment and counseling needs that are revealed in the group. Those who refuse are reassured of being seen individually as soon as a counselor is available.

Step 3: The crisis counselor explores with each group member the nature of the problem. Each is asked to share the reason for coming to the emergency mental health service. Members are specifically asked why they came *today* rather than on another day. This line of questioning usually reveals the precipitating event as well as the person's current coping ability. Some responses might be as follows:

> *Joe:*   I had another argument with my wife last night, and I felt like killing her. I couldn't control myself and got scared. Today I couldn't face going to work, so I thought I'd come in.
>
> *Jenny:*   I've been feeling so depressed lately. The only reason I happened to come in today is that I was talking with my best friend, and she convinced me I should get some help.
>
> *Charles:*   I've been so nervous at work. I just can't concentrate. Today I finally walked off and didn't tell anyone. I'm afraid to face my wife when I get home because we really need the money, so I decided to come here instead.
>
> *Louise:*   I took an overdose of pills last night, and they told me at the hospital emergency room to come in here today for some counseling.

Step 4: Coping ability and resources are explored in detail. The counselor ascertains in each case the degree of danger to self or others. Group members are asked how they have resolved problems in the past. They are invited to share and compare problem areas and ways of solving them:

> *Joe:*   Usually, I go out drinking or something just to keep away from my wife. Maybe if I'd have done that last night, too, I wouldn't have felt like killing her. No, I've never hit her, but I came pretty close to it last night.
>
> *Jenny:*   Usually, it helps a lot to talk to my friend. We both think I should get a less stressful job, but my husband thinks it's too risky to quit right now. No, I've never planned anything in particular to kill myself.

Charles: I find, too, that it helps to talk to someone. My wife has been really great since I've had this trouble on the job. She convinced me to talk with the company doctor. Maybe I could do that tomorrow and get medical leave or something for a while.

Louise: My mother said I had to come in here. They think I'm crazy for taking those pills last night. I feel like you, Joe. I can't stand going back home, but I don't know where else to go. Maybe if someone else could just talk to my folks.

Step 5: Action plans are developed with the members, and members are invited to share ideas:

Joe's plan: An individual assessment is scheduled for later in the afternoon. A call to Joe's wife, asking her to participate in the assessment, is also planned. Joe is extremely tense and uses alcohol to calm his nerves. This, in turn, upsets his wife, so a referral to Alcoholics Anonymous (AA) will be considered after the full assessment.

Jenny's plan: An individual assessment interview is planned for Jenny three days later, as Jenny is depressed but not in crisis or in immediate danger of harming herself. She is also given the agency's emergency number should she become upset between now and her scheduled appointment (see "Assessment of the Suicidal Person" in Chapter 9). Jenny is also given the names and telephone numbers of private psychotherapists accepting referrals.

Charles's plan: He agrees to talk with the company doctor the next day and request medical leave. He will call in the results and return for a detailed assessment and exploration of his problem soon thereafter.

Louise's plan: A telephone call is planned to Louise's parents to solicit their participation in working with the counselor on Louise's behalf. If they refuse to come in, a home visit will be planned within 24 hours.

This example illustrates the function of the crisis assessment group as a useful way to focus helping resources intensely on people whose problems are most urgent without neglecting others. The crisis assessment group rapidly reveals the degree of stress that people are feeling and their ability to cope with problems. It is apparent, for example, that Jenny has a problem with which she needs help, although she is not in crisis.

Mental health agencies with limited counseling resources need to develop techniques and clear coordinating protocols to ensure that those in crisis or in life-and-death emergencies receive immediate attention (see Online Resources). The assessment worker who uses social resources and network techniques also facilitates the use of resources outside the agency and the individual. Charles, for example, is supported in his self-preservation plan to see the company doctor for medical leave; he intends to resolve his problem through counseling.

As is true with crisis groups generally, crisis assessment groups develop rapid cohesion. Members receive immediate help in a busy agency. Sharing their problems voluntarily with others and assisting fellow group members with similar or more difficult problems give people a sense of self-mastery. It also strengthens their sense of community. An appropriately conducted crisis assessment group can lay the foundation for (1) network techniques in each individual's own social milieu, (2) later participation in a crisis-counseling group that may be recommended as part of the total plan for crisis resolution, and (3) participation in self-help groups such as AA, widows' clubs, and Parents-in-Crisis.

Crisis Counseling in Groups

An important facet of crisis intervention is determining when group work is indicated. Counselors should guard against unnecessarily protecting people in crisis from groups. This attitude is often revealed in workers' statements, such as, "I'll see her individually just for a few sessions," or "She's not ready for a group yet." These statements can be interpreted in several ways:

1. A person actually needs individual crisis counseling.
2. A person is so terrified of the prospect of a group experience that he or she is, in fact, not ready.
3. The counselor believes that counseling people individually is always better and that a group approach is indicated only when there is not enough time for individual work.

Consider the following responses to these interpretations:

1. The need for individual crisis counseling does not negate the need for group crisis counseling. If both are indicated, both should be offered simultaneously.
2. If a person is indeed terrified of a group experience, this may suggest an even greater need for it. In the individual sessions preparatory to the group experience, the counselor should convey the expectation that group work will be a helpful process. An overprotective attitude will confirm the person's fear that groups are basically destructive, and this can limit the person's learning of new coping skills.
3. If the counselor believes in group work only as an expedient measure to be taken in certain instances rather than as the intervention of choice, the counselor will not use this effective method of crisis counseling even when its use is indicated.

Group Structure

Other facets of crisis counseling in groups are the structure, content, and conduct of the group itself. Some crisis workers recommend structuring the group to a strict limit of six sessions. A more flexible approach takes into consideration the different coping abilities and external resources available to individuals. In general, group members should be asked to attend sessions once or twice a week (average session length of 1.5 to 2 hours) for a minimum of six sessions, but they might be permitted a maximum of 10 sessions if a particular crisis situation warrants it. Group crisis counseling that extends beyond 10 sessions indicates that (1) the counselor does not recognize the difference between crisis counseling and longer-term therapy, (2) the person in crisis has an underlying, chronic mental health problem that should be dealt with in a traditional group therapy setting, or (3) the person in crisis may be substituting the group meetings for other, more regular social contacts, and the counselor is inadvertently fostering such restricted social engagement by not limiting the number of group sessions.

The content and conduct of the crisis-counseling group are determined by its purpose—resolution of crisis by means of a group process. The sessions therefore focus on the crises identified by group members. Individual histories and feelings not associated with the crisis are restricted from group discussion. There is a continued focus on resolving the crisis that brought the person to the group. All techniques employed in crisis care for individuals should be used: encouraging expression of feelings appropriate to the traumatic event, gaining an understanding of the crisis situation, exploring resources and possible solutions to the problem, and examining social change strategies that might reduce crisis risk in the future (see Chapter 4).

Participating in a crisis group may reduce social isolation through bonds created in the group problem-solving process. Such group solidarity can be an important forerunner of social action taken to prevent future crises. For example, peer support groups are strongly recommended for people with cancer, parents who have lost a child, battered women, or widowed people. Some people, however, have a strong aversion to discussing their problems with strangers and therefore should not be pressed into groups. Cultural norms might also influence people's enthusiasm or unwillingness to engage with a group about their problems.

Admission to and termination of a group can serve as a medium for discussion about the events that are often an integral part of life crises: loss, admission of a new family member by birth of a baby, revelation of minority sexual identity, divorce, unwanted pregnancy, rape, death, or absence of a family member through illness. By providing an opportunity to work through possible feelings associated with familiar personal losses, group counseling can facilitate individual and social growth from a crisis experience. Crisis groups can also be viewed as contemporary substitutes for traditional rites of passage, an idea explored more fully in Chapter 6. In busy crisis and community mental health centers where crisis group work might be a valuable option, the basics of group counseling apply (e.g., defining goals, number of members, time limits, etc.). These principles and strategies are well known by professionally trained providers such as social workers and advanced practice psychiatric nurses.

Counseling Families in Crisis

Group crisis work resembles family crisis work, but scapegoating and established family patterns and roles make helping families in crisis more complex.

Determining who the scapegoat (or identified symptom bearer) is, along with that person's social network, will reveal the purpose of a person's symptoms in maintaining a family's function—unhealthy and maladjusted as the family may appear at times.

Case Example: Julie

School personnel identified Julie, age 15, as a "behavior problem." She violates all the family rules at home. John, age 17, is seen as a "good boy." Through this convenient labeling process, the mother and father can overlook the chronic discord in their marital relationship and child-rearing practices. Julie's mother and father always seem to be fighting about disciplining Julie. It is therefore easy for them to conclude that they would not be fighting if it were not for Julie's behavior problems. Julie becomes very withdrawn, threatens to kill herself, and finally runs away from home to her friend's house.

A naive counselor could simply focus on Julie as the chief source of difficulty in the family. If, however, the counselor were attuned to the principles of human growth, development, and life crises in a social context, the analysis would be different. Julie would be viewed as the symptom bearer for a disturbed family. The entire family would be identified as the client.

Crisis intervention for a family such as Julie's includes the following elements:

1. Julie's mother brings her to the crisis or mental health clinic as recommended by the school guidance counselor.
2. Julie and her mother are seen in individual assessment interviews.
3. A brief joint interview is held in which the counselor points out the importance and necessity of a family approach if Julie is to get any real help with her problem. The mother is directed to talk with her husband and son about this recommendation, with the understanding that the counselor will assist in this process as necessary.
4. Individual assessment interviews are arranged with the husband and son.
5. The entire family is seen together, and a six- to eight-session family counseling contract is arranged.
6. Crisis counseling sessions are conducted with all family members participating. Julie does indeed have a problem, but the family is part of it. For example, Julie's mother and father give conflicting messages regarding their expectations: John is an "ideal boy," and Julie "never does anything right." Julie feels that her father ignores her. The guidance counselor had asked Julie's parents to come to the school for a conference, but they "never had time."

The sessions will focus on helping Julie and her parents reach compromise solutions regarding discipline and expected task performance. The parents are helped to recognize and change their inconsistent patterns of discipline. All family members are helped to discover ways to give and receive affection in needed doses. John and his parents are helped to see how John's favored position in the family has isolated Julie and contributed to her withdrawing and running away.

7. A conference is held after the second or third session with the entire family, the school guidance counselor, and Julie's friend. This conference will ensure proper linkage to and involvement of the important people in Julie's social network.
8. During the course of the family sessions, basic marital discord between Julie's mother and father becomes apparent. They are referred to a marital counselor from a family service agency.
9. Family sessions are terminated with satisfactory resolution of the crisis, as manifested by the family symptom bearer, Julie.
10. A follow-up contact is agreed on by the family and the counselor.

In some families, the underlying disturbance is so deep that the symptom bearer is forced to remain in the scapegoat position. For example, if Julie's father and mother refused to seek help for their marital problems, Julie would continue her role in the basic family disturbance. Unfortunately, these situations often get worse before they improve. For example, if in her desperation Julie becomes pregnant or carries out her suicide threat, the family might be jolted into doing something about the underlying problems that can lead to such extreme behavior.

For children and adolescents in crisis, family crisis counseling is the preferred helping mode in nearly all instances. Bypassing this intervention method for young people does a grave disservice and ignores the concepts of human growth and development as well as the key role of family in this process. Decades ago, Langsley and Kaplan (1968) demonstrated the effectiveness of family crisis intervention in other situations as well (see McKenry & Price, 2000). As already discussed, the widespread practice of prescribing antidepressants and other psychoactive drugs for children is a disturbing example of such disservice. Fortunately, family and pediatric specialty groups, the Federal Drug Administration, and the media are revealing the damaging results of this reductionist approach to complex social and behavioral problems (Elliott, 2006; Waters, 2000; Zito et al., 2000).

When dealing with suicidal persons, family approaches may be lifesaving (see Chapter 10). Figure 5.3 highlights the relationship between crises and chronic problems. It also illustrates:

■ The interface between crisis and longer-term help for families such as Julie's and Ellen's
■ The greater crisis vulnerability of people with chronic problems
■ The inherent limitations of applying only a crisis approach to chronic problems

- The possible threat to life when crisis assistance is unavailable to people with chronic problems
- The consequent need to use a tandem approach to situations that contain elements of both a chronic and a crisis nature

Self-Help Groups

Whereas social network and family groups are typically led by trained mental health professionals, self-help groups emphasize the strengths of the group members themselves. With roots in the consumer movement, self-help groups play an important part in all phases of crisis care: in the acute phases, in prevention, and in follow-up support. Key factors in the success of such groups are the climate of empowerment that is created and the bonding among members that so often occurs. Among self-help groups, AA and Al-Anon are the most familiar. Many self-help groups have adopted the AA 12-step model and should be considered valuable sources of support by professionals working with distressed people.

Grieving people who share an acute loss with others, such as the death of a child from SIDS or the stress of having a child with AIDS, may feel less isolated. The group is also a source of affirmation and information and a potential protection against suicide. Survivors of abuse, for example, can encourage one another to externalize their misfortunes rather than blaming themselves. Self-help groups exist in most communities for practically every kind of problem or health issue (for example, parents of murdered children, incest survivors, families of people with AIDS, mastectomy patients). Although professionals do not usually lead or facilitate such groups, they can help as catalysts and as resources for getting self-help groups started. They can also be a source of referrals. Current information about such groups is available in most hospitals, clinics, police stations, and other community agencies. As a resource for people in crisis and with chronic problems, self-help groups have assumed growing importance in an era of increased consumer awareness of responsibility for one's own health. However, such groups should never become a substitute—at least not because of fiscal constraints—for the comprehensive professional health services to which every community member is entitled.

Summary and Discussion Questions

Individuals, families, and communities interact with one another in inseparable ways. Crises arise out of this interaction network and are resolved by restoring people to their natural place. Attention to these principles can be the key to success in crisis intervention; inattention to the social network is often a source of destructive resolution of crises. In spite of the heavy influence of individualistic philosophies in all helping professions, a social network approach is being used effectively by increasing numbers of human service workers.

1. Despite the evidence for group support in crisis work, consider the sociocultural roots and limitations of individualism in crisis care.
2. Considering the tremendous influence of biological psychiatry on interpretations and treatment modalities for people in crisis, how can nonmedical crisis workers achieve a balanced, collaborative, and evidence-based approach on behalf of people in crisis?
3. Identify an example from your personal or professional experience in which a client in crisis "fell through the cracks," and consider how social network strategies might have beneffited such a client.

References

Allen, K. R., & Baber, K. M. (1994). Issues of gender: A feminist perspective. In P. C. McKenry & S. J. Price (Eds.), *Families and change: Coping with stressful events* (pp. 21–39). Thousand Oaks, CA: Sage.

Antonovsky, A. (1987). *Unraveling the mystery of health: How people manage stress and stay well.* San Francisco: Jossey-Bass.

Berges, I., Dallo, F., DiNuzzo, A., Lackan, N., & Weller, S. C. (2006). Social support: A cultural model. *Human Organization, 65*(4), 429.

Berkman, L. F., & Syme, S. L. (1979). Social networks, host resistance, and mortality: A nine-year follow-up study of Alameda County residents. *American Journal of Epidemiology, 109,* 186–204.

Bishop, E. E., & McNally, G. (1993). An in-home crisis intervention program for children and their families. *Hospital and Community Psychiatry, 44*(2), 182–184.

Boissevain, J. (1979). Network analysis: A reappraisal. *Current Anthropology, 20*(2), 392–394.

Caplan, G. (1964). *Principles of preventive psychiatry.* New York: Basic Books.

Cohen, C. I. (1993). The biomedicalization of psychiatry: A critical overview. *Community Mental Health Journal, 29,* 509–521.

DeNavas-Walt, C., Proctor, B. D., & Smith, J. (2007). U.S. Census Bureau, Current Population Reports. *Income, poverty, and health insurance coverage in the United States: 2006* (pp. 60–233). Washington, DC: U.S. Government Printing Office.

Diller, L. (2007, June 19). Misguided standards of care. *Boston Globe,* A9.

Dowrick, S. (1994). *Intimacy and solitude.* New York: Norton.

Dressler, W. W., Balieiro, M. C., & Dos Santos, J. E. (1997). The cultural construction of social support in Brazil: Associations with health outcomes. *Culture, Medicine, and Psychiatry, 21,* 303–335.

Elliott, G. R. (2006). *Medicating young minds.* New York: Stewart, Tabori & Chang.

Elklit, A., Schmidt-Pedersen, S., & Jind, L. (2001). The crisis support scale: Psychometric qualities and further validation. *Personality and Individual Differences, 31,* 1291–1302.

Evans, M., Boothroyd, R., Armstrong, M., Greenbaum, P., Brown, E., & Kuppinger, A. (2003). An experimental study of the effectiveness of intensive in-home crisis services for children and their families. *Journal of Emotional and Behavioral Disorders, 11*(2), 92–121.

Farrell, S. P., & Deeds, E. S. (1997). The clubhouse model as exemplar. *Journal of Psychosocial Nursing, 35*(1), 27–34.

Fausto-Sterling, A. (2000). *Sexing the body.* New York: Basic Books.

Garrison, J. (1974). Network techniques: Case studies in the screening-linking-planning conference method. *Family Process, 13*, 337–353.

Halleck, S. (1971). *The politics of therapy.* New York: Science House.

Hansell, N. (1976). *The person in distress.* New York: Human Sciences Press.

Hill, R. (1965). Generic features of families under stress. In H. J. Parad (Ed.), *Crisis intervention: Selected readings* (pp. 32–52). New York: Family Service Association of America.

Hoff, L. A. (1990). *Battered women as survivors.* London: Routledge.

Hoff, L. A. (1993). Review essay: Health policy and the plight of the mentally ill. *Psychiatry, 56*(4), 400–419.

Hoff, M. (2005). *Resilience: A paradigm of promise.* Unpublished master's thesis. Fargo: North Dakota State University, Department of Counselor Education.

Johnson, A. B. (1990). *Out of bedlam: The truth about deinstitutionalization.* New York: Basic Books.

Kann, L., Brener, N. D., & Wechsler, H. (2007). Overview and summary: School health policies and program study 2006. *Journal of School Health, 77*(8), 385–397.

Kreider, R. M., & Fields, J. (2005). *Living arrangements of children: 2001 current population reports* (pp. 70–104). Washington, DC: U.S. Census Bureau.

Langsley, D., & Kaplan, D. (1968). *The treatment of families in crisis.* Philadelphia: Grune & Stratton.

Lin, N., Cook, K., & Burt, R. S. (Eds.) (2001). *Social capital: Theory and research.* New York: Aldine de Gruyter.

Loustaunau, M. O., & Sobo, E. J. (1997). *The cultural context of health, illness, and medicine.* New York: Bergin & Garvey.

Luhrmann, T. M. (2000). *Of two minds: The growing disorder in American psychiatry.* New York: Knopf.

Lynch, I., & Tiedje, L. B. (1991). Working with multiproblem families: An intervention model for community health nurses. *Public Health Nursing, 8*(3), 147–153.

Macy, R., Behar, L., Paulson, R., Delman, J., & Smith, S. (2004). Community-based, acute posttraumatic stress management: A description and evaluation of a psychosocial-intervention continuum. *Harv. Rev. Psychiatry, 12*, 217–228.

Maslow, A. (1970). *Motivation and personality* (2nd ed.). New York: HarperCollins.

McCamant, K., & Durrett, C. (1988). *Cohousing: A contemporary approach to housing ourselves.* Berkeley, CA: Ten Speed Press.

McHugh, P. R. (1999). How psychiatry lost its way. *Commentary, 108*(5), 32–38.

McKenry, P. C., & Price, S. J. (Eds.). (2000). *Families and change: Coping with stressful events and transitions.* (2nd ed.). Thousand Oaks, CA: Sage.

McKinlay, J. B., & Marceau, L. D. (1999). A tale of three tails. *American Journal of Public Health, 89*(3), 295–298.

Medoff, P., & Sklar, H. (1994). *Streets of hope: The fall and rise of an urban neighborhood.* Boston: South End Press.

Meyer, I. H., & Schwartz, S. (2000). Social issues as public health: Promise and peril. *American Journal of Public Health, 90*(8), 1189–1191.

Mitchell, S. C. (Ed.). (1969). *Social networks in urban situations.* Manchester, England: Manchester University Press.

More, T. (1965). *Utopia.* London: Penguin Classics. (Original work published 1516.)

Moynihan, D. P. (1965). The Negro family, the case for national action. In L. Rainwater & W. Yancy (Eds.), *The Moynihan Report and the politics of controversy.* Cambridge, MA: MIT Press.

Parad, H. J., & Caplan, G. (1965). A framework for studying families in crisis. In H. J. Parad (Ed.), *Crisis intervention: Selected readings* (pp. 53–74), New York: Family Service Association of America.

Polak, P. (1971). Social systems intervention. *Archives of General Psychiatry, 25,* 110–117.

Seelig, W. R., Goldman-Hall, B. J., & Jerrell, J. M. (1992). In-home treatment of families with seriously disturbed adolescents in crisis. *Family Process, 31*(2), 135–149.

Sommers, T., & Shields, L. (1987). *Women take care: The consequences of caregiving in today's society.* Gainesville, FL: Triad.

Vega, W. A., Kolody, B., Valle, R., & Weir, J. (1991). Social networks, social support, and their relationship to depression among immigrant Mexican women. *Human Organization, 5*(2), 154–162.

Walsh, J. A., & Phelan, T. W. (1974). People in crisis: An experimental group. *Community Mental Health, 10,* 3–8.

Waters, R. (2000, March/April). Generation RX: The risk of raising our kids on pharmaceuticals. *Networker,* 34–43.

Wilson, W. J. (1987). *The truly disadvantaged: The inner city, the underclass, and public policy.* Chicago: University of Chicago Press.

Wolin, S. (1993). *The resilient self: How survivors of troubled families rise above adversity.* New York: Random House.

Yalom, I. D. (1995). *The theory and practice of group psychotherapy* (4th ed.). New York: Basic Books.

Zito J. M., Safer, D. J., dos Reis, S., Gardner, J. F., Boles, M., & Lynch, F. (2000). Trends in the prescribing of psychotropic medications to preschoolers. *Journal of the American Medical Association, 283*(8), 1025–1030.

See Online Resources for additional references.

PART **II**

CRISES RELATED TO DEVELOPMENTAL AND SITUATIONAL TRANSITION STATES

Hazardous life events, both anticipated and unanticipated, were traditionally defined as transitional and situational crises (see Crisis Paradigm figures in chapters). In presenting crises associated with various transitions, Chapter 6 highlights rites of passage and life crises arising from status and role changes through developmental stages of the life cycle. It concludes with the final crisis for all—passage from life to death—and how we can help ourselves and others through this last developmental task. Chapter 7 addresses the theme of passage from health to illness, including the paradigmatic crisis of AIDS in global perspective. Chapter 8 covers passages in occupational status change from employed to unemployed, and residential change from one home or country to another.

危機
CHAPTER **6**

Stress and Change during
Life Passages

How are the terms *transition* or *passage* and *status* and *role change* related? What do they mean for people in crisis? Transition refers to passage or change from one place or stage of development to another. Status designates the place of individuals and groups with respect to their prestige, rights, obligations, power, and authority within a society. People are evaluated socially by their contribution to the common good and by other criteria such as birth, marital alliance, sex, race, age, sexual identity, wealth, and power. One's status is related to but different from one's *role:* status refers to *who* a person is, whereas role refers to *what* a person is expected to *do* within a given sociocultural milieu (Zelditch, 1968, p. 251).

What do these social concepts have to do with people in crisis in the clinical sense? It is, after all, a normal part of human life to grow and develop through childhood, adolescence, middle age, and old age to death. It is also common to marry, give birth, and lose one's spouse. Anthropologists and psychoanalysts for years have referred to these transition states as *life crises* (Erikson, 1963; Freud, 1950; Kimball, 1909/1960). In anthropology, life crisis refers to a highly significant, expectable event or phase in the life cycle that marks one's passage to a new social status, with accompanying changes in rights and duties. Traditionally, such status changes are accompanied by rituals (such as puberty and marriage rites) designed to assist the individual in fulfilling new role expectations and to buffer the stress associated with these critical, though normal, life events. In traditional societies, families and the entire community, led by "ritual experts," are intensely involved in the life passages of individual community members. This *anthropological* concept of life crisis corresponds roughly to the anticipated crises discussed in clinical literature (see "The Origins of Crisis" in Chapter 2).

Crisis in its *clinical* meaning flows from the tradition of Caplan (1964) and others, who emphasize the sudden onset and brief duration of acute emotional upsets in response to identifiable traumatic events. In this sense, adolescence, marriage, giving birth, and entering middle age are *not* crises except in extraordinary circumstances, such as when the bridegroom fails to show up or the expected infant is stillborn—unanticipated traumatic events that accompany the transition. Transition states are critical life phases, not necessarily traumatic but with the *potential* for activating an *acute emotional upset* in the clinical sense. They are *turning points*, social and psychological processes involving the challenge to successfully complete social, developmental, and instrumental tasks—for example:

- Changing social role, such as single to married
- Changing image of self, such as young to middle aged, healthy to sick
- Gathering material resources to support a new family member

As turning points in the developmental process, these life crises fit the classic definition of crisis as a period of both danger and opportunity. They also highlight the importance of the social, cultural, and material resources necessary for individuals to avoid acute emotional upset. Another connection between the anthropological and clinical definitions of crisis is the fact that individuals in acute emotional upset do not exist in a social vacuum; they are members of cultural communities. People in crisis are therefore influenced by social expectations of how to behave and by values guiding their interpretation of expected and unexpected life events, factors that figure strongly in the way one resolves a particular emotional crisis.

Thus, if it is unclear *who* a person is, *what* the person is expected to do, or *how* the person fits into familiar social arrangements based on cultural values, status or role ambiguity is activated. Status and role ambiguity can create so much stress that a person with conflicting or changed roles may withdraw from social interaction or may try to change the social structure to redefine the anxiety-provoking statuses (Douglas, 1966). For example:

- If pregnant teenage girls sense that they are expected to drop out of high school, they are more likely to be poorly educated, unemployed, and dependent on welfare and to marry early, which enhances their potential for future crises.
- If widowed people sense that they are a threat to social groups of married people, they may feel cut off from social support and thereby increase their risk of emotional crisis around traumatic events.
- If children of parents feuding about divorce are not allowed to see their grandparents, they may ask, "Who is my family?" The deprived grandparent may ask, "What have I done wrong?"

Rites of Passage: Traditional and Contemporary

An important means of reducing the stress and minimizing the chaos associated with such role ambiguity is the constructive use of ritual. One of the most dramatic differences between traditional and urban or industrialized societies is the relative importance of ritual and the separation between the sacred and the profane. With an increase in industrialization comes a corresponding increase in secularization and a decrease in sacred ceremonialism. In his classic work, *Rites of Passage*, van Gennep (1909/1960, p. 11) distinguished three phases in the ceremonies associated with an individual's life crises: rites of separation (prominent in funeral ceremonies), rites of transition (important in initiation and pregnancy), and rites of incorporation (prominent in marriage). A complete schema of rites of passage theoretically includes all three phases. For example, a widow is *separated* from her husband by death; she occupies a *liminal* (transitional) status for a time, and finally is *reincorporated* into a new marriage relationship (Goody, 1962).

These rites protect the individual during the hazardous process of life passages, times considered potentially dangerous to the person if not supported by the community. Ritual thus makes public what is private, makes social what is personal, and gives the individual new knowledge and strength (LaFontaine, 1977). For example:

- A person who loses a loved one needs a public occasion to mourn.
- A couple who are intimate and cohabiting desire social approval (typically through marriage).
- A dying person who is anointed has new knowledge of the imminence of death and greater strength to accept death.
- A divorced person needs community support following a failed marriage—in short, a ritual for public recognition and acceptance of a new role.

Rites of passage are not developed to the same extent by all societies (Fried & Fried, 1980). Until recently, it was generally assumed that rites of passage are relatively unimportant in modern societies: public and private spheres of activity and various social roles (such as worker, parent, or political leader) are more clearly separated than in traditional societies and hence less need of ritual specification. However, there is no evidence that people in a secular urban world have less need for ritualized expression during transition states (Kimball, 1909/1960, pp. xvi–xvii). Some contemporary discarding of ritual can be understood in part as a move toward greater freedom of the individual. Ritual can be a powerful mechanism for maintaining the status quo in traditional and contemporary societies (Durkheim, 1915); less ritual implies more personal freedom. Thus, while some rituals protect the individual during stressful transitions, they have a social purpose as well. For example, the traditional Samburu of Kenya, a polygynous gerontocracy (society ruled by elders) kept young men in a marginal position relative to the total society and forbade them to marry until around age thirty, an institution known as *moranhood*. This ritual preserved the concentration of power and wives among the older men (Hoff, 1978; Spencer, 1973).

Another ritual under scrutiny is female genital mutilation, affecting an estimated 100 to 136 million women and girls, most in African, Far Eastern, and Middle Eastern countries. Sometimes referred to as female circumcision, unlike male circumcision, the operation (categorized in four types) damages or destroys a woman's normal sexual response and can cause life-threatening physical complications (see Chapter 1, diversity). Novelist Alice Walker's fictionalized account (1992), *Possessing the Secret of Joy*, has made the practice and its context of gender-based oppression widely visible in the Western world. Canada and the United States have declared the practice illegal (Affara, 2000). The Nigerian Nurses and Midwives Association, Somali immigrant physicians, and other groups worldwide advocate for elimination of the practice and the education of health professionals in how to deal sensitively with women presenting their daughters for the ritual in Western medical settings. However, as with teen pregnancy and similar issues, this culturally embedded practice is complex, controversial, and intricately tied to socioeconomic and educational equity for women worldwide (Boddy, 1998; Ngugi, 1965).

A contemporary negative ritual is the heavy drinking, and sometimes hazing, associated with admission to college campus clubs—a practice under increasing scrutiny over past decades. Despite U.S. college campus efforts to control the purchase and use of alcohol, binge drinking is indulged in by thousands of young people. In a contemporary twist on traditional rites of passage, these young people (not unlike their Samburu brothers or Somali sisters) feel pressured to drink in order to "belong" in a new environment without the usual supports of family and neighborhood. Wherever these destructive rituals occur, students have poorer grades, reduced career motivation, and increased dropout rates—all challenges for school and parents' groups to create positive rituals for students under stress, who have a powerful need to belong.

An inspiring illustration of initiating young people into responsible adulthood is told by Glenda Dubienski, a private school chaplain, about leading Canadian young people to other cultures to explore and assist people much less fortunate than themselves. Here is her synopsis of the result.

Case Example: Cross-Cultural Connecting

Over the past several years I have had the distinct pleasure of taking youth and young adults on mission trips to Asia, Africa, Pacific Islands, and the Caribbean. One of my passions is to connect the "overly privileged" with the "underprivileged." By taking young people out of their comfort zone, living in very rustic conditions, working extremely hard, and exposing them to a wonderfully unique culture, their eyes are opened to the realities of the world and the beauty of diversity. On every trip I have led, at least one-third of the young people have shared during debriefing that they feel as though *they* are the underprivileged. It grieves them to leave our hosts because they have received so much from people who have so little. The friendships they develop overseas are so deep in comparison with those at home. In essence, they feel as though they have been relationally deprived. Needless to say, this type of involvement has opened my eyes to the injustice and economic disparities of our world. It has afforded such wonderful friendships with the dearest people who have suffered tremendously at the hands of others.... I know we can make a difference in their lives (Dubienski, Personal Communication, 2008).

Women and Marriage across Cultures

Many contemporary women worldwide view marriage and especially the ritual of the wedding day as high points in their lives—some viewing themselves as failures if they cannot marry and retain a husband. Caught up in the emotional high of the wedding ritual, with dreams of "living happily ever after," the average bride is unconscious of the social significance of the ritual of being "given away" by her father and relinquishing her own name to assume that of her husband (Chapman & Gates, 1977). Some women willingly interrupt or delay careers to support their families through unpaid and devalued household work. Many are happy and secure in their role and testify that their dreams have come true.

Millions, however, are battered, as the marriage license seems to have been transformed for some into a "hitting license" (Straus, Gelles, & Steinmetz, 1980); they feel trapped and become convenient objects of violence (Dobash & Dobash, 1979; Hoff, 1990); or find themselves poor and rearing their children alone. Many women are left behind for younger women, especially during middle age, when women are considered "over the hill," whereas men become more "distinguished." Often this occurs after women have sacrificed education and career opportunities in order to fulfill the social expectation of building a stable home (see Hyman & Rome, 1996). Among teenage mothers in the United States, Hymowitz (2006) ties their financial inequality to the absence of marriage and a two-parent structured family life for nurturing children toward their role as responsible citizens.

Ritual, then, can serve to maintain society or various subgroups in a state of traditional equilibrium, with each person behaving according to accepted roles. However, maintaining traditional social roles, often reinforced through the negative use of ritual, can exact a considerable price from certain individuals—for example, more heart disease and suicides for men, social isolation or death for adolescents by suicide, and battering or poverty for women. A consideration of ritual reveals a continuum between traditional and contemporary rites of passage, and suggests that people in all times and places need ritual. But what kinds of rituals are needed, and under what circumstances should they take place? How can ritual be helpful for the individual in transition as well as for society?

The Changing Role of Ritual

Ritual holds a paradoxical place in a secularized society. On the one hand, it is viewed as a sign of an earlier stage of social evolution (Moore, 1992). On the other hand, certain rituals are retained without critical examination of their expression in contemporary life. In modern life, three approaches to ritual are observed: (1) ritual is often denied any relevance; (2) some of its most oppressive and destructive aspects are recycled from ancient tradition to include the abuse of alcohol, guns, or cars and medical technology to prolong life; (3) when ritual is observed, it is highly individualized, as in the rite of psychotherapy, in which the 50-minute session and other practices are observed. Such rituals are complemented by medicalization and its focus on individuals rather than groups in modern urban societies.

These interpretations of ritual, however, are in the process of change. Meaningless and destructive rituals are being dropped entirely or are being questioned. For example, many women today retain their last names after marriage, and *both* parents of the bride *and* groom (rather than only the father of the bride) participate in the marriage ceremony. Similarly, with cultural awareness, barbaric rituals, oppression, and violence are no longer seen as the province of any one society, traditional or modern. Looking the other way in the face of human rights violations with a shrug "Oh, that's just their culture" (i.e., *cultural relativism*, see Chapter 1, key concepts regarding diversity) is no longer acceptable.

Our task as crisis workers is to consider the place of ritual during challenging turning points of life, particularly as it relates to crisis prevention. Whether critical life passages also become occasions of emotional crisis will depend on

1. What the individual does to prepare for anticipated transitions
2. The nature and extent of social support available to the individual during turning points
3. The occurrence of unanticipated hazardous events (such as fire, accident, illness, or loss of job) during transitional phases of life, when vulnerability is often greater
4. Our creativity as crisis workers in helping individuals and families develop positive contemporary rites of passage where there are few or none

Traditional and contemporary rites of passage are compared and the continuity between them illustrated in Table 6.1. The successful passage of individuals through critical stages in the developmental process depends on a combination of personal and social factors. Transition states highlight the dynamic relationships among the individual, family, and society (see Individual Family and Community Interaction in Chapter 5). For example, adolescents who choose marriage or parenthood even though they are not ready for those responsibilities may become liabilities to society and may face more complex problems during later stages of development. But the reason they are personally unfit might be traced to inadequate support from adults and to the complex social, economic, and cultural factors that affect adolescents and their families (Leach, 1994). Some legislators and schools favor requiring psychoeducation courses as a condition for a marriage license. Many church groups have required such courses for decades. These contemporary rituals are an attempt to increase marital happiness and prevent the often negative results of divorce, especially for children.

TABLE 6.1 Rites of Passage in Comparative Perspective

Life Passage	Traditional Rites[a]	Contemporary North American Rites	
		Unexamined or Questionable	Newly Emerging or Suggested
Birth	Attended by family and/or midwife, birth occurs in natural squatting position Death risk is high if there are complications	Medicalized birth: pubic shaving, ultrasound, drugs, episiotomy or forceps, horizontal position Absence of family and friends unless specially arranged Death risk in the U.S. is high among developed countries	Natural childbirth aided by husband's or friends' coaching in home or birthing center, attended by midwife with backup medical care for complications Death risk is low when attended by properly trained midwife, and medical backup is available for special cases
Adolescence	Puberty rites	Hazing and binge drinking on college campuses Religious rites of confirmation and Bar and Bat Mitzvah[b] Obtaining driver's licenses[b]	Supervised college initiation Support and education groups in high schools, churches, and colleges, such as those concerning menstruation, sexuality, driving responsibly without drinking, and parenthood Relating traditional religious rites to modern life, for example, Mikvah in Judaism
Intimate relationships: beginnings and endings	Betrothal and marriage rites; required remarriage of widow; or remarriage may be forbidden	Bridal showers; stag parties[b] Traditional marriage rites	Egalitarian marriage ceremony and contract Consciousness-raising groups for men and women regarding traditional versus egalitarian male and female roles Divorce ceremonies Support groups for the divorced or for parents without partners
Middle age	Not generally ritualized; general increase in social value and respect by community; postmenopausal women may be regarded as asexual	Labeling of menopause as "illness"; individual psychotherapy and drugs for depression; estrogen replacement therapy for women Men past youth become more "distinguished"; women are often devalued further	Education and peer support groups for menopausal women Support groups for couples to redefine marriage (or other committed) relationship to avoid "empty nest" and other midlife crises

(continued)

TABLE 6.1 Rites of Passage in Comparative Perspective (continued)

| | | Contemporary North American Rites | |
| | | Unexamined or Questionable | Newly Emerging or Suggested |
Life Passage	Traditional Rites[a]		
Older age	Not generally ritualized; general increase in social value and respect by family and community Infirm elderly are cared for by family	Forced retirement Institutional placement for care	Economic and social policies to support care of elderly at home; respite services for caretakers Senior citizen programs such as part-time or shared jobs Volunteer work
Death	Usually elaborate, extended rituals involving family and entire community	80% die in institutions with restricted family involvement Mortician has become the main "ritual expert" Children often barred from death and burial rituals Prescription of tranquilizers to survivors after death of a loved one	Social support to aid in grief work Hospice care for the dying; support for family to care for dying member at home Support groups for cancer patients Inclusion of children in death and burial rituals Enhancement of funeral director's role to assist with grief work Widow-to-widow and other self-help groups for survivors

[a] These rites vary widely among societies. No attempt is made to summarize them here; they are cited to illustrate continuity with modern practice. For an introduction to traditional transition rituals and further references, see Fried and Fried (1980).

[b] These rites are not always used to their greatest positive potential.

The role of individuals and families during transition states demands the successful completion of several tasks. For instance, among the traditional LoDagaa in Ghana (Goody, 1962), widows are metaphorically buried by being dressed in premarital *fibers* to signify that they are again adolescents without husbands. They are also fed, as a symbolic last supper of husband and wife and as a test of the widow's possible complicity in her husband's death. The widow's acceptance of food is equivalent to an oath to the ancestors of her innocence. The widow cooks porridge and flicks some on her husband's shrine to show that she has not committed adultery. These rituals are dramatic in that they involve not only the individual and the family but also the entire community.

In contrast, in contemporary society there is the stereotype of the widow who ritually sets the table every night for her dead husband. A possible reason for this behavior may be that the widow had no social, public occasion to cook her "last supper." She lacks the necessary community support to separate from her previous role, abandon her private illusion that her husband is still alive, and proceed to a new role without her husband. This example illustrates the tremendous importance of moving beyond the individual and the family to such social creations as widow-to-widow clubs, a contemporary substitute for the elaborate death rituals of traditional societies (see Lopata, 1995).

Golan (1981, pp. 21–22) outlines the specific tasks to be accomplished by individuals and families during transition states. Her division of "material-arrangemental" tasks (such as exploring resources and choices in the new role) and "psychosocial" or "affective tasks" (such as dealing with feelings of loss and longing for the past) corresponds to the emotional, cognitive, and behavioral steps in effective crisis coping discussed in Chapter 4. However, the effectiveness of these individual and family coping strategies greatly depends on the social and cultural setting. If a society is poor in constructive ritual, if familiar and secure routines and supports in an old role are not replaced, and if there is little awareness of the need for social support, even the strongest individuals may be unnecessarily scarred during passage through life's developmental stages. The challenge of moving on to a new stage of development or role becomes a threat: "Will I succeed or fail?" "What will people think if I fail?" "No, I don't think I can face having this baby—not without the help of its father." "Life just isn't worth living if I can't keep on working. I'm worth more dead than alive."

Keeping in mind the traditional and contemporary rites of passage and their relationship to stress and crisis in modern society, we discuss next the hazards and opportunities of these normal passages from birth to death. During these passages, crisis counselors and health and mental health professionals can be thought of as contemporary "ritual experts" (see Crisis Paradigm, Box 3, lower circle).

Birth and Parenthood

Parenthood places continual demands on a person from the time of conception until at least the child's 18th birthday. Parents must adjust to include an additional member in their family group. Such adjustment is especially difficult for first-time parents, even when they assume the role of parenthood willingly and regard their children as a welcome responsibility. The unique pleasure and challenge of bearing and nurturing a child through childhood into adult life usually outweighs the ordinary problems of parenthood.

Some parents fall into their role unwillingly or use it to escape less tolerable roles. Consider, for example, the adolescent who seeks relief from a disturbed family home and uses pregnancy as an avenue of escape, or the couple who may have more children than they can properly care for emotionally and physically. Some women still view themselves as having no other significant role than that of mother and wife. Others do not limit their pregnancies because of religious beliefs forbidding artificial contraception. Still others lack the knowledge and means to limit their pregnancies. Unwanted children and their parents are more crisis prone than others. Emotional, social, and material poverty are important contributors to their crisis vulnerability (see McKenry & Price, 2000).

All parents, whether or not their children were wanted, are under stress and strain in their parental role. Parenthood requires a constant giving of self. Except for the joy of self-fulfillment and watching a child grow and develop, the parent–child relationship is essentially nonreciprocal. Infants, toddlers, and young children need continuous care and supervision. In their natural state of dependency, they give only the needy love of a child who says, in effect, "I am helpless without you, take care of me, protect me."

Some children, in fact, not only are dependent and needy but also for various reasons are a source of great distress and grief to their parents. Their difficult behaviors, for example, trouble at school or drug abuse, often signal trouble in the parents' marriage or in the entire family system. Sometimes parents try to deal with these troubles by themselves, struggling for a long time with whatever resources they have. Often they are ashamed to acknowledge that there is a problem with the child. They view any problem as a reflection of their own failure. Still other parents may not have access to child and family resources for help, either because the resources do not exist or because they cannot afford them. Religion professor Cornell West and economist Sylvia Ann Hewlett (1999) have produced a manifesto, *The War against Parents*, to bridge the race, class, and gender divide in the "family values-government handout" debate.

Chronic problems of parenthood often persist until a crisis occurs and finally forces parents to seek outside help. Common examples of ongoing problems are a child's getting into trouble with the law, running away from home, becoming pregnant during adolescence, truancy, being expelled from school, or making a suicide attempt.

Parents usually seem surprised when these problems occur, but evaluation of the whole family often reveals signs of trouble that were formerly unobserved or ignored. Teachers, recreation directors, pastors, truant officers, and guidance counselors who are sensitive to the needs of children and adolescents can help prevent some of these crises. They should urge parents to participate in a family counseling program *early*, at the first sign of a problem. It is important for counselors and parents to keep in mind that even if preventive programs are lacking, it is never too late to act. An acute crisis situation provides, once again, the opportunity for parents and child to move in the direction of growth and development and for the parents to fulfill their needs for generativity.

Common Crisis Points for Parents

Over the course of parenting, many experience these common crisis points.

Death of a Child. Upon the death of a child, crisis often occurs not only because of the parents' acute loss but also because the death requires parents to reorder their expectations about the normal progression of life to death—that parents usually precede their children in death. Thus, the loss of a child (including an adult child) is like no other death experience. Some claim it is felt more acutely than loss of a spouse. It is also keenly painful to accept the fact that death has cut off the child's passage through life. Besides being a profound loss, death of a child threatens the parents' perception of parenthood and the normal life cycle (Cacace & Williamson, 1996; Walsh & McGoldrick, 1991). And if the child's death was by suicide, the parents' painful loss is even more acute (see Chapter 10, survivors).

The sudden death of infants is known as *crib death*. The exact cause of these deaths is still unknown, hence the medical designation—sudden infant death syndrome (SIDS). With no warning signs, parents or a babysitter will find the infant dead in its crib. They take the infant to the hospital emergency department in a desperate, futile hope of reviving it. The parents or caregiver have fears and guilt that they may somehow have caused the death. The fact that emergency service staff may seem suspicious or appear to blame the parents complicates this crisis. Indeed, the emergency staff must rule out the possibility of child battering, which they cannot do without examination.

Whether or not the child was battered, emergency personnel should withhold judgment. Parents in either case are in crisis and need understanding and support. Those in crisis over SIDS should be offered the opportunity to express their grief in private and with the support of a nurse. Hospital chaplains can often assist during this time and should be called in accordance with the parents' wishes. Parents should also be given information about sleeping position and self-help groups of other parents whose infants died suddenly in their cribs.

Until the 50-year rate increase in SIDS was closely examined, it had been widely assumed that the exact cause of these deaths was unknown. Now Hogberg and Bergstrom's epidemiological and historical research (2000) in Sweden and other Western countries has uncovered the *prone* (lying on the stomach) sleeping position as the missing risk factor in all previous research aimed at finding a cause. It turns out that the 50-year rise in SIDS rates corresponded with the widespread medical advice against the *supine* position (infant lying face up) to prevent swallowing vomitus or the turned-from-side-to-side position—advice popularized by Dr. Spock's and other baby books in the 1960s, 1970s, and 1980s. With the drop in SIDS rates in the mid-1990s, after a gradual shift from prone to supine positions, the study authors refer to SIDS as an "iatrogenic" tragedy, in showing that the misdirected infant care advice was targeted to and accepted by whole populations.

The most widely known and used group for parents whose infants have died is the Sudden Infant Death Syndrome Foundation, a national organization with chapters in all states and major cities. The program includes support from other parents, counseling from maternal-child nurse specialists, education through films, and a speakers' bureau with medical and lay experts on the topic. Education should include information about sleeping position, preferably supine.

The following case example illustrates the crisis of SIDS for parents and shows how negative outcomes of this crisis might have been avoided through crisis intervention by the pediatrician and others.

Case Example: Lorraine

I can't begin to tell you what my life was like before Doris at our counseling center helped me. Six months ago, my second child died from crib death. She was two months old. When Deborah stopped breathing at home, I called the rescue squad. They resuscitated her and took her to the hospital. Deborah was kept in the intensive care unit for two months. Finally, the hospital and doctor insisted that we take her home. When we did, she died the very same day. I was completely grief stricken, especially since I am 41 years old and had waited so long to have a second child. Our other child, David, is seven. I just couldn't accept the fact that Deborah was dead. My husband and the doctors kept telling me to face reality, but I kept insisting on an answer from the pediatrician as to why Deborah had died. I began having chest pains and problems breathing. Several times, my husband called the ambulance and had me taken to the hospital for elaborate heart tests. My doctor told me there was nothing physically wrong with me.

I went home and things got worse. My husband became impatient and annoyed. I worried day and night about doing something wrong with David and eventually causing his death. The school principal finally called me to say that David was having problems at school. I realized I was being overprotective, but I couldn't help myself. The school recommended that we go to a child guidance clinic with David. I resisted and went back instead to my pediatrician and insisted once again on knowing the cause of Deborah's death. The pediatrician was apparently tired of my demands and recommended that I see a psychiatrist. I felt he was probably right, but also felt we couldn't afford a psychiatrist; we had spent so much money on medical and hospital bills during the past year. I became so depressed that suicide began to seem like my only way out. One night, after an attack of chest pain and a crying spell, I was so desperate that I called the suicide prevention center. The counselor referred me to the local counseling center, where I saw Doris.

With Doris's help, I discovered that I was suffering from a delayed grief reaction. Through several counseling sessions, I was able to truly mourn the loss of my child, which I had not really done through all those months of trying to be brave, as my doctor and husband wanted me to be. Doris and I included my husband in some of the sessions. On her recommendation, I finally joined a group of other parents whose infants had died of crib death. I began to understand my fear of causing David's probable death and could finally let go of my overprotectiveness of him.

Although crib death has special features, the death of children in other ways is also traumatic and requires similar support and opportunities for grief work. A self-help group such as Compassionate Friends offers friendship and understanding to bereaved parents after the death of a child, whether by illness, murder, accident, or suicide.

Miscarried or Stillborn Child. The response of a mother at this crisis point is similar to that of a mother giving birth to a handicapped child: anger, loss, guilt, and questioning. Mothers may ask, "Why did this have to happen to me? What did I do wrong? What did I do to deserve this?" Most important in this crisis for parents as a first step in grieving their acute loss is open acknowledgment of the loss—usually through the sensitive and compassionate *disclosure of facts* by medical personnel. Such honest disclosure helps to allay any misplaced tendencies toward self-blame or parental neglect. And since burial of the stillborn child follows soon, clergy representing religion-affiliated parents serve as primary facilitators of the grieving process. Besides hospital polices regarding the disposition of remains, referrals to grief counselors should be made available to bereaved parents.

The discomfort that some health professionals still feel with death and loss is compounded by ethical issues in cases of miscarriage—that is, some hospitals consider a miscarried fetus as just tissue, not a baby. Because many women miscarry without knowing it, some regard all miscarriages as the simple passing of body fluids. An insensitive remark such as, "You can always try again," fails to consider the mother's bonding with the unborn life or that she may not want to try again. A mother needs to mourn this loss within the framework of the meaning the pregnancy had for her and her family, in spite of others' possible dismissals of the event as relatively unimportant.

Similarly, women who have an abortion need to grieve the loss, regardless of the moral and religious conflicts that may accompany the event. Despite continued public controversy over abortion, for most women faced with an unwanted pregnancy, abortion is rarely a matter of good versus evil, but rather the lesser of two evils in the face of daunting odds.

The Medicalization of Birth. The potential crises surrounding birth and parenthood are colored further by the fertility industry and controversy about cesarean births. Traditionally, cesarean birth was selected when life was at risk for the child or mother (less than 10% of births, though the rate of cesareans still exceeds this figure in some U.S. hospitals). There is perhaps no event arising from birth and parenthood that shows more sharply the difference between traditional societies and Western societies. Birth in North America has come to be identified as an elaborate medical event in which mothers turn over the unique birthing process to physicians, drugs, and surgery. The hazards of medicalizing the natural event of birth are increasingly challenged (Jordan, 1993; Mitford, 1993). The development of birthing centers and the increasing use of midwives is an outgrowth of public debate over birth as a natural event (Boston Women's Health Book Collective, 2005; Inch, 1984). Ideally, the management of birth should be in natural settings with trained midwives, with obstetrical consultation available for medical complications during birth to avoid the possible crisis of unnecessary death. Such medical intervention is required in only a small percentage of total births. For most births, medicalization is itself a hazard to be avoided (Jordan, 1993).

Although less common than cesarean birth, assisted reproduction (including in vitro fertilization) is a multibillion-dollar business and is very controversial for some on religious grounds. Deborah Spar (2006) says that tighter government regulation is needed, including a requirement that fertility clinics disclose associated health risks. Since the desire for children is deep-seated and dates to biblical times, most infertile couples describe the in vitro fertilization procedure as harrowing or even of crisis proportions (Lee, 2003).

Another fallout of medical technology's role in parenting is sex selection through prenatal ultrasound requested by some parents with intent of aborting a female child—a practice deeply rooted in a cultural preference for boys. Related factors are a "one-child" policy and inability to afford expensive dowries for brides. This is also a motive for female infanticide. Aside from the moral dimensions of these practices, there is now a shortage of marriageable women in some societies, despite legal banning of prenatal sex selection except for legitimate medical reasons. While various waves of feminism have mitigated some of the economic and other hardships rooted in gender discrimination, much work remains to be done worldwide.

Illness or Behavior Problems of a Child. Similar social support is indicated for parents whose children are seriously ill, have had a serious accident, or are dying. The modern, relaxed visiting regulations in most hospital wards for children have reduced the crisis possibility at this time for both parents and child. Parents are encouraged to participate in their child's care, so that the child feels less isolated and anxious about separation from parents, and the parents feel less threatened about their child's welfare. When behavioral problems are the issue, parents, teachers, and health providers should note the cautions and dangers of using psychoactive drugs as a first-level response, as discussed in Chapter 4 (see also Leach, 1997, and the "Child Screening Checklist," Chapter 3).

Divorce and Single Parenthood

The high rate of divorce in North America has stabilized. The parent who gains custody of the children has the responsibility of rearing them alone, at least until remarriage; the other parent experiences a loss of the children. The loss is more acute if the divorced parents live in different cities or different parts of the country. If the loss is accompanied by a sense of relief, guilt usually follows. To assuage guilt, the relieved parent may shower the children inappropriately with material gifts or accuse the other parent of being too strict, inattentive, or uncaring. This crisis point of parenthood can be anticipated whenever the divorce itself is a crisis for either parent. Divorce counseling can help avoid future crisis.

The increase of no-fault divorce laws and attention to the needs of children in divorce settlements will also help prevent crises for parents, children, and grandparents. Although divorce affects children of all ages, preschoolers are at greatest risk following divorce; boys seem to have a harder time than girls, and the fallout for children generally is worst during the first year of breakup. Cross-cultural studies show that children of divorce worldwide experience problems similar to those of U.S. children (Boey et al., 2003). A study in China found that children of divorce were more likely than other children to make somatic complaints ("my stomach hurts"), demonstrate lower social competence, and behave aggressively (Liu et al., 2000). A study of children in Botswana found that divorce led to economic hardship and feelings of resentment and betrayal among children and mothers (Maundeni, 2000). The following sources of support help children cope with divorce: support of extended family and friends, membership in a religious community, financial security, and intrafamily communication (Rathus, 2006; Rogers, 2004).

However, as already discussed, it is not so much the divorce itself as it is the manner in which parents conduct themselves and the poverty (especially for women) that cause the greatest stress on children of divorced parents (Sidel, 1996). Existing laws do not adequately address the crisis of divorce, as attested by the incidence of child snatching by the parent denied custody. Another problem faced by many mothers is the awarding of custody to fathers on the basis of their greater financial security and attendant access to legal services (which many women cannot afford), even when these fathers have not been the primary caretakers of the children (Chesler, 1986). Although the increasing interest of fathers in parenting their children is to be applauded, to award them custody primarily on a class basis is a cruel punishment of mothers, who have assumed the major burden of child care throughout history. This growing practice highlights the need for social change to address women's economic inequality.

Single Fathers. Fortunately, divorce courts increasingly confer joint custody of children, and more fathers willingly assume both the joys and responsibilities of child care. One result is the growing percentage of fathers (divorced, separated, never married, or widowed) who are raising three or more children under age 18. Among single fathers, 27% have an annual income of $50,000 (U.S. Census Bureau, 2007) compared with the significantly lower income of single mothers.

Fathers who do assume full-time parenting responsibility face stereotypes about that role, struggle with the same issues as single mothers, and have fewer support groups available to them (Wong, 1999). A new group of professionals, certified divorce planners, are available to divorcing parents, who must always remember that they are divorcing each other, not their children. Fathers who parent successfully after divorce are able to distinguish being a father from being an intimate partner, elevate their love for their children over any anger at an ex-partner, prioritize children's needs over adult rights, and fulfill relational aspects of fathering as well as financial responsibility. During custody conflicts, divorce counseling can help prevent such abuses as (1) awarding visitation rights to a father who abused his partner and children and (2) charging a nonabusive father with child molestation as a means of denying him visitation or joint custody rights (see Arendell, 1995).

Teenage Parenthood. The problems and hazards of single parenthood are increased for a teenager with no job and an unfinished education. The infants of teen mothers are also at increased risk of death, battering, and other problems exacerbated by the poverty of most adolescent parents. Increasingly, teenage mothers do not automatically drop out of high school because of pregnancy, do not marry only because they are pregnant, and do not give up their babies. Hospitals and social service agencies are now establishing collaborative programs with high schools, which include an emphasis on health, sex education, parenthood, and career planning.

There is also growing recognition that the prevalence, problems, and hazards of teenage pregnancy will not subside until values and opportunities for women in society change. Counselors and others working with young mothers, many of whom are from low-income or troubled homes, repeatedly note that these girls see mothering as their only chance for fulfillment. Life seems to offer them no prospect of happiness through career or an education. Indeed, there is still widespread social, cultural, and economic reinforcement of the notion that a woman's major value to society is her capacity for motherhood, a view bolstered by Freudian psychoanalytic theory (see Chodorow, 1978). A young woman may sense that she has little chance to contribute anything else to society and says in effect, "But I can produce a baby." In fact, some young women request pregnancy tests not because they fear they are pregnant, but because they wish to gain assurance of their fertility. So even if a girl does not plan to conceive, once pregnant she finally finds meaning in her life; she now will be important and necessary—at least to a helpless infant. Current efforts to reform welfare will probably fail if they do not consider these issues and emphasize the joint responsibility of mothers and fathers for the children they produce (Eyre & Eyre, 1993). In her book, *Marriage and Caste in America*, Hymowitz (2006) notes that marriage may pose a larger social divide than race; in 2006, young two-parent families in the top quintile with postsecondary education had a mean income of $88,000; while the mean income of those in the bottom 20% (mostly single) was only $5,200. Hymowitz attributes the rising inequality of income based on education of single parents and two-parent families, to a reversal of young married couple formation.

Stepfamilies and Adoption

In addition to the high rate of divorce and teen pregnancy in North America is the high rate of remarriage and the increasing presence of blended families. As with any major transition, families in these situations face many challenges and need support through crises in order to reap the potential riches of new family structures while avoiding the pitfalls, especially for children. There is now a growing body of literature on this topic, including the need for community-wide approaches to helping such families.

Adoption is another parenting issue ripe with opportunity and danger for the child, parents, and entire groups. One married woman who could not bear a child and wanted to adopt sacrificed her marriage because her husband wanted no children. A single person desiring parenthood usually faces many more challenges during the adoption approval process than a heterosexual couple with the same desire. Anyone, married or single, who attempts inter-racial adoption in the United States must navigate not only the usual hurdles but also the national debate on the topic. While acknowledging the impor-tance of racial identity, emphasis should be on the common humanity and needs of all children for nurturance and love in a stable family, needs that are rarely met in institutional settings or with frequent shifts between fos-ter families (Bartholet, 1993). Fortunately, more affluent people—whether infertile or not—are pursuing adoptions from among the world's children who need a loving home.

Lesbian and Gay Parenthood

The contemporary stresses of parenthood include those of gay, lesbian, bisex-ual, and transgendered parents. There is probably no group of parents more misunderstood than gay parents. The myth and fear is that gay parents will bring up their children to be gay. Another myth is that gay men are much more likely than straight men to abuse children. As a result, lesbian and gay parents may lose custody of their children for no other reason than their sexual identity. Gay people of both sexes may be denied adoption if their sexual identity is known. For example, community protest in Massachusetts resulted in the removal of a foster child from the home of two gay foster par-ents, only to have the child abused six months later in a "normal" foster home. In case of a medical emergency in a nontraditional family unit without legal status, the nonbiological parent may be denied access to emergency or inten-sive care units if hospital rules state "family only." Crises around gay parent-hood might decline with reflection on the following facts: the vast majority of parents are heterosexual, yet these straight parents have reared millions of gay people. The necessary role models of either sex and sexual identity exist for all children in many social contexts besides the home. Also, the majority of child sexual abusers are heterosexual male relatives (see Blumenfeld & Raymond, 1993).

Surrogate Parenthood

Legal, ethical, and emotional controversy over this technological response to the desire of childless couples for children continues, with proponents citing the Bible in support of their position, and opponents noting that the last time human beings were bred for transfer of ownership was during slavery (Corea, 1985). The parenting issues of infertility and the right of procreation are cited as rationales justifying surrogacy. However, infertility rates are highest among low-income racial minority groups, due in part to greater exposure to various hazards, whereas lower rates among affluent women are traced largely to later age at attempting pregnancy. Surrogate babies, therefore, are usually born to poor women and paid for by affluent white couples. In the United States, the price of a surrogate arrangement is usually many thousands of dollars, while women in poor countries are paid much less or nothing at all. And although procreation is a right, this right cannot be exercised at the expense of the primordial right of a woman to the child she has nurtured and birthed.

The *preventive* approach to the infertility that has spawned surrogacy includes removal of environmental and workplace hazards affecting fertility, and child care provisions that would allow career women to have children at earlier ages without compromising their jobs. The controversy in wealthy countries surrounding this issue has resulted in tighter licensing standards and the banning of surrogate motherhood and sex-selection techniques in Canada (Krishnan, 1994), while in the United States, there is a move toward such federal regulation of birth technology, especially for protecting the rights of children.

The complexity of this issue is compounded by a resurgence of 19th-century *natalism*, which emphasizes the biological reproduction role of women. Natalism's seductive power is dramatized in the stories of two Montreal couples who began in vitro technology; one couple followed through for years at enormous financial and personal cost, whereas the other dropped out in favor of adoption and a more global (versus individualistic) approach to their desire to care for children (see *The Technological Stork*, Canadian Film Board). But among those parents who in good faith choose adoption, after weathering the crisis of infertility, some are confronted with the loss of their adopted child to biological parents, whose rights are almost always favored by courts, sometimes apparently irrespective of the child's best interests. One couple who faced this crisis made meaning out of their loss by successfully advocating for a change in laws that more fairly protects the rights of all concerned in such cases.

Fatherhood in Transition

A discussion of parenthood is incomplete without considering the changing notion of fatherhood, especially in regard to prevention of parent–child crises. The changing role of fathers is related to several factors: (1) the necessity for most mothers to work outside the home, (2) financial and other risks of single parenting to all concerned, (3) increasing realization of the benefits to children of being reared by two parents rather than one, and (4) growing awareness by fathers of what they miss emotionally through marginal involvement in parenting. However, there are strains in this transitional process. Several factors work against contemporary fathers assuming a more active role in child rearing: (1) continued sex-role socialization at home and in school (Sadker & Sadker, 1994), (2) continued gender-based inequality in the paid labor force, (3) the tenacious notion that it is more appropriate for a mother than a father to take time from a job on behalf of family needs (Thurer, 1994), (4) lack of role models for male participation in child care, (5) gender-based stereotypes in such professions as nursing and child development, and (6) some women's continued ambivalence about men's active participation.

Because child care is the only arena in which women routinely have exercised control, it is unlikely that they will readily give it up so long as their limited access to other areas of power continues. Language is a barometer of our success here; for example, we still hear that mothers "take care of their children," whereas fathers "babysit" or "watch" them. In North America and worldwide, the poverty of children usually mirrors the poverty of their mothers. A 1993 United Nations Human Development Report on 33 countries that keep gender-based statistics reveals that no country (including rich nations like Canada, Germany, Switzerland, and the United States) treats women as well as it treats men. A social health index measuring, among other items, child poverty and teen suicide reveals that the United States lags behind Western European countries in policies and practices that address the needs of working parents. For example, Western European countries grant paid work leave for attending to family issues, whereas in the United States many cannot afford to take the unpaid family leave available—and this, only to workers in companies of 50 or more employees (Crittenden, 2001). Poverty and inadequate child care services are not just issues for welfare mothers; they adversely affect increasing numbers of intact families and struggling parents. Some corporations are also realizing greater business returns, more employee satisfaction, and reduced absenteeism as a result of providing child care benefits. As Ruddick (1989) suggests, children, women, men, and the whole social order would benefit by balancing domestic and public work between women and men.

Adolescence and Young Adulthood

Opinion regarding the age span of adolescence varies in different cultures and according to different theorists. The Joint Commission on Mental Health of Children in the United States considered youth up to age 25 in the program it recommended for youth in the 1970s. The extent of adolescence is influenced by such factors as (1) length of time spent in school, (2) age at first marriage, (3) parenthood or the lack of it, (4) age at first self-supporting job, and (5) residence (with or apart from parents). In general, adolescence can be considered in two stages—early and late. Late adolescence overlaps young adulthood, particularly for those who prolong vocational and educational preparation into their early and middle twenties.

Developmental Challenges and Stress

During early adolescence, the major developmental task is achievement of "ego identity" (Erikson, 1963). Adolescents and young adults must give up the security of dependence on parents and accept new roles in society including assuming responsibility in the work world and achieving a capacity for intimacy. The adolescent struggles with the issue of independence and freedom from family. On the one hand, the young person is very much in need of the family's material and emotional support. On the other hand, the young person may resent the continued necessity of dependence on parents. Interdependence—a balance between excessive dependence and independence—is a mark of growth during this stage.

Developmental tasks during late adolescence include finding and adjusting to a place in the world apart from immediate family and developing a capacity for intimacy in one's sex role. These tasks may involve finding and holding a satisfying job; succeeding in college, technical training, or graduate school; and choosing and adjusting to a lifestyle such as marriage or communal living.

Success with the developmental tasks of adolescence depends on what happened during one's infancy and childhood, including transitions such as toilet training, weaning, and starting school. An unhappy childhood is the usual precursor to unhappiness for an adolescent or young adult. Successful completion of the tasks of adolescence or young adulthood can be accomplished only if parents know when to let go and do not prevent the young person from making decisions she or he is capable of making independently. Young people today simultaneously face new opportunities and terrifying threats, often with insufficient support in either instance. Flom and Hansen (2006) note that among youth studied, the seeds of hope were rooted in the soil of current experience and relationships. Those who had maintained interests and involvement, even in the midst of significant trouble, were able to envision future satisfaction, occupational stability, and contribution to the community. In contrast, those with constricted interests and tenuous connections reflected vague, narrow, and unrealistic dreams.

U.S. society has been described as youth oriented. This does not mean that Americans particularly value younger people; instead, it shows a devaluation of older people. In fact, the necessary services for both normal and troubled young people are grossly lacking in many communities. For example, many schools do not have guidance counselors or school social workers. The youthful population in every community should have access to emergency hostels, where young people abused by their parents or seeking refuge from conflict can go. There should be housing for youthful offenders in special facilities with a strong community focus, not with hardened criminals. In addition, all schools should provide suicide prevention programs. The lack of specialized services for disturbed children and adolescents needing psychiatric hospitalization has reached crisis proportions in many places, a problem exacerbated by managed care policies and the misuse of psychotropic drugs on young children (see Chapters 4, 10, and 11).

In their search for identity and meaning, many young people turn to religion for a sense of belonging, with some caught up in age-old religion-inspired wars. Author Iboo Patel in *Acts of Faith* (2007) has written of the positive role of faith and his identity as a Muslim, an Indian, and an American. The Interfaith Youth Core, which he founded in Chicago, is an inspiring account of how informed and idealistic young people can reduce religion-based hatred and reap the fruits of peaceful religious pluralism. His example could be replicated in families and among youth groups worldwide to help heal our divided world.

Sexual-Identity Crisis

Many adolescents today are at increased risk of destructive behaviors toward self and others, and gay, lesbian, bisexual, and transgendered youth are at even greater risk, especially of suicide. Though complex factors intersect during all adolescent crises, homophobia in mainstream North America is commonly assumed to underpin the crises and chronic problems faced by gay youth. Williams (1992, 1986), an anthropologist who has studied among Native people of North American, Pacific, and Southeast Asian cultures, points out how these people revere androgynous members of the community as "higher" because the spirit from which all life (human, animal, plant) emanates has blessed the person with *two* spirits; hence the person is respected as a "double person," with particular roles and contributions to make in religion, the family, the workplace, and the community at large. Thus "difference is transformed—from *deviant* to *exceptional*—becoming a basis for respect rather than stigma" (Williams, 1992, p. 267). From his fieldwork with the Lakota, for example, Williams notes that the *berdache* (androgynous men) are the first choice to become adoptive parents when there is a homeless child—a marked contrast to nearly universal policy in most North American jurisdictions, which forbid such adoption, allegedly to prevent sexual molestation.

Blumenfeld (1992) shows the enormous costs of homophobia to *all*—those who are stigmatized, victimized, and deprived of an opportunity to live peaceful and fruitful lives, as well as those who have accepted the notion that these "different" people are also evil. But the highest price is paid by adolescents during the vulnerable developmental stage of discovering their sexual identity in a homophobic mainstream society and coming to terms with who they are without engaging in self-destructive behaviors. Figure 6.1 illustrates the sexual-identity crisis that many lesbian, gay, bisexual, and transgendered youth experience. It depicts the Crisis Paradigm applied to this at-risk group of adolescents, highlighting both the danger and the opportunity to move beyond homophobia toward a more egalitarian value system, as espoused by many pre-Columbian Native communities (see also Blumenfeld & Lindop, 1994).

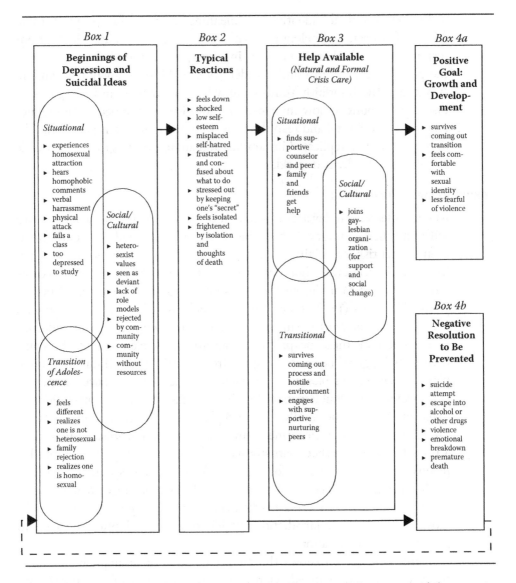

FIGURE 6.1 Sexual-Identity Crisis. Crisis origins, manifestations, and outcomes and the respective functions of crisis care have interactional relationships. The intertwined circles represent the distinct yet interrelated origins of crisis and aids to positive resolution, even though personal manifestations are often similar. The arrows pointing from origins to positive resolution illustrate the *opportunity for growth and development* through crisis; the broken line at the bottom depicts the potential *danger of crisis* in the absence of appropriate aids. The loop between Box 4b and Box 1 denotes the *vulnerability* to future crisis episodes following negative resolution.

Case Example: Robert, a Haitian Youth (as told to a Boston immigrant)

One day while I was riding the T (Boston subway) I was approached by a young man asking for money. Although his clothes were dirty and he looked as though he had not showered that day, something about him made me want to know his history. So I asked him, "If you don't mind, could you tell me how you got in this situation?" He looked at me as though stunned that someone would want to hear *his* story. And so he smiled and explained with a heavy accent that he was originally from Haiti, which we all know is a country in turmoil. His parents wanted to send him to the United States to live with some relatives he had in Boston. Leaving his family and all that he knew behind, Robert left what he called home. He explained that he was still very young—around 13 or 14—and that people do this all the time. Fortunately for him, he finished high school and went to a community college in Boston. Life seemed to be going great. He met a guy friend with whom he explored his sexuality. His relatives did not accept this, due to the fact that homosexuality is considered a huge dishonor to one's family within the Haitian community. Slowly things got worse with his relatives. His uncle would beat him whenever he thought he was going out with his gay friends. Therefore, Robert moved in with his boy-friend. He explained that they never used protection and how they began to use drugs. He was not sure whether it was through sharing needles or the unprotected sex, but somehow he contracted the HIV virus. He gave me the most serious look as he told me that he could never return home and was simply waiting to die.

Let us consider the cross-cultural *commonalities* and *unique* features of Robert's crisis:

- *Commonalities*: (1) As with other immigrants, Robert suffers the loss of his native country and proximity to parents and homeland. (2) Robert struggles with education and jobs in an economy less than supportive and friendly to "outsiders." (3) As with most others in the gay community, Robert experienced a sexual-identity crisis in discovering his homosexuality. (4) Like millions of others, Robert was in crisis on learning he is HIV positive and all that news of this serious illness entails.
- *Unique Features*: (1) The cultural value of the Haitian community regarding homosexual orientation, compared with growing acceptance of gay identity in the United States and Canada, for example. (2) Robert's sense of isolation in realizing that he could not return home to his family of origin, given their values about sexual identity, and feeling abandoned in a foreign culture as he faced the prospect of an untimely death from AIDS.

Helping Young People

Parents, teachers, pastors, youth directors, guidance and residence counsel-ors, primary care providers, and school nurses are in powerful positions to help or hinder young people in their quest for identity and a meaningful place in society. Help may mean simply being available and attentive when a young person is upset and wants to talk; offering information the young person needs in order to make decisions about career, education, or marriage; guiding young people in the use of counseling and other resources when they find themselves in a crisis; or acting as a youth advocate in instances of neglect, abuse, or other injustice.

The crisis intervention principle of doing things *with*, rather than *to* and *for*, troubled people is particularly important when trying to help the young (see Chapter 4). Because a major developmental task of adolescence is finding a unique place and achieving healthy interdependence, a counselor's inattention to this principle can defeat the purpose of the helping relationship. Certainly, a young person in trouble may need a caring adult to help make certain decisions. But the same principle applies here as in work with troubled adults: The troubled person should participate in any decision affecting him or her unless that is clearly impossible under certain circumstances when a counselor should be ready and available to act on the person's behalf. Some adults assume that young people are incapable of making decisions or of accepting responsibility. In contrast, others force adolescents to make decisions and assume responsibilities they may not be ready for. Either attitude causes trouble. Crises and ongoing problems such as drug abuse, delinquency, and violence can often be avoided when young people have the support they need to meet the demands of this phase of development.

Case Example: Nora Staples

Nora Staples, age 17, and her sister, Jennifer, age 16, moved to a large city 300 miles from their home in order to get away from their abusive father. Their elderly grandparents invited Nora and Jennifer to stay with them, despite their cramped living quarters and financial straits. Nora and Jennifer's parents divorced when the children were 11 and 10, respectively. Their mother left the area after the divorce, and the girls had not seen her since. For four years, Nora and Jennifer stayed with an aunt and uncle who lived near their father's home.

When Nora was 15 and Jennifer 14, their father insisted that they live with him. He expected them to cook and keep house, which they did without complaint; they were afraid of what he would do if they rebelled. On weekends, their father went on drinking binges. Every month or two after such a binge, he would put both girls out of the house and lock the door; they would then go back to their aunt and uncle's house for a few days until their father insisted they come home again. The aunt and uncle were finally threatened by the father if they ever took the girls in again. When they heard this, Nora and Jennifer hitchhiked to their grandparents' home.

Two weeks after arrival at her grandparents' home, Nora began talking about shooting herself. The grandmother called a local crisis service and persuaded Nora to talk with the counselor. Indeed, Nora had obtained a gun and was seriously considering suicide. She felt angry with her father, though she had never let him know that. She also felt guilty about leaving him, although she could not bear being with him any longer. Now she felt she was a burden to her grandparents and saw no point in going on. Nora agreed, however, to come to the crisis clinic for counseling to deal with her problem. She also agreed to a plan to dispose of the gun, with the help of her grandparents and the police. Nora's grandparents were helped to deal with their anger and disgust with their son for the way he had treated Nora and Jennifer.

In spite of her problems, Nora managed to graduate from high school with honors at age 17 and was offered a scholarship by a nearby private college. She was undecided about whether to start college immediately or get a job to help support herself while living with her grandparents.

The service plan for Nora and her grandparents included the following:

1. Individual counseling sessions for Nora to deal with her anger and misplaced guilt regarding her father, to help her make a decision about college or work, and to explore alternatives other than suicide as a way out of her despair
2. Family counseling sessions for Nora, her grandparents, and her sister, Jennifer, to help them deal together with their feelings about the situation, to find ways of supporting one another, and to find a solution to the problem of crowded living quarters
3. Collateral conferences with the Department of Family Services to obtain financial support for Nora and Jennifer and to enable the grandparents to find a larger residence

Nora, Jennifer, and their grandparents were also advised of their rights and of resources available to them to press charges of neglect against the father if he came to take the young women away with him, as they suspected he would do within weeks.

By the end of eight individual counseling sessions and six family sessions, Nora was no longer suicidal. She had learned that the scholarship would be available to her the following year if she chose to delay going to college. She therefore decided to stay with her grandparents for a year and get a job to help support herself. One factor in this decision was Nora's realization, through counseling, that she was very resentful of having had to assume so much responsibility for her father and his needs. She said she wanted the chance to live in peace and quiet with a family for a while. She also felt deprived, as a result of her disturbed home situation, of the opportunity to live the way most teenagers do.

Nora gained the strength and courage to file charges against her father when he came to demand that she and Jennifer return to his home. A restraining order was obtained, and he was directed by a family court to make regular support payments to Nora and Jennifer while they continued to live in their grandparents' home. Custody of Nora and Jennifer was vested with their grandparents. A six-month follow-up contact revealed that Nora was much happier and had decided to go ahead with college plans. She was advised of college counseling services available to her should she become upset and suicidal again.

Young women like Nora and Jennifer need special support to avoid crisis during their passage through adolescence. If adolescents come from troubled families, we should pay particular attention to the social and family approaches discussed in Chapter 5. The role of grandparents in such situations is becoming more common as drug abuse, joblessness, poverty, incarceration, and death among parents leave many children—even infants—without the family support they need. Grandparents are not only essential in these cases, but also need extra support themselves as they "weather the storm" of resumed parenting roles during a major transition state of their own

(Minkler & Fuller-Thomson, 1999). Conversely, grandparents who feel useless and discarded may gain a new lease on life by tending to the needs of children within familial and community circles. A loosening of the dominant nuclear family structure, enhancement of extended family roles, and community developments such as cohousing (see Chapter 5) can serve not only distressed children but also the community at large.

But even if family disturbance, rejection, and deprivation are not apparent, many young people complain that they feel that no one is listening to them. Parent effectiveness training should begin in high school and include a focus on listening, loving, and giving, as well as discipline and nonviolent positive control approaches. Adult guidance from schools, churches, and recreation directors should supplement family support with creative approaches (Brendtro, Brokenleg, & Van Bockern, 1990). Hazing tragedies, teenage gangs, binge drinking, and similar negative group associations attest to the tremendous need of young people for peer belonging and acceptance along with adult guidance. Dangerous hazing activities are remarkable for their destructiveness and for their lack of any mature adult influence. Although rites of passage for adolescents are necessary, the challenge is to develop contemporary alternatives that reflect sensitivity to adolescents' simultaneous needs for support, guidance, independence, and group belonging. For example, when considering the threat of HIV-AIDS and of adolescents' continuing abuse of alcohol, groups such as Students Against Drunk Driving or discussion sessions on AIDS and responsible sexual behavior can function as contemporary rites of passage during this critical developmental phase (see Crisis Paradigm, Box 3, lower circle).

Helping a Family in Crisis

More consistent efforts are also needed within social service and mental health agencies for family approaches to the problems of adolescents. The interrelated stresses and crises of parents and their children, along with several intervention strategies, are illustrated in the following example of a family in crisis.

Case Example: The Page Family

Donald Page, 44, and Ann Page, 39, had been married for 20 years and had 4 children—Alice, age 20; Michael, 18; Betsy, 14; and Gary, 9. Donald worked in a local automobile factory. After two years in military service, he returned home as a disabled veteran. Ann worked as a secretary prior to their marriage and returned to work when her husband joined the service. When Donald returned, the Pages moved to a small farm on the outskirts of a large city. They leased the farmland, and Donald stayed at home most of every day doing odd jobs around the farm. He did few routine household chores, even though Ann worked full-time outside the home. The Pages had a bleak social life, and in general their marriage and family life were strained.

The Page children felt isolated because it was difficult to see their friends except during school hours. Alice had a baby at age 17 and dropped out of her junior year in high school. She and her mother quarreled constantly over responsibility for the baby, who lived in the family home. After two years of this fighting, Alice's parents asked her to find a place of her own, which she did. Ann, meanwhile, threatened to report Alice to child protection authorities if she did not start assuming more responsibility for her child. Ann really wanted to keep Alice's baby herself, for she had wanted another child. Alice also talked about giving her baby away to her mother.

Betsy, meanwhile, was reported to be having problems in school, and teachers suspected her of taking drugs. Betsy had been belligerent at home, refusing to do chores and staying out late. Finally, Betsy ran away from home and was returned by police after three days. Donald and Ann were advised by police and school authorities to seek help for Betsy. They did not follow through and continued alone in their struggle to control her behavior. Michael tried to help both Betsy and his parents, but he felt pulled between the two parties. Gary was the "spoiled" child and occasionally asked why everyone was fighting all the time.

When Betsy's school problems heightened, she was threatened with expulsion and a week later ran away again. This time when police found her, she threatened suicide if she was taken home. Police therefore took her to a community mental health emergency service, where she saw a crisis counselor; she begged to be placed in a detention center rather than go back home. After several hours with Betsy, the counselor was able to persuade her that she could help her and her family make things more tolerable at home and that a detention center was no place for a girl her age, at least not until other alternatives had been tried.

Betsy's parents, meanwhile, were called and asked to come to the crisis clinic. Betsy felt hopeless about anything changing at home, though she expressed the wish that somehow things could get better. She particularly hated two situations: (1) her father and mother fighting about what she could and could not do and whom she could and could not see, and (2) her mother's and Alice's constant fighting about Alice's baby. If these situations at home did not change, she said she just wanted to die.

The Pages agreed to a contract for eight crisis counseling sessions that were to involve the entire family, including Alice. One of the sessions was with the parents, Alice, and Betsy only. Another session was with the parents, Betsy, the school guidance counselor, principal, and homeroom teacher. The following goals were established for the counseling sessions:

1. Improve communication among all members of the family and cut out the contradictory messages Betsy was receiving
2. Help family members detect signs of distress among themselves and learn to listen and support one another when troubled
3. Work out a mutually agreeable program of social outlets for Betsy
4. Work out a plan to divide the chores in a reasonable and consistent way among all family members

5. Arrive at an agreeable system of discipline that includes rewards and punishments appropriate to various behaviors
6. Help Alice make satisfying decisions regarding herself and her baby
7. Develop a plan to work cooperatively with Betsy's teachers and the guidance counselor to resolve Betsy's problems in school

Family members agreed on various tasks to achieve these goals. For example, Donald and Ann would set aside some private time each day to discuss their problems and disagreements about discipline—out of the children's range of hearing. Betsy agreed to follow through on certain chores around the house. If she failed to do so, Ann agreed not to pick up after her and to discuss disciplinary measures with Donald. Alice would seek individual counseling to assist her in making a decision about herself and her child.

Two of the counseling sessions were held in the home, which the counselor observed was quite crowded. One result of this meeting was that the family found ways of ensuring individual privacy in spite of cramped quarters.

The threats of Betsy's suicide attempt and school expulsion were crisis points that moved Donald and Ann to work on underlying problems in their marriage. These problems made parenthood more difficult than it might otherwise have been. After eight crisis counseling sessions, the Page family existence was much less disturbed but by no means tranquil. However, Betsy was no longer in danger of being expelled from school, and she at least preferred her home to a detention house. Donald and Ann Page agreed to marriage counseling for themselves after termination of the crisis counseling contract in an effort to make their future years as parents less burdensome. The attention directed to dealing with marriage and family problems may decrease the chance that Betsy will follow in her sister's footsteps and become pregnant out of wedlock (see Weingarten, 1994).

Intimate Relationships: Beginnings and Endings

Because intimacy is basic to the human condition, a break in intimate attachments can lead to crisis. In this section, the beginnings and endings of intimate relationships are discussed briefly as one of the major transition states.

Intimacy as a Basic Need

An intimate relationship refers to any close bond between two people in which there is affection, reciprocity, mutual trust, and a willingness to stand by each other in distress without expectation of reward. The emphasis in this definition is on psychological and social intimacy, although a sexual relationship may also exist. Whether one is married, single, or living with someone of the same or opposite sex, intimate relationships are essential to a happy, productive life. Sexual relationships alone do not necessarily imply intimacy as defined here (see the "Assessment Forms" example in Chapter 3).

Intimate relationships—the social and emotional bonds between people—constitute a significant portion of the fabric of society. Some of the more common of these relationships and intimacies are courtship, marriage, and deeply committed friendships outside marriage. Entering into such a relationship is a major event with important social and psychological ramifications. Common endings include divorce or widowhood. These endings are highly visible, but other, less official, disruptions of close bonds can be equally traumatic and often produce crisis (Doherty, 2006).

At the beginning and ending of an intimate relationship, the people involved undergo a change in role and status: from single to married, from spouse to divorce, from associate to friend, or from friend to forgotten one. When beginning a new intimate relationship, an old, secure role must be abandoned and replaced by a new and unfamiliar one. If the person changing roles is lacking in personal and social resources, taking on a new role may be the source of crisis. Often a role change results in feelings of loss, including mourning what one has given up. When the familiar role of lover, spouse, or trusted friend ends, a sense of insecurity may result. The person may experience crisis because a basic needed attachment is severed and may again face the challenge of role and status change. Transitions into and out of supportive intimate relationships are therefore among the more common occasions of crisis for many people, with adolescents being particularly vulnerable.

Besides couples who begin and end intimate relationships, couples who choose to remain childless also experience strain. Reasons for remaining childless include support for zero population growth, inability to cope with the responsibility of parenthood, or simply choosing a way other than child rearing to make a social contribution. Childless couples often meet with social disapproval from others who assume that the basic purpose of marriage is procreation. In effect, the message is this: You can have intimacy if you assume the social responsibility of producing and rearing children. The National Alliance for Optional Parenthood is working on gradually changing the public's attitude toward childless marriage.

Gay and lesbian couples face similar disapproval, despite the movement to ensure equal rights for gay people. Various countries, municipal and other jurisdictions have legalized gay marriage or civil unions and thereby have guaranteed gay couples the same employment insurance and other benefits traditionally limited to heterosexual couples. Gay men in particular often face additional threats to intimate attachments related to HIV-AIDS.

Excessive Dependence on Intimate Attachments

Because intimacy with others is an integral part of our lives, deep emotion and importance are attached to intimate relationships. Our feelings about these attachments affect our thoughts and behavior. For example, some people have unrealistic expectations of those they love and may behave in unusual ways when the bond is threatened or severed. In contrast, some people have such deep fear of possible rejection that they repeatedly resist offers of friendship, love, and intimacy. Crisis can occur at the beginning of attachments or when the intimate relationship is disrupted, as in divorce, death of a spouse, or betrayal by a friend.

Halpern (1982) discusses "addictions" to people—the excessive need to be attached to someone special—as well as the dynamics of ending such an addiction, which involve breaking away and appreciating the beauty and positive aspects of solitude. Remembering Halpern's maxims and those described in other self-help books can help buffer the crisis potential when breaking out of addictive, codependent, or other destructive relationships; for example,

1. You can live—and possibly live better—without the person to whom you are attached.
2. A mutual love relationship should help one feel better, not worse, about oneself.
3. Guilt is not reason enough to stay in a relationship.
4. Some people die of destructive relationships. Do you want to be one of them?
5. If someone says, "I'm not ready for a relationship," or "I'm not going to leave my spouse," or "I don't want to be tied down," believe it.
6. The pain of ending a relationship, like other crises, will not last forever. In fact, it will not last as long as the pain of sustaining it.
7. We are whole and valuable as individuals apart from particular relationships.
8. When we end a destructive relationship, we open our lives to new possibilities.

Singles, Isolation, and Divorce

Considered within the privacy, intimacy, and community dynamic (see Chapter 5), an excessive dependency on intimacy usually results in a neglect of basic needs for privacy and community. Conversely, attachments to people who are not good for us can be fostered by the threat of social isolation.

Social opportunities, especially for the single person who has moved recently to a new community, are often lacking. In many communities, social events are organized around couple relationships. Consequently, a single person may find it extremely difficult or impossible to feel comfortable in a tightly knit society that demands that people participate as couples. Many communities now have singles organizations, where single people of any age can make friends and enjoy a wide range of social activities. However, despite the existence of these clubs, it is still difficult for a single person to establish satisfying social relationships after changing location. Fortunately, the single state is now being accepted by many as a fulfilling lifestyle, making it easier for the single person to establish social contacts in a new community.

A person who is not single by choice and is unable to make friends easily is likely to be crisis prone. Psychotherapy may be indicated if the person is chronically unhappy or depressed about being single; if living alone, that person is also a greater risk for suicide. In general, the risks of isolation and crisis responses like suicide are greater when the person is single because of divorce, separation, or widowhood (see Buehlman, Gottman, & Katz, 1992).

Divorce is particularly hazardous when the burden of care and support of young children falls entirely on one parent and when older people divorce and their value system has no place for divorce. Until very recently, divorce in the latter category was rare. It is now increasing rapidly and is overwhelmingly initiated by men. The crisis potential of these nonmutual divorce actions is high because of (1) lack of expectation, (2) contradiction of deeply held values, or (3) widespread absence of social support structures for these special groups.

Consider the following example of what divorce can mean to an older person.

Case Example: Helen

Helen, age 64, was not allowed to continue working in the same government agency as her husband, Tom, when they married decades earlier. It was understood and accepted then that a husband should have the advantage of career development, and the wife should tend the home and children. Giving up her fledgling career as a civil servant was not a problem for Helen, as it was also understood and expected that marriage was for a lifetime and that her future economic support was secure. When Helen was 60, Tom, then age 64, left her for a woman 25 years his junior. Helen felt devastated and suicidal, saying over and over to her friends and two adult children that somehow it must have been her fault. She said repeatedly that Tom's death would have been preferable to a divorce.

Helen had a hard time acknowledging to anyone but her family and closest friends that she was divorced. She felt ashamed and frequently referred to herself as a widow. Helen could not understand how her daughter Caroline, also divorced, could be so apparently unruffled by the event. (Caroline had no children, worked as a writer, and preferred her single life.) Helen's only marketable job skill was babysitting. She was also a good gardener and cook but had no paid work experience in these fields. Besides being mateless at age 60, Helen barely escaped homelessness. By a stroke of luck, she obtained the marital home and was able to rent one room so she could pay taxes and utilities. There was no legal provision, however, for her to receive benefits from her husband's pension.

In spite of these hardships, Helen scraped by and came out of her depression after two years. She now takes advantage of senior citizen travel packages and attends adult education classes. She is attractive, charming, and dearly loved by her friends and family, and she acknowledges at times that she may be better off without Tom in spite of occasional loneliness. Two years before, Helen turned down the marriage proposal of a courtly but sickly older man. Although she was fond of this man, she resisted tying herself down to what she anticipated would eventually turn into a nursing role, especially after she had adjusted to her new freedom.

The harsh realities of the single life are contradicted by the stereotypes of swinging singles with a carefree existence. The single state without children does provide greater freedom to pursue one's career or engage in other activities, but the hazards of single parenthood speak for themselves. Every lifestyle has its advantages and trade-offs; for example, greater freedom and less responsibility may be balanced against greater insecurity in old age. Social research in the last century, beginning with Durkheim (1915), consistently reveals that marriage is in fact more advantageous and ego protective for men than it is for women (Martikainen & Valkonen, 1996). But women and men who have never married are better adjusted and are less at risk for suicide than those who have lost a spouse by any means. The hazards to individuals in these transition states would be modified by contemporary rites of passage, such as divorce ceremonies and acceptance into widows' clubs. Lacking such social supports can leave single people in a permanent liminal (transitional) state (van Gennep, 1909/1960), as they are never quite reincorporated into the community in their new role.

Middle Age

The term *middlescence* has been applied to those past adolescence but not yet in senescence. Stevenson (1977, p. 1) identifies two stages in this period of adult life: *middlescence I,* the core of the middle years between 30 and 50, and *middlescence II,* the new middle years, extending from 50 to 70 or 75. This division contrasts with the U.S. Census Bureau and popular opinion, which define middle age as the time between the ages of 45 and 64. Until very recently, little attention has been paid to the middle years except in the negative sense of stereotypes about being over the hill, sexually unattractive, unhappy, and depressed (Anderson & Stewart, 1994). People in midlife are literally caught in the middle: they have major responsibilities for the young and the old. They are the primary figures in society's major institutions: family, business, education, health and social service, religion, and politics. Besides doing most of the regular work of society, they are also its major researchers, with the understandable result that they have focused their research primarily on groups other than themselves.

Because of the relative lack of attention given to the midlife period, it is not surprising that many popular notions about midlife are the result of myth and folklore. Considering also the influence of medicalization, this major life passage is often recast as a "disease" to be "treated." The reality is that most people in midlife

- Are happier than they were when younger
- Lead highly productive and satisfying lives
- Have stable jobs and have met the major challenges of education and parenthood
- Are securely settled in a community in purchased rather than rented housing
- Enjoy a network of satisfying social relationships
- Have more disposable income and financial security than either the young or the old
- Enjoy good health and feel physically and mentally vigorous

In general, middle-agers today have more options than in earlier times because they are healthier. Census data reveal that North American and Western European women who are age 45 can expect to live 35 more years and men, 29 more years. Popular beliefs about middle age lag behind these statistical predictions.

Many, however, experience midlife as a threat. If a person at midlife is married and has children, familiar parenting roles may no longer fill one's day; spousal roles may need redefining. If not single by choice, a middle-ager may see the chances for marriage as decreasing. Men may be threatened by a diminished sex drive and leveling off of career advancement opportunities. Women in careers face the same threat; women without careers must meet the challenge of returning to school or resuming an interrupted career. The onset of menopause may threaten a woman's sense of feminine identity and attractiveness. Both men and women may perceive their lives at middle age as quickly slipping away before they achieve what they want for themselves and others.

The success of men and women in dealing with these midlife changes depends on

- Psychological health and general outlook on life
- Lifelong preparation for this stage of human development
- Social support and economic security

Some people are trapped into the false security of living as though life were an unending fountain of youth. Such people may avoid healthy preparation for the developmental tasks of midlife. Or if they are socially isolated and lack the financial assets necessary to pursue education and leisure activities, midlife can increase their crisis proneness. In spite of the advantages middle-aged people have, this developmental passage is as hazardous as other transitions, though it is not as hazardous as popular stereotypes would have us believe.

Among all the myths associated with middle age, none is more widespread than that of female menopause as a disease. Significant efforts to undo this stereotype include publications such as *Our Bodies, Ourselves* by the Boston Women's Health Book Collective (2005), which has been translated into many foreign languages. It is now widely accepted that menopause is a natural transition state, not a disease, in spite of bodily and mental changes such as hot flashes and a changing view of self past child-bearing age. Not only does menopause not require medical intervention for distress in the majority of cases, but estrogen replacement therapy, so popular in the past, has drastically declined in use due to various complications found from long-term studies. Menopause support groups now sometimes take the place of estrogen replacement therapy during this important transition state. In such groups, women receive factual information and support in coping with the physical, social, and psychological changes accompanying the cessation of menstruation.

Men undergoing the climacteric could benefit from similar support groups. Coming to terms with middle age could influence the behavior of men who cope with changes in themselves by establishing liaisons with younger women.

Old Age

It has been said that we are as old as we feel. Many of the issues discussed regarding middle age apply to old age: psychological outlook, social support, and economic security are critical factors affecting the crisis proneness of older people. The issues concerning retirement, noted in Chapter 8, also apply to many elderly people, and many are at special risk for crisis. For example, minority elders have lower incomes than white elders; three-fourths of elderly people below poverty level are female; older women earn much less than older men; low-income elders are much more likely to have limiting chronic conditions than are high-income elders. Among those wishing to remain in the workforce, some experience age discrimination (Yuan, 2007). With the federal cutbacks in domestic programs since 1981, greater burdens of caring for increasing numbers of elders fall on women (Doress & Siegal, 1987; Pillemer, Moen, Wetherington, & Glasgow, 2000; Sommers & Shields, 1987). Typically, those caring for impoverished and chronically ill women are underpaid, overworked, and overwhelmed.

The needs of elders are being addressed through the work of advocates such as senior legislators, the Gray Panthers, the Older Women's League, the American Association of Retired Persons, and increasing numbers of individuals. A recent emphasis on gerontological research and graduate training programs in universities also can contribute to the long-range welfare of the elderly. Many of the myths about old age are an extension of those about middle age: old age is a disease, and old people are uniformly needy, dependent, and asexual.

Attitudes toward Seniors

Despite increased political advocacy and advances in gerontological research, ageism and stereotypes about old people persist. Cultural values and the policies and practices flowing from them do not change rapidly. Old people are not as highly valued in mainstream North American society as they are, for example, in some Native communities and most non-Western societies. Recent social emphasis on the small nuclear family has virtually displaced the extended family arrangement in most Western societies. Grandparents, aunts, and uncles are rarely integrated into a family home. Most children, therefore, routinely have only two adults (their parents) as role models and supporters. In cases of death, desertion, or divorce, children are even more deprived of adult models. Fortunately, this is changing with attempts to get children and old people together—for example, through nursing home visits by groups of children and other intergenerational volunteer programs in schools. Health attitudes toward aging are also helped by books such as *The Art of Aging* (Nuland, 2007), which highlights the extraordinary rewards of growing old, especially by those with a keen sense of spirituality and life purpose, and who nurture personal relationships and accept the fact that some goals may remain unaccomplished due to physical or mental infirmity.

Older people experience even greater hardship than children do by their exclusion from the nuclear family. They feel—and often are—unwanted. Often they are treated as guests and have no significant role in matters of consequence in their children's families. When older people, because of health or other problems, do live with their grown children, additional tensions arise. The older person may become impatient and irritable with the normal behavior of the grandchildren. Space is sometimes insufficient to give everyone some privacy, or the old person may seem demanding and unreasonable (Killeen, 1990).

Services for Elderly People

Stress can be relieved and crisis situations prevented when special public health and social services are available to families caring for an older person. As a parallel to child care needs, many workers and advocacy groups for elders are demanding inclusion of elder care in benefit packages. Some programs combine child care and elder housing services under a single administrative umbrella, thus fostering important intergenerational contact. In some areas of North America, outreach workers from the public office for aging make regular contacts with older people in their homes. When housekeeping and other services are available, many outreach programs serve a pivotal role toward success in the prized goal of "aging in place" and can help to prevent crises and avoid the institutionalization that many dread.

Where public and affordable private services are lacking, the lives of many older people can take on a truly desperate character (see "Abuse of Older Persons" in Chapter 11). The situation is particularly acute for the older person living alone who (for physical or psychological reasons) is unable to get out. Senior citizen centers now exist in nearly every community. Every effort should be made to encourage older people to use these services. This may be the only real source for keeping active physically and for establishing and maintaining social contacts, and for preventing emotional, mental, and physical deterioration. Some people need help—money and transportation—to get to senior centers or counseling to convince them to use the services. Other services for seniors in many countries include volunteer programs, Lifeline (24-hour security service that alerts police and fire services in emergency situations); Meals on Wheels, which makes and delivers hot meals to the incapacitated; and similar public and private organizations available to the isolated and distressed.

Visiting nurses are another key resource for helping to keep frail elderly people in their homes. Often a nurse can detect stress or suicidal tendencies. Facing demographics of high percentages of older people compared with younger ones able to care for them, there are increasing *all-inclusive care* housing developments providing leveled services from independence to semi-independent, to assisted living, and nursing care—most including fitness centers and some including on-site comprehensive medical care. All agencies for the aging should maintain active contact with the local crisis center for consultation and direct assistance in acute crisis situations to prevent tragic deaths as illustrated in the following case example.

Case Example: Marjorie Jones and Daughter Rose

After the death of her elderly husband, Marjorie Jones was overwhelmed with caring for Rose, her mentally retarded adult daughter. She had resisted neighbors' offers of assistance. After a postal worker became concerned and alerted authorities, she and her daughter were found dead in their trash-filled home in a middle-class neighborhood. The neighbors anguished about what they might have done to avoid this tragedy.

This case suggests the need for more proactive social services following loss, as well as for people caring for any disabled person. It also illustrates the need for community education about how to offer neighborly help or make early referrals without invading the privacy of people who may feel too proud to ask for or receive assistance.

Case Example: Antone Carlton

Antone Carlton, age 77, lived with his wife, Marion, in a run-down section of a city. Antone was nearly blind and had had both legs amputated, due to complications of diabetes. Antone and Marion survived on a poverty-level income. Marion, age 68, was able to take care of Antone. Then she was hospitalized and died of complications following abdominal surgery. Antone was grief stricken. After Marion's death, a visiting nurse came regularly to give Antone his insulin injections and arrange for help with meals.

One day, Antone's house was broken into, and he was beaten and robbed of the few dollars he had. The nurse found Antone with minor physical injuries, but he was also depressed and suicidal. The local crisis center was called and an outreach visit made. The crisis outreach team assessed Antone as a very high risk for suicide. Antone, however, insisted on remaining in his own home. The services of a volunteer group for shut-ins were enlisted for Antone, especially to provide for an occasional visitor. Homemaker services were also arranged. A week later, Antone was beaten and robbed again, but he still refused to move out of his home. The nurse inquired about a senior citizen housing project for Antone. They refused to accept anyone as handicapped as Antone, although he did consider leaving if he could move to such a place. After a third robbery and beating a few weeks later, Antone agreed to move to a nursing home.

Institutional Placement of Elders

In Antone's case, a nursing home placement was a means of resolving a crisis with housing, health care, and physical safety. However, admission to a nursing home is itself an occasion for crisis for nearly every resident. And while some people do well in a nursing home, for many, institutionalization marks the beginning of a rapid decline in physical and emotional health. A new nursing home resident will invariably mourn the loss of his or her own home or apartment and whatever privacy it afforded, no matter how difficult the prior circumstances were. New residents resent their dependence on others, regardless of how serious their physical condition may be. These problems are less acute for those whose health status does not require such complete dependence. A person placed in a nursing home by family members may feel unloved and abandoned. Some families do abandon an old parent, often not by choice but because they cannot handle their own guilt feelings about placing the parent in a nursing home, no matter how necessary that placement might be.

The most stressful time for a nursing home resident is the first few weeks after admission. The new resident's problems are similar to those of people admitted to other institutions: hospitals, detention facilities, or group homes for adolescents. Crisis intervention at this time will prevent many more serious problems later, such as depression, suicidal tendencies, withdrawal, refusal to participate in activities, and an increase in physical complaints. Studies reveal that a significant number of elderly people simply give up after retirement or admission to a nursing home and die very soon thereafter (Richman, 1993). Hopelessness in these cases is the forerunner to death. Elderly people admitted to nursing homes should be routinely assessed for suicide risk. Besides having to deal with feelings of loss, resentment, and rejection, some people placed in nursing homes do not get a clear, honest statement from their family about the need for and nature of the placement. This contributes further to the person's denial of the need to be in the nursing home.

Alzheimer's Disease. The complexity of institutional placement and the family's pain and anxiety are exponentially increased in instances of dementia, particularly Alzheimer's disease (AD), especially when the common tendency toward denial is paramount in it early stages. Some refer to Alzheimer's Disease—the risk of which increases with age—as the cruelest of diseases because cognitive impairment ultimately destroys one's functioning as a whole human being. Losing one's ability for self-care and managing activities of daily living, while also aware in early stages that it is happening and is beyond one's control, can be a truly terrifying and sometimes life-threatening experience. As one highly educated psychologist tearfully said to her friends during diagnostic workups: "I feel like I'm losing my soul." At a later point when dealing with her anger at having an appointed guardian to manage her affairs, she said: "I want to kill him and then myself." While this woman's life was in danger from wandering off in front of running cars, and so forth, by this time in development of the disease, she in fact would have been incapable of the planning necessary for committing either murder or suicide.

The powerful emotional responses to the diagnosis of dementia, especially AD, include: the fear of stigma and devaluation; mourning associated with actual and anticipated losses; and a sense of increased vulnerability of self. Recent advances in diagnostic accuracy have resulted in earlier detection and prospects of slowing the process with medications. This has created a unique opportunity for (1) research to recruit people with dementia early in the course of the disease who are still capable of reflecting on and verbalizing their subjective experiences and service needs; (2) supportive interventions to maximize adaptive coping and quality of life outcomes; and (3) raising public awareness about the disease and the subjective experiences of people with dementia in an attempt to dispel myths and stigmas attached to the disease, and empathize with people affected by it. Ideally, emotional support and other interventions should begin in the diagnostic phase (Aminzadeh, et al., 2007).

Families of persons with AD should avail themselves of the many support and technical sources needed in some cases over years, along with a professional geriatric care manager—if available and affordable—that typically include legal and gerontological nursing specialists (Melillo & Houde, 2005). Not to do so adds to the growing evidence of increasing morbidity and mortality rates among family caretakers of a spouse with AD or other dementias (Liken, 2001).

Nursing staff who are sensitive to this crisis of admission to a nursing care facility—whether for AD or other reasons—are in a key position to prevent some negative outcomes. The newly admitted resident, along with the family, should be provided ample opportunity to express feelings associated with the event. Family members persuaded to be honest with the resident about the situation and not deny reality will feel less guilty and more able to maintain the social contact needed by the resident. Staff should actively reach out to family members, inviting them to participate in planning for their parent's or relative's needs in the nursing care facility. This will greatly relieve the stress experienced by an older person during the crisis of admission and adjustment. It will also reduce staff crises. When families are not included in the planning and have no opportunity to express their own feelings about the placement, they often handle their stress by blaming the nursing staff for poor care. This is a desperate means of managing their own guilt as well as the older person's complaints about the placement.

Besides the crisis of admission, other crises can be prevented when nursing care facilities have (1) activity programs in keeping with the age and sociocultural values of the residents, (2) programs involving the residents in outside community events, and (3) special family programs. Unfortunately, the quality of nursing care facilities frequently reflects a society's devaluation of older people. Funding is often inadequate, which prevents employment of sufficient professional staff.

Retirement and the realization of old age are times of stress but need not lead to crisis. Societal attitudes toward old age are changing, so that this stage of life is now anticipated by more and more people as another opportunity for human growth. In some societies, retired people are called on regularly to work several weeks a year when full-time workers go on vacation. There are many other opportunities in progressive societies for older people to remain active and involved. Many crises in the lives of elderly citizens can be avoided if they are accorded more honor and some postretirement responsibilities.

How we treat our elderly citizens can account for the marked difference in death rituals in traditional and modern urban societies: In modern societies, many people are dead *socially* (by forced retirement or familial rejection) long before physical death occurs. Society needs therefore, only dispose of the body; no rituals are needed to transfer social functions (Bloch, 1971; Goody 1962). This cross-cultural observation invites further consideration of death, the final passage.

Death

Death is the final stage of growth (Kübler-Ross, 1975). It marks the end of life and is the most powerful reminder we have that we have only one life to live and that to waste it would be folly.

Death has been a favorite topic of philosophers, poets, psychologists, physicians, and anthropologists for centuries. Volumes have been written by authors such as Aries (1974), Bertman (1991), Glaser and Strauss (1965), and Mitford (1963). There is even a science of *thanatology* (study of death and dying). Yet death is still a taboo topic for many people, which is unfortunate because it means the loss of death as a "friendly companion" to remind us that our lives are finite. Such denial is the root of the crisis situation that death becomes for many. Vast and important as the subject of death is, consideration of it here is limited to its crisis aspect for health and human service workers.

Attitudes toward Death

Death is not a crisis in itself, but becomes one for the dying person and survivors because of the widespread denial of death as the final stage of growth. As Tolstoy (1886/1960) wrote so eloquently in *The Death of Ivan Ilyich*, the real agony of death is the final realization that we have not really lived our life, the regret that we did not do what we wanted to do, that we did not realize in and for ourselves what we most dearly desired. This fact was borne out in research by Goodman (1981), who compared top performing artists' and scientists' attitudes toward death with a group who were not performing artists or scientists, but were similar in other respects. She found significant evidence that the performing artists and scientists were less fearful of death, more accepting of death, and much less inclined to want to return to earth after their death if they had a chance. Having led full and satisfying lives, they were able to anticipate their deaths with peace and acceptance. They had "won the race with death."

Noted writer and humorist Art Buchwald decided not to let death have the last word. He held court with friends and others and planned his funeral during his final months in hospice. There, in effect, death waited for him as he invited his children and various well-known people like Carly Simon and Tom Brokaw to write eulogies that he included in his last book, *Too Soon to*

Say Goodbye (2006). Here he treats death with his famed sense of humor and offers the living inspiring ways to face life's final loss.

The denial of death, so common in U.S. society, is a far greater enemy than death itself. It allows us to live our lives less fully than we might with an awareness and acceptance of death's inevitability. Through works like those of Buchwald, Sherwin Nuland, and many others, we have made progress in dealing with death openly. However, some health professionals and families still are reluctant to discuss the subject openly with a dying person (see Christakis & Asch, 1995; Ross, Fisher, & MacLean, 2000).

This is changing through the promotion of living wills, advance directives regarding the use of extraordinary treatment, and the public debate about physician-assisted suicide. For many, the assisted-suicide issue is primarily one of maintaining control over one's last days and not suffering unnecessary pain. More and more physicians and nurses are concerned about the influence of technology on the care of the dying and the undertreatment of pain (Solomon et al., 1993), and they avail themselves of courses on death and dying (see Bertman, 1991). Increased public awareness, a more realistic approach to death, and a loosening of denial's grip are now evident as people consider (especially through media attention) the prospect of dying in an institution attached to tubes and with no control over or conscious awareness of the process. As Dubler (1993) notes, the culture of medical institutions must change to accommodate the notion of negotiated death. The Patient Self-Determination Act passed by Congress in 1990 facilitated such change by requiring health care institutions to inform patients of their rights to make advance medical directives. The act encourages people to think about what treatment they wish if terminally ill. It also ensures compliance with their wishes for the kind of death they envision. See Haynor (1998) for detailed information on how health professionals can empower patients and assist them in decision making around advance directive requirements.

Many problems and crises associated with death, dying people, their families, and those who attend them in their last days might be avoided if death were faced more directly. Nurses, physicians, ministers, and family need to become open, communicative companions to those who are dying. Dying patients pay a high emotional price when physicians avoid talking openly with them about their condition. Yet, examples of avoidance cited in Kübler-Ross's classic book, *On Death and Dying* (1969), still occur unless the staff has had extensive sensitization to the needs of dying patients. *How We Die* (Nuland, 1994), written by a physician, is another attempt to break through denial by his blunt account of the physiological process of ending life.

The inability or refusal to come to terms with death is a critical issue for crisis workers in general, not just on behalf of the dying. Why? Because death, as suggested in earlier chapters, is a kind of prototype for *all* crisis experiences—that is, many crises arise directly from the death of a loved one, but all crises and life passages are like a "minideath" in the *loss experience* common to them all. The successful resolution of crisis, then, is crucially connected to the process of coming to terms with loss. Helping others through their losses and helping them find new roles, new relationships, and emotional healing depends heavily on whether we are comfortable with the topic of death and our own mortality. A healthy attitude toward our own death is our most powerful asset in assisting the dying through this final life passage and comforting their survivors.

In a culture without strong ritual and social support around dying, the major burden of positively dealing with death falls on individuals. Crisis workers and health professionals associated with death in their professions can make their work easier by attending courses on death and dying, which are widely offered on college campuses. Sensitization to death and its denial in modern society and to ethical issues such as assisted dying (de Vries, 1999) is also aided by reading literary and other works on the topic (e.g., Fried & Fried, 1980; Goodman, 1981; Goody, 1962; Tolstoy, 1886/1960). Intensive workshops focusing on our own denial of death through sensitizing exercises have provided the stimulus for some to become aware of the preciousness of every moment (Bertman, 1991). Coming to terms with our own death not only can change our life and eventual death but also lays the foundation for assisting others through death.

Helping a Dying Person

In U.S. and Canadian society, instead of dying in institutions such as hospitals, more people are dying in their own homes or in hospice care. Ted Rosenthal, a young poet dying of leukemia, struck out against the coldness and technology that awaited him along with death in a hospital. He tells his remarkable story of facing death and living fully until that time in *How Could I Not Be Among You?* (1973). On learning of his imminent death from leukemia, Rosenthal checked out of the hospital, moved to the country, and did the things he wanted to do before dying.

Dying people who are not able to die in self-chosen circumstances deserve to have the shock of their terminal illness tempered by those who attend them. Crisis intervention for a person who has learned of a diagnosis of fatal illness begins with awareness of one's own feelings about death. Next in the helping process is understanding what the dying person is going through. Family members and everyone working with the dying will recognize the phases of dying as described by Kübler-Ross (1969) from her interviews with over 200 dying patients.

Kübler-Ross identifies five stages of dying: denial, anger, bargaining, depression, and acceptance. All people do not necessarily experience all the stages, nor do these stages occur in a fixed, orderly sequence. Kübler-Ross's work is most useful for sensitizing health and hospice workers to some of the major issues and problems faced by the dying.

1. *Denial.* Typically, denial is expressed with, "No, not me," on becoming aware of a terminal illness. People deny even when they are told the facts explicitly. Denial is expressed by disbelief in X-ray or other reports, insistence on repeat examinations, or getting additional opinions from other doctors. Denial is the basis for the persistence of quack remedies. But denial may be necessary as a delaying mechanism, so the person can absorb the reality of having a terminal illness. During this phase, the person is withdrawn and often refuses to talk. Nurses, physicians, clergy, and social workers must wait through this phase and let the person know that they will still be available when he or she is finally ready to talk. Pressing a person to acknowledge and accept a bitter reality before the person is psychologically ready may reinforce the need for defensive denial. Self-help groups are a contemporary substitute for traditional rites of passage through this important transition state.

2. *Anger.* When denial finally gives way, it is often replaced by anger: "Why me?" This is more difficult for hospital staff and family to deal with than denial, as the person often expresses the anger by accusations against the people who are trying to help. The person becomes very demanding. No one can do anything right. The person is angry at those who can go on living. As frequent targets of anger, it is important for nurses to understand that the anger is really at the person's unchosen fate, not at the nurses. They must support the patient, not retaliate or withdraw, recognizing that the anger must be expressed and will eventually pass.

3. *Bargaining.* Faced with evidence that the illness is still there in spite of angry protests, the person in effect says, "Maybe if I ask nicely, I'll be heard." This is the stage of bargaining, which goes on mostly with God, even among those who do not believe in God. Bargaining usually consists of private promises: "I'll live a good life," or "I'll donate my life and my money to a great cause." During this phase, it is important to note any underlying feelings of guilt the person may have or any regrets that life has not been lived as idealized. The dying person needs someone who can listen to those expressions of regret.

4. *Depression.* During this stage of dying, people mourn the losses they have borne: losses of body image, income, people they loved, joy, or the role of wife, husband, lover, or parent. Finally, they begin the grief of separation from life itself. This is the time when another person's presence or touch of the hand means much more than words. Again, acceptance of one's own eventual death and the ability to be with a person in silence are the chief sources of helpfulness at this time.

5. *Acceptance.* This follows when anger and depression have been worked through. The dying person becomes weaker and may want to be left alone more. It is the final acceptance of the end, awaited quietly with a certain expectation. Again, quiet presence and communication of caring by a touch or a look are important at this time. The person needs to have the assurance that he or she will not be alone when dying and

that any wishes made, such as in advance directives, will be respected. Messages of caring will give such assurance.

Awareness and understanding of our own and of the dying person's feelings are the foundation of care during the crisis of terminal illness and death. Crisis intervention with the families of dying people will also be aided by such awareness and understanding. Because dying alone is a dying person's greatest fear, communication with families is essential. Families should not be excluded from this final phase of life by machines and procedures that unnecessarily prolong physical life beyond conscious life. Family members who help by their presence will very likely become more accepting of their own future deaths. Denial of death and death in isolation do nothing to foster growth.

The Hospice Movement

One of the most significant recent developments aiding the dying person is the hospice movement, founded by a physician, Cecily Saunders (1978), in London in 1967. Sylvia Lack (Lack & Buckingham, 1978), also a physician, extended the hospice concept to the United States. The hospice movement, now taking root worldwide (Saunders & Kastenbaum, 1997), grew out of awareness of the needs of the dying and concern that these needs could not be met adequately in hospitals engaged primarily with curing and acute-care procedures. A main focus of the hospice concept is the control of pain and the provision of surroundings that will enhance the possibility of dying as naturally as possible (Carson & Eisner, 1999). The growing emphasis on palliative-care research and service extends this concept. A groundbreaking work in Canada (Fisher, Ross, & MacLean, 2000) provides guidelines for comprehensive care at the end of life, which, if widely implemented, would go far in alleviating unnecessary pain and preventing emotional crisis during this final life stage (see also Field & Cassel, 1997).

Lack has identified ten components of hospice care (McCabe, 1982, p. 104):

1. Coordinated home care with inpatient beds under a central, autonomous hospice administration
2. Control of symptoms (physical, social, psychological, and spiritual)
3. Physician-directed services (due to the medical nature of symptoms)
4. Provision of care by an interdisciplinary team
5. Services available 24 hours a day, 7 days a week, with emphasis on availability of medical and nursing skills
6. Patient and family regarded as the unit of care
7. Provision for bereavement follow-up
8. Use of volunteers as an integral part of the interdisciplinary team
9. Structured personnel support and communication systems
10. Patients accepted into the program on the basis of health care needs rather than ability to pay

The hospice movement is a promising example of a new awareness of death in modern society and the importance of supporting the rights of the dying. As more people select hospice care, however, the need for respite for families and more hospital-based hospices will also increase (Wegman, 1987). Assistance for the dying person is supported by the "Dying Person's Bill of Rights," adopted by the General Assembly of the United Nations (1975, p. 99):

I have the right to be treated as a living human being until I die.

I have the right to maintain a sense of hopefulness however changing its focus may be.

I have the right to be cared for by those who can maintain a sense of hopefulness, however changing this might be.

I have the right to express my feelings and emotions about my approaching death in my own way.

I have the right to participate in decisions concerning my care.

I have the right to expect continuing medical and nursing attention even though "cure" goals must be changed to "comfort" goals.

I have the right not to die alone.

I have the right to be free from pain.

I have the right to have my questions answered honestly.

I have the right not to be deceived.

I have the right to have help from and for my family in accepting my death.

I have the right to die in peace and dignity.

I have the right to retain my individuality and not be judged for my decision, which may be contrary to beliefs of others.

I have the right to discuss and enlarge my religious and/or spiritual experiences, whatever these may mean to others.

I have the right to expect that the sanctity of the human body will be respected after death.

I have the right to be cared for by caring, sensitive, knowledgeable people who will attempt to understand my needs and will be able to gain some satisfaction in helping me face my death.

Throughout our lives, hazardous events and transitions can be occasions of crisis, growth, or deterioration. So in death, our last passage, we may experience our most acute agony or the final stage of growth. Whether or not we "win the race with death" depends on

- How we have lived
- What we believe about life and death
- The support of those close to us during our final life crisis

Summary and Discussion Questions

Life passages are mini-deaths. In each of these transition states, we leave something cherished and familiar for something unknown and threatening.

We must mourn what is lost in order to move without terror to whatever awaits us. Preparation for transitions—whether from one role to another, one stage of life to another, or from life to death—is helpful in averting acute emotional crisis during passage. To assist us in this all-important life task, we need contemporary ritual experts—that is, mature, caring people who are willing to support and protect us from tumultuous waves that might block our successful passage. These modern-day ritual experts are crisis counselors, members of self-help groups, pastors, health professionals, family, neighbors, and friends—people who care about people in crisis.

1. Consider the possible impact of a year of national/international volunteer service by young people (with vouchers for college) on such problems as drug abuse and violence in affluent societies.
2. From personal or professional experience identify an example of a young person in trouble or crisis and consider what family or group rituals might support young people through the turbulence of adolescence.
3. Since death is a fact of life, consider what can be learned from traditional societies and the role of rituals in one's final days.
4. What are the ethical issues to be considered in prolonging the life of a dying person with no hope of recovery by using advanced medical technology beyond the will of family members?

References

Affara, F. A. (2000). When tradition maims. *American Journal of Nursing, 100*(8), 52–70.

Aminzadeh, F., Byszewski, A., Molnar, F. J. and Eisner, M. (2007). Emotional impact of dementia diagnosis: Exploring persons with dementia and caregivers' perspectives. *Aging & Mental Health, 11*(3), 281–290.

Anderson, C. M., & Stewart, S. (1994). *Flying solo: Single women at midlife*. New York: Norton.

Arendell, T. (1995). *Fathers and divorce*. Thousand Oaks, CA: Sage.

Aries, P. (1974). *Western attitudes toward death from the Middle Ages to the present*. Baltimore, MD: Johns Hopkins University Press.

Bartholet, E. (1993). *Family bonds: Adoption and the politics of parenting*. Boston: Houghton Mifflin.

Bertman, S. L. (1991). *Facing death: Images, insights, and interventions*. Bristol, PA: Hemisphere.

Bloch, M. (1971). *Placing the dead*. London: Seminar Press.

Blumenfeld, W. J. (Ed.). (1992). *Homophobia: How we all pay the price*. Boston: Beacon Press.

Blumenfeld, W. J., & Lindop, L. (1994). *Family, schools, and students' resource guide*. Boston: Safe Schools Program for Gay and Lesbian Students, Massachusetts Department of Education.

Blumenfeld, W. J., & Raymond, D. (1993). *Looking at gay and lesbian life* (2nd ed.). Boston: Beacon Press.

Boddy, J. (1998). Violence embodied? Circumcision, gender politics, and cultural aesthetics. In R. E. Dobash & R. P. Dobash (Eds.), *Rethinking violence against women* (pp. 77–110). Thousand Oaks, CA: Sage.

Boston Women's Health Book Collective. (2005). *Our bodies, ourselves: A new edition for a new era* (8th ed.). New York: Simon & Schuster.

Brendtro, L. K., Brokenleg, M., & Van Bockern, S. (1990). *Reclaiming youth at risk: Our hope for the future.* Bloomington, IN: National Educational Service.

Buchwald, A. (2006). *Too Soon to Say Goodbye.* New York: Random House.

Buehlman, K. T., Gottman, J. M., & Katz, L. F. (1992). How a couple views their past predicts their future: Predicting divorce from an oral history interview. *Journal of Family Psychology, 5*(3/4), 295–318.

Cacace, M., & Williamson, E. (1996). Grieving the death of an adult child. *Journal of Gerontological Nursing, 22*(2), 16–22.

Caplan, G. (1964). *Principles of preventive psychiatry.* New York: Basic Books.

Carson, M., & Eisner, M. (1999). *Caregiving guide for seniors.* Ottawa: Algonquin.

Chapman, J. R., & Gates, M. (1977). *Women into wives: The legal and economic impact of marriage.* Thousand Oaks, CA: Sage.

Chesler, P. (1986). *Mothers on trial: The battle for children and custody.* Seattle: Seal Press.

Chodorow, N. (1978). *The reproduction of mothering.* Berkeley: University of California Press.

Christakis, N. A., & Asch, D. A. (1995). Physician characteristics associated with decisions to withdraw life support. *American Journal of Public Health, 85*(3), 367–372.

Corea, G. (1985). *The mother machine.* New York: HarperCollins.

Crary, D. (2002, November 25). Fathers' rights groups criticize court system. *Boston Globe*, p. A3.

Crittenden, A. (2001). *The price of motherhood: Why the most important job in the world is still the least valued.* New York: Metropolitan Books.

De Vries, B. (Ed.). (1999). *End of life issues: Interdisciplinary and multidimensional perspectives.* New York: Springer.

Dobash, R. P., & Dobash, R. E. (1979). *Violence against wives: A case against the patriarchy.* New York: Free Press.

Doherty, W. (March/April 2006) Couples on the brink. *Psychotherapy Networker*, 31–39, 70.

Doress, P. B., & Siegal, D. L. (1987). *Ourselves, growing older.* New York: Simon & Schuster.

Douglas, M. (1966). *Purity and danger.* London: Routledge.

Dubienski, G. (2008). Personal communication.

Dubler, N. N. (1993). Commentary: Balancing life and death—proceed with caution. *American Journal of Public Health, 83*(1), 23–25.

Durkheim, E. (1915). *Elementary forms of the religious life.* London: Hollen St. Press.

Erikson, E. (1963). *Childhood and society* (2nd ed.). New York: Norton.

Eyre, J., & Eyre, R. (1993). *Teaching your children values.* New York: Simon & Schuster.

Field, M. J., & Cassel, C. K. (Eds.). (1997). *Approaching death: Improving care at the end of life.* Washington, DC: National Academy Press.

Fisher, R., Ross, M. M., & MacLean, M. J. (2000). *A guide to end-of-life care for seniors.* Toronto and Ottawa: University of Toronto and University of Ottawa.

Flom, B. L., & Hansen, S. S. (2006). Just don't shut the door on me: Aspirations of adolescents in crisis. *Professional School Counseling, 10*(1), 88–91.

Freud, S. (1950). *Totem and taboo*. London: Routledge.

Fried, N. N., & Fried, M. H. (1980). *Transitions: Four rituals in eight cultures*. New York: Norton.

General Assembly of the United Nations. (1975). Dying person's bill of rights. *American Journal of Nursing, 75,* 99.

Glaser, B. G., & Strauss, A. (1965). *Awareness of dying*. Hawthorne, NY: Aldine de Gruyter.

Golan, N., (1981). *Passing through transitions*. New York: Free Press.

Goodman, L. M. (1981). *Death and the creative life*. New York: Springer.

Goody, J. (1962). *Death, property, and the ancestors*. London: Tavistock.

Halpern, H. (1982). *How to break your addiction to a person*. New York: McGraw-Hill.

Haynor, P. M. (1998). Meeting the challenge of advance directives. *American Journal of Nursing, 98*(3), 26–32.

Hoff, L. A., (1978). *The status of widows: Analysis of selected examples from Africa and India*. Unpublished master's dissertation, London School of Economics.

Hoff, L. A. (1990). *Battered women as survivors*. London: Routledge.

Hogberg, U., & Bergstrom, E. (2000). Suffocated prone: The iatrogenic tragedy of SIDS. *American Journal of Public Health, 90*(4), 527–531.

Hyman, J. W., & Rome, E. R. (1996). *Sacrificing our selves for love*. Freedom, CA: Crossing Press.

Hymowitz, K. S. (2006). *Marriage and caste in America*. Chicago: Ivan R. Dee.

Inch, S. (1984). *Birth rights*. New York: Pantheon Books.

Jordan, B. (1993). *Birth in four cultures* (4th ed.). Prospect Heights, IL: Waveland Press.

Killeen, M. (1990). The influence of stress and coping on family caregivers' perception of health. *International Journal of Aging and Human Development, 30*(3), 197–211.

Kimball, S. T. (1960). *Introduction: Rites of passage* (A. van Gennep, Trans.). Chicago: University of Chicago Press. (Original French edition published 1909.)

Krishnan, V. (1994). Attitudes toward surrogate motherhood in Canada. *Health Care for Women International, 15*(4), 333–358.

Kübler-Ross, E. (1969). *On death and dying*. New York: Macmillan.

Kübler-Ross, E. (1975). *Death, the final stage of growth*. Englewood Cliffs, NJ: Prentice Hall.

Lack, S., & Buckingham, R. W. (1978). *First American hospice*. New Haven, CT: Hospice.

LaFontaine, J. (1977). The power of rights. *Man, 12,* 421–437.

Leach, P. (1994). *What our society must do—and is not doing—for our children today*. New York: Knopf.

Lee, S. (2003). Effects of using a nursing crisis intervention program on psychosocial response and coping strategies of infertile women during in vitro fertilization. *Journal of Nursing Research, 11*(3), 197–207.

Leach, P. (1997). *Your baby and child: New visions for the '90s*. New York: Knopf.

Levinson, D. J., Darrow, C. N., Klein, E. N., Levinson, M. H., & McKee, B. (1978). *The seasons of a man's life*. New York: Knopf.

Liken, M. (2001). Caregivers in crisis. *Clinical Nursing Research, 10*(1), 52–68.

Liu, X., et al. (2000). Behavioral and emotional problems in Chinese children of divorced parents. *Journal of the American Academy of Child and Adolescent Psychiatry, 39*(7), 896–903.

Lopata, H. Z. (1995). *Current widowhood: Myths and realities*. Thousand Oaks, CA: Sage.

MacPherson, K. (1992). Cardiovascular disease prevention in women and noncontraceptive use of hormones: A feminist analysis. *Advances in Nursing Science, 14*(4), 34–49.

Mahoney, S. (May/June 2006). The secret lives of single women. *American Association of Retired Persons,* 50–74.

Maltas, C. (1992). Trouble in paradise: Marital crises of midlife. *Psychiatry, 55*(2), 122–131.

Martikainen, P., & Valkonen, T. (1996). Mortality after the death of a spouse: Rates and causes of death in a large Finnish cohort. *American Journal of Public Health, 86*(8), 1087–1093.

Masotti, P. J., Fick, R., Johnson-Masottia, A., & MacLeod, S. (2006). Healthy naturally occurring retirement communities: A low-cost approach to facilitating healthy aging. *American Journal of Public Health, 96*(7), 1164–1170.

Matthews, A. K., Hughes, T. L., Johnson, T., Razzano, L. A., & Cassidy, R. (2002). Prediction of depressive distress in a community sample of women: The role of sexual orientation. *American Journal of Public Health, 92*(7), 1131–1138.

McCabe, S. V. (1982). An overview of hospice care. *Cancer Nursing, 5,* 103–108.

McKenry, P. C., & Price, S. J. (Eds.). (2000). *Families and change: Coping with stressful events and transitions* (2nd ed.). Thousand Oaks, CA: Sage.

Melillo, K. D., & Honde, S. C. (Eds.) (2005). *Geropsychiatric and mental health nursing.* Sudbury, MA: Jones and Bartlett Publishers.

Minkler, M., & Fuller-Thomson, E. (1999). The health of grandparents raising grandchildren: Results of a national study. *American Journal of Public Health, 89*(9), 1384–1389.

Mitford, J. (1963). *The American way of death.* New York: Simon & Schuster.

Mitford, J. (1993). *The American way of birth.* New York: NAL/Dutton.

Moore, T. (1992). *Care of the soul: A guide for cultivating depth and sacredness in everyday life.* New York: Walker.

Ngugi, W. (1965). *The river between.* London: Heinemann.

Nuland, S. B. (2007). *The art of aging.* New York: Random House.

Patel, E. (2007). *Acts of faith: The story of an American Muslim, the struggle for the soul of a generation.* Boston: Beacon Press.

Pillemer, K., Moen, P., Wethington, E., & Glasgow, N. (Eds.). (2000). *Social integration in the second half of life.* Baltimore, MD: Johns Hopkins University Press.

Rathus, S. A. (2006). *Childhood voyages in development.* (2nd ed.). Belmont, CA: Thompson Learning.

Richman, J. (1993). *Preventing elderly suicide: Overcoming personal despair, professional indifference and social bias.* New York: Springer.

Rogers, K. N. (2004). A theoretical review of risk and protective factors related to post-divorce adjustment in young children. *Journal of Divorce and Remarriage, 40*(3–4), 135–147.

Rosenthal, T. (1973). *How could I not be among you?* New York: Braziller.

Ross, M. M., Fisher, R., & MacLean, M. J. (2000, June–August). Toward optimal care for seniors who are dying: An approach to care. *Mature Medicine Canada,* 127–130.

Ruddick, S. (1989). *Maternal thinking: Toward a politics of peace.* Boston: Beacon Press.

Sadker, M., & Sadker, D. (1994). *Failing at fairness: How America's schools cheat girls.* New York: Scribner.

Saunders, C. (1978). Hospice care. *American Journal of Medicine, 65,* 726–728.

Saunders, C., & Kastenbaum, R. (Eds.). (1997). *Hospice care on the international scene.* New York: Springer.

Sidel, R. (1996). *Women and children last: The plight of poor women in affluent America.* New York: Penguin Books.

Solomon, M. Z., O'Donnell, L., Jennings, B., Guilfoy, V., Wolf, S. M., Nolan, K., Jackson, B. A., Koch-Weser, D., & Donnelley, S. (1993). Decisions near the end of life: Professional views on life-sustaining treatments. *American Journal of Public Health, 83*(1), 14–23.

Sommers, T., & Shields, L. (1987). *Women take care: The consequences of caregiving in today's society.* Gainesville, FL: Triad.

Spar, D. (2006). *The baby business: How money, science, and politics drive the commerce of conception.* Boston: Harvard Business School Press.

Spencer, (1973). *Nomads in alliance.* Oxford, UK: Oxford University Press.

Stevenson, J. S. (1977). *Issues and crises during middlescence.* Englewood Cliffs, NJ: Appleton-Century-Crofts.

Straus, M. A., Gelles, R. J., & Steinmetz, S. K. (1980). *Behind closed doors: Violence in the American family.* New York: Anchor Books.

Surkan, P. J., Kawachi, I., Ryan, L. M., Berkman, L. F., Carvalho Vieira, L. M. C., & Peterson, K. E. (2008). Maternal depressive symptoms, parenting self-efficacy, and child growth. *American Journal of Public Health, 98*(1), 125–132.

The Technological Stork. New York: The National Film Board of Canada. (No date available.) URL: http://www.nfb.ca. 1-800-542-2164.

Thurer, S. L. (1994). *The myths of motherhood: How culture reinvents the good mother.* Boston: Houghton Mifflin.

Tolstoy, L. (1960). *The death of Ivan Ilyich.* New York: New American Library. (Original work published in 1886.)

U.S. Census Bureau. (2007). Facts for features: Fathers Day, June 17, 2007. Retrieved February 10, 2008 from http://www.census.gov/PressRelease/www/releases/archives/families_households/009842.html

van Dennys, A. (1960). *Rites of passage.* Chicago: University of Chicago Press. (Original French edition published in 1909.)

van Gool, C. H., Kempen, G. I. J. M., Bosma, H., van Boxtel, M. P. J., Jolles, J., & van Ejik, J. T. M. (2006). Associations between lifestyle and depressed mood: Longitudinal results from the Maastricht Aging Study. *American Journal of Public Health, 97*(5), 887–894.

Walker, A. (1992). *Possessing the secret of joy.* Orlando, FL: Harcourt Brace.

Walsh, F., & McGoldrick, M. (Eds.). (1991). *Living beyond loss: Death in the family.* New York: Norton.

Wegman, J. A. (1987). Hospice home death, hospital death, and coping abilities of widows. *Cancer Nursing, 10*(3), 148–155.

Weingarten, K. (1994). *The mother's voice: Strengthening intimacies in families.* Orlando, FL: Harcourt Brace.

West, C., & Hewlett, S. A. (1999). *The war against parents.* Boston: Houghton Mifflin.

Williams, W. L. (1986). *The spirit and the flesh: Sexual diversity in American Indian culture.* Boston: Beacon Press.

Williams, W. L. (1992). Benefits for nonhomophobic societies: An anthropological perspective. In W. J. Blumenfeld (Ed.), *Homophobia: How we all pay the price* (pp. 258–274). Boston: Beacon Press.

Wong, D. S. (1999, July 5). Single fathers embrace role, fight stereotype. *Boston Globe,* pp. A1, A16.

World Health Organization. (1994). *Maternal and child health and family planning: Traditional practices harmful to the health of women and children* (Resolution WHA 47). Geneva: World Health Assembly, 47th.

Yuan, A. S. V. (2007). Perceived age discrimination and mental health. *Social Forces Volume, 86*(1), 291–311.

Zelditch, M. (1968). Status, social. In D. L. Sills (Ed.), *International encyclopedia of the social sciences*. New York: Macmillan and Free Press.

See Online Resources for additional references.

CHAPTER 7

Threats to Health Status and Self-Image

Many have said that if their health is intact, they can endure almost anything else. This is because a change in health status is not only hazardous in itself and potentially life threatening, but poor health status leaves one more vulnerable than otherwise to hazardous events. To avoid a crisis state, all of us need to have

- A sense of physical and emotional well-being
- An image of self that flows from general well-being and acceptance of one's physical attributes
- Some control in everyday life functions and the activities of daily living

These aspects of life are acutely threatened by illness, accidents, surgery, physical or mental handicap, and the uncontrolled use of alcohol and other drugs. Several of our basic needs are in jeopardy when events that are hazardous to health occur. A full crisis experience can be avoided if the threatened person is supported by family, friends, and health workers and receives necessary treatment regardless of financial status. Self-defeating outcomes such as suicide, assault or homicide, mental illness, and depression can also be avoided if appropriate treatment and emotional support are available when threats to health status occur.

People in emotional crisis related to illness, injury, surgery, or handicap rarely come to the attention of crisis specialists or mental health workers in the acute crisis stage. Mental health workers often see people *after* a crisis episode, when they may have become dependent on alcohol or other drugs, lapsed into depression, or experienced other emotional disturbance. This pattern underscores the pivotal role of general health workers such as physicians and nurses in the crisis care process, especially at various entry points to the health care system (see Hoff & Morgan, in press). In addition, many frontline workers such as police, rescue teams, firefighters, and Travelers Aid caseworkers are the first to confront a person injured or in emotional shock from an accident, violent attack, or fire.

Centuries ago, Hippocrates said that it is more important to "know the man who has the disease than the disease the man has." More recent research, along with the human potential movement, documents the intrinsic relationship between mind, body, and spirit. The congressional document *Action for Mental Health* (Congressional Joint Commission on Mental Health and Illness, 1961) and federal legislation that led to pioneering efforts in the community mental health movement in the United States also documented the fact that many distressed people *first* visit physicians or clergy, *not* mental health professionals.

These data underscore a premise of this book, that the crisis response is a *normal*, not pathological, life experience. Yet crisis assessment and intervention in general health care practice are by no means routine. While many health and frontline workers are already doing crisis intervention, some may lack self-confidence because they have no formal training in the field (see Online Resources). They often need reinforcement and confirmation from crisis specialists for work they are doing with distressed people.

This chapter addresses the crisis care process as applied in *general* health care situations when a person is in a status change from health to illness or from physical intactness to handicap. It includes illustrations of how to synchronize rapid assessment and social support with appropriate use of psychotropic drugs for clients who present with high anxiety but who refuse a mental health referral. The strategies apply in doctors' offices; emergency, intensive care, and other hospital departments; primary care settings, and prenatal clinics—in virtually all health and human service settings, including long-term care facilities. The discussion here assumes the underpinnings of general assessment and intervention strategies and life-threatening situations addressed in other chapters, including the use of psychotropic drugs for suicidal persons (see Chapter 10).

Rescue Workers, Nurses, Physicians, and Social Workers in Acute-Care Settings

Crisis situations demanding response are as diverse as the people experiencing them. Health practitioners have numerous opportunities to assist people in crisis because of threats to health, life, and self-image from illness, accidents, and related problems. All human service workers have a responsibility to assist people in crisis, but health care personnel in emergency and acute-care settings are in a particularly strategic position to influence the outcome of high-risk crisis situations. The nature of emergency and acute-care settings, with a focus on lifesaving procedures, precludes the opportunity to assist a person to complete resolution of an emotional crisis originating from threats to health and life. If life is at stake, no one would place the expression of feelings, however intense these may be, before lifesaving measures.

Yet because of the tense atmosphere of emergency medical scenes, it is important to remember that emotional needs do not disappear when physical needs take on life-and-death importance. An appropriate attitude and a sensitivity to the emotional needs of victims and survivors must accompany necessary lifesaving procedures, and a team approach accomplishes this best; the strain on nurses, physicians, and emergency medical technicians would be enormous without teamwork. Staff burnout in these settings is often very high in any case, and the lack of teamwork and staff support, the inappropriate placement of personnel in high-risk work, or the lack of training in crisis intervention frequently contribute to such burnout (Fullerton, McCarroll, Ursano, & Wright, 1992; McCarroll, Ursano, Wright, & Fullerton, 1993; see also Online Resources). Not everyone is suited for crisis work, but those who are should not suffer burnout or develop callous attitudes toward people in life-threatening situations. Acute-care nurses, for example, need the time and opportunity to air their feelings about the person who is comatose for days from a drug overdose. When the patient comes through the critical stage and survival seems certain, many nurses find it difficult to communicate empathetically with such a person.

In cases of cardiac arrest at hospitals, teamwork combines emergency medical work with crisis intervention. Nurses have observed that the emergency code system is so effective that it often brings more staff to the scene than are needed; however, provision is not always made for attending to the emotional needs of anxious family members (Davidhizar & Kirk, 1993). In one hospital, the psychiatric nurses—"surplus" personnel—routinely designate themselves to attend to family members who may otherwise be ignored. Nurses and physicians can be routinely trained to assist in emotional crises as well as medical emergencies (Bertman, 1991).

In general, health care practitioners in primary care, emergency, and acute-care settings need to focus on five key aspects of the crisis care process (discussed in detail in Chapters 3 and 4):

1. Identification of persons at risk through routine inquiry on initial contact
2. Level I assessment (triage) for (a) physical and emotional trauma and (b) risk to life—self and other
3. Empathic, supportive response
4. Safety planning (if assessment reveals risk to life)
5. Linkage, effective referral for Level II assessment, and follow-up

These basics of crisis work in general medical settings are interrelated: the likelihood of a person accepting a referral for crisis counseling, physical refuge, Alcoholics Anonymous (AA), or other service following emergency medical treatment (such as after a suicide attempt, rape, battering, or crisis related to drinking) will often be influenced by the health care worker's attitude and recognition of the complexity of these situations. In short, health practitioners in emergency settings are not usually expected to assist people through *all* phases of crisis resolution. Effective crisis care, however, does require assessing the emotional aspects of events threatening health and life, offering support, and linking people to reliable sources for further assistance (see Chapter 4, George Sloan). In addition to such clinical skills, workers in emergency settings need an up-to-date resource file with procedures to ensure follow-up when referrals are made. Social workers usually coordinate such resources.

The challenge of combining emergency medical treatment and crisis intervention protocols is compounded by the misuse of emergency medical centers for routine prenatal care and common ailments that should be treated in physicians' offices or primary health care settings. On the assumption that health care is a right, not a privilege, and that primary care is less costly than treatment in tertiary settings, some services must be publicly supported (Feingold, 1994; Rachlis & Kushner, 1994).

Crisis Care in Primary Health Care Settings

Since the essential features of formal crisis intervention have not changed much since the era when it was deemed a mere Band-Aid, we have a paradoxical situation. On the one hand, mental health care and crisis intervention are being increasingly cited in health reform policy statements (for example, Fiedler & Wight, 1989). On the other hand, a mind–body split is still evident as many general health practitioners hesitate to deal with emotional issues, citing either discomfort with them or lack of time. Understandably, most nonpsychiatric physicians and nurses do not think of themselves as psychotherapists, yet the psychosocial facet of treatment and care is a given whether the primary health problem is physical or emotional. And therein may lie insight into the paradox. As already discussed, although crisis intervention shares certain techniques with psychotherapy and may have *psychotherapeutic* outcomes if aptly applied, it is not psychotherapy. The social construction of crisis intervention as therapy within a decade of having discounted it as a mere Band-Aid may partially explain the continued reluctance of general health practitioners to incorporate the model into routine health care practice. The medicalization of crisis intervention is one facet of the tradition, especially in North America, where equating "health" care with "medical" care is common (Rachlis & Kushner, 1994; Smith, 1994). There is a need to reclaim the primary prevention model espoused by Caplan (1964) and recast crisis intervention within the public health model, rather than the biomedical model (Feingold, 1994; Navarro, 1994).

The increasing emphasis on primary care and concerns about the escalation of health care costs underscore the inclusion of crisis intervention as an essential element of comprehensive health care. As this book's Crisis Paradigm illustrates, prevention (including through crisis intervention) is less costly than treatment, especially in residential facilities. But crisis and quick-fix drug approaches must not be used *as financially expedient* substitutes for the longer-term care and rehabilitation that some problems require (Hoff, 1993; Johnson, 1990). In many of these primary care situations, crisis assessment, social support, and a referral to a peer support or self-help group, as discussed in Chapter 5, will do. For example, one woman said that her physical and emotional recovery after a mastectomy might have been much more precarious if a nurse had not comforted her when she broke down crying the first time she looked in the mirror. This was the beginning of her grief work around the loss of her breast. The surgical nurse, who was not a psychotherapist, simply understood and responded to the crisis dimensions of the woman's transition in health status and potentially her self-image. People with cancer or another life-threatening illness often say that the shared strength from a support group is what keeps them going as they struggle with the side effects of treatment and, for some, the reality of their final loss.

Hazards to Physical and Emotional Health

Physical illnesses or accidents are often the beginning of a series of problems for an individual as well as for that person's family. A potentially fatal illness can incite the same sense of dread and loss that death itself implies. Besides fear of death, a person's self-image is threatened by serious physical alteration resulting from surgical amputation of a limb, scars from an accident or extensive burns, or HIV/AIDS. If injury and illness result from a disaster of human origins, crisis resolution that avoids despair, revenge, or violence is especially challenging (Sugg & Inui, 1992). People with sexually transmitted diseases (STDs) are also particularly crisis prone; shame, revulsion, ignorance, and fear about such diseases can precipitate marriage breakups, suicidal tendencies, social isolation, self-loathing, and depression. And if a person realizes that an STD may be a forerunner of AIDS and was caused by having unprotected sex, the potential for crisis is increased. This is also true when HIV is transmitted through rape.

If an acutely or chronically ill person also needs hospital or nursing home care, the potential for other crises looms for the individual and his or her family, as discussed in Chapter 6. Hospitals and other institutions can be considered as subcultures in which the longest-term occupants—the staff—know the procedures and rules that prevent chaos and help them do their jobs. The sick person, however, especially one who has never been hospitalized, may experience culture shock, a condition that can occur when the comfort of familiar things is missing—not to mention the dangers of hospital-based infections, which cause thousands of deaths per year in the United States. Because the staff of these institutions become enculturated to their work environment, they may forget that a hospital admission is a temporary detour in the sick person's normal, everyday existence.

Without support in the "foreign" institutional environment, a person's usually successful response to life's ups and downs may be weakened—not unlike being stranded in a foreign country and not knowing the local language. In extreme cases, a person in culture shock feels too surprised and too numbed by a new culture's unfamiliarity to proceed with the successful management of everyday life tasks. Add the fear of the unknown regarding the outcome of treatments, and it is easy to understand why some patients lash out at staff in what may appear to be unreasonable outbursts or manifest other classic signs of culture shock or crisis. Even in transitional or long-term care placements, attention to these crisis manifestations, especially upon admission, can avoid much pain for both client and staff. Complicating this scenario is the potential crisis response of a patient who feels unready for discharge. In an era of escalating health care costs, timely discharge may seem cost-efficient. But premature discharge does not save money and may eventually cost more through readmission or result in family caretaker crisis or an extreme response such as suicide (Hoff, 1993).

In some instances, people's illnesses and the crisis of hospitalization are complicated further by negligence, mishandling, or unethical medical practice (see Brownlee, 2007). When this occurs, in addition to the original illness, the patient (or survivor) must contend with the personal damage inflicted by the people he or she trusted. Patients and families, however, are not the only ones in crisis around these issues. Nursing and medical colleagues face the moral dilemma of collusion in cover-up of negligence. If lawsuits occur, a new series of crises may unfold: joblessness, financial loss, and damage to professional status.

A related issue concerns unnecessary surgery. Although unnecessary elective surgery is under scrutiny for ethical and cost containment reasons, cosmetic surgery (mostly on women) is a booming business in affluent societies despite highly controversial results such as disfigurement and immune system breakdown. Without the profits to be made and the cultural component of women's general concern (and sometimes obsession) with body image, some of the crises related to these health issues might be avoided. Besides having the majority of unnecessary operations, women also receive 50% more prescription drugs than men (Hamilton, Jensvold, Rothblum, & Cole, 1995). This practice is especially significant in view of women's emotional and physical assets: on average, women in industrialized societies live seven years longer than men and are assumed worldwide to be the emotional and social caretakers of others. But many women have insufficient access to care. These facts are linked to the political economy of medicine and to cultural values about women that portray them as less valuable than men and when sick, in need of medical intervention and control (Becktell, 1994; Lugina, 1994).

The issue of surgery as a crisis point is particularly poignant in the case of mastectomy. Increasingly, women who have had mastectomies are referred to self-help groups such as Reach for Recovery, which offer emotional support during this crisis-prone period. However, in many communities, advocacy is needed to ensure such referrals. As the rates of breast cancer steadily grow and research begins to examine possible environmental causes, such as contamination of the food chain by pesticides, it is important to link this personal traumatic event with broader social concerns. Hoskins and Haber (2000) highlight the key role of nurses in education and counseling to reduce the risk of crisis for women and their families during the four phases of adjustment: diagnostic, postsurgical, adjuvant therapy, and ongoing recovery. For each phase, they suggest specific techniques for talking with patients and their partners—for example, for partners in the postsurgical phase: "Many partners of women who have had breast surgery are concerned, as are the women themselves, about how they'll respond to the loss. How have you felt about your partner's losing [part of] her breast?" (p. 29).

Men having surgery on sex organs also need supportive communication and accurate information. Although radical surgery (prostatectomy) has increased dramatically in recent years, there is little evidence that this surgery saves lives, whereas there is evidence of incontinence and impotence following the operation. Since prostate cancer is very slow-growing, most older men with the disease die of other causes. Nurses are in especially strategic positions to encourage male patients to communicate their feelings regarding this sensitive issue and to assist them in making informed decisions about surgery (see O'Rourke, 1999). The crisis for men having such surgery is heavily tinged by the threat to male potency and self-image that is signaled by cancer or surgery affecting sex organs. The hazards of such a diagnosis are compounded because males have been socialized not to cry or to express feelings readily. Together these factors become barriers to early diagnosis of prostate cancer, which is very important in improving survival rates. This is especially important for African American men who have the highest prostate cancer rates. Some physicians recommend that men begin routine screening for prostate cancer at age 50, although the issue is still controversial. Education, as well as communication with the man's sex partner, is important (Shipes & Lehr, 1982). Crisis prevention and intervention can also prevent later problems by timely support during medical and surgical care.

Physicians and advance practice nurses play a pivotal role in such crisis situations. Alex, for example, was upset with the news that his wife intended to divorce him. When his physician diagnosed his cancer of the testicle, he was even more distressed. The physician simply told him to check into the county hospital's psychiatric unit 30 miles away if he continued to feel upset. Instead Alex went home, told his wife what the physician had said, and shot himself in his front yard. Alex had been discussing the impending divorce with a crisis counselor who lived in Alex's community; the physician also practiced there. Even if the physician had no time to listen to Alex, he should have made a local referral. This case illustrates how local crisis specialty services may go unused if effective linkages with health and other frontline professionals are lacking.

If illness, surgery, and hospitalization are occasions of crisis for most adults, they are even more so for children and their parents (Kruger, 1992). Professionals with special training in child development now work in child life departments of many hospitals. They arrange preadmission tours and listen to children's questions and worries, such as the following:

- Sam, age four, has been told by his doctor that a hole will have to be made in his stomach to make him well again. Because the doctor neglected to mention that the hole will also be stitched up again, Sam worries that "the things inside me will fall out."

- Cindy, age nine, sees an intravenous bottle and tubes being wheeled to her bedside. She had once seen the same apparatus attached to her cousin Jeffrey, who later died. As the needle is being inserted, she wonders if she is as sick as Jeffrey was.
- Ken, a junior high school football player, is confined to a traction frame. Unable to dress or wash himself each morning, he suffers acute embarrassment in front of the nurses.
- Darryn, a 7-year-old African American child, with cerebral palsy and in state protective custody, was in a Boston hospital for leg surgery. In the foreign environment of the hospital, strung up in traction, immobile and in pain, he became hysterical when the surgical staff came in for rounds. The night before he had been watching the TV drama, *Roots*, and saw images of the Ku Klux Klan hanging blacks. The medical team, coming in en masse in white uniforms, caused him to panic.

If a child is going to the hospital, child life workers offer the following advice to parents:

1. Accept the fact of the hospitalization.
2. Be honest with your child.
3. Prepare yourself; for example, find out about procedures.
4. Prepare your child, for example, through preadmission get-acquainted tours.
5. Whenever possible, stay with your child.

In addition to these general health care situations, frontline health workers need to increase their vigilance on behalf of victims whose first contact after injury is a health care professional or emergency medical technician (see Chapter 3, triage; Hoff & Rosenbaum, 1994; U.S. Department of Health and Human Services, 1986).

Crisis Response of People in Health Status Transition

To better understand the responses of those who are in pain, are ill, or are hospitalized, some questions must be addressed, such as: How do sick and hospitalized people feel? How do they perceive their illness and its relationship to their beliefs and lifestyle? How do they behave in the "sick role"? The person whose physical integrity, self-image, and social freedom are threatened or actually damaged by these hazards to health shows many of the usual signs of a crisis state (see Chapter 3).

Because a majority of distressed people present first in health clinics, emergency departments, or offices of primary care providers, health care workers' pivotal role in detecting and preventing florid crises therefore cannot be overstated. There are parallels in general medical and psychosocial care. For the client presenting with acute pain, general physical discomfort, or impairment of normal functioning, common responses and questions include, "Tell me where it hurts. When did it begin? Have you taken any medication to relieve the pain? When are the symptoms most bothersome?" Since responses to illness vary cross-culturally, all health professionals should incorporate into medical intake protocols the kinds of questions suggested in Chapter 3, diversity perspectives. This can help to avoid an unfortunate "culture clash," such as occurred between Western physicians' diagnosis and the Hmong parents' beliefs about treatment of "epilepsy" (Fadiman, 1997).

Some clients present with symptoms suggesting *generalized anxiety disorder* (GAD)—a DSM-IV-TR (*Diagnostic and Statistical Manual of Mental Disorders*) Axis I diagnosis. This diagnosis requires three or more of the following symptoms: worry and apprehension, restlessness, easily fatigued, poor concentration, irritability and frustration, muscle tension, sleep disturbance, and mild to moderate transient physical symptoms (Hoff & Morgan, in press). Most of these symptoms overlap with the classical manifestations (biophysical, emotional, cognitive, behavioral) of a person in crisis (see Chapter 3). In addition, given the undisputed connections between stress, crisis, and illness (physical and mental), physicians and advanced practice nurses are challenged with differentiating acute crisis responses (that is, duration of a few days to six weeks) from the longer-standing GAD symptoms (that is, symptoms that are present more days than not over a six-month period). The importance of this differentiation underscores the key role of primary care providers in *preventing* the negative resolution of acute crisis in the form of emotional and mental illness without the hazard of a psychiatric diagnosis (see Chapter 3 regarding DSM-IV-TR diagnosis and managed care, and Link, Struening, Rahav, Phelan, & Nuttbrock, 1997).

In the holistic preventive approach presented in this book, primary care providers are therefore advised as follows regarding clients presenting with acute or chronic anxiety or physical complaints that diagnostic tests rule out as biologically based: instead of concluding with a psychiatric diagnosis of GAD in the biomedical paradigm, assume that the presenting symptoms designate *emotional pain* (from loss, threat, abuse, and so on) and proceed with comments such as, "You seem to be very upset. Can you tell me what's happening?" To the client asking for a tranquilizing prescription: "Of course I can write you a prescription; that will help you feel less anxious, but it won't really solve whatever is troubling you. I think I'd be helping you more if we talked a bit before giving you a tranquilizer to see if maybe a referral for counseling would be the most helpful."

This approach avoids pathologizing essentially *normal* responses to life's ups and downs and sometimes life-threatening events. As evidence of the biomedical versus public health emphasis in the United States, legislative language in states that require parity in health insurance defines all persons benefiting from mental health care as having a "disease." While recognizing that insurance reimbursement in the United States may require a DSM diagnosis, we should remember that the original intent of the DSM was for use by mental health professionals trained in psychopathology and its treatment. Current pressures on primary care providers to use it portends the need for advocacy and policy change that provides coverage for *preventive* psychosocial care, an essential component of which is crisis intervention in primary care settings. Let us review the classical crisis manifestations in reference to health status loss or threat of loss.

Biophysical Response. Besides enduring the pain and discomfort from the disease or injury itself, the person losing health and bodily integrity suffers many of the biophysical symptoms experienced after the loss of a loved one (see "Loss, Change, and Grief Work" in Chapter 4). For example, Parkes (1975) compares the "phantom limb" experience with the "phantom husband" of widows, noting the influence of connections between psychological factors and the nervous system.

Feelings. After an amputation or a diagnosis such as heart disease, AIDS, diabetes, or cancer, people respond with a variety of feelings:

- Shock and anger: "Why me?"
- Helplessness and hopelessness in regard to future normal functioning: "What's left for me now?"
- Shame about the obvious scar, handicap, or reduced physical ability and about dependence on others: "What will my husband think?"
- Anxiety about the welfare of spouse or children who depend on them: "How will they manage at home without me?"
- Sense of loss of bodily integrity and loss of goals the person hoped to achieve before the illness, accident, or trauma from abuse: "I don't think I'll ever feel right again."
- Doubt of acceptance by others: "No one will want to be around me this way."
- Fear of death, which may have been narrowly escaped in an accident or a violent attack by one's partner, or which now must be faced, in the case of cancer: "It was almost the end," or "This is the end."
- Fear that one's sex life is over after diagnosis with prostate cancer: "Am I condemned to lead a celibate life now?"

Thoughts and Perceptions. The fears raised by a serious illness, an accident, or a changed image from the trauma of abuse or from a surgical operation usually color the person's perception of the event itself—that is, understanding the event and how it will affect the future. For example, a young woman with diabetes assumed that she would be cut off from her cocktail party circuit, which she felt was necessary in her high executive position. She lacked knowledge about how social obligations might be synchronized with diabetes.

A person with heart disease may foresee spending the future as an invalid; the reality is that he or she must only change the manner and range of performance. The woman with a mastectomy may perceive that all men will reject her because of the bodily alteration; in reality only some men would do so. A woman who does not have a secure relationship with a man before a mastectomy may experience rejection; we can help such a woman consider the value of a relationship with a man who accepts her primarily for her body.

Women with stable relationships are seldom rejected by their husbands or lovers following a mastectomy.

Behavior. The behavior of people who are ill or suffering from the physical effects of an accident, surgery, or other trauma is altered by several factors. First, hospitalization enforces a routine of dependency, which may be necessary when people are weak, but the routine also keeps the hospital running according to established rules of hierarchy. This hierarchy has little or nothing to do with patient welfare. In fact, rigidity in the hierarchy often defeats the purpose for which hospitals exist—quality care of patients.

The environment of an intensive care unit—the tubes, lights, and electrical gadgets—is a constant reminder to the patient and family members of proximity to death (Kleeman, 1989). Furthermore, a patient's fears, anger, and lack of knowledge about illness, hospital routines, and expectations can elicit the worst behavior from a person who is otherwise cooperative and likable. The rules and regulations governing visitors to these settings present a further hazard to people already in a difficult situation.

Responses of Health Care Personnel. To understand and respond appropriately to the emotional, perceptual, and behavioral responses of people to illness, pain, and hospitalization, sensitivity to cultural differences is essential. For example, when the king of the gypsies was gravely ill in a Boston hospital, his clan came to hold vigil, but were disallowed by official hospital policy on visitors. Staff became alarmed by burgeoning numbers overwhelming physical space of the emergency room and called hospital security as tension rose to a threatening level. A staff member skilled in community relations brokered a compromise, with a few staying close to where the king was moved and the larger contingent moved outside where police assured entrance to the hospital and ambulance lanes. In Roma culture, constant vigil is kept by the sickbed of dying relatives.

The role of culture and value systems in the development of and response to crisis is pivotal in the face of illness, pain, and hospitalization. For example, Zborowski's classic study (1952) of Jewish, Italian, Irish, and other Americans revealed that (1) similar *reactions* to pain by different ethnocultural groups do not necessarily reflect similar *attitudes* to pain and (2) similar reactive patterns may have different functions in various cultures. For instance, typically, Jews' responses to pain elicit worry and concern, whereas Italians' elicit sympathy. Standard texts on health, illness, and healing in cross-cultural perspective offer further discussion of this topic (Conrad & Kern, 1990; Loustaunau & Sobo, 1997).

Nurses, physicians, social workers, chaplains, and others familiar with the common signs of patients in crisis can do much to relieve unnecessary stress and harmful outcomes of the illness and hospital experience. The patient in crisis needs an opportunity to

- Express the feelings related to his or her condition
- Gain an understanding of the illness, what it means in terms of one's values, what limitations it imposes, and what to expect in the future

- Have the staff understand his or her behavior, how it relates to feelings and perceptions of the illness, and how the behavior is related to the attitudes and behavior of the primary care provider or the entire hospital staff
- Communicate with family members, who should be viewed as the "collective patient" (Tolbert-Washington, 2001)

Case Example: Michael and Maria French

Michael French, age 53, had suffered from prostate cancer for several years. During the past year, he was forced to retire from his supervisory job in a factory. The cancer spread to his bladder and colon, causing continuous pain as well as urinary-control problems. Michael became very depressed and highly dependent on his wife, Maria, age 51. Stress for both of them increased. Michael began to suspect Maria of infidelity.

Maria was scheduled to go to the hospital for a hysterectomy for uterine fibroids but repeatedly cancelled the surgery. Her husband always protested her leaving, and at the last minute, she would cancel. Finally, her doctor pressed her to go through with the operation. Because Maria did not look sick to Michael, he felt she was abandoning him unnecessarily. Along with the ordinary fears of anyone facing a major operation, Maria was very worried about her husband's condition when she went to the hospital. However, she was too embarrassed by Michael's accusations of infidelity to discuss her fears with the nurses or with her doctor.

After going to the hospital, Maria received a message from her friend that her husband was threatening to kill her when she came home. He had dismissed their tenants without notice and changed the locks on the doors. The friend, who was afraid of Michael in this state, also called a local community health nurse who, in turn, called a nearby crisis clinic. The nurse had been making biweekly visits to supervise Michael's medication.

Crisis intervention took the following form:

1. The crisis counselor called Maria in the hospital to talk about her concerns and to determine whether Michael had any history of violence or whether guns were available. Michael's accusations of infidelity—which, according to Maria, were unfounded—may have been related to his concern about his forced dependency and to feelings of inadequacy, as he had cancer of the sex gland.
2. The crisis counselor called Michael and let him know that the counselor, Maria, and the neighbors were all concerned about him. Michael accepted an appointment for a home visit by the counselor within the next few hours. He expressed his fears that people were trying to take advantage of him during his wife's absence—his stated reason for dismissing the tenants and changing the locks. Further exploration revealed that he felt inadequate to handle household matters and the tenants' everyday requests, which Maria usually managed.

3. Michael agreed to the counselor's recommendation for a medical-psychiatric-neurological evaluation to determine whether his cancer might have spread to his brain. The counselor explained that brain tumors can contribute to acute emotional upsets or paranoid ideation such as Michael was experiencing.

4. As Michael had no independent means of visiting Maria in the hospital, the counselor arranged for such a visit. The counselor also scheduled a joint counseling session between Michael and Maria after they had had a chance to visit. This session revealed that Michael and Maria each had serious concerns about the welfare of the other. In their two telephone conversations during Maria's stay in the hospital, Michael and Maria had been unable to express their fears and concern. The joint counseling session was the highlight in successful resolution of their crisis. Michael's threat to kill Maria was a once-in-a-lifetime occurrence, triggered by his unexpressed anger at her for leaving him and for the troubles he had experienced during her absence.

5. When Maria returned from the hospital, a joint session was held at the French's home, which included the two of them, the community health nurse, and the friend who had made the original calls (see the social network sections in Chapter 5). This conference had several positive results: (a) it calmed the neighbor's fears for Michael; (b) it broadened everyone's understanding of the reactions people can have to the stress of illness and hospitalizations; (c) the community health nurse agreed to enlist further home health services to relieve Maria's increasingly demanding role of nurse to her husband (Halldorsdottir & Hamrin, 1997); and finally, (d) Michael and Maria agreed to several additional counseling sessions to explore ways in which Michael's excessive dependency on his wife could be reduced. Michael and Maria had never discussed openly the feelings they both had about Michael's progressive cancer (Dunn, 2005; Pruchno & Potashnik, 1989). In future sessions, the Frenches dealt with ways they could resume social contacts with their children and friends, whom they had cut off almost completely.

Preventive Intervention

This case history reveals at least three earlier points at which crisis intervention should have been available to the Frenches:

1. At the time Michael received his diagnosis of cancer
2. When Michael was forced to retire
3. Each time Maria delayed her operation, as well as at the point of Maria's hospitalization

In each of these instances, nurses and physicians were in key positions to help the Frenches through the hazardous events of Michael's illness and Maria's operation. Sessions with the crisis counselor confirmed the fact that the Frenches, like many other people facing illness, received little or no attention regarding the fears and social ramifications of their illnesses and hospitalization.

When Maria expressed to the community nurse her original concern about Michael's early retirement, the nurse might have extended her ten-minute visits to a half hour, thus allowing time for Maria to express her concerns. For example, the nurse might have said, "Maria, you seem really concerned about your husband being home all the time. Can we talk about what's bothering you?" Or the nurse might have made a mental health referral after observing Michael's increasing depression.

The gynecologist attending to Maria's health problems might have explored the reason for her repeated cancellations of the scheduled surgery, saying, "Mrs. French, you've cancelled the surgery appointment three times now. There must be some serious reason for this, as you know that the operation is necessary. Let's talk about what's at the bottom of this." Such a conversation might have led to a social service referral.

The nurse attending Maria before her operation, as well as the community health nurse visiting the home, might have picked up on Maria's concerns about the effect of her absence on Michael. Such a response requires listening skills and awareness of psychological cues given by people in distress.

The nurse might then explain the hospital resources, such as social services or pastoral care—ways of helping Maria explore the problem further.

Case Example: Interview with Maria

Hospital nurse: Mrs. French, you've been very quiet, and you seem tense. You said before that you're not particularly worried about the operation, but I wonder if something else is bothering you.

Maria: Well, I wish my husband were here, but I know he can't be.

Nurse: Can you tell me more about that?

Maria: He's got cancer and isn't supposed to drive. I hated leaving him by himself.

Nurse: How about talking with him by phone?

Maria: I've done that, but all we talk about is the weather and things that don't matter. I'm afraid if I tell him how worried I am about him, he'll think I'm putting him down.

Nurse: Mrs. French, I understand what you're saying. A lot of people feel that way. But you know there's really no substitute for telling people honestly how we feel, especially those close to us.

Maria: Maybe you're right. I could try but I'd want to be really careful about what I say. There's been a lot of tension between us lately.

Nurse: Why don't you start by letting him know that you wish he could be here with you and that you hope things are OK with him at home. (Pause) You said there's been a lot of tension. Do you have anyone you can talk to about the things that are bothering you?

Maria: No, not really.

Nurse: You must feel pretty alone. You know, we have counseling services here in the hospital that could be very useful for you and your husband. I could put you in touch with someone, if you like.

In this brief interaction about a hazardous event such as surgery, the nurse has (1) helped Maria express her fears openly, (2) conveyed her own understanding of Maria's fears, (3) helped Maria put her fears about not communicating with her husband in a more realistic perspective, (4) offered direct assistance in putting Maria in touch with the person most important to her at this time, and (5) made available the resources for obtaining counseling service if Maria so desires.

This type of intervention should be made available to everyone with a serious illness or who experiences the traumatic effects of an operation, burns, or an accident. Putting people in touch with self-help groups, as discussed in Chapter 5, is another important means of reducing the hazards of illness and hospitalization. Such groups exist for nearly every kind of illness or operation a person can have: heart disease, leukemia, diabetes, mastectomy, amputation, and others. Many hospitals also hold teaching and discussion groups among patients while they are still in the hospital. This is an excellent forum in which people can air their feelings with others who have similar problems, gain a better understanding of an illness or operation and how it will affect their lives, and establish contacts with people who may provide lasting social support in the future.

People with HIV/AIDS: Personal, Community, and Global Perspectives

Working with Ted changed my life. I'll never be the same.

Hospice volunteer

It's so humiliating [to be so dependent on people]. I think I'll kill myself.

Twenty-three-year-old man with Kaposi's sarcoma, dying of AIDS

The nurses really want to be here [a hospital AIDS unit in Boston]. Lance [who had no appetite] forced himself to eat one of the chocolate chip cookies I made because, 'You made it just for me.' I almost cried; there was such a bond there.

Psychiatric liaison nurse

I can't move my legs at night, but if I touch even one person, then maybe it will help them be good to my boy, who lost his mother to this horrible disease.

Woman dying of AIDS

These statements from people with acquired immunodeficiency syndrome (AIDS) and those who help them dramatize the *opportunity* and the *danger* of a crisis, which more than many others may symbolize a much larger crisis of the modern world—the persistent and growing inequalities that leave the poor, people of color, women, and culturally marginalized groups disproportionately at risk for AIDS. Of all health-related experiences and potential for crisis, HIV-AIDS is one of the greatest public health catastrophes of modern times, which has been compared to Europe's medieval Black Plague (Stall & Mills, 2006). AIDS is not only a crisis of global proportions, but also is one of the most illustrative of intersections between clinical and public health perspectives in crisis care and the Crisis Paradigm informing this book. It typifies life crises as a whole and cuts across the ramifications of crises already discussed: loss, grief, and mourning; suicide by despairing people with AIDS; antigay violence; social network support; family and community crises; status changes in health, residence, and occupation; and finally, life cycle transitions and death. Sadly, AIDS is a tragic example of how sociocultural risk factors—racism, sexism, poverty, and bias against marginalized groups—cut across populations in wealthy and poor countries. Not only for the individuals and their families confronting AIDS, but for all of us, perhaps no other crisis will present greater danger or opportunity for the human community.

After more than a quarter century of massive mobilization of human, medical, and economic resources, much progress has been made with prevention and antiretroviral therapy, but there are still multimillions infected and countless orphaned children—most in sub-Saharan Africa, Asia, and among the poor worldwide (Landers, 2006; Nyamukapa et al., 2008). The bereaved in South Africa, for example, confront additional stressors uncommon in wealthy countries, such as scarce mental health and social services, government indifference, and extreme hardships of daily living such as lack of food and clean water, inadequate housing, and widespread unemployment. It is self-evident then, that besides medical treatment and psychosocial support, helpers need to address socioeconomic needs as well (Demmer, 2007).

Infected persons in the United States, Canada, and Western Europe are living longer; the death toll from AIDS in these countries has declined dramatically for those treated early (the financially and racially advantaged), and for many of these, infection can be controlled as a chronic disease. The bulk of the transmission in poor countries is by heterosexual contact, with women bearing the brunt of responsibility for protected sex, stigma attached to infection (including shunning by the community), care of a couple's children or dead relatives' children, and the burden of her own illness. But as antiretroviral medications have become more available, life has improved somewhat even for people with HIV-AIDS in sub-Saharan African (Phaladze et al., 2005; Des Jarlass et al., 2006). And while there is progress with prevention, much more needs to be done (Auerbach & Coates, 2000). Despite the dire statistics, there appears to be a paradigm shift to the view that AIDS is not primarily a medical-scientific issue but rather an issue of *justice* and ethical responsibility (Stall & Mills, 2006).

In essence, AIDS is endemic, a view supported in mainstream analysis at international AIDS conferences. The late Jonathan Mann of the International AIDS Center at the Harvard School of Public Health (1993, p. 1379) was prophetic in his statement, which still expresses the dominant analysis of this global crisis:

The central insight gained from over a decade of global work against AIDS is that societal *discrimination* [emphasis added] is fundamentally linked with vulnerability to HIV. The spread of HIV in populations is strongly influenced by an identifiable societal risk factor: the scope, intensity, and nature of discrimination practiced within the particular society. The HIV pandemic flourishes where the individual's capacity to learn and to respond is constrained. Belonging to a discriminated-against, marginalized, or stigmatized group reduces personal capacity to learn and to respond.

Mann stressed that curtailment of AIDS is also in a nation's economic interest (given the cost of caretaking and loss of productive workers), though many now recognize the intrinsic connection between health status and human rights issues. So profound is the pandemic of AIDS that even groups upholding traditional sex roles and norms regarding men's sexual conduct are acknowledging the need for fundamental change on combined fronts: (1) individual responsibility in sexual behavior and (2) social, political, and economic measures directed to the global inequalities affecting the poor and women (predominantly people of color), who are most at risk of infection and its sequelae (Fuller, 1996).

Illustration of the Crisis Paradigm

These perspectives provide support for the overall message that AIDS as a crisis for individuals is intertwined with the sociocultural origins depicted in the Crisis Paradigm informing this book. Let us examine this crisis from the perspective of people with AIDS and those who help them, keeping in mind the link between their personal pain and the underlying social and cultural factors that leave them disempowered and vulnerable. (See standard texts for historical overview and medical and nursing facets, such as Shilts, 1987; Durham & Lashley, 2000; Barth, Pietrzak, & Ramler, 1993; Hughes, Martin, & Franks, 1987; Sande & Volberding, 1995).

Case Example: Daniel

Daniel is a 38-year-old bisexual man who has been diagnosed with AIDS and who has lived for 18 months in a hospice managed by a local AIDS Action Committee (AAC). Pneumocystis pneumonia was the occasion for Daniel's several hospitalizations. He is down from his usual 185 pounds to 130, has periodic bouts of nausea and diarrhea, and has some neurological involvement that affects his gait. Once a successful health care worker and artist, Daniel lost his human service job because of federal cuts in domestic programs and could not find another. Getting AIDS further reduced his employability. He is now without a paid job, receives Social Security disability payments, and is eligible for food stamps.

Daniel says, "When I left the hospital, I had no money, no job, no apartment. I'm still struggling with the VA [Veterans Administration] for the benefits coming to me. If it weren't for AAC, I would have been out on the street. With the trouble I've had getting care, especially an awful case worker, I got a dose of what the elderly and the homeless go through. You know, I say 'forget your cure.' What would I ever want to come back [from death] for? Homelessness? Poverty? I have no regrets. I used to be seen as a pillar of strength; then people saw me as sick and no longer there for them, but slowly they're coming back. So I don't have a regular job anymore, but now I'm a teacher and counselor [helping other people with AIDS], and I work three hours volunteering at a local men's shelter. I also do liaison work at the hospital where I was a patient. Yes, I get weak, but now I do what I can, when I can, and as much as I can. There's not the same pressure as before. As long as I don't set expectations, there's no disappointment."

Case Example: Sophia

Sophia, age 30, has a 4-year-old son whom she placed with relatives as an infant because she could not care for him properly as long as she was addicted to drugs. Although she had symptoms for about four years, Sophia was diagnosed with AIDS only two years ago. She suffers from night sweats, thrush, shingles, chronic fatigue, abscesses, a platelet disorder, and central nervous system involvement, including seizures and memory loss. Through her 12 years of addiction, Sophia worked as a waitress and a prostitute to support her drug habit. "It's hard to realize that all the things I dreamed about if I was drug free can't be now because of AIDS. I thought having a baby would help me get my act together. I was wrong, but I would never hurt my son. I don't take pride in too many things I've done, but I spared Mickey by putting him in a stable environment. I'm not sorry I had Mickey because he's what keeps me going now. If it weren't for him, I probably would have killed myself already. I'm not through doing what has to be done—helping other drug users and letting my son know me better. And I do a lot of talks for doctors and nurses about AIDS.

Mickey and I spend every weekend together. I'm making some videos for him, so he will remember who I was and how much I love him. He knows to say no to drugs. Behind every addict, you know, there is a child, a lover. It's people's responsibility to set aside their biases, to take care. I have my problems, but at least I can care for someone else's pain, maybe because I've been close to pain. Some say they should lock up prostitutes, but don't tell me it's my fault that a man rides around in his Mercedes-Benz looking for sex instead of being faithful to his wife. I have wonderful friends. When the memory problems get worse, I'll give one of them power of attorney because my family judges me very harshly—for my addiction, prostitution, and now AIDS, plus I'm a lesbian—and if I left it to them, they would put out all the people who care about me when I'm dying. None of my family come to see me when I'm in the hospital. It's sad. I've spent half my life finding myself, and now I'm going to die, but I have an opportunity to plan my time and get closure, and that's good."

Daniel and Sophia are at peace; indeed, talking and being with them is an inspiration.[1] Both are doing meaningful work. At his young age, Daniel feels he has accomplished much of his life's work, though he still wants to write his memoirs. Daniel does not seem to be afraid of death. When asked if he would commit suicide if his symptoms included a new crisis point, dementia, he said "No. It could be tough, though, because I've always been very

---

[1] Daniel and Sophia are now dead, but they live on because in spirit they are everyman and everywoman.

independent and self-sufficient. I had to fight like hell to get what I have now, but if it came to the point where I needed more care and they don't respond, well, I'm going anyway." As Daniel's neurological symptoms progressed, his struggle to remain at peace intensified. He also was stressed by the fact that some of his friends could not face the reality of his approaching death, but instead of expressing their pain and impending loss, they either avoided him or made fleeting visits, stating they "didn't have time" to talk. Daniel's occasional angry outbursts toward his friends may also be displacements of the anger he feels about dying, but that is difficult to express because it implies a contradiction to his "caretaker" and "nice guy" image of self. Sophia readily expresses her sadness and pain but says her work is not done yet, so she keeps going and no longer feels like killing herself.

How did Daniel and Sophia arrive at the peace and acceptance they experienced in spite of constant physical pain and the knowledge that they were dying? By what process did Daniel win his "fight like hell" to get where he is? How did Sophia come to manage her ultimate life crisis in a constructive manner and finally give up her addiction to drugs? The Crisis Paradigm illustrates the process of dealing with the crisis of AIDS and how people with AIDS can capitalize on the opportunity of this tragic unanticipated event to arrive at positive resolution and avoid the danger inherent in crisis. The following discussion elaborates on the paradigm, using the AIDS crisis experience and illustrations from the lives of Sophia and Daniel. It shows what people with AIDS have in common with others, such as victims of violence or man-made disaster, whose crises originate primarily from the sociocultural milieu.

Crisis Origins. A diagnosis of AIDS is an unanticipated, traumatic event of overwhelming proportions. Individuals, of course, can modify behaviors such as drug use or unprotected sex that place them at greater risk, especially if a person's cultural heritage is considered in prevention programs (Bayer, 1994; Hirsch et al., 2007; Singer, 1992; Smith, 2007). But without more preventive behaviors, discovery of a vaccine, and alleviating the endemic conditions of poverty, malnutrition, and the widening disparities between rich and poor nations, the global epidemic will claim still more lives. As in the case of other epidemics, history reveals that *public health* measures—not medicines—have had the greatest impact in saving and lengthening lives. Thus, even among groups in the wealthy United States, in the so-called outerclass, education in risk reduction behaviors must be combined with economic and other change; in other words, the intertwined origins of the problem must be addressed simultaneously.

Given the lack of a vaccine or cure for AIDS, only a few years ago, death was the almost certain prediction, and it still is for those uninsured or too poor to afford the expensive treatment and support services for living with AIDS—an increasingly reasonable option for people in wealthy countries. Progress in the United States and Canada with civil rights of the gay community has also alleviated the additional stress affecting sexual minority individuals who are not "out" or whose communities are unfriendly or openly hostile toward such groups. Figure 7.1, Box 1, depicts the intersecting origins of crisis for people with HIV-AIDS, which may apply to the diagnosis of any serious illness in which such factors as stigma (for example, STDs) or sociocultural disadvantage play a key role.

The events that often follow a diagnosis of AIDS—loss of job, home, friends, and sometimes family—are closely tied to sociocultural factors and differ from losses such as temporary homelessness due to a fire or the unexpected death of a loved one from an illness that is not stigmatized (Sontag, 1978). Certainly, individual behaviors are part of the picture, but inattention to family and cultural context will limit the success of individualistic approaches (Bayer, 1994)—a fact exacerbated for socially disadvantaged people (Mann, 1993).

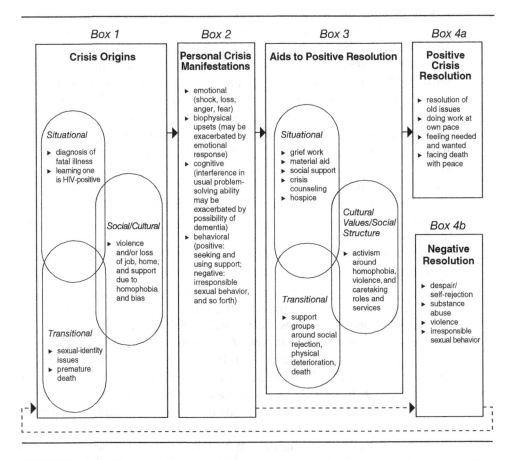

FIGURE 7.1 Crisis Paradigm. Crisis origins, manifestations, and outcomes and the respective functions of crisis care have interactional relationships. The intertwined circles represent the distinct yet interrelated origins of crisis and aids to positive resolution, even though personal manifestations are often similar. The arrows pointing from origins to positive resolution illustrate the *opportunity for growth and development* through crisis; the broken line at the bottom depicts the potential *danger of crisis* in the absence of appropriate aids. The loop between Box 4b and Box 1 denotes the *vulnerability* to future crisis episodes following negative resolution.

Personal Crisis Manifestations

The person afflicted with AIDS will experience most of the common emotional responses to a traumatic life event. Anger springs not simply from being stricken by the ultimate misfortune of facing an untimely death, but also from unfair or violent treatment by a society with limited tolerance for anyone who is different or is perceived as receiving deserved punishment for a deviant lifestyle. Anxiety is felt not only for one's own health and welfare but also for one's lover or previous partners whom one may have infected. *Survivor guilt*, as noted for some disaster survivors in Chapter 13, may also surface for those who have lost partners and loved ones to AIDS. Some may also feel guilt or shame over their gay lifestyle, having incorporated societal homophobia (Blumenfeld, 1992). Sophia says, for example, "I can't take pride in too many things I've done," but she does not wallow in guilt, nor is she ashamed of being a lesbian even though her family condemns her for it.

Denial of the medical facts and the need for behavioral change, especially if accompanied by free-floating anger at being infected, may result in irresponsible sexual behavior and the risk of infecting others. When Sophia learned that cleaning her needles with bleach or practicing safer sex could have prevented her infection, she expressed regrets that she may have infected others, but if she did, it was out of ignorance, not malice. In general, the most ethical approach is to inform a sex partner of one's infection status. Crisis counseling and support are clearly indicated for infected persons who act out their anger by placing others at risk. Sexual decision making is a complex process often not amenable to a simplistic "just say no" approach. Sadness over loss of health and impending death is compounded by fear of losing friends or lovers and the necessary support to face early death.

Anxiety's usual interference in cognitive functioning during crisis may be exacerbated with AIDS because of the fear of dementia. For example, normal forgetting may be interpreted as a first sign. AIDS dementia complex may sometimes be the only sign of AIDS. Sophia clearly planned for this possibility by arranging for a friend to act with power of attorney on her behalf. In the case of Charlie, another person dying with AIDS, flashes of awareness and clarity pierced his general comatose state, so that he could convey his wish not to be kept alive with heroic measures.

In general, the emotional and biophysical stress responses common during any life crisis are exaggerated here because of sociocultural facets of the crisis that are usually beyond the control of an individual to manage alone. In addition, the physical toll that the disease exacts usually includes drastic energy reduction, which in turn increases stress because of inability to engage in physical stress-reduction activities. Table 7.1 summarizes effective and ineffective coping with AIDS and forms the foundation for planning crisis care strategies with the affected person and his or her family, lover, and other network members.

Aids to Positive Crisis Resolution. In spite of Daniel's spirit of independence, he recognized his need for support and accepted it. He said that the

TABLE 7.1 Effective and Ineffective Crisis Coping by Person with AIDS and Family Members

Person in Crisis	Personal Crisis Manifestations	Crisis Coping	
		Ineffective	Effective
Person with AIDS	Emotional	Denial of medical facts and probability of death Repression Depression Hatred of self	Grief work Communication of feelings with caring persons
	Biophysical	Additional stress symptoms of emotional origin	Physical symptoms limited to opportunistic infections Resistance to additional stress symptoms
	Cognitive	Conviction that one is being punished for lifestyle or sexual orientation Failure to accept reality of illness	Recognition and acceptance of the reality and horror of the disease and all that it implies
	Behavioral	Irresponsible sexual behavior placing others at risk Violence Substance abuse	Safer sex practices Preventive health practices: diet, rest, exercise, relaxation Acceptance of love and necessary assistance Preparation for death
Family member of person with AIDS	Emotional	Denial of medical facts Inappropriate self-blame for child's sexual orientation	Grief work Unconditional acceptance regardless of sexual orientation or lifestyle
	Biophysical	Additional stress symptoms of emotional origin Burnout from failure to care for self	Resistance to additional stress symptoms and burnout through self-care and acceptance of support and respite
	Cognitive	Perception of AIDS as a "gay" disease Clinging to myths about contagion, and so forth	Recognition and acceptance of medical facts about AIDS
	Behavioral	Judgment and blaming of person with AIDS Avoidance and withholding of support and love	Expression of caring through communication, hugging, and so forth Material support and assistance with activities of daily living

hospital nurses were wonderful and that friends and his overall attitude helped the most. Daniel also said that he was greatly strengthened by helping his friends face death, an experience common among many people with cancer. One buddy of Daniel's with Boston's AAC said, "Sometimes I feel guilty because it seems like I get more than I give." He also said of standing by a man dying of AIDS, "I've never been so compelled by anything in my whole life. What a gift it was to be able to be with him. Nothing I've done since has been as honest."

What about Sophia? Precisely what did she have or receive that assisted her along the path of constructive coping with AIDS? Sophia tells of being hospitalized for abscesses, violating hospital rules by shooting up drugs on the ward, and leaving the hospital only to collapse shortly afterward. She knew that without treatment she would probably die, but having a drug fix at the time seemed more important. Later she checked back into the hospital and was confronted by the head nurse, who said, "You ruined my day. I can help you, but here are the rules. Are you willing to keep them?" Sophia said, "You know, that nurse did me a real favor. She was furious with me and I don't blame her, but instead of burying her anger, she confronted me and I could tell that she did it because she cared."

These responses highlight the point repeatedly made by people with AIDS and others facing a life-threatening illness: they are not victims and do not want to be treated as victims. For those of us less ready for death than Daniel was, it is important to remember that emotional healing from life's traumatic events requires the individual in crisis to make sense out of the experience and to process it within his or her personal meaning system. For example, when Daniel's immune system became weaker and weaker, he was advised to discontinue volunteer work at the men's shelter to protect himself from further infections. He then replaced his on-site volunteering with a monthly monetary donation out of his meager welfare funds.

Similarly, Sophia found meaning in her suffering and a reason to keep going for the sake of her child, as well as for the influence she had on the drug problem and the help she gave health professionals learning about AIDS. Her lifelong proximity to suffering and pain has apparently heightened her sensitivity to the needs and pain of others. Assistance to Daniel, Sophia, and many like them during crisis is available primarily through groups like the AAC in Boston. They provide housing and hospice care as well as neighborhood people who help as needed with mowing the lawn, keeping the sidewalks clear, and tending the garden. With this kind of assistance, people like Daniel and others in a hospice house are able to live a normal life in the community and face their impending deaths with greater comfort than institutional care would provide. This is the kind of care that should be available everywhere, but it is rare in poor countries where the toll is greatest.

The crisis care strategies that helped Daniel correspond to the interrelated origins of his crisis in situational, transitional, and sociocultural factors.

Together they led to growth and development; for example, he said that getting AIDS was the occasion for him to resolve with his ex-wife old issues around his bisexuality. He is no longer rushed and overworked. He felt needed and wanted by the homeless men and others with AIDS and had a healthy circle of friends, including a cadre of mental health professionals who enjoyed chatting with him. His adjustment to a healthy interdependence allowed him to maintain as much independence as possible, but he did not hesitate to ask for needed help. Daniel said that AIDS forced him to take a "closer, more intense look at life, so now I'm more ready to leave it."

For Sophia, in addition to her educational work with health professionals and the importance of being there for her son as long as possible, she said, "There's a reason for this. I went on the radio and made $53,000 for the AIDS Action Committee. It makes it meaningful. I feel robbed by this disease, but it's an opportunity to plan my time and get closure, and that's good."

Avoiding Negative Crisis Outcomes

For Jesse, one of Daniel's friends with AIDS, things did not go as well, at least temporarily. Jesse had Kaposi's sarcoma. His skin was dying; he was being eaten away. Jesse also had neurological involvement and some beginning symptoms of dementia. He found it humiliating to have people do things for him that he was used to doing for himself. Daniel helped out by putting reminders up around the house to compensate for Jesse's growing mental impairment. One day, Jesse declared to Daniel that he just could not go on any more: "I want to kill myself." Daniel's response was, "Jess, no matter how bad this hits us, let's face it together. I'm in pain, too. You know where I'm at. Let's share it. You're strong. Look at what you've done for others." Jesse did not commit suicide but died in the hospital a few weeks later.

As we examine the interchange between Daniel and Jesse, it is clear that Daniel did not simply talk Jesse out of suicide. First of all, the issue of suicide for people dying of AIDS raises all the ethical issues discussed in Chapter 9. In the case of AIDS, it might be easier for people to favor "rational suicide" than in other crisis situations. Many would argue therefore for the right of people dying with AIDS to commit suicide rather than suffer the horrors of physical and mental deterioration. However, as tragic as AIDS is, Daniel, Sophia, and thousands like them tell us that life can be meaningful and worthwhile in spite of great suffering. If those afflicted with AIDS experience insult added to injury through scorn and violence and then decide to commit suicide, those of us left can well ask whether we have in some sense "manipulated" such suicides (Battin, 1980), even those considered to be rational, through our failure to respond to them with the necessary, nonjudgmental care.

If a person with AIDS or another terminal illness requests assistance in committing suicide, the caretaker or friend must not only be familiar with ethical and legal issues regarding suicide but should consider hidden messages as well. One of those messages may be the inability or unwillingness to tolerate chronic severe pain. Most people dying of cancer do not wish to kill themselves, although some individual and couple suicides have occurred. Perhaps the greatest challenge for supporters of people with AIDS is to help create a milieu that will make it unnecessary for them to choose suicide. It is altogether remarkable and inexcusable that some people in excruciating pain in modern medical facilities still do not receive adequate medication and information about nonpharmacological treatment of chronic pain (Bral, 1998; Caudill, 1994; Fishbain, 1996). And in a global human rights perspective, it is morally reprehensible that for many people with AIDS, medications are either unavailable or unaffordable, even if health professionals are there to administer them. An appropriate environment and care, either at home or in a hospice house, would underscore the love and caring that helps dying people put their material affairs in order; say good-bye to lovers and family after reconciliation and, it is hoped, healing; and be recognized and valued for their place on this earth and thus be ready for life's final stage.

Women and Children with AIDS

Sophia and Daniel illustrate commonalities among people with AIDS: shock, anger, loss, and mourning a shortened life. But women, whether sick with AIDS or as caretakers, face several special issues. For example, because of cultural messages regarding body image, women may experience greater stress around appearance as they deteriorate physically. Women have the additional stress of worrying about becoming pregnant and possibly transmitting the virus to offspring. Fortunately, having her child infected with the AIDS virus was not one of Sophia's many stressors. Women who are HIV-positive generally are advised not to become pregnant. However, although there is support for a sperm-washing procedure for men who wish to have children, there is no corollary support for women with the same desire. Research and prevention trends have also slighted the fact of women's unequal power at personal, family, and social levels worldwide (Bianco, 1992). Women's continued inequality has major implications for risk not only of contracting AIDS from their male partners demanding sex, but also of violence if they urge the use of condoms.

Female prostitutes, perhaps more so than gay men, are scorned by most in society, as Sophia's case amply illustrates. It is therefore easy to scapegoat them for spreading AIDS. In Africa, where AIDS is distributed equally between women and men in the heterosexual population, female prostitutes in particular have been blamed for its transmission, whereas male promiscuity is rarely mentioned. Prostitutes who have AIDS or are HIV-positive already receive discriminatory treatment. Blaming them for AIDS also reveals the double standard regarding prostitution—arresting the women, but rarely their patrons—and the economic disadvantages of women that drive many of them into prostitution in the first place. Similar dynamics operate in regard to the traffic in sex—for example, women who are kidnapped, raped, and sent to places like Japan or Europe and forced into prostitution to service tourists (Barry, 1979). Women like this who get AIDS are in crisis not only because of a fatal illness but primarily because of the worldwide sexual and economic exploitation of women (Bianco, 1992). In other words, their crises around AIDS are primarily of social and cultural origin; essentially, AIDS is a human rights issue calling for structural change (Gollub, 1999).

A problem faced by those prostitutes and many other women who attempt to have safer sex by using condoms is that many men refuse to cooperate (Stevens & Galvao, 2007). When that happens, a woman is at a disadvantage not only because of inadequate female barrier methods but also because she may be physically abused if she asserts herself—a contemporary version of the traditional responsibility for contraception being borne primarily by women. This issue highlights the additional danger presented by AIDS if people ignore the imperative to change stereotypical sex roles and accept equal responsibility for safer sex (Pulerwitz et al., 2001; Wardlow, 2007; Gross, 2006).

If women with AIDS are also intravenous drug users (the largest group of U.S. women with AIDS) and fail to prevent pregnancy, their ability to take care of a child will be even more limited because the problems connected with drug use are added to the debilitating effects of AIDS. Sophia's foresight in this area (and access to resources not available to many poor women) moved her to place her child with a stable family when she was unable to overcome her addiction. In addition, a woman whose child has AIDS will probably feel guilty and angry whether she does or does not have AIDS herself. The millions of orphans in AIDS-devastated countries underscore the double burden of illness and caretaking as AIDS affects women.

Lesbian women, although in the lowest-risk group for AIDS, are nevertheless at risk for the same reasons other women are. Sophia, for example, traces her infection to dirty needles to support her drug habit, not to her lesbian status. Lesbian women are affected by the crisis in other ways as well. As significant others for gay men, some lesbians will suffer the loss of friendships through the deaths of these men. They are similarly affected by antigay discrimination and violence. Lesbians are also concerned if they are considering artificial or self-insemination. Finally, lesbians in the United States are among the majority of AIDS caretakers.

The tragedy of AIDS is even more poignant with respect to children. While an adult with AIDS can come to terms with the inevitability of death and work through the crisis, including its implications for previous and future sexual behavior, children with AIDS obviously cannot. This implies an additional challenge for people with AIDS to prevent pregnancy and for caretakers to treat and care for children with AIDS with extraordinary compassion. Attention should also be paid to the disenfranchised parents who brought them into the world.

A documentary film, *Today the Hawk Takes One Chick*, depicts the wrenching social consequences of the AIDS epidemic in Swaziland. In this small southern African country, urban dwellers have returned to their ancestral land to die, 85% of children have lost both parents, and *gogos* (grandmothers) and nurses wage a daily battle caring for and feeding children and preventing their society's near-total breakdown (Burr, 2008, p. D7). The granddaughter of one *gogo* has just had her second child and attributes her mother's death to "evil spirits." For AIDS prevention and for teens across cultures—some of whom treat their youthful sexuality with reckless abandon—this film might be a powerful addition to parental instruction and in all school-based health education classes.

Similarly poignant and tragic is the fear of HIV infection following rape. Although this double crisis also affects male victims of rape, the majority of rape victims are women. The emotional trauma for such victims is overwhelming, particularly in the face of continuing public attitudes of blaming the crime of rape on its victims and prosecuting very few assailants. If these attitudes prevail, rape victims may continue to blame themselves not only for the rape but also for contracting AIDS; in addition, they must face all that any other person with AIDS confronts in an untimely death.

The Worried Well, Prevention, and HIV Testing

The challenge in this area is to unbundle realistic concern about AIDS from anxiety about various other issues, such as sexual practice or sexual identity. Krieger (1988, pp. 263–264) suggests five steps in a counseling approach to persons with heightened anxiety about AIDS and fears about sexual transmission of AIDS: (1) obtain accurate information, (2) assess fear of prior exposure, (3) learn to protect oneself and others, (4) gather strong peer support, and (5) address related issues, such as homophobia, addictive attachments to dangerous sex, or guilt over sexual or drug use behavior. Everyone working with the worried well and people in high-risk groups for AIDS should be thoroughly familiar with the clues to suicide, risk assessment techniques, and strategies of suicide prevention discussed in Chapters 9 and 10. Of particular note here is the trend among a minority in the U.S. gay community toward laxity in HIV prevention measures since the decline in death rates due to drug therapy. The behavior of the few who intentionally seek HIV infection can best be interpreted as a cry for help, not unlike that of the self-destructive persons described in Chapter 9, who lack other ways of communicating their need for attention. In the gay community, the AIDS epidemic galvanized a sense of community and mutual assistance that was rare before the appearance of AIDS.

This leads to consideration of the controversial issue of testing for HIV infection. If testing were more definitive than it is, opinion might be less divided. Testing reveals infection with the virus but not whether a person has AIDS. Because it takes some time for antibodies to form, even if a person were exposed yesterday, tests might be negative today, thus potentially conveying false reassurance. In general, opinion is equally divided between the advantages and disadvantages of testing. Because a positive test can send psychologically unstable people into panic and possible suicide, testing should be carefully considered in each case. Counseling and ongoing support services for those who either are considering testing or have been tested are therefore essential. Such services are available through groups like the AAC and health centers. Self-testing kits are also available now, although their use is controversial because of concern about access to emotional support when receiving results.

Although the issue of testing will probably remain controversial as long as we lack a vaccine, testing is definitely indicated when pregnancy is being considered for one who has symptoms and a differential diagnosis is needed (Koo et al., 2006). Those who are psychologically healthy enough to deal with the unknown and who have greater tolerance for ambiguity may choose not to be tested. Conversely, people embarking on a new relationship should decide jointly to be tested before engaging in sex.

Caretakers of People with AIDS: Support and Self-Care

We have seen from our examples that Daniel and Sophia have come through the first crises of AIDS to the point of peace and acceptance of eventual death. They managed to do so with a combination of natural and formal crisis care strategies. Others with fewer resources, however, may not face life's final passage to death with peace, fulfillment, and the comfort of family and friends without extraordinary assistance from various caretakers. Caring for others whose needs are very great exacts serious emotional and physical health tolls on family and friends. In hospitals as well, women provide most of the care for the acutely ill and dying; in addition, they face the stress of overwork because of fiscal constraints and health reform measures that leave nurses and low-wage workers vulnerable because of their historical disempowerment within the system (Rachlis & Kushner, 1994). As so often in the past, so now with AIDS, the cost of caring is borne disproportionately by women, regardless of sexual orientation.

In caring for people with AIDS, extraordinary stressors must be dealt with: danger of needle stick infection for nurses and physicians; stigmatization stemming from association with devalued members of society (Goffman, 1963); confrontation with issues of sexual identity, one's own risk of AIDS, and death; assuming power-of-attorney roles; dealing with suicide issues; and finally, simple overload from association with the depths of pain and tragedy surrounding people with AIDS, their families, and lovers. Providing ongoing support for all AIDS crisis workers and family members helps to prevent burnout, compassion fatigue, and the eventual loss of needed staff. Among families as well, the ability to care for a dying loved one varies, requiring that professionals provide what families may not be able to. Caring for an AIDS patient includes the need for a comprehensive system of respite service for families offering care at home, in addition to skilled home nursing assistance (Cadell & Marshall, 2007). The challenge of facing great numbers of new cases worldwide will probably not be met if the general caretaking issue and health care costs are not addressed at a societal level.

Groups in the forefront of the AIDS crisis (SHANTI in San Francisco, Gay Men's Health Crisis in New York City, AIDS Action Committee in Boston) have recognized the stressors on caretakers and have provided support groups and staffing arrangements that offer respite from the stress of caring for dying people. Those working with persons with AIDS—formal and informal caretakers—cite the following factors as most significant for self-care and the prevention of burnout from the constant giving and confrontation with loss and death:

- Participating in support groups
- Being connected to a community of caring people
- Reading, taking time to smell the roses and watch the sunset
- Calling people "when I need them, when they need me"
- Accepting love on both sides unconditionally
- Realizing there is more to life than material riches

As one volunteer says, however, "Caretaking is very painful. Don't go into it if you don't want to grow. By seeing other people's pain, you grow yourself." A study by Cadell and Marshall (2007) revealed how caregiving became a part of the self as well as aspects of the partner. A crisis of meaning followed the loss of the person and relationship that had contributed significance and purpose to life. Fortunately, with public education, the attitudes of church representatives and others have changed toward compassion. For example, ecumenical healing services in various churches are becoming common. People who might otherwise despair under the weight of the AIDS crisis are finding new meaning and community support in these ritual gatherings—examples of contemporary rites of passage (see Figure 7.1, Box 3, lower circle).

Whereas some have the choice of volunteering to work directly with people with AIDS, most families and those in the health and social service professions do not. The global nature of the AIDS crisis and its embeddedness in social disadvantage mean that practically everyone is affected, at least indirectly, and the enormous demands of caretaking require that the burden be shared within the human community. This will probably not happen, however, without learning all we can about AIDS, without attention to caring for ourselves to prevent burnout, and without acceptance of the challenge to grow from humane involvement with the AIDS crisis. Concern about these needs of the caretakers of people with AIDS is expressed in the AAC requirement that volunteers attend support group meetings at least twice a month. Similar support services for caretakers should become a routine part of the total service program if we are to meet the challenge of providing all the care demanded by this ongoing crisis.

One mark of a humane and civilized society is its ability to care for the sick, the "different," and the suffering and dying in a compassionate manner. There is evidence of a paradigm shift that Bianco (1992, p. 61) suggested in her address to the international AIDS conference: "Despite repeated calls and protests by women all over the world, despite international conferences and the United Nations Convention on Elimination of All Forms of Discrimination Against Women, inequality is still ignored when political and social decisions are made. Will AIDS be the detonator needed to end this inequality?"

Jonathan Mann's visionary statement (1993, p. 1379) seems to have inspired the approach many now accept as the most promising: "We are all Berliners—because to the extent that societies can reduce discrimination, they will be able to uproot the HIV/AIDS pandemic, rather than addressing only its surface features. ... The world needs—and is now ready for—a far-reaching transformation of our approach to the global epidemic of AIDS."

Rarely has the world community had such an opportunity through the paradigmatic crisis of AIDS to mobilize together, combine efforts, and reconsider policies and the distribution of national and international resources. Yes, there is danger of compassion fatigue in the face of this crisis. But aside from the horrors of this crisis, AIDS can be viewed as a catalyst to address issues that we might otherwise continue to ignore, such as universal health care, widening inequality between rich and poor nations, the caretaking crisis, and advocacy of equal rights for all (see Farmer, 1999). As the AIDS crisis unfolds into the new millennium for the individuals and families affected around the world, our attempts to understand people with AIDS and communicate compassionately with them and their families can increase the opportunities for personal and community growth and forestall such dangers as suicide, violence, bigotry, and the creation of scapegoats for societal problems and global inequalities.

Crisis Intervention in Mental Institutions, Transitional Housing, and Hostels

As noted in Chapters 2 and 3, admission to a psychiatric facility is often a sign that crises have not been constructively resolved at various points along the way. Whenever possible, crisis hostels and other alternatives to psychiatric hospitalization should be used if a person cannot be helped in the home environment. Although mental hospitals are intended to relieve acute breakdowns or stress situations, they, like general hospitals, can create another kind of crisis.

Case Example: Angela

Angela, age 18, highly suicidal, upset, and dependent on her family, was admitted to the psychiatric service of a private hospital on the advice of a psychiatrist whom the mother had called a few hours earlier. Angela and her mother arrived at the hospital at 3:00 p.m. The admitting nurse stayed with them until 3:30 p.m., when she was scheduled to go off duty. Angela was just beginning to calm down but became very upset again when the nurse left. The nurses were unable to reach the physician to obtain an order for tranquilizing medication. Visiting hours ended meanwhile, and Angela's mother was asked to leave. At this point, Angela became even more upset. The nurse on the evening shift was unable to quiet or console her. By the time an order for tranquilizing medication arrived, Angela's behavior had become uncontrollable, and she was placed in a high-security room, as she became more suicidal. During the process of administering the medication, Angela screamed that she wanted to see her mother. After being told her mother was no longer in the unit, she became more upset; Angela struck and injured the attending nurse and was then placed in four-point restraints.

In this case, the rules and regulations of the hospital and the absence of an efficient call system to obtain doctor's orders for emergency medication clearly contributed to Angela's crisis state, which reached the point of panic. Richardson's study (1987) of inpatients' perceptions of the seclusion-room experience revealed that in 58% of the cases, patients experienced negative interaction with the staff before being secluded; 50% said that seclusion protected them; 58% perceived seclusion as a form of punishment, and 50% said that a different approach would have averted the need for seclusion.

The same principles of crisis intervention already discussed apply in mental institutions and residential settings. The worker should (1) help people express their feelings, (2) help them understand their situation and develop new ways of problem solving, and (3) help them reestablish themselves with family and community resources. The staff in residential facilities should examine their programs and routines to determine whether people become even more upset than they were originally as a result of the rules, thus defeating the purpose of the residential program (Hoff, 2000; Kavanagh, 1988).

For example, most psychiatric facilities routinely search patients on admission for dangerous articles, contraband, and anything that might be used as a weapon. Considering the number of dangerous people now admitted to psychiatric centers instead of prisons and the frequency of attacks on staff (see Chapter 12), such searches seem reasonable. They should not, however, be done without a full explanation to the patient as to the reasons. A person's psychotic condition does not preclude the prospect of experiencing culture shock or eliminate the need for respect and personal integrity, including for those committed involuntarily to a mental institution (Farberow, 1981).

The constraints of managed care, including sometimes the excessive use of chemical restraint as a substitute for longer psychotherapeutic approaches not covered by insurance, may account for the increased rates of violent outburst by psychiatric patients. Such system-produced crisis episodes are compounded if staff use rigid authoritarian approaches—in essence, engage in power struggles with persons already disempowered and vulnerable instead of skilled crisis prevention strategies that are primarily interpersonal. Once health care or other human service workers become enculturated into the minisocieties of bureaucratic agencies, they can easily forget that others may experience culture shock when entering them—not unlike the shock an anthropologist or tourist may feel when entering a foreign country.

Physical and Mental Handicap

Becoming a parent can be a crisis, even if everything occurs as expected. The birth of a handicapped child, however, presents a serious threat to the parents' image of themselves as successful parents. Frequently, the parent asks, "What did I do wrong? What have I done to deserve this?" Parents conclude mistakenly that something they did or failed to do is responsible for their child's handicapped condition.

Because of the strength of the parent–child bond, the child's physical or mental handicap is, in a sense, the parent's handicap as well. The intergenerational and family aspects of handicap suggest that initial and successive crisis points related to birth and the continued care of a handicapped person extend well beyond childhood. The degree of handicap and the level of parental expectation of a normal child are key factors influencing the likelihood of crisis for concerned parents. Handicaps vary greatly. Down syndrome is a mental deficiency with distinctive physical signs: slanting, deep-set eyes that are close together and often crossed; flattened nose; loose muscles; thick, stubby hands; and short stature. Hydrocephalus is characterized by an enlarged head containing excessive fluid. In addition to Down syndrome and hydrocephalus, the range of handicaps varies from gross deformity to minor physical deformity, to developmental disabilities that surface later, such as a learning disability or hypothyroidism.

Initial Crisis Point

In many cases, birth defects are obvious immediately after birth. Sometimes, however, the handicap is not noticed until the child is obviously lagging in normal development. Whenever the handicap becomes known to the parents, the usual response includes anger, disbelief, a sense of failure, numbness, fear for the child's welfare, guilt, and an acute sense of loss—loss of a normal child, loss of a sense of success as parents. The parents' initial reactions of disbelief and denial are sometimes compounded unnecessarily by medical personnel who withhold the truth from them. Seventy to 80% of developmentally disabled children also have physical disabilities, but parents should not be encouraged to believe that when these physical conditions are remedied, the mental condition will be cured as well.

Case Example: Anna

Edgar and Jean took their six-year-old girl, Anna, for kindergarten evaluation. They were told bluntly that she required special education. They were shocked by the news. No psychological or social services had been made available to these parents. Edgar and Jean had tried to ignore their daughter's obvious differences and had not questioned their physician, who was noncommittal. Finally, the grandparents and a sister convinced them to seek guidance from the local Association for Retarded Children.

A child's physical or mental handicap can be a source of crisis for a parent even before the child is born. When medical tests reveal a fetal handicap, parents face the decision of whether or not to abort the fetus. An infant born with devastating brain damage can now be kept alive through advanced medical technology. Like the spouse and children of an elderly parent who is dying, parents of a handicapped infant are caught in the middle of passionate public debates on life-and-death issues such as whether it is morally justifiable to sustain physical life by extraordinary means when brain death is certain (Lynn & Childress, 1991; Solomon et al., 1993). Parents of unborn children who are certain to die now face another moral dilemma—whether to carry the infant to term in order to donate healthy organs to other infants. Sensitive health care workers will make themselves available to parents who need to work through these dilemmas.

Successive Crisis Points

Parents of children who are developmentally disabled or otherwise handicapped can experience crisis at many different times, the most common of which are

- When the child is born
- When the child enters school and does not succeed in a normal classroom
- When the child develops behavior problems peculiar to the handicap
- When the child is ridiculed or sexually abused
- When the child becomes an adult and requires the same care as a child
- When the child becomes an intolerable burden and parents lack the resources to care for him or her
- When it is necessary to institutionalize the child
- When institutionalization is indicated and parents cannot go through with it out of misplaced guilt and a sense of total responsibility
- When the child is rejected by society and parents are reminded once again of their failure to perform as expected
- When parents decide on home-based care instead of the publicly funded institutional care that their child was entitled to, only to discover they are now ineligible for such funds as they plan for guardianship and the continued care of their adult child after their own deaths

The classic signs of crisis are easily identified in most parents of handicapped children.

1. *Feelings.* They deny their feelings and may displace their anger onto doctors, nurses, or each other. They feel helpless about what to do. Essentially, they feel they have lost a child as well as their role as successful parents.
2. *Thoughts.* Expectations for the child are often distorted. The parents' problem-solving ability is weakened; they lack a realistic perception of themselves as parents and sometimes expect the impossible. In short, they deny reality.

3. *Behavior.* Sometimes parental denial takes the form of refusing help. Sometimes help is not readily available, or parents are unable to seek out and use available help without active intervention from others.

The following case illustrates these signs of crisis and the manner in which a maternal health nurse successfully intervened.

Case Example: Mona Anderson

Mona Anderson, age 31, had been married for ten years when she finally became pregnant after many years of wanting a child. Her baby girl was born with Down syndrome. When Mona was tactfully informed of this by the physician and nurse in the presence of her husband, she became hysterical. Initially, she refused to look at the baby. Whenever the nurse attempted to talk with her about the baby's condition, she denied that she could give birth to a "defective child." The nurse allowed her this period of denial but gradually and consistently informed her of the reality of her child's condition. During this time, Mona's husband was also very supportive. Neither he nor the nurse insisted that Mona see the baby before she was ready.

When she felt ready and the nurse brought the baby in, Mona broke down, crying, "All I wanted was a normal baby. I didn't expect a genius." Mona continued to grieve over her loss of a normal child. Gradually, she was able to talk with the nurse about her hopes for her child, her sense of loss, and what she could and could not expect of her baby girl. Although the nurse could not answer all of Mona's or her husband's questions, she referred them to a children's institute for genetic counseling. They were also given the name and number of a self-help group of parents of children with Down syndrome.

The nurse was also helpful to other members of Mona's family who were drawn into the crisis. Mona's sister had a baby two months previously. She concluded, wrongly, that she could not come to visit Mona with her normal baby because such a visit would only remind Mona again of her "abnormal" baby. The nurse counseled the family members against staying away, as it would only support Mona's denial of the reality of her child's condition.

The nurse, in the course of her usual work in a maternity ward, practiced successful crisis intervention by supporting Mona through her denial and mourning periods, offering factual information about the reality of Down syndrome, and actively linking Mona to her family as well as to outside resources that could continue to help in the future. Because hospital stays after delivery now average only 24 to 48 hours, a visiting nurse would also be a key figure in a situation like Mona's. An important source of continued help for these families is the availability of respite care. Other crises associated with birth and parenthood were discussed in Chapter 6.

Besides crises around parenting a handicapped child, any person, child or adult, with a handicap is more vulnerable than others to additional stressors, trauma, and potential crises. For example, physical limitations may prevent one from protecting oneself in cases of domestic dispute, rape, or robbery;

lack of access to public transportation and buildings affects one's mobility, financial security, and other requisites for a healthy self-image. Another vulnerability of people with mental handicaps is that their grief following the loss of a loved one often goes unnoticed. Luchterhand and Murphy (1998) offer guidelines for families and service providers to assist this special population through the grieving process. The alienation and feelings of powerlessness associated with such stressors can also lead to unhealthy coping, such as excessive drinking. Recent federal legislation in the United States has facilitated addressing some of these issues that affect the health, crisis vulnerability, and general welfare of people with disabilities.

Crisis and Intersection with Chronic Health Problems

The abuse of alcohol, other drugs, or food is not a crisis in itself. A common view of these problems is that they are diseases; another view is that they are possible negative outcomes of crisis that leave one with greater vulnerability to future crisis episodes. In either case, the person who abuses substances is engaging in a chronic form of self-destructive behavior (see Chapter 9). The abuse of food by excess eating is sometimes accompanied by bulimia, compulsive gorging followed by self-induced vomiting to avoid weight gain. This is related to excess dieting, which may result in anorexia nervosa, a life-threatening condition of severe weight loss. Because eating disorders are most common among young women, they are increasingly linked to female identity issues and the pressure on young women to conform to cultural images of women's roles and body size. Crises arising from these chronic problems can bring about lasting change in the tendency to abuse food. It can be assumed that when people were in crisis at earlier points in their lives, they lacked the social support and personal strength to resolve the crisis in a more constructive manner. People abusing food, drugs, and alcohol commonly avoid getting help for their problem until another crisis occurs as a result of the addiction itself. Frequently, a crisis takes the form of a family fight, eviction from an apartment, loss of a job, or trouble with the law. Depending on the attitude and skill of helpers at such times, later crises can be the occasion of a turning point (see Chapter 5).

Case Example: Anita

Anita was abused physically and verbally by her husband for years. Her way of coping with the abuse was by overeating to the point of gaining over 100 pounds. When her husband threatened her life, she finally left the violent marriage and sought refuge in a shelter for abused women. This crisis was a turning point, leading Anita to seek help for her compulsive overeating in Overeaters Anonymous, a peer support group similar to Alcoholics Anonymous.

Chronic Self-Destructive Behavior and Crisis Intervention

The opportunity to change a self-destructive lifestyle is often missed. This is due in part to the lack of appropriate long-term treatment facilities and in part to the negative attitudes some hospital and clinic staff hold toward self-destructive people. Careful application of crisis intervention techniques can greatly reduce the sense of defeat experienced by client and staff alike. Crisis principles that apply especially to the person dependent on alcohol or other drugs include the following:

1. Crisis represents a turning point. In this case, a turning away from drugs or food as a means of coping with stress. For example, intravenous drug users are at high risk for AIDS and therefore are offered clean needles, in a nonjudgmental manner, to reduce the risk of transmitting HIV. Users might reach a turning point in their lives through this constructive interaction with health and social service workers.
2. In crisis intervention, we avoid doing things *for* rather than *with* people. Proposed solutions to problems are mutually agreed on by client and staff person. The substance-dependent person will often act helpless and try to get staff to do things for him or her unnecessarily, thus increasing dependency even more. While expressing concern, staff should avoid falling into this rescue trap (see Chapter 4, Figure 4.2, the Victim-Rescuer-Persecutor Triangle).
3. Basic social attachments that have been disrupted must be reinstated or a substitute found to help avoid further crises and more self-destructive behavior. Usually, people who abuse drugs, alcohol, and food are more isolated than most.
4. For all of these reasons, the principles and techniques of social network intervention (see Chapter 5) are particularly helpful in assisting the person in repeated crisis because of *chronic* underlying problems. Although other approaches often yield little progress, clinicians skilled in *social network techniques* point to impressive results.

Failure to observe these points leads to greater dependency of the client and increasing frustration of the staff. These crisis intervention techniques should be practiced in hospitals, transition facilities, primary care offices, and by police and rescue services—wherever the substance-dependent person is in crisis. The use of these techniques would be a first step for many persons toward a life free of these harmful addictions.

Case Example: Emma Jefferson

Emma Jefferson, age 42, had been drinking heavily for about 15 years. When she was 35, her husband divorced her after repeated pleading that she do something about her drinking problem. He also obtained custody of their two children. Emma was sufficiently shocked by this turn of events to give up drinking. She joined AA, remarried at age 37, and had another child at age 38. She had hurried into her second marriage, the chief motive being that she wanted another child.

A year later, Emma began drinking again and was threatened with divorce by her second husband. Emma made superficial attempts to stop drinking and began substituting an antianxiety prescription drug when she felt anxious or depressed. Her second husband divorced her six months later. This time, Emma retained custody of her child, though it was a close fight.

Emma took a job, was fired, went on welfare assistance, and began spending a lot of time in bars. On the urging of a friend, Emma finally decided to seek help for her alcohol and tranquilizer dependency. She gave up drinking but continued a heavy use of the antianxiety drug, sometimes taking as many as six a day. Emma was inconsistent in carrying out plans to reorganize her life to include less dependence on drugs and more constructive social outlets.

One day a neighbor reported to the child protection agency that she believed Emma was neglecting her child and should be investigated. The child protection worker learned that Emma indeed had few social contacts outside the bars and occasionally left her two-year-old child unattended. Emma was allowed to maintain temporary custody of her child with regular home visits by a caseworker to supervise her parenting activity. The threat of loss of her third child was apparently a sufficient crisis to serve as a turning point for Emma. The caseworker urged Emma to seek continued help with her problems from her counselor. Emma finally gave up her dependency on drugs, developed a more satisfying social life, and returned to work. She also made plans for another marriage, this time being more selective in her choice of a partner and less desperately dependent on a man for security.

The crisis of losing her children as a result of chronic dependence on alcohol and drugs led Emma to give up her self-destructive lifestyle. Two divorces resulting from her drug dependency were not enough to make her change. In fact, Emma did not seek available counseling on either of these occasions. She said she was ashamed to ask for help and in any case did not think she could afford it. Other people abusing drugs and alcohol seek help and make changes after serious financial or job failures, threats of imprisonment, or brushes with death, such as delirium tremens (DTs)—a sign of advanced alcoholism—bleeding ulcers, liver damage, or near fatal suicide attempts.

Emma's case illustrates the damaging effects of alcoholism on children. According to the National Institute on Alcoholism and Alcohol Abuse, millions of American minors living at home have at least one alcoholic parent. Besides the daily stresses and crises experienced by these children, many become alcohol dependent themselves. High school and college students in the United States engage in binge drinking at alarming rates. The increasing availability of crisis services and follow-up treatment programs should result in earlier choices toward growth rather than self-destruction for substance-dependent people. There are also increasing numbers of self-help groups for adult children of alcoholics that can be contacted through local AA branches.

Influence of Societal Attitudes and the Crisis in Psychiatry

The values of a given society naturally affect the use of drugs in that society. In the United States, many attitudes toward drug use are contradictory. For example, a drug such as marijuana is often regarded as dangerous, whereas some consider the excessive use of alcohol to be acceptable. A stable, law-abiding citizen can be censored or convicted for the use of marijuana, but if the same person chose to use alcohol, there would be no legal restrictions.

If alcohol is consumed privately with no damage to others, there are no sanctions against its use, even if excessive. Yet those who use alcohol chronically often suffer eventual liver or brain damage. A legal crisis can occur only for the user of alcohol who excessively indulges in public and then damages other people or their property, as in the case of reckless driving. For the drunken person's innocent victims, however, it is different. The U.S. society implicitly supports alcohol abuse as illustrated by the looseness of laws punishing drunken drivers. For the most part, alcoholism has been decriminalized, and the concept of alcoholism as a disease is now widely accepted. However, whether or not alcoholism is a disease, the combination of drinking and driving takes an enormous social toll. The loss and crises of drunk-driving victims and their families are the focus of a concerted effort to stop what has been called a national slaughter on U.S. highways resulting from the abuse of alcohol.

The user of other drugs can experience a crisis simply by the purchase or possession of a substance such as marijuana. In the United States, a few states have changed the drug possession laws for medicinal use, but the use of drugs other than alcohol is still predominantly a political issue. Little effort is made to distinguish between the *user* and the *abuser* of drugs. Many crises, such as arrest and imprisonment of people using illegal drugs, occur by design of the social system. The most egregious U.S. examples of reactionary, punitive, and racially biased approaches to the problem of illegal drug use are the mandatory minimum sentencing laws. The gross disparities in sentences for crack cocaine use (mostly by blacks) and the powdered version (mostly by whites) underscores the continued effects of racism in U.S. society. With good reason, the majority of federal and state judges and many others want to end these counterproductive drug sentencing laws, not just because they are patently unfair, but also because such sentencing is 7.5 times less effective than drug treatment in reducing cocaine consumption (Donnelly & Chacon, 2000; Jackson, 1997).

A public health perspective would focus first on prevention through early education, support of families, and collaborative parent–teacher efforts.[2] Unfortunately, the most serious drug abuse problems receive the least attention. The most widespread and dangerous abuse problems today are alcoholism

---

[2] The U.S. Department of Health and Human Services, the National PTA, and the Center for Substance Abuse Prevention publish an informative and highly practical resource for parents, grandparents, and other caregivers, *Keeping Youth Drug Free*. Contact state departments of public health, or write the National Clearinghouse for Alcohol and Drug Information, P.O. Box 2345, Rockville, Maryland 20847-2345. (Web site: http://ncadi. samhsa.gov)

and the overuse or misuse of prescribed drugs, both of which are legal. As physician Nahill (2000, p. C2) states, although drugs may possess lifesaving properties, the duality of nearly all drugs in use today means that "each pill we swallow carries with it certain risks that we downplay or ignore altogether."

Among the most dramatic examples of adverse consequences are the results of some debatable experimental studies of psychoactive drugs, which prompted the appointment of a presidential commission to study the issue nationally. The questionable research tactics included giving a drug to induce a psychotic episode, withdrawing medications, and obtaining debatable forms of consent. These practices were reported in a four-part investigative journalism piece, "Doing Harm: Research on the Mentally Ill" (Whitaker & Kong, 1998). The report cites the "lure of riches," in that the studies are heavily funded by the pharmaceutical industry. This factor, however, is situated in the larger crisis in American psychiatry, compounded by managed-care preference for psychotropic drug treatment over talking therapies (Dubovsky & Dubovsky, 2007; Luhrmann, 2000).

The story of Ruth illustrates further the complex interplay between acute crisis and chronic social and mental health problems: beatings as a child, feelings of rejection, a troubled marriage, suicide attempts, depression, death of a husband by suicide, and alcohol dependence (see "Stress, Resilience, Crisis, and Illness" in Chapter 2). It also highlights how crisis intervention can be the occasion for a turning point in a chronically troubled life.

Case Example: Ruth

I called the crisis center because I was afraid I'd attempt to take my life again. All my suicide attempts stemmed from feeling rejected, especially by my father. He picked on me and favored my older sister. I couldn't do anything right. Once I stole some money from my mother's purse, so I could buy a gift for my friend (now I think I was trying to buy friendship). My father beat me so that my hands were bleeding; then he made me show my hands to my mother. My mother cried when he beat me, but I guess she was afraid to stop him. When my father was dying, he asked me to forgive him.

I dropped out of school after tenth grade and got a job in a stockroom and later worked as a bookkeeper. I got married when I was 19. Our first five years were beautiful. We had three boys. I loved my husband very much and waited on him hand and foot. We bought a home, and he helped finish it. During the second five years, he started changing and got involved with another woman. My family and everyone knew, but I kept denying it. Then he left for about four months. I made a suicide attempt by turning on all the gas. I didn't really want to die; I just wanted him to stop seeing the other woman and come back to me. He came to pick me up at the hospital, and two weeks later I went over to his girlfriend's house and beat her up. I could have gotten in trouble with the law for that, but she didn't press charges.

After that, we tried to patch things up for about four months, but it didn't work. Then I started seeing other men. We had lots of arguments. I threatened divorce and he threatened to kill himself, but I didn't believe him.

One night, he sat in his car and wouldn't come in to go to bed when I asked him. At 7:00 a.m., my oldest son reported finding Dad dead in his car. I thought it was my fault. Even today, I still tend to blame myself. His parents also blamed me. My father was still alive then, and he and my mother stood by me. After my husband's death, I made another suicide attempt. I was in and out of the hospital several times, but nothing seemed to help in those days.

Three years after my first husband's death, I remarried. We argued and fought, and again I felt rejected. When I was afraid of taking an overdose of aspirin, I called the crisis center and was referred to the local crisis and counseling center near my home. I can't say enough good things about how my counselor, Jim, helped me. After all those years of being in and out of hospitals, having shock treatments, and making several suicide attempts, I'm so glad I finally found the help I needed long ago.

I don't think I'd ever attempt suicide again. I still struggle with the problem of feeling rejected, which I think is the worst thing in the world to go through. Even though I feel I'm on the horizon of something much better, I still have my down days and have to watch that I don't drink too much. But I don't think I'd ever let myself get as down and out as I've been in the past. I've seen that real help is available when I need it.

Summary and Discussion Questions

Health and assistance to people whose health is threatened constitute a major domain of social life. The loss or threat of losing life, limb, or healthy self-image are occasions of crisis for many. Most often, people who are thus threatened come to the attention of general health providers (for example, nurses and physicians) and frontline workers such as rescue teams, caseworkers, and others close to people's daily struggles. AIDS brings into perspective the intersection between personal health, the family, community, and global issues. It typifies life crises as a whole as it touches major themes of the crisis experience: loss, grief, suicide danger, violence, and the need for social support. AIDS reveals starkly the relationship between situational, transitional, and sociocultural origins of crisis as depicted in this book's Crisis Paradigm. The potential of workers in entry points to health and social service systems is enormous, as is the cost savings in human and financial terms when crisis assessment and intervention are routine parts of practice in these settings.

1. Given continuing health disparities based on race, class, and gender, what are the realistic prospects of progress toward ending the AIDS pandemic in the next quarter century?
2. Considering economic and time constraints on health providers, discuss the relevance of the crisis model in preventive mental health, and containment of healthcare costs.
3. In an example from personal or professional experience in which acute and chronic health problems intersect, consider what crisis intervention services might have prevented repeated crisis episodes or chronic mental health o substance abuse problems.

References

Auerbach, J. D., & Coates, T. J. (2000). HIV prevention research: Accomplishments and challenges for the third decade of AIDS. *American Journal of Public Health, 90*(7), 1029–1936.

Barry, K. (1979). *Female sexual slavery.* New York: Avon Books.

Barth, R. B., Pietrzak, J., & Ramler, M. (Eds.). (1993). *Families living with drugs and HIV: Intervention and treatment strategies.* New York: Guilford Press.

Battin, M. P. (1980). Manipulated suicide. In M. P. Battin & D. J. Mayo (Eds.), *Suicide: The philosophical issues* (pp. 169–182). New York: St. Martin's Press.

Bayer, R. (1994). AIDS prevention and cultural sensitivity: Are they compatible? *American Journal of Public Health, 84*(6), 895–898.

Becktell, P. J. (1994). Endemic stress: Environmental determinants of women's health in India. *Health Care for Women International, 15*(2), 111–122.

Bertman, S. L. (1991). *Facing death: Images, insights, and interventions.* Bristol, PA: Hemisphere.

Bianco, M. (1992). How HIV/AIDS changes development priorities. *Women's Health Journal/Isis International, 4,* 58–62.

Blumenfeld, W. J. (Ed.). (1992). *Homophobia: How we all pay the price.* Boston: Beacon Press.

Bral, E. E. (1998). Caring for adults with chronic cancer pain. *American Journal of Nursing, 98*(4), 27–33.

Brownlee, S. (2007). *Overtreated: Why too much medicine is making us sicker and poorer.* New York: Bloomsbury.

Burr, T. (2008, March 20). Small snapshot sheds light on Africa's AIDS crisis. *Boston Globe,* p. D7.

Cadell, S., & Marshall, S. (2007). The (re)construction of self after the death of a partner to HIV/AIDS. *Death Studies, 31*(6), 537–548.

Caplan, G. (1964). *Principles of preventive psychiatry.* New York: Basic Books.

Caudill, M. (1994). *Managing pain before it manages you.* New York: Guilford Press.

Congressional Joint Commission on Mental Health and Illness. (1961). *Action for mental health.* New York: Basic Books.

Conrad, P., & Kern, R. (Eds.). (1990). *The sociology of health and illness: Critical perspectives* (3rd ed.). New York: St. Martin's Press.

Davidhizar, R., & Kirk, B. (1993). Emergency room nurses: Helping families cope with sudden death. *Journal of Practical Nursing, 43*(2), 14–19.

Demmer, C. (2007). Responding to AIDS-related bereavement in the South African context. *Death Studies, 31*(9), 821–843.

Des Jarlais, D. C., Galea, S., Tracy, M., Tross, S., & Viahov, D. (2006). Stigmatization of newly emerging infectious diseases: AIDS and SARS. *American Journal of Public Health, 96*(3), 561–567.

Donnelly, J., & Chacon, R. (2000, February 21). The endless war: A deadly grip. *Boston Globe,* pp. Al, A8–A10.

Dubovsky, S. L., & Dubovsky, A. N. (2007). *Psychotropic drug prescriber's survival guide: Ethical mental health treatment in the age of Big Pharma.* New York: W. W. Norton.

Dunn, S. L. (2005). Hopelessness as a response to physical illness. *Journal of Nursing Scholarship, 37*(2), 148–154.

Durham, J. D., & Lashley, F. R. (2000). *The person with HIV/AIDS: Nursing perspectives* (3rd ed.). New York: Springer.

Fadiman, A. (1997). *The spirit catches you and you fall down.* New York: Farrer, Straus and Giroux.

Farberow, N. L. (1981). Suicide prevention in the hospital. *Hospital and Community Psychiatry, 32*(2), 99–104.

Farmer, P. (1999). Pathologies of power: Rethinking health and human rights. *American Journal of Public Health, 89*(10), 1486–1496.

Feingold, E. (1994). Health care reform—more than cost containment and universal access. *American Journal of Public Health, 84*(5), 727–728.

Fiedler, J. L., & Wight, J. B. (1989). *The medical offset effect and public health policy: Mental health industry in transition.* New York: Praeger.

Fishbain, D. A. (1996). Current research on chronic pain and suicide. *American Journal of Public Health, 86*(9), 1320–1321.

Fleming, P. L., Wortley, P. M., Karon, J. M., DeCock, K. M., & Janssen, R. S. (2000). Tracking the HIV epidemic: Current issues, future challenges. *American Journal of Public Health, 90*(7), 1037–1038.

Fuller, J. (1996). AIDS prevention: A challenge to the Catholic moral tradition. *America, 175*(7), 13–20.

Fullerton, C. S., McCarroll, J. E., Ursano, R. J., & Wright, K. M. (1992). Psychological responses of rescue workers: Fire fighters and trauma. *American Journal of Orthopsychiatry, 32*(3), 371–378.

Gillooly, Jane, director. *Today the Hawk Takes a Chick.* (A documentary film.)

Goffman, E. (1963). *Stigma.* Englewood Cliffs, NJ: Prentice Hall.

Gollub, E. L. (1999). Human rights is a U.S. problem, too: The case of women and HIV *American Journal of Public Health, 89*(10), 1479–1482.

Gross, M. (2006). Bad advice: How not to have sex in an epidemic [Editorial]. *American Journal of Public Health, 96*(6), 964–966.

Halldorsdottir, S., & Hamrin, E. (1997). Caring and uncaring encounters within nursing and health care: From the cancer patient's perspective. *Cancer Nursing, 20*(2), 120–128.

Hamilton, J. A., Jensvold, M. F., Rothblum, E. D., & Cole, E. (Eds.). (1995). *Psychopharmacology from a feminist perspective.* New York: Harrington Park Press.

Hirsch, J. S., Meneses, S., Thompson, B. et al. (2007). The inevitability of infidelity: Sexual reputation, social geographies, and marital HIV risk in rural Mexico. *American Journal of Public Health, 97*(6), 986–996.

Hoff, L. A. (1993). Review essay: Health policy and the plight of the mentally ill. *Psychiatry, 56*(4), 400–419.

Hoff, L. A. (2000). Crisis care. In B. Everett & R. Gallop *Linking childhood trauma and mental illness: Theory and practice for direct service practitioners* (pp. 227–251). Thousand Oaks: CA: Sage.

Hoff, L. A., & Morgan, V. (In press). *Psychiatric & mental health essentials in primary care.*

Hoff, L. A., & Rosenbaum, L. (1994). A victimization assessment tool: Instrument development and clinical implications. *Journal of Advanced Nursing, 20*(4), 627–634.

Hoskins, C. N., & Haber, J. (2000). Adjusting to breast cancer. *American Journal of Nursing, 100*(4), 26–32.

Hughes, A., Martin, J. P., & Franks, P. (1987). *AIDS home care and hospice manual.* San Francisco: AIDS Home Care and Hospice Program, Visiting Nurse Association of San Francisco.

Jackson, D. Z. (1997, May 14). Study strikes a blow against mandatory sentencing for drug crimes. *Boston Globe*, p. A15.

Johnson, A. B. (1990). *Out of bedlam: The truth about deinstitutionalization.* New York: Basic Books.

Kavanagh, K. J. (1988). The cost of caring: Nursing on a psychiatric intensive care unit. *Human Organization, 47*(3), 242–251.

Kleeman, K. M. (1989). Families in crisis due to multiple trauma. *Critical Care Nursing Clinks of North America, 1*(1), 23–31.

Koo, D. J., Begier, E. M., Henn, M. H., Sepkowitz, K. A., & Kellerman, S. E. (2006). HIV counseling and testing: Less targeting, more testing [Editorial]. *American Journal of Public Health, 96*(6), 962–963.

Krieger, I. (1988). An approach to coping with anxiety about AIDS. *Social Work, 33*(3), 263–264.

Kruger, S. (1992). Parents in crisis: Helping them cope with a seriously ill child. *Journal of Pediatric Nursing, 7*(2), 133–140.

Landers, S. (2006). Death and hope [Editorial]. *American Journal of Public Health, 96*(6), 958.

Link, B. G., Struening, E. L., Rahav, M., Phelan, J. C., & Nuttbrock, L. (1997). On stigma and its consequences: Evidence from a longitudinal study of men with dual diagnoses of mental illness and substance abuse. *Journal of Health and Social Behavior, 38,* 177–190.

Loustaunau, M. O., & Sobo, E. J. (1997). *The cultural context of health, illness, and medicine.* New York: Bergin & Garvey.

Luchterhand, C., & Murphy, N. E. (1998). *Helping adults with mental retardation grieve a death loss.* Philadelphia, PA: Brunner/Mazel.

Lugina, H. I. (1994). Factors that influence women's health in Tanzania. *Health Care for Women International, 15*(1), 61–68.

Luhrmann, T. M. (2000). *Of two minds: The growing disorder in American psychiatry.* New York: Knopf.

Lynn, J., & Childress, J. F. (1991). Must patients always be given food and water? In C. Levine (Ed.), *Taking sides: Clashing views on controversial bioethical issues* (4th ed., pp. 118–126). Guilford, CT: Dushkin.

Mann, J. M. (1993). We are all Berliners: Notes from the ninth international conference on AIDS. *American Journal of Public Health, 83*(10), 1378–1379.

McCarroll, J. E., Ursano, R. J., Wright, K. M., & Fullerton, C. S. (1993). Handling bodies after violent death: Strategies for coping. *American Journal of Orthopsychiatry, 63*(2), 209–214.

Nahill, A. (2000, January 3). A doctor's lesson on duality of drugs: Second opinion. *Boston Globe,* p. C2.

Navarro, V. (1994). The future of public health in health care reform. *American Journal of Public Health, 84*(5), 729–730.

Nyamukapa, C. A., Gregson, S., Lopman, B. et al. (2008). HIV-associated orphanhood and children's psychosocial distress: Theoretical framework tested with data from Zimbabwe. *American Journal of Public Health, 98*(1), 133–142.

O'Rourke, M. E. (1999). Narrowing the options: The process of deciding on prostate cancer treatment. *Cancer Investigation, 17,* 349–359.

Parkes, C. M. (1975). *Bereavement: Studies of grief in adult life.* Harmondsworth, England: Penguin Books.

Phaladze, N. A., Human, S., Dlamini S. B. et al. (2005). Quality of life and the concept of "living well" with HIV/AIDS in Sub-Saharan Africa. *Journal of Nursing Scholarship, 37*(2), 120–126.

Pruchno, R. A., & Potashnik, S. L. (1989). Caregiving spouses: Physical and mental health in perspective. *Journal of the American Geriatrics Society, 37,* 697–705.

Pulerwitz, J., Izazola-Licea, J., & Gortmaker, S. L. (2001). Extrarelational sex among Mexican men and their partners' risk of HIV and other sexually transmitted diseases. *American Journal of Public Health, 91*(10), 1650–1652.

Rachlis, M., & Kushner, C. (1994). *Strong medicine: How to save Canada's health care system.* Toronto: HarperCollins.

Richardson, B. K. (1987, July/August). Psychiatric inpatients' perception of seclusion room experience. *Nursing Research, 36,* 234–238.

Root-Berstein, R. S. (1993). *Rethinking AIDS: The tragic cost of premature consensus.* New York: Free Press-Maxwell Macmillan International.

Sande, M. A., & Volberding, P. (Eds.). (1995). *The medical management of AIDS* (4th ed.). Philadelphia: Saunders.

Shilts, R. (1987). *And the band played on.* New York: St. Martin's Press.

Shipes, E., & Lehr, S. (1982). Sexuality and the male cancer patient. *Cancer Nursing, 5,* 375–381.

Singer, M. (1992). AIDS and U.S. ethnic minorities: The crisis and alternative anthropological responses. *Human Organization, 51*(1), 89–95.

Smith, D. J. (2007). Modern marriage, men's extramarital sex, and HIV risk in Southeastern Nigeria. *American Journal of Public Health, 97*(6), 997–1005.

Smith, D. R. (1994). Porches, politics, and public health. *American Journal of Public Health, 84*(5), 725–726.

Solomon, M. Z., O'Donnell, L., Jennings, B., Guilfoy, V., Wolf, S. M., Nolan, K., Jackson, B. A., Koch-Weser, D., & Donnelley, S. (1993). Decisions near the end of life: Professional views on life-sustaining treatments. *American Journal of Public Health, 83*(1), 14–23.

Sontag, S. (1978). *Illness as metaphor.* New York: Farrar, Straus & Giroux.

Stall, R., & Mills, T. C. (2006). A quarter century of AIDS [Editorial]. *American Journal of Public Health, 96*(6), 959–961.

Stevens, P. E., & Galvao, L. (2007). "He won't use condoms": HIV-infected women's struggles in primary relationships with serodiscordant partners. *American Journal of Public Health, 97*(6), 1015–1022.

Sugg, N. K., & Inui, T. (1992). Primary care physicians' response to domestic violence: Opening Pandora's box. *Journal of the American Medical Association, 267*(23), 3157–3160.

Tolbert-Washington, G. (2001). Families in crisis. *Nurse Management, 32*(5), 28–33.

U.S. Department of Health and Human Services. (1986). *Surgeon General's workshop on violence and public health: Report.* Washington, DC: Author.

Wardlow, H. (2007). Men's extramarital sexuality in rural Papua New Guinea. *American Journal of Public Health, 97*(6), 1006–1014.

Whitaker, R., & Kong, D. (1998, November 15–18). Doing harm: Research on the mentally ill [A four-part series], *Boston Globe.* Testing takes human toll [First of four parts], pp. A1, A32–A33. Lure of riches fuels testing [Third of four parts], pp. A1, A34–A35.

Zborowski, M. (1952). Cultural components in responses to pain. *Journal of Social Issues, 8,* 16–30.

See Online Resources for additional references.

CHAPTER **8**

Threats to Occupational and Residential Security

Basic human needs include success in one's ascribed and achieved social roles and a secure, stable dwelling place. Meeting these needs implies

- The ability and opportunity to be creative and productive in a way that is meaningful to us and accepted by others
- Membership in a supportive community that values our presence and contribution
- Enough material supplies to maintain self-sufficiency and protection from the elements

Just as a serious change in health status threatens a person's self-image, so does the ability to be self-supportive. Underscoring the interacting relationships among health, occupational, and general social security, many people—especially in the United States where there is no comprehensive health care system—remain in unfulfilling jobs that can literally make them sick (Illich, 1976) to keep from losing insurance coverage. If they lose their jobs, the loss of insurance as well adds to their stress, fear, and insecurity about the future. In turn, these additional stressors affect one's health status and ability to function at precisely the time of greatest need. When occupation-based stress intersects with domestic issues, depression is not uncommon. This includes stress from overwork by people who cannot afford to build regular leisure time into their lives (Schor, 1993). A study by Barnett and Rivers (1998) reveals that people who occupy multiple roles are more resilient than workaholics, who feel most disillusioned and more easily plunge into depression if something goes wrong on the job, having placed all their eggs in one basket, so to speak. Generally, job security is the fundamental means of maintaining residential security, since housing constitutes most people's major financial liability. The most extreme response to job loss is violence by the dismissed employee against the employer and others, a phenomenon more common in the United States than elsewhere (see Chapter 12, Aggression and Violence).

These intertwined hazards around health, occupational, and residential security are compounded for those with a prior history of mental illness, for victims of violence, especially women and children, and for those forced to flee their home and country because of war or ethnic cleansing. Most people look forward to the comfort and security of returning to a safe dwelling after a day's work or to welcoming co-workers after a vacation or business trip. When occupational and residential status are threatened, however, a person's status may be dramatically changed from

- Home to streets
- Having a job to the unemployment lines or poverty
- A sense of self-sufficiency to unexpected dependency
- A sense of security to uncertainty about where the next meal is coming from or where the next night will be spent: On someone's couch? In a welfare hotel? A shelter? The mean streets? Another country?

The following pages address principles and techniques of crisis intervention we can enact on behalf of people in crisis around work goals, or who suffer occupational and housing losses. People need to mourn the losses that characterize these unanticipated transitions, some of which are life threatening. And they need the hope that comes from advocacy and social change to alleviate the conditions that deprive people of jobs and homes and perpetuate the widening gap between the world's rich and poor.

Occupational Changes

Changes in occupational status include the complex issues that pertain to working, earning money, and maintaining oneself and one's family economically.

Promotion, Success, and Economic Security

Promotion and success are not hazardous events or occasions of crisis for most, but suicide studies reveal that promotion can be the last straw that leads some people to commit suicide. The person promoted to a prestigious position may feel incapable of performing as expected in the new role. An anticipated promotion can also be a crisis point, as a new position brings increased responsibility, higher rank and status, and a change in role relationship among peers. If the move is from ordinary staff worker to a management position, the person may fear loss of acceptance by the peer group he or she leaves.

The combination of losing familiar supportive relationships at work and the challenge of unfamiliar work becomes too much to handle. A person's vulnerability to crisis in these circumstances is affected by several factors:

1. The general openness of communication in the company or agency
2. The person's ability to openly discuss questions and fears with a trusted confidant, because expressing worries about self-confidence, for example, might jeopardize the promotion

3. The person's perception of self and how one should perform in a given role—especially difficult for perfectionists or young adults trying to find a compatible and secure place in the work world

The Success Neurosis and Sex Roles

A crisis stemming from promotion has also been called the *success neurosis*, which is sometimes seen in women who view themselves as occupying second-rate or second-best positions. If they have worked primarily in the role of housewife and mother, they may suddenly become immobilized when other opportunities arise. This can happen even when they have openly expressed a desire for new opportunities.

Crises associated with promotion and success are usually quiet crises. People in this kind of crisis are not acutely upset but feel generally anxious and depressed and express bewilderment about being depressed. They feel disappointed that they cannot measure up to their own expectations; they know they have every reason to be happy. They cannot relate their feelings of depression to their lack of self-confidence and rigid expectations of themselves. A deep fear of failure may lead to the idea of suicide in the event that the person really does fail.

Anxiety, depression, and suicidal thoughts may move a person in this kind of crisis to seek help. Usually, such a person will go to a local crisis clinic or a private therapist. Several crisis counseling sessions are often sufficient for the person to

- Express underlying fears, insecurity, and disappointment with self
- Gain a realistic perspective on his or her abilities
- Grow in self-confidence and self-acceptance
- Use family and friends to discuss feelings and concerns openly rather than viewing such expressions as another failure

---

Case Example: Angie

Angie, age 37, had been doing volunteer work with the mental health association in her community. One of her special projects was helping handicapped people run a confection stand for local Parks and Recreation Department events. Because of the high quality of her work—which she could only acknowledge self-consciously—her friends urged her to open and manage her own coffeehouse. She finally did so, and the project was a glowing success. Angie suddenly found herself in the limelight, a situation she had not anticipated. She could not believe it would last. After a few months, she began feeling tense and depressed and thought vaguely about suicide. She talked with her physician about her problem and was referred to a psychotherapist for help.

Short-term crisis counseling may reveal deeper problems of low self-esteem, rigid role expectations, inflexible behavior patterns, and habitual reluctance to communicate feelings of distress to significant people. Psychotherapy should be offered and encouraged, as these people are high risks for suicide if other crisis situations arise. But in addition to offering individual assistance, as crisis workers and as a society, we need to examine the structures and differential expectations and rewards that place women at greater risk of failing in their career aspirations. For example, executive women (unlike executive men) who want to avoid being derailed from the career ladder typically must jump through two hoops: traditional masculine behavior and traditional feminine behavior (Morrison, White, & Van Velsor, 1987). This is a new version of the old adage, "Women must be twice as good to get half as far." One consequence of such stress might be an obsession with work, to the detriment of a healthy balance between work and other activities. Although women have made progress in traditionally male-dominated professions— for example, law, medicine, and engineering—they are vulnerable to the same gender-based harassment and abuse as women in traditionally female-dominated professions such as nursing (Phillips & Schneider, 1993). Finally, despite their high professional status, they shoulder the same dual burden that most women carry: they still do the bulk of unpaid domestic work such as child care.

The origins of work-related crises can be traced to cultural values and the tradition that men do public work and are paid well for it, whereas women do private work and are not paid at all (Waring, 1990). When women do work outside the home, the majority do so in traditionally female, nurturant or supportive jobs, such as nursing, child care, and clerical work (Foner, 1994; Kavanagh, 1988; Reverby, 1987). Because most women today work outside the home for economic, psychological, and social survival, the points of stress and potential crises are numerous as long as traditional values prevail. The internationally publicized murder trial of au pair Louise Woodward in 1997 underscored the persistence of these values: of the parents, both physicians with active careers, only the mother worked part-time in order to be available more for parenting; yet it was only the *mother* who was publicly vilified for not setting her career aside so she could be at home full-time and eliminate the need for an au pair. For many women, the cost of caring is very high (Facione, 1994; Sommers & Shields, 1987) and will get higher as the number of seniors and people with AIDS increases, unless men assume more equal responsibility for the caring work of society (Rosen, 2007). Crisis counseling or therapy is indicated for individual men and women struggling with these issues. The long-term results, however, will be limited without simultaneous attention directed to the social change strategies relevant to these crises of sociocultural origin (see Chapter 2).

Institutional Barriers to Promotion and Economic Security

Aside from regressive cultural values about men, women, and work, there are institutional barriers to promotion for millions of workers, especially ethnic minorities and poor women (Dujon & Withorn, 1996; Sidel, 1996). Globalization has led to ever widening gaps between the rich and traditionally disadvantaged groups. These social problems can lead to homelessness, child neglect, marital discord, bitterness, withdrawal from the mainstream of social life, substance abuse, suicide, and violence.

Numerous studies (see Chapter 2) underscore the work of Caplan (1964), Hansell (1976), and others documenting the need for intactness of one's social, cultural, and material supplies in order to avoid personal crisis (Perese, 1997; Schmidt, Weisner, & Wiley, 1998). Pearce and McAdoo (1982), writing for the National Advisory Council on Economic Opportunity regarding the "feminization of poverty," point out the differing results of divorce for women and men: the postdivorce poverty of most women is associated with the burden of single parenting and minimal financial support from the children's father, a situation exacerbated in cases of domestic violence.

Despite some exceptions to this pattern and some divorce settlements unfair to men, this situation is dramatized by the fact that within a year of divorce, the standard of living for most women decreases significantly and for men it increases. The largest percentage of poor women and children are members of racial minorities, which underscores the combination of race, gender, and class bias. Labor statistics show that women with children in the United States still earn less than men doing comparable jobs despite the Equal Pay Act passed in 1965 (Crittenden, 2001). To offer psychotherapy or crisis counseling alone, without job training, day care, and advocacy for adequate housing for disadvantaged workers, represents a misunderstanding of the problem, its origins, and its solutions. Rather than recycling these old problems, a fresh look upstream to their source holds the most promise for reducing crisis proneness and long-term negative outcomes for victims of discrimination. Even many in the business community are recognizing that continued wage disparities hurt not only the individuals affected but also business as a whole.

Paid and Unpaid Work

Worldwide, in labor statistics jargon, *work* is defined as paid work. In Africa, for example, a majority of agricultural work is done by women, while globally work at home is not included in official labor force counts (Waring, 1990). As Mollison (1993, p. 15A) states, "The economy would shudder if homemakers stopped doing unpaid work. Families would have to choose between recruiting other unpaid volunteers, hiring replacements, or settling for a life in which unfed, ignorant children and grouchy, unkempt adults struggled for survival under burned-out light bulbs and amid mountains of stinky socks."

In sum, women probably will not achieve equality in the paid workforce until men do an equal share of society's unpaid—but nevertheless very necessary—work (Frieswick, 2007). Statistics compiled for the 1985 United Nations Decade for Women Conference in Nairobi, Kenya, reveal that women do two-thirds of the world's work (not counting unpaid child care), earn one-tenth of the world's income, and own less than one-hundredth of the world's property (Seager & Olson, 1986). As Waring (1990) notes, if women's work "counted," official labor statistics and potentially the entire social landscape could be transformed.

Few would contest the negative—even damaging—outcomes of intergenerational welfare dependency for some recipients (see Schmidt et al., 1998). Results of reform thus far throw into sharp relief the public denigration of women's work in rearing children alone, often following abuse and because some divorced fathers do not pay child support. Success in welfare reform would also link the worldwide correlation of teenage motherhood and general birthrates with equity in women's economic and educational status. Contrary to popular perception, adolescent pregnancy is not just a racial minority issue; rather, it reflects poverty and the increasing unwillingness of teens to defer sexual activity, factors that cross racial boundaries (Desmond, 1994).

Welfare reform acts in the United States during the mid-1990s by many states reveal very mixed results. Among states that enacted a "work-first" policy, in 1999 only 25% of those who had gone from welfare to work were employed at wages above $250 per week for a full year (Albelda, 1999). According to a study by the Educational Testing Service, most welfare recipients lack the education and training needed to escape poverty, but work-first overhaul programs generally do not provide such training. Another reason for "reform" outcomes like this is the lack of affordable child care for poor mothers, while the role of fathers in parenting is virtually unchanged from traditional patterns. As Kuttner (2000) asks, "When was the last time you read an article about the stresses of being a working father?" (p. C7). But when fathers do share equitably in caring for their children, they often suffer more negative repercussions than women do in the workplace, thereby reinforcing the traditional value that child care is really just "women's work."

There is a perverse irony or double standard in expressed values and policy regarding women's work and welfare reform: In the Louise Woodward case, the mother, a physician with a comfortable income from her own and her husband's professional work is expected to stay home full-time to ensure proper child care; whereas poor mothers—many on welfare because of abuse—are expected to work outside the home whether or not child care is available. The hazards of these policies to the education and healthy development of children are great. This neglect of the nation's greatest resource—its children—means that future generations will pay the ultimate price (see Kozol, 2000). A similar double standard is evident in the fact that there is little organized effort by government to reform policies of tax credits to corporations that expand to cheap labor markets, subsidies to wealthy agribusiness originally intended for small farmers, tax-supported outlays to sports clubs and their wealthy players, tax rebates on mortgages for those lucky enough to own a home, and so forth.

Challenges of the Poor and Young Adults toward Occupational Security

Despite these grim results of regressive U.S. social policy affecting children, youth, and society's communal health, the state of Wyoming has implemented a very effective, nonpunitive welfare reform effort in the United

States, although Wyoming's economy lags the rest of the nation. Its 65% reduction in its welfare caseload is attributed to several policy decisions: In a people-to-people small-town approach, caseworkers offer support instead of threats. Their caseloads were reduced, and guidelines replaced rigid rules. Recipients are assured of continued benefits so long as they actively pursue a job, classes in preparing for a job, and opportunities for job training. Overall, the program is "work eventually" instead of "work first" (Grunwald, 1998).

This issue of welfare and *workfare* is especially urgent because it is connected to the hopelessness and apathy of chronically poor people. When the usually booming U.S. economy takes a downturn, groups at the economic bottom, which are mostly untouched during the "good times," are even worse off in the "bad times." A major reason for their fate through both boom and bust economic cycles is that their education in many substandard schools has not prepared them to command a living-wage job in the era of high technology and a globalized economy. The significant dropout rates in U.S. high schools exacerbates risks for future occupational security—a situation that may only worsen without progress toward equality of educational advantage, especially in large inner-city school systems, and where poverty is rampant, as on American Indian reservations. In such a climate, despair and violence flourish. Perhaps in no instance is the link between personal crisis and socioeconomic and cultural factors more dramatically illustrated. The tandem approach discussed in Chapter 12 most aptly applies here: assist individuals through traumatic life events like joblessness and unemployment (often based on race and class status), hold them accountable for violence and child supervision, and *simultaneously* engage them and others to address the roots of their plight (see Chapter 1, Crisis Paradigm, Box 3).

Family and human development research indicates that the transition to adulthood and economic self-sufficiency is more difficult and complicated than in the past. Traditionally, the launch into adulthood was typically marked by mastering a trade, studying for a profession, or assuming direction of a family business; committing to a life partner and raising a family; or in other ways contributing to societal needs. Those broad patterns still hold for most. But, moving from childhood to adulthood is now a more protracted, difficult, and complex mixture of continuing dependency on parents stretching into the twenties and beyond for financial help and a place to live between jobs. Yet not all parents (e.g., the "sandwich" generation caring for parents and securing their own retirement security) have the resources to offer these supports. Still others face even greater demands because their children have physical, mental, or behavioral problems (Conference Summary, 2006; Morrow & Richards, 1996).

Following the 1992 Los Angeles riots, Bondi Gabrel, an ethnic minority owner of an apartment complex in that riot-torn community, could have abandoned his damaged building. Instead he *employed* gang members and provided leadership options and a vision of another lifestyle. Gang members now, instead of vandalizing property, are paid to guard it. When chosen as *person of the week* by a national television network, Mr. Gabrel said, "This is what happens when you invest in people.... We haven't asked for enough." As this example and Medoff and Sklar's account (1994) of the death and life of an urban neighborhood demonstrate, models for such multifaceted approaches are there and need to be widely replicated.

Work Disruption: Safety and Local/Global Economic Factors

Just as promotion, success, or disadvantaged status can be a source of crisis or threat to health, so can disruption or change in work role, especially for a person accustomed to a lifetime of job security. The depression of inner-city neighborhoods is connected to global economic changes and the widespread loss of manufacturing jobs, which had been the mainstay of security for many who are now desperate.

Ethnic minority and immigrant groups are the most affected by the loss of U.S. manufacturing jobs, many of which have been transferred to countries with cheaper labor and looser laws protecting both workers and the environment. Many of these workers have little choice but low-paying service jobs with few benefits and few chances for advancement. Globally, the gap between rich and poor is widening, with reports of exploited and cheaply paid workers (mostly very young women escaping rural poverty) in repetitive and grueling manufacturing jobs. These conditions hark back to those cited from over a century ago in the Merrimack Valley cotton mills of Massachusetts and other New England states, which thrived off cotton extracted by Southern slave labor, and which heralded the beginning of the American industrial revolution.

Western society's attitude toward work, especially in the United States, is highlighted by a tendency to value people in proportion to how much money they earn and to respect them in proportion to the socioeconomic status they derive from their earnings. In other words, many have absorbed the deeply embedded cultural value, "You're worth what you earn." This value system helps fuel the welfare reform debate and the suspicion on the part of the haves that the have-nots are ultimately responsible for their own misfortune and could remedy that misfortune if they simply tried harder. Such judgments fail to account for the complex relationship between most unemployment situations and either global economics or discrimination based on race, gender, age, disability, or ill health. Usually, the unemployed or underemployed in a changing economy are deeply regretful of their position and struggle continually to correct it. These complexities and troubles are compounded for recent immigrants, many of whom have few rights and legal protections and often live in fear of deportation if they make their plight known or are subject to government raids if they are undocumented. Unemployment, then—or the threat of same—whether by firing, layoff, or because of a personal problem like illness, is frequently the occasion of emotional crisis, including violent responses like suicide or murder. While unemployed people must act on their misfortune, they will be much more empowered to do so if they are not inappropriately blamed for their plight.

Regardless of the reasons, the person in crisis because of unemployment is usually in need of a great deal of support. If unemployment originates from personal sources, social support and individual crisis intervention are indicated. However, people who are unemployed because of economic recession or discrimination are less likely to feel hopeless and powerless if they are also put into contact with groups devoted to removing the underlying sources of their stress through social change strategies. This includes policy changes that would prevent corporations from simply closing U.S. plants, laying off hundreds of employees, and moving to a country where labor is cheaper without any collaboration with or consideration of the workers who have built their lives around the company. The primary origin of crisis for a worker thus laid off is the profit motive. The appropriate response, therefore, should include linking such a person to groups advocating labor–management policy change (see Crisis Paradigm). In Germany, for example, workers in an automobile manufacturing plant decided on a four-day workweek so that *none* lost their jobs. Routine protests during meetings of the World Trade Organization, the World Bank, the International Monetary Fund, and the Organization of American States suggest a new era of social change as activists clash with police to demonstrate for fairness to workers and for environmental protection in the face of global trade policies and agreements.

Standards of personal success for most of us hinge on involvement in work that is personally satisfying and of value to the external community. For example, a 55-year-old man in a middle-management position, who is prematurely retired, may begin to drink or may attempt suicide as a way of dealing with the crisis of job disruption. These and other work-related crises are within the common province of personnel directors, occupational physicians and nurses, or anyone the person turns to in distress.

Case Example: Russell and Jenny Owens

Russell Owens, age 52, was a civil engineer employed for 20 years as a research consultant in a large industrial corporation. When he lost his job because of a surplus of engineers with his qualifications, he tried without success to find other employment, even at lower pay. Family financial needs forced his wife, Jenny, age 47, to seek full-time employment as a biology instructor; she had worked only part-time before. Jenny was grateful for this opportunity to advance herself professionally. She always regretted the fact that she had never tried to excel at a job, partly because Russell did not want her to work full-time. Gradually, however, Jenny became resentful of having to support herself, her husband, and their 16-year-old daughter, Gwen, in addition to assuming all responsibility for household tasks. She urged Russell to do at least some of the housework. Because Russell had never helped in this way, except for occasional errands and emergencies, Jenny's expectations struck a blow to his masculine self-image beyond the sense of failure and inadequacy he already felt from his job loss.

Russell also found it difficult to follow Jenny's advice that he seek help with his depression and increasing dependence on alcohol. The strain in their marital relationship increased. Jenny eventually divorced Russell, and he committed suicide. This case illustrates the importance of preventive intervention. Russell's drinking problem and eventual suicide might have been avoided if immediate help had been available to him at the crisis points of job loss and threat of divorce. Such help might also have resulted in a constructive resolution of Jenny's resentment of Russell concerning the housework.

Rural and Urban Occupational Transitions

Similar dynamics are apparent in the farm crisis. Farmers not only face a threat to their source of livelihood but also to their way of life. Although some farm foreclosures can be traced to individual mismanagement, the problem originates in policies that favor unbridled corporate accumulations of agricultural resources and profits at the expense of individual farm families. For example, federal price supports for farm products are cut back because of a "surplus." Yet in New England, where hundreds of Vermont dairy families have been driven off their farms, there is no milk surplus. Rather, the large amounts of milk at issue are from huge corporate farms in California.

It is ironic that in a country of immigrants who fled Europe and prized the opportunity to earn an honest living on the land, people are now in crisis because public policy favors government subsidies to large agribusiness rather than small farmers. No doubt the suicides, alcoholism, violence, and family conflicts arising from the farm crisis will continue unless grassroots efforts and public policy reverse the conditions causing so much pain and despair among the nation's rural citizens. One such grassroots organization is Farm Aid Rural Management in Bismarck, North Dakota. A similar program, the Kitchen Table Alliance, was organized as a countywide community development project in Ontario for farm families in financial, legal, or emotional difficulty or crisis to regain their health and productivity. These groups offer support, advocacy, crisis prevention, and referral for these distressed workers and their families.

Although the farm crisis in North America has abated, similar disruption of a way of life is now occurring in fishing communities worldwide. In poor countries, millions of rural dwellers flock to shantytowns near water, only to continue their grim struggle for survival, often with additional threats of violence in crowded slums or death from tidal waves. The threat in fishing communities is not only to a way of life taken for granted for generations but also to marine life, because overfishing depletes the fish supply. Support and crisis intervention groups like the Kitchen Table Alliance for farmers are crucial to the health and social welfare of affected fishing community members, in order to prevent suicide, violence, and substance abuse as governments and international agencies address the long-term facets of this issue.

Retirement Preparation—Anticipated or Forced

Some people look forward to retirement. Others dread it. For many people, retirement signifies loss of status, a reduced standard of living, and a feeling of being discarded by society. The experience is more pronounced when one is forced to retire at an early age due to illness or other disability. It is a time of stress not only for the retired person but also for family members, especially wives who do not work outside the home. Suddenly, a homemaker has to adjust to having at home all day a husband who may feel worthless and who may have developed few outside interests or hobbies apart from work. Fortunately, these patterns are changing as the population ages, and older persons realize and take advantage of the fact that for many, formal retirement means the continuation, not the end, of a fulfilling life.

The attitude people hold toward retirement depends on the situation they retire to; whether retirement is pleasant or not is also influenced by lifestyle. Key areas of concern in evaluating a person's retirement situation include the following:

1. Does the person have any satisfying interests or hobbies outside of work? For many, work has been their main focus all of their adult lives, and most of their pleasures are work related. For many overworked Americans, this may be a key issue requiring focused preretirement planning.
2. Does the person have a specifically planned retirement project? For example, some people plan to study literature, carpentry, or cooking when they retire. For people of means, Elderhostel offers many such programs.
3. Does the person have a safe and comfortable place to live? This factor is highly influenced by the job issues already discussed.
4. Does the person have enough retirement income to manage without excessive dependence?
5. Is the person in reasonably good health and free to manage without hardship?
6. Has the person been well adjusted socially and emotionally before retirement?

Even if the retired person's circumstances are favorable in all or most of these areas, retirement can still be stressful. We live in a youth-oriented society, and retirement signals that one is nearing or has already reached old age; after that, death approaches.

For some people, retirement is not an issue or occasion for crisis. They may be self-employed and simply keep working at a pace compatible with their needs and inclinations. Such people usually prepare for a reduced pace and have a healthy attitude toward life in each development phase, including old age. A new view of the life cycle suggests three phases: learning, earning, and returning. Thus, instead of retiring, people have an opportunity to return wisdom and other values to society and to have something returned to them after their years of learning, earning, and caring for others.

Those who are crisis prone as a result of retirement should have the assistance accorded anyone experiencing a loss. They need the opportunity to grieve the loss of their former status, explore new ways of feeling useful, and eventually accept their changed roles.

Residential Changes

Moves across country or to a different continent require leaving familiar surroundings and friends for a place with many unknowns. Even though the person moving may have many problems at home, at least he or she knows what the problems are. Pulling up stakes and starting over can be an exciting venture, an occasion for joy and for gaining a new lease on life, or a source of deep distress and an occasion for crisis.

Anticipated Moves

Consider the young woman who grew up in the country and moves to the city for the first time. She asks herself, "Will I find a job? Will I be able to make friends? Will I be unbearably lonely? Will I be safe?" Or the career person looking for opportunities wonders, "Will things be any better there? How will I manage not seeing my family and friends very often?" And last, consider the war refugee or immigrant, who worries, "How will those foreigners accept me? Will I be able to learn the language so I can get along? Who will help me if things go wrong? What if I want to come back and don't have the money?" These questions are more urgent for some would-be immigrants, as nations tighten their borders and entry rules for people intending no harm, but are only seeking a job and a better life for themselves and their children.

These are a few of the many questions and potential problems faced by people who plan a move in hopes of improving their situation. Even in these instances, moving is a source of considerable stress. It takes courage to leave familiar territory, even when the move would free one from many negative situations. No matter what the motive for the move, and despite the anticipation of better things to come, people in this transition state often experience a sense of loss.

To prevent a crisis at this time, the person planning and looking forward to a move should avoid denying feelings of loss. Even when a person is moving to much better circumstances, there is usually the loss of close associations with friends or relatives. As in the case of promotion or success, the would-be mover often does not understand the sense of depression, which is probably related to the denial of feelings and guilt about leaving friends and relatives. Understanding and expressing these feelings helps the person keep an open relationship with friends left behind and frees the person to use and enjoy new opportunities more fully, unburdened of misplaced guilt or depression.

People who plan and look forward to a move are vulnerable to other crises. Once they reach their destination, the situation may not work out as anticipated: the new job may be less enjoyable than the old one; the escape from a violent city to a farm may seem less secure than expected; new friends may be hard to find; envisioned job opportunities may not exist.

Social isolation and the inability to establish and maintain satisfying social attachments can leave a person vulnerable to crises and even suicide. People with satisfying supports can help prevent crises among those who have recently moved but not yet established a reliable social support system. Elderly people, for example, who are moved to a group residential setting have a much improved chance of adjusting well to the change and perceiving it as a challenge if (1) they had a choice in relocation, (2) relocation was predictable and understandable within their meaning system, and (3) they received necessary social support (Armer, 1993). In the cohousing movement discussed in Chapter 5, diversity by age is one of the goals, with some groups reserving a certain number of units (for example, five households out of 25) for persons 55 and older. A planned move of this sort for people who dread living in housing complexes only for old people could do much to avoid a crisis during this major life transition.

Unanticipated Moves

The potential for crisis is even greater for those who do not want to move but are forced to, for example,

- The family uprooted to an unknown place because of a job transfer
- Inner-city dwellers—especially older people—dislocated because of urban renewal and priced out of the housing market
- Victims of disaster moving from a destroyed community
- People evicted because of unpaid rent
- Mental patients who have been discharged to the community without adequate shelter and social support
- Abused women and their children who are forced to leave their homes to avoid beatings or death
- Political or war refugees who must leave their homelands
- Migrant farm workers who must move each year in the hope of earning a marginal subsistence

Globally, many refugees not only have lost family members and property but also face dramatic cultural differences, tripled social burdens, and social isolation. Thousands of teenagers and young people either have no home "safety net," run away from home, or they are simply "on the move." Many young people who run away do so because they are physically or sexually abused, or because they have come out as gay, lesbian, bisexual, or transgendered and are wholly rejected by their families. Often they lack housing, food, and money; many are further exploited sexually or feel forced into prostitution for survival; still others succumb to substance abuse (Greene,

Ennett, & Ringwalt, 1997); in extreme cases they are killed by police for petty stealing and vagrancy.

War refugees who are crowded into camps in neighboring countries face similar hazards—unsanitary conditions, indifference, brutality, and even rape by soldiers and officials. As if these prices of civil and ethnic strife were not enough, some refugees face grim prospects for immigration, depending on race and political considerations of a prospective host country. In the United States, for example, because of immigration quotas negotiated between Congress and the Immigration and Naturalization Service, far fewer African refugees are admitted than are admitted from Asia, Latin America, and Europe. International debates and advocacy continue in an effort to protect refugees who are the most vulnerable and are fleeing from war or persecution (Amnesty International, 2000, p. 21).

There are also groups of people who have been relocated by their own governments. Some of the most dramatic historic examples of such forced relocation and its long-term damaging effects are the destruction of Boston's West End in the 1950s to build Government Center (Gans, 1962); the 1953 dispatching of 85 Inuit people from northern Quebec to the High Arctic, where their families were wrenched apart and they endured extreme hardship and deprivation (Aubry, 1994); and the creation of racially segregated communities in South Africa (Sparks, 1990). As a result of these government actions, Boston's former West Enders are still mourning the loss of their homes, and the Inuit and South African majority are still seeking justice. Finally, there is the ordinary traveler who is en route from one place to another and loses money or belongings or is attacked.

In spite of the crisis potential of moves for many, moving can also be an occasion for growth through success in facing new challenges. Although highly mobile families may have fewer deep friendships, the family unit may feel closer and have a stronger self-concept as a result of successful coping in diverse circumstances. When counseling people with emotional problems related to relocation, psychologists identify four phases in coping with a move: (1) decision making—the less a person contributes to the decision, the more potential there is for trouble, (2) preparation—mastering the many details preceding a move, (3) separation from the old community—including acceptance of the sadness and loss involved, and (4) reinvestment—through involvement in one's new community (Singular, 1983, p. 46). These phases are akin to grief work and the rites of passage discussed in Chapters 4 and 6.

Helping the Migrant

Where is help available for the people in crisis related to migration? Crisis centers and mental health agencies are appropriate for people who are under great stress before a move, as well as those who are anxious and upset afterward. Special programs for stranded youth and for refugees are on the rise. Social service agencies and services for aging persons should also provide anticipatory guidance and crisis counseling to all groups forced to move because of need for asylum or a planned urban housing project they cannot afford. Unfortunately, such support and counseling are either not available or are not offered regularly.

Case Example: Noreen Anderson

Noreen Anderson, age 61, was confined to her apartment with a serious muscle disease. She was forced to retire at age 58 and had felt lonely and isolated since then. She did not have family in the area but did have many friends. However, they gradually stopped visiting her after she had been confined for a year. Now her apartment building was being converted to condominiums that she could not afford. Everyone in the building had moved out except Noreen, who was unable to move without help. Fortunately, Noreen's phone was not disconnected. She called various social service agencies for help and was finally referred to a local crisis center.

An outreach crisis counselor went to Noreen's apartment. She expedited an application through a federal housing agency for a place for Noreen in a senior citizen's housing project. The counselor also engaged an interfaith volunteer agency to help Noreen pack and processed a request for immediate physical supplies through Catholic Charities. Noreen was grateful for the help she received after her several desperate telephone calls, but by this time she was depressed and suicidal. The crisis counselor saw her in her new apartment in the senior citizen's housing project for several counseling sessions. She helped Noreen get in touch with old friends again and encouraged the friends to visit on a regular basis. A number of Retired Senior Citizen Volunteers also visited Noreen, which helped relieve her isolation and loneliness. Noreen was no longer suicidal at the termination of the counseling sessions.

Travelers Aid Family Service. This agency began as the Travelers Aid Society and has been doing crisis intervention work with people in transit for years. It arose from 19th-century social movements formed to help immigrant single women and families find housing and jobs. Caseworkers of this agency see travelers at the peak of their distress. The traveler who calls the agency is often without money or resources and is fearful in a strange city. In extreme cases, the person may have been beaten, robbed, or raped. The agency caseworker gets in touch with relatives; ensures emergency medical services, food, and emergency housing; provides travel money; and ensures the traveler a safe trip home. A close working relationship with 24-hour crisis services has bolstered the agency's preventative and advocacy goals on behalf of families at risk. The relative isolation of this agency often results in the Travelers Aid staff handling suicidal or emotionally upset travelers by themselves, without the support of crisis specialists who should be available.

International Institute and Other Support. The International Institute and special refugee groups are pivotal in helping people in crisis related to immigration. The institute's unique contribution is crisis work with refugees and immigrants who do not know the local language. Inability to speak a country's language can be the source of acute crises related to housing, employment, health, welfare, and legal matters. Institute workers, all of whom speak several languages, assist refugees and immigrants in these essential life areas.

There is an International Institute or comparable agency in nearly all major metropolitan areas, where most refugees and immigrants first settle. Health and social service personnel can refer immigrants who are unaware of this service on arrival. The language crisis is so acute for some immigrants that they may be mistakenly judged psychotic and taken to a mental hospital, or they may have to rely inappropriately on their own children for translation. Intervention by a multilingual person is a critical part of care in such cases. Unfortunately, this important social service agency has low visibility in the community and may not be linked adequately with 24-hour crisis services. Such linkages may become routine as health and crisis services become more comprehensive and cosmopolitan.

The actual and potential crises of immigrants and refugees have become more visible as ethnic conflict and international tensions have grown. People persecuted or sought out for their public protest against injustice seek refuge and political asylum in friendly countries with greater frequency. Cooperation between private and public agencies on behalf of these people is paramount to avoid unnecessary distress and crisis. In addition to legal, housing, language, and immediate survival issues, refugees experience the psychological pain of losing their homeland. No matter how they may have been treated, most people have a strong attachment to their country of birth. Whether this bond is broken voluntarily or by torture and threat to life, refugees need an opportunity to mourn the loss and find substitutes for what was left behind. They also should not have to endure prolonged detention in substandard facilities, which the UN defines as a denial of basic human rights.

Case Example: A Cambodian Woman

Sarong Ty, age 57, is an immigrant to Massachusetts, in the United States. Ms. Sarong was seen in a local Cambodian-directed multiservice health center for her trouble with insomnia, secondary to intrusive thoughts and nightmares. As a survivor of the Cambodian genocide, she arrival in the United States with her children and settled in a Cambodian immigrant community in Massachusetts.

Sarong was the oldest of five girls born to farmers in a remote province of Cambodia. She was 31 years old when the Khmer Rhouge overthrew the Lon Nol government in Cambodia. She and her family lived in a refugee camp for six years. Her father died of malaria in 1975; her mother died of starvation more than a decade later. Married at age 20, Sarong's husband left her for another woman while in the refugee camp. They had eight children, two of whom are incarcerated in Massachusetts for street crime and domestic violence. As sole provider of her eight children, Sarong is unemployed, receives public welfare assistance, and is now raising her 7-year-old grandson whose mother is involved with the drug culture.

Sarong's chief complaint on intake at the Community Health Center was "not having enough money to pay for food, rent, and getting by month to month." At

77 pounds, she is frail and reports eating one meal a day consisting mostly of rice. Her mood was sad, lonely, and angry. She denied alcohol or drug use in past or present, but attended the Addiction Treatment Program for socialization and information about how to protect her grandson from drugs, and to help her daughter-in-law. Sarong has classic symptoms of posttraumatic stress disorder (PTSD), and grieves the loss of her country and extended family. To ease her sorrow, she uses the traditional healing method of coining. She is illiterate in her own language and practices Buddhist meditation.

Let us consider what Sarong has in common with others experiencing crisis, and what is unique about her situation. First, the *commonalities*:

1. Sarong's pain of loss (one of the most common themes of emotional crisis); loss of her family, country, and husband
2. The physical health sequelae of abuse and torture, in her case by the Khmer Rhouge, and Sarong's relocation and extra parenting burden in an adopted new country
3. The similarities of her plight with Nazi Holocaust, Bosnian, Rwandan, Kenyan, and Sudanese survivors of genocide, massacres and ethnic cleansing
4. Intergenerational and cross-cultural conflict in child-rearing practice, minus a marital partner and usual social supports for child rearing
5. Sarong's parenting of grandchildren because her adult children are incarcerated or suffering from addiction or other disabilities

What is *unique* about Sarong's experience? And what are the implications for practice? Sarong's suffering epitomizes the depth of psychological trauma and its impact on physical health as a survivor of torture and genocide by the government of one's own country. (This is unique among Western-raised people in crisis, but not among similar survivors of torture and ethnic cleansing.) A practice lesson from Sarong's suffering is awareness that PTSD results from traumatic events that are well beyond the range of more ordinary or "normal" life crises, or because timely crisis care and social support were lacking at the time of the initial traumatic experience.

One way that refugees and immigrants cope with their loss is to preserve their customs, art, language, ritual celebrations, and food habits. These practices provide immigrants with the security that comes from association with their familiar cultural heritage. Sensitivity of neighbors and agency personnel to immigrants' cultural values, along with control of their own ethnocentrism, can go a long way in helping refugees feel at home. In contrast, members of host countries need particular sensitivity regarding a practice like female genital mutilation, which some immigrants wish to continue. See Chapter 1 regarding this cultural issue and what many groups define as a human rights violation.

Homelessness and Vulnerability to Violence

Some people live in cardboard boxes, ride the subway all night long, or stay in doorways of public buildings until they are asked or ordered by the police to move. Some sleep on steel grates to catch steam heat from below. Some abused women and their children move from shelter to shelter, staying the limit at each because battering may not fit the city's criteria of eligibility for emergency housing; one mother of three finally bought a tent and camped in a city park.

Besides having no secure place to stay, homeless people are frequent victims of rape or robbery of their few possessions; homeless youth are often victims of child prostitution; among the elderly homeless, some are disabled, some are deaf or blind, and some have symptoms of Alzheimer's disease. Contrary to popular perception, a good percentage of the homeless hold low-paying jobs that do not provide enough income to pay inflated rental prices. Many are victims of eviction when apartments are converted to condominiums for upwardly mobile, mostly white professionals. At no time since the Great Depression have homeless people represented such a cross-section of a wealthy Western society. The plight of homelessness in the United States is starkly visible in New Orleans years after hurricane Katrina. Overnight, working men and women, never before without a roof over their heads, found themselves sleeping under the stars in Depression-era conditions while political and business leaders squabble with nonprofit agencies about housing for the poor and disabled who suffered the greatest impact of Katrina (Ratner, 2008).

Among industrialized nations, the most visible and the highest numbers of homeless people are in the United States. As the problem has continued over decades, many worry that homelessness will become institutionalized as a permanent feature of social life. Several factors that help explain the apparent intractability of this problem are (1) the growing disparity between rich and poor, (2) in the United States, the lack of a national health program that includes sufficient coverage for crisis and mental health services, and (3) the continuing bias against the mentally ill and the resulting inadequate transitional housing and support services to prevent homelessness (Hoff, Briar, Knighton, & Van Ry, 1992; Jencks, 1994; Shinn et al., 1998; Weitzman, Knickman, & Shinn, 1992). But the problem is by no means limited to the United States. Worldwide recession and similar bias against the mentally ill occur cross-culturally and in any society where community values are sacrificed in favor of an individualistic paradigm, such as the one that dominates in the United States (Bellah, 1986; Luhrmann, 2000). Perhaps most alarming of all is the fact that homeless people include families with children. For these families, getting to work or school is a maze of buses and subway rides, taking as long as two hours one way, while they await their turn for transfer from temporary housing in a motel to placement in affordable housing that is all too scarce.

Homelessness strips people of their self-respect, denies them basic human rights, and blights the future of a nation's greatest resource—children. The victim-blaming practice of attributing homelessness to personal deficits is not supported by research that corrects the methodological flaws of earlier prevalence studies (Link et al., 1994). This study also suggests that the problem is of greater magnitude than has commonly been assumed. The crisis of homelessness is due primarily to the severe cuts in federal funds to build or rehabilitate low-income housing, and to the overpriced real estate market that is generally free of obligation to include low-income and moderate-income housing in their speculative ventures.

The skyrocketing housing costs well documented in cities like New York, San Francisco, London, and Boston have also affected smaller cities, forcing the average family to spend as much as two-thirds of their income on housing (in contrast to the former U.S. bank affordability standard of approximately 35%, (Bashir, 2002). Haphazard policies and bureaucratic ineptness are also responsible. As Jonathan Kozol (1988) related from his months with homeless people in one of New York's welfare hotels, the city spends $1,900 per month for a family of four, thus supporting enormous profits for a modernized poorhouse. But Kozol's informants wondered why so much money was spent on such hotels rather than designated for rent support in regular housing. Unfortunately, these questions of basic human rights and fair distribution of resources are more relevant than ever.

In the case of the homeless mentally ill, some of whom also have prison records, these problems are all exacerbated. Homeless people with mental illness are victims of failed deinstitutionalization programs and inadequate community planning (Cella, Besancon, & Zipple, 1997; Farrell & Deeds, 1997; Johnson, 1990; Kaplan, 2000; Scheper-Hughes & Lovell, 1986; Walker, 1998).

It would seem a foregone conclusion that what homeless people need is a home—a hallmark of the American dream. Yet despite numerous references to the crisis of affordable housing in large U.S. cities, major responses to this crisis have been essentially reactionary, individualistic, and biomedically focused, rather than being recognized as primarily a social problem demanding a policy response in accord with its social character. Lyon-Callo's (1998) ethnographic exploration of funding concerns dramatically illustrates this point. From his 10 years of work and field study in homeless shelters, Lyon-Callo uncovered a funding focus on tertiary-level sheltering, case management, and "treatment" (that is, changing or reforming) of the "disordered" homeless harbored there. This funding emphasis suppressed efforts to change the dynamics of inequality around jobs and housing that fuel homelessness. Despite rhetoric from public officials regarding the homelessness problem, coalitions of shelter workers and homeless persons themselves who focused on obtaining stable homes have been thwarted by governmental and nongovernmental funders who have shortchanged a primary care focus that addresses the roots of the problem. Progress on this issue demands a both-and, not an either-or, approach, particularly since some psychiatric facilities discharge mental patients to these shelters for lack of other appropriate resources for persons needing continuing mental health service.

One of the most tragic examples of the failure to address the systemic problems fueling homelessness is the 1999 deaths of six firefighters in Worcester, Massachusetts, resulting from their attempt to rescue a homeless couple in an abandoned warehouse; firefighters from across the nation and abroad attended the funerals of these fallen heroes. The homeless young couple, expecting a child, were charged with manslaughter and prosecuted because they failed to report the fire that started from their tipped-over candle during a domestic fight. As emphasized throughout this book, a crisis of social origin demands a social response. In this tragic case, once again, the focus was on individual rather than on the social dimensions of the crisis. In sum, the interrelated social, cultural, and economic factors—along with discrimination based on race, sex, and age—that precipitate crises of homelessness (and in this case, the death of six firefighters in the prime of life) must be addressed in a comprehensive proactive manner.

What, then, is to be done to turn the tide of this grave threat to the basic need for secure housing? What do we do for people who have no place to sleep or who are at risk of dying from exposure to the elements in spite of affluence all around them in the richest country in the world? People often react with embarrassment and discomfort to a homeless person who appears on a doorstep or begs for spare change. But regardless of how charitably people respond to individual appeals for help, the crisis of homelessness in a humane, democratic society entails more than goodwill or charity. Although there is still a tendency to blame the victim, as Ryan's classic book (1971) expounds, people do not choose to be poor or homeless.

Increasingly, grassroots groups and health and governmental agencies are trying to interrupt the vicious cycle of individuals and families forced to navigate between the streets and homeless shelters. Many now emphasize the less costly primary prevention approaches (Bashir, 2002). This includes addressing not only the harmful health effects of inadequate housing, but also the societal and ethical responsibility to meet the shelter needs of everyone, including the most disadvantaged (Buchanan et al., 2006; Freeman, 2002). Further, attorney Thiele (2002) of the Center on Housing Rights and Evictions (COHRE) in Geneva, Switzerland, notes that housing rights are embedded in international law and various UN Conventions such as the Universal Declaration of Human Rights and the Convention on the Rights of the Child.

Another hopeful and empowering example of moving beyond shelter and stopgap measures is the first federally funded farm (in Cape Cod, Massachusetts) to be staffed by residents who have histories of chronic homelessness. Each will have a private room with shared dining and bathroom facilities—reminiscent of the single-room occupancy (SROs) living quarters that were plentiful in most cities before gentrification and the reduction of government housing assistance. Residents must work 35 hours per week at the farm or in neighboring businesses, pay approximately 25%

of their income to rent, commit to teaching newly acquired skills to at least one new arrival, try to get a high school diploma if they do not have one, and abide by the strict rules of no alcohol or drugs (Gaines, 2000).

At the national level, a similar approach called Housing First is gathering momentum across the usually partisan ideological landscape. It is aimed at *ending* homelessness, not merely managing it. A 1999 Republican-controlled Congress endorsed the idea by requiring that HUD (U.S. Department of Housing and Urban Development) allocate at least a third of its homelessness funding toward permanent housing for chronically homeless and disabled persons (Graves & Sayfan, 2007).

We should support individual and communal efforts like these and those of Moshe Dean and others who write for and sell *Spare Change*. In Boston and New England, this newspaper is published by and for homeless people. Individuals who sell the paper for $1 are provided a means for some meager income. There is an international association of "street" newspapers, dedicated to advocacy and social change around this global problem. Such efforts, however, will never be sufficient to avoid further crises of homelessness without a change in public policies affecting housing (see Crisis Paradigm, Box 3, right circle).

Summary and Discussion Questions

To be happy, we need some meaningful work to support ourselves and a secure place to live. Many people are threatened with the loss of these basic necessities—and for refugees, even their homeland. Opportunities to assist people in crisis because of occupational or housing loss cross the social service and health care landscape. Helping people at these initial crisis points can make an enormous difference in the final outcomes of these transition states. Removing the socioeconomic roots of crises, such as unemployment and homelessness, is urgent public business.

1. Given women's gains in pay equity in economically developed societies, what are the primary gender and other reasons why the paid and unpaid work of society is still so widely disparate between men and women?
2. Discuss the realistic prospects of a multipronged public health approach to homelessness beyond the ups and downs of a country's economic stability.
3. Besides the institutional programs available for refugees from political, ethnic, and religious conflict worldwide, consider how individuals might maintain hope and "make a difference," locally and globally, to reduce threats to occupational and residential security.

References

Albelda, R. (1999, May 24). Now we know: "Work first" hasn't worked. *Boston Globe*, p. A13.

Amnesty International. (2000, summer). Pass the refugee protection act. *Amnesty International*, p. 21.

Armer, J. M. (1993). Elderly relocation to a congregate setting: Factors influencing adjustment. *Issues in Mental Health Nursing, 14*(2), 157–172.

Aubry, J. (1994, March 5). Exiled to a forsaken place. *Ottawa Citizen*, pp. 1, B1–B6.

Barnett, R. C., & Rivers, C. (1998). *She works/he works: How two-income families are happy, healthy, and thriving.* Cambridge, MA: Harvard University Press.

Bashir, S. A. (2002). Home is where the harm is: Inadequate housing as a public health crisis. *American Journal of Public Health, 92*(5), 733–738.

Bellah, R. (1986). *Habits of the heart: Individualism and commitment in American life.* New York: HarperCollins.

Buchanan, D., Doblin, B., Sai, T., & Garcia, P. (2006). The effects of respite care for homeless patients: A cohort study. *American Journal of Public Health, 96*(7), 1278–1281.

Caplan, G. (1964). *Principles of preventive psychiatry.* New York: Basic Books.

Cella, E. P., Besancon, V., & Zipple, A. M. (1997). Expanding the role of clubhouses: Guidelines for establishing a system of integrated day services. *Psychiatric Rehabilitation Journal, 21*(1), 10–15.

Conference Summary (2006, October 18 & 19). *Adolescence and the transition to adulthood: Rethinking the safety net for vulnerable young adults.* Chicago: University of Chicago.

Crittenden, A. (2001). *The price of motherhood: Why the most important job in the world is still the least valued.* New York: Metropolitan Books.

Desmond, A. M. (1994). Adolescent pregnancy in the United States: Not a minority issue. *Health Care for Women International, 15*(4), 325–332.

Dujon, D., & Withorn, A. (Eds.). (1996). *For crying out loud: Women's poverty in the United States.* Boston: South End Press.

Facione, N. C. (1994). Role overload and health: The married mother in the waged labor force. *Health Care for Women International, 15*(2), 157–167.

Farrell, S. P., & Deeds, E. S. (1997). The clubhouse model as exemplar. *Journal of Psychosocial Nursing, 35*(1), 27–34.

Foner, N. (1994). *The caregiving dilemma: Work in an American nursing home.* Berkeley: University of California Press.

Freeman, L. (2002). America's affordable housing crisis: A contract unfulfilled. *American Journal of Public Health, 92*(5), 709–715.

Frieswick, K. (2007, March 11). The job without benefits. *The Boston Globe Magazine*, pp. 30–32, 42–44.

Gaines, J. (2000, January 3). Home grown: Farm for homeless planned on Cape. *Boston Globe*, pp. A1, B5.

Gans, H. J. (1962). *The urban villagers.* New York: Free Press.

Graves, F., & Sayfan, H. (2007, June 24). First things first. *The Boston Globe*, pp. E1. E4.

Greene, J. M., Ennett, S. T., & Ringwalt, C. L. (1997). Substance use among runaway and homeless youth in three national samples. *American Journal of Public Health, 87*(2), 229–235.

Grunwald, M. (1998, February 27). Wyoming cuts rolls by putting some heart into welfare reform. *Boston Globe*, pp. A1, A12.

Hansell, N. (1976). *The person in distress.* New York: Human Sciences Press.

Hoff, M. D., Briar, K. H., Knighton, K., & Van Ry, A. (1992). To survive and to thrive: Integrating services for the homeless mentally ill. *Journal of Sociology and Social Welfare, 29*(4), 235–252.

Illich, I. (1976). *Limits to medicine.* Harmondsworth, England: Penguin Books.

Jencks, C. (1994). *The homeless.* Cambridge, MA: Harvard University Press.

Johnson, A. B. (1990). *Out of bedlam: The truth about deinstitutionalization.* New York: Basic Books.

Kaplan, F. (2000, August 23). For mentally ill, jail means care. *Boston Globe,* pp. A1, A8.

Kavanagh, K. J. (1988). The cost of caring: Nursing on a psychiatric intensive care unit. *Human Organization, 47*(3), 242–251.

Kozol, J. (2000). *Ordinary resurrections: Children in the years of hope.* New York: Crown.

Kuttner, R. (2000, February 2). The hidden failure of welfare reform. *Boston Sunday Globe,* p. C7.

Link, B. G., Susser, E., Stueve, A., Phelan, J., Moore, R. E., & Struening, E. (1994). Lifetime and five-year prevalence of homelessness in the United States. *American Journal of Public Health, 84*(12), 1907–1912.

Luhrmann, T. M. (2000). *Of two minds: The growing disorder in American psychiatry.* New York: Knopf.

Lyon-Callo, V. (1998). Constraining responses to homelessness: An ethnographic exploration of the impact of funding concerns on resistance. *Human Organization, 57*(1), 1–20.

Medoff, P., & Sklar, H. (1994). *Streets of hope: The fall and rise of an urban neighborhood.* Boston: South End Press.

Mollison, A. (1993, June 27). Unpaid work by homemakers under scrutiny. *St. Paul Pioneer Press,* p. 15A.

Morrison, A. M., White, R. P., & Van Velsor, E. (1987). Executive women: Substance plus style. *Psychology Today, 21*(8), 18–27.

Morrow, V., & Richards, M. (1996). *Transitions to adulthood: A family matter?* York Publishing Services, Ltd., U.K.: Joseph Roundtree Foundation.

Pearce, D., & McAdoo, H. (1982). *Women and children: Alone and in poverty.* Washington, DC: National Advisory Council on Economic Opportunity.

Perese, E. F. (1997). Unmet needs of persons with chronic mental illnesses: Relationship to their adaptation to community living. *Issues in Mental Health Nursing, 18*(1), 19–34.

Phillips, S. P., & Schneider, M. S. (1993). Sexual harassment of female doctors by patients. *New England Journal of Medicine, 329*(26), 1936–1939.

Ratner, L. (2008). Homeless in New Orleans. *The Nation,* February 25, 13–18.

Reverby, S. (1987). *Ordered to care.* Cambridge: Cambridge University Press.

Rosen, R. (2007, March 12). The care crisis. *The Nation,* 11–16.

Ryan, W. (1971). *Blaming the victim.* New York: Vintage Books.

Scheper-Hughes, N., & Lovell, A. M. (1986). Breaking the circuit of social control: Lessons in public psychiatry from Italy and Franco Basaglia. *Social Science and Medicine, 23*(2), 159–178.

Schmidt, L., Weisner, C., & Wiley, J. (1998). Substance abuse and the course of welfare dependency. *American Journal of Public Health, 88*(11), 1616–1622.

Schor, J. B. (1993). *The overworked American: The unexpected decline of leisure.* New York: Basic Books.

Seager, J., & Olson, A. (1986). *Women in the world: An international atlas.* New York: Simon & Schuster.

Shinn, M., Weitzman, B. D., Stojanovic, D., Knickman, J. R., Jimenez, L., Duchon, L., James, S., & Drantz, D. H. (1998). Predictors of homelessness among families in New York City: From shelter request to housing stability. *American Journal of Public Health, 88*(11), 1651–1657.

Sidel, R. (1996). *Women and children last: The plight of poor women in affluent America.* New York: Penguin Books.

Singular, S. (1983). Moving on. *Psychology Today, 17,* 40–47.

Sommers, T., & Shields, L. (1987). *Women take care: The consequences of caregiving in today's society.* Gainesville, FL: Triad.

Sparks, A. (1990). *The mind of South Africa: The story of the rise and fall of apartheid.* London: Mandarin.

Thiele, B. (2002). The human right to adequate housing: A tool for promoting and protecting individual and community health. *American Journal of Public Health, 92*(5), 712–715.

Walker, C. (1998). Homeless people and mental health: A nursing concern. *American Journal of Nursing, 98*(11), 26–32.

Waring, M. (1990). *If women counted: A new feminist economics.* San Francisco: Harper San Francisco.

Weitzman, B. C., Knickman, J. R., & Shinn, M. (1992). Predictors of shelter use among low-income families: Psychiatric history, substance abuse, and victimization. *American Journal of Public Health, 82*(11), 1547–1550.

See Online Resources for additional references.

PART **III**

SUICIDE, VIOLENCE, AND CATASTROPHIC EVENTS

The Crisis Paradigm presented in Part 1 links the origins of crisis with their possible outcomes. Part 2 addressed the more predictable crises that may follow normal life cycle development phases, and the potential for crisis when threats to health status, and occupational and residential security occur. In this part, violence is discussed, both as an origin of and a response to crisis. Violence toward oneself and others is a major, life-threatening factor for individuals, families, and whole communities in many stressful situations. Chapters 9 and 10 focus on assessing and helping people who respond to crisis by suicide or other forms of self-destructiveness. Chapters 11 and 12 deal with violence toward others, including the crises of both victims and perpetrators of violence. In Chapter 13, violence affecting entire communities—disaster—is traced to natural and human sources. Because the effects of violence are so destructive for many and are often irreversible, the theme of prevention is reemphasized regarding crises that originate from violence.

Part III

SUICIDE, VIOLENCE, AND CATASTROPHIC EVENTS

CHAPTER 9

Suicide and Other Self-Destructive Behavior
Understanding and Assessment

Some people respond to life crises by suicide or other self-destructive acts. George Sloan, whose case was noted in previous chapters, tried to kill himself in a car crash when he saw no other way out of his crisis (see Figure 9.1, Box 4b).

A Framework for Understanding Self-Destructive Behavior

Suicide is viewed as a major public health problem and leading cause of death in many countries. Suicide among adolescents and young adults continues as a serious problem. The highest rates of suicide in the United States are among older white males (Moscicki, 1999, p. 41). Adolescent suicides constitute about 20% of all suicides nationwide. Among black men, American Indian, and Alaska Natives, however, the highest rates occur between ages 20 and 29 (Moscicki, p. 41). This suggests racial minority groups' continuing struggle with devastating social and individual circumstances. There is a strong association between suicide risk and bisexuality in males, which is only recently commanding research attention (Remafedi, French, Story, Resnick, & Blum, 1998). Homosexuals are estimated to account for 30% of adolescent suicides, despite constituting only 5 to 10% of the general population (Remafedi, Farrow, & Deisher, 1991). The rate of suicide for all ages and groups in the United States is about 12 per 100,000 (approximately 30,000 annually) and has remained relatively constant over several decades (National Center for Health Statistics, 2004).[1]

In the United States, firearms are the suicide method of choice for both men and women, whereas the second most common method used by men is hanging

---

[1] Only those statistical figures reflecting broad trends or changes are cited here. For current official government statistics in the U.S. and internationally, readers are referred to Internet sources, e.g., Centers for Disease Control (CDC) and the World Health Organization (WHO).

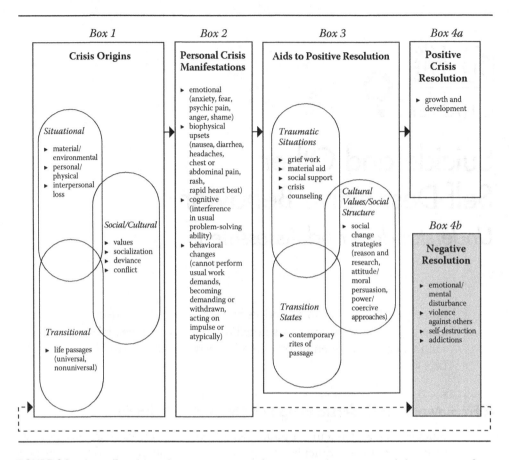

FIGURE 9.1 Crisis Paradigm. Crisis origins, manifestations, and outcomes and the respective functions of crisis care have interactional relationships. The intertwined circles represent the distinct yet interrelated origins of crisis and aids to positive resolution, even though personal manifestations are often similar. The arrows pointing from origins to positive resolution illustrate the *opportunity for growth and development* through crisis; the broken line at the bottom depicts the potential *danger of crisis* in the absence of appropriate aids. The loop between Box 4b and Box 1 denotes the *vulnerability* to future crisis episodes following negative resolution.

and by women is poisoning. White women's rates peak at around age 50, whereas rates for nonwhite women remain low and fairly constant through old age.

Suicide attempts occur at least 10 times more frequently than suicides, with a total of approximately 300,000 annually. Among adolescents, particularly females, the attempt rate may be 20 to 50 times higher. Many of these adolescents have been physically or sexually abused. Stephens's research (1985, 1987) on suicidal women reveals strong links to conflict and abuse in intimate relationships. She suggests that women with histories of exaggerated passivity may be at greater risk of suicide than those who are rebellious. Women have higher rates of depression than men, which is commonly attributed to socioeconomic disparities (Badger, McNiece, & Gagan, 2000). However, research remains to be done on why greater numbers of women who are abused or otherwise disadvantaged do *not* kill themselves.

Internationally, the wide range of suicide rates further reveals the complexity of the suicide problem. In Canada, the age-adjusted suicide rate is 13.6. In England, France, Italy, Denmark, and Japan, the rates for men are consistently higher than for women. England has the lowest rate for older people, Hungary the highest rates in the world, and Italy the lowest rate for the young. In most European countries, the rates are lowest among those of Catholic tradition (Kerkhof & Clark, 1993; United Nations, 1996). In Japan, the rate for women between 15 and 24 is half that for men (McGinnis, 1987, p. 25), whereas in India, for every 100 suicides, 70 are women, and in rural China, female suicides outnumber those of males (Conner et al., 2007). World Suicide Prevention Day occurred on September 10, 2007. In the year 2000, approximately one million people died by suicide, a "global" mortality rate of 16 per 100,000. Over the past several decades, suicide rates have increased by 60% worldwide, although some of this increase may be attributed to more accurate reporting related to public health attention to the issue. Suicide is among the three leading causes of death for both sexes aged 15 to 44 (WHO [World Health Organization], retrieved 2008).

Because reporting systems differ widely, there are probably more suicides than are reported. Cultural taboos, insurance policies, and other factors strongly influence the reporting of suicide. Some coroners, for example, will not certify a death as suicide unless there is a suicide note. However, everyone who commits suicide does not leave a suicide note. Research supports the claim that the compilation of suicide statistics, like suicide itself, is a social—not strictly scientific—process affected by cultural, social, and economic considerations (Atkinson, 1978). In Japan, there are no religious or state laws banning suicide; hence, a significant number of Internet-assisted group suicides occur (Samuels, 2007).

All these factors contribute to the lack of accurate and comprehensive data. Statistics about suicide, therefore, should be used primarily as an indicator of trends, not as a substitute for sensitive interpersonal work with suicidal people. For example, because suicide rates among adolescents and ethnic minority groups have increased the most dramatically in recent years, greater public attention is warranted than earlier, lower rates seemed to indicate.

Suicide as a response to crisis is used by all classes and kinds of people with social, mental, emotional, and physical problems—possibly including our relatives and neighbors. In short, people of every age, sex, religion, race, sexual identity, and social or economic class commit suicide. Perhaps most important of all, in the ethic of most world religions, suicide is generally considered the most stigmatizing sort of death, while suicide prevention is a major public health goal (Wasserman, 2004).

In this and the following chapter, suicide and self-destructive behavior are discussed in the contexts of the Judeo-Christian value system and the development of social science, crisis theory, and public health. The discussion assumes the psychosociocultural perspective presented in earlier chapters, with particular emphasis on themes of growth and empowerment despite the specter of death as a response to psychic pain during crisis. Inasmuch as suicide has occurred since the beginning of recorded history—the similar age-old response of distressed and despairing people—the holistic, preventive model of this book contrasts with the current widespread tendency to treat suicide primarily as a result of mental disorder (see Figure 9.1, Box 4b). This is not to disclaim what contemporary psychiatry offers; rather, the intent is to avoid "pathologizing" a phenomenon that is much more complex than is implied by a diagnosis such as subclinical depression or major depressive disorder (MDD). Suicide most often occurs during periods of socioeconomic, family, and individual crisis situations (WHO, retrieved 2008).

Suicide universally conveys the value that "death is preferred over life," making this discussion relevant in cross-cultural terms as well. However, particular belief systems will influence how and why suicide occurs and is interpreted in various non-Western societies. For a fuller cross-cultural discussion of suicide, see Counts (1987), Farberow (1975), and the journal *Crisis*.

Perspectives, Myths, and Feelings about Self-Destructive People

Nearly everyone has had contact with self-destructive people. Some of us have relatives and friends who have committed suicide or made suicide attempts. We know others who slowly destroy themselves by excessive drinking or abuse of other drugs. Among the readers of this book, a certain percentage will have responded to a life crisis by some kind of self-destructive act. For example, the suicide rates among physicians and dentists are some of the highest among occupational groups. Also, narcotic addiction, as a way of coping with stress, and with professional access to drugs, occurs among some physicians and nurses. It is a tragedy that those whose main work is service to others may find it difficult to ask for help for themselves when in crisis. All too often, physicians and nurses, particularly those who are in direct contact with people who have cut their wrists, attempted to kill themselves in a car crash, or overdosed on pills, will attempt to drown their own troubles in alcohol. These are only a few of the many consequences of self-destructive incidents commonly addressed by emergency service personnel.

Volunteers and other workers in suicide and crisis centers are another group that has frequent contact with self-destructive people. About 20% of callers to these centers are in suicidal crisis. Counselors and psychotherapists also work with self-destructive people.

These workers, as well as other people, have varying degrees of knowledge about suicide and self-destructive people. Unfortunately, myths and misleading beliefs about suicidal people are widespread. The following are some of the most common myths and facts about suicide (Motto, 1999; Shneidman, 1981, pp. 213–214):

Myth: People who commit suicide have a psychiatric illness; they are "crazy."
Fact: Diagnosable mental illness is not the dominant factor in most suicides, although people who commit suicide are usually in emotional turmoil. (See this

chapter's "Assessment of the Suicidal Person" section for the suicide–depression link.)

Myth: Good circumstances—a comfortable home or a good job—prevent suicide. This view is revealed in the surprised expression following the suicide of a talented student: "He had everything going for him."

Fact: Suicide cuts across class, race, age, and sex differences, although its frequency varies among different groups in society.

Myth: When gay, lesbian, bisexual, and transgendered people recognize the "sinfulness" of their lives, most of them kill themselves.

Fact: Although a significant number of this group commit suicide or make suicide attempts, they do so most often because of the prejudice, hatred, and sometimes violence they have endured from mainstream society.

Myth: People who talk about suicide are not a serious risk for suicide.

Fact: People who die by suicide almost invariably talk about suicide or give clues and warnings about their intention through their behavior, even though the clues may not be recognized at the time.

Myth: People who threaten suicide, superficially cut their wrists, or do not succeed with other attempts are not at risk for suicide.

Fact: The majority of people who succeed in killing themselves have a history of previous suicide attempts. All threats and self-injury should be taken seriously. Not to do so may precipitate another attempt.

Myth: Talking about suicide to people who are upset will put the idea in their heads. This myth prevails as a misguided protection for those who do not know how to help and therefore are uncomfortable bringing up the subject.

Fact: Suicide is much too complex a process to occur as a result of a caring person asking a question about suicidal intent.

Myth: People who are deeply depressed do not have enough energy to commit suicide.

Fact: The energy level of another person is subjective and difficult to assess. People may kill themselves when depressed or following improvement; frequent and repeated assessment is therefore indicated, regardless of the level of depression.

Some of these myths can probably be recognized among ourselves, family, friends, and associates. Even among health professionals, these ideas are more common than one would expect.

Professional *suicidologists* (those trained in the study of suicide and suicide prevention) believe that suicide prevention is everybody's business—a difficult order considering how many unfounded beliefs about suicide still persist. But often, even nurses and physicians may resist dealing with self-destructive people by telling themselves, "That's somebody else's job." To be fair, people can hardly deal with something they know little about, and there are a number of difficulties in trying to learn more about self-destructive people:

- Cultural taboos against suicide
- Strong feelings about suicide and other self-destructive acts
- Limitations of doing research on human beings

- The intrinsic difficulty of examining the self-destructive process in those who commit suicide because study is limited to determining the probable reasons for suicide from survivors closely associated with the person

In spite of these limitations, research and direct work with self-destructive persons have yielded promising results. *Suicidology,* the study of suicide and suicide prevention, is still by no means an exact science. Yet the scientific practices developed in the past few decades are a considerable advancement over responses based on myths and taboos. Knowledge alone, however, does not guarantee the use of that knowledge. Many misguided perceptions about self-destructive people and responses to them persist because of intense feelings about suicide, death, and dying. What are some of the most common feelings people have about a self-destructive person? And why are these feelings particularly intense in the helper–client interaction?

As we interact with or observe self-destructive people, we may feel sadness, pity, helplessness, desire to rescue, anger, or frustration. Some of these feelings are mirrored in the following comments:

Curious bystander: "Oh, the poor thing."
Friendly neighbor: "What can I possibly do?"
Family: "Why did she have to disgrace us this way?"
Health provider: "I can't stand wasting my time on these people who are just looking for attention."

After a suicide, several feelings are common among survivors: *anxiety* that something they did or did not do caused the suicide; *relief,* which is not uncommon among family members or therapists who have exhausted themselves trying to help the suicidal person; or *guilt,* which often follows feelings of disgust or relief that the desperate person has died.

Understanding these feelings and their sources is crucial if we are to keep them from becoming impediments to helping distressed people find alternatives to suicide. Our feelings about suicide and responses to self-destructive persons can be clarified from three perspectives: social, psychological, and cultural.

Social Perspective

Physicians, nurses, and other providers are often frustrated in working with self-destructive people. This can be traced, in part, to the socialization these professionals receive in their role of helping the sick person return to health. Success in this role depends partly on whether patients behave according to expectations of people in the "sick role." Parsons (1951, pp. 436–437) identified the following exemptions and responsibilities associated with the sick role:

1. Depending on the nature and severity of the illness, the person is exempt from normal social responsibility. This implies that the illness has been legitimized by a "mandated labeler," usually a physician (Becker, 1963; see also Chapter 3). Such legitimation gives moral approval to being

sick and prevents people from using sickness inappropriately for secondary gains (Ehrenreich & Ehrenreich, 1978).

2. The sick person is expected to accept help and depend as necessary on the caregiver; it is understood that the person cannot improve merely by an act of will.

3. The person is obligated to want to get well as expeditiously as possible.

4. The person must seek technically competent help and cooperate with the helper.

This concept of the sick role is unproblematic if applied to acute illness such as appendicitis or extreme pain caused by kidney stones. In fact, the study of persons with precisely such acute physical conditions resulted in Parsons's sick role formulation. However, the concept is inadequate if applied to chronic illnesses or to any condition with significant social, psychological, or cultural components—in short, any condition in which lifestyle or a willful act, such as smoking, drinking, or sexual contact by the individual, is directly related to the malady.

If so-called social illnesses do not fit the traditional sick role–helper model, think of the model's limitations when applied to a person who is self-destructive. Not only do suicidal people defeat the medical role of fostering and maintaining life, but self-injury appears to flout deliberately the natural instinct to live. The self-destructive person is requesting, directly or indirectly, a departure from the usual roles of patient and health service provider. If such providers deal with suicidal people according to rigid role expectations, the helper–patient relationship can lead to conflict. And if helping is limited to a medical approach when the problem is as philosophical, religious, and social as it is medical, the trouble that health professionals have when working with suicidal persons becomes more understandable. Attention to these social and sick role concepts is particularly relevant in a time-constrained health care system that provides limited insurance coverage for "talk" therapies.

Psychological Perspective

Role conflicts are complicated further if helpers have an unrecognized or excessive need to be needed or to rescue the self-destructive person. Not only is the helper denied the fulfillment of traditional role expectations, but the suicidal person says, in effect, "I don't need you. How can you save me when I don't even want to save myself?" This is a very good question, considering what we know about the failure of psychotherapy without the client's voluntary collaboration.

The most complex manifestation of the social-psychological roots of conflict with suicidal people is in the victim-rescuer-persecutor triangle discussed in Chapter 4. Of all the phases of crisis work, it is most important here that we are sensitive to a person's need for self-mastery, as well as to our own need to control any rescue fantasies we might have. Not to do so could result in a vicious cycle of results that are exactly the opposite of our intentions:

- Our misguided rescue attempts are rejected.
- We feel frustrated in our helper role.
- We persecute the suicidal person for failing to cooperate.
- The suicidal person feels rejected.
- The suicidal person repeats the self-injury.
- The helper feels like a victim.

Preventing and interrupting the victim-rescuer-persecutor cycle is one of the most challenging tasks facing the crisis worker, especially in dealing with self-destructive people. The social network strategies discussed in Chapter 5 are particularly helpful in this task.

Cross-Cultural Perspective

Self-destructive behavior takes on added meaning when placed in cultural-historical perspective. Suicide and self-destructive behavior have been part of the human condition from the beginning of time. Views about it—whether it is honorable or shameful—have always varied. In the Judeo-Christian tradition, neither the Hebrew Bible nor the New Testament prohibits suicide. Jews (defenders of Masada) and Christians (martyrs) alike justified suicide in the face of military defeat or personal attack by pagans. Later, however, suicide took on the character of a sinful act.

Over the centuries, we have seen suicide considered first from a religious standpoint and more recently from a legal and medical perspective as well. Today these three major social institutions overlap in their interpretations of suicide. In spite of professionals' and civil libertarians' sophistication about the topic, suicide is still largely taboo. Now suicide is seen less as a moral offense than as a socially disgraceful act, a response to crisis, or a manifestation of psychiatric illness.

When we view suicide in social, psychological, and cultural perspective, our beliefs and feelings about it are not surprising. We are, after all, members of a cultural community with distinct values about life, ourselves, and other people, as well as views about how people should behave. These cultural facts of life are even more complex when considering the multiethnicity of North American and European societies and the current emphasis on preserving one's unique cultural heritage. It is impossible for us to know in detail the beliefs and customs of cultures to which we have had little direct exposure. What we can do, however, is educate ourselves about ethnocentrism and refrain from imposing our values on others (see Chapters 1 and 4). For example, in some belief systems the idea of an afterlife is meaningless, whereas for others suicide might be precisely the avenue toward a better life after reincarnation.

It is easier to accept and deal with our feelings if we remember that they have historical roots and are complicated by contemporary socialization to professional roles. Failing to recognize this can prevent us from being helpful to self-destructive people, which places an especially heavy burden on emergency and rescue personnel. Human service workers need an opportunity to express and work through their feelings about self-destructive behavior. Dealing with feelings and their origins, then, is a basic step in a worker's acquiring the knowledge and skills necessary to help people in suicidal crisis. Team relationships, peer support groups, and readily accessible consultation are some of the avenues that should be available to people working with suicidal persons.

Ethical Issues Regarding Suicide

Closely related to coping with feelings about self-destructive behavior are our positions on the right to die and the degree of our responsibility for the lives of others. In professional circles of suicidology, philosophy, and psychiatry, and among the general public, the following are hotly debated topics (Battin & Mayo, 1980; Humphrey, 1992; Richman, 1992):

- The right to die by suicide
- The right to physician-assisted suicide
- The right and the responsibility to prevent suicide
- The right to euthanasia and abortion (related topics)

Several ethical and legal questions have implications for the crisis worker.

- How do we respond to a person's declaration: "I have the right to commit suicide, and you don't have the right to stop me"?
- If our own belief system forbids suicide, how might this belief influence our response to such a person?
- If a person commits suicide, whose responsibility is it?
- If we happen to believe the suicidal person alone is responsible, why do we often feel guilty?
- What is the ethical basis for depriving a person of normal, individual rights by commitment to a mental health facility to prevent suicide?
- What do we do if someone close to us requests our assistance in committing suicide?

The intent of these questions is not to persuade the reader to give up cherished beliefs or to impose a libertarian view about suicide. Rather, it is to provide an ethical and clinical basis for dealing with the issues without either abandoning our own beliefs or imposing them on others.

Some workers may confuse suicide prevention efforts with a distorted sense of obligation to prevent any and all suicides whenever physically possible and by whatever means possible. The term *distorted* is used to emphasize these facts:

1. It is physically impossible to prevent suicide in some instances unless we place a person in a padded cell and strip him or her of all clothing. This

does not mean that suicide is inevitable; it means that if psychological aid and social support are lacking, physical protection alone is inadequate.

2. Forced physical protection attacks a person's basic need for mastery and self-determination and may result in the opposite of what is intended in the long run, even though suicide may be prevented in the short run. Such suicide prevention efforts may (a) impose on others the belief that people do not have the right to commit suicide or (b) result in the worker's unresolved "savior complex."

These beliefs and unconscious conflicts often accompany a lack of scientific knowledge about self-destructive behavior and the skills needed to assess suicidal risk. The results may promote rather than prevent suicide through practices such as these:

1. *Placing a hospitalized or imprisoned suicidal person in physical isolation.* This is done to allow closer observation, but it increases the person's sense of abandonment, which for someone suicidal, is already acute.

2. *Committing a suicidal person involuntarily to a psychiatric facility.* This practice assumes the belief that others know what is best for a suicidal person. This can be an attack on the person's sense of dignity and self-worth, yet mental health laws in many states and provinces may encourage the practice among those working in public agencies or mental health professions. There is often little awareness that extreme restriction of individual freedom is a counterproductive power play that can give the suicidal person one more reason to choose death over life—as jail and prison suicides readily attest.

3. *Engaging in punitive practices or discounting the seriousness of self-injury.* When this occurs, the self-destructive person feels attacked and more worthless than ever.

The hidden function of these practices is probably the expression of anger against the self-destructive person for violating the suicide taboo and for frustrating the worker's helping role. The suicidal person has little or no ability to understand such messages. He or she already has an overdose of emotional pain or self-hatred. Rejection by helpers or prison custodians as they carry out their service responsibilities can only increase a person's self-destructiveness.

Opinions differ regarding the issue of responsibility to save others, the right to determine one's own death, and differentiating between adults and children in regard to rights and responsibilities. The *ethical* and *legal* aspects of certain issues must be distinguished. For example, many people believe that suicide is ethically acceptable in certain circumstances, but regardless of personal beliefs, it is illegal in the United States and in most other countries to assist another in the act of suicide. The passage in Oregon of a ballot measure regarding physician-assisted suicide is an exception to this rule. Other states are considering similar legislation. In contrast, although abortion is legal in the United States, people differ about whether it is ethically or morally acceptable. Crisis workers must consider the relevance of theoretical debates to their everyday interaction with suicidal people. The following case analyses illustrate some of the ethical questions.

Case Example: Rachel's "Right" to Commit Suicide

Rachel, age 69, lived with her daughter and son-in-law and was dying of cancer. The community health nurse learned that she was considering suicide. In fact, Rachel spoke openly of her right to kill herself, although she had no immediate plan. Basically, Rachel felt she was a burden to her daughter. Although the daughter had voluntarily invited Rachel to live in her home, she acknowledged the extra stress of caring for her mother. After the nurse worked with the daughter and explored her feelings regarding her dying mother, the relationship between the daughter and mother improved. The daughter was put in touch with a respite service for families of cancer patients. Rachel was no longer suicidal and decided not to exercise her right.

This case demonstrates the philosophical dilemma posed by rational versus "manipulated" suicide (Battin, 1980). Among the rank and file of health and social service workers, the idea of manipulation is commonplace, especially with respect to suicidal people. But several things are noteworthy about this usage. When someone is unsuccessful in a suicide attempt, the assumption is that the person is inappropriately trying to *manipulate* the staff, a family member, or others. The term therefore has a moral connotation. Yet human service workers often do not acknowledge that manipulation is common in all social life. For example, the average person manipulates to get a larger salary, a different work shift, or better housing. When considering the right to commit suicide, we need to examine whether we, as members of a suicidal person's social world, have manipulated a person into "choosing" suicide. A person like Rachel can be manipulated into suicide through material and social circumstances and through ideology.

Rachel's case illustrates (1) her social circumstances, highlighted by her relationship with her daughter and changed through home health care given to the daughter, and (2) her ideology—that is, her belief about her value as an older person dying of cancer. As her view of herself changed, from feeling nonproductive and worthless to feeling valuable in the eyes of her daughter and herself, she stopped arguing about her right to commit suicide. The argument about the right to die, then, becomes moot if the reasons for choosing suicide are the failure to (1) relieve intolerable pain, (2) provide relief to family caretakers, and (3) critically examine a value system that holds no place for the "nonproductive" old, ill, or disabled. Despite continuing trends to pathologize suicide, it is useful to recall Jourard's (1970) definition of suicide as "an invitation [from social network members] to die." Rachel's case suggests that the right-to-commit-suicide argument can cloak hidden social processes and values at work. Paradoxically, acknowledging a person's right to commit suicide can have a curious suicide prevention effect. Even if our own belief system disallows such a right, it is empowering (and therefore life promoting) to respect and acknowledge others' beliefs.[2]

Case Example: Diane—Young Adult Suicide

Diane, a college student, age 22, resisted all alternatives to suicide as proposed by a crisis counselor. She learned she was pregnant, was rejected by her lover, and could not share her distress with her parents or friends. Abortion was not an acceptable alternative to her. She feared that continuing the pregnancy would mean failure to graduate. The counselor agreed with Diane's assertion of her basic right to commit suicide, but expressed regret if Diane were to follow through on that decision during the peak of her crisis. This acknowledgment seemed to give Diane a sense of dignity and control over her life and a new will to live, even though the only resource she perceived at the moment was the counselor.

This and other examples of distressed youth invite us to consider the alarming increase in adolescent suicides. We could profitably ask ourselves the following questions:

■ What are our children telling us about the life and the world we have created for them if they choose death over life at a time when life has just begun?
■ Have we "manipulated" our children into suicide by creating a material and social world and value system in which they do not feel it is worth living?
■ If we acknowledge the "right" of a young person to commit suicide, do we ignore a larger question about reasons for hope or despair among young people?

Case Example: John—Mental Health Commitment

John, age 48, was placed in a mental health facility against his will when he became highly suicidal after his wife had divorced him. He also had a serious drinking problem. John had two very close friends and a small business of his own. The main reason for hospitalizing John was to prevent him from committing suicide. John found the hospital worse than anything he had experienced. He had no contact with his friends while in the hospital. After two weeks, John begged to be discharged. He was no longer highly suicidal but was still depressed. John was discharged with antidepressant medicine and instructed to return for a follow-up appointment in one week. He killed himself with sleeping pills (obtained from a

---

[2] Current debates on voters' ballots about physician-assisted suicide and action intersect with people's concerns about the adequacy of health and social services during terminal illness and their dread of the prospect of "high-technology" death in institutions, which is discussed at length in Chapter 6.

private physician) and alcohol two days after discharge. The staff of the mental hospital did not understand how they had failed John.

John's case represents the complexity of the debate between a commitment to protect against suicide and infringement on the right to self-determination. Mental health laws in North America include provisions for involuntary commitment for observation, evaluation, and treatment of persons considered a serious danger to themselves, either by overt suicidal behavior or by neglect of necessary self-care. But as the paralyzed hero of a movie by the same title put it, "Whose life is it, anyway?" He was speaking of his resistance to the treatment that kept him alive. Even though suicide can be seen as rational in certain circumstances, John's decision could also be seen as "not in his own best interest." Cases like John's reveal the ethical basis for depriving a person of personal freedom in the name of suicide prevention and treatment. In this case, John had friends and by objective standards something to live for, even though he could not see that when he killed himself. It could be argued, therefore, that extreme rescue action by helpers is justified (see Bongar et al., 1998).

John's eventual suicide, though, illustrates the care that must be taken in implementing mental health laws on behalf of suicidal people. First of all, the decision to commit a person must be based on a thorough assessment. Second, even if John had been found to be a serious risk for suicide, involuntary hospitalization seemed to contribute to rather than prevent John's suicide. Hospitalization is indicated for suicidal people only when natural social network resources (such as John's friends) are not present. This case is analyzed further in "Team Analysis Following a Suicide" in Chapter 10.

Some people choose suicide even after considering the alternatives with caring people. Public and controversial examples include the planned suicide of artist Jo Roman in the United States and the case of Sue Rodriguez in Canada. Roman's suicide plans and discussion with her family and friends were aired on national public television, followed by an interdisciplinary panel discussion of the issues by authorities on the topic.

Case Example: Paul—Rational Suicide?

Paul, age 64, had chronic heart disease. He had been depressed since his wife's death 3 months earlier. When he was laid off from his job, he became suicidal and talked with his doctor. Paul's doctor referred him to a community mental health center for therapy. He received individual and group psychotherapy and antidepressant drugs. After 3 months, Paul's depression lifted somewhat, but he was still unconvinced that there was anything left to live for. He had been very dependent on his wife and seemed unable to develop other satisfying relationships, even through the support group for widowed people that he had joined. Paul killed himself by carbon monoxide poisoning after terminating therapy at the mental health center.

Paul's situation does not imply that suicide is inevitable. Instead it suggests the rationality of Paul's decision to commit suicide rather than live in circumstances to which he apparently could not adjust. However, Paul's case also shows us what can be done to help lonely older people find alternatives to suicide, even though these alternatives may be rejected. The people who tried to help Paul can take comfort in the fact that they acted humanely on his behalf, although they may still feel regret. But we must recognize our limitations in influencing the lives of other people (see "Support and Crisis Invention for Survivors" in Chapter 10).

Rational suicide as well as assisted suicide continue as points of discussion in professional and lay circles—including the periodic efforts to test these issues in the voting booth, as states consider laws similar to the one passed in Oregon.

Case Example: Dennis—Rational Suicide?

Dennis, age 33, held a good job as a university professor when he was diagnosed with AIDS. Initially, Dennis was overwhelmed with shock, rage, and despair. He had been successful in his career, enjoyed a supportive circle of friends, and was comfortable with his gay identity. He had decided to kill himself, but after surviving an antigay physical attack and helping two of his friends cope with a similar episode of violence, he became involved in a local activist group and no longer felt suicidal. Dennis reserves for himself, though, the possibility of suicide at a future time if AIDS progresses to the point of dementia for him.

Dennis's case illustrates the importance of control and self-determination for anyone in crisis. Although we need to respect the decisions of people like Dennis, we must be particularly careful in reference to AIDS not to proffer rational suicide as a substitute for our humane response to this worldwide crisis (see Chapter 7).

The following is offered as a practical guideline to helpers with respect to rights and responsibilities regarding suicide: Each person has the final responsibility for his or her own life. This includes the right to live as one chooses or to end life. We have a communal responsibility to do what we reasonably can to help others live as happily as possible. This includes preventing suicide when it appears to be against a person's own best interests—for example, when suffering from major depression without the benefit of treatment. It also involves examining values and social practices that inadvertently lead people to choose suicide only because they are socially disadvantaged and see no other way out. This same principle applies to the issue of euthanasia and assisted suicide: for many, the ethical concern is the "slippery slope" that is too close to the Nazi experience of exterminating people on grounds of ethnicity, religion, sexual identity, or perceived "uselessness" in a society that is bigoted or lacks policies guaranteeing equal access to health and social services (see Fuller, 1997; U.S. Public Health Service, 1999). And if ethical arguments do not support legalized physician-assisted suicide, neither does an economic argument. Emanuel and Battin (1998) found that in the wealthy United States, total end-of-life health care expenditures would be reduced by only 0.07% if physician-assisted suicide were legalized. The choice of assisted suicide in these instances is not truly free. Our social responsibility does not require that we prevent a suicide at all costs. We need to recognize that misguided savior tactics can result in suicide if overbearing help is interpreted as control. However, workers in human service professions such as nursing, medicine, mental health, and law enforcement have an additional responsibility: they should learn as much as they can about self-destructive people and advocate strongly to help despairing people find alternatives to suicide.

Characteristics of Self-Destructive People

To be understood is basic to the feeling that someone cares, that life is worth living. When someone responds to stress with a deliberate suicide attempt, those around the person are usually dismayed and ask *why*. The wide range of self-destructive acts adds to the observer's confusion; there are many overlapping features of self-destructive behavior. For example, Mary, age 50, has been destroying herself through alcohol abuse for 15 years, but she also takes an overdose of sleeping pills during an acute crisis.

The majority of adolescents who harm themselves or have thoughts about self-harm have had serious personal, emotional, or behavioral problems during this period. A study by Evans, Hawton, & Rodham (2005) revealed that self-harm thoughts might reflect a stage of adolescence in which the person's concept of one's own mortality is developing, rather than a sign that something is seriously wrong; on the other hand, those who harmed themselves or had thoughts of doing so, had fewer people with whom they felt able to talk about things that really bothered them. They were also more likely to report emotion-focused strategies such as having an alcoholic drink or getting angry instead of talking with someone who could help to sort things out. All told, adolescents' self-harm thoughts usually reflect major distress and the need for caring adults who will facilitate healthy, nondestructive coping.

Volumes have been written about suicide—by philosophers, the clergy, psychiatrists and psychologists, nurses, and crisis specialists. Academics and researchers have profound discussions and varied opinions regarding the process, meanings, morality, and reasons involved in the act of self-destruction. While these debates continue, the focus in this book is on the *meaning* of self-destructive behavior and the importance of understanding and reaching out to those in emotional pain (see O'Carroll, 1993; Shneidman, 1993). Suicidology founder Edwin Shneidman calls this emotional pain *psychache*, the "hurt, anguish, or ache that takes hold of the mind. It is intrinsically psychological; it is the . . . pain of negative emotions, such as guilt, shame, anguish, fear, panic, anger, loneliness, helplessness. . . . Suicide occurs when the psychache is deemed to be unbearable and when death is actively sought in order to stop the unceasing flow of intolerable consciousness" (1999, pp. 86–87).

Precise definitions and a clear understanding of such behavior are complex and difficult to achieve. However, in spite of academic differences, most people agree that self-destructive behavior signals that a person is in turmoil or "perturbation" (Shneidman, 1976, p. 53). We can enhance our effectiveness in working with suicidal people by becoming familiar with several aspects of self-destructive behavior and with intervention practices widely accepted by experts:

- The range and complexity of self-destructive behavior
- Communication and the meaning of self-destructive behavior
- Ambivalence and its relevance to suicide prevention
- The importance of assessing for suicidal risk
- Sensitivity to ethical and cultural issues as an aid to understanding, assessment, and appropriate intervention

Self-Destructiveness: What Does It Include?

Self-destructive behavior includes any action by which a person emotionally, socially, and physically damages or ends his or her life. Broadly, the spectrum of self-destructiveness includes biting nails, pulling hair, scratching, cutting one's wrist, swallowing toxic substances or harmful objects, smoking cigarettes, banging one's head, abusing alcohol and other drugs, driving recklessly, neglecting life-preserving measures such as taking insulin, attempting suicide, and committing suicide (Farberow, 1980; Menninger, 1938).

At one end of the spectrum of self-destructiveness is Jane, who smokes but is in essentially good emotional and physical health. She knows the long-range effects of smoking and chooses to live her life in such a way that may in fact shorten it. However, Jane would hardly be regarded as suicidal on a lethality assessment scale. Smoking by Arthur, who has severe emphysema, is another matter. His behavior could be considered a slow form of deliberate self-destruction. At the other end of the spectrum is James, who plans to hang himself. Unless saved accidentally, James will most certainly die by his own hand.

There are four broad groups of self-destructive people, which are outlined below.

1. *Those Who Commit Suicide.* Suicide is defined as a fatal act that is self-inflicted, consciously intended, and carried out with the knowledge that death is irreversible. This definition of suicide generally excludes young children because a child's conception of death as final develops around age ten (Pfeffer, 1986). Self-destructive deaths in young children are usually explained in terms of learning theory; the child learns—often by observing parents—that physical and emotional pain can be relieved by ingesting pills or banging one's head.

   Classically defined, suicide is one of four modes of death; the others are natural, accidental, and homicidal. Shneidman (1973, p. 384) emphasizes the role of intention in an individual's death and proposes a reclassification of death as (a) intentioned, (b) subintentioned, and (c) unintentioned. If full information is not available about the person's intentions, it is difficult to determine whether the act is suicidal or accidental. Suicide is not an illness or an inherited disease, as popular opinion and some professional practice seem to imply.

2. *Those Who Threaten Suicide.* This group includes those who talk about suicide and whose suicidal plans may be either very vague or highly specific. Some in this group have made suicide attempts in the past; others have not. Note that only suicidal people threaten suicide; all suicide threats should be taken seriously and considered in relation to the person's intention and social circumstances.

3. *Those Who Make Suicide Attempts.* A suicide attempt is any nonfatal act of self-inflicted damage with self-destructive intention, however vague and ambiguous. Sometimes the individual's intention must be inferred from behavior. Technically, the term *suicide attempt* should be reserved for those actions in which a person attempts to carry out the *intention* to die but for unanticipated reasons, such as failure of the method or an unplanned rescue, the attempt fails, as was the case with George Sloan, Chapter 3. Other self-destructive behavior can more accurately be defined as *self-injury*. The neutral term self-injury should be substituted for the term *suicide gesture*, as the latter suggests that the behavior need not be taken seriously or that the person is "just seeking attention."

Some suicidal persons are in a state of acute crisis—in contrast to some who are chronically self-destructive—and therefore experience a high degree of emotional turmoil. As discussed in Chapter 3, people in crisis may experience a temporary upset in cognitive functioning. This upset can make it difficult for a person to clarify his or her intentions, or it may interfere with making wise decisions. This feature of the crisis state is the basis for the general wisdom of delaying serious decisions such as getting married, selling one's house, or moving to a foreign country while in crisis. Certainly, then, it is similarly unwise to make an irrevocable decision such as suicide when in a state of emotional turmoil and crisis.

The ambiguity arising out of the crisis state should not be confused with a psychotic process, which may or may not be present. Nor should one subscribe to the prevalent myth that "only a crazy person could seriously consider, attempt, or commit suicide." Loss of impulse control influences some suicide attempts and completed suicides. In the large majority of instances, however, self-destructive behavior is something that people consciously and deliberately plan and execute.

4. *Those Who Are Chronically Self-Destructive.* People in this group may habitually abuse alcohol or other drugs and are often diagnosed with personality disorders. For many First Nations people, self-destructive behaviors are embedded in the abject poverty, unemployment, and other results of colonialism and the near destruction of Native

American cultures. The complex relationship between multiple self-harm episodes and suicide risk is discussed further in "Assessment of the Suicidal Person" later in this chapter. Other people may destroy themselves by the deliberate refusal to follow life-sustaining medical programs for such conditions as heart disease or diabetes. Still others engage in high-risk lifestyles or activities that bring them constantly in the face of potential death. Such individuals seem to need the stimulation of their risky lifestyles to make life seem worth living. These behaviors are not, of course, explicitly suicidal. However, individuals who engage in them may become overtly suicidal. This complicates whatever problems already exist.

When considering chronic self-destructiveness, Maris's concept of *suicidal careers* (1981, pp. 62–69) is relevant. In this framework, suicide can be seen as "one product of a gradual loss of hope and the will and resources to live, a kind of running down and out of life energies, a bankruptcy of psychic defenses against death and decay" (p. 69). Or as Shneidman (1987) puts it, "People reach 'the point of no return' in response to unendurable psychological pain."

It is important to distinguish here between self-destructive persons and those who engage in self-mutilating activity (for example, cutting, scraping, and bruising), which generally has no dire medical consequences, although some may end up killing themselves. Unlike suicidal behavior, self-mutilation is not characterized by an intent to die. Rather, it is a way of coping and is usually employed by women. Many of these women are survivors of extreme childhood sexual abuse who have internalized their oppression (see Burstow, 1992, pp. 187–220; Everett & Gallop, 2000; Hoff, 2000).

The Path to Suicide

Suicidal behavior can be viewed on a continuum or as a *highway leading to suicide*. The highway begins with the first suicide threat or attempt and ends in suicide. As in the case of any trip destined for a certain end point, one can always change one's mind, take a different road to another destination, or turn around and come back. The highway to suicide can be conceived either as a short trip (acute crisis) or as a long trip—chronic self-destructiveness extending for years or over a lifetime. But in either case, it suggests that suicide is a process involving

- One's perception of the meaning of life and death
- Availability of psychological and social resources
- Material and physical circumstances making self-destruction possible (for example, when a gun or pills are available or when a bedridden, helpless person is capable of self-destruction only through starvation)

The continuum concept is also useful in understanding suicides that appear to result from impulsive action, as sometimes happens with adolescents.

Even with adolescent suicides, though, examination and hindsight usually reveal a process including, for example, alienation, an acute loss, developmental issues, family conflict, abuse, depression, self-doubt, and cynicism about life.

A destiny of suicide is not inevitable. Whether one continues down the highway to suicide depends on a variety of circumstances. People traveling this highway usually give clues to their distress, so the suicide continuum can be interrupted at any point: after a first attempt, a fifth attempt, or as soon as clues are recognized. Much depends on the help available and the ability of the suicidal person to accept and use help. It is never too late to help a despairing person or to change one's mind about suicide.

Lacking help, some suicidal persons try to relieve their pain by repeated self-injury; each time, their gamble with death becomes more dangerous. As they move along the suicide highway repeating their cries for help, they are often labeled and written off as manipulators or attention seekers. This usually means that professional helpers and others regard them as devious and insincere in their demands for attention. Some conclude that a person who was really serious about suicide would try something that "really did the job." Such a judgment implies a gross misunderstanding of the meaning of a suicidal person's behavior and ignores the person's real needs.

Individuals who are thus labeled and ignored will probably continue to injure themselves. The suicidal episodes typically become progressively more serious in the medical sense, signaling increasing desperation for someone to hear and understand their cries for help. They may also engage in the "no-lose game" as they plan the next suicide attempt (Baechler, 1979). The no-lose game goes something like this: "If they (spouse, friend, family) find me, they care enough and therefore life is worth living. (I win by living.) If they don't find me, life isn't worth living. (I win by dying.)"

The suicide method chosen is usually lethal but includes the possibility of rescue, such as swallowing pills. No-lose reasoning is ineffective in instances when one cannot reasonably expect rescue (for example, a family member rarely checks a person at 2:00 a.m.). It nevertheless indicates the person's extreme distress and illustrates the logic of the no-lose game.

The Messages of Self-Destructive People

Despite differing explanations for suicide, most people agree that self-destructive acts are a powerful means of communicating; suicidal people are trying to tell us something by their behavior. Interrupting the suicide continuum depends on understanding and responding appropriately to messages of psychic pain, distress, or despair.

Most individuals get what they need or want by simply asking for it. Or friends and family are sensitive and caring enough to pick up the clues to distress before the person becomes desperate. Some people, however, spend a lifetime trying to obtain, without success, what they need for basic survival and happiness. This may be because they cannot express their needs directly, either because their needs are insatiable and therefore unobtainable or because others do not listen and try to meet their needs. Finally, these people give up and attempt suicide as a last effort to let someone know that they are hurting and desperate.

Typically, then, suicidal people have a history of unsuccessful communication. Their problems with communication follow two general patterns, which are outlined below.

1. In the first pattern of communication problems, people habitually refrain from expressing feelings and sharing their concerns with significant others. People in this group use the "stiff upper lip" approach to life's problems. Men socialized to be cool and rational in the face of adversity and women socialized to be the social and emotional experts for everyone but themselves contribute to the withholding of feelings. This kind of failure in communication is typified by the following:

    a. A successful businessman, who obtains a promotion, is threatened by his fear of not being able to handle his new responsibilities and kills himself.
    b. A mother of five children, who works devotedly and without complaint for her children and husband and is considered an ideal mother, one day kills two of her children and then herself.
    c. A boy, age 17, who is an honor student, plans to go to law school, and is the pride of his parents and the school, is found dead of carbon monoxide poisoning in the family car.

    In each of these cases, the response is great shock and consternation: "He seemed to have everything. I wonder why. There doesn't seem to be any reason." Yet hindsight usually reveals that there were clues. Subtle changes in behavior, along with a tendency to repress feelings, should be regarded as quiet cries for help. The messages of these suicidal people are less explicit, and there often is no history of suicidal behavior. Caring others, therefore, need great sensitivity; they need to encourage the suicidal person to share life's joys, troubles, and suicidal fantasies without feeling like an "unmanly" man, a "failure" as a wife and mother, or a "sissy" as an adolescent. Lacking invitations to share and live instead of die, these people's despair may be forever unexpressed in the eternity of death.

2. The second pattern of communication problems is less subtle than the first. People in this group typically include those who threaten suicide or have actually injured themselves. Their suicidal messages are quite direct and are often preceded by other cries for help (Farberow & Shneidman, 1961). Consider, for example, an adolescent girl's signals that something is wrong:

    Age 11: sullenness and truancy from school
    Age 12: experimentation with drugs
    Age 13: running away from home

Age 14: pregnancy and abortion
Age 15: first suicide attempt

After a person's first suicide attempt, family members and other significant people in the individual's life are usually shocked. They often are more disturbed by a suicide attempt than by anything else the person might have done. Typically, a parent, spouse, or friend will say, "I knew she was upset and not exactly happy, but I didn't know she was that unhappy." In other words, the first suicide attempt is the most powerful of a series of behavioral messages or clues given over a period of time.

We should all be familiar with suicidal clues or cries for help, such as

- "You won't be seeing me around much anymore."
- "I've about had it with this job. I can't take it anymore."
- "I'm angry at my mother. She'll really be sorry when I'm dead."
- "I can't take any more problems without some relief."
- "I can't live without my boyfriend. I don't really want to die; I just want him back or somebody in his place."
- "I can't take the pain and humiliation [from AIDS, for example] anymore."
- "There's nothing else left since my wife left me. I really want to die."

Behavioral clues may include making out a will, taking out a large life insurance policy, giving away precious belongings, being despondent after a financial setback, or engaging in unusual behavior.

Studies reveal that a majority of persons who commit suicide have made previous attempts, or have given other significant clues of their suicidal intent (Brown & Sheran, 1972; Shneidman & Farberow, 1957; see Online Resources for later research supporting this foundational work). These behavioral, verbal, and affective clues can be interpreted in two general ways: (1) "I want to die," or (2) "I don't want to die, but I want something to change in order to go on living," or "If things don't change, life isn't worth living. Help me find something to live for."

It is up to the interested helping person to determine the *meaning* of suicidal behavior and to identify clues in the distressed person's words and attitudes. This is done not by inferring the person's meaning, but by *asking*, for example,

- "What do you mean when you say you can't take your problems anymore? Are you thinking of suicide?"
- "What did you hope would happen when you took the pills (or cut your wrists)? Did you intend to die?"

There is no substitute for *simple, direct communication* by a person who cares. Besides providing the information we need in order to help, it is helpful to the suicidal person. It tells the person we are interested and concerned about her or his motives for the contemplated suicide. Often self-destructive people have lacked the advantages of communicating directly about their feelings all of their lives.

Unfortunately, many people lack the knowledge or resources to respond helpfully to a suicidal person. The self-destructive person is often surrounded by others who potentially could help but whose own troubles prevent them from providing what the self-destructive person needs. Some families are so needy that the most they can do is obtain medical treatment for the suicidal person. This situation is not helped by the fact that 24-hour crisis services are not accessible in some communities.

Some would-be helpers fail to communicate directly about suicide in the false belief that talking to the person about suicide intentions may trigger such ideas if the person does not already have them. The process of deciding to commit suicide is much more complicated than such reasoning implies. A person who is not suicidal will not become so as a result of a question from someone intending to help. In fact, experience reveals that suicidal people are relieved when someone is sensitive enough to respond to their despair and help protect them from themselves.

For three reasons, then, communication is crucial in our work with people who respond to crisis by self-destructive behavior.

1. It is a key element in discerning the *process* of self-destruction (understanding).
2. It is the most effective means of ascertaining the person's *intention* regarding death (assessment of risk).
3. It is an essential avenue for *helping* the person feel reconnected to other human beings and find a reason to live (crisis intervention).

Ambivalence: Weighing Life and Death

Suicidal people usually struggle with two irreconcilable wishes—the desire to live and the desire to die. They simultaneously consider the advantages of life and death, a state of mind known as *ambivalence*. As long as the person has ambivalent feelings about life and death, it is possible to help the individual consider choices on the side of life. Suicide is not inevitable. People can change their minds if they find realistic alternatives to suicide. The concept of ambivalence is basic to the purpose of suicide prevention and crisis work; those who are no longer ambivalent do not usually come to an emergency service, see their physician, or call crisis hotlines.

Case Example: Sally

Sally, age 16, made a suicide attempt by swallowing six sleeping pills. In medical terms, this was not a serious attempt. Although she contemplated death, she also wanted to live. She hoped that the suicide attempt would bring about some change in her miserable family life, so that she could avoid the last resort of suicide itself. Before her suicide attempt, Sally was having trouble in school, ran away from home once, experimented with drugs, and engaged in behavior that often brought disapproval from her parents.

All of these behaviors were Sally's way of saying, "Listen to me! Can't you see that I'm miserable, that I can't control myself, that I can't go on like this anymore?" Sally had been upset for several years by her parents' constant fighting and playing favorites with the children. Her father drank heavily and frequently was away from home. When Sally's school counselor recommended family counseling, the family refused out of shame. Sally's acting out was really a cry for help. After her suicide attempt, her parents accepted counseling. Sally's behavior improved generally, and she made no further suicide attempts.

If Sally had not obtained the help she needed, it is probable that she would have continued down the highway to suicide. The usual pattern in such a case is that the attempts become medically more serious, the person becomes more desperate, and finally he or she commits suicide. Helping the ambivalent person move in the direction of life is done by understanding and responding to the meaning of the person's behavior.

Assessment of the Suicidal Person

Communication leads to understanding, which is the foundation for decision and action. Helping suicidal people without understanding what their behavior *means* and without ascertaining the degree of suicide risk is difficult. *Suicide risk assessment* is the process of determining the likelihood of suicide for a particular person. *Lethality assessment* refers to the degree of physical injury incurred by a particular self-destructive act. Sometimes these terms are used interchangeably. *Suicide prediction* is "not very precise or useful" (Maris, 1991, p. 2) and according to psychiatrist Motto (1991, p. 75) should probably be eliminated from scientific terminology. The main focus here is to provide clinicians with guidelines about the risk of suicide that are based on clinical experience and on empirical and epidemiological findings. Clinical assessment tries to answer this question: What is the risk of death by suicide for *this individual* at *this time*, considering the person's life as a whole?

Some workers use lethality assessment scales, which are primarily research tools, to assess suicidal risk. Most of these scales are not very effective (Brown & Sheran, 1972), and are too lengthy and time-consuming in a crisis situation. Motto (1985, p. 139) states, "The use of a scale has never been intended to predict suicide, but simply to supplement clinical judgment at the time an evaluation is done." Nor can a rating scale ever substitute for a clinician's sensitive inquiry (Motto, 1991)—for example, "Can you tell me what's happening to cause you so much pain?" The problem with most scales is that they do not exclude the nonsuicidal population—a pivotal point revealed in the pioneering research by Brown and Sheran (1972). For example, let us consider depression as a predictive sign. A large number of people who commit suicide (approximately 60%) have been diagnosed as depressed; however, the majority of depressed people do not commit suicide. Of the 20 million or so persons with a depressive disorder, only 0.1% commit suicide; Jacobs (2000, p. 32) notes the striking fact that 99.9% of persons diagnosed annually with depression do not commit suicide. Similarly, the majority of people who commit suicide have made previous suicide attempts, yet 8 out of 10 people who attempt suicide never go on to commit suicide. These statistics do not invite complacency; they simply indicate the complexity of suicide risk assessment, the limits of psychiatric diagnostic criteria, and the fact that something changed for a particular person at risk—for example, a cry for help was heard.

The Importance of Assessing Suicide Risk

The importance of suicide risk assessment can be compared with the importance of diagnosing a cough before beginning treatment. Effective assessment of suicide risk should accomplish the following:

- Cut down on guesswork in working with self-destructive people
- Reduce the confusion and disagreement that often occur among those trying to help suicidal people
- Provide a scientific base for service plans for self-destructive people
- Ensure that hospitalization of suicidal persons is used appropriately
- Decrease a worker's level of anxiety in working with suicidal persons

Failure to assess the degree of suicide risk results in unnecessary problems, such as failure to institute follow-up counseling following emergency medical treatment for self-injury. Another problem arising out of guesswork about suicide risk is unnecessary hospitalization. It is inappropriate to hospitalize a suicidal person when the degree of suicide risk is very low and other sources of protection are available. A person who hopes, by a suicide attempt, to relieve isolation from family may feel even more isolated in a psychiatric hospital. This is especially true when community and family intervention are indicated instead.

Sometimes health providers hospitalize suicidal people because of their own anxiety about suicide. Unresolved feelings of guilt and responsibility about suicide usually precipitate such action. Conversely, hospitals can be places in which isolation can be relieved and suicide prevented when social supports in the community are lacking. As with personal factors, assumptions about the presence or absence of social supports should not be made without a systematic social assessment (see Chapters 3 and 5).

Signs that Help Assess Suicide Risk

Risk assessment techniques are based on knowledge obtained from the study of completed suicides. Such research is among the most difficult of scientific studies (Maris, 1991), but the study of completed suicides has explained much about the problem of risk assessment. Maris et al. (1992), Brown and Sheran (1972), and others have identified signs that help us assess the degree of risk for suicide. The *most reliable indicators* help us distinguish people who commit suicide from the population at large and also from those who only attempt suicide. These signs, however, have their limitations. For instance, there is not enough research on suicide to warrant general conclusions about suicide for different population groups. One should never be overconfident in applying signs to a suicidal person. It is impossible to predict suicide in any absolute sense; the focus for clinicians should be on assessing *immediate* and *long-term risk*. However, attention to the known signs of suicide risk is a considerable improvement over an approach based on myth, taboo, and unresearched guesswork. The chaos of a crisis situation and anxiety about suicide can be reduced by thoughtful attention to general evidence-based principles.

The following material regarding signs that help us assess suicide risk is summarized from the seminal works of Alvarez (1971), Brown and Sheran (1972), Brown and Harris (1978), Durkheim (1897/1951), Farberow (1975), Furst and Huffine (1991), Hendin (1982), Litman (1987), Maris (1981, 1992), and Shneidman (1985). Over the years since Edwin Shneidman's 1960s inauguration of suicidology as a field of scientific clinical study, the classic signs of suicide risk have varied little. These principles for assessing suicide risk apply to *any* person in *any* setting contacted through *any* helping situation: telephone, office, hospital, home, work site, jail, nursing home, school, or pastoral care. *Functional* assessment (emotional, cognitive, behavioral) is the focus, although psychiatric *pathology* may be present in some instances. The discussion is based on research in Western societies; suicide signs and methods vary in other cultural settings (see the World Health Organization Web site, http://www.who.int). Sensitivity to these differences, however, is important in helping various immigrant and ethnic groups in distress in North America.

Suicide Plan. Studies reveal that the majority of persons who die by suicide deliberately planned to do so. Without a high-lethal plan with available means, suicide cannot occur. In respect to the plan, people suspected of being suicidal should be asked several direct questions concerning the following subjects.

1. *Suicidal Ideas.* "Are you so upset that you're thinking of suicide?" or "Are you thinking about hurting yourself?"
2. *Lethality of Method.* "What are you thinking of doing?" or, "What have you considered doing to harm yourself?"

   High-lethal methods include:
   Shooting
   Hanging
   Barbiturate and prescribed sleeping pills
   Jumping
   Drowning
   Carbon monoxide poisoning

Aspirin (high dose) and acetaminophen (Tylenol)
Car crash
Exposure to extreme cold
Antidepressants

Low-lethal methods include:

Wrist cutting
Nonprescription drugs (excluding aspirin and acetaminophen [Tylenol])
Tranquilizers (antianxiety agents)

The helper should also determine the person's knowledge about the lethality of the chosen method. For example, a person who takes 10 tranquilizers with the mistaken belief that the dose is fatal is alive more by accident than by intent.

3. *Availability of Means.* "Do you have a gun? Do you know how to use it? Do you have ammunition? Do you have pills?" Lives have often been saved by removing very lethal methods such as guns and sleeping pills. A highly suicidal person who calls a crisis center is often making a final effort to get help, even while sitting next to a loaded gun or a bottle of pills. Such an individual will welcome a direct, protective suggestion from a telephone counselor, such as, "Why don't you put the gun away?" or "Why don't you throw the pills out, and then let's talk about what's troubling you." When friends and family are involved, they too should be directed to get rid of the weapon or pills. In disposing of lethal weapons, it is important to engage the suicidal person actively in the process, keeping in mind that power ploys can trigger rather than prevent suicide. If trust and rapport have been established, engaging the suicidal person is generally not difficult to do.

4. *Specificity of Plan.* "Do you have a plan worked out for killing yourself?" "How do you plan to get the pills?" "How do you plan to get the gun?" A person who has a plan that is well thought out—including time, place, and circumstances—with an available high-lethal method is an immediate and very high risk for suicide. We should also determine whether any rescue possibilities are included in the plan—for example, "What time of day do you plan to do this?" or "Is there anyone else around at that time?" We should also inquire about the person's intent. Some people really do intend to die; others intend to bring about some change that will help them avoid death and make life more livable.

We can seldom discover a person's suicide plan except through direct questioning. Someone who believes in the myth that talking about suicide may suggest the idea will hesitate to ask direct questions. The suicide plan is a less important sign of risk in the case of people with a history of impulsive behavior. This is true for some adults and for adolescents in general, who are inclined to be impulsive as a characteristic of their stage of development.

History of Suicide Attempts. In the North American adult population, suicide attempts occur 8 to 10 times more often than actual suicide. Among adolescents, there are about 50 attempts to every completed suicide. Most people who attempt suicide do not go on to commit suicide. Usually, some change occurs in their psychosocial world that makes life more desirable than death. But it is also true that the majority of people who kill themselves have made previous suicide attempts. A history of suicide attempts (65% of those who have completed suicide) is especially prominent among suicidal people who find that self-destructive behavior is the most powerful means they have of communicating their distress to others. Those who have made previous high-lethal attempts are at greater risk for suicide than those who have made low-lethal attempts.

Another historical indicator is a change in method of suicide attempt. A person who makes a high-lethal attempt after several less lethal attempts that elicited increasingly indifferent responses from significant others is a higher risk for suicide than a person with a consistent pattern of low-lethal attempts. This is particularly true in the case of suicidal adolescents. Suicide attempts as a risk factor should also be considered in relation to depression. Among the 929 severely depressed patients in the Collaborative Depression Study, suicide attempt was not a predictor of suicide within one year, but was a predictor of suicide within 2 to 10 years (Fawcett, 2000, p. 38). This finding underscores a pivotal point in suicide prevention work—the need to *reassess* for suicide risk.

We should also determine the outcome of previous suicide attempts—for example, "What happened after your last attempt? Did you plan any possibility of rescue, or were you rescued accidentally?" A person living alone who overdoses with sleeping pills and then has unexpected company and is rescued is alive more by accident than by intent. This person falls into a high-risk category for future suicide if there are other high-risk indicators as well. Suicide risk is also increased if the person has a negative perception of a psychiatric hospital or counseling experience. This finding underscores the importance of extreme caution in employing mental health laws to hospitalize suicidal people against their will for self-protection.

Resources and Communication with Significant Others. Internal resources consist of strengths, problem-solving ability, and personality factors that help one cope with stress. External resources include a network of persons on whom one can rely routinely as well as during a crisis. Communication as a suicide sign includes (1) the statement to others of intent to commit suicide and (2) the disruption of bonds between the suicidal person and significant others. A large number of people who finally commit suicide feel ignored or cut off from significant people around them, some to the point of feeling there are no significant people in their lives. This is extremely important in the case of adolescents, especially regarding their attempts to communicate with their parents. Research suggests that most adolescents who kill themselves are at odds with their families and feel very misunderstood or have experienced various external stressors (Berman & Jobes, 1991; Evans, Owens, & March, 2005; Goldston et al., 2008).

Institutionalized racism and the unequal distribution of material resources in the United States appear to contribute to the rapidly increasing rate of suicide among minority groups. This is especially true among young people (under 30 years) who realize early in life that many doors are closed to them. Their rage and frustration eventually lead to despair, suicide, and other violent behavior. An example of violence that is closely linked to suicide is *victim-precipitated homicide.* In this form of homicide, the person killed is suicidal, but instead of committing suicide, the victim incites someone else to kill, thus precipitating the homicide (see Parent, 1998, for a discussion on when such deaths involve police).

Others may have apparent resources, such as a supportive, caring spouse, but the conviction of their worthlessness prevents them from accepting and using such support. This is especially true for suicidal people who are also extremely depressed. Adequate personality resources include the ability to be flexible and to accept mistakes and imperfections in oneself. Some people who kill themselves seem to have happy families, good jobs, and good health. Observers therefore assume that these people have no reason to kill themselves. Research by Breed (1972) reveals that this kind of person perceives himself or herself in very rigid roles imposed by culture, sexual identity, or socioeconomic status. A typical example is the middle-aged male executive who rigidly commits himself to success by climbing up the career ladder in his company. A threatened or actual failure in this self-imposed and rigid role performance can precipitate suicide for such a person.

Such perceived failure is usually gender specific—work failure for men (Morrell, Taylor, Quine, & Kerr, 1993) and family or mate failure for women (Stephens, 1985). Other research, however, suggests that a woman might commit suicide in response to "superwoman" demands that she be both the perfect, unpaid domestic worker and the perfect paid public worker (Hoff, 1985). Investigation of completed suicides reveals that a person with rigid role perceptions commits suicide after receiving, for example, a long-anticipated promotion, an event that leads the person to doubt his or her ability to fulfill higher expectations (Perrah & Wichman, 1987). Such rigidity in personality type is also revealed in the person's approach to problem solving. The individual sees narrowly, perceiving only one course of action or one solution to a problem—suicide. This has sometimes been described as telescopic or *tunnel vision* (Shneidman, 1987, p. 57). Such people typically are candidates for psychotherapy to help them develop more flexible approaches to problem solving. We should recognize this rigidity as a possible barrier in our efforts to help suicidal people consider alternatives. A person of this type whose personal and social resources are exhausted and whose only remaining communication link is to a counselor or helping agency is a high risk for suicide.

Research and clinical experience suggest that workers should look not only at such signs of risk but also at the complex *patterning* of signs (Brown & Sheran, 1972; Farberow, 1975), in concert with clinical judgment (Motto,

1991). *Let us apply this evidence to the pattern of the signs considered previously. If the person (1) has a history of high-lethal attempts, (2) has a specific, high-lethal plan for suicide with available means, (3) lacks both personality and social resources, and (4) cannot communicate with available resources, the immediate and long-range risk for suicide is very high, regardless of other factors.* Attempts at precise measurement of a scale are of little value if one has inadequate information about these critical signs. The risk increases, however, if factors such as those discussed next are also present.

Sex, Age, Race, Marital Status, and Sexual Identity. The suicide ratio among North American men and women is approximately three males to one female, although female suicides are increasing at a faster rate than male suicides. Among children between the ages of 10 and 14, the suicide rate averages 0.8 per 100,000. Because suicide implies an understanding of death as irreversible, in the case of children below the age of 10, designating suicide as a cause of death should be done cautiously. Surely there is psychic pain, but a child's *learned* self-destructive behavior may be more accurate. Older Americans, especially white males, are disproportionately likely to die by suicide. Among blacks, Chicanos, and First Nations people, the suicide rate reaches its peak under the age of 30.

The overall suicide rate among white persons is three times that among black persons. However, among young, urban, African American men between 20 and 35 years of age, the rate is twice that of white men the same age. In Native North American communities, the suicide rate varies from group to group. In general, suicide rates are increasing among adolescents and racial minority groups and among youth experiencing sexual-identity crisis.

If a person is separated from a spouse, widowed, or divorced, the risk of suicide increases. Those who are married or who have never been married are at less risk. This seems related to the loss factor among suicidal people but does not seem to apply to two specific groups—older, married, white men who are simply tired of living and married black people who have lost a love relationship. See Motto (1991) regarding limitations of statistical data to predict suicide in particular individuals. (See www.cdc.gov for current rates.)

Recent Loss. Loss or the threat of loss of a spouse, parent, status, money, or job increases a person's suicide risk. Loss is a very significant suicide indicator among adolescents. Loss should also be kept in mind as a common theme in most people's experience of crisis (see "Loss, Change, and Grief Work" in Chapter 4).

Physical Illness. Studies reveal that many people who kill themselves are physically ill. Many suicide victims have been under medical care or have visited their physician within 4 to 6 months of their death. The visit to a physician does not necessarily imply that the person is physically ill. However, it highlights the fact that a large number of people with any problem seek out either physicians or the clergy. In the case of suicidal people, the visit may be their last attempt to find relief from distress.

These facts suggest the influential role primary care providers can have in preventing suicide if they are attentive to clues. This includes alertness to older adults' tendency to somatize depression. The provider's failure to ascertain the suicide plan or to examine the depression disguised by a complaint with no physical basis often leads to the common practice of prescribing a psychotropic drug without listening to the person and making a referral for counseling. Such a response by a physician or advanced practice nurse can be interpreted by the individual as an invitation to commit suicide (see Chapter 7). The possibility of suicide is even greater if a person receives a diagnosis that affects his or her self-image and value system or demands a major switch in lifestyle—for example, AIDS, degenerative neurological conditions, heart disease, breast cancer, amputation of a limb, or cancer of the sex organs (see Hoff & Morgan, in press; Rodin, 2000).

Drinking and Other Drug Abuse. Drinking increases impulsive behavior and loss of control and therefore increases suicide risk, especially if the person has a high-lethal means available. Alcohol also reduces the number of sleeping pills needed for a lethal overdose. Among those diagnosed with alcoholism, a significant number die by suicide. Often adolescents who die by suicide were involved in drug or alcohol abuse before their death. People with liver damage from alcohol abuse may die from a low-lethal method like wrist cutting because of interference with the normal clotting time.

Physical Isolation. If a person is isolated both emotionally and physically, risk of suicide is greater than if he or she lives with close significant others. In Durkheim's classic work (1897/1951), *egoistic suicide* occurs among people who feel they do not belong to society; *anomic suicide* occurs among people who cannot adjust to change and social demands. Approval by others of our performance in expected roles is one of our basic human needs. The lack of such approval leads to social isolation.

Negative reactions from significant people are incorporated into the hurt and painful sense of self. Rejection from significant others can lead to a conviction of worthlessness. When this happens, people believe that others also see them as worthless. People who suffer from discrimination are at risk for egoistic suicide. However, studies indicate that once minority groups and women achieve equality and better conditions, their risk for anomic suicide will increase. If white society or male dominance can no longer be blamed, the person may internalize failure. This process can lead to suicide. As one black person put it, "Being on the ground floor left no room to jump." Thus, upward mobility may increase suicide risk.

A person who is physically alone and socially isolated is often a candidate for hospitalization or other extraordinary means to relieve isolation. In such cases, hospitalization can be a lifesaving measure.

Unexplained Change in Behavior. Changes in behavior, such as reckless driving and drinking by a previously careful and sober driver, can be an indicator of suicide risk. It is particularly important to observe behavior changes in adolescents, as these changes are often clues to inner turmoil. Again, direct communication about observed behavior changes can be a lifesaving measure, signaling that someone cares and is sensitive to another's distress, even though talking about it initially may seem impossible.

Depression. Depressed people may experience sleeplessness, early wakening, slowed-down functioning, weight loss, menstrual irregularity, loss of appetite, inability to work normally, disinterest in sex, crying, and restlessness. Feelings of hopelessness are an even more important indicator of suicidal danger than depression (Beck, Steer, Beck, & Newman, 1993; Bertolote et al., 2003). Those with bipolar illness, especially early in the illness, are also at risk (Solomon, Keitner, Miller, Shea, & Keller, 1995). Depressed adolescents are often overactive (agitated depression); they may fail in school or withdraw from usual social contacts. Although not all people who kill themselves show signs of depression, enough suicide victims are depressed to make this an important indicator of risk. This is particularly true for the depressed person who feels worthless and is unable to reach out to others for help. Because most depressed people do not kill themselves (Fawcett, 2000, p. 38) and because a useful predictor must distinguish between the *general population* and those who make *suicide attempts*, we should refrain from declaring depression as a significant predictor of suicide. That said, *depression is a significant avenue for opening direct discussion of possible suicide plans:* "You seem really down. Are you so depressed that perhaps you've considered suicide?"

Social Factors. Social problems such as family disorganization, a broken home, and a record of delinquency, truancy, and violence against others increase a person's risk of suicide. Many adolescents who kill themselves had prior physical fights with their families. A person with a chaotic social background is also likely to follow the suicide attempt pattern of significant others. Suicide risk also increases for people who are unemployed or forced to retire or move, especially when these upsets occur during a developmental transition stage. Among women who attempt suicide, many have a history of sexual or other abuse (Hoff, 2000; Stephens, 1985).

Psychosis. Some people falsely believe that only a mentally ill person could commit suicide. If an individual with a thought disorder hears voices directing him or her to commit suicide, the risk of suicide is obviously increased. However, the number of individuals who fall into this category is extremely small. Risk may also increase following remission if the person interprets effective treatment as freedom from illness and then discontinues antipsychotic medication only to have the perception of being "cured" dashed by another psychotic episode (Motto, 1999, pp. 227–228). People who are diagnosed as psychotic should routinely be assessed for suicide risk according to the criteria outlined in this section.

Table 9.1 illustrates how signs of suicide risk help distinguish people who kill themselves from those who injure themselves non-lethally and from the general population. In the next section, the pattern of these signs is described in a typology of suicide risk.

TABLE 9.1 Signs Comparing People Who Complete or Attempt Suicide with the General Population

Signs	Suicide	Suicide Attempt	General Population
Suicide plan[a]	Specific, with available, high-lethal method; does not include rescue	Less lethal method, including plan for rescue; risk increases if lethality of method increases	None, or vague ideas only
History of suicide attempts[a]	65% have history of high-lethal attempts; if rescued, it was probably accidental	Previous attempts are usually low lethal; rescue plan included; risk increases if there is a change from many low-lethal attempts to a high-lethal one	None, or low lethal with definite rescue plan
Resources[a] Psychological Social	Very limited or nonexistent; or person *perceives* self with no resources	Moderate, or in psychological and/or social turmoil	Either intact or able to restore them through nonsuicidal means
Communication[a]	Feels cut off from resources and unable to communicate effectively	Ambiguously attached to resources; may use self-injury as a method of communicating with significant others when other methods fail	Able to communicate directly and nondestructively for need fulfillment
Recent loss	Increases risk	May increase risk	Is widespread but is resolved nonsuicidally through grief work, and so forth
Physical illness	Increases risk	May increase risk	Is common but responded to through effective crisis management (natural and/or formal)
Drinking and other drug abuse	Increases risk	May increase risk	Is widespread but does not in itself lead to suicide
Physical isolation	Increases risk	May increase risk	Many well-adjusted people live alone; they handle physical isolation through satisfactory social contacts
Unexplained change in behavior	A possible clue to suicidal intent, especially in teenagers	A cry for help and possible clue to suicidal ideas	Does not apply in absence of other predictive signs

Signs	Suicide	Suicide Attempt	General Population
Depression	60% have a history of depression	A large percentage are depressed	A large percentage are depressed
Social factors or problems	May be present	Often are present	Widespread but do not in themselves lead to suicide
Psychosis	May be present	May be present	May be present
Age, sex, race, marital status, sexual identity	Statistical predictors that are most useful for identifying whether an individual belongs to a high-lethal risk group, not for clinical assessment of individuals	May be present	May be present

ᵃ If all four of these signs exist in a particular person, the risk for suicide is very high regardless of all other factors. If other signs also apply, the risk is increased further.

Typology of Suicidal Behavior: Assessing Immediate and Long-Range Risk

People tend to classify the seriousness of self-destructive behavior according to whether there is immediate danger of death. A person might engage in several kinds of self-destructive behavior at the same time. For example, an individual who chronically abuses alcohol may threaten, attempt, or commit suicide—all in one day. We should view these behaviors on the continuum noted earlier; all are serious and important in terms of life and death. The difference is that for some the danger of death is *immediate*, whereas for others it is *long-range*. Still others are at risk because of a high-risk lifestyle, chronic substance abuse, and neglect of medical care.

Distinguishing between immediate and long-range risk for suicide is not only a potential life-saving measure, it is also important for preventing or interrupting a vicious cycle of repeated self-injury. If immediate risk is high, and we do not uncover it in assessment, a suicide can result. Conversely, if immediate risk is low, as in medically nonserious cases of wrist slashing or swallowing a few sleeping pills, but we respond medically as though life were at stake while failing to address the *meaning* of this physical act, we run the risk of *reinforcing* self-destructive behavior. In effect, we say through our behavior, "Do something more serious (medically), and I'll pay attention to you." In reality, medically nonserious self-injury is a life-and-death issue—that is, if the person's cries for help are repeatedly ignored, there is high probability that eventually the person will accept the invitation to do something more serious and actually commit suicide. The Collaborative Depression Study (Fawcett, 2000) affirms this decades-long clinical observation.

The following section assists in assessing suicide risk by means of a structured guide, as presented in Chapter 3 (see Table 9.2). Examples illustrate the application of risk criteria to people at low risk, moderate risk, and high risk. This assessment guide highlights the importance of the patterns of signs and the use of clinical judgment, along with a database—not simply a mechanical rating—in evaluating suicidal risk (Motto, 1991).

Low-Risk Suicidal Behavior. This includes verbal threats of suicide with no specific plan or means of carrying out a plan. This category also includes self-injury by a person who knows that the effects of the method do not involve physical danger or clearly provides for rescue. Ambivalence in low-risk behavior tends more in the direction of life than death.

The immediate risk of suicide is low, but the risk of an attempt, a repeat attempt, and eventual suicide is high, depending on what happens after the threat or attempt. The risk is increased if the person abuses alcohol and other drugs. Social and personal resources are present but problematic for people in this behavior group.

TABLE 9.2 Lethality Assessment Tool: Self

Key to Risk Level	Danger to Self	Typical Indicators
1	No predictable risk of suicide now	Has no suicidal ideation or history of attempt, has satisfactory social support system, and is in close contact with significant others
2	Low risk of suicide now	Has suicidal ideation with low-lethal methods, no history of attempts or recent serious loss, has satisfactory support network, no alcohol problems, basically wants to live
3	Moderate risk of suicide now	Has suicidal ideation with high-lethal method but no specific plan or threats. Or has plan with low-lethal method, history of low-lethal attempts; for example, employed female, age 35, divorced, with tumultuous family history and reliance on psychotropic drugs for stress relief, is weighing the odds between life and death
4	High risk of suicide now	Has current high-lethal plan, obtainable means, history of previous attempts, is unable to communicate with a significant other; for example, female, age 50, living alone, with drinking history; or black male, age 29, unemployed and has lost his lover, depressed and wants to die
5	Very high risk of suicide now	Has current high-lethal plan with available means, history of suicide attempts, is cut off from resources; for example, white male, over 40, physically ill and depressed, wife threatening divorce, is unemployed, or has received promotion and fears failure

Note: Adapted from specifications for use of forms discussed in Chapter 3.

Case Example: Sarah

Sarah, age 42, took six sleeping pills at 5:00 p.m. with general knowledge of the drug's lethal capacity (about one-third of a lethal dose) as a way to just "get away from it all" through sleep. When her husband found her sleeping at 6:00 p.m. the next day, he had at least some message of her distress. Sarah is troubled by her marriage and has a limited social circle (her husband never liked any of her friends). She is employed part-time as a secretary. She really wants a divorce but is afraid she cannot easily make it on her own. Sarah also takes an antidepressant drug every day. She has not made any other suicide attempts.

Suicide risk for Sarah: Sarah's immediate risk of suicide is low (risk rating: 2). The risk of repeat suicide attempts is moderate to high, depending on what Sarah is able to do about her problem.

Moderate-Risk Suicidal Behavior

This includes verbal threats with a plan and available means more specific and potentially more lethal than those involved in low-risk behavior. Also included are attempts in which the possibility of rescue is more precarious. The chosen method, although it may result in temporary physical disability, is not fatal, regardless of whether or not there is rescue. Ambivalence is strong; life and death are seen more and more in an equally favorable light. The immediate risk for suicide is moderate. The risk for a repeat suicide attempt and eventual suicide is higher than for low-risk behavior if emotional pain is not relieved and no important life changes occur after the attempt or revelation of the suicide plan. The risk is significantly increased in the presence of chronic alcohol or other drug abuse.

Case Example: Susan

Susan, age 19, came alone in a taxi to a local hospital emergency department. She had taken an overdose of her antidepressant prescription (three times the usual dose) a half hour earlier. Susan and her 3-year-old child, Debbie, live with her parents. She has never gotten along well with her parents, especially her mother. Before the birth of her child, Susan had a couple of short-lived jobs as a waitress. She dropped out of high school at age 16 and has experimented off and on with drugs. Since the age of 15, Susan has made four suicide attempts. She took overdoses of nonprescription drugs three times and cut her wrists once. These attempts were assessed as being of low lethality.

At the emergency department, Susan had her stomach pumped and was kept for observation for a couple of hours. She and the nurses knew one another from emergency service visits after her other suicide attempts. She was discharged with a recommendation that she seriously consider previous referrals for follow-up counseling. This emergency department did not have on-site crisis or psychiatric consultants. While there, Susan could sense the impatience and disgust of the staff. A man with a heart attack had come in around the same time. Susan felt that no one had the time or interest to talk with her. Twice before, Susan had refused referrals for counseling, so the nurses assumed that she was hopeless and did not really want help.

Suicide risk for Susan: Susan is not in immediate danger of suicide (risk rating: 3). She does not have a high-lethal plan and has no history of high-lethal attempts, although overdosing on a prescription antidepressant signifies a change toward increased risk. As already noted, most antidepressants are considered high-lethal methods, depending on the particular drug and the age and weight of the patient. In general, *a lethal dose is 10 times the prescribed dose*. Susan's overdose of three times the prescribed dose therefore falls in the moderate-risk category. Best practice includes calling local poison control centers when there is any question about dosage and lethality. Susan's personal coping ability is poor. She used drugs and failed in school, but she is not cut off from her family, despite their disturbed relationship. She has not suffered a serious personal loss. However, because there is no follow-up counseling or evidence of any changes in her troubled social situation, she is at risk of making more suicide attempts in the future. If such attempts increase in their medical seriousness, Susan's risk of eventual suicide also increases significantly. On the ambivalence scale, life and death may begin to look the same for Susan if her circumstances do not change.

High-Risk Suicidal Behavior

This includes a threat or a suicide attempt that would probably be fatal without accidental rescue and sophisticated medical or surgical intervention. Such behavior also includes instances when a suicide attempt fails to end in death as expected, such as in a deliberate car crash. Another example is a threat that will be carried out unless a potential rescuer, such as a friend, family member, or crisis worker, can convince the person that there are good reasons to go on living. Ambivalence in high-risk behavior tends more in the direction of death than life.

The present and long-range risk of suicide is very high unless immediate help is available and accepted. Chronic self-destructive behavior increases the risk even further.

Case Example: Edward

Edward, age 41, had just learned that his wife, Jane, had decided to get a divorce. He threatened to kill himself with a gun or carbon monoxide on the day she filed for the divorce. Jane's divorce lawyer proposed that their country home and the 20 adjoining acres be turned over completely to Jane. Edward told his wife, neighbors, and a crisis counselor that his family and home were all he had to live for.

Indeed, all Edward could afford after the divorce was the rental of a single shabby room. He and Jane have four children. Edward also has several concerned friends but does not feel he can turn to them, as he always kept his family matters private. Jane's decision to divorce Edward has left him feeling like a complete failure. He has several guns and is a skilled hunter. A major factor in Jane's decision to divorce Edward was his chronic drinking problem. He had threatened to shoot himself eight months earlier after a violent argument with Jane when he was drinking, and Jane kept urging him to get help from AA.

Several strong signs of high risk can be identified in Edward's case.

1. He has a specific plan with an available high-lethal means—the gun.
2. He threatened suicide with a high-lethal method eight months previously and is currently communicating his suicide plan.
3. He is threatened with a serious interpersonal loss and feels cut off from what he regards as his most important social resources, his family and home.
4. He has a rigid expectation of himself in his role as husband and provider for his family. He sees himself as a failure in that role and has a deep sense of shame about his perceived failure.
5. His coping ability is apparently poor, as he resorts to the use of alcohol and is reluctant to use his friends for support during a crisis.
6. He is also a high risk in terms of his age, sex, race, marital status, and history of alcohol abuse.

Suicide risk for Edward: Edward is in immediate danger of committing suicide (risk rating: 5). Even if he makes it through his present crisis, he is also a long-range risk for suicide because of his chronic self-destructive behavior—abuse of alcohol and threats of suicide by a readily available, high-lethal means.

Case Example: Barbara

Barbara, age 77, is noted in the nursing care facility for her disagreeable personality and suspiciousness of staff and other residents. She has diabetes, heart disease, and asthma, the symptoms of which are exacerbated when she has an unpleasant encounter with others. Barbara has been moved to several different wings of the institution because staff "can take only so much of her." After her last move, Barbara refused to eat or receive visits from other residents, resisted taking her medication, and said she just wanted to die. Barbara has a daughter and son-in-law who see her every few months. She also attends religious services routinely, the only activity she has continued.

Suicide risk for Barbara: Barbara is a high risk for suicide both immediately and in the future (risk rating: 4). The outcome of her self-destructive behavior will depend on how staff and her family understand and respond to her distress. On the ambivalence scale, unless her circumstances change, Barbara will probably continue to see death as more desirable than life (see Moore, 1997).

Case Example: Shirley

A woman went to visit her mother, Shirley, at a psychiatric facility, though she was advised on arrival not to see her mother at that time; Shirley was hearing voices telling her to kill herself and had therefore been placed in a special room with restraints. Her treatment consisted of psychotropic drugs and periodic checks by staff members. After the staff convinced the daughter that a visit would not benefit Shirley, the daughter asked to be allowed to see her mother through the peek hole, unobserved by her mother. The daughter had had a dream about her mother dying and told the psychiatrist she would not be able to forgive herself if her mother did die and she had not seen her. The psychiatrist refused, claiming then to be protecting the daughter.

Suicide risk for Shirley: Shirley is an immediate and long-range risk for suicide (risk rating: 5). Shirley's physical restraint decreased her immediate risk; however, it is now known that social isolation only promotes suicidal tendencies. Hallucinations directing her to kill herself also increase risk. The long-range probability of suicide by Shirley is further increased by the coercive measures used and by the psychiatrist's refusal to allow a caring daughter to visit. The immediate and long-range risks of these suicidal behaviors in relation to ambivelence and rescue plan are summarized in Table 9.3.

Understanding and Assessing Risk in Special Populations

This chapter describes the wide range of people who are self-destructive and need help. The general principles of assessment apply to all people who are actually or potentially suicidal—the old, the young, different ethnic and sexual-identity groups, institutionalized people, the unemployed, prisoners, the educated, patients in medical and surgical wards, and psychotic and nonpsychotic persons in psychiatric settings. Still, trends and issues in the suicidology field suggest the need to highlight the special needs of adolescents, distinct ethnic groups, and suicidal people in hospitals and other institutions.

Young People

As we have seen, suicidal behavior is a cry for help, a way to stop the pain when nothing else works. Unnecessary death by suicide is a tragedy regardless of age, gender, class, race, or sexual identity and regardless of variations in suicide rates among these different groups. But suicidal death by those

TABLE 9.3   Suicide Risk Differentiation

Suicidal Behavior		Ambivalence Scale	Rescue Plan	Immediate Risk	Long-Range Risk	
Low risk	Life	Desires life more than death	Present	Low	High	
Moderate risk		Life and death seem equally desirable	Ambiguous	Moderate	High	Depending on immediate response, treatment, and follow-up
High risk	Death	Desires death more than life	Absent, or rescue after past attempts was accidental	Very high	High	

who have barely begun life's journey is particularly poignant—for the victims themselves, their families, and all of society. The tragedy of youth suicide must not be missed in statistical comparisons with other at-risk groups. Young people who kill themselves not only prefer death over life, but they are telling us in powerful behavioral language that they do not even want to try out the society we have created for them. The question is *why*. What can we do to prevent these premature deaths? And how is youth suicide related to other problems, such as substance abuse, violence against others, and entrenched social problems?

Increased public attention to these questions has resulted in a recent surge in literature on the topic (for example, Berman & Jobes, 1991; Deykin & Buka, 1994; Holinger, Offer, Barter, & Bell, 1994; Leenaars & Wenckstern, 1991). As already discussed, the general criteria for assessing risk of suicide are similar for adolescents and adults, except for adolescents' greater tendency toward imitation and impulsivity as seen in cluster suicides. However, the issues are complex, and the answers are not always clear. Recognition of the individual developmental, familial, and societal factors that interact in self-destructive youth will enhance the understanding and empathic communication necessary for risk assessment and suicide prevention among young people. Providers face a challenging ethical issue involving confidentiality and parental rights when a young person divulges suicidal intentions but does not want the listener or school authority to inform his or her parents. (See Chapter 10, "Young People," for suggestions regarding this ethical dilemma.)

Teens in North America and other industrial societies today feel great pressure to avoid failure in a social milieu that is very achievement oriented, while facing employment uncertainties affected by global economic shifts and turmoil. As a distinct and increasingly prolonged phase in the life cycle, adolescence exaggerates the challenge of finding one's place in the world, while cultural messages emphasize that anything can be had in modern society if one only works hard and takes advantage of opportunities. This means, among other things, that traumatic life events, such as failing an exam or the breakup of a relationship, are perceived as disasters by at-risk teens. Furthermore, the brutal reality for many is that individual efforts are not enough to overcome obstacles such as race and class divisions, which are deeply embedded in the social structure and cultural values. This is particularly true for black and Hispanic urban males in the United States, who face disproportionately high unemployment rates, and for Native youth on reservations, whose futures are even more bleak. Development of the Tribal Colleges system portends some relief for Native Americans.

Complicating teenagers' lives today are the flux and change occurring throughout many societies, particularly in traditional roles for women and men. All adolescents face normal role confusion and sexual-identity issues, but family instability and the frequency of divorce create additional stresses for children. Thousands of teens also encounter problems with alcoholism, violence, and incest. (Chapter 11 discusses in greater detail the relationship between victimization and self-destructiveness. See also Figure 2.2 in Chapter 2.) Many suicidal runaway teens are victims of these family problems. Considered together, these factors make a teenager's hopelessness and disillusionment with planning a career and entering adult life understandable.

This is not to suggest that living in an era of global change and unrest causes teen suicide. Rather, an attitude of cultural pessimism, financial uncertainties, and a widening gap between rich and poor combine with individual stressors, family, and other social factors to create a climate from which many teens today will want to escape (see Chapters 1 and 2 on crisis origins). These issues are elaborated further in Chapters 6, 11, and 12.

Distinct Ethnic and Sexual Identity Groups

The tragedy of suicide among ethnic minority and Native groups in U.S. society is often hidden behind the predominant presence of the white majority. Consideration of context and culture in their full complexity is essential in suicide prevention among specific ethnic groups (Duarte-Velez & Bernal, 2007). A study with young Native Americans revealed that most participants did not seek help because of the lack of perceived need for help, embarrassment and stigma, and feelings of loneliness, fear, and hopelessness (Freedenthal & Stiffman, 2007). Suicidal behavior and help seeking vary among cultural groups, including different vulnerability and protective factors, differing interpretations of the behavior, and different resources and options for help (Goldston et al., 2008). For example, high levels of involvement in Latino culture may serve as a protective factor (Uman, Taylor, & Updegraff, 2007).

Similarly, research about suicide among gay, lesbian, bisexual, and transgendered people has been neglected in favor of the heterosexual majority. Social and cultural factors have been cited as the origin of many crises, especially among those disadvantaged by the economic, political, ethnic, and related factors stemming from personal and institutionalized racism and homophobia (Berlin, 1987; Hendin, 1987; Nisbet, 1996; Remafedi, 1994; Remafedi et al., 1998; Russell, 2003; see also Chapter 6). Understanding and assessing individual pain and suicide risk in these instances is incomplete without attention to the cultural context of this pain. It is incongruous to speak of the right of disadvantaged people to commit suicide when the basic rights of life are not enjoyed on an equal basis. Our common humanity demands a renewed effort to combine understanding of individuals in crisis with keen sensitivity to the social and political origins and ramifications of these crises (see Figure 9.1, the right circle in Boxes 1 and 3).

People in Hospitals and Other Institutions

Finally, a number of people are in institutions because they are suicidal or for other reasons: illness, infirmity, crime, or behavioral problems. Admission to an institution is often a crisis in itself. Not infrequently, the culture shock experienced in this process is so extreme that suicide seems the only way out. Osgood's (1992) research supports the relationship between adverse environmental factors (for example, frequent staff turnover) and suicidal behavior and death in long-term care facilities, as in the case example of Barbara. Such factors also contribute to the greater frequency of suicide in temporary holding centers than in prisons. Often a person already suicidal feels so disempowered by the experience of institutionalization that suicide is the single action that says, "I am in charge of my life (and death)."

Preventing suicide, self-injury, and indirect self-destruction in institutions demands that:

- We do not use hospitals as a "catchall" to prevent suicide.
- We abandon the notion that when a patient is under a physician's care, responsibility for intelligent assessment and intervention by others ceases.
- We recognize that the general principles of suicidology and risk assessment apply equally to institutionalized and other people. If physical and social isolation and powerlessness increase suicidal risk, people in hospitals and other institutions who are isolated and powerless are at increased suicide risk (Farberow, 1981; Haycock, 1993).
- We correct the appalling policy failures that have resulted in many thousands of suicidal and mentally ill persons being contained and abused in U.S. prisons instead of receiving the psychiatric treatment they need (Earley, 2006).

Despite decades of knowledge about therapeutic milieu, public placards declaring patients' rights, and experience with the fact that authoritarian attitudes and power tactics in institutional settings are always counterproductive, it is shocking to read and hear about abusive approaches to distressed people in institutions, some of which result in violent retaliation against staff (see Chapter 12).

This discussion of special population groups and the previous case examples is continued in the next chapter.

Two final points about the assessment of suicide risk must be noted.

1. *Suicide risk assessment is an ongoing process.* A person at risk should be reassessed continually. If important social and attitudinal changes occur as a result of a suicide attempt, the person who is suicidal today may not be suicidal tomorrow or ever again. The opposite is also true: a crucial life event or other circumstance can drastically affect a person's view of life and death. Someone who has never been suicidal may become so.
2. *Suicide risk assessment is an integral aspect of the crisis assessment process.* No assessment of a person who is upset or in crisis can be considered complete if evaluation of suicide risk is not included. See Chapter 3 for interview examples of how to incorporate these suicide risk assessment principles and techniques into routine crisis and mental health practice in emergency settings and elsewhere.

Summary and Discussion Questions

Suicide and self-destructive behavior are extreme ways in which some people respond to crisis. The pain and turmoil felt by a self-destructive person can be compared with the confusion and mixed feelings of those trying to help. People destroy themselves for complex reasons. Understanding what a self-destructive person is trying to communicate is basic to helping that person find alternatives to suicide. Assessment of suicide risk is a difficult task, but it is made possible by recognition of signs that portend the likelihood of suicide for particular individuals. Assessment of suicide risk is an important basis for appropriate response to self-destructive people.

1. In historical perspective, identify the interrelated issues of suicide prevention and basic human rights.
2. Consider evidence-based risk assessment in the context of biomedical psychiatry: What are the advantages and disadvantages?
3. Why should clinicians and others take seriously even a low-lethality type of suicide attempt? Or are such attempts really just "gestures"?
4. Identify a family or friendship situation in which danger of suicide was suspected, what was done or not done in response, and the reasons why.

References

Alvarez, A. (1971). *The savage god.* London: Weidenfeld and Nicolson.

Atkinson, J. M. (1978). *Discovering suicide: Studies in the social organization of death.* Pittsburgh, PA: University of Pittsburgh Press.

Badger, T. A., McNiece, C., & Gagan, M. J. (2000). Depression, service need, and use in vulnerable populations. *Archives of Psychiatric Nursing, 14*(4), 173–182.

Baechler, J. (1979). *Suicide.* New York: Basic Books.

Battin, M. P. (1980). Manipulated suicide. In M. P. Battin and D. J. Mayo (Eds.), *Suicide: The philosophical issues* (pp. 169–182). New York: St. Martin's Press.

Battin, M. P., & Mayo, D. J. (Eds.). (1980). *Suicide: The philosophical issues.* New York: St. Martin's Press.

Beck, A. T., Steer, R. A., Beck, J. S., & Newman, C. F. (1993). Hopelessness, depression, suicidal ideation, and clinical diagnosis of depression. *Suicide & Life-Threatening Behavior, 23*(2), 120–129.

Becker, H. (1963). *Outsiders: Studies in the sociology of deviance.* New York: Free Press.

Berlin, I. N. (1987). Suicide among American Indian adolescents: An overview. *Suicide & Life-Threatening Behavior, 17*(3), 218–232.

Berman, A. L., & Jobes, D. A. (1991). *Adolescent suicide: Assessment and intervention.* Washington, DC: American Psychological Association.

Bertolote, J. M., Fleischmann, A., De Leo, D., & Wasserman, D. (2003). Suicide and mental disorders: Do we know enough? *British Journal of Psychiatry, 183*(5), 382–383.

Bongar, B., Berman, A. L., Maris, R. W., Silverman, M. M., Harris, E. A., & Packman, W. L. (1998). *Risk management of suicidal patients.* New York: Guilford Press.

Breed, W. (1972). Five components of a basic suicide syndrome. *Suicide & Life-Threatening Behavior, 2,* 3–18.

Brown, G. W., & Harris, T. (1978). *The social origins of depression.* London: Tavistock.

Brown, T. R., & Sheran, T. J. (1972). Suicide prediction: A review. *Suicide & Life-Threatening Behavior, 2,* 67–97.

Burstow, B. (1992) *Radical feminist therapy: Working in the context of violence.* Thousand Oaks, CA: Sage.

Conner, K. R., Phillips, M. R., & Meldrum, S. C. (2007). Predictors of low-intent and high-intent suicide attempts in rural China. *American Journal of Public Health, 97*(10), 1842–1846.

Counts, D. A. (1987). Female suicide and wife abuse: A cross-cultural perspective. *Suicide & Life-Threatening Behavior, 17*(3), 194–204.

Deykin, E. Y., & Buka, S. L. (1994). Suicidal ideation and attempts among chemically dependent adolescents. *American Journal of Public Health, 84*(4), 634–639.

Duarté-Vélez, Y. M., & Bernal, G. (2007). Suicide behavior among Latino and Latina adolescents: Conceptual and methodological issues. *Death Studies, 31*(5), 435–455.

Durkheim, E. (1951). *Suicide* (2nd ed.). New York: Free Press. (Original work published 1897.)

Early, P. (2006). *Crazy: A father's search through America's mental health madness.* New York: Berkeley Books.

Ehrenreich, B., & Ehrenreich, J. (1978). Medicine and social control. In J. Ehrenreich (Ed.), *The cultural crisis of modern medicine* (pp. 39–79). New York: Monthly Review Press.

Emanuel, E. J., & Battin, M. P. (1998). What are the potential cost savings from legalizing physician-assisted suicide? *New England Journal of Medicine, 339*(3), 167–172.

Evans, E., Hawton, K., & Redham, K. (2005). In what ways are adolescents who engage in self-harm different in terms of help-seeking, communication and coping strategies? *Journal of Adolescence, 28,* 573–587.

Evans, W. P., Owen, P., & Marsh, S. C. (2005). Environmental factors, locus of control, and adolescent suicide risk. *Child and Adolescent Social Work Journal, 22*(3–4), 301–319.

Everett, B., & Gallop, R. (2000). *The link between childhood trauma and mental illness: Effective interventions for mental health professionals.* Thousand Oaks, CA: Sage.

Farberow, N. L. (Ed.). (1975). *Suicide in different cultures.* Baltimore, MD: University Park Press.

Farberow, N. L. (Ed.). (1980). *The many faces of death.* New York: McGraw-Hill.

Farberow, N. L. (1981). Suicide prevention in the hospital. *Hospital and Community Psychiatry, 32*(2), 99–104.

Farberow, N. L., & Shneidman, E. S. (Eds.). (1961). *The cry for help.* New York: McGraw-Hill.

Fawcett, J. (2000). The complexity of suicide. Grand rounds: Suicide: Clinical/risk management issues for psychiatrists. *CNS Spectrums Academic Supplement: The International Journal of Neuropsychiatric Medicine, 5*(2, Suppl. 1), 38–41.

Freedenthal, S., & Stifferman, A. R. (2007). "They might think I was crazy": Young American Indians' reasons for not seeking help when suicidal. *Journal of Adolescent Research, 22*, 58–77.

Fuller, J. (1997). Physician-assisted suicide: An unnecessary crisis. *America, 177*(2), 9–12.

Furst, J., & Huffine, C. L. (1991). Assessing vulnerability to suicide. *Suicide & Life-Threatening Behavior, 21*(4), 329–344.

Goldman, S., & Beardslee, W. R. (1999). Suicide in children and adolescents. In D. G. Jacobs (Ed.), *The Harvard Medical School guide to suicide assessment and intervention* (pp. 417–442). San Francisco: Jossey-Bass.

Goldston, D. B., Molock, S. D., Whitbeck, L. B., Murakami, J. L., Zayas, L. H. & Hall, G. C. H. (2008). Cultural considerations in adolescent suicide prevention and psychosocial treatment. *American Psychologist, 63*(1), 14–31.

Haycock, J. (1993). Double jeopardy: Suicide rates in forensic hospitals. *Suicide & Life-Threatening Behavior, 23*(2), 130–138.

Hendin, H. (1982). *Suicide in America.* New York: Norton.

Hendin, H. (1987). Youth suicide: A psychosocial perspective. *Suicide & Life-Threatening Behavior, 17*(2), 151–165.

Hoff, L. A. (1985). [Review of the book *Suicidal women: Their thinking and feeling patterns.* By C. Neuringer & D. Lettieri (1982). New York: Gardner Press.] *Suicide & Life-Threatening Behavior, 15*(1), 69–73.

Hoff, L. A. (2000). Crisis care. In B. Everett & R. Gallop, *The link between childhood trauma and mental illness: Effective interventions for mental health professionals* (pp. 227–251). Thousand Oaks, CA: Sage.

Hoff, L. A., & Morgan, V. (In press). *Psychiatric & mental health essentials in primary care.*

Holinger, P. C., Offer, D., Barter, J. T., & Bell, C. C. (1994). *Suicide and homicide among adolescents.* New York: Guilford Press.

Humphrey, D. (1992). Rational suicide among the elderly. *Suicide & Life-Threatening Behavior, 22*(1), 125–129.

Jacobs, D. G. (2000). The complexity of suicide. Grand rounds: Suicide: Clinical/risk management issues for psychiatrists. *CNS Spectrums Academic Supplement: The International Journal of Neuropsychiatric Medicine, 5*(2, Suppl. 1), 32–33.

Jourard, S. M. (1970). Suicide: An invitation to die. *American Journal of Nursing, 70*(2), 269, 273–275.

Kerkhof, A. J. F. M., & Clark, D. C. (1993). Stability of suicide rates in Europe. *Crisis, 14*(2), 50–51.

Leenaars, A. A., & Wenckstern, S. (1991). *Suicide prevention in schools.* Bristol, PA: Hemisphere.

Litman, R. E. (1987). Mental disorders and suicidal intention. *Suicide & Life-Threatening Behavior, 17*(2), 85–92.

Maris, R. W. (1981). *Pathways to suicide.* Baltimore, MD: Johns Hopkins University Press.

Maris, R. W. (1991). Assessment and prediction of suicide: Introduction [Special issue]. *Suicide & Life-Threatening Behavior, 21*(1), 1–17.

Maris, R. W. (Ed.). (with Berman, A. L., Maltsberger, J. T., & Yufit, R. I.) (1992). *Assessment and prediction of suicide.* New York: Guilford Press.

McGinnis, J. M. (1987). Suicide in America—moving up the public health agenda. *Suicide & Life-Threatening Behavior, 17*(1), 18–32.

Menninger, K. (1938). *Man against himself.* Orlando, FL: Harcourt Brace.

Moore, S. L. (1997). A phenomenological study of meaning in life in suicidal older adults. *Archives of Psychiatric Nursing, 11*(1), 29–36.

Morrell, S., Taylor, R., Quine, S., & Kerr, C. (1993). Suicide and unemployment in Australia. *Social Science & Medicine, 36*(6), 749–756.

Moscicki, E. (1999). Epidemiology of suicide. In D. G. Jacobs (Ed.), *The Harvard Medical School guide to suicide assessment and intervention* (pp. 40–51). San Francisco: Jossey-Bass.

Motto, J. A. (1985). Preliminary field testing of a risk estimation for suicide. *Suicide & Life-Threatening Behavior, 15*(3), 139–150.

Motto, J. A. (1991). An integrated approach to estimating suicide risk. *Suicide & Life-Threatening Behavior, 21*(1), 74–89.

Motto, J. A. (1999). Critical points in the assessment and management of suicide risk. In D. G. Jacobs (Ed.), *The Harvard Medical School guide to suicide assessment and intervention* (pp. 224–238). San Francisco: Jossey-Bass.

Nisbet, P. A. (1996). Protective factors for suicidal black females. *Suicide & Life-Threatening Behavior, 26*(4), 325–341.

O'Carroll, P. (1993). Suicide causation: Pies, paths, and pointless polemics. *Suicide & Life-Threatening Behavior, 23*(1), 27–36.

Osgood, N. (1992). Environmental factors in suicide in long-term care facilities. *Suicide & Life-Threatening Behavior, 22*(1), 98–106.

Parent, R. B. (1998). Suicide by cop: Victim-precipitated homicide. *Police Chief, 65*(10), 111–114.

Parsons, T. (1951). Social structure and the dynamic process: The case of modern medical practice. In *The social system* (pp. 428–479). New York: Free Press.

Perrah, M., & Wichman, H. (1987). Cognitive rigidity in suicide attempters. *Suicide & Life-Threatening Behavior, 17*(3), 251–255.

Pfeffer, C. R. (1986). *The suicidal child.* New York: Guilford Press.

Remafedi, G. (Ed.). (1994). *Death by denial: Studies of gay and lesbian teenagers.* Boston: Alyson.

Remafedi, G., Farrow, J. A., & Deisher, R. W. (1991). Risk factors for attempted suicide in gay and bisexual youth. *Pediatrics, 87*(6), 869–875.

Remafedi, G., French, S., Story, M., Resnick, M. D., & Blum, R. (1998). The relationship between suicide risk and sexual orientation: Results of a population-based study. *American Journal of Public Health, 88*(1), 57–60.

Richman, J. (1992). A rational approach to rational suicide. *Suicide & Life-Threatening Behavior, 22*(1), 130–141.

Rodin, G. M. (2000). Psychiatric care for the chronically ill & dying patient. In H. H. Goldman (Ed.), *Review of general psychiatry* (pp. 505–512). New York: Lange Medical Books/McGraw-Hill.

Russell, S.T. (2003). Sexual minority youth and suicide risk. *American Behavioral Scientist, 45*(9), 1241–1257.

Samuels, D. (May 2007). Let's die together. *The Atlantic,* 92–98.

Shneidman, E. S. (1973). Suicide. *Encyclopaedia Britannica.* (Reprinted in *Suicide & Life-Threatening Behavior, 11,* 198–220.)

Shneidman, E. S. (1976). *Suicidology: Contemporary developments.* Philadelphia: Grune & Stratton.

Shneidman. E. S. (1981). Suicide. *Suicide & Life-Threatening Behavior, 11,* 198–220.

Shneidman, E. S. (1985). *Definition of suicide.* New York: Wiley.

Shneidman, E. S. (1987). At the point of no return. *Psychology Today, 21*(3), 54–58.

Shneidman, E. S. (1993). Some controversies in suicidology: Toward a mentalistic discipline. *Suicide & Life-Threatening Behavior, 23*(4), 292–298.

Shneidman, E. S. (1999). Perturbation and lethality: A psychological approach to assessment and intervention. In D. G. Jacobs (Ed.), *The Harvard Medical School guide to suicide assessment and intervention* (pp. 83–97). San Francisco: Jossey-Bass.

Shneidman. E. S., & Farberow, N. L. (Eds.). (1957). *Clues to suicide.* New York: McGraw-Hill.

Solomon, D. A., Keitner, G. I., Miller, I. W., Shea, M. T., & Keller, M. B. (1995). Course of illness and maintenance treatments for patients with bipolar disorder. *Journal of Clinical Psychiatry, 56*(1), 5–13.

Stephens, B. J. (1985). Suicidal women and their relationships with husbands, boyfriends, and lovers. *Suicide & Life-Threatening Behavior, 15*(2), 77–90.

Stephens, B. J. (1987). Cheap thrills and humble pie: The adolescence of female suicide attempters. *Suicide & Life-Threatening Behavior, 17*(2), 107–118.

Uman, A. J., Taylor, A., & Updegraff, K. A. (2007). Latino adolescents' mental health: Exploring the interrelations among discrimination, ethnic identity, cultural orientation, self-esteem, and depressive symptoms. *Journal of Adolescence, 30,* 549–567.

United Nations. (1996). *Prevention of suicide: Guidelines for the formation and implementation of national strategies.* New York: Author.

U.S. Public Health Service. (1999). *Surgeon general's call to action to prevent suicide.* Washington, DC: Author.

Wasserman, D. (2004). Evaluating suicide prevention: Various approaches needed. *World Psychiatry, 3*(3), 153–154.

WHO. http://www.who.int/mentalhealth/prevention/suicide/suicideprevent/en/. Retrieved February 7, 2008.

CHAPTER **10**

Helping Self-Destructive People and Survivors of Suicide

Several agencies or helpers are usually needed to provide distinct facets of service for suicidal people. All, however, should be aware of what constitutes comprehensive care for this at-risk population and establish linkages that actually work for clients.

Comprehensive Service for Self-Destructive People

A key theme of this book is the universality of crisis throughout history and at various points of an individual's life cycle. But negative or destructive outcomes of crisis are neither universal nor inevitable—thus underscoring a public health and preventive approach to the topic. In the case of suicidal persons, prevention efforts have often failed as an integral part of comprehensive health and social service. The U.S. Department of Health and Human Services, Public Health Service, has published the *National Strategy for Suicide Prevention: Goals and Objectives for Action* (2001). Internationally, other countries have published similar national strategies. Everyone who threatens or attempts suicide should have access to all the services the crisis calls for. Three kinds of service should be available for all at risk of killing themselves:

1. Emergency medical treatment
2. Crisis intervention
3. Follow-up counseling or therapy

Emergency Medical Treatment

Emergency medical treatment is the obvious response to anyone who has already made a suicide attempt. Unfortunately, this is still all that is received by some people who attempt suicide. Everyone—friend, neighbor, family member, passerby—is obligated by simple humanity to help a suicidal person obtain medical treatment. First aid can be performed by police, volunteers in fire departments, rescue squads, or anyone familiar with first-aid procedures.

Any time a person is in immediate danger of death, the police should be called because police and rescue squads have the greatest possibility of ensuring rapid transportation to a hospital. If there is any question about the medical seriousness of the suicide attempt, a physician should be called. The best way to obtain a medical opinion in such cases is to call a local hospital emergency service. In large communities, a physician is always there; in small ones, a physician is on call.

Most communities also have poison control centers, usually attached to a hospital, which should be called when the lethality level of the drug is not certain. The amount of a drug necessary to cause death depends on the kind of drug, the size of the person, and the person's tolerance for the drug in cases of addiction. Sleeping pills are the most dangerous.

In general, *a lethal dose is 10 times the normal dose.* In combination with alcohol, only half that amount can cause death. Aspirin is also much more dangerous than is commonly believed. One hundred five-grain tablets can cause death; less is needed if other drugs are also taken. Tylenol (acetaminophen), an aspirin substitute, is even more dangerous, as it cannot be removed from body tissue by dialysis. Tranquilizers (antianxiety agents) are less dangerous; antidepressant drugs, however, can be used as a suicide weapon.

Some suicidal people have gone through hospital emergency rooms, intensive care and surgical units, and on to discharge with no explicit attention paid to the primary problem that triggered the suicide attempt. The urgency of medical treatment for a suicidal person can be so engrossing that other aspects of crisis intervention may be overlooked. For example, if a person is in a coma from an overdose or is being treated for injuries from a car crash, a careful suicide risk assessment may be forgotten after the person is out of physical danger. Great care should be taken in emergency situations to ensure that this does not happen.

If a person whose suicide attempt is medically serious does not receive follow-up counseling, the risk of suicide within a few months is very high. Medical treatment, of course, is of primary importance when there is danger of death. Still we should remember that the person's physical injuries are a result of the suicide attempt; treating those injuries is only a first step. The attitude of hospital emergency department staff can be the forerunner of more serious suicide attempts or the foundation for crisis intervention and acceptance of a referral for follow-up counseling. (See Chapter 4, George Sloan, regarding collaborative service planning.) Emergency and primary care providers should also carefully consider the appropriate use of drugs for suicidal people in crisis, as discussed in Chapter 4, because prescribed drugs are one of the weapons used most frequently for suicide.

Crisis Intervention

People who threaten or attempt suicide as a way of coping with a crisis usually lack more constructive ways of handling stress. The crisis intervention principles presented in Chapters 4 and 5 should be used on behalf of self-destructive persons. Several additional techniques are important for a person in suicidal crisis:

1. *Relieve isolation.* If the suicidal person is living alone, physical isolation must be relieved. If there is no friend or supportive relative with whom the person can stay temporarily and if the person is highly suicidal, that individual should probably be hospitalized until the active crisis is over.

2. *Remove lethal weapons.* Lethal weapons and pills should be removed by the counselor, a relative, or a friend, keeping in mind empowerment issues and the active collaboration of the suicidal person in this process. If caring and concern are expressed and the person's sense of self-mastery and control is respected, he or she will usually surrender a weapon voluntarily, so it is safe from easy or impulsive access during the acute crisis. While avoiding power tactics or engaging in the heated debate regarding gun control, all human service providers should calmly inform an acutely distressed person and the family of this sobering fact: Suicide risk increases fivefold and homicide risk increases threefold when there is a gun in the home (Boyd & Moscicki, 1986; Kaplan, 1998).

3. *Encourage alternate expression of anger.* If the person is planning suicide as a way of expressing anger at someone, we should actively explore with the individual other ways of expressing anger short of paying with his or her life. For example, "I can see that you're very angry with her for leaving you. Can you think of a way to express your anger that would not cost you your life?" or "Yes, of course she'll probably feel bad if you kill yourself after the divorce. But she most likely would talk with someone about it and go on with her life. Meanwhile you've had your revenge, but you can't get your life back." If anger at the crisis worker or therapist is connected to the suicide threat, a similar empathetic but not indifferent response is called for: "Of course I'd feel bad, but not guilty. So I'd like to continue working with you around the pain you have even though you're disappointed right now with our progress."

4. *Avoid a final decision about suicide during crisis.* We should assure the suicidal person that the suicidal crisis—that is, seeing suicide as the only option—is a *temporary* state. We should also try to persuade the person to avoid a decision about suicide until all other alternatives have been considered during a noncrisis state of mind, just as other serious decisions should be postponed until the crisis is over.

A cautionary note about contracts is in order here. The *no-suicide contract* is a technique employed by some therapists, crisis workers, and primary care providers in which the client promises to refrain from self-harm between sessions and to contact the therapist if contemplating such harm. Since this controversial issue emerged in the crisis and suicidology literature, there is growing consensus on this point: Such contracts offer neither special protection against suicide nor legal protection for the therapist (Clark & Kerkhof, 1993; Drew, 2001; Reid, 1998). No-suicide contracts may convey a false sense of security to an anxious provider. This is because any value the contract may have flows from the *quality of the therapeutic relationship*—ideally, one in which the therapist conveys caring and concern about the client. In no way should a contract serve as a convenient substitute for the time spent in empathetic listening, crisis intervention with the suicidal person, and in careful planning of therapeutic alternatives to self-destruction. Contracts are no more than a mechanistic "quick fix" by time-pressured providers if not incorporated into an overall service plan as discussed here and in Chapter 4. This should include such specifics as relieving isolation, finding substitutes for losses, and developing concrete plans and actions to control impulsive behavior—for example, calling a crisis hotline or asking a friend to join in a favorite recreation activity.

5. *Reestablish social ties.* We should make every effort to help the suicidal person reestablish broken social bonds. This can be done through family crisis counseling sessions or by finding satisfying substitutes for lost relationships. Active links to self-help groups such as Widow to Widow or Parents Without Partners clubs can be lifesaving (see Chapter 5).

6. *Relieve extreme anxiety and sleep loss.* If a suicidal person is extremely anxious and also has been unable to sleep for several days, he or she may become even more suicidal. To a suicidal person, the world looks bleaker and death seems more desirable at 4:00 a.m. after endless nights of sleeplessness. A good night's sleep can temporarily reduce suicide risk and put the person in a better frame of mind to consider other ways of solving life's problems.

In such cases, it is appropriate to consider medication on an emergency basis (Bongar, Maris, Berman, & Litman, 1992). This should never be done for a highly suicidal person, however, without daily crisis counseling sessions. Without effective counseling, the extremely suicidal person may interpret such an approach as an invitation to commit suicide. An antianxiety agent will usually suffice in these instances and thus improve sleep, as anxiety is the major cause of sleeplessness. Antidepressants, in contrast, are more dangerous as a potential suicide weapon. If medication is needed, the person should be given a *one- to three-day supply at most*—always with a return appointment scheduled for crisis counseling.

Sometimes nonmedical crisis counselors need to seek medical consultation and emergency medicine for a suicidal person. In such cases, the counselor must clearly advise the consulting physician of the person's suicidal state and of the recommended limited dose of drugs. This is particularly important when dealing with physicians who lack training in suicide prevention or who seem hurried and disinterested. Some practitioners accustomed to using medication in treatment programs may recommend psychotropic medication during crisis; however, these drugs are indicated only if a person is too upset to be engaged in the process of problem solving (see Chapter 4). Nonchemical means of inducing sleep should be encouraged. This assumes a thorough assessment and an effort to apply various psychosocial strategies before prescribing drugs. Crisis workers should never forget that many suicide deaths in North America are caused by *prescribed* drugs. Sadly, Rogers's (1971) account of drug abuse is even more applicable today than decades ago.

Crisis assessment is never more important than when working with a self-destructive person. It determines our immediate and long-range response to the individual. A person who is threatening or has attempted suicide is either in active crisis or is already beyond the crisis and is at a loss to resolve it any other way.

Not everyone who engages in self-injurious acts is in a life-and-death emergency. Anyone distressed enough to be self-destructive to any degree should be listened to and helped; however, if the suicide attempt is medically nonserious, the counselor's response should not convey a life-and-death urgency. This does not mean that the person's action is dismissed as nonserious. Rather, the underlying message of the behavior—its psychosocial dynamics—should receive priority attention. To do otherwise may inadvertently lead to further suicide attempts. A helper reinforces self-destructive behavior by a dramatic and misplaced medical response while ignoring the problems signaled by the self-destructive act. For example, while suturing a slashed wrist, the physician and nurse should regard the physical injury neutrally, with a certain sense of detachment, and focus—in an empathic tone—on the *meaning* of self-injury: "You must have been pretty upset to do this to yourself. What did you hope would happen when you cut your wrists?"

Persons at all levels of suicide risk warrant a helping response, while differentiating between the types of response. Emergency measures are used when there is immediate danger of death from a medically serious failed suicide attempt. If the risk of death is long-range, the therapeutic approach should be long-range as well. If the attempt is medically nonserious, we should avoid using only medical treatment or a life-and-death approach. People in these risk situations need professional help to resolve crises constructively rather than by self-destructive acts.

Follow-Up Service for Suicidal People

Beyond crisis care, all self-destructive persons should have the opportunity to receive counseling or psychotherapy as an aid in solving the problems that led them to self-destructive behavior (Bongar et al., 1992). People who respond to life crises with self-destructive behavior often have a long-standing pattern of inadequate psychological and social coping. Individual or group psychotherapy, therefore, is frequently indicated. Drug treatment for clinical depression may also be indicated.

Counseling and Psychotherapy

Psychotherapy is the proper work of specially trained people, usually clinical psychologists, psychiatric nurses, psychiatrists, and psychiatric social workers. Others qualified to do counseling may be clergy and mental health counselors. The main concern is that the counselor or psychotherapist is properly trained, licensed, and supervised (see Online Resources).

Counseling should focus on resolving situational problems and expressing feelings appropriately. The person is helped to change various behaviors that are causing discomfort and that he or she is conscious of without deep probing. Psychotherapy involves uncovering feelings that have been denied expression for a long time. It may also involve changing aspects of one's personality and deep-rooted patterns of behavior, such as an inability to communicate feelings or inflexible approaches to problem solving. People usually engage in psychotherapy because they are troubled or unhappy about certain features of their personality or behavior.

In general, counseling or psychotherapy should be made available to the suicidal person. It is particularly recommended for crisis-prone people who approach everyday problems with drug and alcohol abuse and other self-destructive behaviors. Such people have difficulty expressing feelings verbally, and self-destructive acts become an easier way to communicate. People who are extremely dependent or have rigid expectations for themselves combined with inflexible behavior patterns are also good candidates for psychotherapy. A severely depressed, suicidal person should always have follow-up counseling or psychotherapy. When hospitalization is also indicated for seriously suicidal persons, health practitioners should observe carefully the standards of care for hospitalized people who are at risk of harming themselves (see Bongar, Maris, Berman, Litman, & Silverman, 1993).

Counseling and psychotherapy can take place on an individual or group basis, in outpatient and inpatient settings. A group experience is valuable for nearly everyone, but it is particularly recommended for the suicidal person who has underlying problems interacting socially and communicating feelings. For adolescents who have made suicide attempts, family therapy should frequently follow family crisis counseling. Marital counseling should be offered whenever a disturbed marriage has contributed to the person's suicidal crisis. These therapies can be used in various combinations, depending on the needs of the individual and family.

Whether conducted in a group or individually, counseling and psychotherapy goals should be directed toward

■ Correcting psychological and social disturbances in the person's life
■ Improving the person's self-image
■ Finding satisfactory social resources
■ Developing approaches to problems other than self-destructive behavior
■ Discovering a satisfying life plan

Crisis counselors should keep in mind that a satisfying and constructive resolution of a crisis is an excellent foundation for persuading people to seek follow-up counseling or psychotherapy for the problems that made them crisis prone in the first place. However, since the crisis experience is time-limited, if people in crisis are placed on waiting lists, they will find other ways to resolve their crises. If such people are suicidal, the chances of a tragic outcome are greatly increased. This is because, with or without our help, the pain of the crisis state compels one to move toward resolution—positive or negative. If waiting lists prevent people from getting help at the time they need it and later appointments are not kept, we should examine the adequacy of our service arrangements rather than conclude that the client was not motivated for therapy (see Online Resources).

Drug Treatment for Depression and Other Problems

Because of the regular introduction of newly approved drugs, health providers authorized to prescribe must keep current on this topic through other sources (for example, Dubovsky & Dubovsky, 2007; Garcia & Ghani, 2000). Here the focus is limited to the intersection of prescription drugs with suicidal danger, especially for those without specialty training in psychopharmacology.

Antidepressants are not emergency drugs. However, these drugs may be used successfully for some suicidal persons who experience severe, recurring depression. Classic drugs for treating depression include selective serotonin reuptake inhibitors, tricyclic antidepressants, and monoamine-oxidase inhibitors (McIlroy, 2001). Successful response to antidepressant therapy is highly variable, and debate about the use of psychotropic drugs continues (Brownlee, 2007). This may be due in part to the unclear demarcation between reactive depression and major depressive episodes, formerly called endogenous depression. Thus, although some people respond favorably to antidepressant treatment, research and controversy continue regarding dosage and the efficacy of such treatment in preventing suicide (Kurdyak et al., 2007; Salzman, 1999, p. 373). In addition, there is no compelling evidence that antidepressant treatment, even with safer psychotropic agents, has reduced suicidal risk (Baldessarini, 2000, p. 34), whereas the risk of overdosing on antidepressants is well established (Baldessarini & Tondo, 1999, p. 356.) The success of antidepressant agents in persons with bipolar illness is significantly related to the timing of suicidal behavior, which occurs most often during the early course of illness (Baldessarini, 2000, p. 35). It is now well established that the greatest success of drug treatment occurs when used in combination with psychotherapeutic approaches (Dubovsky & Dubovsky, 2007; Solomon, Keitner, Miller et al., 1995). This principle is of the utmost importance when considering the use of psychotropic drugs for children and adolescents, where family and school-based approaches are pivotal for safety and therapeutic outcomes (Elliott, 2006). For persons with major affective disorder, especially bipolar illness, lithium is preferred for its protective effect against suicidal behaviors (Baldessarini & Tondo, 1999, p. 357).

Antidepressants should be used sparingly or not at all for a person who is going through normal grief and mourning (Worden, 1991, p. 54). They also should not be used when the person is suffering from a reactive depression; grief work and crisis counseling are indicated instead, except when the person does not respond to interpersonal interventions (p. 31). A reactive depression occurs when a person in crisis because of a loss does not express normal feelings of sadness and anger *during* the crisis and later reacts with depression (sometimes called a *delayed grief reaction*). Psychotherapy is indicated for such persons.

Classic symptoms of a major depressive episode, lasting at least two weeks, include weight loss, early morning wakening, loss of appetite, slowed-down body functions, sexual and menstrual abnormality, crying spells, anhedonia (lack of pleasure in life), and extreme feelings of worthlessness. The symptoms usually cannot be related to a conscious loss, specific life event, or situation. The assumption, therefore, is that the depression arises from sources within the person—that is, is biologically based; whereas in reactive depression one is aware of the loss or depressing situation (see "Loss, Change, and Grief Work" in Chapter 4). Even among people who are genetically predisposed to depression, social factors usually play a significant role in alleviating symptoms (Brown & Harris, 1978; Cloward & Piven, 1979). For example, depression in the women studied by Brown and Harris was significantly associated with their economic circumstances and large numbers of children—less money and more children meant greater depression.

Antidepressant drugs are dangerous and should be prescribed with extreme caution for suicidal persons (Bongar et al., 1992; McIlroy, 2001). When taken with alcohol, an overdose of drugs can easily cause death. People using these drugs can experience side effects, such as feelings of confusion, restlessness, or loss of control. Persons with symptoms of borderline personality disorder can have an increase in self-destructive behaviors while treated with antidepressants (Salzman, 1999, p. 379). A review of clinical trials examining the effectiveness of antidepressants revealed that 94% of positive results found themselves into print, while FDA analysis showed that only 51% were positive, thus revealing bias in publishing decisions and potential adverse effects for drug prescribers and their patients (Turner et al., 2008). This study prompted U.S. Congressional legislation expanding the depth of information to be submitted to the public database operated by the National Library of Medicine.

Another problem with antidepressant drugs is that they take so long to work. Ten to 14 days elapse before depression lifts noticeably, even though the person sleeps better as a result of the sedative side effect. This delayed action should be explained carefully, because most people expect to feel better immediately after taking a drug. And during the pretherapeutic phase, a suicide could occur as a result of confusion and agitation, which are additional drug side effects.

Another danger of suicide occurs after the depression lifts during drug treatment. This is especially true for the person who is so depressed and physically slowed down that he or she did not previously have the energy to carry out a suicide plan. Because of all these factors, it is critical to use antidepressant drugs in combination with psychotherapy or psychiatric hospitalization for a depressed person who is highly suicidal, especially if the individual is also socially and physically isolated.

Crisis counselors should always remember that antidepressants are not emergency drugs. These drugs should usually not be prescribed for a highly suicidal person during the acute crisis state unless the individual is hospitalized. The crisis counselor should routinely ask what drugs the person in crisis is taking or possesses. The prescription of *any* drug as a substitute for effective counseling is irresponsible. Not only can some of these drugs increase agitation and sometimes provoke suicidal ideation and subsequent litigation (Breggin & Breggin, 1994; Bongar et al., 1992), but the unwarranted prescription of drugs can also lead to serious drug-related problems (Duncan, Miller, & Sparks, 2000). Although conscientious therapists recognize this principle, today in the United States their best clinical judgment may be overruled by managed care policies. The results (for example, effects on developing brains) remain to be seen, especially for the young children now being treated with antidepressant and other drugs never evaluated for use with children (Elliott, 2006; Zito et al., 2000). Waters (2000, pp. 42–43) describes this as a national uncontrolled experiment that portends the cruel and unnecessary outcomes similar to other mass experiments (for example, thalidomide for pregnant women) in which the gold standard of medical research, the controlled trial, was ignored.

Case Example: Jack

Jack, age 69, a widower living alone, had seen his physician for bowel problems. He was also quite depressed. Even after complete examination and extensive tests, he was obsessed with the idea of cancer and was afraid that he would die. Jack also had high blood pressure and emphysema. Months earlier, he had had prostate surgery. His family described him as a chronic complainer. Jack's doctor gave him a prescription for an antidepressant drug and referred him to a local mental health clinic for counseling. Jack admitted to the crisis counselor that he had ideas of suicide, but he had no specific plan or history of attempts. After two counseling sessions, Jack killed himself by carbon monoxide poisoning. This suicide might have been prevented if Jack had been hospitalized. He lived alone, and in the cultural milieu promoting "take pill, feel better," he probably expected to feel better immediately after taking the antidepressant even though the delayed reaction of the drug had been explained. An alternative might have been to prescribe a drug to relieve his anxiety about cancer in combination with a plan to live with relatives for a couple of weeks.

Intervention with Self-Destructive People: Case Examples

The following cases are continued from Chapter 9. They illustrate the resolution of ethical dilemmas regarding suicide, as well as planning for emergency, crisis, and follow-up services for self-destructive people at various levels of risk for suicide.

The Right-to-Die Dilemma

The right-to-die dilemma is illustrated in the case of Rachel.

Case Example: Rachel

Rachel, age 69, is dying of cancer and feeling suicidal (see Chapter 9).

Rachel: This cancer is killing me. I have nothing to live for.
Nurse: You sound really depressed, Rachel.
Rachel: I am. I'm a burden to my daughter. I don't want to live like this anymore.
Nurse: You mean you're thinking of suicide, Rachel?
Rachel: Yes, I guess you could say that. At least I don't want to go on living like this. Yes, I want to die, and no one can stop me. I'm old and I'm sick. If there is a God, I'm sure I wouldn't be punished. How could any God expect me to go on living with this? Yes, I want to die. It's my right.
Nurse: I know you feel old and I know you're sick, and I agree, Rachel, that you have the right to determine your own life. But I'd feel bad if you acted on that now, Rachel, when you're feeling so depressed and like such a burden to your daughter. I'd really like to help you find some other way—(Rachel interrupts.)
Rachel: There's no other way that I can see. I've thought about it a lot. I don't know exactly what I'd do, but I'd figure something out. I just don't know how things could change for me. After all, my daughter's got her own life.
Nurse: Rachel, I'd like to go back to something you said earlier. You seem to feel you're a burden to your daughter. Can you tell me some more about that? (The conversation continues.)

Other possible elements of a service plan for Rachel include the following:

1. Continue problem exploration on a one-to-one basis.
2. Talk with daughter (with Rachel's consent) after exploring the "burden" issue further with Rachel.
3. Have a joint session with Rachel and her daughter (see Chapter 5).
4. Arrange for evaluation of her pain-control medication.
5. Continue weekly visits.
6. Explore home health respite service for daughter.

Some persons, many of whom are much older than Rachel, must spend their final years in long-term care facilities, either because their family may not be able to care for them or because they are the last of their family still alive. In such cases, compassionate care and ethical norms regarding the slippery slope of legally assisted suicide are crucial. Such a person may recognize and accept the sincerely given care of staff, but may also "know" that the end is near and simply not want to eat anymore. Palliative care, not extraordinary lifesaving measures, should be the norm in these cases (Carson, Eisner, Kartes, & Kolga, 1999; see also Kaplan, Adamek, & Calderon, 1999).

Low-Risk Suicidal Behavior

The case of Sarah illustrates low-risk suicidal behavior.

Case Example: Sarah

Sarah, age 42, is troubled by her marriage (see Chapter 9).

Emergency medical intervention: Medical treatment for Sarah is not indicated because pills are absorbed from the stomach into the bloodstream within 30 minutes. The dose of six sleeping pills is not lethal or extremely toxic. Other medical measures, such as dialysis, are therefore not indicated.

Crisis intervention: Crisis counseling should focus on the immediate situation related to Sarah's suicide attempt and decision making about her marriage.

Follow-up service: In follow-up counseling, Sarah can examine her extreme dependency on her marriage, her personal insecurity, her limited social life, and her dependency on drugs as a means of problem solving. Sarah might also be linked to a women's support group that focuses on career counseling and the midlife transition faced by women (see Chapter 6).

Moderate-Risk Suicidal Behavior

Susan's case illustrates moderate-risk suicidal behavior.

Case Example: Susan

Susan, age 19, has a history of repeat suicide attempts (see Chapter 9).

Emergency medical intervention: Treatment for the overdose is stomach lavage (washing out the stomach contents).

Crisis intervention: Crisis counseling for Susan should include contacts with her parents and should focus on the situational problems she faces: unemployment, conflicts with her parents, and dependence on her parents.

Follow-up service: Because Susan has had a chaotic life for a number of years, she could benefit from ongoing counseling or psychotherapy, if she so chooses. This might include exploration of continuing her education and improving her employment prospects. Family therapy may be indicated if she decides to remain in her parents' household. Group therapy is strongly recommended for Susan.

High-Risk Suicidal Behavior

Edward, Barbara, and Shirley are all at high risk for suicide.

Case Example: Edward

Edward, age 41, is facing divorce and threatening to shoot himself (see Chapter 9).

Emergency medical intervention: No treatment is indicated as no suicide attempt has been made. Depending on Edward's level of engagement in crisis counseling, an antianxiety agent may be indicated for temporary stabilization, as discussed in Chapter 4.

Crisis intervention: Remove guns (and alcohol, if possible) or have wife or friend remove them *with* Edward's collaboration. Arrange to have Edward stay with a friend on the day his wife files for divorce. Try to get Edward to attend a self-help group, such as Alcoholics Anonymous (AA), and to rely on an individual AA member for support during his crisis. Arrange frequent crisis counseling sessions for Edward, including daily telephone check-in during the acute phase.

Follow-up service: Edward should have ongoing psychotherapy, both individually and in a group, focusing on his alcohol dependency and his rigid expectations of himself; therapy should help Edward find other satisfying relationships after the loss of his wife by divorce.

Case Example: Barbara

Barbara, age 77, is in a nursing home and is refusing to eat (see Chapter 9).

Emergency medical and crisis intervention: Barbara should be assigned to a nurse or other staff person she trusts, who can persuade her noncoercively to take her medication and to eat. Her daughter and son-in-law should be called and urged to visit immediately, so Barbara has some evidence that someone cares whether she lives or dies. A stable staffing arrangement should be instituted; further moving of Barbara to different wings of the nursing facility should be avoided. A trusting, caring relationship can thereby be established with at least one or two staff members, which is necessary for understanding what makes Barbara upset and suspicious.

Follow-up service: Organize problem-solving and service-planning meetings with Barbara, her daughter and son-in-law, the chaplain, and the nursing staff who have worked with Barbara most closely—her social network (see Chapter 5). Examine the rotation practices and support system for staff, which gives temporary "relief" from troublesome residents like Barbara. Frequent rotations exacerbate the underlying insecurity of an older person who has decreased ability to adjust to environmental changes and disruptions in staff–resident relationships.

Case Example: Shirley

Shirley, age 55, is acutely suicidal and psychotic in a psychiatric setting (see Chapter 9).

Emergency medical and crisis intervention: Institute routine precautions with regard to sharp objects, belts, and so on (see Bongar et al., 1993). Assign a staff member for one-to-one care of Shirley. Place Shirley in a bedroom arrangement that is close to the nurses' station, with at least one other patient in the room. Do *not* place her in physical isolation. Since social isolation is a key suicide risk factor, it is imperative that psychiatric service providers finally eliminate this practice, which continues under the presumed guise of "therapy" or "protection." A return to the principle of "therapeutic milieu" promulgated by Maxwell Jones in Britain and the United States after World War II (Bloom, 1997) could be a significant factor in preventing the suicide of patients like Shirley and compensate for any negative effects during and following institutional containment. *Therapeutic milieu* means that the *total* environment is part of therapy: e.g., staff attitudes and interaction, physical arrangement of furniture, proximity of nurses' station, meals in a group setting, etc. It includes engaging patients or other volunteers to assist in offering support and protection to Shirley during her acute psychotic episodes, contacting relatives and encouraging frequent visits.

Follow-up service: Family meetings are recommended to encourage ongoing support and help prevent future psychotic and suicidal episodes; drug therapy can help alleviate thought disorder and depression. Institute daily ward meetings in which patients' acute suicidal episodes can be discussed openly and dealt with cooperatively among all residents. Develop staff in-service training programs on suicide prevention as a means of critically examining and eliminating destructive, authoritarian, and inhumane measures such as isolation and physical restraint of suicidal people.

Suicide Prevention and Intervention with Special Populations

As noted in Chapter 9, certain groups in contemporary society are at special risk of suicide. These groups need particular service programs commensurate with their assessed needs.

Young People

The tragedy of youth suicide has commanded international attention at several levels recently. In the United States, the National Institute of Mental Health (NIMH) convened a task force on youth suicide in several locations to address the problem. The *Surgeon General's Call to Action to Prevent Suicide* (U.S. Public Health Service, 1999) affirms the continued need for attention to youth suicide. Since the occurrence of cluster suicides, the National Committee on Youth Suicide has been formed, with a focus on suicide education in schools and colleges. The American Association of Suicidology (AAS) and the Canadian Association of Suicide Prevention (CASP) have information about model school suicide prevention programs. The AAS also publishes a newsletter for survivors.[1]

In general, suicide prevention programs for young people focus on educational and support activities for the youth themselves, their parents, and their teachers (Leenaars & Wenckstern, 1991). Pastors, recreation workers, school nurses, physicians, and police officers should also receive such education. Intervention in community settings should include drop-in services, where

1

troubled youth can receive individual help without being stigmatized and can be referred to peer support groups or family counseling services. School health programs, counseling agencies, and local crisis and suicide prevention centers usually collaborate on such programs. The reeducation and developmental approach used by Brendtro, Brokenleg, and Van Bockern (1990) is distinguished internationally for its focus on (1) recognizing (rather than pathologizing) that the troubled behavior of many youth originates from their alienation and (2) assisting them in restoring broken bonds with family and community—bonds that often are severed because of policies that are not friendly to the needs of children. This developmental and community-based approach is particularly relevant for addressing the self-destructive behaviors of alienated American Indian youth living on reservations (May et al., 2005). Canada et al. (2006) also highlight the need for school counselors' sensitivity to diverse backgrounds of students in multicultural societies.

If suicidal young people are referred to mental health and psychiatric agencies, the treatment of choice should include the family in an active way (Richman, 1986). This is particularly true for an adolescent still living with parents. The adolescent's cry for help might otherwise be misunderstood; often the problem is related to family issues, or the adolescent depends on the family for necessary support during this hazardous transition state (see Chapters 5 and 6). In the case of suicidal college students still dependent on but not living with parents, it is crucial not only to recognize clues to suicide but also to explore the person's manifest and possible latent messages: "I don't want my parents to know" (manifest); "I'm too ashamed to tell my parents that I just can't cope with all these pressures in college" (latent). The counselor's obligations are threefold: (1) to form a therapeutic alliance with the young person as a context for nonauthoritarian parental involvement; (2) to facilitate engaging the person's parents in a way that honors the young person's developmental tasks around dependency; and (3) to remember that confidentiality pledges do not apply in instances of life-or-death risk among dependent persons.

Suicide prevention programs that focus their activities primarily on depression may miss their target (Motto, 1999, p. 225; Shaffer, 1993, p. 172). A study by Garrison, McKeown, Valois, and Vincent (1993) reveals powerful relationships among suicidal behavior, aggression, and alcohol use, especially by high school males.

Suicide prevention for young people should include the following elements:

■ Providing a suicide prevention information program each semester for students in junior and senior high schools and colleges, including cards listing warning signs, myths and facts about suicide, and emergency telephone numbers
■ Training students in communication skills, including role playing and modeling of reaching out to others
■ Developing suicide prevention curriculum packets to be used by faculty
■ Conducting special information programs for parents

- Providing drop-in centers staffed by trained persons sensitive to the special needs of adolescents
- Offering information packets for gay, lesbian, bisexual, and transgendered youth (see Lease et al., 2005)
- Being aware of the Internet as a resource for befriending and as a challenge and risk in care of social isolation (Bale, 2001; Mehlum, 2001)

Although many communities now have such programs (Kann, Brener, & Wechsler, 2007; Leenaars & Wenckstern, 1991; Webb, 1986), denial of suicide by school authorities and failure to provide *prevention* and *postvention* programs still occur despite the international efforts noted previously. Basic knowledge about crisis vulnerability during adolescence is also either absent or ignored. For example, the story of a highly publicized suicide of an 18-year-old university student revealed the university's claim that 18-year-olds are "adults," with no apparent recognition that late adolescence extends to the early twenties for those still in school, not married, and not yet financially independent (not to mention the fact that they are experiencing the hazardous transition from home to college). In school-based programs, students are trained to become peer counselors for classmates who feel left out, lonely, and depressed. Such programs include role playing real-life crises and exploring dramatically how to avert tragedy. Opportunities for grief work have also become common in schools following loss of a classmate or friend through suicide, accident, or violence (Collins & Doolittle, 2006).

Distinct Ethnic and Sexual Identity Groups

Besides the general principles of helping suicidal people, some other points should be kept in mind with respect to individuals in these groups.

1. *In agencies routinely serving people with language, cultural, and other differences, staff should be recruited from the distinct communities served.* This does not mean that a distressed person can only be helped by someone from the same ethnic or sexual identity group. But having some staff from the same community provides a resource for special problems related to different belief systems and lifestyles. It also helps avoid the appearance of discriminatory practices, which can be a barrier to accepting help. In cases of immigrants who speak rare languages, International Institute staff can be called on to assist (see Chapter 8). Communication with respect to process, intention, and helping is pivotal during suicidal crises; human bonds formed through language, culture, lifestyle, and sexual identity are therefore crucial (Blumenfeld & Lindop, 1994). In Massachusetts, a 1993 Governor's commission developed the Safe Schools Program for Gay and Lesbian Youth in response to increased incidence of suicidality in this group. The program includes education

and support strategies for school personnel and student peers aimed at preventing suicide and protecting civil rights.

2. *The suicidal crises of people in these groups may be strongly linked to their disadvantaged social position.* When this appears to be the case, the social change strategies discussed in Chapter 2 are a particularly important aspect of follow-up after crisis intervention. For example, a poor, immigrant woman with three small children became suicidal each time she was threatened with having her heat cut off because she could not pay the bill. To offer this woman only crisis counseling without linking her to social support, financial aid, and social action groups would not approach the social roots of the problem. In Boston, for example, there is an organization called the Coalition for Basic Human Needs, a welfare rights group. Gay rights organizations are also becoming increasingly visible in their advocacy work for civil rights. People in crisis because of discriminatory treatment should be linked to such groups or at least be informed that they exist on their behalf (see Chapter 9, Figure 9.1, right circle, Box 3).

People in Hospitals and Other Institutions

People in crisis, like other human beings, have a need for self-mastery and control of their lives. Sensitivity to this need is an important element of positive crisis resolution. People in crisis who are suicidal not only do not lose their need for self-determination but also frequently feel powerless to solve their problems except by the ultimate act of self-determination—suicide. As Shirley's case (see Chapter 9) illustrates, staff members in institutions should examine various approaches to suicidal people intended to protect them from suicide, but which may result in exactly the opposite.

Although physical restraint and isolation may prevent *immediate* self-injury, these methods may actually *increase* the long-term suicide risk. Such results are especially probable if the physical measures are carried out with authoritarian attitudes and an absence of communication, warmth, and genuine concern. People who already feel powerless may interpret such harsh, outmoded practices as another attack on their self-esteem and ability to control their lives. As Farberow (1981, p. 101) states, people in hospitals (and other institutions) "are continually impressed with a sense of powerlessness; their lives must conform to a schedule designed essentially for the convenience of staff. Most things happen *to* them, not because of or *for* them; other people continually make the most important decisions about their lives." Ottini (1999) describes an intensive program (built on psychoanalytic and crisis concepts) designed to address the weaknesses of psychiatric inpatient services for suicidal adolescents (see also Berman, Coggins, Zibelin, Nelson, & Hannon, 1993; Osgood, 1992).

Many people expect institutionalized people to conform to the sick role, but it is unrealistic to conduct our practice within this framework for suicidal people. The problem of expecting suicidal people to fit the traditional sick role is exacerbated if there is no systematic effort to include family or other social contacts in hospital treatment programs. Once institutionalization has taken place, a person's natural social community is often forgotten. Or if the person is suicidal because such community support is lacking, it takes a special effort by hospital staff to help develop substitute support systems, such as transitional housing services, prior to discharge. In addition, admission to institutions is frequently the occasion of suicidal impulses based on culture shock for people not acculturated to institutions through routine work or residence.

Attention to these points can help prevent self-injury and suicides in hospitals and other institutions as well as reduce angry patients' attacks on staff and the high rate of suicide after discharge from mental hospitals. See Farberow's work (1981) and Bongar et al. (1993) for additional recommendations and standards for suicide prevention in hospitals.

Suicide prevention in holding centers and correctional institutions presents similar but even more complex problems (Haycock, 1993). A study in the Netherlands (cited in Kerkhof & Clark, 1993) revealed four types of stressors faced by prisoners: (1) problems with relatives or the problems of relatives, (2) legal process issues, (3) conflicts with staff or other inmates, and (4) issues of drug abuse. In one sense, the isolation cell is like an instrument of death. Yet relieving the physical isolation of a suicidal inmate may expose the person to possible abuse or attack by fellow inmates. Correctional treatment specialists and mental health practitioners working within the criminal justice system are challenged to advocate for more stringent adherence to suicide prevention protocols (Tripodi & Bender, 2006).

The crisis of suicide in jails and prisons is gaining attention. A unique program, Lifeline, is operated by staff of the Samaritans in Boston. Similar to the Prisoner Befriender program in several prisons in the United Kingdom, Lifeline is conducted in the county jail. Inmates—including murderers, arsonists, and rapists—receive special training to work as befrienders of the lonely and depressed. Besides reducing the number of suicides in this jail, the program is noted for its benefits to the befriending inmates: They have the satisfaction of saving others' lives and of feeling useful and appreciated for their caring (McGinnis, 1993).

Halleck's (1971) concern about chronic self-destructiveness among inmates is more relevant than ever, as various nations, including the United States, are cited by Amnesty International for cruel and unusual treatment of prisoners. He suggests that prisoners' repeated suicide attempts are a symptom of conditions in the institution that bear examination and reform (see Chapter 12). A related problem is the extensive use of psychotropic drugs on prisoners, with no psychotherapy services available for most (Earley, 2006). As crime and prison populations in the United States soar, suicide attempts are probable as long as real prison reform lags, and primary prevention of crime takes a back burner in policy circles.

Helping Survivors in Crisis

When a suicide occurs, it is almost always the occasion of a crisis for survivors: children, spouse, parents, other relatives, friends, crisis counselor, therapist, and anyone else closely associated with the person who has committed suicide. The term *survivor* in the suicidology literature properly refers to those left after *completed suicides*, not to those who survive a suicide attempt. The usual feelings associated with any serious loss are felt by most survivors of a suicide—sadness that the person ended life so tragically and anger that the person is no longer a part of one's life.

In addition, however, survivors often feel enormous guilt, primarily from two sources:

1. The sense of responsibility for not having prevented the suicide. This is especially true when the survivors were very close to the person who has died.
2. The sense of relief that some survivors feel after a suicide. This happens when relationships were very strained or when the person had attempted suicide many times and either could not or would not accept the help available.

A common tendency among survivors of suicide is to blame or scapegoat someone for the suicide. This reaction often arises from a survivor's sense of helplessness and guilt about not having prevented the suicide. Deeply held beliefs about suicide also contribute to this response. Some survivors deny that the suicide ever took place because they have no other way to handle the crisis. This often takes the form of insisting that the death was an accident.

Case Example: Denial of Suicide

One couple instructed their 9-year-old daughter, who was a patient in the pediatric ward, to tell the hospital supervisor that her older brother had died of an accident. (The supervisor knew the family through the hospital psychiatric unit.) The parents had insisted that he be discharged from psychiatric care, even though he was highly suicidal and the physician advised against it. A few days later, the boy shot himself at home with a hunting rifle. These parents were apparently very guilt ridden and went to great lengths to deny the suicide.

Various authors (Dunne, Dunne-Maxim, & McIntosh, 1987; Cain, 1972) have documented problems that can occur throughout survivors' lives if they do not have help at the time of the crisis of suicide. A study by Farberow, Gallager-Thompson, Gilewski, and Thompson (1992) revealed that suicide survivors among bereaved elderly people received significantly less support than those whose spouses died by natural death; men received less support than women did. Reed and Greenwald (1991) found that survivor–victim *attachment* and the quality of the relationship are more important in explaining grief reactions than the survivor's status (that is, the relationship between the survivor and the suicide, such as father and daughter or husband and wife). Problems for survivors include depression, serious personality disturbances, and obsession with suicide as the predestined fate for oneself, especially on the anniversary of the suicide or when the survivor reaches the same age.

The tragic effect of suicide is particularly striking in the case of children after a parent's suicide. In studies of child survivors, some of the symptoms found were learning disabilities, sleepwalking, delinquency, and setting fires (Cain & Fast, 1972). Crisis counseling should therefore be available for all survivors of suicide. Shneidman (1972) calls this *postvention*, an effort to reduce some of the possible harmful effects of suicide on the survivors. Making such support available, however, presents a special challenge, particularly in settings such as schools (Wenckstern, 1991).

Team Analysis Following a Suicide

Some people commit suicide while receiving therapy or counseling through a crisis center, mental health agency, or private practitioner or while receiving hospital or medical care. In these cases, the counselor, nurse, or physician is in a strategic position to help survivors. Unfortunately, workers often miss the opportunity for postvention because they may be struggling with the same feelings that beset the family. It is more effective to deal with the family immediately than to wait for an impasse to develop, but if staff members have not dealt with their own feelings, they may avoid approaching family survivors.

The most useful preventive measure is for helpers to learn as much as they can about suicide and about constructive ways of handling the feelings that often accompany working with self-destructive people. There will always be strong feelings following a suicide. However, anyone with a realistic concept of the limits of responsibility for another's suicide can help other survivors work through their feelings and reduce the scapegoating that often occurs.

In counseling and health care settings, a counselor or nurse should immediately seek consultation with a supervisor after a suicide occurs. Team meetings are also important, as they provide staff with an opportunity to air feelings and evaluate the total situation. For example, team analysis of John's case (Chapter 9) illustrates how easy it is to forget a person's natural place in the world and to fail to draw on social resources once the patient is in an institutional subculture. John's friends were never contacted, nor was a peer support source like AA considered. Involuntary commitment for self-protection, although well intentioned, was not enough. Analysis of this case sharpened the staff's awareness that the sense of isolation and powerlessness often experienced in mental health facilities may increase rather than decrease suicide risk. Through open discussion, staff members were able to acknowledge that John's suicide might have been prevented with a different approach to intervention, including helping him reestablish himself socially after a serious interpersonal loss (see Chapter 5). If suicide prevention efforts are based on established standards in suicidology, the staff is less likely to feel guilty, and malpractice suits are less likely (Bongar et al., 1993). In addition, self-examination and hindsight after a suicide usually yield knowledge that can be applied on behalf of others (Hoff & Resing, 1982).

Team meetings also provide a forum for determining who is best able to make postvention contact with the family. If the counselor who has worked most closely with the victim is too upset to deal with the family, a supervisory person should handle the matter, at least initially. In hospitals or mental health agencies in which no one has had training in basic suicide prevention and crisis counseling, outside consultation with suicidologists or crisis specialists should be obtained whenever possible.

Support and Crisis Intervention for Survivors

Most suicides do not occur among people receiving help from a health or counseling agency. This is one reason many survivors of suicide get so little help. In some communities, there are special bereavement counseling programs or self-help groups, such as Widow to Widow clubs, to help survivors of suicide. Ideally, every community should have an active outreach program for suicide survivors as a basic part of comprehensive crisis services (see Online Resources). Survivors are free to refuse an offer of support, but such support should be available.

A parent survivor, Adina Wrobleski, is one of the pioneers in developing survivors' grief groups, having formed such a group in 1982 following the suicide of her teenage daughter in the metropolitan Minneapolis area. Since then, many similar groups have been established. Wrobleski's work is significant in two respects: (1) following the suicide of her daughter, there were no peer support groups available to her and her husband; and (2) survivors of suicide do not necessarily need professional therapy as much as they need support from people who have experienced the same kind of loss. This point has been illustrated by groups such as the SIDS Foundation and various self-help groups for health and social problems, such as AA and groups for mastectomy patients (see Chapters 5 and 7).

In the absence of these avenues of help, survivors of suicide can still be reached by police, clergy, and funeral directors, if such caretakers are sensitive to survivors' needs. These key people should take care not to increase survivors' guilt and denial, recognizing how strong the suicide taboo and scapegoating tendency can be. The least one can do is offer an understanding word and suggest where people might find an agency or person to help them through the crisis. See Grollman's classic work (1977) regarding the role of clergy with survivors.

Techniques for helping survivors of suicide are essentially the same as those used in dealing with other crises. A survivor should be helped to:

1. Express feelings appropriate to the event
2. Grasp the reality of the suicide
3. Obtain and use the help necessary to work through the crisis (sometimes including the survivor's own suicide crisis). A survivor who depended

on the suicide victim for financial support may also need help in managing money and housing, for example.

Helping Child and Parent Survivors of Suicide

A surviving spouse with young children, including preschoolers as young as three or four, usually needs special help explaining to them that their parent has committed suicide. People tend to hide the facts from children in a mistaken belief that they will thus be spared unnecessary pain. But adults often fail to realize that children usually know a great deal more than adults think they know. Even without knowing all the facts surrounding a death, children are likely to suspect that something much more terrible than an accident has occurred. If the suicide is not discussed, the child is left to fill in the facts alone—and to do it with fantasies even more frightening than the real story would be. For example, a child may fear that the surviving parent killed the dead parent or that the child's own misbehavior caused the parent's death. The child may have unrealistic expectations that the dead parent will return: "Maybe if I'm extra good, Daddy will come back." What children do not create in their fantasy lives will often be filled in by information from neighborhood and school companions. Some child survivors also suffer from jeers and teasing by other children about the parent's suicide.

Survivors should explain the death by suicide clearly, simply, and in a manner consistent with the child's level of development and understanding. The child should have an opportunity to ask questions and express feelings. The child needs to know that the surviving parent is also willing to answer questions in the future, as the child's understanding of death and suicide grows. A child should never be left with the impression that the issue is closed and is never to be discussed again.

Parents might explain suicide to child survivors as follows:

"Yes, Daddy shot himself. No, it wasn't an accident; he did it because he wanted to."

"Mommy will not be coming back anymore. No, Mommy didn't do it because you misbehaved last night."

"No one knows exactly why your daddy did it. Yes, he had a lot of things that bothered him."

Surviving parents who cannot deal directly with their children about the other parent's suicide have usually not worked through their own feelings of guilt and responsibility. In these cases, parents need the support and help of a counselor for themselves as well as for their children. Parents often do not understand that serious consequences can arise from hiding the facts from children. Counseling should include an explanation of the advantages of talking openly with children about the suicide.

In some cases, a child is completely aware that the parent committed suicide, especially if there were many open threats or attempts of suicide.

Sometimes a child finds the dead parent or has been given directions by the other parent to "call if anything happens to Mommy" (Cain, 1972). If the suicidal person was very disturbed or abusive prior to committing suicide, the child may feel relief. In all of these cases, surviving children may feel guilt and misplaced responsibility for the death of their parent. They may become restless and fearful and refuse to sleep in their own beds. Parents will usually need the assistance of a crisis worker, a child guidance counselor, or a pastor to help a child through this crisis. Crisis intervention programs for such children are far too uncommon.

A study by Andrews and Marotta (2005) involving grieving children generated two categories of information about the role of spirituality as relationship, containment, connection, and play for comforting grieving children—what children need and are able to know for themselves, and what adult family members and counselors need to remember and do when in the presence of a grieving child. Children will gravitate toward what they need, especially if they are allowed and encouraged to create a new connection with the deceased through a caring adult, peer, pet, or even a toy; are invited to choose a linking object; and are given the opportunity for metaphorical play. These aspects of spirituality are pervasive and foster an environment for comforting children through their grieving.

Parents who survive a child's suicide—no matter the child's age—face related and very wrenching psychic challenges. First, the universal natural instinct of parents is the protection of their children and hope for their future well-being and success (abuse and violence as discussed in the next chapter are radical and tragic departures from this sociocultural norm). Second, in the natural order of things, parents expect to *precede*, not follow their children's deaths. Thus, the immediate and sometimes lifetime questions are: What did I/we do wrong? How did we fail? Why didn't he/she tell us what was going wrong so that we could have helped? Without a survivors group or help of a grief counselor, some parent survivors may struggle with these questions for years.

And indeed, there is no such thing as a "perfect" parent or one who has not made one or more mistakes in child rearing. However, as discussed in Chapter 1 (resilience), most children survive even terrible childhood odds (even outright abuse)—some because they resolve not to repeat their parents' mistakes, and others despite their imperfect parents. Further, beyond parents' best intentions and efforts on behalf of their children, the reasons for a teen or adult child's suicide may never be known. This is because, despite the clues cited in Chapter 9 that may reveal suicidal intent, in some cases the centuries-old decision to commit suicide is buried forever in the soul of particular individuals whose depths others (including parents and therapists) have not been able to plumb or understand. Counseling can help these survivors move beyond guilt and responsibility for another's self-inflicted death and end the search for reasons the person took with him or her into oblivion.

One parent survivor of an adult child who committed suicide had also survived the loss of a spouse only a few months earlier, following years of support and caretaking of the spouse through protracted treatment of cancer. Had the spouse still been alive, this parent survivor said their child's suicide might have ended their marriage in a search for what the other might have done wrong to explain the suicide. The acute grief and search for answers described by this parent survivor included contemplation of suicide following the process of death investigation, the funeral, etc. This survivor decided to go on living in part for the sake of another child and grandchildren, and finally found a measure of peace and healing through literary sources, selling the family home, and moving away to heal in a simple life and the embrace and beauty of nature.

Additional Outreach to Survivors

Help for survivors of suicide has always been one of the goals of the suicide prevention movement. Such work is important but difficult to carry out. Many people, including those in some coroners' offices, tend to cover up the reality of a suicide. When denial occurs in families and information about suicide is lacking, some parents may go to extraordinary lengths to conceal the real cause of a suicidal death in the mistaken belief that suicide "runs in families." Ironically, if such a belief is passed on to children, it may have intergenerational results as a "self-fulfilling prophecy." The suicide taboo in modern times continues, despite a growing acceptance of the morality of suicide in certain instances (Battin & Mayo, 1980; see also "Ethical Issues Regarding Suicide" in Chapter 9).

One means of reaching a large number of survivors is through coroners' offices. Every death is eventually recorded there. In Los Angeles County, follow-up investigation is done on all suicide deaths as well as equivocal deaths (those in which suicide is suspected but not certain). This is done through the "psychological autopsy"—that is, an intensive examination to determine whether the death was by suicide and if it was, to uncover the probable causes (Litman, 1987). Information for the psychological autopsy is obtained from survivors and from medical and psychiatric records.

Research is the primary purpose of the psychological autopsy; however, it is an excellent means of getting in touch with survivors who are not in contact with a crisis center, physician, or mental health agency. Survivors are, of course, free to refuse participation in such postmortem examinations. Experience reveals, however, that the majority of survivors do not refuse to be interviewed and welcome the opportunity to talk about the suicide. This is especially true if they are contacted within a few days of the suicide, when they are most troubled with their feelings. Many survivors use this occasion to obtain some help in answering their own questions and dealing with possible suicidal inclinations following a suicide. Some people find the "official" interview an acceptable context in which to talk about an otherwise taboo subject. It thus provides an ideal opportunity for the interviewer to suggest follow-up counseling resources to the survivor. If weeks or months pass, survivors may resent the postmortem interview. By that time, they have had to settle their feelings and questions on their own and in their own way, which may include denial and resentment. A delayed interview may seem like the unnecessary opening of an old wound.

Various suicide prevention and crisis centers offer survivor counseling programs. Many communities, however, still do not have formal programs available to survivors of suicide. Obviously, a great deal of work remains to be done in this important area.

Summary and Discussion Questions

People who get help after a suicide attempt or other self-destructive behavior may never commit suicide. Much depends on what happens in the form of emergency, crisis, and follow-up intervention. However, when suicide does occur, survivors of suicide usually are in crisis and are often neglected because of cultural taboos and the lack of aggressive outreach programs for them. Children, spouses, and parents who lose a loved one by suicide are especially vulnerable if they do not receive support during this crisis. This is an area of great challenge for crisis program staff.

1. Consider in your particular community what suicide prevention services are available and publicly promoted. If there are none, why?
2. Discuss with a family member, classmate, or other suicide survivor the enormous challenge of dealing directly with a suicidal death.
3. In sociocultural perspective, identify factors that may contribute to youth suicides in wealthy societies like the United States and Canada.

References

Andrews, C. R., & Marotta, S. A. (2005). Spirituality and coping among grieving children: A preliminary study. *Counseling and Values, 50,* 38–50.

Baldessarini, R. J. (2000). The complexity of suicide. Grand rounds: Suicide: Clinical/risk management issues for psychiatrists. *CNS Spectrums Academic Supplement: The International Journal of Neuropsychiatric Medicine, 5* (2, Suppl. 1), 34–38.

Baldessarini, R. J., & Tondo, L. (1999). Antisuicidal effect of lithium treatment in major mood disorders. In D. G. Jacobs (Ed.), *The Harvard Medical School guide to suicide assessment and intervention* (pp. 355–371). San Francisco: Jossey-Bass.

Bale, C. (2001). Befriending in cyberspace: Challenges and opportunities. *Crisis, 22*(1), 10–11.

Battin, M. P., & Mayo, D. J. (Eds.). (1980). *Suicide: The philosophical issues.* New York: St. Martin's Press.

Berman, A. L., Coggins, C. C., Zibelin, J. C., Nelson, L. F., & Hannon, T. (1993). Inpatient treatment planning. *Suicide & Life-Threatening Behavior, 23*(2), 162–168.

Bloom, S. L. (1997). *Creating sanctuary: Toward the evolution of sane societies.* New York: Routledge.

Blumenfeld, W. J., & Lindop, L. (1994). *Family, schools, and students' resource guide.* Boston: Safe Schools Program for Gay and Lesbian Students, Massachusetts Department of Education.

Bongar, B., Maris, R. W., Berman, A. L., & Litman, R. E. (1992). Outpatient standards of care and the suicidal patient. *Suicide & Life-Threatening Behavior, 22*(4), 453–478.

Bongar, B., Maris, R. W., Berman, A. L., Litman, R. E., & Silverman, M. M. (1993). Inpatient standards of care and the suicidal patient: Part I: General clinical formulations and legal considerations. *Suicide & Life-Threatening Behavior, 23*(3), 245–256.

Boyd, J. H., & Moscicki, E. K. (1986). Firearms and youth suicide. *American Journal of Public Health, 76*, 1240–1242.

Breggin, P., & Breggin, G. R. (1994). *Talking back to Prozac: What doctors won't tell you about today's most controversial drug.* New York: St. Martin's Press.

Brendtro, L. K., Brokenleg, M., & Van Bockern, S. (1990). *Reclaiming youth at risk: Our hope for the future.* Bloomington, IN: National Educational Service.

Brown, G. W., & Harris, T. (1978). *The social origins of depression.* London: Tavistock.

Brownlee, S. (2007). *Overtreated: How too much medicine is making us sicker and poorer.* New York: Bloomsbury.

Cain, A. C. (Ed.). (1972). *Survivors of suicide.* Springfield, IL: Thomas.

Cain, A. C., & Fast, R. (1972). Children's disturbed reactions to parent suicide: Distortions of guilt, communication, and identification. In A. C. Cain (Ed.), *Survivors of suicide* (pp. 93–111). Springfield, IL: Thomas.

Canada, M., Heath, M. A., Money, K., Annandale, N., Fischer, L., & Young, E. L. (2006). Crisis intervention for students of diverse backgrounds: School counselors' concerns. *Brief Treatment and Crisis Intervention, 7*, 12–24.

Carey, B. (2008, January 17). Study indicates bias in drug trial reporting for antidepressants. *Boston Globe,* p. A20.

Carson, M., Eisner, M., Kartes, L., & Kolga, C. (1999). *A care-giving guide for seniors.* Ottawa: Algonquin Publishers.

Clark, D. C., & Kerkhof, A. J. F. M. (1993). No-suicide decisions and suicide contracts in therapy. *Crisis, 14*(3), 98–99.

Cloward, R. A., & Piven, F. F. (1979). Hidden protest: The channeling of female innovations and resistance. *Signs: Journal of Women in Culture and Society, 4*, 651–669.

Collins, W. L., & Doolittle, A. (2006). Personal reflections of funeral rituals and spirituality in a Kentucky African American family. *Death Studies, 30*, 957–969.

Drew, B. L. (2001). Self-harm behavior and no-suicide contracting in psychiatric inpatient settings. *Archives of Psychiatric Nursing, 15*(3), 99–106.

Dubovsky, S. L., & Dubovsky, A. N. (2007). *Psychotropic drug prescriber's survival guide.* New York & London: W. W. Norton.

Duncan, B., Miller, S., & Sparks, J. (2000, March/April). Exposing the mythmaking. *Networker,* 25–33, 52–53.

Dunne, E., Dunne-Maxim, K., & McIntosh, J. (Eds.). (1987). *Suicide and its aftermath.* New York: Norton.

Earley, P. (2006). *Crazy: A father's search through America's mental health madness.* New York: Berkley Books.

Elliott, G. R. (2006). *Medicating young minds.* New York: Stewart, Tabori, & Chang.

Farberow, N. L. (1981). Suicide prevention in the hospital. *Hospital and Community Psychiatry, 32*(2), 99–104.

Farberow, N. L., Gallager-Thompson, D., Gilewski, M., & Thompson, L. (1992). Changes in grief and mental health of bereaved spouses of older suicides. *Journal of Gerontology, 47*(6), 357–366.

Garcia, G., & Ghani, S. (2000). Pharmacology update: Newer medications and indications used in psychiatry. *Primary Care Practice, 4*(2), 207–220.

Garrison, C. Z., McKeown, R. E., Valois, R. F., & Vincent, M. L. (1993). Aggression, substance use, and suicidal behaviors in high school students. *American Journal of Public Health, 83*(2), 179–184.

Grollman, E. (1977). *Living—when a loved one has died.* Boston: Beacon Press.

Halleck, S. (1971). *The politics of therapy.* New York: Science House.

Haycock, J. (1993). Double jeopardy: Suicide rates in forensic hospitals. *Suicide & Life-Threatening Behavior, 23*(2), 130–138

Hoff, L. A., & Resing, M. (1982). Was this suicide preventable? *American Journal of Nursing, 82*(7) 1106–1111. (Also reprinted in B. A. Backer, P. M. Dubbert, & E. J. P Eisenman, Eds., 1985. *Psychiatric/mental health nursing: Contemporary readings,* pp. 169–180. Belmont, CA: Wadsworth.)

Kann, L., Brener, N. D., & Wechsler, H. (2007). Overview and summary: School health policies and program study 2006. *Journal of School Health, 77*(8), 385–397.

Kaplan, M. S. (1998). Firearm suicides and homicides in the United States: Regional variations and patterns of gun ownership. *Social Science & Medicine, 46*(9) 1227–1233.

Kaplan, M. S., Adamek, M. E., & Calderon, A. (1999). Managing depressed and suicidal geriatric patients: Differences among primary care physicians. *Gerontologist, 38*(4), 417–425.

Kerkhof, A. J. F. M., & Clark, D. C. (1993). Suicide attempts and self-injury in prisons. *Crisis, 14*(4), 146–147.

Kurdyak, P. A., Juurlink D. N., & Mamdani, M. M. (2007). The effect of antidepressant warnings on prescribing trends in Ontario, Canada. *American Journal of Public Health, 97*(4), 750–754.

Lease, S. H., Horne, S. G., & Noffsinger-Frazier, N. (2005). Affirming faith experiences and psychological health for Caucasian lesbian, gay, and bisexual individuals. *Journal of Counseling Psychology, 52*(3), 378–388.

Leenaars, A. A., & Wenckstern, S. (Eds.). (1991). *Suicide prevention in schools.* Bristol, PA: Hemisphere.

Litman, R. E. (1987). Mental disorders and suicidal intention. *Suicide & Life-Threatening Behavior, 17*(2), 85–92.

May, P. A., Serna, P., Hurt, L., DeBruyn, L. M. (2005). Outcome evaluation of a public health approach to suicide prevention in an American Indian Tribal Nation. *American Journal of Public Health, 95*(7), 1238–1244.

McGinnis, C. (1993). *Lifeline: A training manual.* Boston: Suffolk County Jail.

McIlroy, A. (2001, April 25). Antidepressant overdoses can kill, research shows. *Globe and Mail,* p. A 9.

Mehlum, L. (2001). The Internet and suicide prevention. In O.T. Grad (Ed.), *Suicide risk and protective factors in the new millennium* (pp. 223–227). Ljubljana, Slovenia: Cankarjev dom.

Motto, J. A. (1999). Critical points in the assessment and management of suicide risk. In D. G. Jacobs (Ed.), *The Harvard Medical School guide to suicide assessment and intervention* (pp. 224–238). San Francisco: Jossey-Bass.

Osgood, M. (1992). Environmental factors in suicide in long-term care facilities. *Suicide & Life-Threatening Behavior, 22*(1), 98–106.

Ottini, J. (1999). Suicide attempts during adolescence: Systematic hospitalization and crisis treatment. *Crisis, 20*(1), 41–48.

Reed, M. D., & Greenwald, J. Y. (1991). Survivor-victim status, attachment, and sudden death bereavement. *Suicide & Life-Threatening Behavior, 21*(4), 385–401.

Reid, W. J. (1998). Promises, promises: Don't rely on patients' no-suicide/no-violence "contracts." *Journal of Practical Psychiatry and Behavioral Health, 4*(5), 316–318.

Richman, J. (1986). *Family therapy of suicidal individuals.* New York: Springer.

Rogers, M. J. (1971). Drug abuse: Just what the doctor ordered. *Psychology Today, 5,* 16–24.

Salzman, C. (1999). Treatment of the suicidal patient with psychotropic drugs and ECT. In D. G. Jacobs (Ed.), *The Harvard Medical School guide to suicide assessment and intervention* (pp. 372–382). San Francisco: Jossey-Bass.

Shaffer, D. (1993). Suicide: Risk factors and the public health. *American Journal of Public Health, 83*(2), 171–173.

Shneidman, E. S. (1972). Foreword. In A. C. Cain (Ed.), *Survivors of suicide.* Springfield, IL: Thomas.

Solomon, D. A., Keitner, G. I., Miller, I. W., Shea, M. T., & Keller, M. B. (1995). Course of illness and maintenance treatments for patients with bipolar disorder. *Journal of Clinical Psychiatry, 56*(1), 5–13.

Tripodi, S. J., & Bender, K. (2006). Inmate suicide: Prevalence, assessment, and protocols. *Brief Treatment and Crisis Intervention, 7,* 40–54.

Turner, E. H., Matthews, A. M., Linardatos, E., Tell, R. A., & Rosenthal, R. (2008). Selective publication of antidepressant trials and its influence on apparent efficacy. *New England Journal of Medicine, 385*(3), 252–260.

U.S. Department of Health and Human Services, Public Health Services. (2001). *National strategy for suicide prevention: Goals and objectives for action.* Washington, DC: Author.

U.S. Public Health Service. (1999). *Surgeon general's call to action to prevent suicide.* Washington, DC: Author.

Wasserman, D. (2004). Evaluating suicide prevention: Various approaches needed. *World Psychiatry, 3*(3), 153–154.

Waters, R. (2000, March/April). Generation RX: The risk of raising our kids on pharmaceuticals. *Networker,* 34–43.

Webb, N. D. (1986). Before and after suicide: A preventive outreach program for colleges. *Suicide & Life-Threatening Behavior, 16*(4), 469–480.

Wenckstern, S. (1991). Suicide postvention: A case illustration in a secondary school. In A. A. Leenaars & S. Wenckstern (Eds.), *Suicide prevention in schools* (pp. 181–196). Bristol, PA: Hemisphere.

Worden, J. W. (1991). *Grief counseling and grief therapy* (2nd ed.). New York: Springer.

Zito J. M., Safer, D. J., dosReis, S., Gardner, J. F., Boles, M., & Lynch, F. (2000). Trends in the prescribing of psychotropic medications to preschoolers. *Journal of the American Medical Association, 283*(8), 1025–1030.

The Crisis of Victimization by Violence

Victimization by violence knows few, if any, national, ethnic, religious, or other boundaries (Levinson, 1989; United Nations, 1996b).[1] The United States has some of the highest homicide rates in the world. In spite of civil rights legislation, nationally and internationally, violence continues apace—from domestic to community and global arenas, and often originating from bias based on gender, race, religion, disability, and sexual identity. Abused immigrants usually face triple jeopardy because of social isolation, language barriers, and fear of deportation if they seek help.

Violence as a Human Rights Issue

The United Nations has convened international meetings on the topic and the United Nations Decade for Women conferences feature numerous workshops on the worldwide problem of violence against women. The last such conference was in 1995 in Beijing, People's Republic of China, with about 36,000 women attending. Beijing Plus 5 convened in New York in June 2000 to assess the progress of member nations toward the goals of the 1995 platform for action (UN, 1996b). Although progress is evident, much work remains to achieve women's equality and freedom from abuse worldwide (see Beijing +5) . It is noteworthy that after sponsoring these international conferences every 10 years over several decades, since the 1995 Beijing conference no similar conference has been convened—this, as the rape of girls and women as the "spoils of war" in Darfur continues despite Sudan's constitution regarding accountability for such crimes, international publicity, and efforts by non-governmental organizations (NGOs) and various aid groups.

Canada has demonstrated extraordinary leadership on this topic, supporting numerous projects as well as five federally funded research centers (Ross, 2001). Canada is the first country to pass a federal, mandatory arrest law for batterers, and the first in which men in the private sector have taken national leadership in a white ribbon campaign to end violence against women and

---

[1] Only those statistical figures reflecting changes in broad trends are cited here. For current official government statistics in the United States and internationally, readers are referred to Internet sources, e.g., the U.S. Department of Justice, the United Nations, and the World Health Organization (WHO).

to institute training criteria for health and social service professionals on violence issues (Hoff, in press; see also Online Resources).

In the United States, the U.S. Surgeon General's Workshop on Violence and Public Health Report (1986) was convened in 1985 to emphasize the fact that victims' needs, treatment of assailants, and prevention of violence should command much greater attention from health and social service professionals than it has until recently. A significant recommendation in the U.S. government's publication report of this conference (1986), was that all publicly licensed professionals (physicians, nurses, social workers, and psychologists) should be trained and *examined* on the topic of violence and victimization as a condition of licensure. Since then, there has been progress on many fronts (for example, the 1999 American Association of Colleges of Nursing position paper; the 1994 research of Tilden et al.), although much is left to be done before curriculum coverage of this topic is considered *essential* for graduation, not incidental according to faculty interest (see Hoff, in press). The historical neglect of victimization, especially in the domestic arena, underscores the value placed on family privacy and the myth that the family is a haven of love and security. Neglect of victimization also points to several related issues:

- Social values regarding children, how they should be disciplined, and who should care for them
- Social and cultural devaluation of women and their problems
- A social and economic system in which elderly citizens often have no worthwhile place
- A social climate with little tolerance for minority group sexual orientation
- A legal system in which it is difficult to consider the rights of victims without compromising the rights of the accused
- A knowledge system that historically has interpreted these problems in private, individual terms rather than in public, social ones (Mills, 1959)

This and the following chapter address these issues from the psychosociocultural and public health perspectives that inform this book. The focus is on prevention, crisis intervention, and the interconnections of violence across the life span. The prevention and early intervention emphasis here is based on extensive interdisciplinary work with survivors, revealing the risk of serious and often long-term medical and mental health sequelae when support and crisis counseling are lacking at the time of victimization by violence (Hoff, 2000). For a discussion of comprehensive psychosocial and psychotherapeutic care beyond crisis, readers are referred to texts such as Burstow, 1992; Campbell, 1998; Everett and Gallop, 2000; Figley and Nash, 2005; Herman, 1992; Rrynearson, 2006; Wiehe, 1998; and Wilson, 2006.

This chapter addresses the various categories of abuse and violence, primarily from the perspective of the victim. Chapter 12 addresses violence from the perspective of the assailant, as well as that directed against police, health and human service workers, and others. The two chapters are companion pieces, as the topics overlap; for example, many assailants have been victimized themselves.

Reflecting a major theme of crisis theory (Hoff, 1990), the term *victim-survivor* is used to acknowledge victimization but to simultaneously convey an abused person's potential for growth, development, and empowerment—a status beyond the dependency implied by the term *victim* alone (Burstow, 1992; Mawby & Walklate, 1994). The terms *violence* and *abuse* are used interchangeably.

Theories on Violence and Victimization

Earlier theories to explain violence and its prevalence fall into three categories: (1) psychobiological, (2) social-psychological, and (3) sociocultural (Gelles & Straus, 1979). Today most violence scholars reject analytical frameworks such as sociobiology, which serve to maintain violence as a private matter. Instead violence is now widely interpreted in psychological, sociological, and feminist terms (Dobash & Dobash, 1998). The position taken in this book is that violence is predominantly a *social* phenomenon, a means of exerting *power* and *control* that has far-reaching effects on personal, family, and public health worldwide (Dobash & Dobash, 1979; Hoff, in press; Yllo & Bograd, 1987). In addition, the book's holistic framework implies a continuum between so-called family violence and other forms of aggression. Finally, while controversy continues between feminist and mainstream theorists and activists (Gelles & Loseke, 1993), the focus here is on bridge building and the common concerns of those who teach and practice violence prevention and who work with victim-survivors and their assailants in diverse settings. An either-or position is rejected in favor of complementary feminist, sociocultural, and public health perspectives that emphasize the intersections among gender, class, race, and other social categories that may figure in the experience of particular victims or assailants. In feminist theory, this approach is called *socialist feminism*. As readers examine their own positions vis-à-vis feminist and mainstream theories of violence, it is important to note that there is no such thing as a monolithic feminism. See Hoff (1990) and Segal (1999).

Accordingly, the term *family violence* is avoided on the grounds that it obscures the fact that most perpetrators in families are men, and most victims are children and women of all ages. One of the continuing controversies about violence concerns the rates of men's and women's violence (Kurz, 1993; Straus, 1993). The argument centers on the alleged methodological flaws of the Conflict Tactics Scale used in the national surveys conducted by Straus and colleagues in 1980 (see Johnson, 1998). The term *family violence* also deflects attention from the sociocultural roots of abuse, which extend beyond the family to deeply embedded cultural values and traditional social structures that disempower women and children particularly.

Many professionals and laypersons have accepted psychological or medical explanations of violence (see violence in the workplace and forensic psychiatry, Chapter 12). Common sentiments include (1) "only a sick man could beat his wife"; (2) child abuse is a syndrome calling for "treatment" of disturbed parents; (3) John W. Hinckley should have been "treated," not punished, for violently attacking President Reagan; (4) a "crazed madman" was responsible (and by implication, not accountable) for highly publicized terrorist attacks; (5) "temporary insanity" sometimes excuses murder (even though juries are becoming more skeptical about this plea); and (6) women who kill their abusers are victims of the "battered woman syndrome."

Public debate about biomedical approaches to social problems is increasing (Luhrmann, 2000; Warshaw, 1989). There is growing acceptance of the view that attention to violent persons and their victims in predominantly individual terms is at best incomplete and at worst does little to address the roots of violence. This view is in accord with the crisis paradigm of this book: Crises stemming from violence should be treated with a *tandem* approach, taking both individual and sociocultural factors into account. A person in crisis because of violence will experience many of the same responses as persons in crisis from other sources. And similar intervention strategies, such as listening and decision counseling, are called for during the acute crisis phase. However, attention to the social and cultural origins of crises stemming from violence is important in designing prevention and follow-up strategies that avoid implicitly blaming the victim (Ryan, 1971; Hoff, 1990). Indeed, the implications of a sociocultural framework are even more critical when considering crises originating from violence than when dealing with crises from other sources (see Chapter 2). For victims of violence, a strictly individual or biopsychiatric approach can compound the problem rather than contribute to the solution (Stark, Flitcraft, & Frazier, 1979).

There is no single cause of violence. Rather, there are complex, interrelated *reasons* that some individuals are violent and others are not. In cases of violence against children, intimate partners, and elders, for example, psychological, cultural, and socioeconomic factors are often present together, forming the *context* in which violence as a means of control seems to thrive. Children, many seniors, and often wives are economically dependent on their caretakers and in most cases are physically weaker than their abusers. Caretakers of children and older people are often stressed psychologically by difficult behaviors and socioeconomically by a lack of social and financial resources to ease the burdens of caretaking. In cases of woman battering and sex-role stereotyping, psychological and economic factors intersect at both ends of the social class continuum: poor women are less able to survive on their own, and some women who earn more than their husbands are more vulnerable to attack in a nonegalitarian marriage.

Violence toward others, then, is one way a person can respond to stress and resolve a personal crisis at the same time. For example, a person with low self-esteem who is threatened by the suspected infidelity of a spouse may react with violence. A violent response is not inevitable though; it is *chosen* and may be influenced by such factors as an earlier choice to use alcohol and other drugs. The choice of violent behavior to control another person is influenced by the social, political, legal, and belief and knowledge systems of the violent person's cultural community. The element of choice implies an interpretation of violence as a moral act—that is, violence is *social action* engaged in by human beings who by nature are rational and conscious. Through socialization, humans become responsible for the actions they choose in various situations.

However, consciousness may be clouded and responsibility mitigated by social and cultural factors rooted in the history of human society. Under certain circumstances, a person may be excused from facing the social consequences of his or her behavior, as in cases of self-defense or when a violent act is considered to be irrational. This does not mean that every violent act is a result of mental illness and that the perpetrator should therefore be "treated," as suggested by a popular conception of violence. Nor does it mean that violence can be excused on grounds of racial or economic discrimination; this would suggest that the moral stature of disadvantaged groups is below the standard of responsible behavior. Given the poverty, unemployment, and other tragic results of social inequalities endured by many people—mostly racial minority groups—perhaps in no other instance is the tandem approach to crisis intervention more relevant: violent *individuals* are held accountable for their behavior, while the political and socioeconomic *context* in which much violence occurs is also addressed. In other words, an individual can be held accountable, can be restrained or rehabilitated, and at the same time the factors that have contributed to the person's vulnerability to choosing aggressive behaviors in the first place can be addressed. This principle applies regardless of gender or race.

Another troubling aspect of a simplistic interpretation of violence is the tendency toward "solutions" in the form of revenge, as suggested, for example, by U.S. voters' choice of capital punishment. To describe violence as a moral act rather than a disease does not imply support of revenge as an appropriate response. As responses to the complex problem of violence, treatment and revenge represent opposite extremes. As in the case of race or gender, excusing violent acts on the basis of psychiatric illness suggests that violent human beings are somewhat less than human, are generally incapable of judging and acting according to the consequences of their behavior, and are driven by uncontrollable, aggressive impulses. In contrast, revenge—in the form of capital punishment, inhumane prison conditions, or a failure to provide economic and other opportunities for learning to change a violent lifestyle— implies a departure from the moral foundations of society.

Violence and our response to its victim-survivors and perpetrators can be interpreted in a multifaceted perspective: moral, social-psychological, legal, and medical. *Violence can be defined as an infraction of society's rules regarding people, their relationships, and their property.* It is a complex phenomenon in which sociocultural, political, medical, and psychological factors touch both its immediate and chronic aspects. Functioning members of a society normally know a group's cultural rules and the consequences for violating them. Those lacking such knowledge generally are excused and receive treatment instead of punishment. Others are excused on the basis of self-defense or the circumstances that alter one's normal liability for rule infractions. A moral society would require restitution to individual victims from those not excused and would design a criminal justice system to prevent rather than promote future crime. *A truly moral approach to violence* would also avoid reform practices that discriminate on the basis of race, gender, class, or sexual identity, practices that create a climate in which crime flourishes with the implicit support of society (Brown & Bohn, 1989; Handwerker, 1998).

Decisions about crisis and follow-up approaches to victims and perpetrators of violence demand a critical examination of the theories and research supporting such practice, an examination not undertaken until recently. This theoretical overview applies to the topics in this and the following chapter. It assumes a continuum between what happens between family members and intimates and the larger sociocultural factors affecting them. In the following discussion, social-psychological and sociocultural theories will be examined as they apply to crises stemming from violence in respect to

- Prevention
- Intervention during crisis
- Follow-up service (psychosocial care and psychotherapeutic treatment)

Each of these topics is important, but the discussion in these two chapters will focus on assessment and intervention, with general reference to the preventive and follow-up strategies necessary for a long-range political and social approach that will reduce crises stemming from violence (see Figure 11.1, right circles, Boxes 1 and 3).

Victimization Assessment Strategies

Providers in various entry points to the health and social service system should incorporate questions about possible victimization trauma into their routine assessments. Bell, Jenkins, Kpo, and Rhodes (1994) state that protocols for such assessments should be mandated by law. In Chapter 3, a triage tool (Exhibit 3.1) was introduced for risk-to-life (victimization, suicide, assault/homicide) questions to incorporate into all intake questionnaires across health care settings. It is replicated here as Exhibit 11.1 for easy reference by readers focused on victim/survivor care, and serves as a baseline for assessing level of trauma from victimization (Table 11.1). This tool, the suicide risk tool (Chapter 9), and the assault/homicide tool (Chapter 12), are part of the Comprehensive Mental Health Assessment guide discussed in Chapter 3, and underscore the interrelationships among violence, victimization, and suicide (see Hoff & Rosenbaum, 1994). Questions about suicide and assault potential and resource depletion should be included in health and social service assessment protocols because these problems are often secondary to the primary problem of abuse; also, suicide and assault risk may signal the severity of trauma from victimization. As the triage questions in Exhibit 3.1 suggest, such routine inquiry could prevent suicide or murder as desperate responses to victimization trauma. For an abuse assessment screen

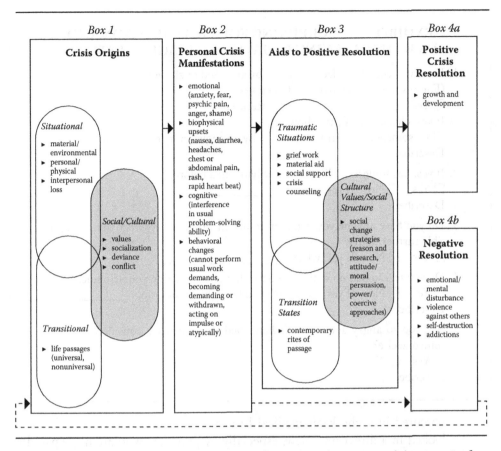

FIGURE 11.1 Crisis Paradigm. Crisis origins, manifestations, and outcomes and the respective functions of crisis care have interactional relationships. The intertwined circles represent the distinct yet interrelated origins of crisis and aids to positive resolution, even though personal manifestations are often similar. The arrows pointing from origins to positive resolution illustrate the *opportunity for growth and development* through crisis; the broken line at the bottom depicts the potential *danger of crisis* in the absence of appropriate aids. The loop between Box 4b and Box 1 denotes the *vulnerability* to future crisis episodes following negative resolution.

designed specifically for use by health professionals working with women, see Soeken, McFarlane, Parker, and Lominack (1998).

As in the case of suicide risk assessment, *no crisis assessment is complete without ascertaining risk and trauma from victimization and assault.* Work with battered women, for example, has uncovered the repeated revelation by survivors seeking help: "No one asked." As the study by Sugg and Inui (1992) suggests, physicians, nurses, and others have moved beyond their traditional fear of opening Pandora's box by inquiring about abuse. Just as health assessments now include routine questions about smoking and drinking, so should victimization and violence assessment be routine for anyone in emotional distress or whose symptoms do not readily suggest a medical diagnosis (Hoff & Morgan, in press). In response to national campaigns, screening in primary care protocols for intimate partner and other types of abuse is now common in many U.S. and Canadian health care agencies. Yet such screening is often

---

EXHIBIT 11.1 SCREENING FOR VICTIMIZATION AND LIFE-THREATENING BEHAVIORS: TRIAGE QUESTIONS

1. Have you been troubled or injured by any kind of abuse or violence? (For example, hit by partner, forced sex)
   ☐ Yes ☐ No ☐ Not sure ☐ Refused
   If yes, check one of the following:
   ☐ By someone in your family? ☐ By an acquaintance or stranger?
   Describe:

2. If yes, has something like this ever happened before?
   ☐ Yes ☐ No If yes, when? _____
   Describe:

3. Do you have anyone you can turn to or rely on now to protect you from possible further injury?
   ☐ Yes ☐ No If yes, who? _____

4. Do you feel so bad now that you have thought of hurting yourself/suicide?
   ☐ Yes ☐ No If yes, what have you thought about doing? _____
   Describe:

5. Are you so angry about what's happened that you have considered hurting someone else?
   ☐ Yes ☐ No
   Describe:

---

obscured in a check-off medical history form where it can easily be overlooked in a direct interview, especially by providers who are unprepared to explore further if the client checked "yes" about abuse or safety in a routine intake questionnaire. On the other hand, lengthy screening tools may be counterproductive in busy emergency and primary care settings (Coker et al., 2007). The best recommendation for use of more in-depth tools is for frontline and primary care providers to make referral to crisis counselors based on information obtained from the five-question triage tool (Exhibit 11.1).

Once victimization status is identified, it should be followed by in-depth assessment (preferably by mental health professionals with backgrounds in victimology who are also sensitive to gender issues) to ascertain the extent of trauma and the victim-survivor's response (see also Burstow, 1992; Campbell & Humphreys, 1993; Everett & Gallop, 2000; Herman, 1992; van der Kolk, 1987).

Child Abuse

The tragedy of child abuse continues, while public debate about related values and social issues escalates.

The Problem

Child abuse can be physical, emotional, verbal, or sexual—any acts of commission or omission that harm or threaten to harm a child (Cook & Bowles, 1980).

TABLE 11.1   Victimization Assessment Tool

Key to Risk	Level of Victimization	Typical Indicators
1	No experience of physical violence or abuse	No memory of violence recently or in the past.
2	Experience of abuse/ violence with minor physical and/or emotional trauma	Currently, verbal arguments that occasionally escalate to pushing and shoving or mild slapping. History *may* include past victimization that is no longer problematic or for which a solution is in process.
3	Experience of abuse/ violence with moderate physical and/or emotional trauma	Abused several times a month in recent years, resulting in moderate trauma/emotional distress (for example, bruises, no threat to life, no weapons). History *may* include past victimization that is still somewhat problematic (for example, a sexual abuse incident/ overture by a parent or stepparent over 2 years ago).
4	Experience of abuse/ violence with severe physical and/or emotional trauma	Violently attacked (for example, rape) or physically abused in recent years, resulting in physical injury requiring medical treatment. Threats to kill, no guns. History *may* include serious victimization (for example, periodic battering, incest, or other abuse requiring medical and/or psychological treatment).
5	Life-threatening or prolonged violence/ abuse with very severe physical and/or emotional trauma	Recent or current life-threatening physical abuse, potentially lethal assault or threats with available deadly weapons. History *may* include severe abuse requiring medical treatment, frequent or ongoing sexual abuse, recent rape at gun- or knifepoint, or other physical attack requiring extensive medical treatment.

The biblical expression "spare the rod and spoil the child" suggests a long history of child abuse. De Mause (1975) has written that the "helping mode" in caring for children is of very recent origin and was preceded historically by often widely accepted infanticide and rampant cruelty toward children. The institution of Good Samaritan laws is a legal response to those practices. Although the natural helplessness of children inspires most adults to aid and protect them, societies have found it necessary to have specific laws to protect children. These laws also protect physicians, nurses, and social workers from prosecution for slander when they report suspected child abuse to authorities.

Case Example: Richard

A young mother with four children felt overwhelmed trying to care for her 5-year-old hyperactive child, Richard. The woman's husband was employed as a hospital maintenance worker but found it difficult to support the family. The family could not obtain public assistance although their income was just above the level to qualify even for food stamps. The mother routinely spanked Richard with a strap several times during the day. By evening, the child was even more hyperactive, so the mother sometimes put him to bed without feeding him. The father and mother mutually approved of this form of disciplining Richard. A neighbor reported the parents of suspected abuse after observing the mother chase and verbally abuse Richard on the street, with a strap poised to spank him.

Child abuse happens in well-to-do families and poor families, in cities, suburbs, and rural areas. No one knows exactly how many children are abused each year because many cases are not reported. Besides the estimated 2 to 4 million abused and neglected children, 2000 to 4000 deaths occur annually in the United States at the hands of parents and caretakers. One or both parents or siblings may be involved. In her study of women who killed their children, Korbin (1987) uncovered a dynamic similar to the "cry for help" noted in suicidal people. If their network of relatives and professionals had responded to their behavioral pleas for help, these women would have been "secretly relieved," and perhaps fatal abuse would have been avoided.

There is disagreement on just what child abuse is. Most people agree that some kind of discipline is necessary and that a swat or controlled spanking for playing with fire or running in front of cars is not the same as child abuse. But it is difficult to persuade the average North American that a child can be brought up without physical punishment, in spite of research supporting the negative effects of such punishment (Greven, 1990; Mer, 2005).

The tragic reality of child abuse gained national attention in North America with the works of Kempe and Heifer (1980) in pediatrics and Gil (1970) in social science; work on childhood sexual abuse followed (for example, Bagley & King, 1990; Everett & Gallop, 2000; Finkelhor, 1984). Most clinicians and researchers challenge single-factor approaches, embracing instead an "ecological" interactive theory and preventive practice in response to the problem.

A tragedy related to child abuse is that of runaway children: Nearly half of American runaways leave home because of incest or physical neglect (Saylors & Daliparthy, 2006). The majority are never reported missing by their parents; most are from white, middle-class families; thousands disappear each year, many dying of disease, exploitation, and malnutrition (Powers & Jaklitsch, 1989; Russell, 1986). Childhood sexual abuse is also associated with young adults' initiation into injection drug use (Ompad et al., 2005), while some children and teens are lured into abusive relationships through the Internet (Flanagan, 2007). The toll of unsupervised Internet use in the form of child exploitation is yet to be revealed.

Case Example: Linda

Linda, age 15, had never told anyone about her father's repeated visits to her room, where he sexually abused her over a 4-year period. Linda did not tell her mother because she thought her mother already knew and approved of what was happening. Linda looked forward to leaving home and marrying her boyfriend, age 19. One night her boyfriend raped her; afterward she went into the bathroom and took 20 of her mother's sleeping pills. If her mother had not heard her crying and taken her to the hospital for emergency treatment, Linda would have died.

When dealing with individual cases of child abuse or neglect, especially if the parents were abused themselves or problems with alcohol are involved, it is easy to lose sight of the evidence that child abuse is rooted in the fabric of many societies:

1. There is long-standing evidence that the use of violence (such as harsh discipline) not only hinders parent–child trust, but also trains a person for violence (Gil, 1970; Straus, Gelles, & Steinmetz, 1980). Thus, while parents using violent forms of discipline may interpret their behavior as an act of love and concern for the child, the child is likely to absorb early on the value that violence is a socially approved form of problem solving. The embeddedness of the spare-the-rod philosophy was dramatized in the 1999 acquittal of a Boston father whose strapping of his child was defended on religious grounds. More disturbing than the incident itself is the expressed view of large numbers of Americans who support such a court decision.

2. Economic hardship and stress can often be traced to unequal social opportunities in the United States. The first (and thus far only) national survey on domestic violence (Straus et al., 1980) suggests a clear association between economic disadvantage and child abuse; the difficulty of providing basic necessities as well as special medical and social services for handicapped or sick children is a source of extraordinary parental stress that continues unabated. Such stress is exacerbated by the plight of homelessness and its unique burden on children (see Chapter 8).

3. Child care, though necessary for the continuation of society, is socially devalued, as revealed in several practices in the United States: (a) the failure to provide adequate child care for wage-earning parents, (b) the low pay scales for those who do provide child care, (c) the continuing acceptance of child rearing as predominantly the responsibility of mothers, (d) a backlash by childless couples protesting the meager employee tax benefits afforded parents (as compared with Western Europe, for example).

In her classic work, Miller (1986) suggests that if men and women wish to have children, they should also figure out how to take care of them so that the children have the benefit of paternal as well as maternal upbringing (see "Birth and Parenthood" in Chapter 6). However, people who choose to be childless should recognize and support in alternative ways the "work" of child rearing as a necessity that not only guarantees a society's continuity but also benefits *all* its members—including the childless.

Child Witnesses to Violence and Murder

Nationally, over three million children are at risk of witnessing violence between their caretakers or murder in the community (Adams, 2006; Bogat et al., 2005; Clements et al., 2003; Harpaz-Roten et al., 2007). These data underscore the importance of collaboration among police, the family, and mental health professionals in protecting children from such trauma. The Federal Bureau of Investigation (FBI) estimates that men in prison for abuse or even murder of their partners have an average of two or three children each. The adverse effects on children of witnessing violence or just living in a violent home are now viewed as a form of child abuse resulting in many of the same symptoms as if the children were directly abused themselves. However, many children and adolescents are amazingly resilient in the face of maltreatment and abuse (Collishawa et al., 2007), while some become activists in violence prevention. A child's trauma from witnessing a parent's murder is almost beyond comprehension—not to mention retraumatization in custody cases in which the imprisoned murderer wants to see his children (see Stephens, 1999). Legislation in Massachusetts denies visitation rights in such cases.

Some of the symptoms of child witnesses include withdrawal from friends and activities, sleep disturbances, physical aches and pains, hypervigilance, worrying about the safety of loved ones, hyperactivity, and trouble concentrating, which may be revealed in a loss of skills learned earlier. Support and early intervention with these "silent" victims (Groves, Zuckerman, Marans, & Cohen, 1993) is central to preventing more serious problems later. A Massachusetts Department of Youth Services study of child witnesses revealed dramatic increases in their risk of suicide and abuse of alcohol and other drugs as well as committing sexual assault and other crimes (Henning, Leitenberg, Coffey, et al., 1996; Taylor, Zuckerman, Harik, & Groves, 1994).

Moving from a domestic to an international arena, consider this account of trauma among Kosovo's "children of war":

> You can't see the damage in Jeton's eyes or the shy smile he gives a stranger. . . . He doesn't sleep, he is easily frightened. . . . It [a mortar shell] exploded in the garden. His grandmother, trying to find cover, was hit. The blast knocked out electricity. The family cowered in deep darkness inside their home. They heard Arifa Hasani, 57, a matriarch of five children and 10 grandchildren, gasping in the hallway. Jeton's uncle lit a lighter. In the flickering glow, Jeton saw his bloodied grandmother, dying (Sennott, 1999, pp. A1, A31).

Children in other conflicts (Rwanda, Darfur, Kenya) are similarly traumatized. To those who seem to know only violence as a solution to human conflict, one could ask: Are ethnic hatred and the desire for power and control really worth the sacrifice of a nation's future—its children?

Refuges for battered women have traditionally included special support for the child witnesses of violent relationships, whether domestic or political.

For children who remain in a home where violence persists and the battered parent is either unable or unready to leave, however, every effort should be made to provide special services. Primary care and emergency service personnel are in strategic positions to advocate for such services. Boston Medical Center (BMC), for example, has a publicly supported program, the Child Witness to Violence Project, which abused women should be informed about when receiving medical treatment of injuries at BMC or through public education and outreach efforts.

Big Brothers–Big Sisters programs can be part of alternative support programs. Because many of the child's symptoms may appear in school performance or behavior problems, teachers and school nurses should network with special services for child witnesses. Such collaborative community-based efforts are greatly preferred to removing a child from the home in cases of continued parental violence. Although the intention is to protect the child by such removal, to do so can leave the child with the same kind of guilt that incest survivors usually experience when they, rather than the perpetrators, are removed—that is, they may blame themselves for the disruption (Saunders, 1999).

Preventive Intervention

Preventive strategies are always important in crisis intervention, but they are particularly urgent concerning the tragedy of child abuse. A focus on the social origins of this problem is critical. Preventive intervention includes the following:

1. Critically examining child-rearing practices and incorporating nonviolent approaches to discipline into high school curriculum courses for boys and girls (Brendtro, Brokenleg, & Van Bockern, 1990; Eggert, 1994).
2. Instituting social and political action to relieve the economic hardship and poverty of many families.
3. Instituting social and political action to address substandard child care programs and develop family policies appropriate to the resources and ideals of a nation.
4. Using consciousness raising and education to stress the advantages to individuals and to society of having children reared in an egalitarian fashion by mothers and fathers, as well as by extended family, foster grandparents, and others.
5. Examining government child protection agencies systematically to ensure that children's problems are adequately attended to before abuse occurs.
6. Instituting public education programs on child abuse and providing in-service training programs for school nurses, teachers, and others working with children.
7. Developing hotlines and drop-in centers for children and adolescents as additional supports and outlets for troubled youth.

8. Instructing children that they own the private parts of their bodies and reassuring them that they have no obligation to satisfy the sexual desires of parents, relatives, or others. This includes lifting the veil of denial about the sources of greatest danger: immediate family, other relatives, or friends, with biological fathers being the single largest group of sexual abusers. The Children's Trust Fund in Boston, for example, educates parents, children, and staff through Talking About Touching, a child personal safety program.

9. Renewing commitment to improving the mental health of children as an aid to resisting seduction (Conte, Wolf, & Smith, 1987)—for example, by working with police officers to teach children how to detect and resist would-be abductors.

10. Examining the societal values and economic arrangements that support the idea so many teenage mothers have absorbed—that their most important contribution to society and means of feeling valuable is to produce a baby, irrespective of their emotional, social, and economic ability to care for a child. (A related value is the near disregard of responsibility by teenage, unmarried fathers; see Eyre & Eyre, 1993.)

11. Considering the incalculable pain of children and the thoughtless sacrifice that war demands of these innocents. (Child protection needs to be undertaken on a global scale by adults who wage war on ethnic and other grounds.)

All these preventive strategies demand that we take the time to discover why so many of our children are being abused and neglected. A shift "from care to prevention" was highlighted in the U.S. Surgeon General's Workshop on Violence and Public Health Report (1986). The fact that Newberger's testimony (1980) before the U.S. House of Representatives is as relevant today as it was decades ago speaks to work still to be done; Newberger emphasized the need to address exploitative sex, isolation, poverty, and a cultural climate that supports violence if we are serious about preventing child abuse and neglect.

Legal and Crisis Intervention

Everyone should be aware of the signs of possible child abuse, such as:

- Repeated injury to a child with unconcern on the part of the parent(s) or with unlikely explanations
- Aggressive behavior that implies a child's cry for help
- Neglected appearance
- Overly critical parental attitude
- Withdrawal, depression, and self-injury (especially with incest)

The serious effects of child abuse include physical handicaps, emotional crippling (an abused child may never be able to love others), homelessness, psychiatric illness, antisocial or violent behavior later in life, self-destructiveness, and death (Everett & Gallop, 2000; Helfer & Kempe, 1991).

Suspicions of child abuse must be reported to child protection authorities, although we should be cautious about making unsubstantiated accusations. A related concern, primarily in longer-term therapy situations, is the controversial "false-memory syndrome" and "therapist-induced memories." Despite this controversy, it is important to *believe* children's stories about abuse. All parents make mistakes; it is the crisis of child abuse and the pattern of abuse that must be reported. In cases of incest, the crisis for the child as well as for the entire family occurs when "the secret" is revealed (Herman, 1981). (See Chapter 6 regarding allegations of abuse in child custody battles.)

We can assume that most parents have the welfare of their children at heart. When parents do not appear to be concerned for the welfare of their children, they must be confronted with the reality that children as well as parents have rights. When abuse is suspected, everyone who knows the child must realize that a parent's rights are not absolute. "Minding one's own business" is inappropriate when child abuse is involved, although many people use that as an excuse for not reporting what they suspect.

Teachers are in a strategic position to help an abused child; the school is often the only recourse open to the child (Hillman & Solek-Tefft, 1988). Although teachers are not trained to deal with disturbed parents, they are responsible for reporting suspected child abuse to child protective authorities. Parents who are abusive or who are afraid of losing control should be encouraged to seek help on their own by contacting Parents Anonymous, a self-help organization in the United States and England. Hotlines for parents, children, and others concerned about child abuse can be contacted through any crisis or mental health agency or by simply dialing the operator. In mental health and social service settings, early signs of child abuse can often be uncovered through family-focused assessment, as discussed in Chapters 3 and 5. The Child Screening Checklist (Chapter 3, Exhibit 3.4) can guide such assessment.

Child abuse is a crisis for the parent as well as for the child; the abused child is often one whose behavior or special needs cause extreme stress, even for the most forbearing parent. Parents in crisis are, unfortunately, sometimes overlooked by health personnel attending a battered child. The tragic situation of treating a helpless, beaten child makes it very difficult for nurses and physicians to recognize the equally great need of the battered child's parents. Whether parents bring the abused child to the clinic or hospital themselves or whether they are reported by nurses, teachers, or neighbors, parents are usually guilt ridden and shaken by the experience. In most cases, they are fearful for the child's life, remorseful about their uncontrolled rage, fearful of treatment at the hands of the law (including loss of custody), and fearful of future outbursts of uncontrollable anger.

If nurses, physicians, and social workers can overcome their own aversion and feelings of rejection, the crisis can become a turning point in parents' lives. Understanding the emotional needs of abusive or neglectful parents is important for doing crisis intervention with them; abusers often have the following characteristics:

- Inability to understand and communicate with children
- Emotional immaturity
- Generally disturbed lives
- Unhappy marriage
- Stress related to economic, unemployment, and housing problems
- Feelings of inadequacy in their role as parents
- Frequent life crises as well as drug and alcohol problems
- Deprived or abused childhood
- Unrealistic and rigid expectations of their children
- Minimal or inadequate parenting skills

Crisis intervention in instances of child abuse includes:

1. Encouraging the parent to express feelings appropriate to the event.
2. Actively engaging the parent in planning medical care for the child—a corrective emotional experience that moves the parent in the direction of doing something constructive for the child, as would be appropriate in Richard's case.
3. Enlisting the parents' cooperation with child protection authorities, who have been appropriately informed by a health professional. This includes correcting the parents' probable perception of the government authorities as punitive. In reality, the people representing such authorities are generally concerned and will help parents carry out their parental responsibilities. This point is important for preventing further tragedies, such as murder of the children by a father accused of incest, as is possible in the case of Linda.
4. Avoiding the removal of an incest victim instead of the assailant from the home. Removing the victim perpetuates the notion that she or he is responsible for the abuse and for the breakup of the family, and also alienates the child from the mother (Evans et al., 2003; Herman, 1981).
5. Referring the parents to self-help groups such as Parents Anonymous or Parents in Crisis, where they can share their feelings and get help from other parents in similar situations, as would be helpful for the parents of both Richard and Linda (see Chapter 5).
6. Instituting job training and day-care services in cases of economic strain and when a mother is overwhelmed with the care of several children at home by herself, as is the case with Richard's mother.
7. Providing concrete suggestions of nonviolent alternatives to physical discipline, such as "time out" or thinking time for the child, and non-violent stress management techniques for parents. There are excellent books on this topic written specifically for parents (for example, Canter & Canter, 1988; Hillman & Solek-Tefft, 1988; McEvoy & Erickson, 1994).

Follow-Up Service

Follow-up for children abused by their parents or others should include referral of parents to a counseling agency where they can receive more extensive help concerning the underlying emotional and social problems that led to the crisis. Child protection services can facilitate parent counseling if they do not offer it themselves. Role modeling, home supervision, and parent effectiveness training are other services that should be available to these parents. Some child survivors of abuse, physical and sexual, may need extensive psychotherapeutic treatment for healing the devastating pain of such exploitation (see Everett & Gallop, 2000).

These suggestions for prevention and referral for longer-term treatment by specialists should be incorporated into the protocols of all primary-care providers and frontline crisis workers, including complete documentation of medical examinations for possible legal action (Hoff & Morgan, in press). It is never too late to consider ways to eliminate pain and the unnecessary death of our children and to reduce this tragic waste of a nation's most precious resource.

Rape and Sexual Assault

Rape is a violent crime, not a sexual act. Because of people's attitudes toward the crime of rape, the crisis of rape victims has not received appropriate attention until recently. Feminists and others who have become sensitized to the horrors of this crime against women are slowly bringing about necessary changes in a legal system that often cause double victimization of the person who has been attacked. Although most rape victims are female, male victims of rape are sometimes even more reluctant than women to report the rape and seek help.

Among gay, bisexual, and transgendered men, partner abuse is one of the most serious health issues. The incidence of abuse among gay men mirrors the rate for straight women—between 25 and 33%. Gay, lesbian, bisexual, and transgendered (GLBT) people may be isolated from family because of their sexual orientation or gender identity, and thus lack this supportive resource if in crisis. Also, there are fewer domestic violence services, and in some places no services, for GLBT people. GLBT people may be reluctant to use mainstream services because of fears of staff homophobia or of being outed. Or, because of myths and misconceptions, staff of mainstream agencies may respond inappropriately; for example, the police may see violence as mutual combat and arrest both partners. Also, the GLBT community's struggle to acknowledge partner abuse makes it harder for them to turn to their own community for support (Gay Men's Domestic Violence Project, http://www. gmdvp.org; see also Chapter 6, sexual identity crisis).

In a widely publicized rape conviction, the defense attorney outraged the public by declaring on national television that the conviction would never have occurred if he had been allowed to enter into testimony the history of the victim's sex life. Similarly, there was public outcry against a judge who let an admitted rapist off with a light sentence for raping a 5-year-old girl because of the girl's "precocious sexual behavior."

If a woman is sexually abused or raped by her physician, the chances of successful prosecution are further reduced because (1) the social and political influence of the medical profession is enormous, (2) the average woman thus abused has been seduced into believing the action is part of medical practice, (3) the woman is often afraid to report the incident and cannot imagine that this could happen to anyone but herself, and (4) the woman may have absorbed the message that she invited the rape or did something wrong. This point applies to any professional who violates a position of trust and power (Burgess & Hartman, 1989).

Only recently in North America has rape in marriage been recognized legally as an offense. The cultural notion of woman as the property and appropriate object of man's violence and pleasure still lingers (Russell, 1982). Fortunately, research findings and public education have changed the attitudes of most physicians, nurses, and police. This is significant when considering the threat to life accompanying many rapes and the great number of acquaintance rapes (mostly female). In date rape, it is often assumed that if a woman says no she does not mean it, and that in some way she invited the attack (Levy, 1991). This issue is complicated when women have drunk too much and are victimized by a gang of rapists. The woman's intoxication is used as an excuse to exploit her; college women are particularly vulnerable to such attacks. These are reported least often because of the continued tendency to excuse rapists on grounds of their *victims'* behavior. Sometimes even the female friends of raped women make public, victim-blaming statements—for example, "If she hadn't stayed out so late, it probably wouldn't have happened" (students in a college class on sexual assault). One interpretation of such behavior is that it is a potential victim's means of gaining some control and reducing her own vulnerability: "If I don't stay out too late or drink too much, I won't get raped." In Warshaw's (1988) study of college students, 50% of the men had forced sex on women but did not define it as rape, and only 33% said that under no circumstances could they rape a woman.

We should not, however, be surprised at these responses in a culture in which women are often considered fair game. Recently, psychiatric and general health personnel have responded to the research regarding attitudes of health professionals toward rape victims. These workers are developing rape crisis intervention programs in hospital settings based on principles of equality and a rejection of popular myths about rape.

The fallacy of blaming a woman for her attack because she was "dressed too provocatively" or "out on the street alone" becomes clear in the analogy of a well-dressed man who is robbed of his wallet: No one would say he was robbed because of what he wore. Regarding women who are raped while out at night, we might consider Golda Meir's response to the curfew proposal for Israeli women at risk of attack: Let the men who are raping be curfewed instead. Unfortunately, and cross-culturally, victim-blaming is still alive as cited in regular news stories in which clergy, political leaders, and others either look the other way, or state publicly that victims—rather than rapists—are responsible for the centuries-old sexual crimes committed against women and even children.

Another popular myth about rape is that the victim "enjoys rape" and that the average woman entertains fantasies of being raped. This myth was evident at the dawn of a new millennium by a mental health professional at a conference when he proclaimed, there are two kinds of rape—real rape and those who want it. This notion is reinforced by popular movies such as *Last Tango in Paris*, by hard-core and soft-core pornography, and by advertising images in which women are depicted as appropriate objects of male violence. These myths about rape stem from the persistent interpretation of rape as a sexual event (Thornhill & Palmer, 2000) rather than an act of violence. Societal attitudes, then, play a major part in the outcome of a rape crisis experience. When rape victims are blamed rather than assisted through this crisis, it is not surprising that they blame themselves and fail to express feelings appropriate to the event, such as anger. Such attitudes also impede the process of long-term recovery (Braswell, 1989).

There is still much to be done to change public attitudes, reform institutional responses to sexual-assault victims, and dismantle the widespread belief that women and girls who are raped are "asking for it." It is instructive to note that many victims fail to report sexual assault because of fear, their perception that police are ineffective, and the threat of further victimization by authorities (Buzawa & Buzawa, 1996). Also, some victims do not seek monetary compensation available through U.S. court-based victim assistance programs because payment was either inadequate or denied altogether.

Rape as the Spoils of War

Rape as a common crime of war is finally being recognized and prosecuted in the United Nations war crimes tribunal in The Hague. From a human rights perspective, rape as the spoils of war is a gender-based crime, as documented by the United Nations war crimes tribunal and by Brownmiller (1975) in her historical account.

The crime of rape has continued over centuries, is still a very visible phenomenon during wars worldwide, but only now is being addressed in the United Nations court in The Hague. During the 1990s Bosnian war, at least 20,000 women on all sides were raped. Figures from the conflicts in Rwanda and Darfur are still to be recorded. Over the ages, the alleged rationale was to satisfy the sexual needs of men on the battlefield, or simply act on the culturally embedded license of men to use and abuse women with few or no legal consequences for their behavior. A woman who testified in the United Nations court said that she and scores of other women were raped in classrooms and apartments, while her detained children became ill from unsanitary conditions. This woman's testimony about damage to her health included sexually transmitted disease, insomnia, severe anxiety, and reproductive dysfunction (Socolovsky, 2000). Women survivors of the Rwandan genocide who are raising children begotten when they were raped as teenagers speak of their struggle to reconcile their traumatic memories with a mother's natural love of a child conceived by the rape.

A refugee woman from Cameroon and then Liberia, Canada, and the United States describes a triple trauma—she watched her son die at the hands of soldiers, as her hands and feet were tied. She was then beaten to persuade her to talk about her husband, and finally placed in a corner and repeatedly raped (Hartigan, 1999). This woman suffered the additional trauma of social stigma for having been raped, because such women in her culture—as in others—are viewed as unmarriageable. As is true of many survivors of violence, this woman found meaning and healing in telling her story—another small step toward ending the worldwide plague of war in general and violence against women in particular.

Preventing Rape and Sexual Assault

Long-range strategies to prevent rape include dismantling the myths and centuries-old norms that promote the double victimization of women. Such a campaign should cover education, health, social service, and criminal justice systems worldwide, as well as the public at large.

At the individual level, a woman whose life is threatened can do little or nothing to prevent sexual assault. In some cases, however, women can lessen their chances of attack by training themselves to be street-smart—alert at all times to their surroundings when outside. Potential victims should remember that even though crime may appear to be random, the would-be criminal has a plan. That plan includes attacking a person who appears to present the greatest chance of success for the crime with the least amount of trouble. Women and children on the street who are alert and make this evident therefore have, to some extent, equalized the criminal–victim relationship. Signals of an escape plan may be as simple as looking around frequently or carrying a pencil flashlight—cues that alert a would-be attacker that you are not an easy target. The attacker does not know what else you may possess— perhaps mace or karate expertise—and generally will not take unnecessary chances with people who appear prepared to resist. Alertness at home is also important. For example, a 56-year-old woman was raped in her home by a man posing as a delivery man, in spite of a highly organized neighborhood patrol on her street.

Self-defense training is also useful as an immediate protection strategy. It provides physical resistance ability as well as the psychological protection of greater self-confidence and less vulnerability. However, women should not rely on self-defense excessively because (1) it may lead to a false sense of security and neglect of planning and alertness, and (2) some attackers are so fast and overpower the victim so completely that there may be no opportunity to put self-defense strategies to work.

Preventing the sexual assault of children includes not leaving children unattended, instructing them about not accepting favors—including car rides—from strangers, and keeping communication open, so that a child will feel free to confide in parents about a threat or attack. Just as important is public education about the dangers from those closest to us, a grim reality that is difficult for many to acknowledge.

Crisis Intervention

There is no question that people who have been raped are in crisis. They feel physically violated, are in shock, and are afraid to be alone. They may fear for their lives or that the rapist will return. Sometimes they feel shame and blame themselves for being attacked. They may or may not feel angry, depending on how much they feel responsible for their victimization. These feelings lead to a temporary halting of their usual problem-solving ability or delay in reporting the crime. Rape is sometimes accompanied by robbery and abandonment at the location where the victim was taken by the rapist. Such a series of events further reduces the victim's normal problem-solving ability. Holmstrom and Burgess (1978) have described the crisis and treatment of rape victims; Brownmiller (1975) deals with the historical and anthropological aspects of rape. Emergency and police personnel are referred to these works for more information about rape—that it is a serious crime, that the *victims* of this crime should not also be the defendants, and that medical center protocols should reflect these concepts.

If a sexual assault has occurred, friends, family, strangers, the police, and agency staff are sometimes able to offer immediate crisis assistance to the victim. The rape victim may hesitate to ask family and friends for help, especially in cases of date or acquaintance rape. One woman raped orally when she was a teenage virgin waited 25 years to share her story with anyone because when it occurred, the legal definition of rape was limited to vaginal penetration. While she suffered all the well-known signs of rape trauma, she did not know she was "raped." Rape crisis counselors cite similar stories after widespread publicity about certain rapes.

Helpers should actively reach out in the form of crisis intervention in every instance of sexual assault, regardless of type, the victim's gender, or the victim's sexual identity. The chance of being asked for such help and our success in offering it during crisis depend on our basic attitudes toward rape and our knowledge of what to do. Family members or friends who are unsure of how to help should seek assistance and support from a rape crisis center. The following is quoted from the public information card of the Manchester, New Hampshire, Women's Crisis Line. It contains essential information that anyone (including victims themselves) can use if someone has been raped. Similar information cards are available at hospital rape crisis intervention programs and in police departments.

What to Do If You Have Been Raped

Emotional considerations: A rape is usually traumatic. Call a friend and/or Manchester Women Against Rape (MWAR) for support. A trained MWAR volunteer can provide information, support, and referral, and is willing to accompany you to the hospital, police, and court.

Medical considerations: Get immediate medical attention. Take a change of clothing along to the emergency service of a hospital or to a private physician (the police will provide transportation if you need it). The exam should focus on two concerns: medical care and the gathering of evidence for possible prosecution. You will have a pelvic examination and be checked for injuries, pregnancy, and venereal disease. Be prepared to give enough details of the attack for the exam to be thorough. Follow-up tests for venereal disease and pregnancy about 6 weeks later are also important.

Legal considerations: Do not bathe, douche, or change clothes until after the exam; that would destroy evidence you will need if you should later choose to prosecute. Try to recall as many details as possible. Call the police to report the crime. Be prepared to answer questions intended to help your case, such as: Where were you raped? What happened? Can you identify the rapist?

If the victim-survivor does come to an emergency medical facility, emergency personnel should listen to the victim and offer emotional support while carrying out necessary medical and legal procedures. Victims should be advised that there are standard protocols for these procedures that are legally required if charges are to be filed. They should be linked with crisis counseling services. Some hospital emergency departments are staffed with such counselors, and many cities have rape crisis services with crisis hotlines or women's centers. Special services are also becoming more common for rape survivors among GLBT groups. Where specialized services do not exist, rape victims should be offered the emergency services of local mental health agencies, which exist in nearly every community.

Crisis counseling by telephone for the rape victim is illustrated in Table 11.2, an interview example.

Follow-Up Service

Women and men who have been raped usually describe it as the most traumatic experience of their life. It should not be assumed, however, that the experience will damage the person for life. Whether permanent damage occurs depends on two factors: (1) the resources available for working through the crisis and not blaming oneself for the crime, and (2) the person's precrisis coping ability. A victim who has a supportive social network and a healthy self-concept will probably work through the crisis successfully, find meaning in the suffering, and go on to assist others, as have many worldwide. For victim-survivors in such circumstances, crisis counseling

TABLE 11.2 Telephone Crisis Counseling for a Rape Victim

Characteristics of Crisis and Intervention Techniques	Case Example: Telephone Interview between Victim and Crisis Counselor	
Establishing personal human contact	*Counselor:*	Crisis Center, may I help you?
	Elaine:	I just have to talk to somebody.
	Counselor:	Yes, my name is Sandra. I'd like to hear what's troubling you. Will you tell me your name?
Upset, vulnerable, trouble with problem solving	*Elaine:*	I'm Elaine. I'm just so upset I don't know what to do.
Identifying hazardous event	*Counselor:*	Can you tell me what happened?
	Elaine:	Well, I was coming home alone last night from a party. It was late (chokes up, starts to cry).
	Counselor:	Whatever it is that happened has really upset you.
	Elaine:	(continues to cry)
Expressing empathy, encouraging expression of feeling	*Counselor:*	(waits, listens, Elaine's crying subsides) It must be really hard for you to talk about.
Self-blaming	*Elaine:*	I guess it was really crazy for me to go to that party alone. I should never have done it ... on my way into my apartment, this man grabbed me (starts to cry again).
Identifying hazardous event	*Counselor:*	I gather he must have attacked you.
Self-blame and distorted perception of reality	*Elaine:*	Yes! He raped me! I could kill him! But at the same time, I keep thinking it must be my own fault.
Encouraging appropriate expression of anger instead of self-blame	*Counselor:*	Elaine, I can see that you're really angry at the guy, and you should be. Any woman would feel the same, but Elaine, you're blaming yourself for this terrible thing instead of him.
Self-doubt, unable to use usual social support	*Elaine:*	Well, deep down I really know it's not my fault, but I think my parents and boyfriend might think so.
Obtaining factual information, exploring resources	*Counselor:*	In other words, you haven't told them about this yet, is that right? Is there anyone you've been able to talk to?
Feels isolated from social supports	*Elaine:*	No, not anyone. I'm too ashamed (starts crying again).
Expressing empathy	*Counselor:*	(listens, waits a few seconds) I can tell that you're really upset.
Failure in problem solving	*Elaine:*	(continues crying) I just don't know what to do. I feel like maybe I'll never feel like myself again.
Expressing empathy, assessing suicide risk	*Counselor:*	This is a serious thing that's happened to you, Elaine. I really want to help you. Considering how upset you are and not being able to talk with your family and your boyfriend, is there a possibility that you've thought of hurting yourself?

(continued)

TABLE 11.2   Telephone Crisis Counseling for a Rape Victim (continued)

Characteristics of Crisis and Intervention Techniques	Case Example: Telephone Interview between Victim and Crisis Counselor
Suicidal ideas only, is reaching out for help	*Elaine:* Well, the thought has crossed my mind, but no, I really don't think I'd do that. That's why I called here. I just feel so dirty and unwanted—and alone—I know I'm not really a bad person, but you just can't believe how awful I feel (starts crying again).
Expressing empathy, involving Elaine in the planning	*Counselor:* Elaine, I can understand why you must feel that way. Rape is one of the most terrible things that can happen to a woman (waits a few seconds). Elaine, I'd really like to help you through this thing. Can we talk about some things that you might do to feel better?
Feels distant from social resources	*Elaine:* Well, yes, I know I should see a doctor, and I'd really like to talk to my boyfriend and my parents, but I just can't bring myself to do it right now.
Supporting Elaine's decision, direct involvement of counselor, exploring resources	*Counselor:* I'd recommend, Elaine, that you see a doctor as soon as possible. Do you have a private doctor?
Decision	*Elaine:* Yes, I'll call and see if I can get in.
	Counselor: And if you can't get in right away, how about going to a hospital emergency service as soon as possible?
	Elaine: OK, I'll do that.
Obtaining factual information	*Counselor:* Elaine, I gather you didn't report this to the police. Is that right?
Helplessness, feeling isolated	*Elaine:* I didn't think it would do any good, and besides, just like with my boyfriend, I was too ashamed.
Obtaining factual information	*Counselor:* Were your clothes torn, and do you have any bruises from the rape?
	Elaine: No, not that I'm aware of. I just feel sore all over, so maybe I do have some bruises I can't see. I probably shouldn't have taken a bath before going to the doctor, but I felt so dirty, I just couldn't stand it.
Reinforcing decision, suggestion to reconsider reporting	*Counselor:* It's really important, Elaine, that you see your doctor soon. You may also want to reconsider reporting the rape to the police.
	Elaine: I guess maybe you're right.
Exploring continued crisis counseling possibility	*Counselor:* Elaine, considering how bad you feel about this and that you don't feel up to talking with your parents and your boyfriend yet, would you like to come in to see a counselor and talk some more about the whole thing?
Needs help in reestablishing contact with significant people in her life	*Elaine:* Not really … anyway, I really feel better now that I've talked with you. But I still can't really face my parents and boyfriend.

Characteristics of Crisis and Intervention Techniques	Case Example: Telephone Interview between Victim and Crisis Counselor	
Encouraging further expression of feeling with significant others, paving way for this through crisis counseling	*Counselor:*	This is a lot to handle all at one time. I'm sure you're going to continue feeling upset, especially until you're able to talk with your boyfriend and parents about it. That's one of the things a counselor can help you with. A counselor can also help you take a second look at the pros and cons of reporting or not reporting the rape to the police.
Mutually agreed-on plan	*Elaine:*	I guess maybe it's a good idea. I do feel better now, but I've been crying off and on since last night, and maybe I'll start crying all over again after I hang up. Besides, I called in sick today because I couldn't face going to work. So I guess I'll stay home tomorrow too and come in and talk to somebody. What time?
Establishing concrete plan mutually arrived at by Elaine and counselor	*Counselor:*	How about 10 o'clock?
	Elaine:	That's OK, I guess.
	Counselor:	How are you feeling right now, Elaine?
	Elaine:	Like I said before, quite a bit better.
Reinforcing of plan	*Counselor:*	Elaine, I'm really glad you called and that you're going to see a doctor and come here to see someone too. Meanwhile, if you get upset and feel you want to talk to someone again, please call, as there's always someone here, OK?
	Elaine:	OK, I will. Thanks so much for listening.

will usually suffice, and long-term therapy is not indicated. Without support and healthy precrisis coping, though, psychological scarring can occur—for example, becoming paranoid about all men or having difficulty with sexual intimacy. This danger is increased by a rape trial in which the defense lawyer succeeds in making the victim rather than the rapist appear to be the criminal or by one's partner and others joining the defense in blaming the victim for the attack (Estrich, 1987). In these cases, survivors of rape will probably need longer-term therapy.

In an era of fiscal constraint and short-staffed social services, vigilance and advocacy are indicated to ensure the continuation of special services to rape victims. As the AIDS crisis continues, additional services are needed to assist the victim through not only the trauma of rape but also the possible additional crisis of infection by HIV (see Chapter 7). Peer support groups of others who have been abused are also helpful. The difficulty of undoing the damage of sexual assault highlights the importance of preventing rape in the first place.

Finally, in regard to child victims, it is important not to project our own shock and horror about the crime onto the child. The child should be treated and supported in proportion to her or his own trauma and perception of the event, physical and psychological, not in proportion to our adult view of the attack. Protection, sympathy, and anger are in order, but should not be expressed in a way that might cripple a child's future development and normal interaction with others.

Woman Abuse and Battering

Abused women say they do not expect us to rescue them. Rather, they want health and crisis workers to be there for them and offer support as they seek safety, healing, and a life without violence. They want us to listen to their terror and dilemmas, as the following vignettes depict.

Vignettes from the Lives of Battered Women

One time when he beat me I started to fight back. . . . He threw kerosene around me and threatened to put a match to it. . . . I never fought back again . . . just kept trying to figure out what I was doing wrong that he would beat me that way. There were some good times together, like when we talked about going to college, and somehow I just kept hoping and believing he would change.

Before I came to this shelter, I had no idea so many other women were going through the same thing I was. . . . I used to think the only way out of my situation would be a tragic one—to kill either myself or him. I'd go to my friend's or mother's house, but I just couldn't make ends meet. I didn't have a babysitter, money, or the physical and mental strength. . . . I was depressed about everything. My mother stuck it out for 40 years. I didn't believe in divorce; I believed in marriage. Basically, it was my religion and need for financial support [that kept me from leaving earlier]. (Hoff, 1990, pp. 31, 69)

Traditionally, it was often assumed that a woman was beaten because the man was drinking, unemployed, or otherwise under stress, or that the woman provoked his behavior by saying the wrong thing or failing to meet his whimsical demands. If, for example, a man beat his wife while she was pregnant, it was because "women are so emotional during pregnancy." It was also claimed that women did not leave violent relationships because they were not sufficiently motivated and ignored the resources they had. Such conclusions were drawn in spite of the fact that when the same women sought help from the police, family, friends, or health or social service professionals, they received little assistance or were blamed by their confidants. A "resource" is hardly a resource if it provides a negative response to a woman in crisis.

Teen mothers and Native American victims of domestic violence face double jeopardy because of their developmental stage, social isolation, and/or cultural factors hindering their access to needed support (Antle et al., 2007; Saylors & Daliparthy, 2006; Sussex & Corcoran, 2005; Zolotor et al., 2007). Rates of interpersonal violence among immigrant women in the United States and Canada are influenced by poverty and the presence or absence of family ties in their host country; and in the absence of such ties, some may engage in risky behaviors such as alcohol consumption, thus increasing the risk of intimate partner violence (Hyman et al., 2006; Raj & Silverman, 2003).

Now, works such as Dobash and Dobash (1998), Hoff (1990), Schechter (1982), and Stark and Flitcraft (1996) reveal that legal, health care, and religious institutions have supported and given tacit approval to woman battering through actions such as:

1. *Defining assault on one's wife as a misdemeanor, whereas the same assault on a stranger is a felony* and then failing to hold violent men accountable even at this level. This situation is changing with better police training. Several class action suits brought against large police jurisdictions for failure to arrest and act on abuse prevention laws have also helped to effect change.

2. *Diagnosing a battered woman as mentally ill and psychiatrically excusing a violent man.* This practice was uncovered in 1979 by Stark et al. (1979) in a study of 481 battered women using the emergency service of a metropolitan hospital. In this study, "medicine's collective response" to abuse was found to contribute to a "pathological battering syndrome," actually a socially constructed product in the guise of treatment (pp. 462–463). Problems such as alcoholism and depression were treated medically, masking the political aspects of violence. The abused woman was psychiatrically labeled, suggesting that she was personally responsible for her problems, and violent families were treated to maintain family stability. The researchers state that medical and psychiatric agencies historically have played a major role in the violence related to the political and economic constraints of a patriarchal authority structure (see also Hilberman, 1980; Warshaw, 1989).

3. *Underestimating how staying in a violent relationship for "the sake of the children"* is a losing plan not only for the couple, but also for the damaging effects of the violence on the children (see Bograd, 1984).

4. *Failing to enforce laws that require equal pay and job opportunities,* making it very difficult for women to support themselves and their children alone.

5. *Failing to provide enough refuge facilities and emotional support for battered women in crisis,* claiming budget constraints and privacy issues between the woman and her husband.

6. *Failing to consider the powerful and complex obstacles a woman faces* when she tries to free herself from violence and blaming the victim instead.

Thanks to massive public and professional education campaigns, today most medical and mental health professionals have abandoned the traditional search to uncover what the woman is doing to "provoke" her husband, although the inclusion of effective protocols in primary care is by no means routine (Hoff & Morgan, in press). Yet domestic partner murders continue. At the beginning of each year, the *Boston Globe* publishes the names of persons (mostly female) killed in the past year by their partners, with little variation in trends over the years—disheartening to say the least, in view of decades of public education on the issue.

Although traditional responses to partner abuse are damaging enough to women, they are not complimentary to men either. Maintaining simplistic explanations of this complex problem implies that men are less than moral beings. It suggests that they are essentially infants, driven largely by impulse and not responsible for their actions. Hoff's (1990) study supports earlier research (Dobash & Dobash, 1979; Stark et al., 1979) and provides new insights into the *process* of violence between spouses. It suggests that violence occurs not merely as a stress response but as a complex interplay between conditions of biological reproduction and economic, political, legal, belief, and knowledge systems of particular historical communities. These interacting systems produce a *context* in which cultural values, the division of labor, and the allocation of power operate to sustain a climate of oppression and conflict. In such a climate, violence against women flourishes, suggesting a link worldwide between the *personal* trouble of individual battered women and the *public* issue of women's status (PAHO/WHO [Pan American Health Organization/World Health Organization], 2003; London School of Hygiene and Tropical Medicine, 2003).

Prevention

Sociocultural interpretations of why men are violent with their mates and why many women stay in abusive relationships aid our understanding of the problem (Adams, 2007). How, though, can this understanding help us deal constructively with the woman who repeatedly calls police and repeatedly receives emergency medical treatment but does not leave the relationship? This cyclic aspect of violence is one of the most complex issues facing police, nurses, physicians, and others trying to help abused women. There is probably nothing more frustrating for a concerned helper than the situation illustrated in the following example.

Case Example: Staying in an Abusive Relationship

A woman calls a hotline, afraid for her own life and worried that she might kill her husband if he returns. She says she wants to come to the shelter and wants to know how she can get there, as she has no money. She agrees to a plan to have police come and take her to a designated place to meet the shelter staff member. The woman never shows up. On follow-up, the shelter volunteer learns that when the police arrived, the woman had changed her mind.

Even people who are sympathetic to the plight of women and eager to help are ready to give up in the face of such apparent resistance to being helped. Such situations make it tempting to blame the victim and assume that if a woman did not like to be beaten, she would take advantage of available help. A helper can avoid falling into this trap by (1) remembering that the issue is much larger than the immediate crisis of a particular woman and (2) realizing that the woman has reasons for staying, whether or not the helper understands or agrees with those reasons. Some of these reasons might be (1) fear of the unknown and how she can manage without her husband's financial support, (2) continued hope and belief that the man will act on his frequent promises and stop beating her, and (3) fear of retaliation—even murder—after she leaves the shelter unless she leaves the area permanently. The experience of women in shelters reveals that some men employ elaborate detective strategies to find a woman who has left. Some who find a woman in a shelter threaten to harm all the shelter residents unless the woman returns. This is why many shelters maintain a secret location.

The complexity of the problem is illustrated further by an analysis of what happens after the first time a woman is beaten. She faces a difficult situation: The first violent incident usually is very shocking to her ("How could he do this to me?") and is followed by the man's elaborate promises never to do it again. The woman believes him and decides not to leave. This apparently rational decision is reinforced by positive, valued aspects of the relationship, which the woman wishes to salvage. When the man beats her a second time, he not only has broken his promise but also has distorted her trust and belief in his word into justification for beating her again ("If she didn't think it was all right for me to beat her, she'd leave"). The cycle is reinforced by the man's blaming his behavior on the woman—she doesn't cook right, dress right, or respect him—which she increasingly absorbs and believes and which eventually takes an enormous toll on her self-esteem. This complex interactional process underscores the importance of preventing violence in the first place (Hoff, 1990). Once this cycle begins, it is very difficult to interrupt. Our prevention efforts therefore should focus on the following:

1. *Reinforcing and educating police, health, and social service workers about abuse protection acts,* which in some countries define partner abuse as a crime punishable by law. Through the battered women's movement, these laws have been updated in the United States and Canadian provinces, while crime legislation in these and other countries describes battering as a gender-based civil rights violation (United Nations, Beijing Women's Conference, 1996a). Legal information about battering can be obtained from local shelters, the police, and government offices concerned with this issue.
2. *Examining educational, social, and religious programs for their implicit support of violence* through socialization of boys and men to aggressive behavior and girls and women to passive, dependent behavior (see classic work

by Broverman, Clarkson, Rosenkrantz, & Vogel, 1970). This process reinforces the view of wives as appropriate objects of violence.

3. *Instituting campaigns to end the marketing of pornography* and other products of popular culture that portray women as objects and glorify violence against them.

4. *Enforcing the Equal Pay Act*, passed in the United States in 1967, and *improving child care and economic and educational services for women*, so that financial and educational disadvantages do not prevent them from leaving violent relationships.

5. *Instituting communitywide consciousness-raising groups for men and women* and focusing on ways to promote egalitarian marriage or other partnerships and break out of dominant or excessively dependent behavior patterns.

These and other "upstream" preventive strategies should be carried out in tandem with immediate intervention for women in acute crisis (see Figure 11.1, Box 3). (For a detailed discussion of the obstacles faced by abused women and ways these can be removed, see Campbell, 1998.) However, it is important to recognize both the commonalities and differences in woman abuse as it occurs in various cultures (Hoff, in press). Prevention efforts and crisis intervention must therefore be framed in cultural context without dismissing the seriousness of such abuse with "Oh, that's just how they treat women there"—a blatant example of "cultural relativism;" that is, excusing certain behaviors although they constitute a violation of basic human rights (see Chapter 1, on diversity).

Cross-Cultural Example: East Africa

Jane, now age 50 and living in Canada, was the first wife of James and in her twenties when he periodically beat her. She has four children and had no publicly recognized marriage (her husband refused civil, church, and traditional marriage rituals). Jane was one of three children of her father's second wife, who basically abandoned the second wife's family on grounds that his newly adopted Christian religion disallowed polygyny. Jane, her mother, and her siblings were taken in by a women's religious order. Jane was provided with a good education, began studying nursing, but dropped out to marry James at age 19. Jane described the emotional stress and pain from physical and emotional abuse she suffered over several years, while always hoping that if her marriage were legalized the abuse would stop. After her father's death, she sought help from an uncle in her quest for public recognition of her marriage, but to no avail. Between beatings on the slightest pretext, James felt entitled to sexual access to Jane (and Jane felt she owed it) whenever he desired. When James finally left her to live full-time with his younger second wife, Jane worked in a government office as a secretary to support herself and her children. As school fees kept rising in response to the World Bank–directed restructuring of the country's debt, a Western European benefactor helped with the education of her four children. Her pain and struggles were exacerbated by poverty and limited social support from her extended family. Yet when a brother and his wife died of AIDS, despite his indifference to her, cultural tradition left Jane with the responsibility of raising his orphaned children. Following all her child-rearing responsibilities, a relative in Canada assisted her in obtaining a visa to move there with him. Today she is free of abuse and happily employed as a home health aide for an ailing older couple.

Jane's psychic trauma from abuse and the attendant socioeconomic struggles she endured are very similar to those of other abused women worldwide, including in wealthy countries like the United States. But there are some unique features of her situation and that of many immigrant women in the United States, Canada, and Western European countries.

1. There is a traditional belief that Jane owed sexual access even to a violent husband when he came to visit unannounced. (Some contemporary women in Canada and the United States may also be further victimized by this traditional norm of wifely duty.)
2. There is a tradition in Jane's ethnic group of turning to one's family of origin in the event of marital conflict or violence. This tradition among some African groups includes the demand by a woman's father that the violent husband return the family's "bride price" as an incentive to stop his violence.
3. In Jane's case, help from her father was unavailable in that he had abandoned Jane's mother and her four children based on his Christian religion's marriage rules. Her brother refused to stand in for her father, which left her with no one to defend her rights, even if her rights as a second wife had been recognized in a civil or traditional marriage, which James refused to act on despite Jane's pleas.
4. When this brother and his wife both died of AIDS, tradition also demanded that Jane (the only surviving relative) assume responsibility for rearing his children.
5. Seeking refuge in a shelter in a rural African community is not an option for a woman like Jane, even if such services existed, which they rarely do except in some large urban areas. Even in some Western European countries until recently, battered women sought refuge in convents, where abusive husbands were allowed to visit out of the tradition of the husband's entitlement to access to his wife, regardless of his behavior.

When working with abused women like Jane as well as in wealthy Western countries, we need to beware of recommending counseling that is not explicitly tied to advocacy for gender and economic equality, and respect for, even when disagreeing with, traditional values. In instances of public transgression of basic human rights, we should share information in a factual way. Without such an approach, counseling can result in pathologizing vs.

empowering an abused woman, especially considering victim-blaming such as occurs regarding rape. A profeminist approach emphasizing empowerment is essential in assisting a woman like Jane to avoid self-blame, depression, and/or suicide in response to her plight. An aside here is recognition that Western in-your-face-style feminism is often not well received in other cultures—not to mention some sub-cultures in the West. In contrast, the "human rights" perspective of the United Nations is usually more acceptable, as thousands of women from across the globe observed firsthand at the international UN Women's Conferences in Beijing (1995) and Nairobi (1985).

Crisis Intervention

Assistance during crisis should be available to women from family and friends. However, relatives and friends often view marital violence as a private issue and are reluctant to get involved. They may also be afraid of getting hurt themselves or making things worse.

The least a relative or friend can do is to put a woman in touch with local crisis hotlines, which have staff prepared to deal with the problem. Because many battered women call the police and contact emergency medical resources, putting these women in touch with crisis workers is the first and most important thing emergency workers can do after providing medical treatment and safety planning.

Two factors, however, may impede the accomplishment of this task: Some women do not acknowledge the cause of their physical injuries, or they provide a cover-up story. There are several reasons for this: (1) the woman may have been threatened by her mate with a more severe beating if she reveals the beating; (2) she may simply not be ready to leave for her own reasons; (3) she may sense the judgmental or unsympathetic attitude of a physician or nurse and therefore not confide the truth. Because of social isolation, prejudice, and fear of deportation, immigrant minority and refugee women who are abused usually face additional impediments to receiving help (Bui & Morash, 1999; Jang, Lee, & Morello-Frosch, 1991; Perilla, 1999). (See also Campbell, 1998, "Part VI: Culturally Specific Clinical Interventions.")

Sensitivity to these factors will help us interpret a woman's evasiveness about her injuries and recognize the implausibility of a cover-up story. Besides physical injuries, a battered woman will show other signals of distress or emotional crisis, as discussed in Chapter 3, and may present with aches and pains or vague symptoms not traceable to specific medical causes (Dutton et al., 2006; Sugg & Inui, 1992). Medical and nursing staff members who use a crisis assessment tool can more accurately identify and appropriately respond to a battered woman in crisis (see Exhibit 11.1 and the service forms in Chapter 3). As is true in dealing with a person at risk of being suicidal, it is appropriate to question a woman directly, which will probably result in her being relieved to know that someone is caring and sensitive enough to discern her distress. And as with suicidal people, if a woman refuses to acknowledge the battering, her refusal may have more to do with our attitude than with her willingness to disclose (Hoff, in press).

The important techniques to remember in these situations are (1) withhold judgment, (2) offer an empathic, supportive response, (3) assist the woman with safety planning, and (4) provide the woman with information—a card or brochure with the numbers of hotlines and women's support groups. This seemingly small response is central to the process of the woman's eventual decision to leave the violent relationship. The reason to have confidence in the value of such a response is that a woman feels empowered if she believes others respect her decision, even if it is to stay in the violent relationship for the time being. She also needs explicit recognition from us that ultimately it is *her* decision that makes the difference and that she can take credit for the decision. Because abused women often feel powerless and disrespected, we should convey to them that they are in charge of their lives (see Chapter 12 and Pence & Paymar, 1986, for details regarding the *power and control wheel*). When a woman *believes* this, it becomes a premise for her eventual action. Thus, although a woman may not be ready for more than emergency medical treatment, at least she has the necessary information if she decides to use it in the future. (See Figure 11.2.)

These principles apply to police officers as well as health workers, and raise the controversial question of mandatory reporting of domestic violence (as is required in *all* cases of child abuse or neglect). Such mandatory reporting laws for abused adults exist in four states: California, Colorado, Rhode Island, and Kentucky. Central to this controversy is the issue of empowerment as expressed by female emergency department patients (Rodriques et al., 2001). Nearly half of non-English-speaking patients opposed mandatory reporting on grounds of protecting autonomy and sociopolitical factors like fear of deportation. Mandatory reporting might also be counterproductive in providing a "quick fix" or loophole in the important process of emergency department health professionals linking abused women to crisis and follow-up mental health services.

It is also important to assure abused women that they are not responsible for their victimization, no matter what the person who battered them says to the contrary (see Chapter 2, Figure 2.2). To do this, we must be convinced that except in self-defense, violence is not justified no matter what happens in the interaction or the relationship. Even when used in self-defense, a return of violence often escalates rather than decreases the violence (see "Assessing the Risk of Dangerousness, Assault, and Homicide" in Chapter 12). In addition, we should not assume that battered women are routinely in need of therapy; this could add a psychiatric label to an already heavy burden (Stark et al., 1979). If a woman is suicidal, the principles and techniques discussed in Chapters 9 and 10 apply.

Once a woman is treated for physical trauma and resolves the dilemma of what to do next, she may be faced with the crises of finding emergency housing, caring for her children, and obtaining money. If a community does not have a safe home network or emergency shelter, if a woman cannot stay with relatives, and if she has no money, she may have little choice but to return to the violent situation. In such instances, crisis care providers should assist her

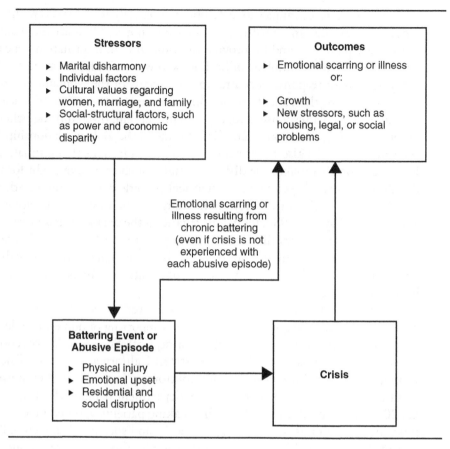

FIGURE 11.2 Interactive Relationships Among Stress, Crisis, and Possible Illness in a Battering Situation. The arrows suggest the interactional relationships among *stress, crisis,* and *illness.* Trouble and stressors in a marriage can lead to positive or negative outcomes through several different routes, depending on personal, social, and economic circumstances.

in developing a survival plan that includes, for example, having a bag packed and getting a key to a friend's house in case of acute danger. We also need to remember that in rural isolated communities, secure shelters may be nonexistent, or that a woman needing protection (as in Jane's case) is expected to rely on kinship or tribal networks.

When a woman decides to leave, up-to-date abuse prevention laws require police to accompany her to her home to get her children, legal documents, and whatever possessions she can bring to an emergency housing situation. Once the woman is in a shelter or linked to a support group network, further assistance is available to deal with legal, housing, and other aspects of the crisis (NiCarthy, 1989). In many countries, such assistance has been made possible by national coalitions. The 1995 Beijing Women's Conference and the 2000 Beijing Plus 5 Conference proceedings are valuable sources for organizing such coalitions and action groups (see United Nations, 1996b).

Almost invariably, when a woman is battered, her children are affected as well (as discussed in the child abuse section). An important element of helping a mother in crisis, as well as her children, is making child care services available. The mother needs time away from her children to deal with housing and other problems. The children are often highly anxious and in need of a stable, calming influence as well as appropriate physical outlets and nonviolent discipline (see Humphreys, 1998).

Follow-Up Service

When an abused woman has successfully dealt with the crisis aspect of her situation, the biggest decision she faces is whether or not to leave her partner permanently. Some women take months, even years, to make this decision, even after living in a safe environment for some time. One woman said: "I had to *practice* how to leave." Peer support groups of other women who have been battered and have broken out of violent relationships are probably the most valuable resource for a woman at this time. Such groups are important for several reasons:

1. If a woman decides to return to her partner, hoping for a change, and the battering continues, it is important that she knows there are people who will not judge her for her decisions.
2. Many women come to shelters convinced that they are psychologically disturbed and in need of a therapist. They have absorbed the message that the battering occurred because of something wrong with them. When they begin to feel strong and in charge of their lives, they may discover that a therapist is not needed after all and that other women can help them in ways they had not imagined. This discovery is a significant contrast to the traditional view of other women as "competition" in what many perceive as the all-important life task of catching and holding a man. Finding alternatives to therapy occurs most often in shelters or support groups that actively encourage women to assume charge of their lives. It also happens through the process of decision making and taking action to obtain housing, money, and legal services. Observing women in responsible, independent, collaborative, and caring roles in shelter staffing also seems to help. After feeling powerless for so long, a woman does not need a program that dictates every hour and detail of her life.
3. These support experiences may provide the basis for abused women to join, if they wish, a wider network of women working on the larger social, political, and economic aspects of stopping violence against women. A woman's positive experience of support while in crisis is the best preparation for possible involvement in such social change activity (see Crisis Paradigm, Figure 11.1 Box 3.)

If women request therapy, referrals should be made to therapists working from a woman's perspective (for example, Burstow, 1992; Everett & Gallop, 2000; Mirkin, 1994). Therapy may be indicated if, after crisis intervention and social network support, a woman continues to be depressed and suicidal or finds herself unable to make decisions and break out of patterns of dependency and self-blame (see Counts, 1987; Stephens, 1985). When the violent marriage and abuse of the children have left damaging scars, family therapy is indicated.

Other aspects of follow-up include:

- An opportunity for the woman to grieve and mourn the loss of a relationship if she finally decides to leave (see "Loss, Change, and Grief Work" in Chapter 4)
- For women who wish to marry again, a group in which to examine and share with others the complex aspects of avoiding relationships that may lead to a repeat of excessive dependency and violence
- Parent effectiveness groups to explore nonviolent ways of dealing with children

Crisis Counseling with an Abused Woman

The preventive, crisis, and follow-up aspects of helping abused women should be practiced with a view to their vital connectedness. This triple approach to the problem may not only help end the pain and terror of women who are attacked but may also remove the negative consequences of violence for children, men, and the entire society (Hoff, 1990). The following case is an example of how crisis counseling with a battered woman might proceed.

Case Example: Sandra Le Claire

Sandra Le Claire is a 22-year-old woman who is currently separated from her abusive husband of 5 years. She came to the United States from a country where French was her second language after her native tongue; Sandra is now learning English. She is the mother of two small children, ages 2 and 5. She does volunteer work for pay and is in the process of applying for public assistance. Her husband has been her sole source of financial support, and since their separation 9 months ago, his support has been sporadic at best. Sandra's visit today is one of several she has made to an emergency department. She presents with cuts and bruises about her face and across her chest and two black eyes, which are swollen shut— all as a result of a beating by her husband. Sandra says this beating was the culmination of an argument over her husband's lack of financial support to her and her children. She has never been willing to press charges against her husband out of fear, as he has threatened to kill her; nor has she ever retaliated with violence herself. She has been drinking more frequently and heavily and is becoming increasingly depressed and despondent about her situation. Sandra has suicidal ideation but denies having a specific plan, although in the past she has thought about taking an overdose of Tylenol when upset with her husband. She says her children have not witnessed any of the abusive episodes.

Sandra became pregnant at age 16 after moving to Boston with her parents, and quit high school to get married. She grew up in poverty, the youngest of five children with an alcoholic father and a born-again, churchgoing mother. Sandra viewed her marriage as a way out.

Although her father worked steadily, he did not earn enough money to support both his family and his drinking. Her mother did not believe in divorce. She raised the children and largely ignored her husband's drinking, sustaining many beatings herself at his hands. Though Sandra feels supported by her mother, who helps her with child care, she does not feel understood. Her mother believes God will provide. She tells Sandra it is just a phase that men go through and that things will improve for Sandra, as they have for her, since Sandra's father has grown less violent over the years. Sandra is not sure she can wait.

Since English is her third language, Sandra has problems with getting financial aid because she cannot complete the forms. Her abusive husband is also a drinker. Sandra had no drinking problem prior to abuse.

Session 1

Using the Comprehensive Mental Health Assessment form presented in Chapter 3, the problems and issues Sandra faces could be summarized as follows:

- Safety
- Suicidality
- Problem solving
- Financial support
- Substance use and abuse
- Goals and decisions regarding marriage
- Social support

Exhibit 11.2 illustrates these issues and the action plan that Sandra and the crisis worker developed as a service contract (as presented in Chapter 4) in her first crisis counseling session. Such a session would occur following initial assessment and referral by a triage nurse and the physician or nurse practitioner treating Sandra's injuries. Typically, the full crisis assessment is done by a crisis team member, usually in liaison with triage nurses and physicians. At Boston Medical Center, for example, this function is carried out by psychiatric nurses; at the Ottawa General Hospital, crisis counseling is done by social workers. Crisis counseling as illustrated here is also done by family practice physicians and advanced practice nurses across specialties (see Hoff

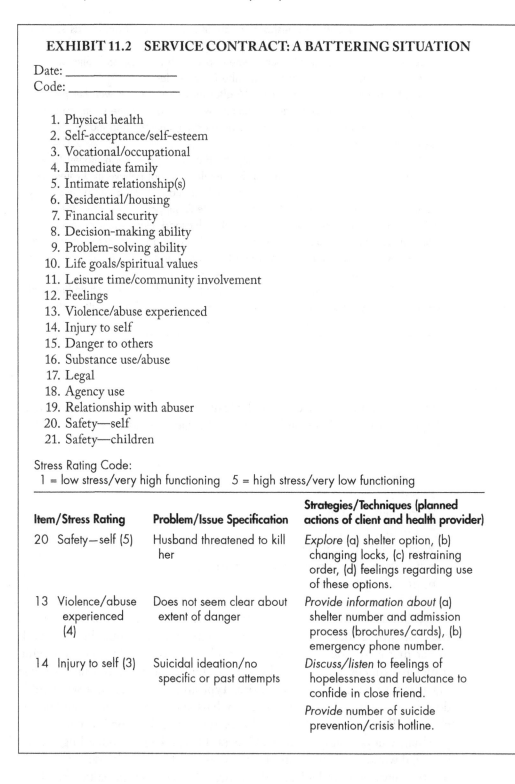

EXHIBIT 11.2 SERVICE CONTRACT: A BATTERING SITUATION

Date: _____

Code: _____

1. Physical health
2. Self-acceptance/self-esteem
3. Vocational/occupational
4. Immediate family
5. Intimate relationship(s)
6. Residential/housing
7. Financial security
8. Decision-making ability
9. Problem-solving ability
10. Life goals/spiritual values
11. Leisure time/community involvement
12. Feelings
13. Violence/abuse experienced
14. Injury to self
15. Danger to others
16. Substance use/abuse
17. Legal
18. Agency use
19. Relationship with abuser
20. Safety—self
21. Safety—children

Stress Rating Code:
1 = low stress/very high functioning   5 = high stress/very low functioning

Item/Stress Rating	Problem/Issue Specification	Strategies/Techniques (planned actions of client and health provider)
20 Safety—self (5)	Husband threatened to kill her	*Explore* (a) shelter option, (b) changing locks, (c) restraining order, (d) feelings regarding use of these options.
13 Violence/abuse experienced (4)	Does not seem clear about extent of danger	*Provide information about* (a) shelter number and admission process (brochures/cards), (b) emergency phone number.
14 Injury to self (3)	Suicidal ideation/no specific or past attempts	*Discuss/listen* to feelings of hopelessness and reluctance to confide in close friend.
		Provide number of suicide prevention/crisis hotline.

12	Feelings (4)	Increasingly depressed	*Sandra agrees* to (a) call/reconnect with friend within 3 days, (b) dispose of her supply of Tylenol, (c) call hotline if very despondent and feeling impulse to take pills.
7	Financial security (4)	Husband/abuser is sole source of support	*Explore* Sandra's ambivalence regarding financial aid versus continued attempt to obtain support from husband.
		Has language trouble with welfare forms	*Review* the welfare application forms to ascertain Sandra's understanding.
16	Substance use/abuse (3)	Never drank before battering	*Discuss* feelings about referral to substance abuse treatment program.
		Now drinking more frequently	*Provide* names, dates, places of local accessible programs.
			Sandra agrees to (a) choose and phone one source, (b) keep a journal record of drinking context and other possible options when upset.
9	Problem-solving ability (3)	Uses alcohol and considers drug overdose in response to abuse	*Agree to discuss* other two priority items (goals/decisions about marriage and social support) during second or later session.
			Engage Sandra in decision counseling around abuse and safety issues.
			Explore alternative coping devices.
21	Safety—children (3)	No direct witnessing but living in climate of violence	*Protect* children from witnessing conflict situation.
			Discuss adverse effect of domestic violence on healthy development.
			Identify protective measures for children in conflict situations.

Signatures: Client _____ Crisis Worker _____

& Morgan, in press). Although Session 1 focuses on assessment and developing a service contract, it does not conclude without an explicit plan around safety issues (items 14, 20, and 21) that might need implementation between Sessions 1 and 2.

The following are illustrations of how crisis counseling might proceed on behalf of Sandra. In general, the sessions are balanced between *structure*, an aid to making order out of the chaos of trauma, and *openness*, which facilitates compassionate regard and empowerment. Typically, there would be 6 to 10 sessions, with attention to the interface between crisis and chronic problems, as discussed in Chapter 5.

Session 2

In the second session, the counselor would set out these plans and goals:

- Explore feeling state and urgent issues, including effects of abusive climate on children
- Review safety and progress with action planned from last session
- Examine barriers to progress with planned action
- Identify any new problems
- Negotiate new or revised action plan for problem solving

The following progress notes and action plan might come out of the session:

Progress Notes
- Feels less despondent and suicidal
- Does not want to go to a shelter, at least not now
- Discussed women's support group as alternative
- Feels ambivalent about restraining order on husband
- Drinking about the same
- Did not call substance abuse treatment source
- Did not go to welfare office; would like someone to go with her

Action Plan
- Continue crisis intervention plan for suicide prevention
- Continue journal regarding drinking pattern; rethink calling AA or other treatment source
- Call advocate and arrange visit to welfare office; also discuss nature of battered women's support group during outing to welfare office with advocate

Remaining Sessions

Each of the remaining sessions would include

- Identification of any urgent issues, particularly safety of self and children
- General review of mood
- Review of progress with previous action plan

- Identification of any new problems and barriers to progress
- Decision counseling around any issues identified
- Negotiated plan for next steps, strategies, and actions regarding problems, including time and place of next appointment

Possible Problems, Issues, and Barriers to Progress

As crisis counseling proceeds with Sandra, new problems and issues may emerge—for example:

Indecision and ambivalence about divorce. Sandra may say, "I don't want to be one of those welfare mothers," or "If only he'd get some help for his drinking," or "Maybe if I were just more patient when he gets angry."

Action plan: Listen to feelings and fears; discuss pros and cons regarding separation, divorce, and future safety; explore level of financial support (husband, welfare, self); consider possibility of job training; discuss self-blame and issue of accountability for violence.

Need for social support. Sandra feels lonely, wishes her mother were more understanding; advocate gave her information about a battered women's support group, but she does not feel like going; would rather be able to communicate better with her mother; feels ashamed to have her problem known beyond her family.

Action plan: Explore feelings of shame; reconsider calling AA as an alternative source of support; explore possibility of a joint session with mother to air issues, goals, and possible further support.

Abuse of Male Partners

This discussion is incomplete without attention to the controversial issue of male partner abuse. Women as well as men can be violent; not to acknowledge this fact is equivalent to viewing women as less than moral beings, in the same way that excusing male violence implies that men are less than moral beings. Women, like men, should be held accountable for their behavior.

It has been suggested that the "real" domestic problem is husband battering and that the reason it is still hidden is because it is too much of an assault on the male ego to acknowledge the shame of having been beaten by a woman. A national survey in the United States on domestic violence revealed that in *numbers* of violent acts—*not in quality or context*—women and men were approximately equal (Straus, 1993; Straus et al., 1980). This statistical finding, however, needs to be qualified: When women are violent, it is primarily in self-defense, and their attacks generally are not as dangerous or physically injurious as those of men. Since then, survey research has been refined (for example, Johnson, 1998), and there is progress in undertaking nonexploitative research on this topic. In addition, when women kill their mates, it is usually after years of abuse, and they do so less frequently than men kill their wives (Browne, 1987; Jones, 1980). Even during pregnancy, rates of battering by partners who should be protecting women are as high as

25%, while most women do not retaliate with violence (McFarlane, Parker, Soeken, & Bullock, 1992).

The pattern of injustice and violence used primarily in self-defense should be kept in mind in trials of women who kill abusive husbands. Rather than medicalizing the woman's case by using a contrived insanity plea, women should have a fair trial on self-defense grounds when the evidence points in that direction. The suggestion that husband beating is more rampant than wife battering covers up the roots of violence against women in traditional social structures and the low socioeconomic status of women that allows violence to flourish worldwide (PAHO/WHO, 2003). To claim an equal problem of husband battering belies reality, especially as it is revealed in emergency settings and in the differences in physical strength between most men and women. The majority of men are physically more capable of inflicting injury than are women. In addition, men who are beaten have much more freedom to leave because of their socioeconomic advantage in society and relative freedom from child care. Men who are abused by their partners should nevertheless receive the same medical care and social support as that recommended for women.

Battering of Lesbian, Gay, Bisexual, and Transgendered Partners

Prevention and intervention strategies for abused heterosexual partners apply to those in GLBT relationships. The stigma of GLBT is added to the stigma of domestic violence. Asking for help necessitates "outing" oneself to law enforcement officers, health care providers, etc. who may or may not be tolerant of "alternative lifestyles." The threat of an intimate partner outing one's mate if he or she reveals abuse or attempts to leave the relationship can be a powerful tool of control. Possible consequences of losing child custody/ visitation, job, and family alienation are serious deterrents to such revelation. There are few, if any, resources such as shelters for battered gay men and transgendered individuals. Additional factors to be considered arise from the bias and social isolation faced by most of these couples; individuals in these relationships usually rely more heavily than others on their partners for emotional support and companionship. As discussed in Chapter 5, excessive dependency in any intimate relationship may be the source of additional stressors that constitute the context in which abuse occurs. In addition, gay men are more vulnerable than lesbian women or heterosexual men to violence from strangers or associates who are motivated explicitly by antigay bias or homophobia (Greenwood et al., 2002).

The extraordinary stress experienced by couples in alternative lifestyles is compounded by stereotypes and the bias that keeps them isolated in the first place. One such stereotype is that all lesbians are feminists, and because a battering lesbian partner has violated the feminist agenda of nonviolence, she is thereby deemed less deserving of help. Another stereotype is that women become lesbians because they have been victims of sexual abuse. In reality, not all lesbian women are feminists, and some feminists are just as homophobic as others are. In fact, many women were sexually abused as children; most of them are heterosexual. Finally, because GLBT people are members of a larger cultural community just as others are, why would they be exempt from having absorbed the pervasive message of violence as a control strategy and a solution to conflict resolution? Their disadvantaged social position may result in greater sensitivity to issues of abuse generally, but they face even greater odds in avoiding violence than the general population.

To provide appropriate service for victims in alternative lifestyles, it is imperative that crisis workers examine attitudes that can prevent battered GLBT partners from disclosing their plight and receiving the help needed. In general, the legacy of victim-blaming experienced by battered women is exacerbated with regard to those in sexual orientation minority groups (Renzetti, 1992). Major cities in Canada and the United States now have publicly established groups addressing violence among these minority groups—for example, in Boston, the Violence Recovery Program at the Fenway Community Health Center. State and provincial offices for victim assistance can provide information about local services for these groups.

Abuse of Older Persons

Attention to abuse of older people[2] has gained increasing international attention (MacLean, 1995; McDonald et al., 1991; Pillemer & Wolf, 1986). Elder abuse includes willful infliction of physical injury or debilitating mental anguish, financial exploitation, and unreasonable confinement or deprivation of necessary care and services. Earlier, public attention was focused on abuse and substandard care in nursing homes. In spite of the prevalence of institutional care of some older people in the United States, the majority of seniors (95%) live alone or with family or other caretakers. The victims are overwhelmingly female, with most naming their spouse as the attacker and a significant number naming a son or daughter as the aggressor (Pillemer & Finkelhor, 1987). Although abuse and neglect may occur in institutions, legal protections limit such abuse. In private settings, legal protections are more difficult to enforce because of civil rights and family privacy. This discussion is particularly relevant to community health nurses, home health aides, pastors, and other professionals offering consultation and supervision on behalf of older people cared for at home.

Why are elders abused? As already noted, there are parallels between battered children and abused seniors: (1) they are in a dependent position for survival; (2) they are presumed to be protected by love, gentleness, and caring; and (3) they are a source of emotional, physical, and financial stress

---

[2] The terms *older persons*, *elders*, and *seniors* are used interchangeably.

for the caretaker, particularly if the older person is physically or mentally impaired (Sommers & Shields, 1987).

Several other factors can be identified in tracing the roots of elder abuse. Inattention to these factors can form obstacles to prevention, crisis intervention, and follow-up service for older people at risk.

1. *Social factors.* In the contemporary nuclear family structure, there is often no social, physical, and economic room for elders. For example, death rituals in traditional African societies include transfer of social responsibility held by the deceased (Goody, 1962; see Chapter 6). In modern societies, an older person's body may linger long after social death occurs. Responsibility for the care of older people is complicated by the trend of women working outside the home while maintaining major responsibility for unpaid work at home. Residential complexes, such as the Erikson communities, support independent, assisted-living, and long-term care in a coordinated framework. For many older people, this is an increasingly common option in the United States and Canada.

2. *Cultural factors.* U.S. society is noted for idolizing youth. The cultural emphasis on economic productivity tends to eclipse elders' contributions of wisdom, life experience, and often continued work. Consequently, seniors often lack status, respect, and similar rewards that are taken for granted in other societies. The culture of violence as it affects children and women flows over to seniors as well; older, abused women are referred to as "forgotten victims." In spite of elders' increasing political influence, ageism is still rampant, particularly with respect to older women (Doress & Siegal, 1987).

3. *Economic factors.* The poverty of many old people is an almost inevitable result of the social and cultural factors noted previously. Strong economic motives for protecting children often do not extend to seniors. In the United States, the Family Medical Leave Act allows for some time compensation to family caretakers of the 95% of elders living in the community, but it does not begin to cover the tremendous financial and social burdens of long-term care.

4. *Psychological factors.* One of the normal features of growing old is a decreased capacity to control impulses and adjust to change. A lifelong pattern of inflexibility can result in a demanding, unpleasant personality in old age. Considering also the interaction between physical dependence and fear of retaliation, elder abuse can remain hidden for some time. Elders abused by adult children—not unlike battered women—will feel deep shame and try to account for the abuse in terms of their own failure as parents. They say, in effect, "What kind of a parent am I that my own child would turn on me in my helplessness and old age?"

5. *Legal factors.* Civil liberties in democratic societies protect one's right to privacy, self-determination, and the refusal of services. Although most jurisdictions now have adult protective service authorities, not

all require mandatory reporting of suspected elder abuse cases, as they do in cases of suspected child abuse. These factors, combined with an abused elder's shame and fear of retaliation, constitute formidable barriers to dealing effectively with elder abuse.

Prevention, Crisis Intervention, and Follow-Up Service

As with other crises, prevention, crisis intervention, and follow-up are interrelated and demand awareness of the origins of the crisis. Preventive measures related to the sociocultural and economic aspects of elder abuse suggest an examination of values regarding older people. Social and political changes affecting seniors are also needed, such as provision of tax and insurance benefits for families who would care for an older person at home if they could add a room to their house and obtain home health care assistance without serious financial hardship. Psychologically, we can reduce the risk of elder abuse by preparing for the social, economic, and physical realities of later life (see Chapter 6 for a detailed discussion). As we prepare for old age, it is wise to remember that old people with unpleasant personalities are the same as young people with unpleasant personalities, except that changing undesirable habits can be more challenging as we grow older.

Crisis intervention for older people at risk of abuse demands careful application of the assessment, planning, and intervention strategies discussed in Chapters 3, 4, and 5, with particular attention to social network approaches. Emergency medical care and crisis intervention for abused elders are complicated for two reasons:

1. *Mental incapacity or confusion on the part of the elder.* State and provincial departments of mental health and elder affairs have standard protocols for these cases. Involuntary commitment or appointment of a legal guardian requires clear and convincing evidence that the adult in question is cognitively impaired and that an emergency exists. When these legal actions are taken, they should be based on the principle of *least-restrictive alternative* and the guarantee of civil liberties.
2. *Misplaced emergency care or crisis intervention.* Carelessness in this area of care for older people or the use of inappropriate savior tactics can alienate family members, who may be needed in the long term. Considering shame, possible retaliation, and the dynamics of family loyalty, follow-up after the emergency as well as future crisis intervention will be very difficult if family members are alienated. Unless foster care is readily available, great care must be taken to prevent further complicating an already difficult situation. Thus, although laws now exist for reporting elder abuse, similar to the Good Samaritan laws protecting children, overzealous action on these laws should not become the occasion for precipitating more trouble.

In both situations, primary care providers treating older persons in crisis or presenting with mental confusion need to carefully ascertain whether neuropsychiatric symptoms and cognitive incapacities can be traced to drug reactions or the interactive effects of the medications prescribed for some. In these complex cases, consultation should be sought from gerontology and psychopharmacology specialists (see Melillo & Houde, 2005).

Application of Intervention and Follow-Up Principles

The following example reveals the intersection of caretaker stress and elder abuse. It also shows the importance of careful teamwork in responding to such abuse.

Case Example: Martha

Martha, age 82, suffered from crippling arthritis and heart disease. She was visited regularly in her daughter's home by a home health aide, who bathed her three times a week. The rest of the time her daughter, Jane, age 55, gave her medicine and helped Martha out of bed into a chair when she had time. Jane worked full-time as a legal secretary. Jane's husband, Robert, age 63, was home most of the day. He had been on disability support for 10 years, after seriously injuring his back doing construction work. For the most part, Robert felt useless, although he did help with shopping and laundry. The disabilities of both her mother and husband left Jane feeling very stressed.

The home health worker discovered black-and-blue marks on Martha's chest and back and suspected that abuse was occurring. Her attempts to talk to Martha about this were met by silence. The aide reported her observation to the visiting nurse, who in turn consulted a social worker. (The nurse had known this family for over a year and visited the home approximately once a month in a supervisory, coordinating, and teaching capacity). The nurse then called Jane and suggested she be seen by the social worker to discuss the problems of taking care of her mother. Even though the nurse did not directly mention the suspicion of abuse, Jane felt threatened, refused to act on the suggestion, dismissed the nurse and home health aide, and hired a private nurse to care for Martha around the clock to "prove" she was not neglectful of her mother. This move was a great financial burden for the family. Three months later, Jane again requested service for her mother from the home health agency.

Several things seem very clear in this example: (1) Everyone concerned appeared to be well intentioned; (2) Jane was alienated by the approach used by the nurse; and (3) the problem was complicated by an inappropriate intervention strategy. The nurse seemed to lack confidence in her ability to take on a key role in intervention; she assumed that a social worker was the more appropriate person to act, in spite of her own year-long relationship with the family.

Success in dealing with sensitive issues like these depends very much on the quality of the relationship between the caregiver and the recipient. If the nurse had recognized this, she would not have suggested what Jane interpreted as an accusation that she neglected her mother. Instead the nurse might have used other intervention and follow-up strategies.

1: After hearing the aide's report, the nurse could have planned an extra visit to the home to spend some time with Martha and Jane individually to further assess the situation. To facilitate communication about the issue, the nurse might have bathed Martha herself once as a way of gaining her confidence. A concerned rather than an accusatory approach to Jane might have resulted in Jane's revealing voluntarily the stress and exasperation she experienced in carrying out her multiple responsibilities. Their conversation might have proceeded as follows:

Nurse: How are things going, Jane, with all the things you have to juggle these days? I know that Terri, the aide, has been coming in three times a week. Do you think you're getting all the help you need?

Jane: Well, it's hard, but somehow I'm managing. On the days I have to get Mother out of bed myself, I sometimes feel like a nervous wreck. She screams with pain when I touch her. I can't stand the thought of putting Mother in a nursing home, but sometimes I don't know.

Nurse: So it seems things are pretty rough for you, Jane? I was in to see your mother this week while Terri was bathing and dressing her, and I noticed several black-and-blue marks. [Nurse tries to keep the aide's relationship with the family intact.] She wouldn't talk about it though, so I'm wondering whether things are getting too difficult for you and if maybe we could be of more help to you.

Jane: If you're thinking I hit my mother, well, I didn't. A couple of times I might have handled her kind of roughly; she's really frail and thin, you know. But I certainly never hit her. After all, she's my mother.

Nurse: This is a really touchy thing to talk about, Jane, and I don't mean to accuse you of anything. I know it must be very difficult at times. What I'm suggesting is that we work on this together to be sure both you and your mother get what you need. I know that you want the best possible care for your mother, and it seems like Robert's disability might wear on you, too. Can you tell me more about the problems you have in taking care of your mother?

Problem exploration continues in this vein; the session ends with agreement to talk again the next week to work on the problem that had been uncovered. It never becomes explicit whether Jane did or did not abuse her mother. It is not a good strategy to try to prove that abuse occurred when the old person is refusing to talk and the caretaker is denying it. It is more important to focus on the underlying issues related to abuse.

2: If, after this, the nurse still does not feel confident about proceeding, she might consult the agency social worker or Adult Protective Services but not abruptly turn the problem over to someone else.

3: The nurse might also talk with Jane's husband to see whether he might become more helpful with household tasks.

4: After exploring the problem with everyone concerned, a social network conference might be indicated (see Chapter 5). This would include Martha, Jane, Robert, Terri, and possibly a social worker consultant and a representative from respite services, which should be discussed as one avenue of relief for Jane.

As the proportion of elders in the population increases, there is hope for favorable political change for elder affairs. With increasing public sensitivity to the problems of seniors, we may devise more creative ways to foster the conditions for peace, safety, and health and for social services during the later years. Changes are already occurring with New Age families, the foster grandparent program, intergenerational housing experiments, and comprehensive health and other services delivered in home settings. The latter include, for example, around 10 people of various ages, with 60% over 60, living in a large, ordinary family home. Each person has a separate room; other areas and general tasks are shared communally. Elders who participate in these programs feel socially useful, with beneficial effects for physical and mental health and less chance of violence directed against them.

Battering and Abuse of Parents and Teachers by Children or Their Parents

The abuse of infirm and dependent elders by adult children differs from another aspect of violence in families—the physical abuse of parents by their minor children. A U.S. national survey by Straus et al. (1980) revealed that almost 10% of children ages 3 to 18 have attacked their parents. Clinicians and others note the increasing number of parents and teachers who fear attacks by children and adolescents. Parricide, the most extreme form of parental assault, is usually associated with severe parental sexual and physical abuse of the child (Mones, 1993).

Some abusive teenagers may be responding to parents who are excessively permissive and indulgent. Some parents act from the misguided belief that acceding to a child's demands for extra privileges and material things will result in the child's improved behavior. A common example is paying children for performing tasks that should be a normal contribution to the common good by every household member who benefits from the whole. A more extreme example is buying an adolescent a luxury car for the good behavior that should be expected without elaborate rewards. Experience in mental health practice with out-of-control adolescents suggests that actual results are exactly opposite those anticipated by parents from their indulged children. The probable reason is that the adolescent feels insecure and entrapped when forced, through lack of parental authority and leadership, to assume an independent role before feeling developmentally ready.

Parents experiencing abuse by their children are in a catch-22 dilemma: As with their elder counterparts, confronting the situation implies an admission of failure at parenting; not confronting it reinforces the child's misplaced sense of omnipotence and need to control others. Preventive strategies are similar to those discussed for child and elder abuse: At the societal level, fostering nonviolent solutions to child rearing and greater respect for seniors can reinforce parental authority. Crisis and follow-up strategies include parent effectiveness training or, if necessary, family therapy. In addition, parents should have access to help during crisis without shame or denial of the problem. Crisis intervention planning with such families should feature nonviolent tactics that a child can use when angry at a parent. Parents, too, need alternatives to giving in to children who behave like dictators (Charney, 1993).

Parents, however, are not the only ones abused by violent children. For years, teachers have been terrorized, raped, knifed, and attacked in other ways (Walker, 1993). The same issues are at play here: social and cultural approval of violence, poverty, racism, loss of respect for parental and other authority, and the need to listen to children. The widespread neglect of inner-city public schools and the disadvantages to students who attend them must also be remedied if we wish to stem the large-scale loss of disaffected, traumatized, and burned-out teachers. Poorly supported schools cannot be solely responsible for the intellectual and moral training of children (Long & Wilder, 1993).

Even more shocking, when school officials attempt to engage parents in dealing with children who have assaulted teachers, are instances of a parent or even a grandparent assaulting the teacher, as if to say without discussion of the context and details: "My child is innocent. You must have provoked the attack." Just as there is no perfect parent, there are imperfect teachers dealing with extraordinary social stressors and demands while also trying to teach. Civilized societies have moved beyond barbaric practices such as caning schoolchildren, and have child protection policies in place. But while parents need to be vigilant about possibilities of sexual and physical abuse, and other betrayals of trust in schools, churches, and any agency or program working with children, an unexamined assumption by parents of the teacher's or other adult's guilt fails to address the problem. Dealing with the complex personal, family, and sociocultural issues associated with violence in schools demands a collaborative school, family, and community approach, minus the negative example of adult violence in response to an out-of-control or misbehaving child.

In many communities, a violence prevention curriculum has been instituted (Eggert, 1994). Teens are taught nonviolent approaches to conflict resolution, and troubled teens and their families are referred to hotlines and other crisis intervention services (see Brendtro et al., 1990, for an educational and developmental approach to troubled youth). In Massachusetts, the Department of Public Health has published a booklet aimed at schools for the prevention of bullying, which is seen as an early warning sign of antisocial or even criminal behavior, but is often ignored despite the psychological damage it inflicts.

Other Sources of Victimization

In addition to abuse from one's own family or spouse, there are many other sources of violent crime. Public opinion polls reveal continued concern about crime—especially the dramatic incidents of school and college shootings. People are angry and afraid. They blame their unease on the media, the courts, television, stressed families, pornography, the economy, drugs, poor housing conditions, indifference to the poor, racial tension and discrimination, poverty, youth gangs, the police, easily available handguns, and the disintegration of the American family. In the United States, there are nearly as many firearms as there are people, along with widespread denial of scientific evidence showing that the presence of guns *decreases* rather than increases safety. The significantly lower rates of homicide and other assaults in Canada and Western European countries are attributed to stringent gun control laws and related cultural factors. However, despite repeated public outrage and national mourning over children killing children, the prospects of reducing gun-related deaths in the United States appear grim when considering the deeply embedded place of guns in American culture.

No doubt, each of the factors mentioned plays some part in this complex problem. Fear of crime seems to generate chronic stress, worry, paranoia, and a sense of helplessness. If no arrests are made or criminals receive light sentences or acquittals, victims and the general public often feel that no one cares or that there is no justice. These feelings can lead to alienation, revenge, and a sense of callousness and insensitivity to others. This may account for the popularity among Americans of the death penalty and for the support of prosecuting violent adolescents in adult courts. However, there are reconciliation movements beginning among the relatives of some murder victims— for example, Crime Victims for a Just Society. Although generally shunned by survivors who seek solace in the death penalty, those seeking alternatives to the death penalty point out that vengeance is a dead end that does not deal with anger and grief.

Victim Assistance after a Crime

What is the ordinary citizen's role in assisting victims of crime? In France, such assistance is mandated by law; in the United States, it is not. Should we intervene on the victim's behalf or ignore a crime? In a frequently cited case in New York City, Kitty Genovese was attacked decades ago late one night while people in at least a dozen households listened to her screams. Nobody went to help or even bothered to call the police from the safety of their own homes. In contrast today, many groups of people are organizing neighborhood patrols and other means of coming to the aid of people victimized by crime. Every would-be helper faces the dilemma of whether and how to intervene in a crime. A basic principle of crisis intervention is to protect oneself from getting hurt while assisting others. Although some people voluntarily sacrifice their lives for others, such a sacrifice is neither expected nor demanded. Not intervening out of fear for one's own safety is fair enough. But not to mobilize police on behalf of a victim is a failure to meet the obligations implicit in our common humanity.

There is now a specialty field called *victimology*, complete with journals and professional conferences. Yet at the practical level, many victims of crime still seem cruelly shortchanged in the criminal justice, emergency medical, and crisis service systems. Through federal task forces and the advocacy and lobbying of the National Organization for Victim Assistance (NOVA), many communities now have victim assistance programs, as do some crisis centers. In general, however, there are no constitutional protections for victims, although there is progress toward training of police and emergency medical personnel in meeting the special needs of victims, including instances of communitywide trauma. NOVA and its state-level counterparts have been instrumental in improving this situation, particularly through crisis response teams and victim advocacy during court proceedings. Federal legislation has supported the development of victim witness and assistance programs in the United States. These include the development of self-help groups, the training of victim advocates, and a plan for financial assistance to victims. The U.S. government executive branch even established a national toll-free hotline number for domestic violence victims: 1-800-799-7233. Similar programs have been instituted in Canada, England, and other countries.

Funding of victim assistance programs is a continuing struggle, as funds are often focused on programs that try to understand and reform the criminal. This is not to say that criminals' needs should be ignored, but the rights of victims should be no less protected than the rights of defendants in a fair justice system. Indeed, the visibility of victims and their needs benefit even the criminal, as some restorative justice programs show (see Chapter 12).

Greater attention, meanwhile, should be focused on the needs of victims in emergency medical, police, and criminal justice systems. Victims are people in crisis who should have the advantage of being listened to and helped by workers who are sensitive, knowledgeable, and skilled in crisis intervention. However, emphasizing crisis service does not mean that we should neglect lifesaving physical treatment in a hospital trauma unit. While medical and legal needs are met, psychosocial needs can be addressed as well. Victims therefore need a bill of rights—for example, the right to

- Be informed of the release of a prisoner who has previously harmed them. Most jurisdictions now oblige psychotherapists, for example, to warn potential murder victims of would-be assailants' plans for release (VandeCreek & Knapp, 1993).

- Receive information about protection services.
- Be secure in a court waiting room that is separate from defendants.
- Receive restitution of stolen or damaged property.
- Receive social and psychological support in working through the crisis.

The international attention currently focused on this problem is a hopeful sign for this facet of crisis care.

Summary and Discussion Questions

People in crisis because of the violence of others suffer emotional and physical injury and are disrupted from their place in society if the violence is from a family member or intimate. In addition to assistance for individual victims of violence, social change strategies are paramount in addressing the culturally embedded values and social practices from which so much violence originates worldwide. Such a tandem approach may eventually reduce the tragic effects of violence for individuals, their families, and society as a whole.

1. Consider and discuss with family and peers the multicultural and political factors that seem to evade influence of the worldwide attention that has been directed to stemming the tide of interpersonal violence.
2. Identify an example and discuss the essentials of care for a traumatized person to move beyond "victimhood" as a lifetime identity.
3. In global perspective, consider the role of the Internet as both an instrument of violence and its prospects for cross-cultural violence prevention.
4. A prominent feeling among people working with victims is *vicarious traumatization* and a feeling of helplessness. What are the best protections against this happening? Should one simply withdraw or change jobs?

References

Adams, C. M. (2006). The consequences of witnessing family violence on children and implications for family counselors. *The Family Journal: Counseling and Therapy for Couples and Families, 14*(4), 334–341.

Adams, D. (2007). *Why do they kill? Men who murder their intimate partners.* Nashville: Vanderbilt University Press.

American Association of Colleges of Nursing. (1999). *Position paper: Violence as a public health problem.* Washington, DC: Author.

Antle, B. F., Barbee, A. P., Sullivan, D., Yankeelov, P., Johnson, L., & Cunningham, M. R. (2007). The relationship between domestic violence and child neglect. *Brief Treatment and Crisis Intervention, 7*, 364–382.

Bagley, C., & King, K. (1990). *Child sexual abuse: The search for healing.* New York: Routledge.

Beijing +5 Process and Beyond. (2000). Retrieve at UN.org.womanwatch.

Bell, C. C., Jenkins, E. J., Kpo, W., & Rhodes, H. (1994). Response of emergency rooms to victims of interpersonal violence. *Hospital and Community Psychiatry, 45*(2), 142–146.

Bogat, G. A., DeJonghe, E., Levendosky, A. A., Davidson, W. S., & von Eye, A. (2005). Trauma symptoms among infants exposed to intimate partner violence. *Child Abuse & Neglect, 30,* 109–125.

Bograd, M. (1984). Family systems approaches to wife battering: A feminist critique. *American Journal of Orthopsychiatry, 54*(4), 558–568.

Braswell, L. (1989). *Quest for respect: A healing guide for survivors of rape.* London: Pathfinder Press.

Brendtro, L. K., Brokenleg, M., & Van Bockern, S. (1990). *Reclaiming youth at risk.* Bloomington, IN: National Educational Service.

Broverman, I. K., Clarkson, F E., Rosenkrantz, P. S., & Vogel, S. R. (1970). Sex-role stereotypes and clinical judgments of mental health. *Journal of Consulting and Clinical Psychology, 34,* 1–7.

Brown, J. C., & Bohn, C. R. (1989). *Christianity, patriarchy, and abuse: A feminist critique.* New York: Pilgrim Press.

Browne, A. (1989). *When battered women kill.* New York: Free Press.

Brownmiller, S. (1975). *Against our will.* New York: Simon & Schuster.

Bui, H. N., & Morash, M. (1999). Domestic violence in the Vietnamese immigrant community: An exploratory study. *Violence Against Women, 5*(7), 769–795.

Burgess, A. W., & Hartman, C. (Eds.). (1989). *Sexual exploitation of patients by health professionals.* New York: Praeger.

Burstow, B. (1992). *Radical feminist theory: Working in the context of violence.* Thousand Oaks, CA: Sage.

Buzawa, E. S., & Buzawa, C. G. (1996). *Domestic violence: The criminal justice response.* Thousand Oaks, CA: Sage.

Campbell, J. C. (Ed.). (1998). *Empowering survivors of abuse: Health care for battered women and their children.* Thousand Oaks, CA: Sage.

Campbell, J. C., & Humphreys, J. H. (1993). *Nursing care of survivors of family violence.* St. Louis: Mosby-Year Book.

Canter, L., & Canter, M. (1988). *A proven step-by-step approach to solving everyday behavior problems* (Rev. ed.). Santa Monica, CA: Lee Canter & Associates.

Charney, R. (1993). Teaching children nonviolence. *Journal of Emotional and Behavioral Problems, 2*(1), 46–48.

Clements, P., Faulkner, M., & Manno, M. (2003). Family-member homicide: A grave situation for children. Topics in *Advanced Practice Nursing eJournal, 3*(3). Retrieved at http://www.medscape.com/viewarticle/458064. September 6, 2005.

Coker, A. L., Flerx, V. C., Smith, P. H., Whitaker, D. J., Fadden, M. K., Williams, M. (2007). Partner violence screening in rural health care clinics. *American Journal of Public Health, 97*(7), 1319–1325.

Collishawa, S., Pickles, A., Messer, J., Rutter, M., Shearer, C., & Maughana, B. (2007). Resilience to adult psychopathology following childhood maltreatment: Evidence from a community sample. *Child Abuse & Neglect, 31,* 211–229.

Conte, J. R., Wolf, S., & Smith, T. (1987, July). *What sexual offenders tell us about prevention: Preliminary findings.* Paper presented at the Third National Family Violence Conference, Durham, NH.

Cook, J. V., & Bowles, R. T. (Eds.). (1980). *Child abuse.* Toronto: Butterworths.

Counts, D. A. (1987). Female suicide and wife abuse: A cross-cultural perspective. *Suicide & Life-Threatening Behavior, 17*(3), 194–204.

Dangor, Z., Hoff, L. A., & Scott, R. (1998). Woman abuse in South Africa: An exploratory study. *Violence Against Women: An International Interdisciplinary Journal, 4*(2), 125–152.

De Mause, L. (1975). Our forebears made childhood a nightmare. *Psychology Today, 8,* 85–88.

Dobash, R. P., & Dobash, R. E. (1979). *Violence against wives: A case against the patriarchy.* New York: Free Press.

Dobash, R. E., & Dobash, R. P. (Eds.) (1998). *Rethinking violence against women.* Thousand Oaks, CA: Sage.

Doress, P B., & Siegal, D. L. (1987). *Ourselves, growing older.* New York: Simon & Schuster.

Dutton, M. A., Green, B. L., Kaltman, S. I., Roesch, D. M., Zeffiro, T. A., & Krause, E. D. (2006). Intimate partner violence, PTSD, and adverse health outcomes. *Journal of Interpersonal Violence, 21*(7), 955–968.

Eggert, L. L. (1994). *Anger management for youth: Stemming aggression and violence.* Bloomington, IN: National Educational Service.

Estrich, S. (1987). *Real rape: How the legal system victimizes women who say no.* Cambridge, MA: Harvard University Press.

Evans, M., Boothroyd, R., Armstrong, M., Greenbaum, P., Brown, E., & Kuppinger, A. (2003). An experimental study of the effectiveness of intensive in-home crisis services for children and their families: Program outcomes. *Journal of Emotional and Behavioral Disorders, 11*(2), 92–121.

Everett, B., & Gallop, R. (2000). *Linking childhood trauma and mental illness: Theory and practice for direct service practitioners.* Thousand Oaks, CA: Sage.

Eyre, J., & Eyre, R. (1993). *Teaching your children values.* New York: Simon & Schuster.

Figley C. R., & Nash, W. P. (Eds.). (2005). *Combat stress injury.* New York: Routledge.

Finkelhor, D. (1984). *Child sexual abuse: New theory and research.* New York: Free Press.

Flanagan, C. (July/August 2007). Babes in the woods. *Atlantic Monthly,* 116–133.

Gelles, R. J., & Loseke, D. R. (Eds.). (1993). *Current controversies on family violence.* Thousand Oaks, CA: Sage.

Gelles, R. J., & Straus, M. A. (1979). Determinants of violence in the family: Toward a theoretical integration. In W. R. Burr et al. (Eds.), *Contemporary theories about the family* (Vol. 1, pp. 549–581). New York: Free Press.

Gil, D. (1970). *Violence against children.* Cambridge, MA: Harvard University Press.

Goody, J. (1962). *Death, property, and the ancestors.* London: Tavistock.

Greenwood, G. L., Relf, M. V., Huang, B., Pollack, L. M., Canchola, J. A., & Catania, J. A. (2002). Battering victimization among a probability-based sample of men who have sex with men. *American Journal of Public Health, 92*(12), 1964–1969.

Greven, P. (1990). *Spare the child: The religious roots of punishment and the psychological impact of physical abuse.* New York: Knopf.

Groves, B. M., Zuckerman, B., Marans, S., & Cohen, D. (1993). Silent victims: Children who witness violence. *Journal of the American Medical Association, 269*(2), 262–264.

Handwerker, W. P. (1998). Why violence? A test of hypotheses representing three discourses on the roots of domestic violence. *Human Organization, 57*(2), 200–208.

Harpez-Rotem, I., Murphy, R. A., Berkowitz, S., Marans, S., & Rosenheck, R. A. (2007). Clinical epidemiology of urban violence: Responding to children exposed to violence in ten communities. *Journal of Interpersonal Violence, 22*(11), 1479–1490.

Hartigan, P. (1999, June 16). "It's like I had this war in me." *Boston Globe,* pp. E1, E4.

Helfer, R., & Kempe, R. S. (1987). *The battered child* (4th ed.). Chicago: University of Chicago Press.

Henning, K., Leitenberg, H., Coffey, P., Turner, T., & Bennett, R. T. (1996). Long-term psychological and social impact of witnessing physical conflict between parents. *Journal of Interpersonal Violence, 11*, 35–51.

Herman, J. (1981). *Father–daughter incest*. Cambridge, MA: Harvard University Press.

Herman, J. (1992). *Trauma and recovery: The aftermath of violence*. New York: Basic Book.

Hilberman, E. (1980). Overview: One "wife-beater's wife" reconsidered. *American Journal of Psychiatry, 137*, 1336–1347.

Hillman, D., & Solek-Tefft, J. (1988). *Spiders and flies: Help for parents and teachers of sexually abused children*. San Francisco: New Lexington Press.

Hoff, L. A. (1990). *Battered women as survivors*. London: Routledge.

Hoff, L. A. (In press). *Violence and abuse issues: Cross-cultural perspectives for health and social services*. London: Routledge.

Hoff, L. A. (2000). Interpersonal violence. In C. E. Koop, C. E. Pearson, & M. R. Schwartz (Eds.), *Critical issues in global health* (pp. 260–271). San Francisco: Jossey-Bass.

Hoff, L. A., & Morgan, V. (In press). *Psychiatric & mental health essentials in primary care*.

Hoff, L. A., & Rosenbaum, L. (1994). A victimization assessment tool: Instrument development and clinical implications. *Journal of Advanced Nursing, 20*(4), 627–634.

Holmstrom, L. L., & Burgess, A. W. (1978). *The victim of rape: Institutional reaction*. New York: Wiley.

Humphreys, J. (1998). Helping battered women take care of their children. In J. C. Campbell (Ed.), *Empowering survivors of abuse: Health care for battered women and their children* (pp. 121–137). Thousand Oaks, CA: Sage.

Hyman, I., Forte, T., Du Mont, J., Romans, S., & Cohen, M. M. (2006). The association between length of stay in Canada and intimate partner violence among immigrant women. *American Journal of Public Health, 96*(4), 654–659.

Jang, D., Lee, D., & Morello-Frosch, R. (1991). Domestic violence in the immigrant and refugee community: Responding to the needs of immigrant women. *Response to the Victimization of Women and Children, 13*(4), 2–7.

Johnson, H. (1998). Rethinking survey research on violence against women. In R. E. Dobash & R. P. Dobash (Eds.), *Rethinking violence against women* (pp. 23–51). Thousand Oaks, CA: Sage.

Jones, A. (1980). *Women who kill*. Austin, TX: Holt, Rinehart and Winston.

Kempe, H., & Helfer, R. E. (Eds.). (1980). *The battered child* (3rd ed.). Chicago: University of Chicago Press.

Korbin, J. E. (1987, July). *Fatal child maltreatment*. Paper presented at the Third National Conference on Family Violence, Durham, NH.

Kurz, E. (1993). Physical assaults by husbands: A major social problem. In R. J. Gelles & D. R. Loseke (Eds.), *Current controversies on family violence* (pp. 88–103). Thousand Oaks, CA: Sage.

Levinson, D. (1989). *Family violence in cross-cultural perspective*. Thousand Oaks, CA: Sage.

Levy, B. (1991). *Dating violence: Young women in danger*. Seattle: Seal Press.

London School of Hygiene and Tropical Medicine. (2003). The health risks and consequences of trafficking in women and adolescents. London: Author.

Long, N. J., & Wilder, M. T. (1993). From rage to responsibility: A massaging numb values life space interview. *Journal of Emotional and Behavioral Problems, 2*(1), 35–40.

Luhrmann, T. M. (2000). *Of two minds: The growing disorder in American psychiatry.* New York: Knopf.

MacLean, M. (Ed.). (1995). *Abuse and neglect of older Canadians.* Toronto: Thompson Educational Publishing.

Mawby, R. I., & Walklate, S. (1994). *Critical victimology.* London: Sage.

McDonald, P. L., Hornick, J. P., Robertson, G. B., & Wallace, J. E. (1991). *Elder abuse and neglect in Canada.* Toronto: Butterworths.

McEvoy, A., & Erickson, E. (1994). *Abused children: The educator's guide to prevention and intervention.* Holmes Beach, FL: Learning Publications.

McFarlane, J., Parker, B., Soeken, K., & Bullock, L. (1992). Assessing for abuse during pregnancy. Severity and frequency of injuries and associated entry into prenatal care. *Journal of the American Medical Association, 267*(23), 3176–3178.

Melillo, K. D. & Houde, S. C. (2005). *Geropsychiatric and mental health nursing.* Boston: Jones and Bartlett Publishers.

Miller, J. B, (1986). *Toward a new psychology of women* (Rev. ed.). Boston: Beacon Press.

Mills, C. W. (1959). *The sociological imagination.* Oxford: Oxford University Press.

Mirkin. M. P. (Ed.). (1994). *Women in context: Toward a feminist reconstruction of psychotherapy.* New York: Guilford Press.

Mones, P. (1993). Parricide: A window on child abuse. *Journal of Emotional and Behavioral Problems, 2*(1), 30–34.

Newberger, E. (1980). *New approaches needed to control child abuse.* Presented before the Subcommittee on Select Education of the Committee on Education and Labor. Washington, DC: U.S. House of Representatives.

NiCarthy, G. (1989). *You can be free: An easy-to-read handbook for abused women.* Seattle: Seal Press.

Ompad, D. C., Ikeda, R. M., Shah, N., Fuller, C. M., Bailey, S., & Morse, E. (2005). Childhood sexual abuse and age at initiation of injection drug use. *American Journal of Public Health, 95*(4).

PAHO/WHO [Pan American Health Organization/World Health Organization]. (2003). *Violence against women: The health sector responds.* Washington, DC: Author.

Pence, E., & Paymar, M. (1986). *Power and control: Tactics of men who batter.* Duluth: Minnesota Program Development.

Perilla, J. L. (1999). Domestic violence as a human rights issue: The case of immigrant Latinos. *Hispanic Journal of Behavioral Sciences, 21*(2), 107–133.

Pillemer, K. A., & Finkelhor, D. (1987). *The prevalence of elder abuse: A random survey.* Durham, NC: Family Violence Research Program.

Pillemar, K. A., & Wolf, D. (1986). *Elder abuse: Conflict in the family.* Westport, CT: Auburn House.

Powers, J., & Jaklitsch, B. (1989). *Understanding survivors of abuse: Stories of homeless and runaway adolescents.* San Francisco: New Lexington Press.

Raj, A., & Silverman, J. G. (2003). Immigrant South Asian women at greater risk for injury from intimate partner violence. *American Journal of Public Health, 93*(3), 435–438.

Renzetti, C. M. (1992). *Violent betrayal: Partner abuse in lesbian relationships.* Thousand Oaks, CA: Sage.

Report: U.S. Department of Health and Human Services. (1986). *Surgeon General's workshop on violence and public health.* Washington, DC: Author.

Rivera, C. (1995, April 26). U.S. child abuse report declares health crisis. *Boston Globe*, p. 3.

Rodriguez, M. A., McLoughlin, E., Nah, G., & Campbell, J. C. (2001). Mandatory reporting of domestic violence injuries to the police: What do Emergency Department patients think? *Journal of the American Medical Association, 286*(5), 580–583.

Ross, M. (2001). *Nursing education and violence prevention, detection, and intervention: Report.* Ottawa: Health Canada, Family Violence Prevention Unit.

Russell, D. E. H. (1986). *Secret trauma: Incest in the lives of girls and women.* New York: Basic Books.

Ryan, W. (1971). *Blaming the victim.* New York: Vintage Books.

Rynearson, E. K. (Ed.). (2006). *Violent death: Resilience and intervention beyond the crisis.* New York: Routledge.

Sanders, S. (2008). *Understanding personal resilience.* New York: Routledge.

Saunders, C. I. (1999). Finding a better way. *Boston Sunday Globe*, pp. D1–D2.

Saylors, K., & Daliparthy, N. (2006). Violence against native women in substance abuse treatment. American Indian and Alaska Native mental health research. *Journal of the National Center, 13*(1), 32–51.

Schechter, S. (1982). *Women and male violence.* Boston: South End Press.

Segal, L. (1999). *Why Feminism? Gender, Psychology, Politics.* New York: Columbia University Press.

Sennott, C. M. (1999, April 18). For Kosovo's children of war, the wounds of trauma run deep. *Boston Sunday Globe*, pp. A1, A31.

Socolovsky, J. (2000, April 26). Rape victim testifies against Serb soldiers. *Boston Globe*, p. A17.

Soeken, K. L., McFarlane, J., Parker, B., & Lominack, M. C. (1998). The abuse assessment screen: A clinical instrument to measure frequency, severity, and perpetrator of abuse against women. In J. C. Campbell (Ed.), *Empowering survivors of abuse: Health care for battered women and their children* (pp. 195–203). Thousand Oaks, CA: Sage.

Sommers, T., & Shields, L. (1987). *Women take care: The consequences of caregiving in today's society.* Gainesville, FL: Triad.

Stark, E., & Flitcraft, A. (1996). *Women at risk: Domestic violence and women's health.* Thousand Oaks, CA: Sage.

Stark, E., Flitcraft, A., & Frazier, W. (1979). Medicine and patriarchal violence: The social construction of a "private" event. *International Journal of Health Services, 9*, 461–493.

Stephens, B. J. (1985). Suicidal women and their relationships with husbands, boyfriends, and lovers. *Suicide & Life-Threatening Behavior, 15*(2), 77–90.

Stephens, D. L. (1999). Battered women's views of their children. *Journal of Interpersonal Violence, 14*(7), 731–746.

Straus, M. A. (1993). Physical assaults by wives: A major social problem. In R. J. Gelles & D. R. Loseke (Eds.), *Current controversies on family violence* (pp. 67–87). Thousand Oaks, CA: Sage.

Straus, M. A., Gelles, R. J., & Steinmetz, S. K. (1980). *Behind closed doors: Violence in the American family.* New York: Anchor Books.

Sugg, N. K., & Inui, T. (1992). Primary care physicians' response to domestic violence: Opening Pandora's box. *Journal of the American Medical Association, 267*(23), 3157–3160.

Sussex, B., & Corcoran, K. (2005) The impact of domestic violence on depression in teen mothers: Is the fear or threat of violence sufficient? *Brief Treatment and Crisis Intervention, 5*, 109–120.

Taylor, L., Zuckerman, B., Harik, V., & Groves, B. M. (1994). Witnessing violence by young children and their mothers. *Developmental and Behavioral Pediatrics, 15*(2), 120–123.

Thornhill, R., & Palmer, C. (2000). *A natural history of rape.* Cambridge, MA: MIT Press.

Tilden, V. P., Schmidt, T. A., Limandri, B. J., Chiodo, G. T., Garland, M. J., & Loveless, P. A. (1994). Factors that influence clinicians' assessment and management of family violence. *American Journal of Public Health, 84*(4), 628–633.

United Nations. (1996a). *Report on the world's women 1995: Trends and statistics.* New York: Author.

United Nations. (1996). *The Beijing declaration and the platform for action.* New York: Author.

VandeCreek, L., & Knapp, S. (1993). *Tarasoff and beyond: Legal and clinical considerations in the treatment of life-endangering patients* (Rev. ed.). Sarasota, FL: Professional Resource Press.

van der Kolk, B. A. (1987). *Psychological trauma.* Washington, DC: American Psychiatric Press.

Walker, H. M. (1993). Anti-social behavior in school. *Journal of Emotional and Behavioral Problems, 2*(1), 20–24.

Warshaw, C. (1989). Limitations of the medical model in the care of battered women. *Gender and Society, 3*(4), 506–517.

Warshaw, D. (1988). *I never called it rape.* New York: HarperCollins.

Wen, P. (2005, January 10). Sale of spanking tool points up larger issue. *Boston Globe,* p. B1, B4.

Wiehe, V. R. (1998). *Understanding family violence: Treating and preventing partner, child, sibling, and elder abuse.* Thousand Oaks, CA: Sage.

Wiehe, V. R., & Richards, A. L. (1995). *Intimate betrayal.* Thousand Oaks, CA: Sage.

Wilson, J. P. (Ed.) (2006). *The posttraumatic elf: Restoring meaning and wholeness to personality.* New York: Routledge.

Yllo, K., & Bograd, M. (Eds.). (1987). *Feminist perspectives on wife abuse.* Thousand Oaks, CA: Sage.

Zolotor, A. J., Theodore, A. D., Coyne-Beasley, T., & Runyan, D. K. (2007), Intimate partner violence and child maltreatment: Overlapping risk. *Brief Treatment and Crisis Intervention 7*, 305–321.

危機 CHAPTER 12

The Violent or Abusive Person
Individual and Sociocultural Factors

The theoretical overview in Chapter 11 introduced the concept of a continuum between violence against intimates and family members and the violence pervading the larger sociocultural milieu. Thus, violence against intimate partners is no longer regarded as a private matter between the couple but is now recognized as a major public health issue. One of the reasons for connecting what happens behind closed doors to the public domain is to avoid transferring the legacy of individual victim blaming to the level of family blaming. As noted in the last chapter, much personal misery can be traced to family dynamics, neglect, and patterns of harsh discipline or outright abuse and violence. But families do not exist in a social or cultural vacuum. In families, children absorb values from their parents that support aggression and violence as solutions to problems. The parents' behavior has been reinforced by policies and media celebrations that nourish, if they do not outrightly condone, aggression as a norm in social life.

Aggression and Violence: A Contextual versus Adversarial Approach

An axiom of victims' rights organizations is that victims deserve the same justice as their accusers and assailants, as amply supported in the last chapter. Yet in addition to academic debates about "family" versus "feminist" research, there are polarizations, even within advocacy and feminist communities, that do not advance the common goal of reducing violence and caring for victims. For example, women are portrayed *either* as victims *or* as having "made it" on equal terms with men. Of course, many women have made it, but the fact remains that millions of women worldwide are victimized and most of the assailants are men (PAHO/WHO [Pan American Health Organization/World Health Organization], 2003).

This chapter focuses on the perpetrators of violence and abuse—the crises of assailants and their sociocultural underpinnings—and suggests that attention to perpetrators forms part of a comprehensive program to reduce violence. Some would argue that programs for perpetrators deflect from the more urgent need of refuge for victims. Violence is a major public health problem as well as a criminal justice issue. At worst, an either/or position damages both victim-survivors and assailants; at best, it constitutes empty polemics. It is therefore not a question of whether we (1) *either* provide refuge and care for battered women *or* provide treatment programs for their batterers, (2) *either* hold parents accountable for the violent and abusive behavior of their children *or* offer parent effectiveness training and socioeconomic support to parents unduly burdened with the task of parenting, or (3) *either* teach inner-city youth anger management skills *or* address the sociocultural and economic roots of their anger. Essentially, either/or debates are adversarial and reflect the power component of violence itself. These counterproductive arguments have surfaced anew just as progress has appeared in respect to understanding male violence (Adams, 2007). Criminal justice and mental health professionals argue about who should direct programs for violent and abusive men. The question of whether such programs should be directed *either* by criminal justice professionals *or* by mental health professionals is another either/or argument that usually goes nowhere (Bennett & Piet, 1999).

From the perspective of health and human service providers who deal with such crises, it is clear that a contextual *both/and* approach offers more than an either/or polarity. A long history of human service organizations reveals that when staff members are divided along ideological and programmatic lines, clients are the ones who suffer the most severe consequences by falling through system cracks. As staff members thus "drop the ball" on difficult questions, almost always they will be picking it up later in a vicious cycle of client recidivism for failing to work toward consensus on controversial issues and postcrisis social service planning. One group cannot do everything; a particular discipline or person cannot be all things to all survivors or perpetrators of abuse. But greater coordination could mend some of the serious systemic problems that can trigger repeat or new crisis responses. And in the case of violence and victimization, the life-and-death consequences as well as the long-term health, financial, and social consequences are enormous in both human and financial terms.

Sociocultural, Criminal Justice, Crisis Theory, and Public Health Perspectives

Violence has historically been a concern primarily of police and specialized psychiatric and crisis personnel. Indeed, most research on assessing risk of violence has focused on psychiatrically disturbed persons presumed as the main perpetrators of violence (Monahan & Steadman, 1994). The idea of a mental illness–violence link is deeply embedded in U.S. popular culture and international media coverage of horrifying violence such as school shootings and the September 11, 2001 terrorist attacks. Readers are referred to the extensive Internet and scientific journal accounts of these highly publicized acts of public violence and death.

Here the focus is a brief overview of what is already known about suicide and other violence, and what can be relearned about the mental health–crime interface and the place of prevention at individual, community, and institutional levels. The Virginia Tech and 9/11 events are highlighted in illustrating basic principles of risk assessment and crisis care, plus the dangers of either overlooking obvious clues to distress or interpreting political action as "psychopathology." The intent is not to blame, but to heed Santayana's adage: "Those who do not know history are doomed to repeat it," or this Arab piece of wisdom: "Fortunate are those who learn from others' mistakes; unfortunate are those who must learn from their own mistakes." Yet despite our best knowledge, skills, and intentions, the prevention of violence is fraught with privacy and civil rights issues, plus the indisputable fact that we may never be able to plumb the motives of some people who first kill others, then themselves.

Virginia Tech and School Violence

On April 16, 2007, a 23-year-old Virginia Tech student killed two students in a dormitory, then killed 30 more (mostly students) 2 hours later in a classroom building. His suicide brought the death toll to 33, making the shooting rampage the worst of its kind in U.S. history. Here is a brief summary of what was already known and might have prevented these deaths:

- Over some period of time, the student shooter provided e-mail and other clues to his distress. Although fellow students reached out to him, adults and classmates apparently did not know how to take further steps in response to his clues of loneliness and distress. Significantly, it was the student's creative writing teacher who sensed most accurately this student's distress. Yet systematic information and frontline action plans for crisis response are not routinely made available to faculty members who are not crisis or mental health professionals.
- He had been psychologically evaluated, revealing "mental health" problems. After one episode of psychiatric treatment, he was discharged with mental health professionals' estimate of no suicidal or homicidal danger, and no formal follow-up care.
- Despite the student's psychiatric history, he was easily able to purchase guns over the Internet with no background checks or constraints on these purchases.
- Nationwide, colleges and universities have instituted tighter police security measures and immediate notification to student bodies of potential danger. Yet college communities are vulnerable to results of national policies regarding easy availability of guns, and a culture of "reaction" after the fact versus comprehensive prevention and crisis care programs that often take second place in identification and follow-up of students in distress or crisis.
- In a comparable situation of a failing student threatening (through the Internet) murder of the faculty member in response to his grade, the

frightened teacher was ignored through various chains of reporting. Since this student was in fact failing all his courses, the apparent assumption was this: He will soon be "out of here" and then he will be someone else's problem. But since colleges are not impregnable fortresses—nor should they be in a "free" society—there seems little awareness that this failure to offer counseling and career advice for such students might result in a student returning to campus in murderous revenge.

■ Suicidology and crisis experts have long known that threats of suicide following murder (plus for some, a history of being physically abused and/or bullied) increase the risk of dangerousness to others. Yet this knowledge and need for systematic incorporation of life-threatening risk assessment into routine health and mental health protocols has yet to reach many primary care and other health providers (see Chapters 3, 9 and 11).[1]

September 11, 2001: Understanding and Pathologizing Violence

It is one thing to recognize the interface between violence and a particular individual's personal turmoil and psychic pain. On the other hand, a university professor offers this dramatic example of the deep-seated tendency to interpret political and culturally tinged violence as evidence of psychopathology.

In a graduate class on politics and culture in health affairs on September 12, 2001, the teacher facilitated student discussion of the attack, their fears, and attempts to make meaning of the event, much as many American people asked, "Why do they hate us so much?" (A few years later, survivors of the London and Madrid transit bombings asked similar questions.) The grief and psychological pain was almost palpable. One student, trying to grapple with the enormity and rarity of such an event on American soil, said: "I can only think that at the moment of impact [on the World Trade Center] they lost their minds... they were insane."

Fellow students and the teacher were stunned at this analysis. The gently led discussion concluded as follows:

1. It is something of an affront to all persons with diagnosable mental illness to suggest that the pilots whose own lives ended along with the victims were psychotic. That is, psychosis by definition includes serious impairment of normal cognitive and emotional functioning, which also affects behavior. The attackers met none of these criteria. Rather, they systematically planned and prepared for the attack over time, including obtaining legitimate U.S. visas and taking lessons in U.S.-licensed schools for flying jet aircraft. The night before, they stayed outside of Boston, presumably to avoid detection, their planned site for flight

---

[1] Researchers and university Student Affairs personnel are invited to contact the author regarding collaboration in further use of a pilot-tested survey tool on student stress and crisis providing a database for planning crisis prevention, intervention, and mental health services for college students. See Online Resources.

takeoff from Logan International Airport. Such deliberately planned and carefully executed actions are not typical of psychotic persons.

2. Violence in most instances is a conscious action directed toward exerting power and control, which is contrary to some popular conceptions. This case and those in London and Madrid are examples of "holy war" or what some describe as a "clash of civilizations" rooted in many earlier "holy wars" such as the medieval Crusades.

3. These global, mostly religious-based clashes are extensively addressed elsewhere and are beyond the scope of this book, except to note research (Friedman, 2006) that the presumed "sea of psychotic violence" is clearly unfounded (Pies, 2008).

4. Unfortunately, the question "Why do they hate us so much?" is afforded much less attention than more wars in response, resulting in many thousands more deaths and the untold suffering of millions. Such deaths and widespread suffering could be avoided if diplomacy were valued more, and if the everyday person and leaders attended to this lesson from research and crisis care on intimate partner violence: *Violence as a response to violence begets more violence.* (See Chapter 4, communication in crisis prevention and resolution.)

Violence and Abuse in the Workplace and Forensic Psychiatry

One of the first principles in crisis work is safety—for ourselves, our clients, significant others, and the general public. Moving from the global to everyday work life, violence as an occupational health hazard has gained public attention (Casteel et al., 2007; Levin, Hewitt, & Misner, 1992; Lipscomb & Love, 1992; Merchant & Lundell, 2001). Police officers, health, mental health, crisis, and other workers make up a special category of victims. Among women who died as a result of workplace trauma, 41% were homicide victims (Jenkins, Layne, & Kisner, 1992). The killing of police officers is particularly demoralizing and frightening because it shows disrespect for the very people dedicated to ensuring public safety. The issue is compounded when officers are victims of violence but there is no certainty that a crime has been committed. This potentially dangerous situation in crisis work embroils us in the controversial relationship between crime and mental illness (forensic psychiatry) (Pies, 2008). Despite numerous debates on this topic, the distinctions between crime and mental illness are blurred with respect to life crises and our response to them; police, security personnel, and other workers are often caught in the middle. With greater skills in applying risk assessment knowledge in the workplace, many instances of workers' injuries from violence might be avoided.

Mental patients are probably no more violent than they were in the past, and their rates of violence are comparable to those of the general public (Friedman, 2006). Yet nurses and others may be getting hurt more often by patients who should never have been admitted to a mental health facility in the first place. This assertion is based on overwhelming evidence that life is becoming increasingly medicalized. Nowhere are the consequences of medicalization potentially more dangerous than when this social trend is applied to violent behavior; for example, when a violent criminal is classified as mentally ill and assigned to medical rather than penal supervision. Research findings (Melick et al., 1979, p. 235) during early phases of community mental health development in the state of New York are still relevant today: "The reason that a case does not reach trial [for criminal justice versus mental health dispositions] probably has as much to do with the strength of the prosecutor's case as it does with the mental state of the defendant."

The medicalization of crime may also be related to overcrowded prisons and empty mental hospitals, conditions that have been created through the process of deinstitutionalization (Johnson, 1990). The replacement of state-owned space in mental hospitals by private hospital psychiatric units, buttressed by managed care and support of the biomedical approach to treatment (Luhrmann, 2000), exacerbates the argument for medicalizing criminal behavior. But apart from the public debate on this topic, health professionals and others should critically examine the trend to interpret life's problems in an "illness" framework (Hoff, 1993). For example, it is still common to refer to a man who has sexually molested dozens or even hundreds of children as "sick," despite a record of stellar job performance and stable family life.

It is certainly true that some people who commit crimes are mentally deranged, therefore entitling them to leniency before the law. Many insanity pleas, however, leave much room for doubt. Insanity is a *legal*, not a mental health, concept. Our difficulties in dealing with this issue in the United States are complicated by a criminal justice system that often denies a decent standard of treatment to criminals. The humanitarian impulse of most people is to spare even a violent person an experience that seems beyond the just desserts of the crime. It is paradoxical, then, that the tendency to treat a person rather than hold him or her responsible for violent behavior exists in concert with the movement to assert the rights of mental patients (Capponi, 1992). We cannot have it both ways. One cannot, on the one hand, exercise the freedom to reject treatment and hospitalization for behavioral disorders and, on the other hand, plead temporary insanity when one then fails to control violent impulses and commits a crime (or in psychiatric settings, assaults a staff member who may or may not press criminal charges). The following cases illustrate this point, as well as the need for mental health and health professionals to examine their misplaced guilt feelings when they hold clients accountable for their violent behavior.

Case Example: Connie

Connie, age 51, was being treated in a private psychiatric facility for a drinking problem and depression following a divorce. A mental status examination revealed that Connie was mentally competent and not suffering from delusions or other thought disorders, though she was very angry about her husband's decision to divorce her because of her drinking problem. When Connie, therefore, decided to check out of the residential treatment facility against medical advice, there was no basis for confining her involuntarily, according to any interpretation of the state's mental health laws. A discharge planning conference was held, at which follow-up therapy sessions were arranged through a special program for alcoholic women. Connie failed to keep her counseling appointments. One week after leaving the psychiatric unit, Connie attempted to demolish her former husband's car by crashing her own car into it. She endangered the lives of other people by driving on sidewalks, where pedestrians successfully managed to escape her fury. Connie was arrested and taken to jail. Two mental health professionals involved with her case were called to testify. The defense attorney was incredulous that the mental health professionals (both female) did not plead with the judge to commit Connie to a mental health facility rather than to jail. The judge clearly seemed to prefer committing Connie to the psychiatric unit where she had been treated but was assured (against the protests of the defense attorney) that her mental status and physical capacity provided no basis on which to keep her from being a further menace to society.

Case Example: Eric

Eric, age 28, was employed but distressed over interpersonal relationships on the job. He came to a group therapy session, and shortly after the session began, he got up and swung his clenched fists, first at one of the therapists. Then he swung at other clients, while making threatening statements. Eric had apparently had something to drink, as the smell of alcohol was on his breath. But as he swung his fists at people, he seemed very controlled; he came just an inch or so from their noses. The therapists and other clients were unable to persuade Eric to stop his violent, threatening behavior and therefore called the police. Eric was taken to the nearby jail. The senior therapist meanwhile, feeling overwhelmed with guilt about her client being in jail, reviewed the mental health laws to ascertain grounds for having Eric transferred from jail to a mental health facility. She reported the incident to the executive director (a psychiatrist) and explored with him the idea of having Eric committed for treatment. The psychiatrist replied, "Treated for what? Threatening you and the other clients?" The therapist revised some of her traditional ideas about "treating" people for violent behavior rather than holding them accountable for it.

These cases suggest a spillover of violence from home to workplace, as well as its sociocultural context. A biomedical versus public health response to workplace violence may help perpetuate the problem if the larger social ramifications of the issue remain unaddressed. Obviously, this takes us well beyond the individual crisis worker's responsibility. Yet our safety in the work setting and our common humanity in a violent society demand such a two-pronged approach to this serious issue (see Arnetz & Arnetz, 2001).

As noted regarding danger assessment discussed later in this chapter, too often the signs of impending assault or homicide are either not recognized or are ignored until it is too late, as documented in widely publicized massacres at schools and worksites. Crisis- and violence-prevention specialists should extend their expertise to human resource personnel in public and private institutions. The layperson needs to know that murder does not occur in a cultural or social vacuum; it does not "just happen." Rather, it is planned, although impulse may play a part. The humane treatment of workers when delivering news of discipline or layoff is another violence-prevention measure needing attention, if for no other reason than self-interest. Some fired workers who are treated like criminals—whatever the reason for job termination—come back to terrorize their former workplace with all-too available guns or explosives.

Fortunately, the days of assaulted health workers having to absorb their injury and emotional trauma as "part of the job" appear to be coming to an end (O'Sullivan et al., 2008). Research has uncovered the relationship of workplace injury to gender, race, and class factors, as well as to the work environment itself—for example, inadequate staffing and lack of structured supervisor support. Guidelines from the Occupational Safety & Health Administration and labor union action portend the prospect of redressing the neglect of many victimized workers who have been largely on their own in the process of recovering from the trauma of such mostly preventable violence (Jenkins et al., 1992; Levin et al., 1992; Lipscomb & Love, 1992; Miller, 1999; Rosen, 2001; Runyan, 2001).

Crisis Intervention Training

As we consider the question of why crisis workers and others are injured, killed, or threatened on the job, the focus in this section is not on what to do if attacked, but on why known crisis intervention strategies are not used or why they may be ineffective. Research by Melick, Steadman, and Cocozza (1979) suggests that three factors are related to this issue that are still relevant today: (1) the lack of crisis intervention training, (2) the widespread absence of appropriate collaboration among police, hospital security personnel, and mental health professionals, and (3) the social trend toward the medicalization of life's problems.

Several strategies could reduce the hazard of workplace violence: (1) routine application of danger assessment techniques, (2) implementation of the principles and strategies for creating a therapeutic milieu, and (3) use of social network techniques and community-based services to defuse highly anxious and hostile behavior by nonchemical means (Cowan et al., 2003; Dyches et al., 2002). Staff members in these highly charged situations also need to reserve time and energy for considering the impact of managed care policies on treatment of the seriously and persistently mentally ill. Some of the results of these policies include the current focus on pharmacological treatment and very brief hospital care and the reduced staffing by skilled professionals; in response, staff may then resort to more authoritarian approaches to disruptive behavior, which in turn escalates tension and violence potential among patients.

It is true that the standards of crisis intervention training among health and mental health workers are far from being met. Years ago the American Association of Suicidology recommend a minimum of 40 hours of training for all frontline and specialty crisis workers—nurses, physicians, police, and mental health professionals (Hoff & Wells, 1989). While the level of exposure to risk is relatively stable, and many workers have had some crisis intervention training, there appears to be more work-related violence, and a health or mental health professional could be a paragon of perfection in crisis intervention practice and still be injured or killed on the job. Why?

Traditionally, nurses and psychiatric professionals have been taught that if they are hurt by mentally disturbed people, it is probably because they missed cues to rising anxiety levels or they antagonized or otherwise dealt inappropriately with the disturbed person. For example, when mental health professionals use chemical or physical restraint before trying time-tested interpersonal approaches, retaliative attacks on the staff are often the result. As already noted, mental health and criminal justice professionals have worked to dispel the myth that all mental patients are dangerous; only a small percentage are. Psychiatric facilities usually have precise protocols for preventing and responding to violence among mental patients. Police procedures are also precise and comprehensive. A basic principle in both disciplines is to avoid force and physical restraint except for protecting oneself and others. This interpretation is strongly supported by Bard's (1972) precedent-setting research and subsequent training for New York City (NYC) police officers. The number of NYC police injuries and deaths on the job were significantly reduced as a result of the application of crisis intervention techniques and tightening linkages with mental health professionals, especially in family disturbance calls. These techniques have been expanded to deal with terrorists through hostage negotiation strategies.

Details of hostage negotiation are beyond the scope of this book or the skills expected of an ordinary crisis worker. The highly sophisticated developments in this field, however, point to the importance of collaborative use of knowledge between police and behavioral science fields in responding to certain crises. Everyone who is even remotely involved with hostage situations—such as when a mentally ill relative holds a child hostage and threatens to commit murder and then suicide if a rescue is attempted—must recognize that offers by civilians to "handle him because I know him better than anyone" can backfire and need thorough investigation. Even police officers chosen for hostage negotiation are carefully screened on several counts, including their professional success in handling general crisis situations. Everyone should also be familiar with ways to reduce the chances of injury or murder. Crisis intervention alone is not enough to prevent violence. Another critical aspect of preventing victimization concerns collaboration between police and mental health professionals, especially when the boundaries of these institutions overlap (Baracos, 1974). The example later in the chapter involving Arthur illustrates the tragic results of failure in such collaboration.

Assessing for Risk of Dangerousness, Assault, and Homicide

As emphasized in Chapter 3, crisis intervention training includes assessment for risk of assault and homicide. As in the case of suicide risk assessment, there is no absolute prediction of homicide risk. The topic itself is highly controversial; Monahan (1981, p. 6), for example, cites three criticisms regarding prediction in forensic work:

1. It is empirically impossible to predict violent behavior.
2. If such activity could be forecast and averted, it would, as a matter of policy, violate the civil liberties of those whose activity is predicted.
3. Even if accurate prediction were possible without violating civil liberties, psychiatrists and psychologists should decline to do it because it is a social control activity at variance with their professional helping role.

Whereas prediction of violence is an issue in forensic work, *assessment of violence potential* can be a matter of life or death in domestic, occupational, and clinical settings. The clinical assessment of risk for dangerousness, assault, and homicide is an inherent aspect of police officers' and health and crisis workers' jobs. And the average citizen is always calculating safety maneuvers when in known risk areas. This is not the same as making an official prediction of risk as part of the court-requested psychiatric or psychological examination of persons who are detained for crimes and who plead insanity (Halleck, 1987). Although assessment of dangerousness by crisis workers is far from an exact science, health and social service workers do not have to rely *only* on their experience or guesswork. As one hospital trainer put it: "There's nothing out there [but my own experience]." Unfortunately, this person had no exposure to basic risk assessment strategies from either formal or in-service education programs. This individual is relying on "guesswork" instead of drawing on crisis, psychiatric, and criminal justice theory and organized data gained through skilled communication with at-risk clients and significant others (see Hoptman et al., 1999; Monahan & Steadman, 1994). Assessment should be based on principles and data, not merely on guesswork.

Based on Monahan's (1981) research, risk assessment criteria include:

1. *Statistics*, for example, men between the ages of 18 and 34 commit a much higher percentage of violent crimes than older men or women of any age. Statistical indicators, however, should be viewed with the same caution as they are in suicide risk assessment (see Chapter 9).
2. *Personality factors*, including motivation, aggression, inhibition, and habit. For example, once a habit of response to upsets by verbal threats and physical force is established, it lays a foundation for further, potentially lethal violence.
3. *Situational factors*, such as availability of a weapon or behavior of the potential victim.
4. *The interactions* among these variables.

Toch (1969) claims that the *interaction* factor is a crucial influence on violence. There are several stages in the interactional process. First, the potential victim is classified as an object or a potential threat—essentially, a dehumanization process. Based on this classification, some action follows, after which the potential victim may make a self-protective move. Whether or not violence occurs depends on the interaction of such variables as the effectiveness of the victim's self-protection or the would-be attacker's interpretation of resistance as an "ego" threat demanding retaliation. Establishing a bond, therefore, between victim and attacker can counteract dehumanization and thus serve to prevent an attack, although that strategy should not be relied on in all cases. This is the basis for a widely held principle in crisis intervention and hostage negotiation: *time* and keeping *communication* channels open (rather than precipitous action, taunts, or threats) are to the benefit of the negotiator and can save the lives of victims, terrorists, and suicidal persons.

Clearly, assessing danger is no simple matter, but lives can be saved by taking seriously the fact that only potentially dangerous people make threats of assault or homicide. A careful read of newspaper accounts of murders reveals, almost invariably, verbal and other cues by the assailant that were either ignored or misinterpreted as not being serious. Thorough training in crisis assessment and intervention is paramount, therefore, for professionals and others who work with disturbed or potentially violent people. This includes always inquiring about the *meaning* of verbal threats that too many times are dismissed by family, friends, and associates. Health and social service providers should educate their clients and the general public about this safety issue.

Case Example: Margie

Margie, age 35, had filed for divorce on the grounds of her husband's jealousy and abusive behavior. In the parking lot where she worked, he took her hostage and threatened to first kill her and then himself. As Margie's estranged husband, armed with a revolver, drove her across the state for several hours, she accommodated his desire to "talk," to the point that he trusted her when she asked to go to the ladies' room while they were in a restaurant. On her way to the restroom, she was able to whisper her plight to a waitress, who quickly called the police. As she cowered beneath a stairwell, the police arrested her husband at the restaurant table. The time and communication principle that Margie so astutely applied most likely saved her life.

Case Example: Arthur

A mentally disturbed man, Arthur, age 61, was brought to a hospital emergency department by two police officers for psychiatric examination at the request of his wife. Arthur had a history of paranoid delusions and at this time was accusing his wife of infidelity, though he threatened no harm to her. Arthur's wife had committed him three times before when he refused to seek treatment. This time, as he was getting out of the car, Arthur grabbed one officer's gun and shot him. The other officer in turn shot Arthur, who died instantly. The police officer died a few hours later. Although Arthur had a history of mental disturbance, he had no lethal weapons at the time of the police investigation. It was also learned after the deaths that this man's history of mental disturbance had never included violence, although he did get very angry each time his wife had him hospitalized.

Arthur's case suggests that if police officers had not been required to perform the tasks of mental health professionals—assessing danger and performing crisis intervention with an acutely disturbed mental patient—two deaths might have been avoided. As it was, the community in which this double tragedy occurred had no mobile crisis outreach capacity. The same situation prevails in other communities, to the point that police, by default, often perform the high-risk mental health work that should be carried out in collaborative arrangements with mental health professionals. Many officers resent this situation, and with justification, as mental health professionals are often unavailable for such collaboration with police in cases such as Arthur's. If mobile crisis outreach teams are not available, police officers should have 24-hour access to telephone consultation regarding mental patients. Such arrangements between police and mental health professionals skilled in crisis intervention should exist in every community (see Online Resources). The need has become more urgent because of managed care and deinstitutionalization of mental patients, often with inadequate community support (Earley, 2006; Hoff, 1993; Johnson, 1990). Mental patients are at great risk for all sorts of crises, often with no one available to help but police officers.

In addition, crisis intervention training for police should be routine. Some officers may resist such training, claiming that a police officer should spend more time preventing crime. However, 80% of an average officer's time is spent in service or domestic calls. Ignoring this reality is foolhardy and can cost officers' lives. In England, where police officers are not armed, and gun availability to laypersons is much more stringently controlled than in the United States, the "service" orientation of officers is more easily promulgated and upheld (Sully, 2000).

Even if officers are not physically injured in hostage or other crisis situations, they and their families can suffer psychological trauma that may require weeks or months for recovery. Reactions similar to those of disaster victims are common (see Chapter 13). Recognizing these reactions and the need for support, the FBI and police departments are making special services available to officers who are involved in shooting and other highly traumatic incidents.

When the indicators of dangerousness described in Table 12.1 and the assessment tool described in Chapter 3 were introduced routinely in crisis and counseling clinics in western New York, staff were astounded at how many clients were entertaining violent fantasies. But crisis workers in that public mental health system also noted the clients' openness to receiving help in dealing with their anger and violent impulses. The next section discusses

TABLE 12.1 Assault and Homicidal Danger Assessment Tool

Key to Danger	Immediate Dangerousness to Others	Typical Indicators
1	No predictable risk of assault or homicide	Has no assaultive or homicidal ideation, urges, or history of same; basically satisfactory support system; social drinker only
2	Low risk of assault or homicide	Has occasional assault or homicidal ideation (including paranoid ideas) with some urges to kill; no history of impulsive acts or homicidal attempts; occasional drinking bouts and angry verbal outbursts; basically satisfactory support system
3	Moderate risk of assault or homicide	Has frequent homicidal ideation and urges to kill but no specific plan; history of impulsive acting out and verbal outbursts while drinking, on other drugs, or otherwise; stormy relationship with significant others with periodic high-tension arguments
4	High risk of homicide	Has homicidal plan; obtainable means; history of substance abuse; frequent acting out against others, but no homicide attempts; stormy relationships and much verbal fighting with significant others, with occasional assaults
5	Very high risk of homicide	Has current high-lethal plan; available means; history of homicide attempts or impulsive acting out, plus feels a strong urge to control and "get even" with a significant other; history of serious substance abuse; also with possible high-lethal suicide risk

safety issues for police and crisis workers as well as criteria for such assessment, followed by elaboration of these themes with respect to three major categories of abusive and violent assailants: (1) the international increase in violence and antisocial behavior among young people; (2) violence and abuse in the workplace; and (3) programs for men who batter and emotionally abuse their female partners.

Besides their usefulness in standard criminal justice and police work, the criteria for assessing the degree of danger and the risk of assault apply in a number of situations:

1. In crisis, emergency, mental health, and forensic services
2. In the event that a worker is threatened with violence or is being taken hostage
3. In all domestic disputes

The third situation in this list would apply, for instance, when an abused woman is in imminent danger of being taken hostage or murdered. Such danger is heightened in relationships in which a man acts as though he owns his wife, as when he says, "If I can't have you, no one can." Most battered women are already aware of the danger they face, but for those who are not, for whatever reason, a crucial part of safety and crisis intervention planning for her includes a frank discussion of the potential for assault or homicide. While acknowledging that violent people can learn other ways, past violent behavior is still a powerful indicator of future behavior. And as the triage questions in Exhibit 11.1 (Chapter 11) indicate, routine screening for assault and homicide potential is gender neutral; therefore, the abused woman's own potential for assaulting or killing her assailant following abuse must also be ascertained.

Application of Assault and Homicide Risk Assessment Criteria

Translated into everyday practice, the following criteria are helpful as guidelines to assess the risk of assault or homicide:

- History of homicidal threats
- History of assault
- Current homicidal threats and plan, including information on the Internet
- Possession or easy availability of lethal weapons
- Use or abuse of alcohol or other drugs
- Conflict in significant social or clinical relationships—for example, infidelity, threat of divorce, labor–management disputes, authoritarian approaches to mental patients
- Threats of suicide following homicide

Assault and homicide risk assessment is illustrated in Table 12.1. This assessment is excerpted from the Comprehensive Mental Health Assessment tool presented in Chapter 3. Consider the case of Arthur (earlier in this chapter): Suppose that Arthur had been seen at home by two crisis outreach specialists and no guns were available. According to the criteria cited, Arthur was a low risk for assault or homicide, with a rating of 2 at most. His anxiety level increased as he was forcibly taken to a hospital; guns were available and the risk of homicide increased dramatically. It seems reasonable to suggest that both Arthur and the officer might be alive today if Arthur and his wife had the advantage of skilled crisis assessment and intervention from mental health professionals, preferably in their home. Similar dynamics can operate in psychiatric settings when a show of force is used before other measures are exhausted; staff members (most often nurses) risk being injured by mental patients who already feel disempowered by rigid hospital rules or forced chemical restraint. In Margie's case (earlier in this chapter), the homicide risk was very high, 5 on the scale, and the necessity of collaboration with police was obvious because the husband was armed.

The Crisis of Youth Violence

Aggressive, antisocial, and violent behavior among children and adolescents is gaining international attention. Overall crime rates in the United States and Western Europe have declined sharply for several years, while dramatic shootings by school children have captured international attention. Bullying and mobbing—usually child-on-child aggression—continue to create terror in schools and have even been associated with suicide (Hoover & Juul, 1993). Youth violence has moved parents, social scientists, journalists, legislators, and others to debate and deep soul-searching about the cultural climate and other factors that have spawned these tragedies. Research on bullying in Europe traces such behavior to a combination of factors in the home (for example, inconsistent discipline, abuse, alcohol), the school (more antisocial behavior in the worst schools), and the individual victims and perpetrators, underscoring this book's premise of the *interactional* character of aggression and its sequelae. Paralleling adult patterns, the majority of bullying and antisocial behavior is perpetrated by males against both males and females (Ellickson, Saner, & McGuigan, 1997; Hoover & Juul, 1993, p. 28; Walker, 1993, p. 21). As Sadker and Sadker (1994, p. 198) point out, however, families begin the process by raising boys according to the cultural ideal of being active, aggressive, and independent; schools inadvertently collude in rewarding their aggressiveness by "going the extra mile" with attention and resources for the nation's future male leaders, as destined by tradition.

Factors Contributing to Youth Violence

In the United States, behavioral specialists assert that antisocial behavior by children should be viewed as a national emergency. For example, young children who bring weapons to school today may become future school dropouts, batterers, and rapists. Given the cultural norms, perhaps the most surprising thing is that there is not more violence. As a paradoxical commentary on the influence (or failure?) of the women's movement, many young girls and women use their newly found "freedom" to adopt the aggressive, bullying, and violent norms of men, including arming themselves in the illusion of self-protection (Morgenstern, 1997; Webster, Vernick, Ludwig, & Lester, 1997; Wright, Wintemute, & Rivara, 1999). The incidence of violence by teenage girls is rising (one of every four juveniles arrested is female), although female rates of homicide are far behind those for boys (Buzawa & Buzawa, 1996; Chesney-Lind, 1997; Cotten et al., 1994). While some men are discovering the pleasures and growth potential of assuming the parenting and nurturing roles traditionally dominated by women, some women choose violence. They have yet to learn from the plight of battered women that violence begets more serious violence (Hoff, 1990). In their classic work, educators and youth workers Brendtro, Brokenleg, and Van Bockern (1990, pp. 6–7) trace the discouragement and alienation of youth at risk to four ecological hazards:

1. *Destructive relationships*, as experienced by the rejected or unclaimed child, who is hungry for love but unable to trust, and expects to be hurt again
2. *Climates of futility*, as encountered by the insecure youngster, crippled by feelings of inadequacy and a fear of failure

3. *Learned irresponsibility*, as seen in the youth whose sense of powerlessness may be masked by indifference or defiant, rebellious behavior
4. *Loss of purpose*, as portrayed by a generation of self-centered youth, desperately searching for meaning in a world of confusing values

These hazards are intertwined with contemporary parenting and family life—among poor families, inadequate time and resources for effective parenting; among some privileged families, excessive material indulgence and permissiveness that leave a child with few boundaries and skills to control behavior and a vacuum around life's larger meaning beyond consumerism (see Dubienski, 2008).

In the United States, in view of such factors as racism, the powerful gun lobby, and the pauperization of mothers who are raising children alone in an inequitable labor market, not only must "teachers, parents, and peers" (Walker, 1993, p. 23) influence antisocial children, but policymakers, church leaders, and all who care about the future of humanity must look "upstream" to discover why children are lost to violence and despair (DuRant, Cadenhead, Pendergast, Slavens, & Linder, 1994; Holinger, Offer, Barter, & Bell, 1994; Way, 1993; West, 1994). In a study of violence and recurrent trauma among young black men, Rich and Grey (2005) present a model with positive prospects of interrupting the pathway to repeated injuries by violence. As Marian Wright Edelman (1994, p. 6) said following a survey commissioned by the Children's Defense Fund and the Black Community Crusade, "This poll confirms what black leaders already know—that we have a major black child crisis, the worst since slavery."

In response to the crisis of youth violence, which is primarily sociocultural in origin, will we invent yet another medicalized explanation like "urban stress syndrome" to excuse assailants and neglect victims? Or will we examine social environments we have created or allowed to fester as a plague that threatens the lives of all who dwell there? Many youthful offenders have had no support in healing from childhood trauma (Holinger et al., 1994; Mendel, 1994). Our homes and schools have many untold numbers of children who have witnessed violence. Will people make connections among values (Dionne, 1999; Eyre & Eyre, 1993), the proliferation of guns, and the shocking increase of children killing children—and others?

Again, this is not an either/or dichotomy. Mitigating circumstances must be considered in judging individual cases, but excusing violent action does nothing to facilitate the growth and resiliency that distressed people, including alienated youth, are capable of when supported through crisis. Previous victimization by peers and/or parents are strong predictors of youth violence. Paul Mones (1993, p. 32), an attorney specializing in the defense of children who have killed their parents, notes that the most common trigger event before parricide is the child's despair after receiving no help when they finally report abuse to an adult. While facing the enormous challenge of youth violence, it is crucial to remember that we are *influenced* by our past, not *determined* by it. Further, with social support, individuals who have endured almost unimaginable cruelty have lived to tell their stories of endurance and survival.

Clearly, youth violence cuts across class, race, and gender boundaries. Despite continued disparity in educational and other resources between racial minority groups and the white majority, it is noteworthy that in the vast majority of recent school shooting tragedies, the assailants were white boys from a range of socioeconomic classes. These highly publicized instances of youth violence tend to obscure the statistical decline in youth crime rates, including school-based violence, over the past several years. But nonstatistical examination of these dramatic examples of youth violence reveals the complexity of factors influencing each case; in many instances, social alienation, bullying and harassment by classmates, and mental health problems were evident but not attended to with preventive measures such as recognizing and responding to the meaning of supposedly "idle" verbal threats or unusual behaviors.

Protective factors aiding in child resilience include extended family support networks, family connectedness, and family religious beliefs. Another protective factor is fostering schools and communities that care for and value all children, set high expectations for all, and invite active school and community participation. Together, these factors can assist alienated youth to change the path they are on.

Crisis Prevention and Intervention Programs

Despite the grim picture of youth violence, the tide may be turning; crisis intervention and anger management programs are being developed in many schools and special treatment settings for disturbed youth. Leona Eggert (1994), for example, has developed a guide for teachers, school nurses, and others working with adolescents and young adults. Fritz Redl developed the Massaging Numb Values Life Space Interview to help aggressive students, many with histories of abuse, who become overwhelmed with guilt and remorse about their destructive behavior (Long & Wilder, 1993). Holden and Powers (1993) describe a therapeutic crisis intervention program developed at Cornell University. The four phases in this model—*triggering, escalation, crisis,* and *recovery*—correspond roughly to the phases of crisis development originally put forth by Caplan (see Chapter 2), with a particular focus on observing behavioral cues in young people. At the institutional or ecological level, Watson, Poda, Miller, Rice, and West (1990) offer step-by-step guidelines to prevent and manage a range of school emergencies, including violence. Such ecological approaches include the active involvement of parents and the entire community to provide safety and a hopeful future for its most vulnerable citizens.

In their hope-inspiring book, *Reclaiming Youth at Risk*, Brendtro et al. (1990) draw on values of a traditional Native society of North America, the Lakota Sioux, in their application of the medicine wheel, with its four spokes depicting *belonging, mastery, independence,* and *generosity*. To many Native peoples, the number four has sacred meaning. They see the person standing in a circle (a symbol of life) surrounded by the four directions—the requisites for a child to feel whole, competent, and cherished as a member of the community. An inspiring example of work toward that end is the Louis D. Brown Peace Institute in Boston, founded by his mother, Clementina Chery, in memory of her son Louis who was killed in a shootout at age 15. Louis was a gentle boy who was working to bring others to their full potential. In her son's absence, peace has become Clementina Chery's career; that is, promoting individual and community healing, and what she calls the seven principles of peace: love, unity, faith, hope, courage, justice, and forgiveness (Walker, 2008, p. B1).

The tradition in which the entire community assumes responsibility for its children is highlighted by a widely publicized case of tribal justice. Two 17-year-old boys of the Tlingit Nation in Alaska, who were convicted of robbing and beating a man, were turned over to their village by a judge in Washington state. Village elders meted out justice in the form of a year to 18-month exile on Alaska's uninhabited islands. The intent was for the boys to reflect on their behavior, observe the power of natural beauty, and emulate the basic skills taught by their elders—something offenders rarely learn in a locked cell. Holland (1994) shares similar hopeful themes among the people of Soweto, South Africa, who are trying to reclaim their heritage after the devastating effects of apartheid.

A central theme in these programs is that controlling, authoritarian responses by adults to aggressive behavior is part of the problem, not the solution. This is because much of youth violence springs from a history of abuse, neglect, and behaviors that control rather than nurture, direct, and foster growth through love and consistent nonviolent discipline. Inconsistent discipline, or conflicting messages from parents and other adults, leaves children confused, directionless, and anxious.[2] Many young people act out aggressively because they feel disempowered and alienated in a society that does not meet their needs. But as frightening as youth aggression and violence can be, it is crucial to remember a major theme in this book: *violence begets violence* (Carlsson-Paige & Levin, 2008; Charney, 1993; Tierney, Dowd, & O'Kane, 1993).

There are many models of effective intervention with troubled youth, and many professionals and others are skilled at using them. Outcome studies of programs such as skills training in anger management, though questioned by some, suggest that youthful participants respond positively to them (Ferrell & Meyer, 1997; Jenkins & Bell, 1992, p. 79). Certainly, at-risk youth can learn and benefit from nonviolent responses to conflict situations. But if they see no hope of escape from racism and a neglected social milieu, their individual tactics to avoid violence may be very short-lived. The greater challenge, then, is in the primary prevention domain of changing socioeconomic and

---

[2] For practical manuals and videos dealing with prevention of aggression and violence among youth, readers are referred to the National Educational Service at 800-733-6786 or 812-336-7700. Readers can also call the National Youth Violence Prevention Resource Center toll-free hotline at 1-866-SAFEYOUTH (723-3968) or see their Web site at http://www.safeyouth.org.

other factors—including a cultural climate glorifying violence—that severely shortchange young people, a nation's most precious resource (see Chapter 11, Figure 11.1, Box 3).

Men Who Batter and Emotionally Abuse Women

The programs that are now being developed and implemented for dealing with batterers are possible because of the evolution in our thinking about how we view these offenders. The most successful programs combine community intervention with criminal justice efforts.

Views on Battering and Batterers

Early work in the violence literature depicted wife battering as the norm in marriage and batterers as incorrigible, with character disorders or a problem with alcohol that excused them from accountability. Gondolf's research (1987) with violent men reveals four types of batterers—sociopathic, antisocial, chronic, and sporadic. Gondolf suggests that sociopathic batterers need continual restraint to stem their violence, whereas those with antisocial behaviors need a variety of coordinated interventions. In a controversial experimental study, Sherman and Berk (1984) found that arrest had the greatest impact on reducing recidivism (repeat battering) as compared with mediation and crisis intervention. Edleson and Tolman (1992, p. 132), citing later studies, note that community intervention such as the Minneapolis Intervention Project *combined with* criminal justice efforts may offer more protection to women. Similar findings have been reported in Canada, despite its aggressive arrest laws (MacLeod, 1989).

This view is supported by Klein's (1994) study of 664 men who were issued civil restraining orders by the Quincy, Massachusetts court. Reliance on such orders alone did not prevent more abuse, especially among younger, unmarried abusers with prior criminal records who also abused alcohol. Klein, chief probation officer of the Quincy court, asserted, "These male batterers look like criminals, act like criminals, and re-abuse like criminals" (p. 111). The majority of men in this study who re-abused were not arrested and if arrested were not sentenced to jail or probation supervision. Another finding with particular relevance for those who ask, "Why doesn't she leave?" was that many of the victims had either divorced or physically separated from their abusers—suggesting how little control women have in preventing re-abuse (p. 113). Klein's study supports earlier critiques of the criminal justice system, which has failed to treat domestic violence as criminal behavior. Newspaper accounts also reveal that restraining orders have not prevented the murders of women. In fact, clinical work with abused women reveals that they are perhaps in greatest danger after filing for a restraining order, particularly in cases in which the woman's partner feels that he owns her and is now confronted with an external force threatening his need to control her. This underscores the need for caution in persuading a woman to seek court protection, and for trusting the woman's own judgment of the man's potential for violence and the contextual factors that may inflame him.

Programs for Violent Men

Moving beyond the debate about whether batterers should receive treatment or serve time in jail, the both/and approach discussed earlier should generally be the norm, even when the women who have been battered (especially those intent on salvaging their relationship and marriage) just want the violence to stop, by whatever means. To carry out that approach, the health and criminal justice aspects of domestic violence must be synchronized, culturally sensitive, and include systematic follow-up through probationary and court systems. In the public health and crisis prevention framework of this book, any program for men who batter must include three facets:

1. The need to assess and reassess their potential for further assault or homicide, as suggested in Table 12.1
2. The importance of holding the perpetrator accountable for his violent behavior, regardless of mental pathology and any excuses, such as that the woman's behavior provoked him to violence
3. Focus on the *roots* of the problem, *power and control* over one's partner, not just "anger management," since anger is a "trigger" not usually used except against the intimate partner

These program elements imply regular supportive contact with the woman who was abused and is possibly still at risk, particularly if she has filed a restraining order and in instances when men present themes of jealousy, desperation, and ownership of their partner (Meloy, 1992).

Court-mandated counseling has led to a proliferation of batterer programs illustrating a variety of intervention systems (Gondolf, 1999; Lee, Green, & Rheinscheld, 1999). Despite progress in evaluating the effects of these programs, results are still mixed (Adams, 2007; Babcock & Steiner, 1999). However, those who have developed standards for and researched batterer programs assert that accountability and victim safety are central, regardless of competing perspectives (Austin & Dankwort, 1999; Bennett & Piet, 1999). Outcome measures of effectiveness across four programs that Gondolf evaluated included re-assault rates (recidivism), rates of men making threats, and victims' assessment of quality of life since the abuser completed a treatment program. The longest, most comprehensive program demonstrated the lowest re-assault rate; this 9-month program of weekly group counseling also includes an extensive clinical evaluation, in-house substance abuse treatment, individual psychotherapy for emotional and mental problems, and casework with women partners (Gondolf, 1999, pp. 44–45). Since effective programs are designed to confront and diffuse power and control dynamics, short "anger management" can be dangerous, especially to the abused spouse, if led by someone without knowledge and expertise about this core feature of violence (Dempsey, 2003).

Some mental health professionals object to the standardization and certification of these programs, based on their view of domestic abuse as a psychiatric disorder or a biologically based dysfunction (Bennett & Piet, 1999).

The flaw in this argument is similar to that held until recently regarding mental patients' assaults against health workers. Interpreting the assaults as the expected expression of aggression originating from the patient's psychopathology led to this conclusion: Assaulted workers are not entitled to justice; rather, they should accept their victimization as "part of the job."

There is nevertheless a move toward certification and regulation of batterer programs across the United States and Canada; standards have been enacted in 21 states and 3 provinces, and several more (five states and three provinces) have drafts of standards (Adams & Cooke, 2003). Groups establishing these programs acknowledge the need for mental health service such as cognitive-behavior therapy, but they define battering as a learned behavior—*not* pathology—that is used to intimidate and control the victim (Bennett & Piet, 1999). The polarizing arguments between mental health and criminal justice professionals appear as a microcosm of the larger debate regarding biomedical and psychotherapeutic approaches to therapy (Luhrmann, 2000). The American Psychological Association asserts that psychologists should set standards (Bennett & Piet, p. 12). Meanwhile, in Massachusetts, the batterers certification program is under jurisdiction of the Department of Public Health, in keeping with the global definition of violence as a public health problem.

Today in the United States and Canada, most programs are modeled after the Domestic Violence Intervention Project developed by Ellen Pence and colleagues in Duluth, Minnesota. This model is informed primarily by profeminist principles that define woman battering and sexual violence in terms of power and control (Kurz, 1993; Pence & Paymar, 1986; Yllo, 1993). In the *power and control wheel* central to this model, eight spokes depict the ways in which men use violence to maintain power and control of women:

- Intimidation—smashing things, displaying weapons
- Emotional abuse—putting the woman down, making her think she is crazy
- Isolation—controlling what she does, where she goes
- Minimization of abuse—denying, blaming, making light of the abuse, saying she caused it
- Exploitation of children—using visitation to harass her
- Assertion of male privilege—treating her like a servant
- Economic abuse—giving her an allowance, taking her money
- Coercion and threats—threatening to leave or commit suicide

In most programs for men who batter, group counseling is the preferred mode (Adams, 2007; Edleson & Tolman, 1992), usually including other men who have been violent in the past but are no longer violent. This approach underscores the premise that violence is not inevitable but is learned and reinforced through parenting practices and its pervasiveness in the sociocultural milieu. Couples counseling and family systems approaches are highly controversial (Bograd & Mederos, 1999), as they tend to obscure violence as the primary problem in the use of such terms as *transaction* and imply the counselor's "neutrality" in regard to criminal behavior. If couples counseling is used, safety, ownership of responsibility for violence, and a *prior* intention of reconciliation must first be established (Edleson & Tolman, 1992, pp. 88–107).

Although programs for batterers and refuges for victims must be supported, these are only secondary and tertiary measures; essentially they are our reactive approaches to a problem that would be much less costly in financial and human terms if primary prevention were more valued and promoted, as discussed later in this chapter.

Crises of People Prosecuted for Violence

Many people believe that the perpetrators of crime have a clear advantage over their victims. Aside from the issue of accountability for violent behavior, we should remember that violent people or those who are apprehended for a crime, especially if they go to jail, are also in crisis—the parents who have beaten their child to death; the rapist; the woman batterer; the 18-year-old who goes to jail after a first offense of breaking and entering with intent to rob; the middle-class man who has sexually abused a child; the mother who loses custody of her children when she goes to prison for a minor drug offense, shoplifting, or prostitution; and the murderer.

In addition to the trauma of being arrested and incarcerated, the prisoner may experience extreme shame, desertion by family, or panic over homosexual advances. Or the prisoner may suffer from chronic mental illness and if awaiting the death penalty may lack adequate legal council because of poverty. A three-part investigative series ("A System Strains, and Inmates Die") describes Massachusetts prisons as the "new madhouse" in which 25% of inmates are mentally ill, with high rates of suicide and suicide attempts—some linked to sadistic treatment by guards lacking necessary training and themselves strapped in a volatile dynamic with inmates that rivals accounts from ancient dungeons (Healy et al., 2007; Latour et al., 2007; Saltzman et al., 2007). These works complement Pete Earley's (2006) one-year investigation of the Miami-Dade County jail and its dreaded ninth-floor psychiatric cell block, and cry out for another serious try at mental health and prison reform.

For mothers of young children, imprisonment may also result in permanent loss of custody of their children. With the increased number of women prisoners, space and other conditions are often more deplorable than they are in overcrowded men's prisons. Suicides are more likely in short-term detention facilities during the height of crisis when there is great uncertainty about one's fate; in long-term holding centers, they are often related to prison conditions.

Let us consider the crises of those prosecuted for crimes in the context of public policy and statistical data on U.S. prisoners. Since the 1970s, the number of inmates in federal and state prisons and jails increased dramatically with construction of new prisons—a major industry in Texas, for example. Many are there for drug offenses and disparity in sentencing (as in the powder or crack cocaine issue) resulting in disproportionate numbers of young black males in prison and leaving many black households fatherless. Many of these prisoners have not completed high school, were unemployed prior to sentencing, or were under the influence of alcohol or other drugs at the time of their offense. There are similar dramatic increases in the number of persons on probation or parole, with a disproportionate number being young black males. Rates of incarceration in the United States are the second highest in the world, behind Russia. Women are more likely than men to be in prison for nonviolent crimes, as sentencing becomes harsher, and newborns of pregnant prisoners are usually separated from their mothers.

Crisis Intervention with Assailants and Those Threatening Violence

All of the principles of crisis intervention apply to the violent or potentially violent person in prison, the home, or the workplace. The application of these principles to aggressive, antisocial, or violent people can help ensure safety of self and others. They are summarized as follows:

1. Keep communication lines open. As long as a person is communicating, violence usually does not occur.
2. Facilitate communication between a disgruntled employee or patient, for example, and the person against whom he or she is threatening violence. While hospital security personnel have designated crisis intervention roles, health workers' premature engagement of a security officer may backfire if excessive physical force is used to gain control of a potentially dangerous situation. Remembering the principle that "violence begets more violence," when physical containment is indicated, humane and respectful behavior is fundamental to safety.
3. Develop specific plans—*with* the dangerous person—for nonviolent expression of anger, such as time-out, jogging, punching a pillow, or calling a hotline, whether at home or in a psychiatric or substance abuse treatment unit.
4. Communicate by telephone or behind closed doors whenever possible when dealing with an armed person, especially until rapport is established and the person's anxiety subsides. This includes applying the risk assessment criteria as in Table 12.1.
5. If dangerous weapons are involved, collaborate with police for their removal whenever possible; implement emergency policies and procedures for appropriate application of force by a security officer or police, and by mobilizing a team effort to warn fellow workers. Failure to work in teams can be life threatening.
6. Insist on administrative support and emergency backup help; refuse any assignment that requires working alone in high-risk settings, for example, psychiatric wards or crisis outreach visits.
7. Make hotline numbers and emergency call buttons readily available.
8. Examine social and institutional factors influencing violent behavior, for example, harsh authoritarian approaches to employee relations, which may trigger revenge and violence by an upset patient or a disgruntled

worker; failure to help disturbed persons seek professional help as an alternative to violence; and rigid structures and rules for geriatric and psychiatric patients.

9. Warn potential victims of homicide, based on risk assessment and the principles of the Tarasoff case (see *Tarasoff v. The Regents of the University of California*, 1976; VandeCreek & Knapp, 1993). A general guideline for warning potential victims is a rating of "moderate—3, or "high—4 or 5" on the risk assessment tool (Table 12.1).

10. Remember that a violent person who is also threatening suicide is a greater risk for homicide.

11. Conduct follow-up. Engage in social and political activity to prevent violence.

Several factors, however, may become obstacles to providing aid to these people in crisis: (1) the sense of contempt or loathing one may feel toward a criminal or patient who has threatened a health or social service worker, (2) the fear of the prisoner or other person threatening violence, and (3) the need to work within the physical and social constraints of the detention setting or workplace where one does not anticipate interaction with disturbed or violent persons. People working in these settings, therefore, must assess and deal with crises according to the circumstances of their particular situations. The works of Adams (2007), McGinnis (1993), Meloy (1992), and Tavris (1983) are particularly recommended.

Follow-Up Service

Specialists in criminal justice cite the problem of recidivism among people convicted of crimes. The ex-offender is stripped of status and community respect and often has been exposed to conditions that harden and embitter rather than rehabilitate. Considering the dire financial straits of the ex-prisoner—a situation that frequently was present before incarceration—along with a lack of job skills, discrimination in employment, and the absence of follow-up programs, it is not difficult to understand why crime becomes a career for some.

Advocates of prison reform and various church groups are working to bring about long-term change in the conditions that seem to breed rather than prevent crime. For the nonviolent offender (more than half the American prison population), alternatives to jail sentencing are being tried in many states—a penalty system used in Native communities and in Europe for years. These less costly and more effective options include (1) community service, such as working in parks and public buildings; (2) restitution, a sanction that is particularly appealing because it takes into account the person most directly affected by the crime—the victim; (3) intermittent confinement, a strategy that spares total disruption of work and family; and (4) intensive probation, that is, no more than 25 persons per probation officer. These humane approaches should be weighed against the thousands of dollars spent each year to keep a person in prison.

Signposts of Restorative Justice

The mandatory minimum drug sentencing laws of 1986 have played a major role in the imprisonment of young black males and the 400% increase of incarcerated women in the United States (Cooper, 1999). These laws, the widening gap between the privileged and the disadvantaged, and policies emanating from the legacy of slavery and racism in the United States contribute to the counterproductivity of punitive versus rehabilitative measures. Instead of a criminal justice system emanating from revenge and punishment, as in "three strikes and you're out," which often does not fit the crime, let us consider the principles and signposts of restorative justice. As Zehr and Mika (1997) state, "Crime wounds. . . . Justice heals." We are working toward restorative justice when we

1. focus on the *harms* of wrongdoing more than the rules that have been broken,
2. show equal concern and commitment to *victims and offenders*, involving both in the process of justice,
3. work toward the restoration of *victims*, empowering them and responding to their needs as they see them,
4. support *offenders* while encouraging them to understand, accept, and carry out their obligations,
5. recognize that while *obligations* may be difficult for offenders, they should not be intended as harms and they must be achievable,
6. provide opportunities for *dialogue*, direct or indirect, between victims and offenders as appropriate,
7. involve and empower the affected *community* through the justice process, and increase its capacity to recognize and respond to community bases of crime,
8. encourage *collaboration* and *reintegration* rather than coercion and isolation,
9. give attention to the *unintended consequences* of our actions and programs,
10. show *respect* to all parties, including victims, offenders, and justice colleagues. (Reprinted with permission from the Mennonite Central Committee.)

Case Example: Mennonite Forgiveness after Shooting[3]

Charles Carl Roberts IV, a non-Amish milk-truck driver who lived nearby in Bart Township, Pennsylvania, entered the one-room school around 10:00 a.m. on October 2, 2006 armed with several weapons and other hardware, which he used to bind 10 female schoolchildren and barricade the door.

---

[3] Most Mennonites and Amish have common historical roots dating to the Anabaptist movement in Europe, which took place at the time of the Reformation. Amish and Mennonites are Christian fellowships; they stress that belief must result in practice. Differences among various Amish and Mennonite groups have always been ones of practice rather than basic Christian doctrine.

Shortly after police arrived, alerted by a teacher who had been allowed to leave with 15 male students and three other women, the execution-style shootings erupted. Three girls and Roberts, who committed suicide, were killed. Two more children died in area hospitals and five remained hospitalized on October 4, four with critical wounds and one in serious condition.

The night after the shootings at West Nickel Mines Amish School, southeast of Lancaster, more than 100 Amish adults and schoolchildren gathered at New Holland for a 2-hour session with several counselors. They hoped to start sorting out the tragedy and allay their children's fears about returning to their own one-room schools. "We shared coping ideas, how to talk with their children," said one Mennonite counselor. "What impressed me was the strong sense of community in that group.... We sang hymns, we prayed together, cried together." The counseling meeting, organized by local Amish leaders, included affirmations of love for children in Amish families (*Mennonite Weekly Review*, October 4, 2006).

The public's disgust at this heinous crime turned to amazement as reports began to circulate about how the Amish community was dealing with the tragedy. For example, within hours of the shooting, Amish leaders sought out and consoled the family of the gunman (who was not Amish); as donations poured in from around the world, the Amish decided that a portion should go toward providing for the wife and children of the gunman; almost immediately, the Amish (including parents of the slain and wounded girls) expressed their forgiveness toward the gunman (retrieved from DannyColemanBlogSpot).

These issues regarding violence, its prevention, and restorative justice speak to the social change strategies in Box 3 of the Crisis Paradigm Figure 11.1 (see also Griswold, 2007).

The Families of Prisoners

Inmates and ex-offenders are not alone in their distress. Historically, their families, especially children, are also neglected. Although there are generally fewer women than men in prison, at least a quarter of a million U.S. children have mothers who are incarcerated. Families not only lose a spouse, parent, or child to prison but may also lose a source of income and status in the community. Poverty, loneliness, and boredom are just a few of the problems faced by these families. Those who attempt to sustain relationships find that prison regulations (such as body searches of visitors and lack of privacy) or societal pressure and personal circumstances thwart their efforts. Children of imprisoned parents feel sadness, anxiety, guilt, and anger. If a divorce occurs during or following imprisonment, the post-release problems of the ex-offender are increased.

To address the crises of prisoners' families, more self-help groups such as Families and Friends of Prisoners in Dorchester, Massachusetts, are needed. This group provides moral support, counseling, information, and inexpensive transportation to state and federal prisons. Similar groups, such as Aid to Incarcerated Mothers, focus on the special needs of mothers and children.

Information about these groups is available through public health departments, coalitions for abused women, and the Internet.

Primary Prevention of Crime and Antisocial Behavior

Chapter 1 presented a general picture of primary prevention as it pertains to life crises, emphasizing the public health and community-wide action necessary if we are to prevent stressful events and situations from escalating into full-blown crises. Here this approach is explicated with particular reference to crises of both victims and perpetrators of violence and antisocial behavior. Clearly, as long as loopholes exist in the criminal justice system's response to battering, refuges are no less than lifesaving for many women. Similarly, residential treatment programs for out-of-control youth are necessary. But the very fact that an entire system of residential programs for battered women has been established speaks to the tendency, especially in the United States, toward *reactive* rather than *preventive* approaches. History reveals that all societies establish rules for how to treat deviant members.

Criminal justice system loopholes and refuges for victims beg for an alternative approach. Instead of forcing victims to live like fugitives, with the additional burden of single parenting, what if *perpetrators* were required to leave and receive counseling in alternative housing as an incentive to stop their violent behavior? Perhaps when the cultural milieu and would-be offenders are saturated with the message of non-tolerance for violence—in the next generation, we hope—the present refuges for victims might be retrofitted for perpetrators instead. The fruits of such a policy recommendation (Hoff, 1990) are underscored by a study in 29 cities documenting that the lives saved by the shelter system are mostly those of men; that is, murders are prevented because women receive help through hotline, shelter, and legal services before reaching the point of using deadly force against their abusers. However, if the male partners do not receive help, they are more likely to kill the women (Dugan, Nagin, & Rosenfeld, 2001; Masters, 1999). In other words, refuges for abused women are just that—an emergency resource, not primary prevention.

But how do we get beyond emergency measures? We certainly will not get there without the community-wide endeavors generally intrinsic to a primary approach to health care (Hoff, in press). Such measures have already been suggested in the section on youth violence; more strategies follow.

Personal and Social-Psychological Strategies

When sincerely addressing the issue, individuals may become overwhelmed by the pervasiveness of violence and withdraw out of a sense of helplessness, self-protection, burnout, or what is sometimes referred to as *vicarious traumatization*—internalizing the psychic pain their victimized clients share with empathetic providers. It is important therefore to focus on selected actions and obtainable goals. These may include

1. Adopting nonviolent language in everyday social interaction
2. Using nonviolent ways of disciplining children; attending parent effectiveness training groups to assist with difficult child-rearing challenges
3. Attending self-defense courses as a means of bolstering self-confidence and providing a substitute for arming oneself; avoiding violence as a response to violence
4. Reading about and attending continuing education courses on nonviolent conflict resolution in personal relationships
5. Avoiding sex-role stereotyping in child rearing and other interactions with children
6. Organizing neighborhood patrols and systematic ways of watching out for one another
7. Providing employees with violence prevention information and emergency protocols, including how to recognize and respond humanely to an upset or disgruntled worker with antisocial tendencies
8. Remembering that since violence and victimization are deeply rooted in sociocultural, economic, and political contexts, individual efforts *alone*, while necessary, are not sufficient to address the problem.

Sociopolitical Strategies

These strategies are most successful when combined with personal and social-psychological approaches on the premise that people need grounding in information and self-confidence in order to stand firm against obstacles in the political arena. Among the most obvious are these:

1. *Educating the public through schools, community organizations, and churches.* How many people who have attended church, synagogue, or mosque, for example, have heard a sermon condemning violence against women and children or have sponsored programs to explicitly address such issues? Probably not many have done so. Abused people often turn to clergy for help, and many religious leaders are now responding to the unique opportunity they have in preventing violence. And how many nurses, for example, who conduct childbirth and parenting classes routinely include strategies to deal nonaggressively with a demanding, finicky, or special-needs infant?
2. *Contacting legislators and organizing for a change in laws that may be outdated or otherwise do not address the issues local people confront.* In the United States, this includes addressing the powerful gun lobby.
3. *Using advocacy and systematic organizing around racial and economic justice.* This includes seeking equality in educational opportunities and addressing the media influence on violence (see Sorenson, Peterson, & Berk, 1998).

Professional Strategies

In the United States, the Surgeon General's report (Report, 1986) recommended that all licensed professionals be required to study and pass examination questions in violence prevention and the treatment of various victims of violence. As a complement to this public policy statement, individual professionals can exert leadership and advocacy within their own groups for curriculum and in-service program development to systematically address this topic. At present, such educational endeavors are incidental at best (Ross, Hoff, & Coutu-Wakulczyk, 1998; Tilden et al., 1994; Woodtli & Breslin, 2005). In Canada, the federal government has published a document entitled *Violence Issues: An Interdisciplinary Curriculum Guide for Health Professionals* (Hoff, 1995), which covers education about violence prevention and service for victims and assailants in a life-span perspective (see Hoff, in press). This document is addressed to the following disciplines: dentistry, medicine, nursing, occupational therapy, pharmacy, physical therapy, psychology (clinical), and social work. The American Association of Colleges of Nursing (1999) has produced a position paper underscoring the need for inclusion of violence content in all nursing education programs. Similar programs have been developed for criminal justice professionals in North America and other countries.

The vast knowledge already available to professionals must be combined with personal strategies in order to

- Widely disseminate new knowledge about this poignant topic to the public
- Change the values and attitudes that have served as fertile soil for nurturing violent and antisocial behavior
- Affect broad policies and functioning of social institutions through the political process necessary to bring about needed change

Summary and Discussion Questions

The crisis of increasing violence, especially among the young, is gaining international attention, while more and more health professionals and educators are joining grassroots community groups to address the crisis. Because children and youth are a nation's most precious resource, few crises command more urgent attention, not only for the sake of the assailants and their victims but also for the future of a nation. Sociopolitical responses must be joined with assistance to the individuals and families affected by violence.

1. In historical and cultural perspective, what is the most probable explanation for continued violence at individual, domestic, and global levels?
2. Identify an example of school or workplace violence and consider what institutional and individual strategies might have prevented the incident.
3. Compare and contrast burnout, vicarious traumatization, and hopelessness about prospects of turning the tide on violence.

References

Adams, D. (2007). *Why do they kill: Men who murder their intimate partners*. Nashville, TN: Vanderbilt University Press.

Adams, D., & Cooke, M. (2003, spring/summer). Attending a Certified Batterer Intervention Program: A fictionalized account. *Victim Impact, 4*(1), 12–13.

American Association of Colleges of Nursing. (1999). *Position paper: Violence as a public health problem*. Washington, DC: Author.

Arnetz, J. E., & Arnetz, B. B. (2001). Violence towards health care staff and possible effects on the quality of patient care. *Social Science and Medicine, 52*, 417–427.

Austin, J. B., & Dankwort, J. (1999). The impact of a batterers' program on battered women. *Violence Against Women, 5*(1), 25–42.

Babcock, J., & Steiner, R. (1999). The relationship between treatment, incarceration, and recidivism of battering: A program evaluation of Seattle's coordinated community response to domestic violence. *Journal of Family Psychology, 13*(1), 46–59.

Baracos, H. A. (1974). Iatrogenic and preventive intervention in police–family crisis situations. *International Journal of Social Psychiatry, 20*, 113–121.

Bard, M. (1972). *Police, family crisis intervention, and conflict management: An action research analysis*. Washington, DC: U.S. Department of Justice.

Bennett, L., & Piet, M. (1999). Standards for batterer intervention programs: In whose interests? *Violence Against Women, 5*(1), 6–24.

Bograd, M., & Mederos, F. (1999). Battering and couples therapy: Universal screening and selection of treatment modality. *Journal of Marital and Family Therapy, 25*(3), 291–312.

Brendtro, L. K., Brokenleg, M., & Van Bockern, S. (1990). *Reclaiming youth at risk: Our hope for the future*. Bloomington, IN: National Educational Service.

Buzawa, E. S., & Buzawa, C. G. (1996). *Domestic violence: The criminal justice response*. Thousand Oaks, CA: Sage.

Caplan, G. (1964). *Principles of preventive psychiatry*. New York: Basic Books.

Capponi, P. (1992). *Upstairs in the crazy house*. Toronto: Penguin Books.

Carlsson-Paige, N., & Levin, D. (2008). *Taking back childhood: Helping your kids thrive in a fast-paced, media-saturated, violence-filled world*. New York: Hudson Street Press.

Casteel, C., Peek-Asa, C., Smith, J., Goldmacher, S., O'Hagan, E., Blando, J. et al. (2007). *Assault rates among hospital employees before and after the release of two California health care initiatives*. National Injury and Violence Prevention Research Conference, October 10–11, Columbus, Ohio.

Charney, R. (1993). Teaching children nonviolence. *Journal of Emotional and Behavioral Problems, 2*(1), 46–48.

Chesney-Lind, M. (1997). *The female offender: Girls, women, and crime*. Thousand Oaks, CA: Sage. Chicago Legal Aid to Incarcerated Mothers. [http://www/c_l_a_i_m.org/factsheet.htm]. 1997.

Cowin, L., Davies, R., Estell, G., Berlin, T., Fitzgerald, M., & Hoot, S. (2003). De-escalating aggression and violence in the mental health setting. *International Journal of Mental Health Nursing, 12*, 64–73.

Cotten, N. U., Resnick, J., Browne, D. C., Martin, S. L., McCarraher, D. R., & Woods, J. (1994). Aggression and fighting behavior among African-American adolescents: Individual and family factors. *American Journal of Public Health, 84*(4), 618–622.

Dempsey, K. (2003, spring/summer 2003). Do batterer programs "work"? *Victim Impact, 4*(1), 6–7, 11.

Dionne, E. J. (1999, September 20). Our exceptionally violent nation. *Boston Globe,* p. A13.

Dubienski, G. (2008). Personal communication.

Dugan, L., Nagin, D., & Rosenfeld, R. (2001). *Explaining the decline in intimate partner homicide: The effects of changing domesticity, women's status, and domestic violence resources.* Paper presented at the 1997 meeting of the American Society of Criminology.

DuRant, R. H., Cadenhead, C., Pendergast, R. A., Slavens, G., & Linder, C. W. (1994). Factors associated with the use of violence among urban black adolescents. *American Journal of Public Health, 84*(4), 612–617.

Dyces, H., Biegel, D., Johnsen, J., Guo, S., & Min, M. (2002). The impact of mobile crisis services on the use of community-based mental health services. *Research on Social Work Practice, 12*(6), 731–751.

Earley, P. (2006). *Crazy: A father's search through America's mental health madness.* New York: Berkley Books.

Edelman, M. W. (1994, May 27). Poll finds pervasive fear in blacks over violence and their children. *Boston Globe,* p. 6.

Edleson, J. L., & Tolman, R. M. (1992). *Intervention for men who batter: An ecological approach.* Thousand Oaks, CA: Sage.

Eggert, L. L. (1994). *Anger management for youth: Stemming aggression and violence.* Bloomington, IN: National Educational Service.

Ellickson, P., Saner, H., & McGuigan, K. A. (1997). Profiles of violent youth: Substance use and other concurrent problems. *American Journal of Public Health, 57*(6), 985–991.

Eyre, J., & Eyre, R. (1993). *Teaching your children values.* New York: Simon & Schuster.

Ferrell, A. D., & Meyer, A. L. (1997). The effectiveness of a school-based curriculum for reducing violence among urban sixth-grade students. *American Journal of Public Health, 87*(6), 979–984.

Friedman, R. A. (2006). Violence and mental illness—How strong is the link? *New England Journal of Medicine, 355*(20), 2064–2066.

Gondolf, E. (1987). *Research on men who batter.* Bradenton, FL: Human Services Institute.

Gondolf, E. (1999). A comparison of four batterer intervention systems: Do court referral, program length, and services matter? *Journal of Interpersonal Violence, 14*(1), 41–61.

Griswold, C. L. (2007). *Forgiveness: A philosophical exploration.* Cambridge, MA: Harvard University Press.

Halleck, S. L. (1987). *The mentally disordered offender.* Washington, DC: American Psychiatric Press.

Healy, B., Latour, F., Saltzman, J., & Farragher, T. (2007, December 9). A system strains and inmates die. *Boston Globe,* p. A1, A18–A19.

Healy, B., Latour, F., Saltzman, J., & Farragher, T. (2007, December 10). Breakdown: Left in uncertain hands, a haunted life ends tragically. *Boston Globe,* p. A1, A6–A7.

Hoff, L. A. (1990). *Battered women as survivors.* London: Routledge.

Hoff, L. A. (1993). Review essay: Health policy and the plight of the mentally ill. *Psychiatry, 56*(4), 400–419.

Hoff, L. A. (1995). *Violence issues: An interdisciplinary curriculum guide for health professionals* [in English and French]. Ottawa: Health Canada, Health Services Directorate.

Hoff, L. A. (In press). *Violence and abuse issues: Cross-cultural perspectives for health and social services.* London: Routledge.

Hoff, L. A., & Wells, J. O. (Eds.). (1989). *Certification standards manual* (4th ed.). Denver: American Association of Suicidology.

Holden, M. J., & Powers, J. L. (1993). Therapeutic crisis intervention. *Journal of Emotional and Behavioral Problems, 2*(1), 49–52.

Holinger, P. C., Offer, D., Barter, J. T., & Bell, C. C. (1994). *Suicide and homicide among adolescents.* New York: Guilford Press.

Holland, H. (1994). *Born in Soweto.* Harmondsworth, England: Penguin Books.

Hoover, J. H., & Juul, K. (1993). Bullying in Europe and the United States. *Journal of Emotional and Behavioral Problems, 2*(1), 25–29.

Hoptman, M. J., Yates, K. F., Patalingug, M. B., Wack, R. C., & Convit, A. (1999). Clinical prediction of assaultive behavior among male psychiatric patients at a maximum-security forensic facility. *Psychiatric Services, 50*(11), 1461–1466.

Jenkins, E. J., & Bell, C. C. (1992). Adolescent violence: Can it be curbed? *Adolescent Medicine: State of the Art Reviews, 3*(1), 71–86.

Jenkins, L., Layne, L. A., & Kisner, S. M. (1992). Homicide in the workplace: The U.S. experience, 1980–1988. *American Association of Occupational Health Nursing Journal, 40*(5), 215–218.

Johnson, A. B. (1990). *Out of bedlam: The truth about deinstitutionalization.* New York: Basic Books.

Klein, A. (1994). *Re-abuse in a population of court-restrained male batterers after two years: Development of a predictive model.* Unpublished doctoral dissertation, Law, Policy, and Society Program, Northeastern University, Boston.

Kurz, D. (1993). Physical assaults by husbands: A major social problem. In R. J. Gelles & D. R. Loseke (Eds.), *Current controversies on family violence* (pp. 88–103). Thousand Oaks, CA: Sage.

Latour, F., Rezendes, M., Healy, J., Saltzman, J., & Farragher, T. (2007). Left in uncertain hands, a haunted life ends tragically. *Boston Globe,* pp. A1, A6–A7.

Lee, M., Green, G. J., & Rheinscheld, J. (1999). A model for short-term solution-focused group treatment of male domestic violence offenders. *Journal of Family Social Work, 3*(2), 39–57.

Levin, P. E., Hewitt, J. B., & Misner, S. T. (1992). Female workplace homicides: An integrative research review. *American Association of Occupational Health Nursing Journal, 40*(5), 229–236.

Lipscomb, J. A., & Love, C. C. (1992). Violence toward health care workers: An emerging occupational hazard. *American Association of Occupational Health Nursing Journal, 40*(5), 219–228.

Long, N. J., & Wilder, M. T. (1993). From rage to responsibility: A Massaging Numb Values LSI. *Journal of Emotional and Behavioral Problems, 2*(1), 35–40.

Luhrmann, T. M. (2000). *Of two minds: The growing disorder in American psychiatry.* New York: Knopf.

MacLeod, L. (1989). *Wife battering and the web of hope: Progress, dilemmas, and visions of prevention.* Ottawa: Health and Welfare Canada. National Clearinghouse on Family Violence.

Masters, B. A. (1999, March 15). Women's shelters save mostly men. *Boston Globe,* p. A3.

McGinnis, C. (1993). *Lifeline: A training manual.* Boston: Suffolk County Jail.

Melick, M. E., Steadman, H. J., & Cocozza, J. J. (1979). The medicalization of criminal behavior among mental patients. *Journal of Health and Social Behavior, 20*, 228–237.

Meloy, R. (1992). *Violent attachments*. Northvale, NJ: Aronson.

Mendel, M. P. (1994). *The male survivor*. Thousand Oaks, CA: Sage.

Merchant, J. A., & Lundell, J. A. (2001). Violence intervention research workshop, April 5–7, 2000, Washington, DC. Background, rationale, and summary. *American Journal of Preventive Medicine, 20*(2), 135–140.

Miller, L. (1999). Workplace violence: Prevention, response, and recovery. *Psychotherapy, 36*(2), 160–169.

Monahan, J. (1981). *Predicting violent behavior: An assessment of clinical techniques*. Thousand Oaks, CA: Sage.

Monahan, J., & Steadman, H. J. (Eds.). (1994). Violence and mental disorder: Developments in risk assessment. Chicago and London: University of Chicago Press.

Mones, P. (1993). Parricide: A window on child abuse. *Journal of Emotional and Behavioral Problems, 2*(1), 30–34.

Morgenstern, H. (1997). Editorial: Gun availability and violent death. *American Journal of Public Health, 87*(6), 899–900.

O'Sullivan, M. et al. (2008). It's part of the job: Healthcare restructuring and the health and safety of nursing aides. In L. McKee, E. Ferlie, and P. Hyde (Eds.), *Organizing and reorganizing: Power and change in health care organizations* (pp. 99–111). Houndmills, Basingstoke, Hampshire, U.K.: Palgrave MacMillan.

PAHO/WHO [Pan American Health Organization/World Health Organization]. (2003). *Violence against women: The health sector responds*. Washington, DC: Author.

Pence, E., & Paymar, M. (1986). *Power and control: Tactics of men who batter*. Duluth: Minnesota Program Development.

Pies, R. (2008, February 25). Mentally ill unfairly portrayed as violent. *Boston Globe*, pp. C1, C3.

Report: U.S. Department of Health and Human Services. (1986). *Surgeon General's workshop on violence and public health*. Washington, DC: Author.

Rich, J. A., & Grey, C. M. (2005). Pathways to recurrent trauma among young black men: Traumatic stress, substance use, and the "Code of the Street." *American Journal of Public Health, 95*(5), 816–824.

Rosen, J. (2001). A labor perspective of workplace violence prevention: Identifying research needs. *American Journal of Preventive Medicine, 20*(2), 161–168.

Ross, M., Hoff, L. A., & Coutu-Wakulczyk, G. (1998). Nursing curricula and violence issues: A study of Canadian schools of nursing. *Journal of Nursing Education, 37*(2), 53–60.

Runyan, C. W. (2001). Moving forward with research on the prevention of violence against workers. *American Journal of Preventive Medicine, 20*(2), 169–172.

Sadker, M., & Sadker, D. (1994). *Failing at fairness: How America's schools cheat girls*. New York: Scribner.

Saltzman, J., Rezendes, M., Healy, B., Latour, F., & Farragher, T. (2007). Guards, inmates a volatile dynamic. *Boston Globe*, pp. A1, A14–A15.

Sherman, L. W., & Berk, R. A. (1984). The specific deterrent effects of arrest for domestic assault. *American Sociological Review, 49*(4), 261–272.

Sorenson, S. B., Peterson, J. G., & Berk, R. A. (1998). New media coverage and the epidemiology of homicide. *American Journal of Public Health, 88*(10), 1510–1514.

Sully, P. (2000). Society, violence and practice program at City University, London, personal communication.

Tarasoff v. The Regents of the University of California. (1976). 551 P. 2d 334. Also in 131 California Reporter 14. Supreme Court of California.

Tavris, C. (1983). *Anatomy of anger*. New York: Simon & Schuster.

Tierney, J., Dowd, T., & O'Kane, S. (1993). Empowering aggressive youth to change. *Journal of Emotional and Behavioral Problems, 2*(1), 41–45.

Tilden, V. P., Schmidt, T. A., Limandri, B. J., Chiodo, G. T, Garland, M. J., & Loveless, P. A. (1994). Factors that influence clinicians' assessment and management of family violence. *American Journal of Public Health. 84*(4), 628–633.

Toch, H. (1969). *Violent men*. Hawthorne, NY: Aldine de Gruyter.

Vande Creek, L., & Knapp, S. (1993). *Tarasoff and beyond: Legal and clinical considerations in the treatment of life-endangering patients* (Rev. ed.). Sarasota, FL: Professional Resource Press.

Walker, A. (2008, April 8). A mother's peace plan. *Boston Globe*, p. B1.

Walker, H. M. (1993). Anti-social behavior in school. *Journal of Emotional and Behavioral Problems, 2*(1), 20–24.

Watson, R. S., Poda, J. H., Miller, C. T., Rice, E. S., & West, G. (1990). *Containing crisis: A guide to managing school emergencies*. Bloomington, IN: National Educational Service.

Way, D. W. (1993). I just have a half heart. *Journal of Emotional and Behavioral Problems, 2*(1), 4–5.

Webster, D. W., Vernick, J. S., Ludwig, J., & Lester, K. J. (1997). Flawed gun policy research could endanger public safety. *American Journal of Public Health, 87*(6), 918–921.

West, C. (1994). *Race matters*. New York: Vintage Books.

Woodtli, A., & Breslin, E. (2002). Violence-related content in the nursing curriculum: A follow-up national survey. *Journal of Nursing Education, 41*(8), 340–348.

Wright, M. A., Wintemute, G. J., & Rivara, E. P. (1999). Effectiveness of denial of handgun purchase to persons believed to be at high risk for firearm violence. *American Journal of Public Health, 89*(1), 88–90.

Yllo, K. (1993). Through a feminist lens: Gender, power, and violence. In R. J. Gelles & D. R. Loseke (Eds.), *Current controversies on family violence* (pp. 47–62). Thousand Oaks, CA: Sage.

Zehr, H., & Mika, H. (1997). *Restorative justice signposts*. Akron, PA: Mennonite Central Committee.

危機

CHAPTER 13

Violence and Crisis from Disaster

The natural world is both a nurturing home and a source of potential destruction. The sun warms us. The beauty of foliage, seacoasts, forests, plains, and mountains satisfies our aesthetic needs and inspires us to write, sing, and love one another. Yet these same elements have the capacity to destroy us if we do not protect ourselves from nature's violent forces. For example, we must build shelters to prevent freezing in a snowstorm. We are also in danger if we misuse or destroy nature's resources, for instance, by the uncontrolled burning of coal, which causes acid rain and destroys lakes and the creatures that live in them.

As human beings, we can see and respond to the differences and connections between natural elements and ourselves. Our ability to rationally construct our social and material world allows us to contain the forces of nature for our own protection. The natural world yields much of what we need for survival; yet the victims of fires, floods, hurricanes, tidal waves, earthquakes, and snowstorms provide ample evidence of nature's destructive potential in spite of great technological attempts to decipher nature's mysteries and direct them for human ends.

How do people respond to disasters of natural origin, as compared with those of human origin? Why are disasters of human origin, such as Love Canal and Hiroshima, not usually viewed as a form of violence? What can individuals and groups do to reduce our vulnerability to disasters from natural and human sources? Listening to survivors will help us answers these questions about disaster, whether from natural or human sources:

- What happens to disaster victims?
- How does disaster affect the quality of our everyday lives?
- With technological advances, what can we realistically anticipate about our quality of life on earth?
- Will we ultimately destroy our planet and ourselves?

I wonder why I remain. I want God to take me too.

I managed to drag myself out, but my mother and father were buried. My mother was unrecognizable. She was all burnt.

For 97 hours and 33 minutes, Er meditated, thought, and prayed. And then his prayers were answered. Before dawn Saturday, he was pulled from beneath 15 feet of debris by a Turkish rescue team. By Sunday, the elation of his rescue had faded. He learned of the deaths of his wife and daughter as he listened to his son being interviewed on television. . . . Surrounded by friends and family, Er said, "I'm going to try to make the most of it. I want to deserve a happy life with the people I love." (5th edition, 2001).

Harlan [an elementary school janitor] thrived on the children, and he was a humble and special man, the closest thing to a saint that anyone would know. . . . [Three days after the flood] Harlan hanged himself in his home, itself damaged by the flood.

"We are out here like pure animals. We don't have help," said a pastor outside the New Orleans Convention Center, where corpses lay in the open and evacuees complained that they were dropped off and given no food, water, or medicine.

A relative who flew from the United States to Hurricane Mitch survivors in Honduras said it was like the country had stepped back in time about a hundred years. Children as young as thirteen suddenly became the head of their little nuclear family.

These are a few of the reactions of victims and survivors of floods and other disasters worldwide. The December 26, 2004 tsunami, one of the deadliest natural disasters in history, killed more than 225,000 in 11 countries, with Indonesia, Sri Lanka, India, and Thailand the hardest hit. The August 29, 2005 Hurricane Katrina, with approximately 2000 U.S. lives lost, was the deadliest in nearly a century. It prompted widespread and ongoing criticism of federal, state, and local government response in a wealthy nation that had pioneered developing professional disaster response protocols. Together, the Asian tsunami and Hurricane Katrina have drawn international attention to what can still be learned and applied in disaster prevention and response, and in public consciousness regarding the seemingly ever-widening gap between rich and poor as a factor in whether and when a disaster strikes.

Natural and Accidental Disaster: Prevention and Aid

One can only guess at the extent to which a disaster such as flood, fire, or earthquake affects the people who experience it. Although global media networks beam a disaster's devastating effects to our television screens, the depth of the tragedy is private and immeasurable. Although the negative consequences of disaster are not always clear, some research suggests long-term stress responses (Erikson, 1994; Gist & Lubin, 1989). Preventive measures and help for survivors are therefore of great importance. What do we need to know about disaster and its victims in order to help? The nature and duration of a disaster, plus individual factors such as age, general personality stability, and religion, affect the victim's response. Disaster is a perilous event that for most falls outside the range of everyday life experience or challenges. Since a disaster usually occurs rapidly and is completely unexpected, the results are shocking. It shatters one's assumptions about the order and security of daily life, depending on type of loss: home, country, intact family, memorabilia, health, and means of livelihood.

Writing about Central America's Hurricane Mitch, the deadliest storm there in over 200 years, and the Catholic Charities relief effort, Doolin and Collins (1998, p. A19) ask:

> Why should we help? As a nation and people blessed with so much, our assistance can lessen the victims' suffering. Food will feed the hungry. Water will quench their thirst. Medicine will aid the sick. But, most important, our assistance will bring what is most needed, and that is hope.
>
> Albeit from different perspectives, both the Truman-era "Good-Neighbor" policy for Central America and the parable of the Good Samaritan ask the question: Who is my neighbor? Last week, we saw their faces. This week they still need us. Next week they will need us even more.

Fortunately, tragedies such as Hurricane Katrina, the tsunami, and Hurricane Mitch happen rarely—or not at all—to most people. Most of our expectations of disaster are formed in the abstract; while observing on television the tragedies of others, denial often serves to tell us, "This couldn't happen to me." Public consciousness and public health efforts are promising, however, since the 1990s were declared the International Decade for Natural Disaster Reduction (Logue, 1996). Overall, our lack of experience with disaster, along with the suddenness, lack of preparation, and unexpectedness with which most disasters strike, greatly reduces the opportunity for escape and effective problem solving.

Yet in a poor country, Turkey, the bulk of the devastation caused by the 1999 earthquake that left 13,000 dead and 200,000 homeless was attributed largely to substandard housing and lax regulation of building codes. As Ahmet Mete Isikara, director of the Bosphorus University's earthquake research center said, "Earthquakes don't kill, badly constructed buildings kill" (Marcus, 1999, p A26). Had a similar level quake (as measured on the Richter scale) occurred in, say, wealthy San Francisco, there would have been far fewer deaths and less material damage from crumbled buildings, only because of differential national wealth and government regulation of building codes.

Technological and Political Factors Affecting Aid to Victims

Rescue operations and assistance with physical necessities occur in disaster-stricken communities throughout the world. Foreign countries, the International Red Cross, and religious and other organizations assist in such relief work following devastating disasters. A country's ability to respond is also related to the amount and quality of its resources, technological developments, and the bureaucratic functioning of its government.

The uncontrolled forces of nature may not seem to differentiate between rich and poor, north and south, or between white people and those of color, but the effects of these forces differ. Widespread flooding in the United States, for example, is less frequent and results in fewer lives lost than it did years ago because of the resources and technology available for good prevention programs—building dams, for example. But a poor country still has difficulty preventing massive floods that take thousands of lives. A poor nation also has fewer government resources for assisting survivors. Similarly, fires of the proportion of the Cocoanut Grove disaster, which claimed 492 lives in Boston in 1942, are rare today because political action has facilitated enforcement of building safety regulations. Federal aviation policy has likewise been tightened to prevent jetliner crashes due to faulty technology or nonenforcement of safety codes.

However, news accounts of disasters worldwide repeatedly emphasize the difference between rich and poor countries' access to resources for preventing, or at least warning of, impending disaster. Presidents of poor countries often plead for technical assistance to warn people of impending disaster so they can take measures to avoid injury. Natural disasters, of course, should always be expected. However, the effects of population growth and land use management decisions are illustrated in the difference in disaster mortality over a 100-year period: the 1876 Bay of Bengal typhoon killed 100,000 people, whereas the 1970 East Bengal cyclone killed 200,000 (Logue, 1996, p. 1208). The devastation wreaked by Hurricane Mitch in Central America can properly be defined as an ecological disaster of human origins in that its greatest damage in floods and mud slides occurred in deforested areas (Goldoftas, 1998). Absent economic policies regarding globalization, the debts of poor countries payable to the World Bank, and the widening gap between rich and poor, Central America's poor people who are vulnerable to future disasters will nevertheless out of necessity eke out a living from the remaining forested areas.

Consider also the contrast in flood damage and compensation in a rich nation, the United States, and a poor nation, Bangladesh. As Fauzia E. Ahmed, South Asia coordinator of Oxfam America, offers the following assessment.

Hurricane Andrew claimed 20 lives. Last year, a hurricane with no name struck Bangladesh, killing 138,000 people. Both hurricanes had winds of 140 miles per hour. But why was one hurricane approximately 7000 times more lethal? The answer is poverty. Bangladesh has 300 shelters for hurricanes. It needs 5000, which could be built for less than the cost of one C-17 military cargo aircraft.

When Hurricane Andrew came to Miami, it found a ghost town. Most people had fled to shelters. In Bangladesh, hundreds of thousands of people tried to run as a huge wall of water advanced on them. Abdul, a survivor, told me, "My two children could not run fast enough. The wave caught up with them and they died. The roar of the sea was so great I could not even hear their cries for help."

There was also tremendous psychological devastation. In Miami, a businessman died of a heart attack after seeing his business reduced to rubble. In Bangladesh, mothers were forced to choose which children to save. They will somehow have to go on living with the consequences of this choice. "I had four children," one mother told me. "But I only have two hands. With one hand I grasped a tree and held my 6-month-old baby with the other. I had to watch my three other children drown because I could not save them."

In Florida, there was insurance for homeowners. The Federal Emergency Management Agency dispensed money for the cleanup. In Bangladesh, there was no compensation for people who lost their livestock—which was often the sum total of all their worldly possessions.

Bangladesh is a nation where there are more riverways than dirt tracks and more dirt tracks than paved roads. In good times, fishermen live off the water. In hurricanes, the water drags them to their death. The overall lack of quality roads makes it impossible for relief supplies to reach people in remote areas.

In Florida, the warning system and evacuation plan worked. Bangladesh's 80 percent illiteracy rate makes it difficult for many citizens to understand storm warnings. In Bangladesh, illiteracy runs highest among women. The majority of the dead in the hurricane with no name were women. Despite all this, people were resilient and struggle to help one another. Women talked of searching for food and finding some rice buried in the sand. A 13-year-old boy found his father's body and gave him proper burial rites. He felt proud that he was able to do his duty toward his father. The media did not report this. In Florida, pictures were shown on TV of neighbors helping each other. Reporters interviewed survivors, asking them how they hoped to return to normal lives. But in Bangladesh, the media showed only dead bodies and masses of dark-skinned people begging for food. Fourteen million people were made homeless, but the media left them as nameless as the hurricane.

This sort of coverage led to absurd queries. Why do these stupid people live in a disaster-prone area? Are there too many people in Bangladesh already? Nobody is asking why 44 million people crowd into hurricane-prone counties from Texas to Maine.

The truth is, death like this does not have to be inevitable in the developing world. What is more important: One C-17 airplane or enough shelters to keep 138,000 people from floating away? (Ahmed, 1992, p. 15)

This account of disaster in a rich and a poor country also describes what shocked most Americans and the world about Hurricane Katrina striking New Orleans and the U.S. Gulf coast. The class and race divide rooted in U.S. history and current affairs was laid bare for all to see: The majority of victims and survivors were poor people of color where million-dollar mansions are erected while many others are homeless or still waiting for assistance to either rebuild a modest home or move back to other decent housing in New Orleans. This is not to discount the hundreds of hours of work done (and continuing) by scores of volunteers and church groups from across the country to assist in Hurricane Katrina relief effort. But it underscores a major theme of this book: the sociocultural origins of many crises and the importance of looking "upstream" to collaborate in prevention of all sorts. And indeed, the theoretical roots of crisis theory cited in Chapter 1 stem from early disaster studies and war veterans (see preventing posttraumatic stress, this chapter).

In short, material, financial, and human resources play a key part in preventing disasters from natural or accidental causes. These economic, political, and technological conditions highlight the continued need for international programs of aid and cooperation in the distribution and use of natural and human resources. Bureaucratic and political rivalries can result in further tragedy and loss of life. Technology, public health, and effective political organizations are central to controlling nature, responding to health hazards during disaster, and aiding disaster victims with material and other resources. The social and behavioral sciences have also contributed to the reduction in human error and accidental disaster through, for example, research on perception and reaction times of pilots and air traffic controllers.

Psychological and Other Factors

In the psychological realm, confronting the unhealthy mechanism of denial is central to preventing victimization by natural disaster. Because a natural disaster is a dreaded experience, most people deny that it could happen to them, even when they live in high-risk areas for floods, tornadoes, or earthquakes. People use denial as a means to go on living normal lives while under more or less constant threat of disaster. Escape and problem solving are also affected by the extent of a person's denial, although some may be in special circumstances that prevent them from hearing the warnings.

Case Example: Martin and Evelyn Schoner

Martin Schoner, age 70, and his wife, Evelyn, age 68, had lived all their lives in a valley neighborhood in Wilkes-Barre, Pennsylvania. The Schoners had both been retired for several years; Martin as a men's clothing merchant, Evelyn as a nurse. They enjoyed the activities of their retirement years, including occasional babysitting for their five grandchildren. They and their two children exchanged visits frequently.

The evening before the flood, Martin was admitted to the hospital for chest and stomach discomfort. When Evelyn left her husband at the hospital that evening, they still did not know his diagnosis, nor did they have any suspicion that disaster was imminent. Meanwhile, flood warnings were being broadcast by radio and television. Evelyn, however, heard none of these. She went to bed as usual, only to be awakened at 5:00 a.m. by a telephone call from a friend advising her of the flood and the need to leave her house quickly. She immediately packed a bag and drove to her friend's house. A few hours later, she learned on the radio that houses in her neighborhood were filled with water up to the second floor. She was unable to reach her husband; the hospital was also flooded and the patients were evacuated. Both Martin and Evelyn were beside themselves with fear and worry, for each had no idea of the whereabouts of the other.

One of Evelyn's special concerns was Martin's medical condition. She still did not know if his symptoms signaled serious heart trouble. As it turned out, Martin's symptoms were from food poisoning. He had been moved to a local college that was converted into a temporary shelter; seriously ill patients were moved to another hospital. Martin, however, was so upset and worried about his wife that rescue workers finally sent a hospital chaplain to talk with him. Martin stated afterward that he found it a tremendous relief to pour out his worry to a sympathetic listener, who helped him through a good cry without embarrassment or shame. Evelyn had no way of knowing these facts because public communication networks were not operating.

Two days later, Evelyn finally learned from a friend that Martin was at the college emergency shelter. Evelyn went to pick him up; they stayed for a few days together at their friend's house before returning to their neighborhood to assess the damage. When they returned, they were grief stricken over the loss of their possessions and the destruction of the home they had treasured. Evelyn was particularly upset. She kept repeating, "If only I had known that this was going to happen, I would have moved at least some of our precious things upstairs or packed them up to take with me."

Martin and Evelyn, with the help of their friend, decided to stay in the neighborhood and rebuild their home with federal aid. In the aftermath of the crisis, Martin gained a new lease on life despite the tragedy. He no longer had any empty hours in his days; he single-handedly took the job of repairing the flood damage and refinishing the house. He became a source of support and encouragement for others in the neighborhood. Evelyn felt the flood left an indelible mark on her. She seemed unable to stop grieving over the loss they had suffered. Evelyn also stated, "If only our minister hadn't been out of town at the time, I would have had someone to talk to when it happened." Martin and Evelyn did not know that specially trained crisis counselors were available to survivors of the disaster. This highlights the fact that communication in a disaster-stricken community is often inadequate.

Martin, Evelyn, and their neighbors live in fear of another flood; they have no assurance that adequate precautionary measures have been taken to prevent a recurrence. They decided, however, to take a chance and live their last years in the neighborhood they love, with the resolution that should another flood occur, they will move away once and for all.

In contrast to the Schoners, there was little time to prepare for the Asian tsunami or Hurricane Mitch in Central America. A Honduran woman and her family were quickly swept away in their house by the merged sea and river created by the hurricane. When the river tore through the house, it also tore away her entire family, leaving her as the sole survivor after being rescued from a makeshift raft she had constructed out of tree roots, branches, and a piece of scrap. A woman in Mozambique also responded to imminent flood danger by flight to a tree, where she lived above raging waters for four days and gave birth to her baby. She and her daughter were rescued by helicopter; the rescue team included a medic who cut the umbilical cord.

It is difficult for anyone who has not experienced a flood to imagine that heavy rain alone can produce enough water to break a dam, merge a river and sea into a single body of water, and flood a whole city, region, or several countries as in the tsunami. People are used to associating certain results with certain causes. When cause and effect are unfamiliar, denial is likely. But when reality strikes, and some survive, reckoning with profound loss is the next ordeal. As we hear and read accounts of recovery from unimaginable losses, however, the face of human resilience offers an ideal for all as we confront everyday stressors and crises. It also underscores the subjectivity of the crisis experience and that emotional recovery is linked to the *meaning* each attaches to stressful life events, plus social and other resources to assist recovery. One may say, "It must have been God's will" and just keep going one step at a time. Another may "curse the darkness" (or the government) and slide into serious depression.

Preventive Intervention

It is impossible to prepare for the crisis of disaster the way one can prepare for transition states such as parenthood, retirement, or death. However, we can act on a community-wide basis before disaster strikes. This is particularly important in communities at high risk for natural disasters. Such preparation is a form of psychological immunization. There are several things a community can do to prepare for possible disaster:

1. Make public service announcements during spring rains or tornado seasons, urging people not to ignore disaster warnings.
2. Broadcast educational programs on television, dramatizing techniques for crowd control and for helping people who are panic-stricken or in shock.
3. Review public safety codes to ensure adequate protection against fire in public gathering places such as restaurants, theaters, and hospitals.
4. Make public service announcements, urging people to take first-aid courses with local Red Cross and fire departments.
5. Broadcast educational programs on radio, television, and the Internet to acquaint people with social agencies and crisis services available to them in the event of disaster.
6. Offer crisis intervention training for mental health and social service workers as an addition to their traditional skills.
7. Institute an upgraded program of disaster preparation by medical, public health, and welfare facilities, including mechanisms for community coordination of disaster rescue services. (In communities with an excellent medical disaster plan, survivors are likely to have adequate medical and health care during and after floods.)
8. Develop plans for support of disaster relief workers, who themselves are usually shocked and numbed from the experience. For example, workers assigned to recover human remains from an airplane wreckage (typically emergency medical and fire-fighting personnel) can tolerate only a few hours at a time confronting the horror. They need time-out

and an opportunity to process what they have witnessed with a crisis or mental health counselor.

9. Ensure that local authorities for disaster prevention and response have up-to-date copies of field manuals and other resources available through Web sites of federal offices—for example, in the United States, the Public Health Service and the National Institute of Mental Health (NIMH).

These preparations will not prevent the devastating effects of a disaster, but they may reduce the impact of the trauma and help people live through the experience with less physical, social, and emotional damage than they might otherwise suffer.

Individual Responses to Disaster

Reactions to the stress and trauma of a disaster are not unlike reactions to transition states such as migration or loss of a loved one through death. They also resemble responses to victimization by crime (see Chapter 11). Tyhurst's classic works (1951, 1957a, 1957b) identify three overlapping phases in disaster reaction. These are similar to the four phases in the development of a crisis state noted by Caplan (see Chapter 2).

Impact

In this period, the person is hit with the reality of what is happening. In catastrophic events, the impact period lasts from a few minutes to one or two hours. The concern of disaster victims during the impact phase is with the immediate present. An automatic stimulus–response reaction occurs, with the catastrophe as stimulus. Victims are struck later with wonder that they were able to carry on as well as they did, especially if they finally break down under the full emotional impact of the experience. During the impact phase, individual reactions to the disaster fall into three main groups:

1. Ten to 25% of the victims remain calm and do not fall apart. Instead they assess the situation, develop a plan of action, and carry it through.
2. Seventy-five percent of the victims are shocked and confused. They are unable to express any particular feeling or emotion. The usual physical signs of fear are present: sweating, rapid heartbeat, upset stomach, and trembling. This is considered the normal reaction to a disaster.
3. Another 10 to 25% become hysterical or confused or are paralyzed with fear. These victims may sit and stare into space or may run around wildly. The behavior of this group is of most concern for rescue workers and crisis counselors who may be on the scene during emergency operations.

Evelyn Schoner (earlier in this chapter), caught in the Wilkes-Barre flood because she did not hear the warnings, had the first type of reaction during the impact phase. When she finally received the warning telephone call, she packed her bag and drove to safety. She had no difficulty doing this, even though she ordinarily depended heavily on her husband when in distress, and he was in the hospital. Evelyn stated, "It really only hit me afterward, that everything I treasured was lost. I just had to drive away and leave everything behind. You don't know what that's like—saving precious things all your life, then all of a sudden they're gone, even the photographs of our family." We cannot accurately predict which people will fall into the third group of reactors to disaster. However, prediction criteria (see Chapter 3) indicate that the following types of people are particularly vulnerable to crisis or emotional disturbance following acute stress from a disaster:

- The elderly who have few physical resources and a reduced capacity to adapt to rapid change
- Those who are already coping with stress in self-destructive or unhealthy ways, such as taking solace in alcohol or other drugs
- Those who are alone and friendless and who lack physical and social resources that they can rely on in an emergency

People with complicated grief have high rates of suicidal ideation even after adjusting for comorbid depression, a finding that supports the importance of screening bereaved individuals for risk of suicide (Neria et al., 2007).

During the San Fernando Valley earthquake, mental health staff at the Los Angeles County–Olive View Medical Center observed that some acutely disturbed mental patients reacted more rationally than usual during the acute phase of the quake, demonstrating the human capacity for resilience—even with a psychiatric illness. For example, they helped rescue fellow patients (Koegler & Hicks, 1972). In Mozambique, a couple and their three children were perched in a tree for a day and night before the water subsided. In Armero, Colombia, rescue workers dug with their bare hands and bailed out water with tin cans to save a 13-year-old girl trapped beneath a cement slab. These incidents reveal the commonly observed heroism and humanity of disaster victims, despite personal pain and loss. People rise dramatically to the occasion and mobilize resources to help themselves and others.

Recoil

During this phase, there is at least a temporary suspension of the initial stressors of the disaster. Lives are no longer in immediate danger, although other stressors such as cold or pain from injury may continue. Often, however, more floods follow the first one, and aftershocks follow earthquakes. During the recoil phase, survivors are typically en route to friends' homes, or they have found shelter in community facilities set up for the emergency. They may look around for someone to be with. They want to be cared for, to receive a cup of coffee or a blanket. Chilled survivors of an earthquake, for example, huddle in makeshift camps and tent cities, lighting fires to keep warm. The disaster experience leaves some survivors with a childlike dependency and need to be with others. In this phase, survivors gradually become aware of the full impact of what they have experienced. Both women and men may break down and weep. Survivors have their first chance to share the experience with others. Their attention is focused on the immediate past and how they managed to survive. This phase has the greatest implication for crisis workers helping the survivors.

The focus during Phase 2, *recoil*, should be on practical help, listening, problem solving, and sincere presence for those who may or may not wish to share their experience with a stranger (that is, a *debriefer*) rather than with fellow survivors and members of their own community—in essence, the basics of traditional crisis care. In a similar vein, we should question media intrusion, or what some call "ambulance chasing." Yes, of course the sharing of feelings with a good listener can foster healthy crisis resolution after disaster. But when a media person or "debriefing" stranger asks "How do you feel [about what happened]," many may interpret the question as either stupid or a privacy invasion, as if to say the "normal" feelings of shock and overwhelming grief around catastrophic events should be self-evident. Some people in crisis may just want to preserve a brave public face, have a good cry in private, and only talk about it later, and then only with a trusted family member or friend, or perhaps a therapist who already knows them.

Posttrauma

During this period, survivors become fully aware of the losses they have sustained during the impact phase: loss of home (for some, even country), financial security, personal belongings, and particularly loved ones who may have died in the disaster. In this phase, much depends on a person's age and general condition. As one survivor put it, "A disaster can bring out the best and the worst in a person." Those who are too old to start over again find their loss of home and possessions particularly devastating. Older people who prize the reminders of their children and their earlier life feel robbed of what they have worked for all their lives. Anger and frustration follow. If loved ones have died in the disaster, grief and mourning predominate.

Murphy (1986, p. 339) cites studies of bereavement suggesting that the recovery period varies from several months to several years and is subjectively defined. Murphy found that among survivors who lost a loved one in a close relationship to the Mount Saint Helens volcanic eruption, bereavement was intense and prolonged, especially if they perceived the disaster as preventable. Some survivors may feel overwhelming guilt over the death of loved ones: "Why me? Why was I spared and not she?" Many survivors, such as a tsunami fisherwoman, describe the horror of listening to screams, of watching people being swept past them to their deaths, and of being helpless to save them. Lifton and Olson (1976) have described this reaction as "death guilt." Survivors somehow feel responsible for the death of their relatives or others they were unable to save. They cannot quite forgive themselves for living, for having been spared. At the same time, they may feel relief at not being among the dead. This, in turn, leaves them feeling guiltier.

During this third phase, survivors may have flashbacks, reactive depressions, anxiety reactions, and dreams in which they relive the catastrophic experience. Some agencies report increased numbers of hospital admissions for emotional disturbances following disaster. Children typically are afraid to be alone and afraid to go to sleep in their own beds. Lifton and Olson (1976) report that when survivors perceive a disaster as a reflection of human callousness, rather than an act of God or nature, the psychological effects are more severe and long lasting. This posttraumatic phase may last for the rest of a person's life, depending on that individual's predisaster state, the extent of loss, the help available during the disaster, and whether the disaster was natural or from human origins (Richman, 1993). (See Leon, Poole, & Kloner, 1996 and Epstein, 1995, who cite increased morbidity and mortality figures following disaster.)

A small group of disaster survivors give up. These people remain despondent and hopeless for the rest of their lives: "I don't think I'll ever be the same. I just can't get over it." Most survivors, however, are resilient. They gather together and reconstruct their lives, their homes, and their community, as accounts from New Orleans and Southeast Asia attest, often despite meager public assistance. Although a number of people in flood-prone areas move to higher elevations, many others rebuild their homes in the same location, even though there is no guarantee against further flooding. This is particularly true for older people, who find it too costly to start over and who want to keep the comfort of a familiar neighborhood, even though they have lost everything else.

Rescue and crisis workers have the most influence during the impact and recoil phases (Joseph, Yule, Williams, & Andrews, 1993), whereas mental health workers may play a key role during the posttraumatic phase for the small percentage who manifest severe depression, for example, or who may have a recurrence of previous psychiatric illness (see Matthieu & Ivanoff, 2006; Tucker, Pfefferbaum, Nixon, & Foy, 1999). As noted throughout this book, crisis intervention—available at the right time and in the right place—is the most effective means of preventing later psychiatric disturbances. The availability of crisis assistance to individuals, however, is intricately tied to the community response to disaster.

Community Responses to Disaster

The most immediate social consequence of a disaster is the disruption of normal social patterns on which all community members depend (Tyhurst, 1957a). The community suffers a social paralysis. People are separated from family and friends and spontaneously form other groups out of the need to be with others.

When disaster strikes, large numbers of people are cut off from public services and resources that they count on for survival. These can include water—one of the first resources to go in the event of a flood—electricity, and heat. People scramble for shelter, food, and water. Traffic controls are out, so accidents increase. In flooded areas, many people fall in the slippery mud and break limbs, thus placing more demands on hospital staff. Often hospitals are flooded out, and all patients must be transferred to other facilities. Schools and many businesses close, creating further strain and chaos in homes and emergency shelters.

Disaster can bring out the worst in people. Some take advantage of the disorder to loot and steal; some business owners take advantage of the occasion to profit from others' misfortune by inflating the prices of necessary supplies. Because normal communication networks are either destroyed or are very limited, rumors abound and panic and chaos increase. Communication problems and physical distance also make information about relief benefits difficult to disseminate. This causes resentment among those who feel they did not receive a fair share of the benefits. Assisting survivors through the bureaucratic maze of many relief organizations is one of the most helpful things crisis workers can do. Residents who are not even on the scene of the disaster can be affected by media generalizations and sensationalistic reports.

In most instances, disasters are instrumental in bringing the people of a neighborhood closer together for support and recovery. During the impact period of a disaster, there is greater cohesion among community members; later, people follow up on their individual concerns, comfort children and others, and assist with rebuilding or applying for grants and loans (Evans & Oehler-Stinnett, 2006.) People must rely on one another for help and support during a disaster in a way that was not necessary before. During the Rapid City flood, for example, a group of professionals were attending a conference on death and dying. A call was put out to the conference participants to assist families who had lost loved ones. The helpers reported that many friends had already turned out to help the bereaved families and that there was no special need for mental health professionals. Following the World Trade Center disaster, various employers sponsored crisis care for survivors (Boscarino et al., 2005).

During the impact and recoil stages of a disaster, community control usually passes from elected government officials to professionals who direct health, welfare, mental health, and public order agencies. Elected officials have the important function of soliciting assistance for the community from state, federal, and sometimes international resources. The community's priorities are rapidly defined by professional leaders, and an emergency health and social service system is quickly established. This emergency network focuses on

- Preservation of life and health—rescue activities, inoculations, treatment of the injured
- Conservation and distribution of resources—organization of emergency shelters and distribution of supplies such as water, food, and blankets
- Conservation of public order—police surveillance to prevent looting and accidents arising out of the chaos and the scramble for remaining resources

■ Maintenance of morale—dispatching mental health, welfare, and pastoral counselors to assist the panic-stricken and bereaved during the acute crisis phase

Material, social, and psychological services should be available for as long as they are needed.

In summary, a community's response to disaster and human resilience are affected by the quality of leadership; survivors' accessibility to rescue and follow-up services; and the political and economic factors embedded in a community's vulnerability to disasters—whether from natural or human origins.

Factors Affecting Recovery of Survivors

Tyhurst (1957a) notes that the nature and severity of reactions to disaster and the process of recovery are influenced by several factors:

1. *The element of surprise.* If and when warnings are given, they should be followed by instructions in what to do. Warnings followed by long silences and no action plan can heighten anxiety and lead to the commonly observed denial of some residents that a disaster is imminent.
2. *Separation of family members.* Children are particularly vulnerable to damaging psychological effects if separated from their families during the acute period of a disaster (Durkin, Khan, Davidson, Zaman, & Stein, 1993). Families should therefore be evacuated as a unit whenever possible.
3. *Outside help.* Reasonable recovery from a disaster requires aid from unaffected areas. Because military forces have the organization, discipline, and equipment necessary for dealing with a disaster, their instruction should include assisting civilians during disaster.
4. *Leadership.* As in any crisis situation, a disaster demands that someone have the ability to make decisions and give direction. The police, the military, and physicians have leadership potential during a disaster. Their training should include preparation to exercise this potential appropriately.
5. *Communication.* Because failures in communication give rise to rumors, it is essential that a communication network and public information centers are established and maintained as a high priority in disaster work. Much impulsive and irrational behavior can be prevented by the reassurance and direction that a good communication network provides.
6. *Measures directed toward reorientation.* Communication lays the foundation for the re-identification of individuals in family and social groups. A basic step of reorientation is the registration of survivors, so that they can once again feel like members of society. This also provides a way for relatives and friends to find one another.
7. *Evacuation.* In any disaster, there is a spontaneous mass movement to leave the stricken area. Planned evacuation will prevent the panic that

results when people find their escape blocked or delayed. Failure to attend to the psychological and social problems of evacuation can result in serious social and interpersonal problems.

Resources for Psychological Assistance

Federal aid for reconstruction has been available to communities stricken with disaster for many years. Since 1972 in the United States, aid for victims' psychological needs and rituals for mourning are also routine. The significance of the NIMH policy to offer crisis services is twofold. First, it demonstrates the need for outside mental health assistance in times of disaster to supplement local resources. Local mental health workers may be disaster victims themselves and may be temporarily unable to help others in distress. Second, it confirms that the ability of people to help others in crisis is strongly influenced by their prior skill or training in crisis intervention. In most communities, the special federal aid for crisis intervention supplements crisis services offered by other groups. For example, Catholic, Jewish, Mennonite, and other religious groups traditionally offer help to disaster-stricken communities.

It is probably impossible to have an oversupply of crisis intervention services for people struck by a disaster. However, community mental health agencies must have prior crisis intervention skills in order to mobilize the resources necessary when a disaster occurs. Health and mental health workers, along with other community caretakers, must know how to put these crisis intervention skills to use when a disaster strikes. As there is little or no time to prepare for the disaster, there is no time to prepare as a crisis worker once a disaster is imminent. Workers must be ready to apply their knowledge, attitudes, and skills in crisis intervention.

In spite of much progress in this area and the United Nations declaration of the 1990s as the International Decade for Natural Disaster Reduction (Logue, 1996), as reconstruction after Hurricane Katrina amply attests, more long-term planning is needed to better meet the psychological, material, and social needs of disaster victims.

Help during Impact, Recoil, and Posttrauma Phases

The helping process during disaster takes on distinctive characteristics during the disaster's impact, recoil, and posttrauma phases. Table 13.1 illustrates the kind of help needed and who is best suited to offer it during the three phases of a disaster. The table also suggests the possible outcomes for disaster victims if help is not available in each of the three phases.

Crisis Intervention and Follow-Up Service

The basic principles of crisis intervention should be applied on behalf of disaster victims. As the debate on CISD (critical incident stress debriefing) (discussed later in this chapter) illustrates, however, crisis care should be embedded in the natural context of practical problem solving, not in a

TABLE 13.1   Assistance during Three Phases of Natural Disaster

	Help Needed	Help Provided by	Possible Outcome if Help is Unavailable
Phase I: Impact	Information on source and degree of danger	Communication network: radio, TV, public address system	Physical injury or death
	Escape and rescue from immediate source of danger	Community rescue resources: police and fire departments, Red Cross, National Guard	
Phase II: Recoil	Shelter, food, drink, clothing, medical care	Red Cross Salvation Army Voluntary agencies such as colleges to be converted to mass shelters Local health and welfare agencies Mental health and social service agencies skilled in crisis intervention Pastoral counselors State and federal assistance for all of the above services	Physical injury Delayed grief reactions Later emotional or mental disturbance
Phase III: Posttrauma	Physical reconstruction Social reestablishment Psychological support concerning aftereffects of the event itself; bereavement counseling concerning loss of loved ones, home, and personal property	State and federal resources for physical reconstruction Social welfare agencies Crisis and mental health services Pastoral counselors	Financial hardship Social instability Long-lasting mental, emotional, or physical health problems

formal counseling framework. During and after a disaster, people need an opportunity to

- Share the experience at their own pace and express their feelings of fear, panic, loss, and grief
- Become fully aware and accepting of what has happened to them
- Resume activity and begin reconstructing their lives with the social, physical, and emotional resources available

To assist victims through the crisis, the crisis worker should

- Listen with concern and empathy; ease the way for the victims to tell their tragic story, weep, and express feelings of anger, loss, frustration, and despair
- Help the survivors accept the reality of what has happened a little bit at a time—perhaps by simply staying with them during the initial stages of shock and denial, accompanying them to the scene of the tragedy, and supporting them when they are faced with the full impact of their loss
- Assist victims in making contact with relatives, friends, and other resources needed to begin the process of social and physical reconstruction—perhaps by making telephone calls to locate relatives, accompanying people to apply for financial aid, and giving information about social and mental health agencies for follow-up services

In group settings where large numbers are housed and offered emergency care, those who are panic-stricken should be separated from the rest and given individual attention to avoid the contagion of panic reactions. Assigning these people simple, physical tasks will move them in the direction of constructive action. Any action that helps victims feel valued as individuals is important at this time. Yet in spite of massive efforts to help survivors of disaster, it may be impossible to prevent lifelong emotional scarring among those who live through the experience, depending on age, predisaster emotional stability, and so forth. Crisis and bereavement counseling can at least reduce some negative effects and should be available to all victims.

No local community can possibly meet all of the physical, social, and emotional needs of its residents who are disaster victims. In the United States, it is now routine to provide federal funds for crisis services and physical reconstruction in communities that are struck by disaster. This is necessary even when local mental health, welfare, and health workers are trained in crisis intervention. In most disasters, the need is too great for the local community to act alone, especially because some of its own human service workers (police officers, nurses, clergy, and counselors) will themselves be among the disaster victims.

In summary, individual responses and the needs of natural disaster victims, as in other crisis situations, vary according to psychological, economic, and social circumstances. Natural disaster victims seem to have something in common for coping with this kind of crisis: They interpret these tragedies as acts of God, or fate, or bad luck—and thus beyond anyone's control. Accounting for an event from a common viewpoint is an important aspect of constructive crisis coping at the *cognitive* level. *Emotional* coping can then occur through grief work and can be followed by *behavioral* responses to rebuild lives. The victims' interpretation of these crises as natural and beyond their control is the basis for the hope felt by survivors of natural disasters in spite of enormous suffering. It is the reason they can rise from the rubble and begin a new life; it lets them move beyond the emotional pain and gain new strength from the experience. This element of disaster response and recovery constitutes the greatest distinction between natural disasters and those occurring from human indifference, neglect, or design.

Critical Incident Stress Debriefing: Crisis Care Values and Cautions

Mental health professionals trained in grief work, crisis intervention, and assessment of psychopathology will be careful not to pathologize what is essentially a normal response to an event that is beyond the range of events experienced by most people (see Neria et al., 2007; Zunin & Zunin, 1991). Caution is also in order with respect to formalized debriefing (CISD) after disaster, especially for survivors who might interpret structured debriefing as a sign they are going crazy.

Regehr's (2001) review of research evidence on this debated topic suggests that the highly ritualized CISD process incorporates into a very formal structure the basic elements of crisis intervention long known from the work of crisis theory pioneers like Tyhurst (1957b), Caplan (1964), and others discussed in Chapter 1 of this text. While the debate on debriefing continues those formally trained as psychotherapists and or in victimology studies know about the potential damage of eliciting expression of deep psychological trauma prematurely or without appropriate follow-up and support during the aftermath of divulging certain feelings such as shame and rage.

Further, Regehr's review suggests evidence of secondary trauma or "vicarious traumatization" among some CISD participants from hearing other participants' graphic descriptions. In a related cautionary note, Jacobs et al. (2004) discuss the personality characteristics of some emergency personnel conducting CISD sessions: high need for control, a need for immediate gratification, and a strong need to be needed (see Chapter 4, Figure 4.2, Victim-Rescuer-Persecutor Triangle).

Adapting CISD in its subset, Critical Incident Stress Management (CISM), Mitchell (2003) summarizes established crisis care strategies and implies with the term *management* a theme from medical practice. That is, "managing" diabetes or heart disease, for example—as is well known in medical circles—will almost inevitably fail if evidence-based treatment sidelines the patient's own role in "managing" his or her illness. "Management" suggests control and taking charge, but means little without the active collaboration of those "managed"—as corporate and other leaders have experienced.

Disasters from Human Origins

Nature's potential for violence seems small beside the destructive possibilities for disaster caused by human beings. In Bhopal, India, a gas leak at a chemical plant killed 2000 and disabled tens of thousands more. Besides the 300 dead and 10,000 evacuated because of the Chernobyl nuclear accident in the former Soviet Union, radioactive fallout affected people and animals thousands of miles away, and illness and death from the accident are still being counted, even as the plant is finally being dismantled. Survivors of the underground gold mine explosion near Yellowknife in the Northwest Territories, Canada, cite the tragedy as proof of the need for reform of labor–management relations. Famines in Ethiopia, Mozambique, and Somalia, though apparently "natural," can also be traced to human origins (Wijkman & Timberlake, 1984). By most accounts, the inferno that killed at least 80 people in a religious compound in Waco, Texas, could have been avoided. Ethnic cleansing and tribal wars in the former Yugoslavia, Rwanda, and Kenya are the most recent man-made disasters creating incalculable misery and loss of life; the systematic slaughter of people in Rwanda is being compared with the Nazi Holocaust and Cambodian genocide in the war crimes category. *Environmental racism*, a term applied to placing toxic waste dumps in communities where ethnic minority groups live, and in poor countries, surely takes its toll—with cleanup and restitution yet to occur in many places.

Human potential for both good and evil seems limited only by the technology we create. For example, a child can be saved through a liver transplant; amputated hands can be replaced; energy from the sun can be collected and stored; but technology also made it possible for the Nazis to perform inhuman experiments on Jews and others in concentration camps and for most of the population of Hiroshima and Nagasaki to be destroyed. While many enjoy the benefits of scientific knowledge, others suffer. For example, in the United States, the Love Canal disaster was a prototype for the 1980 Superfund law enacted by Congress as the public health response to hazardous waste sites (Logue, 1996).

Three years after Hurricane Katrina, New Orleans is still struggling to recover from infrastructure losses, physical and mental illness, and housing deficits (Ratner, 2008; Siegal, 2007). Major assistance has been offered through nongovernmental organizations (NGOs), professional groups, and volunteers (McCabe, 2006; Stevens, 2006). However, the United States has spent less on Hurricane Katrina than most expected, while it spends about $10 billion per month on the Iraq war. In contrast, considering the difference in scale of destruction and lives lost (compared with Hurricane Katrina), in the Asian tsunami, through massive safe water campaigns and international aid providers (some already established in the infrastructure, such as Oxfam and church relief groups), epidemics among tsunami refugees were avoided—a testament to preventive public health measures. Oxfam and others cite this effort as "a story of aid done right" (*Oxfam America*, 2006, p. 14).

"Aid done right" also bears consideration of assumptions carried by Western mental health disaster practitioners—a main assumption being the belief that it helps to talk about our problems and another that respects an autonomous independent self. The tsunami volunteers (most of whom were survivors themselves) agreed that it was helpful to talk about the event, but also had concerns about burdening others with their accounts. The social ecology of societies influences who gets help and who does not. Volunteers who came from other areas of the world would stay for short periods of time and then leave, often without exit or follow-up plans. We should consider these issues when working with victim-survivors from other cultures who have different worldviews and value systems (Hobfoll et al., 2006; Miller, 2006; see also CISD discussion, later in this chapter).

What Lois Gibbs (1982, p. 1), a Love Canal resident turned activist, wrote a quarter century ago applies poignantly to the long-term fallout for Hurricane Katrina survivors:

> *Ask Those Who Really Know!*
> Ask the Victims of Love Canal why they need immediate,
>   permanent relocation, and why some will refuse to leave their
>   motel rooms once funds are cut off.
> Ask the innocent victims of corporate profits.
> The reasons are simple. We cannot lead a normal life, we:
>   Cannot go in our basements because of contamination from
>   Love Canal.
>   Cannot eat anything from our gardens because of soil
>   contamination.
>   Cannot allow our children to play in our yards because of
>   contaminated soils.
>   Cannot have our children attend school in the area—two have
>   been closed due to Love Canal contamination.
>   Cannot breathe the outside air—because of air contamination
>   we are now in hotels.
>   Cannot become pregnant—miscarriage rate is state defined:
>   45%. Homeowners' survey: 75%.
>   Cannot have normal children—because of 56% risk of birth
>   defects.
>   Cannot sell our homes. Love Canal was not mentioned in our
>   deeds; who wants a contaminated house?
>   Cannot get a VA or FHA loan in Love Canal; even the
>   government is reluctant.
>   Cannot have friends or relatives visit us on holidays; they're scared
>   it's unsafe.
>   Cannot have our pregnant daughters, or our grandchildren
>   visit: it's unsafe for them.
> We need your support and your help to end the suffering of men,
>   women, and especially children of Love Canal. We have lost our
>   constitutional rights of life, liberty and the pursuit of happiness.
>   Justice for all but not Love Canal Victims.
> We cannot live at Love Canal—we cannot leave Love Canal.

The disastrous effects of violence from natural and human sources can be described in both personal and social terms. Although people have now moved back to Love Canal, this highly publicized disaster holds lessons for other communities still struggling against toxic waste and development issues. For example, the Hurricane Katrina disaster has been linked to the deliberately building on wetlands; left in their natural flood protection role instead of building on them might have spared the hurricane's worst damage.

An analysis of disaster by Lifton and Olson (1976) is classic in depicting survivors' psychological recovery, depending on whether the disaster's origins are natural (as in an "act of God") or man-made, and therefore preventable. In Buffalo Creek, West Virginia, a mining corporation carelessly dumped coal waste, which formed artificial dams that eventually broke and caused dozens of deaths. Buffalo Creek residents knew that the dam was considered dangerous and that the mining corporation had neglected to correct the problem. When loved ones, homes, and the natural environment were destroyed, survivors concluded that the mining company regarded them as less than human. In fact, one of the excuses offered by the company for not correcting their dangerous waste disposal method was that fish would be harmed by alternative methods. The survivors' feelings of devaluation were confirmed by their knowledge of the coal company's proposal of hasty and inadequate financial settlements. The physical damage to the community was never repaired, either by the company or through outside assistance. Residents are constantly reminded of the disaster.

Unlike the Rapid City community described earlier, Buffalo Creek survivors did not respond to the disaster with community rejuvenation borne of the tragedy. Lifton and Olson (1976) attribute this tremendously different response to the disaster's human (rather than natural) origin. Even though the mining company was forced to pay $13.5 million in a psychic damage suit, Buffalo Creek residents said they and their community could never be healed. Considering genetic, health, and material damage such as that suffered by Love Canal residents, monetary compensation becomes practically meaningless. Money cannot repair such losses. *Prevention of* and *learning from* such tragic neglect seem the only reasonable responses.

The reactions of Buffalo Creek and Love Canal survivors are similar to those observed among survivors, including children, of Hiroshima, the Nazi Holocaust, and other wars (Lifton, 1967). Quoting Luchterhand (1971), Lifton and Olson (1976) state, "As the source of stress shifts from indiscriminate violence by nature to the discriminate oppression by man, the damage to human personality becomes less remediable" (p. 10). Survivors of planned disaster—including war—feel that their humanity has been violated. Their psyches are bombarded to such a degree that their capacity for recovery is often permanently damaged.

In a related category are victims and survivors of technological disaster, an increasing occurrence worldwide. As people demand more goods and energy, technical errors occur, and more toxic wastes are produced. The most outstanding international examples are the Bhopal and Chernobyl disasters. At least 7000 people died in the Indian Bhopal industrial calamity; it took years for the 500,000 survivors to negotiate compensation and to bring to trial the plant officials, who were charged with manslaughter. On a less dramatic scale are the increasing numbers of people exposed to occupational hazards, as evidenced by increasing rates of infertility, especially among low-paid workers (predominantly people of color) at work and in the least protected environments (de Castro et al., 2008). Central to the emotional recovery of persons exposed to such hazards are the concepts of *meaning* and *control*.

Preventing Posttraumatic Stress Disorders

As discussed in Chapter 2, emotional recovery seems to require that trauma- tized people be able to incorporate events into their meaning system and to maintain at least some perception of control. If a situation seems beyond one's control, self-blame may be used as a way to cope with the event (O'Sullivan et al., 2008).

Thus, if the origin of trauma or prolonged distress is external—that is, if people are exposed to occupational hazards or are victims of disasters traced to negligence—it is important that victims attribute responsibility to its true sources rather than to themselves. Interpreting a person's anger and demand for compensation as a "dependency conflict" or in other psychopathologi- cal terms is a form of blaming the victim. Instead, such traumatized peo- ple should be linked to self-help and advocacy groups through which they might channel their anger into constructive action for necessary change—in this case, improved safety standards on the job or social change regarding toxic waste (Hoff & McNutt, 1994; Silverstein, 2008). (See also Chapter 11, Figure 11.1, Box 3, right circle). This is not to say that prior psychopatholo- gies do not play a role in some injury claims, but these should not be used to obscure the fact that injurious exposure reduces some people to joblessness, ill health, and poverty.

Many of these ideas are now being examined in studies of *posttraumatic stress disorder* (PTSD), a controversial and much-published concept describ- ing a chronic condition that may occur *months or years* after an original trauma that falls outside the normal range of life events, such as during a war or in a concentration camp or from terrorist bombings (unlike the relatively short crisis response time after other distressful events). (See Baronowski, Gentry & Schultz, 2005; Hobfoll et al., 2006; McCarroll, Ursano, & Fullerton, 1993; Peterson, Prout, & Schwarz, 1991). When the DSM-IV-TR (*Diagnostic and Statistical Manual of Mental Disorders*) diagnostic criteria of PTSD are rel- evant to those with histories of childhood abuse (physical or sexual) or other interpersonal violence, it is termed *complex PTSD* (Everett & Gallop, 2000). Although PTSD has some features common to clinical depression, panic disorder, and alcoholism, its increasing prevalence underscores the impor- tance of crisis intervention and grief work for all traumatized people in addi- tion to renewed efforts to prevent abuse and trauma in the first place (see Miller, 1999; Pfefferbaum et al., 2006).

Aside from the original formulation of PTSD in the DSM, some now routinely apply the term to what historically in crisis theory evolved from the "shell shock" of war. Despite these conceptual issues regarding PTSD, it is wise and humane to provide all combat veterans what they need (without a psychiatric label) when suffering from what should be considered a "normal" response after exposure to the extraordinary horrors of war—experiences falling well beyond the ordinary range of the average person's life. Even more shocking than the liberal use of the PTSD diagnosis is delay in mental health services and substituting the DSM diagnosis of PTSD with that of *personality disorder* (by definition, "preexisting" their military service) by psychiatric professionals as a justification to deny disability benefits to veterans (Priest & Hull, 2007; Sennott, 2007).

Besides veterans themselves, special attention is needed for the children of parents deployed to war, which entails three areas of boundary ambiguity: routines, responsibilities, and reintegration of a parent upon return (Huebner et al., 2007). This study revealed adolescent behavioral changes and a lower threshold for emotional outbursts. Depression and anxiety were common and related to ongoing uncertainty about the status of the deployed parent. During deployment, adolescents were required to assume and then relinquish various roles and responsibilities, thereby adding confusion regarding their place in the family system—suggesting that reunion with the deployed parent was more difficult than actual absence. Adolescents were also acutely aware of changes in the emotional state and personal resilience of the nondeployed parent. (See Lasser & Adams, 2007 for examples of groups assisting people exposed to the trauma of war.)

The world knows about the atomic bombs dropped in Japan, the Nazi Holocaust, the Cambodian genocide, and the mass murders and rapes in Rwanda and Darfur. War and environmental pollution are planned disasters that bring about physical, social, and emotional destruction of immeasurable proportions. Some survivors of Hiroshima describe the horror (WGBH Educational Foundation, 1982, pp. 4–6):

> People who were laying there and dying and screaming and yelling for help and the people who were burned were hollering, "I'm so hot, please help me, please kill me" and things like that and . . . it was terrible. (Mary)

> We had a hospital near our place and many, many hundreds of injured people came to the hospital and there weren't too many adequate medical supplies and there were some doctors there, some nurses there, but they didn't have enough medicine to take care of all the people. And these people were thirsty and hurt and dying and all night long I could hear them calling, "mother, mother," and it sounded to me like ghosts calling out in the middle of the night. (Mitsuo)

> In the Japanese tradition, you're supposed to look for your family. I walked for three weeks, every single day, looking for my grandparents and my brother. It was a feeling of real loneliness and looking at the devastation of the whole city wondering why God left me here alone. You know, why didn't he take me too. At the time, yeah, I did want to go too. I felt they should have . . . I should have gone too instead of being left alone. (Florence)

On August 6, 1945, the first atomic bomb was dropped on Hiroshima. Three days later, Nagasaki was bombed. Six days later, World War II was over.

Over 80% of the people within one kilometer of the explosion died instantly or soon afterward. By December 1945, the number of dead in Hiroshima and Nagasaki was over 200,000. By 1950, another 140,000 people had died from the continuing effects of radiation exposure; since then, 100,000 more people have died from radiation-related cancer. Before and during the same war, millions of Jews, gypsies, homosexuals, mentally retarded people, and others viewed as undesirable by the Nazis were systematically exterminated in what many consider the most horrible crime in the history of the world.

When Japanese-American victims of the atomic bomb declared themselves as survivors, insurance companies withdrew their health and life insurance policies, and employers discriminated against them. Nightmares, flashbacks, and fear for themselves and their children were common among these survivors. Finally, these survivors formed the Committee of Atomic Bomb Survivors in the United States to gain medical benefits from the U.S. government.

Responses to terrorist attacks in the global community are similar to the impact, recoil, and posttrauma experienced by other disaster survivors. The responses vary according to episode—that is, brief, long-term, repeated, and prolonged exposure. An extreme and powerful threat overwhelms peoples' usual coping mechanism and sense of safety and security. All affected by terrorism typically assess their old values and beliefs about themselves, the world around them, spirituality, and human nature. In this process, people either integrate the experience into their existing values and beliefs or accommodate and develop new ones. Those who cannot integrate or accommodate will most likely present with physical and psychological symptoms that may be unexplainable. Terrorism and grief should be viewed as connected and similar, but uniquely different and distinct. Outcomes of terrorism are affected by personal, predisposing, peridisposing, postdisposing, and protective factors. Three nonlinear phases make up the terrorist grief and recovery process: (1) disequilibrium—the immediate aftermath; (2) denial—outward adjustment; and (3) integration—coming to terms (Jordan, 2005).

Vietnam War veterans also finally succeeded in gaining veterans' benefits for health damage they believe resulted from exposure to the defoliant Agent Orange, damage affecting at least 250,000 U.S. families. For many Vietnam veterans, America's most unpopular war still rages; many still feel that the loss of life and limb, accepted as necessary in earlier wars, was not justified in a war that most believe should never have been fought. Veterans of the Gulf War (Desert Storm) have had a much shorter struggle. They have been given compensation for damages that they believe to have resulted from exposure to as-yet-unidentified agents during warfare, based on testimony in Congress from sick veterans and their advocates. Veterans of the Iraq War face similar challenges in obtaining care (Kors, 2008).

Maintaining or regaining health (*salutogenesis*) and avoiding illness are greater challenges when the crisis originates from sociocultural sources—in this case, disasters of human origin. This is because the emotional healing process requires, among other things, that people answer for themselves the question, "Why did this happen to me?" If the answer is, "It was fate," "It was God's will," or "That's life; some bad things just happen," people are able to recover and rebuild their lives, especially with social support. But if the answer can be traced to one's gender, race, sexual identity, or other prejudice; to neglect or hatred from individuals, groups, or corporations (as in environmental pollution); to ethnic cleansing; or to any other human origin, the persons affected must receive a message of caring and compensation to counteract the devastating effects of such malevolent actions. Otherwise a person's sense of coherence, including comprehensibility, meaningfulness, and manageability (Antonovsky, 1987, pp. 17–19), is shaken; the person tends to absorb the blame and devaluation implied by others' neglect or outright damage. This process is similar to the downward spiral to depression and possible morbidity discussed in Chapter 2 (Figure 2.2), which can occur when survivors of violence are blamed for their plight. Follow-up service for *individual* survivors of man-made disaster includes particular attention to the meaning of these traumas in cross-cultural perspective.

Those meanings are often associated with social and political action, especially prevention efforts that can benefit other people. Working with survivors of the September 11, 2001 attack, researchers Ai et al. (2005) recommend more research on spirituality as a coping tool, and how working with clients of different religious beliefs helps them use their value systems to recover from traumatic violence. For a source that trauma survivors and their families may find helpful, see the *PTSD Workbook*, which Williams and Poijula (2002) dedicated to survivors of the September 11, 2001 terrorist attacks. Inspiring examples of international collaboration and making meaning out of man-made disasters include:

- Fundraising by a group of Boston women to build and staff schools for girls after the Rwanda genocide
- Physician Paul Farmer's leadership to provide surviving Rwandans medical and related services—including mentoring American medical students in delivering cross-cultural health care
- A Boston woman who lost a family member in the 9/11 attack found meaning in using her survivor funds to build a school for girls in Afghanistan
- Tulane University students fanning out across New Orleans to assist with the unfinished work of rebuilding after Hurricane Katrina, and aligning the lessons from Katrina with their formal courses

Human Resilience and Learning from Disaster

Vietnam veterans are still trying to rebuild their lives after a generation of being made scapegoats for a nation's guilt and shame about a war they were not personally responsible for starting, while many Iraq veterans embark on a similar journey. Holocaust survivors have formed awareness groups as resources for support and the preservation of history. Atomic bomb survivors say their sacrifice was worthwhile, if only the bomb is never used again. First

Nations people are fighting for their cultural survival as well as against the destruction of the environment, which they view as a crime against the harmony that should exist between nature and human beings (Mousseau, 1989). Lois Gibbs's story (1982) about the Love Canal tragedy moved a nation to awareness of similar hazards in numerous other communities. Not unlike the parent survivors of teenage suicide, these survivors are trying to find meaning in their suffering by sharing the pain and tragedy of their lives to benefit others. The survivors of human malice, greed, and prejudice tell us something about ourselves, our world, and the way we relate to one another and the environment.

Yet more than 100 years after the American Civil War, over a half-century after the Holocaust, and decades after the Vietnam War, we still have

- Racially motivated violence and institutionalized racism across the United States
- Crimes with apparent anti-Semitic and other ethnic, religious, and political motives, from Boston to London, Madrid, Bosnia, Haiti, Rwanda, and the Middle East
- A systematic attempt to declare the Holocaust a "myth"
- Repeated famines in African countries that can be traced to war and to the widening gap between the haves and have-nots of the world (Wijkman & Timberlake, 1984)
- An international nuclear capacity continuing apace for destruction more than one million times the power of the atomic bomb dropped on Hiroshima

To meet the challenges of these potentially destructive forces, there are now national and international debates about nuclear proliferation, regional wars, and arms trade that are unparalleled in the history of the human race in their importance to our ultimate survival. But the social, political, religious, and psychological ramifications of national and international crises and chronic problems are complex, controversial, and passionately debated. People are deeply divided, for example, in their views about

- Whether or how ethnic cleansing should be stopped
- What the division of government spending should be between domestic and defense needs
- Whether the environmental crisis is as serious as some claim

These issues will probably be argued for a long time, but the following facts remain:

- Many crises can be traced to social, economic, and political factors of local and global origins.
- Children are pressing their teachers for answers about crime and environmental threat.

- Fear about nuclear accidents and environmental pollution has increased since the Chernobyl disaster.
- Effective crisis intervention cannot be practiced without considering the sociocultural context of the crisis.

It is imperative that individual and public crises be understood in terms of their human meaning (Mills, 1959). Public issues should be debated and acted on, not abstractly, but in terms of their impact on each of us—you, me, our families and friends, and others. Not only is there a dynamic interplay between public and private life, but in both realms our sensitivity to others' perceptions and value systems regarding controversial issues can foster cooperation and prevent conflict.

Each person's unique perception of traumatic events is central to understanding and resolving a crisis. Without communication, we cannot understand another's interpretation of an event or issue, and we may become a hindrance to constructive crisis resolution. The differences in interpretations of personal, social, and political problems are as diverse as the community members themselves. Unquestionably, communication is the key to uncovering these interpretations and thus understanding people in crisis and instituting appropriate care. A person tells of a traumatic experience through emotional display, behavior, and verbal communication—Hansell's "crisis plumage" (1976). Responses are often embedded in cultural differences. If there is no caring and supportive listener, the chances of a constructive crisis outcome are diminished.

But although listening is necessary, it is not sufficient if the crisis did not originate from individual circumstances. Social and political actions are pivotal to a positive crisis outcome if the origin of the crisis is social and political (see Figure 11.1, Crisis Paradigm, Box 3, right circle). Individuals traumatized from these sources are more real than the casualty figures reported on the evening news make them seem.

- Richard, a refugee from Rwanda with recurrent nightmares, is someone's husband, father, son, and brother. He is 48 years old and lives on Locust Street in a town of 45,000 people.
- Shigeko is an atomic bomb survivor who has had 26 operations on her face and lips and is glad that she is alive and that her son is not ashamed of her appearance.
- Jane, age 5, lives near a hazardous waste site and has toxic hepatitis.

These people and many others like them tend to get lost in statements of "statistically significant" incidences (of cancer, deformed children, or other medical problems), scientific jargon, and "investigative procedures" for determining whether corrective action is in order. This process of generalizing does not seem to apply to real people. The abstractness, along with the grossness of the figures of 10 million victims of the Holocaust, nearly 500,000 dead from atomic bomb blasts—contributes to denial and psychic numbing for the average person. The numbers, the destruction, and the sheer horror are unimaginable for most of us. To defend ourselves against the terror, we deny and try to convince ourselves that there is nothing we personally can do about these global issues.

Although the Cold War is officially over, there are still stockpiles of nuclear arms sufficient to destroy the planet several times over, and additional nations are testing nuclear devices even as the United Nations Security Council debates how to deal with one regional crisis after another in which thousands of innocent civilians (many of them children) are slaughtered or wounded by warring factions. As Apfel and Simon (1994, p. 72) note,

> If we decide it is the responsibility of the enemy's leadership to take care of its own children, then we can more easily go ahead with our bombing program. If we decide children anywhere in the world are also our children, we can less easily bomb. We distance ourselves and say that children who are far away are not our children, and if they suffer it is because their leaders and their parents are irresponsible.

In the spirit of violence prevention and Ruddick's thesis (1989) regarding "maternal practice," it is reasonable to suggest that if men and women shared equally in the everyday tasks of caring for children and learned the conflict-resolution tactics demanded by nonviolent parenting, they would insist that more resources be spent to promote peace and conserve lives and resources than are presently spent on war and destruction (Goodman & Hoff, 1990).

From a safe distance, it is relatively easy to think of our enemies as less than human and therefore worthy of destruction. As in our attitudes toward the homeless, deinstitutionalized mental patients, and unwed mothers, our enemies are distant; they belong to groups and are the responsibility of the state or church. When they are thus objectified, we do not have to think of them as someone's sister, brother, child, father, mother, or friend.

Our worst enemies are people like ourselves: they eat; sleep; make love; bear children; feel pain, fear, and anger; communicate with one another; bury their dead; and eventually die. Statistics and machines will never be a substitute for human interaction, just as rating scales can aid but not displace clinical judgment in evaluating individual suicide risk. As Albert Einstein said, "Peace cannot be kept by force. It can only be achieved by understanding."

In a particular crisis situation, if we do not *communicate*, for example, with a suicidal person, we will not understand why death is preferable to life for that individual and therefore may be ineffective in preventing suicide. If we take the time to *talk* with and *listen* to a person in crisis, we are less likely to suggest or prescribe a drug as a crisis response. Similarly, at the national and international levels, if we keep communication open and foster political strategies to handle crises, there is less likelihood of resorting to physical force for solving problems. Human communication, then, is central to our survival—as individuals and as a world community.

Our ethnocentrism is nevertheless often so strong, and greed and power motives are often so disguised that the average person may find it difficult to think of disasters occurring from human design as a form of violence. Victims of disasters and other traumas of human origin, however, feel violated. They have experienced directly the destruction of their health, their children, their homes, their sense of security, their country, their hopes for the future, and their sense of wholeness and worth in the human community.

In many ways, the poignant testimonies and tragic lives of the victims of ethnic, class, and political conflicts speak for themselves. Still, two of the most painful aspects of their crises are that they feel ignored and often cannot receive even material compensation for their enormous losses. People suffering from these policies feel denied. A hopeful sign of policy change is the international response to the Asian tsunami, while some countries reduced the debt burden of disaster-struck poor countries. Another hopeful sign is advocacy for forgiving these debts altogether, in that they accrued around global economic policies developed with the major advantage going to rich countries.

If we have not listened, or if we have been silent when we should have spoken, convinced that we have nothing to say about public issues, perhaps we should reexamine what Nobel Peace Prize recipient Albert Schweitzer said in 1954: "Whether we secure a lasting peace will depend upon the direction taken by individuals—and, therefore, by the nations whom those individuals collectively compose." Survival is too serious to be confined to partisan politics, the government, or liberal versus conservative debates. Every citizen—and certainly crisis workers—should be informed on the critical issues confronting the human race (see Ekins, 1992; Foell & Nenneman, 1986; Hoff & McNutt, 1994). Therapist-claimed "neutrality" is a concept that will not do in cases of crisis originating in sociocultural and political sources. From caring for various victims, we have learned that people traumatized by violence need *explicit public acknowledgment* that what happened to them is wrong.

When confronted with the enormity and horror of disaster from human sources, denial is understandable. Although we may feel helpless and powerless, in fact, we are not. The opinions of officials and professionals are not necessarily wiser or more lifesaving than those of ordinary citizens. Lois Gibbs, in describing why she wrote *Love Canal: My Story* (1982), emphasizes the fact that as an average citizen with limited education and almost no funds, she was able to fight city hall and the White House and win! Every country has someone like Lois Gibbs, who, in the face of unnecessary and preventable suffering, joins with others to make a difference for themselves, their families, and the world.

Murray Levine, a community psychologist, wrote in his introduction to Gibbs's story (1982, pp. xii–xviii), reasons why her story and others like it should be told; he also illustrated crisis and preventive responses to a disaster of human origins:

1. Lois Gibbs is in many respects a typical American woman—a mother of two children and a housewife. In response to crisis and challenge, she courageously "transcended herself and became far more than she had been."
2. Her story informs us of the relationship between citizens and their government and shows that the government's decisions about a problem are not necessarily in the interests of ordinary people whose lives are threatened by these decisions.
3. Lois Gibbs's story is one of "inner meanings and feelings of humans," a story that "provides a necessary and powerful antidote to the moral illness of those cynics and their professional robots who speak the inhuman language of benefit-cost ratios, who speak of the threat of congenital deformities or cancers as acceptable risks."

In conclusion, the differences between disasters of natural and human origin are striking: The uncontrolled, violent forces of nature (fire, water, wind, and temperature), destructive as they are, are minuscule in comparison with disasters from human sources. The possible crisis outcomes for the victims are also markedly different, with enormous implications for prevention. As discussed, technology has been a double-edged sword, sometimes the cause of disaster, sometimes the cure. Through technology and public health planning, much has been done to harness some of the destructive potential of nature. Natural disaster–control technology, land management policies, and resources for aid to victims should now be shared more widely in disaster-prone areas of the world. Concerning disaster from human sources, however, we have been much less successful in directing and controlling conflict and indifference toward the health and welfare of others. This is unfortunate but not hopeless. Violence is not inevitable (Lifton, 1993); it results from our choices, action, and inaction (see Figure 11.1, Crisis Paradigm, Box 3, right circle).

In the discussion of understanding people in crisis in Chapter 2, emphasis was placed on the examination of crisis origins. In the case of disasters of human origin, such an examination inevitably leads us into the most pressing social, political, and economic questions facing humankind. After hearing the voices of survivors of nuclear bombs, of Love Canal, of the concentration camps, of genocides, or of still another war or ethnic cleansing, the crisis worker may well begin to question the social and political choices that led to these disasters. The broad view suggested by these questions is important for the crisis worker to develop in tandem with individualized crisis intervention strategies. Without it, the helper may begin to perceive the task of helping victims of man-made disasters as an exercise in futility. Frustration, loss of effectiveness, and burnout may replace the understanding, sensitivity, and problem-solving ability that the crisis worker should bring to this task.

Coming full circle, and keeping our gaze on both the risks and potential for growth that crisis portends, let us consider this: Among the many origins of personal crisis, man-made disaster presents not only the greatest *danger* across cultures, but also the greatest *opportunity* to make a difference for individuals, families, communities, and whole nations affected by such devastating and preventable crises.

Summary and Discussion Questions

Disaster is experienced as a crisis unlike any other that a person will ever live through. Victims may face a threat to their lives and may lose loved ones, homes, and personal belongings in a single stroke. Many spend the rest of their lives mourning these tragic losses and trying to rebuild their homes and lives. Rescue services, crisis intervention, and follow-up care for physical, emotional, and social rehabilitation are necessary for all survivors. Although financial aid for physical restoration and rehabilitation has been available for years, crisis counseling services are a newer phenomenon on the disaster scene. Communities will be better equipped to handle the emotional crisis related to the disaster experience when health and social service workers, as well as other caretakers, are prepared in advance with skills in crisis care. The urgency of preventing disasters of human origin is self-evident.

1. In response to disaster, typically there is an outpouring of local and global aid. What can be done to foster greater connection and public consciousness between such crisis care and multifaceted disaster prevention?
2. Finding meaning in critical life events is central to emotional recovery. Discuss the spiritual and other factors underpinning this facet of crisis care during and following disaster.
3. Formal crisis theory and practice arose from responses to disaster survivors and war veterans, and from ego psychology and preventive psychiatry. Consider the status of the crisis field today from the perspective of resilience, hope, and primary care.
4. After the Nazi Holocaust, many repeated the phrase "never again." How do we explain the genocides (e.g., in Cambodia and Rwanda) that have occurred since then?

References

Ai, A. L., Cascio, T., Santangelo, L. K., & Evans-Campbell, T. (2005). Hope, meaning, and growth following the September 11, 2001, terrorist attacks. *Journal of Interpersonal Violence, 20*(5), 523–548.

Ahmed, F. E. (1992, September 1). The Bangladesh hurricane has no name. *Boston Globe*, p. 15.

Antonovsky, A. (1987). *Unraveling the mystery of health: How people manage stress and stay well.* San Francisco: Jossey-Bass.

Apfel, R. J., & Simon, B. (Eds.). (1994). *Minefields in the heart: Mental life of children of war and communal violence.* New Haven, CT: Yale University Press.

Baum, A., Fleming, R., & Singer, J. E. (1983). Coping with victimization by technological disaster. *Journal of Social Issues, 39*(2), 117–138.

Boscarino, J., Adams, R., & Figley, C. (2005). A prospective cohort study of the effectiveness of employer-sponsored crisis interventions after a major disaster. *International Journal of Emergency Mental Health, 7*(1), 9–22.

Baranovsky, A. B., Gentry, J. E., & Schultz, D. F. (2005). *Trauma practice: Tools for stabilization and recovery.* Cambridge, MA: Hogrefe.

Caplan, G. (1964). *Principles of preventive psychiatry.* New York: Basic Books.

de Castro, A. B., Gee, G. C., & Takeuchi, D. T. (2008). Workplace discrimination and health among Filipinos in the Unites States. *Research and Practice, 98*(3), 520–526.

Doolin, J., & Collins, M. (1998, November 10). Face to face with the suffering in Central America. *Boston Globe,* p. A19.

Durkin, M. S., Khan, N., Davidson, L. L., Zaman, S. S., & Stein, Z. A. (1993). The effects of a natural disaster on child behavior: Evidence for post-traumatic stress. *American Journal of Public Health, 83*(11), 1549–1553.

Ekins, P. (1992). *A new world order: Grassroots movements for global change.* New York: Routledge.

Epstein, P. R. (1995). Emerging diseases and ecosystem instability: New threats to public health. *American Journal of Public Health, 85,* 168–172.

Erikson, K. (1994). *A new species of trouble.* New York: Norton.

Evans, L., & Oehler-Stinnett, J. (2006). Children and natural disasters: A primer for school psychologists. *School Psychology International, 27*(1), 33–55.

Everett, B., & Gallop, R. (2000). *Linking childhood trauma and mental illness: Theory and practice for direct service practitioners.* Thousand Oaks, CA: Sage.

Foell, E., & Nenneman, R. (1986). *How peace came to the world.* Cambridge, MA: MIT Press.

Gibbs, L. (1982). *Love canal: My story.* Albany: State University of New York Press.

Gist, R., & Lubin, B. (Eds.). (1989). *Psychosocial aspects of disaster.* New York: Wiley.

Goldoftas, B. (1998, December 11). Hurricane Mitch's deadly ally. *Boston Globe,* p. A35.

Goodman, L. M., & Hoff, L. A. (1990). *Omnicide.* New York: Praeger.

Hansell, N. (1976). *The person in distress.* New York: Human Sciences Press.

Hobfoll, S. E., Canetti-Sisim, D., & Johnson, R. J. (2006). Exposure to terrorism, stress-related mental health symptoms, and defensive coping among Jews and Arabs in Israel. *Journal of Consulting and Clinical Psychology, 74*(2), 207–218.

Hoff, M., McNutt, J. D. (Eds.). (1994). *The global environmental crisis: Implications for social welfare and social work.* Aldershot, England: Avebury.

Huebner, A. J., Mancini, J. A., Wilcox, R. M., Grass, S. R., & Grass, G. A. (2007). Parental deployment and youth in military families: Exploring uncertainty and ambiguous loss. *Family Relations, 56,* 112–122.

Jacobs, J., Horne-Moyer, L., & Jones, R. (2004). The effectiveness of critical incident stress debriefing with primary and secondary trauma victims. *International Journal of Emergency Mental Health, 6*(1), 5–14.

Jordan, K. (2005). What we learned from 9/11: A terrorism grief and recovery process model. *Brief Treatment and Crisis Intervention, 5,* 340–355.

Joseph, S., Yule, W., Williams, R., & Andrews, B. (1993). Crisis support in the aftermath of disaster. *British Journal of Clinical Psychology, 32*(Part 2), 177–185.

Kizzier, D. (1972). *The Rapid City flood.* Lubbock, TX: Boone.

Koegler, R. R., & Hicks, S. M. (1972). The destruction of a medical center by earthquake. *California Medicine, 116,* 63–67.

Kors, J. (2008, September 18). How the VA abandons our vets. *The Nation,* 13–21.

Lasser, J., & Adams, K. (2007). The effects of war on children: School psychologists' role and function. *School Psychology International, 28*(1), 5–10.

Leon, J., Poole, W. K., & Kloner, R. A. (1996). Sudden cardiac death triggered by an earthquake. *New England Journal of Medicine, 334*, 413–419.

Lifton, R. J. (1967). *Life in death*. New York: Simon & Schuster.

Lifton, R. J. (1993). *The protean self: Human resilience in an age of fragmentation*. New York: Basic Books.

Lifton, R. J., & Olson, E. (1976). The human meaning of total disaster: The Buffalo Creek experience. *Psychiatry, 39*, 1–18.

Logue, J. N. (1996). Disasters, the environment, and public health: Improving our response. *American Journal of Public Health, 86*(9) 1207–1210.

Luchterhand, E. G. (1971). Sociological approaches to massive stress in natural and man-made disasters. *International Psychiatry Clinic, 8*, 29–53.

Marcus, A. (1999, August 19). Amid din of heavy equipment, rescuers strain to hear voices of the trapped. *Boston Globe*, p. A26.

Matthieu, M. M., & Ivanoff, A. (2006). Using stress, appraisal, and coping theories in clinical practice: Assessments of coping strategies after disasters. *Brief Treatment and Crisis Intervention, 6*, 337–348.

McCabe, C. (2006, winter). After the hurricanes. *Oxfam Exchange*, 8–12.

McCarroll, J. E., Ursano, R. J., & Fullerton, C. S. (1993). Symptoms of posttraumatic stress disorder following recovery of war dead. *American Journal of Psychiatry, 150*(12), 1876–1877.

Miller, J. (2006). Waves amidst war: Intercultural challenges while training volunteers to respond to the psychosocial needs of Sri Lankan tsunami survivors. *Brief Treatment and Crisis Intervention, 6*, 249–365.

Miller, L. (1999). Treating posttraumatic stress disorder in children and families: Basic principles and clinical applications. *American Journal of Family Therapy, 27*(1), 21–24.

Mills, C. W. (1959). *The sociological imagination*. Oxford: Oxford University Press.

Mitchell, J. (2003). Major misconceptions in crisis intervention. *International Journal of Emergency Mental Health, 5*(4), 185–197.

Mousseau, M. (1989). *The medicine wheel approach to dealing with family violence*. Dauphin, Manitoba, Canada: West Region Child and Family Services.

Murphy, S. A. (1986). Status of natural disaster victims' health and recovery 1 and 3 years later. *Research in Nursing and Health, 9*, 331–340.

Neria, Y., Gross, R., Litz, B., Maguen, S., Insel, B., Seirmarco, G. et al. (2007). Prevalence and psychological correlates of complicated grief among bereaved adults 2.5–3.5 years after September 11th attacks. *Journal of Traumatic Stress, 20*(3), 251–262.

O'Sullivan, M. et al. (2008). It's part of the job: Healthcare restructuring and the health and safety of nursing aides. In L. McKee, E. Ferlie, & P. Hyde (Eds.), *Organizing and reorganizing: Power and change in health care organizations* (pp. 99–111). Houndmills, Basingstoke, Hampshire, U.K.: Palgrave MacMillan.

Oxfam America. (2006, Winter). A story of aid done right. *Oxfam Exchange, 6*(1), 14. Author.

Peterson, K. C., Prout, M. F., & Schwarz, R. A. (1991). *Post-traumatic stress disorder: A clinician's guide*. New York: Plenum.

Pfefferbaum, B., North, C. S., Doughty, D. E., Pfefferbaum, R. L., Dumont, C. E., & Pynoos, R. S. (2006) Trauma, grief and depression in Nairobi children after the 1998 bombing of the American embassy. *Death Studies, 30*, 561–577.

Priest, D., and Hull, A. (2007, December 2). Mental health problems still stigmatized in the military. *Boston Globe*, p. A23.

Ragehr, C. (2001). Crisis debriefing groups for emergency responders: Reviewing the evidence. *Brief Treatment and Crisis Intervention, 1*, 87–100.

Ratner, L. (2008, September 15). New Orleans redraws its color line. *The Nation*, 21–26.

Richman, N. (1993). After the flood. *American Journal of Public Health, 83*(11), 1522–1523.

Ruddick, S. (1989). *Maternal thinking: Toward a politics of peace.* Boston: Beacon Press.

Schwartzman, R., & Tibbles, D. (2005). Rhetorical dimensions of the post-September eleventh grief process. Central States Communication Association convention, April 18, 2005.

Sennott, C. M. (2007, February 11). Told to wait, a marine dies. *Boston Globe*, pp. A1, A10.

Siegel, M. (2007, September 10/17). Trauma in New Orleans. *The Nation*, 4–5.

Silverstein, M. (2008). Getting home safe and sound: Occupational safety and health administration at 38. *American Journal of Public Health, 98*(3), 416–423.

Stevens, E. (2006, winter). Tsunami survivors rebuild. *Oxfam Exchange*, 11–12.

Tucker, P., Pfefferbaum, B., Nixon, S. J., & Foy, D. W. (1999). Trauma and recovery among adults highly exposed to a community disaster. *Psychiatric Annals, 29*(2), 78–83.

Tyhurst, J. S. (1951). Individual reactions to community disaster. *American Journal of Psychiatry, 107*, 764–769.

Tyhurst, J. S. (1957a). Psychological and social aspects of civilian disaster. *Canadian Medical Association Journal, 76*, 385–393.

Tyhurst, J. S. (1957b). The role of transition states—including disasters—in mental illness. In *Symposium on preventive and social psychiatry.* Washington, DC: Walter Reed Army Institute of Research and the National Research Council.

WGBH Educational Foundation. *Survivors* [Public television documentary]. (1982). Boston: Author.

Wijkman, A., & Timberlake, L. (1984). *Natural disaster: Acts of God or acts of man?* London: International Institute for Environment and Development.

Williams, M. B., & Poijila, S. (2002). *The PTSD Workbook: Simple, effective techniques for overcoming traumatic stress symptoms.* Oakland, CA: New Harbinger Publishers.

Zunin, L. M., & Zunin, H. S. (1991). *The art of condolence: What to write, what to say, what to do at a time of loss.* New York: HarperCollins.

Glossary

ambivalence: The feeling of two irreconcilable wishes, e.g., love and hate, or a suicidal person weighing the advantages of life over death.

basic attachments: Essential needs; a stable arrangement of transactions between ourselves and our environment, such as physical necessities of life, self-identity, group belonging, social role, meaning, etc.

burnout: A chronic condition manifested by cynicism, anger, resentment, and emotional exhaustion, usually stemming from work-related stressors. People suffering from burnout often do not connect their feelings and behavior with the chronic stress they are under.

cohort specificity: Refers to a group of people sharing a common factor such as the same age, gender, role, a distinct or particular situation, e.g., male with breast cancer, newlywed as widow.

conflict: A fight or power struggle for control, or a hostile encounter, usually involving a clash of opinions and divided interests; may lead to violence or crisis.

contextual purity: How an event relates to other dimensions and people, e.g., if a public figure is caught in an illegal sex scandal, it impacts reputation, family, career, criminal justice system, etc.

crisis: A state of acute emotional upset in which one's usual problem-solving ability fails; occurs in response to an identifiable traumatic event, e.g., accident, victimization, death of a loved one, divorce.

crisis assessment: The first of four basic steps in crisis care—ascertaining the stressful or hazardous event, its origins, the precipitating factor, the person's vulnerability and response to what happened, and resources aiding positive crisis resolution.

crisis counseling: An aspect of the crisis management and resolution process focusing on the emotional, cognitive, and behavioral ramifications of the crisis. A crisis worker with formal preparation in counseling techniques carries out this process. Typically it is limited to only a few sessions (6 to 10).

crisis intervention: That aspect of the crisis care process focusing on immediate response to and resolution of an urgent problem—with particular attention to its life-threatening aspects—through use of personal, social, environmental, spiritual, and sometimes material resources.

crisis management: Consists of the entire process of working through one's crisis to its endpoint of resolution; implies the active collaboration between the person or family in crisis and a human services provider.

crisis origins: The roots of a problem leading to crisis; an important facet of the crisis assessment process; can be classified as situational, transitional, and/or social-cultural.

crisis paradigm: See **paradigm**.

crisis stabilization: A term usually referring to the short-term treatment (12 to 72 hours) of acute psychiatric emergency situation in a hospital setting, in which chemical restraint is often applied. Crisis counseling and a follow-up treatment plan are instituted when the disturbed person is more tranquil and can be engaged in problem solving.

crisis worker: Anyone with the knowledge, skills, and attitudes required to assist a person or family in crisis (e.g., police officer, mental health professional, clergy, nurse, physician, social worker).

critical incident stress debriefing (CISD): A structured debriefing typically conducted for groups after a disaster or other incident, such as a school shooting, to ascertain people's immediate response to the event and need for psychological and other aid. See **traumatic stress debriefing**.

cultural relativism: Making a judgment about the acceptability of certain actions that are different or *relative* to a particular culture, circumstances, etc., e.g., excusing violence toward women as "part of their culture" in contrast to defining violence in a universal human rights framework.

culture shock: An experience of mental and emotional agitation when suddenly thrust into a strange situation or environment in which ordinary cultural supports are lacking, e.g., arriving alone in a foreign country and not knowing the local language; admission to the distinct "culture" of a hospital.

discrimination: Actions or policies that show partiality or unfairness based on ethnicity, gender, class, age, sexual identity, or other characteristics that signify diversity or disadvantage in terms of power and influence.

disease: A pathological condition that can be objectively verified through observation, physical examination, and laboratory findings.

diversity: A state of being different in relation to culture, beliefs, ethnicity, language, sexual identity, etc.

emergency: An unforeseen combination of circumstances, often of a life-or-death nature, calling for immediate action; it may or may not result in emotional crisis.

emergency psychiatry: A branch of medicine that deals with acute behavioral disturbances related to severe cognitive impairment, emotional instability, or dysfunction in daily living and self-care. It includes crisis intervention but also implies the need for distinct *medical* intervention such as psychotropic medication or admission to an inpatient psychiatric facility. Elements of its practice are carried out by various members of the traditional mental health professions: psychiatry, psychiatric nursing, social work, clinical psychology.

equilibrium: A state of balance between conflicting or competing desires or forces; a concept related to homeostasis and maintaining emotional control in everyday functioning and when facing stressful circumstances.

ethnicity: Refers to ethnic classification or affiliation, and is tied to the notion of shared origin and culture.

ethnocentrism: The emotional attitude that one's own ethnic group, nation, or culture is superior to that of others.

formal crisis care: That part of the helping process carried out by health and other human service providers on behalf of a person or family in crisis. Also known as crisis intervention.

gentrification: A socioeconomic development term referring to the displacement of urban dwellers—usually poor—by more affluent groups, the "gentry" or people of higher social class. Often entails residential crisis for those displaced.

hazardous event: A deeply disturbing occurrence or situation that sets in motion a series of reactions that may culminate in acute crisis.

homeostasis: The tendency to maintain stability or equilibrium; e.g., for one at risk of crisis, a need to maintain control of one's normal cognitive, emotional, and behavioral functioning. In psychoanalytic theory, maintaining balance between the id, ego, and superego facets of personality.

horizontal violence (also, lateral violence): Refers to abusive and harmful words or action directed at one's colleagues or own cultural group. A concept best understood in the framework of "oppressed group behavior" (Freire, P. [1989]. *Pedagogy of the oppressed.* New York: Continuum); i.e., people who feel angry, uninformed, and/or powerless to change their disadvantaged circumstances may lash out at one another, or against persons even more powerless than themselves.

iatrogenesis: A concept referring originally to disorders or injury caused by medical treatment, but now applied to injuries originating from any health, mental health, or social service provider's action or neglect.

ideology: A way of thinking or system of ideas stemming primarily from political, economic, or social values, and speculation, in contrast to theories based on scientific evidence and philosophical reasoning.

illness: A concept related to disease but distinguished by its subjective character and cross-cultural variation; i.e., one may "feel" ill without objective verification of "disease." Illness may be used to excuse oneself from responsibilities that cannot otherwise be negotiated, or as a social control device, as in "psychiatric labeling."

insanity: A legal concept denoting mental illness or cognitive impairment to the extent that the person is incapable of the judgment and corresponding behavior that legally is considered normal. It constitutes the basis for excusing a person of accountability for such behavior, usually on historical and related evaluation data obtained by a licensed mental health professional—a psychiatrist or clinical psychologist.

natural crisis care: That part of the helping process carried out by a friend or family member on behalf of a person in crisis.

paradigm: A model for explaining a complex process or idea that is accepted by most people in an intellectual community. In this book, based on research and clinical experience, a paradigm depicts the crisis experience from origin through resolution; understanding this experience serves as an underpinning for natural and formal intervention across a range of hazardous events and transition states to promote growth and avoid negative crisis outcomes such as substance abuse or violence toward self and others.

posttraumatic stress disorder (PTSD): A psychiatric term describing a chronic condition that may occur years after experiencing a trauma that is outside the normal range of life events. The term originated from work with survivors of concentration camps and the Vietnam War. The occurrence of posttraumatic stress often signifies that crisis care was inadequate when the traumatic event was first experienced. The term *traumatic stress* signifies the essential "normality" of emotional response to horrific events, although psychiatric "disorder" may follow in the absence of early supportive response.

pathogenesis: Tracing the development of a disease; a counterpoint to examining what keeps people healthy (**salutogenesis**).

precipitant: An often minor event or trigger that sets off a crisis state; "the straw that broke the camel's back."

primary health care: Refers to the first or entry point to the health care system, with the emphasis on education and early detection of health problems and the pivotal role of primary care providers to coordinate the often complex facets of health service delivery. It assumes the psychosocial aspect of any health problem. It is a key concept in crisis care for its emphasis on preventive mental health and timely response to self-injury, abuse, and other critical life events.

protective factors: Conditions in families and communities that increase the health and well-being of children and families; they provide a buffer against stress and crisis vulnerability.

psychosocial health care: The element of human service that recognizes and addresses the psychological and social factors inherent in most health, illness, and crisis phenomena.

psychotherapist: Someone specially trained (and with a minimum of a master's degree) to help people resolve underlying psychological and psychiatric problems. Includes persons working with a license: psychiatrist, clinical or counseling psychologist, licensed social worker, advanced practice psychiatric nurse.

psychotherapy: A helping process directed toward changing a person's feelings and patterns of thought and behavior. In contrast to crisis intervention's focus on problem solving around hazardous events, it involves uncovering unconscious conflict leading to symptoms of distress.

reductionism: A common term in the social sciences that refers to "reducing" to a *single* factor an explanation for a *complex*, multifactor phenomenon; e.g., violent behavior can be a "caused" by mental incompetence, as in the expression after a crime: "Only a crazy person could do something like that."

resilience: The ability to recover quickly and thrive following setbacks or serious upsets; a dynamic process that results in psychological and social adaptation in the context of significant adversity.

salutogenesis: Examining what leads to health and healthy behavior (in contrast to what leads to illness—**pathogenesis**).

self-destructive behavior: Any act or neglect which results in physical, social, or emotional harm or death; e.g., neglect of medicine, substance abuse, direct self-injury.

social network: May consist of a person's family, friends, neighbors, relatives, employer, teacher, bartender, hairdresser—anyone with whom a person has regular social intercourse.

stereotyping: Refers to an unvarying pattern of thinking and pigeonholing a person or group in a box (often based on ethnicity or other diversity) that does not allow for individuality or critical judgment.

stress: Tension, strain, or pressure caused by various stressors (physical, social, psychological, cultural) and resulting in physiological changes in the organism (e.g., ulcers, heart disease), and affecting one's social and psychological functioning and job performance; unrelieved stress leaves one vulnerable to crisis.

suicide: Self-intended, self-inflicted death.

suicide attempt: An attempt to die; implies *intention* to die, although death may not occur because of nonlethal method or unintended rescue.

suicide gesture: A term often used to describe a low-lethal suicide attempt. It suggests a judgment that the distressed person was "not really serious" or was "just seeking attention." It should be avoided in crisis care because it can result in failure to ascertain the *meaning* of the self-harm behavior.

trauma: The subjective experience of an unusually stressful event that often involves a realistic danger of death.

traumatic stress debriefing: The first step in the crisis management process, initiated as soon as possible after a critical event such as a suicide in school or by a hospital patient, police and emergency medical response at a crime scene, or loss by disaster. It typically involves listening, opportunity for catharsis, emotional and material support, psychoeducation about normal crisis response, and linkage to follow-up crisis counseling or psychiatric services based on assessed needs. Sometimes referred to as **critical incident stress debriefing (CISD)**.

vicarious traumatization: The feeling of distress and psychological trauma experienced especially by persons working with victims or survivors of violence and abuse whose job entails listening with empathy to a particularly gruesome story of violence, or to similar stories of clients repeated over hours, days, or months in a job. It refers to the absorption of the trauma into one's own psyche, which without attention to its source and appropriate support and self-care, can lead to burnout and other psychological or social problems.

violence: Social action that inflicts harm on another, or even death, and for which one is accountable, except in cases of self-defense or insanity.

vulnerability: Susceptible to physical or emotional harm.

Author Index

Subject Index

American Association of Suicidology (AAS), 32
Androgyny, Native appreciation of, 195
Anger
    in AIDS, 245
    in bereavement, 127
    encouraging alternate expressions, 343
    as stage of dying, 215, 216
Anger management approach, limitations for
        batterers, 446–447
Anhedonia, 348
Anomic suicide, 324
Anorexia nervosa, 259
Anticipated moves, 280–281
Anticipated states, 38
Anticipatory prevention, 27
Antidepressant drugs, 347
    controlling supply in self-destructive people, 344
    danger for suicidal persons, 348
    delay in efficacy, 348
    as suicide weapons, 342
Antiretroviral medications, 240
Antisocial behavior, primary prevention, 453–455
Anxiety
    among suicide survivors, 300
    in crisis experience, 86
    during developmental transition states, 40
    physical symptoms, 87
    relieving in self-destructive people, 344
Asian tsunami, xvii, 462, 467, 479–480, 489
Aspirin, as suicide weapon, 342
Assailants
    crisis intervention with, 449–450
    follow-up service, 450
Assault
    applying risk criteria, 440
    assessing risk of, 436–440
    double standards for, 395
Assault and Homicidal Danger Assessment Tool, 439
Assault risk, 79, 82
Assessment, 31, 32
    individuals and families, 1
    links to planning, 116
    in primary care, 137
    process, 79
    through group work, 162
Assessment forms, 98
    assessment worksheet, 100
    child screening checklist, 104–105
    initial contact sheet, 98–100
    interview summary, George Sloan example, 100
Assessment interviews, 93–96
    assessment forms, 98–205
    comprehensive crisis assessment in, 96
    example, 94–95
    record systems in, 96–97
Assessment levels, 79, 82
    Level I, risk to life, 79–80
    Level II, comprehensive mental health assessment, 81
Assessment worksheet, 100
    George Sloan example, 101–104
Assisted-living communities, 412

Assisted reproduction, 187–188
Assisted suicide, 214, 303, 308, 309
    in AIDS, 248
At-promise paradigm, 10, 33
At-risk paradigm, 33
Attachments. *See* Seven basic attachments
Atypical behavior, in crisis situations, 91

B

Bangladesh hurricane, 464, 465
Bargaining, as stage of dying, 215, 216
Basic attachments, 495
Battered women, 179, 394, 439. *See also* Abused
        women
    diagnosing as mentally ill, 395
    refuge and care for, 428
    vignettes, 394
Battered women shelters, 16. *See also* Abused women
Battered women syndrome, 372
Batterers, 445. *See also* Abusive men
    four types of, 445
    mandatory arrest, 369
    treatment programs for, 428
Befrienders International, 16
Behavior problems
    in children, 188
    in handicapped children, 257
Behavioral changes, and suicide risk, 324–325, 326
Behavioral responses, 90–91
Bereavement reactions, 126–127
    following disaster incidents, 470
Bereavement work, 11, 126–128
Bhopal disaster, 478, 481
Bicultural concepts, 18
Big Brothers-Big Sisters programs, 381
Binge drinking, 261
Biological psychiatry, 170
    dominance of, 154
Biophysical responses, 86–88, 234
Bipolar disorder, and obsession with diagnostic labels, 71
Birth, 183–184
    medicalization of, 187–188
    as rite of passage, 181
Bisexuality, and suicide risk, 295, 334
Blame, internalization of, 49
Blended families, 190–191
Bosnian war, rape crimes, 387
Breakdown, 4, 5
    emotional or mental, 51
Buffalo Creek mining disaster, 481
Building codes, 464
    and natural disaster impacts, 463
Bulimia, 259
Bullying prevention, 418, 441
Burnout, 46, 453
    in acute-care settings, 227
    defined, 495
    prevention in AIDS caretakers, 253
    prevention in service workers, 7, 23
    protecting clinicians from, 117

C

Cambodian genocide, 483
Canada, mandatory arrest for batterers in, 369
Caretaking burden
    and origins of violence, 372
    on women, 147
Catastrophic events, 293. *See also* Natural disasters
Catharsis, 9, 22
Causal models, limitations, 38, 47, 48
Certified divorce planners, 189, 190
Cesarean births, 187–188
Chemical tranquilization, 134
Chernobyl disaster, 478, 481, 487
Child abuse, 376
    accountability *vs.* treatment options for
            perpetrators, 428
    and child removal from home, 381, 384
    child witnesses to violence and murder, 380–381
    follow-up service, 385
    legal and crisis intervention, 382–384
    and origins of parricide, 416
    parallels with elder abuse, 411
    parental needs in, 383
    preventive intervention, 381–382
    the problem, 376
    signs of, 382
    suggesting nonviolent alternatives, 384
    as trigger of parricide, 442
Child care, 148
    and family crisis, 147
    lack of affordable, 274
    need for, in domestic violence situations, 403
    social devaluation of, and violence, 379
Child poverty, 193
Child Screening Checklist, 100, 104–105
Childhood sexual abuse, 378
Childless couples, 203
    devaluation of child care by, 379
Children
    with AIDS, 249–251
    behavior problems, 188
    dangers of psychiatric labeling, 72
    death of, 184–186
    effect of parent suicide, 359, 362
    explaining parental suicide to, 361
    family crisis counseling for, 168
    handicapped, 255
    illness, surgery, and hospitalization crises,
            231–232
    illness or behavior problems, 188
    of imprisoned parents, 452
    inadequate counseling and psychiatric services
            for, 134
    lack of specialized services for disturbed, 194
    miscarried or stillborn, 187
    misuse of psychotropic drugs in, 194, 349
    sex selection, 188
Children of divorce, 188, 189
Chronic care, 15–16
Chronic crisis, 83
Chronic health problems, crisis and, 259–264

Chronic problems, *vs.* crises and intervention
        strategies, 155
Chronic stress, 46, 51, 83
Civil rights movement, and origins of record system, 98
Civil rights violations, 118
Client-centered records, 100
Client empowerment
    decision counseling and, 116–118
    facilitating, 119
Client independence, 28
Codependence, 204
Cognitive behavior approach, in decision counseling, 117
Cognitive impairment, 211–212
Cohesion, developing in crisis assessment groups, 164
Cohort specificity
    and crisis development, 44
    defined, 495
Cohousing approach, 145, 146, 200
    and needs for privacy, intimacy, community, 150
Cold War, 488
Collaboration, in developing crisis intervention plan,
        122
Commonalities, role in crisis care, 19–20
Communication
    in crisis work, 109
    and disaster recovery, 474
    importance in disaster prevention and mitigation, 467
    nature and purpose, 109–110
    and rapport, 112–114
    and relationships, 112–114
    role in disaster survival, 488
    role in violence prevention, 437
    by self-destructive people, 315–316
    and suicide prevention, 315, 321
    and suicide risk, 321–323, 326
    trust-risk factors in, 114
Community, *vs.* privacy and intimacy, 150–152
Community-based services, 98
Community-based treatment, 72
Community crises, 11, 148–150
Community mental health, 13–14
Community service, 450
Compassion fatigue, 254
Complex PTSD, 482
Comprehensive crisis care, 63
Comprehensive Mental Health Assessment (CMHA),
        xvii, 16, 81
    use in battering cases, 405
Comprehensive mental health record systems, 97–98
Conflict, 495
Consensus theory, 12
Contact USA, 16
Contextual purity, 48
    and crisis development, 44
    defined, 495
Continuum perspective, 28–30
Coping strategies, 45, 81
    assessing through group work, 162
    effective and ineffective, 92
        in AIDS, 246
    exploring in group work, 163
    family and community factors influencing, 91–93